(Continued on back endsheets)

Concise Dictionary of American Literary Biography

Broadening Views, 1968-1988

Concise Dictionary of American Literary Biography

Broadening Views, 1968-1988

A Bruccoli Clark Layman Book
Gale Research Inc.
Detroit, London

Advisory Board for
CONCISE DICTIONARY
OF AMERICAN LITERARY BIOGRAPHY

The paper used in this publication meets the minimum requirements
of American National Standard for Information Sciences—Permanence
Paper for Printed Library Materials, ANSI Z39.48-1984. ∞™

Copyright © 1989
Gale Research Inc.
835 Penobscot Bldg.
Detroit, MI 48226-4094

ISBN 0-8103-1823-7 (vol. 6)

Printed in the United States of America

Published simultaneously in the United Kingdom
by Gale Research International Limited
(An affiliated company of Gale Research Inc.)

Contents

Plan of the Work

The six-volume *Concise Dictionary of American Literary Biography* was developed in response to requests from high school and junior college teachers and librarians, and from small- to medium-sized public libraries, for a compilation of entries from the standard *Dictionary of Literary Biography* chosen to meet their needs and their budgets. The *DLB*, which comprises over ninety volumes as of the end of 1987, is moving steadily toward its goal of providing a history of literature in all languages developed through the biographies of writers. Basic as the *DLB* is, many librarians have expressed the need for a less comprehensive reference work which in other respects retains the merits of *DLB*. The *Concise DALB* provides this resource.

This series was planned by a seven-member advisory board, consisting primarily of secondary school educators, who developed a method of organization and presentation for selected *DLB* entries suitable for high school and beginning college students. Their preliminary plan was circulated to some five thousand school librarians and English teachers, who were asked to respond to the organization of the series and the table of contents. Those responses were incorporated into the plan described here.

Uses for the Concise DALB

Students are the primary audience for the *Concise DALB*. The stated purpose of the standard *DLB* is to make our literary heritage more accessible. *Concise DALB* has the same goal and seeks a wider audience. What the author wrote; what the facts of his life are; a description of his literary works; a discussion of the critical response to his works; and a bibliography of critical works to be consulted for further information: These are the elements of a *Concise DALB* entry.

The first step in the planning process for this series, after identifying the audience, was to contemplate its uses. The advisory board acknowledged that the integrity of *Concise DALB* as a reference book is crucial to its utility. The *Concise DALB* adheres to the scholarly standards established by the parent series. Thus, within the scope of major American literary figures, the *Concise DALB* is a ready reference source of established value, providing reliable biographical and bibliographical information.

It is anticipated that this series will not be confined to uses within the library. Just as *DLB* has been a tool for stimulating students' literary interests in the college classroom–for comparative studies of authors, for example, and, through its ample illustrations, as a means of invigorating literary study–the *Concise DALB* is a primary resource for high school and junior college educators. The series is organized to facilitate lesson planning, and the contextual diagrams (explained below) that introduce each entry are a source of topics for classroom discussion and writing assignments.

Organization

The advisory board further determined that entries from the standard *DLB* should be presented complete–without abridgment. Their feeling was that the utility of the *DLB* format has been proven, and that only minimal changes should be made.

The advisory board further decided that the organization of the *Concise DALB* should be chronological to emphasize the historical development of American literature. Each volume is devoted to a single historical period and includes the most significant literary figures from all genres who were active during that time. Thus, the volume that includes modern mainstream novelists Saul Bellow, Bernard Malamud, and John Cheever will also include poets who were active at the same time–such as Allen Ginsberg, Lawrence Ferlinghetti, and John Berryman–and dramatists who were their contemporaries–such as Tennessee Williams, Arthur Miller, and William Inge. It should be noted that the volume of the *Concise DALB* that includes these authors comprises thirty-six entries, while the volumes in the standard *DLB* covering the same period include some four hundred author biographies. The *Concise DALB* limits itself to major figures, but it provides the same coverage of those figures as the *DLB* does.

The six period volumes of the *Concise DALB* are *Colonization to the American Renaissance, 1640-1865; Realism, Naturalism, and Local Color,*

1865-1917; The Twenties, 1917-1929; The Age of Maturity, 1929-1941; The New Consciousness, 1941-1968; Broadening Views, 1968-1988. The sixth volume will also contain a comprehensive index by subjects and proper names to the entire *Concise DALB.* (As in the standard *DLB* series, there is a cumulative index to author entries in each *Concise DALB* volume.)

Form of Entry

The form of entry in the *Concise DALB* is substantially the same as in the standard series, with the following alterations:

1) Each entry has been updated to include a discussion of works published since the standard entry appeared and to reflect recent criticism and research of interest to the high school audience.

2) The secondary bibliography for each entry has been selected to include those books and articles of particular interest and usefulness to high school and junior college students. In addition, the secondary bibliography has been annotated to assist students in assessing whether a reference will meet their needs.

3) Each entry is preceded by a "contextual diagram"–a graphic presentation of the places, literary influences, personal relationships, literary movements, major themes, cultural and artistic influences, and social and economic forces associated with the author. This chart allows students–and teachers–to place the author in his literary and social context at a glance.

It bears repeating that the *Concise DALB* is restricted to major American literary figures. It is anticipated that users of this series will find it advantageous to consult the standard *DLB* for information about those writers omitted from the *Concise DALB* whose significance to contemporary readers may have faded but whose contribution to our cultural heritage remains meaningful.

Comments about the series and suggestions about how to improve it are earnestly invited.

A Note to Students

The purpose of the *Concise DALB* is to enrich the study of literature. In their various ways, writers react in their works to the circumstances of their lives, the events of their time, and the culture that envelops them (which are represented on the contextual diagrams that precede each *Concise DALB* entry). Writers provide a way to see and understand what they have observed and experienced. Besides being inherently interesting, biographies of writers provide a basic perspective on literature.

Concise DALB entries start with the most important facts about writers: What they wrote. We strongly recommend that you also start there. The chronological listing of an author's works is an outline for the examination of his or her career achievement. The biographies that follow set the stage for the presentation of the works. Each of the author's important works and the most respected critical evaluations of them are discussed in *Concise DALB*. If you require more information about the author or fuller critical studies of the author's works, the annotated references section at the end of the entry will guide you.

Illustrations are an integral element of *Concise DALB* entries. Photographs of the author are reminders that literature is the product of a writer's imagination; facsimiles of the author's working drafts are the best evidence available for understanding the act of composition–the author in the process of refining his work and acting as self-editor; dust jacket and advertisements demonstrate how literature comes to us through the marketplace, which sometimes serves to alter our perceptions of the works.

Literary study is a complex and immensely rewarding endeavor. Our goal is to provide you with the information you need to make that experience as rich as possible.

Acknowledgments

This book was produced by Bruccoli Clark Layman, Inc. Karen L. Rood is senior editor for the *Dictionary of Literary Biography* series. Laura Ingram was the in-house editor.

Production coordinator is James W. Hipp. Systems manager is Charles D. Brower. Photography supervisor is Susan Todd. Penney L. Haughton is responsible for layout and graphics. Copyediting supervisor is Joan M. Prince. Typesetting supervisor is Kathleen M. Flanagan. William Adams and Michael D. Senecal are editorial associates. The production staff includes Rowena Betts, Anne L. M. Bowman, Nancy Brevard-Bracey, Joseph M. Bruccoli, Teresa Chaney, Patricia Coate, Marie Creed, Allison Deal, Holly Deal, Sarah A. Estes, Brian A. Glassman, Willie M. Gore, Cynthia Hallman, Kristine Hartvigsen, Susan C. Heath, Mary Long, David Marshall James, Kathy S. Merlette, Laura Garren Moore, Philip R. Moore, Sheri Beckett Neal, and Jack Turner. Jean W. Ross is permissions editor.

Walter W. Ross and Jennifer Toth did the library research with the assistance of the reference staff at the Thomas Cooper Library of the University of South Carolina: Lisa Antley, Daniel Boice, Faye Chadwell, Cathy Eckman, Gary Geer, Cathie Gottlieb, David L. Haggard, Jens Holley, Jackie Kinder, Marcia Martin, Jean Rhyne, Beverly Steele, Ellen Tillett, Carol Tobin, and Virginia Weathers.

Concise Dictionary of American Literary Biography

Broadening Views, 1968-1988

Concise Dictionary of American Literary Biography

Elizabeth Bishop

This entry was updated by Brett C. Millier (Middlebury College) from the entry by Ashley Brown (University of South Carolina) in DLB 5, American Poets Since World War II.

Places	Nova Scotia Paris	Florida Brazil	New England
Influences and Relationships	Marianne Moore Robert Lowell May Swenson	George Herbert Wallace Stevens	Gerard Manley Hopkins
Literary Movements and Forms	"Closed Form" Poets		The Elegy
Major Themes	The Interaction of Man and Beast	Geography Moral Choice	Dislocated Perspective Loss
Cultural and Artistic Influences	Jazz / The Blues Impressionist Painting	Brazilian Music and Culture	Portuguese Language Protestant Hymns
Social and Economic Influences	Political Unrest in Brazil	The Presidency of John F. Kennedy	Poverty

BIRTH: Worcester, Massachusetts, 8 February 1911, to Gertrude Bulmer and William Thomas Bishop.

EDUCATION: A.B., Vassar College, 1934.

AWARDS: Houghton Mifflin Poetry Award, 1945; Guggenheim Fellowship, 1947; Consultant in Poetry (Library of Congress), 1949-1950; Lucy Martin Donnelly Fellowship (Bryn Mawr College), 1951; National Institute of Arts and Letters Award, 1951; Shelley Memorial Award, 1953; *Partisan Review* Fellowship, 1956; Pulitzer Prize for *Poems: North & South—A Cold Spring*, 1956; Amy Lowell Fellowship, 1957; Chapelbrook Foundation Fellowship, 1960; Academy of American Poets Fellowship, 1964; LL.D., Smith College, 1968; National Book Award for *The Complete Poems*, 1970; Order Rio Branco (Brazil), 1971; LL.D., Rutgers University, 1972; LL.D., Brown University, 1972; Harriet Monroe Poetry Award (University of Chicago), 1974; *Books Abroad* / Neustadt International Prize for Literature, 1976; National Book Critics Circle Award for *Geography III*, 1977.

DEATH: Boston, Massachusetts, 6 October 1979.

BOOKS: *North & South* (Boston: Houghton Mifflin, 1946);
Poems: North & South—A Cold Spring (Boston: Houghton Mifflin, 1955; London: Chatto & Windus, 1956);
Brazil, by Bishop and the editors of *Life* (New York: Time / *Life* World Library, 1962; London: Sunday *Times*, 1963);
Questions of Travel (New York: Farrar, Straus & Giroux, 1965);
Selected Poems (London: Chatto & Windus, 1967);
The Ballad of the Burglar of Babylon (New York: Farrar, Straus & Giroux, 1968);
The Complete Poems (New York: Farrar, Straus & Giroux, 1969; London: Chatto & Windus, 1970);
Geography III (New York: Farrar, Straus & Giroux, 1976);
The Complete Poems, 1927-1979 (New York: Farrar, Straus & Giroux, 1983);
The Collected Prose, edited by Robert Giroux (New York: Farrar, Straus, & Giroux, 1984).

OTHER: Alice Dayrell Brant, *The Diary of "Helena Morley,"* translated, with an introduc-

tion, by Bishop (New York: Farrar, Straus & Cudahy, 1957; London: Gollancz, 1958);
An Anthology of Twentieth-Century Brazilian Poetry, volume 1 edited by Bishop and Emanuel Brasil, contains translations by Bishop (Middletown, Conn.: Wesleyan University Press, 1972).

Elizabeth Bishop started publishing poems in the mid 1930s, but her reputation as one of the best American poets has emerged rather slowly. She never rushed into print, and only in her last years did she give public readings of her work. One can think of few other writers who so steadily refused to exploit their "personalities"; yet in her poems a very distinctive voice and attitude can always be sensed. She was honored in several ways, and in 1976 she was the first American writer and the first woman to receive the *Books Abroad* / Neustadt International Prize for Literature, chosen by an international jury of writers who convened at the University of Oklahoma. And in the following year the poet Anthony Hecht, writing in the London *Times Literary Supplement*, said that "Hers is about the finest product our country can offer the world; we have little by other artists that can match it. . . ."

Elizabeth Bishop was born in Worcester, Massachusetts, on 8 February 1911. Her parents, Gertrude Bulmer and William Thomas Bishop, were of Canadian descent; her father's family was from Prince Edward Island, her mother's from Nova Scotia. Because her father died when she was eight months old, she was brought up by her mother and then her maternal grandparents, who lived in Nova Scotia. Her mother was placed permanently in a mental institution when the child was five years old. Many years later Miss Bishop wrote a story, "In the Village," about her mother's collapse. But in that version the event takes place among the many vivid details of a summer day; an entire community is evoked; and the mother's scream that hangs over the village is only the focal point of a complex human situation, a domestic tragedy that is recollected in tranquillity. (The story, originally published in the *New Yorker* in 1953, eventually became the centerpiece of Miss Bishop's 1965 collection of poems, *Questions of Travel*, and is included in *The Collected Prose* [1984].)

Although she continued to spend her childhood summers in Nova Scotia, a place to which she often returned in her poems, Miss Bishop lived most of her childhood in Boston and had

Elizabeth Bishop (Gale International Portrait Gallery)

her formal schooling at Walnut Hill School, Natick, Massachusetts, between 1927 and 1930. By that time she had already given herself something of a literary education through her wide, haphazard reading. In an interview conducted in 1965 (*Shenandoah*, Winter 1966) she recalled some of the books of her girlhood:

> I was crazy about fairy tales–Anderson, Grimm, and so on. Like Jean-Paul Sartre (as he explains it in *Les Mots*), I also read all kinds of things I didn't really understand. I tried almost anything. When I was thirteen, I discovered Whitman, and that was important to me at the time. About that time I started going to summer camp and met some more sophisticated girls who already knew Emily Dickinson and H.D. and Conrad and Henry James. One of them gave me Harriet Monroe's anthology of modern poets. That was an important experience. (I had actually started reading poetry when I was eight.) I remember coming across Harriet Monroe's quotations from Hopkins, "God's Grandeur" for one. I quickly memorized these, and I thought, "I must get this man's work." In 1927 I saw the first edition of Hopkins. I also went through a

Shelley phase, a Browning phase, and a brief Swinburne phase. But I missed a lot of school and my reading was sporadic.

Elizabeth Bishop's years at Vassar College (1930-1934) marked the beginning of her literary career. Her fellow students included Mary McCarthy, Eleanor Clark, and Muriel Rukeyser, all of whom would soon begin to publish poems or stories in the best little magazines of the period and who would all become well-known writers. In 1934 she met Marianne Moore through the Vassar College librarian and began a friendship that was to last almost forty years. Miss Bishop's poetry has sometimes been compared to Moore's, and undoubtedly there are resemblances–the extraordinary gift of observation, the "understated" wit, even certain subjects. But Miss Bishop's range is larger in that she has more kinds of approaches to her subjects; Marianne Moore was only one of her influences.

In 1935, having finished college, Miss Bishop began the travels that were such an important part of her life. She first went to Brittany and then stayed on through the winter in Paris.

The next year she traveled in North Africa and Spain, and in 1937 she visited Key West for the first time. After another period in Europe she settled temporarily in Florida and eventually bought an old house in Key West. This was to be home for the next several years. Meanwhile her poems began appearing in *Partisan Review, Poetry*, and other periodicals, and by 1941 she had already published about twenty-five, enough to compose a small book. But there was no urgency about her work, and during the years of World War II her production was small. She spent most of 1943 in Mexico, where she happened to meet the Chilean poet Pablo Neruda, and added Spanish to her languages. Most of these places—Paris, North Africa, and especially Key West—provided occasions for her poems. It was not till 1946, however, that she brought out her first collection, *North & South*.

The book was published by Houghton Mifflin as part of its first annual poetry award. It was also very well received. Randall Jarrell, who was the best reviewer of poetry in those days, put her book in a category with new works by William Carlos Williams and Robert Graves, and he drew special attention to "The Fish" and "Roosters": "two of the most calmly beautiful, deeply sympathetic poems of our time...." Indeed, "The Fish" is still the most frequently anthologized of her poems, partly because of Jarrell's enthusiasm. "She is morally so attractive," Jarrell wrote, "because she understands so well that the wickedness and confusion of the age can explain and extenuate other people's wickedness and confusion, but not, for you, your own."

There is a kind of general movement from North to South in the book, and the first poem, "The Map" (1935), although it is mainly concerned with maps as aesthetic objects, not just guides to geographical locations, almost inevitably presents a part of the world familiar to the author:

> The shadow of Newfoundland lies flat and still.
> Labrador's yellow, where the moony Eskimo
> has oiled it. We can stroke these lovely bays,
> under a glass as if they were expected to blossom,
> or as if to provide a clean cage for invisible fish.

This poem, which so obviously has the "calmly beautiful" quality that Jarrell mentions, uses the most natural kind of word order. Elizabeth Bishop always insists on the same order of words in poetry that one would use in a good sentence of English prose (she follows Marianne Moore in

this procedure), and she uses a capital letter at the beginning of a verse line only if a sentence begins at that point.

The earliest poems in the book, including "The Map," are mostly in the mode of wit or ironic fantasy—the author seldom brings herself directly into them—but their indirection of method does not mean that they lack a human subject of great interest. "The Man-Moth," for instance, started out from a newspaper misprint for the word *mammoth*. The printing error suggested a strange creature that Miss Bishop used as a way of apprehending the eerie life of the modern city, such as the experience of riding the subway:

> Each night he must
> be carried through artificial tunnels and dream recurrent dreams.
> Just as the ties recur beneath his train, these underlie
> his rushing brain. He does not dare look out the window,
> for the third rail, the unbroken draught of poison,
> runs there beside him. He regards it as a disease
> he has inherited the susceptibility to. He has to keep
> his hands in his pockets, as others must wear mufflers.

This fantasy—some would call it almost Kafkaesque—has a special poignancy among the early poems. No wonder that the poet herself continued to cherish it, and in 1962, when asked to contribute a favorite poem to an anthology (*Poet's Choice*, edited by Paul Engle and Joseph Langland), she offered this one with a brief comment about the misprint that got her started: "An oracle spoke from the page of the *New York Times*, kindly explaining New York City to me, at least for the moment."

Miss Bishop was alert to the different kinds of poetry being written during the 1930s; by this time an American poet could go off in several directions. Having lived for a year in the Paris of André Breton, she was well aware of surrealism, a literary and artistic mode that was practiced there more successfully than it usually was in England and the United States. It is not surprising that several of her poems with Parisian settings (such as "Sleeping on the Ceiling" and "Cirque d'Hiver") are to some extent surrealist. Her real triumph in this mode is "A Miracle for Breakfast" (1937), a strict sestina that deploys the end words through six different arrangements in as many stanzas:

At six o'clock we were waiting for coffee,
waiting for coffee and the charitable crumb
that was going to be served from a certain balcony,
–like kings of old, or like a miracle.
It was still dark. One foot of the sun
steadied itself on a long ripple in the river.

This poem, which at first seems mostly artifice and which certainly carries through an elaboration of method, is about a real subject–hunger. It is written from the point of view of the hungry, and the reader who attends carefully to the details of language (for instance the variations on "the charitable crumb") will see that the strict sestina form is precisely what builds up the effect of hallucination. This is a poem with a social conscience, in its own way a response to the Depression of the 1930s, but it is not like any other American poem of the period. In some ways it resembles the early films of René Clair, such as *Le Million*, which Miss Bishop would have seen in Paris or New York, but its manner, its voice, is hers. Had she wished to, she could have practiced the surrealist mode at length–it seemed to come rather easily to her–and about this time she published several stories that bear out her interest in it. But she had other ways of presenting her subjects.

Miss Bishop's years in Key West were rewarding. In her 1965 interview she looked back on them with some pleasure:

I can't say Key West offered any special advantages for a writer. But I liked living there. The light and blaze of colors made a good impression on me, and I loved the swimming. The town was absolutely broke then. Everybody lived on the W.P.A. I seemed to have a taste for impoverished places in those days. But my Key West period dwindled away. I went back for winters till 1949, but after the war it wasn't the same.

At least six poems from this period seem to have had their inception in Florida, beginning with the poem of that title ("The state with the prettiest name, / the state that floats in brackish water . . ."). This group alone would illustrate something of Miss Bishop's range; it includes "Roosters," "Jerónimo's House," "Seascape," "Little Exercise," and "The Fish."

"Jerónimo's House" is very much a Key West poem. The speaker, in what might be considered the author's first dramatic monologue, is a member of the poor Cuban colony on the island; his fragile house is hardly even a shelter from the hurricanes that will batter the place. But out of his poverty he builds up a quiet "rage for order" (to borrow Wallace Stevens's phrase from a famous poem about Key West). The homeliest details contribute to this state of mind, which is what the poem is finally about: the "little / center table / of woven wicker / painted blue," the "little dish / of hominy grits / and four pink tissue- / paper roses." The speaker says with charming modesty:

Also I have
      hung on a hook,
an old French horn
      repainted with
aluminum paint.
      I play each year
in the parade
      for José Marti.

Miss Bishop was also being modest when she said that she had "a taste for impoverished places in those days." There is something humane, even compassionate in her treatment of the subject; Jerónimo is neither idealized nor patronized. It may be that her few years at Key West, when it was still an isolated place difficult to approach except by sea, gave her a sense of community that she had not found in the great cities where she had lived temporarily. To go from "The Man-Moth" to "Jerónimo's House" gives one this impression.

"Jerónimo's House" is a new kind of poem in another way: its versification. Miss Bishop now began to practice a kind of controlled free verse (there is no other term for it) that descended from a few early poems by Wallace Stevens, such as "The Snow Man" and "The Death of a Soldier." (There is a brilliant discussion of this topic in Yvor Winters's *Primitivism and Decadence*, 1937.) The norm is usually a set number of stresses in each line; in "Jerónimo's House" there are usually two stresses (sometimes the stresses are light); the number of unstressed syllables is variable. This system, if one can call it that, allows for a high degree of "naturalness" in the rhythm, but the movement is always controlled. A good place to see how this works is "Roosters," the most ambitious poem in *North & South*.

This poem is a kind of mini-epic of Western history as it was formulated by Hegel: ancient, medieval, and modern. But the form is cyclical because we start with some real roosters (probably in Key West), whose "uncontrolled, traditional cries" are gradually presented in a mock-heroic way, and before long we are back in the world of the *Iliad* and its late Bronze-Age warriors. When the fighting subsides, we move to the long stretch of the Christian era in which "St. Peter's sin," his denial of Christ, is symbolized in the traditional way by the crowing of the cock. The presentation of the subject on an "old holy sculpture" is one of Miss Bishop's most brilliant passages. As intense religious belief gradually plays out, the rooster survives as a symbol on weather vanes. Then we return to the backyard where we started; the roosters are replaced by the sun, "faithful as enemy, or friend."

Miss Bishop has sustained her subject through forty-four stanzas. Her formal model was a secular poem by the baroque poet, Richard Crashaw, called "Wishes to his supposed mistress." Crashaw's stanza form must have been his invention, and it starts out thus:

> Who e'er she be,
> That not impossible she
> That shall command my heart and me;

The pattern, although unusual, perhaps unique, is altogether regular: triplets in which iambic lines move from dimeter to trimeter to tetrameter. The effect of the triplet, which could be somewhat heavy in English verse, is softened by the varying length of the lines. Crashaw's poem is a splendid exercise in late Renaissance poetics. Miss Bishop's adaptation of the stanza form is by way of controlled free verse: lines of two, three, and four stresses:

> Chríst stands amázed,
> Péter, two fíngers ráised
> to surprísed líps, bóth as if dázed.

Winters in *Primitivism and Decadence* explains that the scheme of free verse can be somewhat varied in its pattern; not every line has to conform. Occasional secondary stresses, inevitable in an accentual language like English, certainly occur. The philosopher John Dewey said of "Roosters" when it was first published in the *New Republic* in 1941, "Well, Elizabeth, you've got these rhymes in threes very well." The rhymes are occasionally half rhymes, according to well-established modern practice. The poem is altogether a stunning performance, in which "wit" in the seventeenth-century sense is carried forward in a twentieth-century idiom. Marianne Moore, her mentor at this time, objected to the stanza form and actually rewrote the poem. For the first time the

younger poet began to refuse Moore's heavy-handed suggestions, and the two became friends and equals.

In a rather different manner is the suite of four poems called "Songs for a Colored Singer" (1944), the first of which was admired by Jarrell when he reviewed *North & South*. Anne R. Newman (*World Literature Today*, Winter 1977) has made the observation that "the four poems make a fine statement of what we now call the black experience." Certainly they are one of the most authentic renditions of black idiom written by a white author; they can be set beside a few stories by Flannery O'Connor and Eudora Welty for comparison. Miss Bishop divulged, in her 1966 interview, that she was thinking of a specific singer when she wrote the poems: "I think I had Billie Holiday in mind. I put in a couple of big words just because she sang big words well–'Conspiring root,' for instance." That comment surely explains the exquisite humor of these lines in the second poem:

> I'm leaving on the bus tonight.
>   Far down the highway wet and black
>   I'll ride and ride and not come back.
>   I'm going to go and take the bus
>   and find someone monogamous.

It is also likely that these very American poems–the blues idiom adapted to the printed page–were suggested by a group of poems by W. H. Auden, "Four Cabaret Songs for Miss Hedli Anderson," which Miss Bishop would have known from his volume *Another Time* (1940). Hedli Anderson, who married the poet Louis MacNeice, may have suggested some details of the poems by her manner of singing, but Auden's songs (which were set to music by Benjamin Britten) were almost parodies of popular song idiom to begin with, just as English popular song of the 1930s was already a kind of imitation of American. Auden gradually let his "Cabaret Songs" go out of print, and one can easily make the claim that Elizabeth Bishop's "Songs"–at least the first two–are superior. Auden was just playing with the idiom.

After *North & South* was published, Miss Bishop gradually consolidated her position as a leading poet of her generation. In 1947 she was awarded a Guggenheim Fellowship. In 1949-1950 she was the Consultant in Poetry at the Library of Congress, and the year after that she was awarded a fellowship by Bryn Mawr College. In November of that year, 1951, she started on

PINK DOG   4.

The sun is blazing and the sky is blue.
Umbrellas clothe the beach in every hue.
Naked, you trot across the avenue.

Oh, never have I seen a dog so bare!
Naked and pink, without a single hair...
Startled, the passersby draw back and stare.

Of course they're mortally afraid of rabies.
But you're not mad. You have a case of scabies,
a terminal one, I'd say. Where are your babies?

—In what slum have you hidden them, poor bitch,
A nursing mother, by those hanging teats,
(in what slum have you hidden them, poor bitch?

                                        its

Didn't you know? It's been in all the papers,
to solve this problem, how they deal with beggars?
They take them out and throw them in the tidal rivers.

Yes, idiots, paralytics, parasites,
go bbbbing in the ebbing sewage, nights,
out in the psuburbs, where there are no lights.

If they do this to anyone who begs,
drunk, drugged, or sober, with or without legs,   drugged, drunk or sober,
what might they do to bare, four-legged dogs?

In the cafés and on the   corners   mostly
the joke is going round that all the beggars
who can afford them, now wear life-preservers.

In your condition you would not be able
to get away   even to dog-paddle,   even to float, much less to dog-paddle
                        this time of year.
Ash Wednesday's coming; Carnival is here.
What samba will you dance? What will you wear?

The Carnival's of course degenerating
—radios, Americans, or something,
have ruined it completely. They're just talking.

Carnival is always wonderful!
A depilated dog will not look well.
Get dressed! Get dressed and dance at Carnival!

Corrected typescript for one of Bishop's poems inspired by her travels in Brazil (courtesy of Alice Methfessel) what was to be her longest and perhaps most important voyage, around the world. Her ship's first stop was Rio de Janeiro, where she visited a friend, Lota de Macedo Soares, and stayed for sixteen years.

Meanwhile she continued to write poems and occasionally prose, sometimes based on visits to Nova Scotia or childhood memories of that locale. Outstanding among these is "At the Fishhouses" (1947), which might be put beside Paul Valéry's "Le cimetière marin" or Stevens's "The Idea of Order at Key West" or (to name a neglected American poem) Howard Baker's "Ode to the Sea." All of these meditations move slowly in the grand manner toward a large statement about existence or knowledge. Miss Bishop builds up her statement and her manner very gradually. Indeed she is almost disarmingly informal at times, and midway she introduces herself thus:

> One seal particularly
> I have seen here evening after evening.
> He was curious about me. He was interested
>   in music;
> like me a believer in total immersion,
> so I used to sing him Baptist hymns.
> I also sang "A Mighty Fortress Is Our God."

Like the other great marine poems, "At the Fishhouses" is based on an opposition between land and sea. It is accordingly arranged in two large sections of forty lines and thirty-seven lines: a setting on land, from which there is a glimpse of the sea, and then the sea itself. Between these sections is a short stanza of six lines in which the transition from land to sea begins. Starting with these facts, one could make a rather extended analysis of the rhetoric of the poem. For instance, the first section is written entirely in the present tense. Although the experience is authentic–Elizabeth Bishop revisiting a decaying fishing village in Nova Scotia–the author carefully suppresses the pronoun *I*, though she is clearly present. The old man repairing nets is, like a character in a poem by Wordsworth, the focus of attention. Then, in the passage about the seal quoted above, the author briefly introduces herself as she makes the transition to the past tense. But this episode lasts only a dozen lines before she moves back to the present. As the large statement begins to emerge in the last part of the poem, the characteristic pronoun becomes *you* or *we;* that is, the reader is drawn into the statement. But at the same time the mood becomes subjunctive ("If you should dip your hand in, / your

wrist would ache immediately"). Only at the end of the poem, when the statement rounds it out, does the mood return to indicative:

> It is like what we imagine knowledge to be:
> dark, salt, clear, moving, utterly free,
> drawn from the cold hard mouth
> of the world, derived from the rocky breasts
> forever, flowing and drawn, and since
> our knowledge is historical, flowing, and flown.

The grand manner of the poem (written in the language of the times as Miss Bishop would naturally use it) is thus secured by traditional rhetorical devices, especially the deploying of tenses and grammatical moods. Miss Bishop, who studied both the old poets and the moderns, was altogether aware of these things, and in her 1965 interview she said:

> the use of the present tense helps to convey this sense of the mind in action. Cummings does this in some poems. Of course poets in other languages (French especially) use the "historical present" more than we do. But that isn't really the same device. But switching tenses always gives effects of depth, space, foreground, background, and so on.

In 1955 Miss Bishop assembled seventeen poems (including "At the Fishhouses") under the heading of *A Cold Spring* to add to her first collection, and her new book was published as *Poems: North & South–A Cold Spring*. It was awarded the Pulitzer Prize in 1956. By this time she had settled into her life in Brazil, and, having learned Portuguese, she began to take an interest in the literature of the country. Much of her activity during the next decade or so was devoted to translating and introducing certain Brazilian writers to the North American public. She worked on and off for three years translating a book called *Minha Vida de Menina (My Life as a Little Girl)*, a diary kept in the 1890s by a young girl who called herself "Helena Morley." She was still living, as Senhora Alice Brant, in Rio de Janeiro when Elizabeth Bishop first went there, and indeed the translator was acquainted with her author, who is described in the introduction to the American edition. The book had been published in Portuguese in 1942 and became a kind of classic (it is still widely sold), especially after it was recommended to the public by the French novelist Georges Bernanos, a refugee in Brazil during World War II. It presents the day-to-day life in

Diamantina, a remote mining town in the interior of Brazil. In her introduction Miss Bishop remembers in some detail a trip that she made to Diamantina for her "research," and the introduction itself is a fine piece of prose. Marianne Moore said in a review (*Poetry*, July 1959): "The attitude to life revealed by the Diary, Helena's apperceptiveness, and innate accuracy, seem a double portrait; the exactness of observation in the introduction being an extension, in manner, of Miss Bishop's verse and other writings. . . ."

A bit to one side of Miss Bishop's main work, but bearing her name, is the book on Brazil commissioned by Time Inc. and published by *Life* World Library in 1962. It is a handsome, illustrated book that in some ways remains a good introduction to the country (although it is not up-to-date on recent political changes), but Miss Bishop's original text was considerably altered by the editors of *Life*, who in fact are listed as collaborators. She tended to disown the book, and in an interview with the poet George Starbuck she said, "I can't remember too much of that book; rather, I choose not to."

Then Miss Bishop turned to Brazil's poets. In 1963 she brought out three of the eighteen sections of João Cabral de Melo Neto's poetic drama, *The Death and Life of a Severino*, in *Poetry* magazine. Cabral de Melo Neto is a sophisticated poet whose language is deceptively simple, but Miss Bishop conveys the special qualities of the original remarkably well, as in this passage:

> We are many Severinos
> and our destiny's the same:
> to soften up these stones
> by sweating over them,
> to try to bring to life
> a dead and deader land,
> to try to wrest a farm
> out of burnt-over land.

She did her best work in translation, however, with several poems by Carlos Drummond de Andrade, Brazil's greatest poet. In 1965 she published one of these poems, called "Travelling in the Family," in *Poetry*. This has become a classic of contemporary translation; it was soon published in anthologies in England. Robert Penn Warren used lines from it as the epigraph of his poem sequence *Audubon: A Vision*, and now it is actually included as one of Miss Bishop's selections in the large anthology of American literature edited by Cleanth Brooks, R. W. B. Lewis, and Warren. Miss Bishop herself included all her transla-

tions of Brazilian verse in *The Complete Poems* (1969). After that she edited the first volume of *An Anthology of Twentieth-Century Brazilian Poetry* (1972) with a young friend, Emanuel Brasil, and she contributed many additional translations to that.

All of this work in translation and prose writing was a background to the approximately twenty poems that Miss Bishop wrote about her life in Brazil, all included in *The Complete Poems, 1927-1979* (1983). The main group appeared in the volume called *Questions of Travel*. Although they had been written at various times during the preceding fifteen years, her arrangement of them was not chronological at all. The first one, "Arrival at Santos," came originally toward the end of *A Cold Spring* (part of the 1955 volume) but was moved to the later book. It describes, amusingly, the author's landing in Brazil in November 1951, and it is frankly done from the tourist's point of view, with her "immodest demands for a different world." At the end of the poem the author says simply: "We leave Santos at once; / we are driving to the interior." She could hardly know then that this was to be home for many years.

The next poem could not be more different. The verbal tapestry called "Brazil, January 1, 1502" is an attempt to recapture the visual experience of another age: how the strange new landscape in the tropics looked to the Portuguese when they first arrived in their caravels at the site of Rio de Janeiro. That is the significance of the date in the title. (These early adventurers mistakenly thought this was the mouth of a great river–hence Rio de Janeiro, or River of January.) But the stately, lush texture born of the landscape and the poem is violated, and at the end Miss Bishop presents the Portuguese thus:

> Directly after Mass, humming perhaps
> *L'Homme armé* or some such tune,
> they ripped away into the hanging fabric,
> each out to catch an Indian for himself–
> those maddening little women who kept calling,
> calling to each other (or had the birds waked up?)
> and retreating, always retreating, behind it.

The next poem, "Questions of Travel," is one of Miss Bishop's most personal responses to her experience; in a way it is a credo. Written about four years after she took up residence in Brazil, it records (along the way) waterfalls, hummingbirds, trees, the sound of a mechanic's wooden clogs in a filling station along the road, a "baroque" bird cage made of bamboo. What a pity it would have been, she says, not to have known these things, not to have traveled. And then at the end she speculates on the whole matter of travel and asks herself the large question:

> *"Continent, city, country, society:*
> *the choice is never wide and never free.*
> *And here, or there . . . No. Should we have stayed*
> *at home,*
> *wherever that may be?"*

The random phenomena that she encountered were familiar because she frequently drove over such a road on the way to a house that she shared with Lota Soares near Petrópolis, the old imperial summer capital, a small city that lies in the mountains above Rio. The next five poems probably take place in or near this house, which was called "Samambaia," after a fern that grows in many parts of Brazil. (The house is described in Ashley Brown's essay in the *Southern Review*, Spring 1977.) The two most impressive poems are "Manuelzinho" (the diminutive for Manuel) and "The Armadillo." The first is a dramatic monologue in which Lota Soares speaks, identified as "A friend of the writer," but it is mainly concerned with the character who gives his name to the poem; it is the most developed work of portraiture that Miss Bishop had written up to that time. Manuelzinho is a maddening "half squatter, half tenant" on the speaker's property, "the world's worst gardener since Cain." The speaker tries to make her peace with him, and that is what the poem is about. But at the end all she can say is,

> You helpless, foolish man,
> I love you all I can,
> I think. Or do I?
> I take off my hat, unpainted
> and figurative, to you.
> Again I promise to try.

"The Armadillo," which is dedicated to Robert Lowell, takes place during a festive season that is celebrated in June—the feast of São João, which comes at the winter solstice in Brazil. But the public festivity only provides the enveloping action for the poem—for instance, the illegal fire balloons that float above the community and could do considerable damage. This is a poem of rather intense and private perception. A fire balloon does fall on an owls' nest up the mountainside behind the house:

> a glistening armadillo left the scene,
> rose-flecked, head down, tail down,
>
> and then a baby rabbit jumped out,
> *short*-eared, to our surprise.

The author generalizes the specific instance: one of the few occasions when she lifts her voice, as it were:

> *Too pretty, dreamlike mimicry!*
> *O falling fire and piercing cry*
> *and panic, and a weak mailed fist*
> *clenched ignorant against the sky!*

"The Armadillo" was first published in 1957, and it was soon taken up by Lowell as the general model for his poem, "Skunk Hour" (from *Life Studies*, 1959), which he dedicated to Miss Bishop.

The remaining Brazilian poems in *Questions of Travel* are set in various places where the author lived or traveled. "The Riverman" is a poem of the Amazon. In a headnote Miss Bishop explains that she drew some details of the poem from *Amazon Town* (1958), by the famous American anthropologist Charles Wagley. But the details are completely absorbed by the poem, which is a dramatic monologue in 158 lines with only five stanzaic divisions. The riverman, according to the headnote, "decides to become a *sacaca*, a witch doctor who works with water spirits," and when the moon is out and he has drunk some sugarcane brandy, he imagines that Luandinha, a river spirit, has approached him. This poem is a sustained achievement in which the whole life of the great river is caught up, and its rhythm has much to do with its success: three stresses in most lines:

> When the moon burns white
> and the river makes that sound
> like a primus pumped up high—
> that fast, high whispering
> like a hundred people at once—
> I'll be there below . . .

The poet James Merrill, one of Miss Bishop's many admirers, said of this poem, "Wonderful, fluid, pulsing lines—you hardly feel the meter at all."

More familiar rhythms can be felt in "The Burglar of Babylon," a modern ballad that deliberately echoes the traditional ballad idiom. This poem is set in a section of Rio de Janeiro that lies

*Elizabeth Bishop in her later years (courtesy of
Alice Methfessel)*

beneath the hill of Babylon, which at one time
was almost covered with rickety slum dwellings.
There a young criminal named Micuçu ("a burglar and killer, / An enemy of society") was hunted down by the police; the manhunt lasted two
days. This journalistic melodrama actually happened; from the apartment where she was then
staying Miss Bishop watched the soldiers and the
army helicopters. This whole part of Rio is
brought into the poem: the slum people, the rich
on their terraces, the bathers on Copacabana
beach, women going to the market. The subject
could have been treated in many ways; it could
have been the occasion for a social protest poem,
and indeed the general plight of the poor is the enveloping action:

On the fair green hills of Rio
    There grows a fearful stain:
The poor who come to Rio
    And can't go home again.

There's the hill of Kerosene,
    And the hill of the Skeleton,
The hill of Astonishment,
    And the hill of Babylon.

So Miss Bishop ends the poem just as she begins
it. Here she translates literally the names of the
hills where the poor live; the juxtaposition of the
names has a sharp, almost grotesque effect in English. On the other hand she does not sentimenta-
lize the young criminal, and the poem is as much
comic as otherwise. But there is something compassionate about her presentation. This poem may
be the finest of all modern ballads, and it is certainly more humane than such poems by Auden
as "Victor" and "Miss Gee." It is, finally, a completely accessible poem that even a child could understand to some degree on a first reading.

Elizabeth Bishop's happiness in Brazil gave
her Nova Scotia childhood back to her as material for poetry and prose. These poems, and a

few others, are collected in the "Elsewhere" section of *Questions of Travel*. They are in a sense introduced by the story "In the Village," the centerpiece of the book. The most remarkable poem here, though, is the last of all, "Visits to St. Elizabeths," dated 1950 and drawn from Miss Bishop's visits to Ezra Pound in the famous mental institution during her year in Washington as Consultant in Poetry. The rhythms are emphatic, because the poem is based on the nursery rhyme called "This Is the House that Jack Built," and the author follows the cumulative effect of the original, with twelve stanzas that run from one to twelve lines. The effect is accelerando, as in music, and the sentences grow longer and more breathless as she nears the last stanza. (In the actual musical setting by the composer Ned Rorem, this tendency is perhaps exaggerated.) Pound is never named, but his case is so well known that the reader could hardly think of anyone else. He is, in successive stanzas, "tragic," "talkative," "honored," "old, brave," "cranky," and so on; but at the end Miss Bishop slows down the feeling, if not the tempo, with "wretched." When asked about Pound in the 1965 interview, she commented, "I think I've said all I want to in that poem. I admired his courage enormously; he proved his devotion to literature during those thirteen years [in St. Elizabeths Hospital]."

Miss Bishop's life in Brazil was disrupted by the illness and suicide of Lota Soares. Greatly saddened and hurt, she returned to the United States to live for most of the time. Before she left Brazil she bought a ruined colonial house in Ouro Preto, Minas Gerais; its restoration preoccupied her during this period, and she lived there when she could be in Brazil as late as 1972. By that time she had begun teaching at Harvard (usually the fall term each year), and in 1974 she moved to an apartment on the waterfront in Boston. This became home most of the time, though she spent her summers in a much-loved house on North Haven Island, Maine. She died suddenly in October 1979.

The Complete Poems appeared in 1969, and it received the National Book Award. It was "complete" only to 1969, however, because Miss Bishop continued to publish poems, and *Geography III*, which came out at the end of 1976, is one of the high points of her career. It won the National Book Critics Circle Award. Although it contains only ten poems (one of them a translation from her friend Octavio Paz, the Mexican poet), at least three of them are substantial and impor-

tant. In various ways they tend to circle back to the scenes and experiences that the author used earlier in her work. "In the Waiting Room," for instance, has the very young Elizabeth (named for the first time in her poetry) in Worcester, Massachusetts, in February 1918. She was seven years old that month. The waiting room is adjacent to a dentist's office where her Aunt Consuelo is keeping an appointment. While the child is looking at the *National Geographic* (whose photographs of highly exotic places and people perhaps anticipate the author's future life), she is shocked back to the present moment:

> Suddenly, from inside,
> came an *oh!* of pain
> —Aunt Consuelo's voice—
> not very loud or long.
> I wasn't at all surprised;
> even then I knew she was
> a foolish, timid woman.
> I might have been embarrassed,
> but wasn't. What took me
> completely by surprise
> was that it was *me*:
> my voice, in my mouth.
> Without thinking at all
> I was my foolish aunt,
> I—we—were falling, falling,
> our eyes glued to the cover
> of the *National Geographic*,
> February, 1918.

The little scream here is not nearly so devastating as the mother's scream that hangs over the Nova Scotia village in the story already referred to, but it is equally penetrating. Here, in the waiting room, once the *National Geographic* has been put aside, there is no real community as there is in the story, no vivid summer's day filled with common sensations. The child can see only "shadowy gray knees, / trousers and skirts and boots / and different pairs of hands / lying under the lamps." Thrown back on her own instincts, she experiences a kind of existential shock of identity. Miss Bishop evidently thought well of this poem. In 1974 the poet Richard Howard asked her to choose a favorite poem for his anthology *Preferences*. This was her choice; and she paired it with George Herbert's "Love Unknown," which she had previously admired for its "naturalness."

"In the Waiting Room" and most of the other late poems have a prose sense about them; that is, one might think that Miss Bishop has versified experiences that she could have put down in prose. She always admired writers like Leo Tolstoy and Flannery O'Connor as much as she admired any poet. On the other hand a late poem like "Night City" (as seen from a plane) is as surrealistic as any of her poems of the 1930s. As she dealt more closely with her own experience, though, the "naturalness" increased; perhaps one could apply this remark to the whole range of her work. "The Moose" has a high degree of "naturalness," and yet there is something visionary about it. Although it was first published in 1972, not long after the author read it at Harvard, she later told George Starbuck that she had had it on her mind if not her desk for a long time: "I started that, I hate to say how many years ago, probably twenty. I had the beginning, the incident with the moose, it really happened; and the very end; and the poem just sat around." Indeed, in August 1947 she had written a letter to Marianne Moore describing the original incident.

"The Moose" recalls a bus trip through Nova Scotia and New Brunswick ("narrow provinces / of fish and bread and tea"). Through twenty-eight stanzas the details of the trip are recreated: the landscape, the houses, the bus stops, a sunset, the passengers' random conversation, fatigue, sleep. A temporary community emerges among strangers (as it could not among the people in the waiting room). Suddenly the bus stops; the driver turns off the lights:

> A moose has come out of
> the impenetrable wood
> and stands there, looms, rather,
> in the middle of the road.
> It approaches; it sniffs at
> the bus's hot hood.

And the vision emerges. Another poet would have elevated the style at this point and taken the subject beyond the "natural" level at which it has existed, but Miss Bishop has the courage to check this tendency. Her characters, including her observer (there is no *I* in the poem), feel a "sweet sensation of joy," but they are not ecstatic. The bus moves on; at the end there is only "a dim / smell of moose, an acrid smell of gasoline." This poem is as accessible as "The Burglar of Babylon," and it has made its way into many anthologies. It is a masterpiece of construction–the sentences played off against the stanzaic structures, the rhyming that varies from stanza to stanza–the work of a poet in full command of her resources.

"Crusoe in England" at first looks like a "literary" poem derived from a familiar source, but it incorporates as much precise observation as any-

thing that Miss Bishop wrote. In her interview with Starbuck she interestingly revealed that she, too, had once visited a desert island, Aruba ("–long before it was a developed 'resort.' I took a trip across the island and it's true that there are small volcanoes all over the place"). Miss Bishop perhaps uses Crusoe, now wiser and more complicated than he is in Daniel Defoe's novel, as an indirect way of reviewing her own experience. The poem that she created for him is one of the most spacious pieces that she wrote. In a fine essay on the poetry of this period, Lloyd Schwartz says:

> "Crusoe in England" is the most emotionally exhaustive study of a single character in all of Elizabeth Bishop's poetry–even more impressive because it is the result of a capacity for total empathy. And it is all the more moving because the concerns of the character, of "Crusoe," are so directly connected to the concerns Elizabeth Bishop expresses in her own voice.

Elizabeth Bishop published four more poems between *Geography III* and the end of her life, each remarkable in its way. One is an elegy for her friend Robert Lowell, whose death in 1977 had saddened her. The poem is called "North Haven" and recalls landscape that both poets had loved and written about, coastal Maine:

> You left North Haven anchored in its rock,
> afloat in mystic blue . . . And now–you've left
> for good: You can't derange, or re-arrange,
> your poems again. (But the Sparrows can
>   their song.)
> The words won't change again. Sad friend, you
>   cannot change.

At the time of her death she was the most honored of living American poets, honored most of all by other poets–John Ashbery, James Merrill, Anthony Hecht, and others, as she was acclaimed a generation ago by Randall Jarrell and Robert Lowell. After her death her publishers collected all her poems, including juvenilia and translations, in the *The Complete Poems, 1927-1979*. The following year, her editor, Robert Giroux, edited *The Collected Prose*.

Interviews:
"An Interview with Elizabeth Bishop," *Shenandoah*, 17 (Winter 1966): 3-19;

George Starbuck, "The Work!: A Conversation with Elizabeth Bishop," *Ploughshares*, 3, no. 3/4 (1977): 11-29.

References:

Ashley Brown, "Elizabeth Bishop in Brazil," *Southern Review*, 13 (Autumn 1977): 688-704.
  Describes the poet's life and work in Brazil from 1951 to 1967.

Randall Jarrell, *Poetry and the Age* (New York: Knopf, 1953), pp. 234-236.
  Jarrell's oft-quoted review of Bishop's first book, *North & South*.

Robert Dale Parker, *The Unbeliever: The Poetry of Elizabeth Bishop* (Champagne: University of Illinois Press, 1988).
  A study of Bishop's poetry as it developed, in the tradition of other American poets.

Lloyd Schwartz and Sybil P. Estess, eds. *Elizabeth Bishop and Her Art* (Ann Arbor: University of Michigan Press, 1983).

Collects all major scholarship on Bishop to date, excerpts numerous reviews and commentaries, and includes a section, "In Her Own Words," of excerpts of Bishop's own reviews and essays. Major essays by David Kalstone, Helen Vendler, Robert Pinsky, David Lehman, Penelope Laurans, Alan Williamson, Bonnie Costello, Lloyd Schwartz, and Willard Spiegelman.

Anne Stevenson, *Elizabeth Bishop* (New York: Twayne, 1966).
  The first full-length study of Bishop's life and work.

Thomas Travisano, *Elizabeth Bishop: Her Artistic Development* (Charlottesville: University Press of Virginia, 1988).
  A study of the changes in Bishop's poetry over the course of her career.

World Literature Today, special issue on Elizabeth Bishop, 51 (Winter 1977).
  Presents a variety of material on Bishop.

Ray Bradbury

This entry was updated by Gary K. Wolfe (Roosevelt University) from his entry in DLB
8, Twentieth-Century American Science Fiction Writers.

Places	Hollywood Waukegan, Ill.	The American Southwest	Mexico
Influences and Relationships	Edgar Rice Burroughs Edgar Allan Poe Jules Verne	Robert Heinlein Henry Kuttner August Derleth	Walt Whitman L. Frank Baum
Literary Movements and Forms	Pulp Science Fiction "Lyric" Short Story Satire	Fantasy Fiction American Romanticism	Midwestern Regionalism
Major Themes	Childhood and Nostalgia Space Travel	Alienation The Nature of Evil The Supernatural	Technology as a Dehumanizing Force
Cultural and Artistic Influences	Science and Technology	Science Fiction Movies	
Social and Economic Influences	Censorship ("Bookburning") Small-Town Life	The Threat of Nuclear War The Depression	Racism Illegal Immigration McCarthyism

See also the Bradbury entry in DLB 2, American Novelists Since World War II.

BIRTH: Waukegan, Illinois, 22 August 1920, to Leonard Spaulding and Esther Moberg Bradbury.

MARRIAGE: 27 September 1947 to Marguerite McClure; children: Susan, Ramona, Bettina, Alexandra.

AWARDS: Selected best author of 1949 by National Fantasy Fan Federation; Benjamin Franklin Magazine Award for "Sun and Shadow," 1954; National Institute of Arts and Letters Award in Literature, 1954; California Literature Medal Award, Fiction Gold Medal for *Fahrenheit 451*, 1954; Boys Club of America Junior Book Award for *Switch on the Night*, 1956; Academy Award nomination and Golden Eagle Film Award for *Icarus Montgolfier Wright* (screenplay), 1963; Mrs. Ann Radcliffe Award, 1965 and 1971; Writers' Guild of America West Valentine Davies Award, 1974.

BOOKS: *Dark Carnival* (Sauk City, Wis.: Arkham, 1947; abridged edition, London: Hamish Hamilton, 1948);
The Martian Chronicles (Garden City, N.Y.: Doubleday, 1950); revised as *The Silver Locusts* (London: Rupert Hart-Davis, 1951);
The Illustrated Man (Garden City, N.Y.: Doubleday, 1951; revised edition, London: Rupert Hart-Davis, 1952);
The Golden Apples of the Sun (Garden City, N.Y.: Doubleday, 1953; revised edition, London: Rupert Hart-Davis, 1953);
Fahrenheit 451 (New York: Ballantine, 1953; abridged edition, London: Rupert Hart-Davis, 1954);
Switch on the Night (New York: Pantheon, 1955; London: Rupert Hart-Davis, 1955);
The October Country (New York: Ballantine, 1955; London: Rupert Hart-Davis, 1956);
Dandelion Wine (Garden City, N.Y.: Doubleday, 1957; London: Rupert Hart-Davis, 1957);
A Medicine for Melancholy (Garden City, N.Y.: Doubleday, 1959); revised as *The Day It Rained Forever* (London: Rupert Hart-Davis, 1959);
The Small Assassin (London: New English Library, 1962);
Something Wicked This Way Comes (New York: Simon & Schuster, 1962; London: Rupert Hart-Davis, 1963);

Ray Bradbury around the age of twenty-five

R is for Rocket (Garden City, N.Y.: Doubleday, 1962; London: Rupert Hart-Davis, 1968);
The Anthem Sprinters and Other Antics (New York: Dial, 1963);
The Machineries of Joy (New York: Simon & Schuster, 1964; abridged edition, London: Rupert Hart-Davis, 1964);
The Vintage Bradbury (New York: Vintage, 1965);
The Autumn People (New York: Ballantine, 1965);
Twice 22 (Garden City, N.Y.: Doubleday, 1966);
Tomorrow Midnight (New York: Ballantine, 1966);
S is for Space (Garden City, N.Y.: Doubleday, 1966; London: Rupert Hart-Davis, 1968);
I Sing the Body Electric! (New York: Knopf, 1969; London: Rupert Hart-Davis, 1970);
The Wonderful Ice Cream Suit and Other Plays (New York: Bantam, 1972; London: Hart-Davis, MacGibbon, 1973);

The Halloween Tree (New York: Knopf, 1972; London: Hart-Davis, MacGibbon, 1973);

Zen and the Art of Writing and the Joy of Writing (Santa Barbara, Cal.: Capra Press, 1973);

When Elephants Last in the Dooryard Bloomed (New York: Knopf, 1973; London: Hart-Davis, MacGibbon, 1975);

Pillar of Fire and Other Plays (New York, Toronto & London: Bantam, 1975);

Long After Midnight (New York: Knopf, 1976);

Where Robot Mice and Robot Men Run Round in Robot Towns (New York: Knopf, 1977; London: Hart-Davis, MacGibbon, 1979);

The Stories of Ray Bradbury (New York: Knopf, 1980);

Death is a Lonely Business (New York: Knopf, 1985).

PLAY PRODUCTIONS: *The Meadow*, Hollywood, Huntington Hartford Theatre, March 1960;

Way in the Middle of the Air, Hollywood, Desilu Gower Studios, August 1962;

Yesterday, Today, and Tomorrow, Hollywood, Desilu Gower Studios, June 1963;

The World of Ray Bradbury, Hollywood, Coronet Theater, October 1964;

The Wonderful Ice Cream Suit, Hollywood, Coronet Theater, February 1965;

Dandelion Wine, New York, Lincoln Center, April 1967;

The Anthem Sprinters, Beverly Hills, Beverly Hills Playhouse, October 1967;

Any Friend of Nicholas Nickleby's is a Friend of Mine, Hollywood, Actor's Studio West, August 1968;

Christus Apollo (cantata), by Jerry Goldsmith, text by Bradbury, Los Angeles, Royce Hall, University of California, December 1969;

Leviathan '99, Hollywood, Samuel Goldwyn Studio, Stage 9 Theater, November 1972;

Madrigals for the Space Age, by Lalo Schifrin, text by Bradbury, Los Angeles, Dorothy Chandler Pavilion, February 1973;

Pillar of Fire, Fullerton, California State College, Little Theatre, December 1973.

MOTION PICTURES: *It Came From Outer Space*, screen story by Bradbury, Universal, 1953;

Moby Dick, screenplay by Bradbury and John Huston, Warner Bros., 1956;

Icarus Montgolfier Wright, by Bradbury and George C. Johnson, Format Films, 1963;

An American Journey, U.S. Government, 1964;

Picasso Summer, by Bradbury and Ed Weinberger, Warner Bros. / Seven Arts, 1972;

Something Wicked This Way Comes, Walt Disney Studios, 1983.

OTHER: *Timeless Stories for Today and Tomorrow*, edited by Bradbury (New York: Bantam, 1952);

The Circus of Dr. Lao and Other Improbable Stories, edited by Bradbury (New York: Bantam, 1956).

PERIODICAL PUBLICATIONS:
FICTION
"Hollerbochen's Dilemma," *Imagination!* (1938);

"The Piper," *Futuria Fantasia*, no. 4 (1940);

"Pendulum," by Bradbury and Henry Hasse, *Super Science Stories*, no. 3 (November 1941);

"Bright Phoenix," *Magazine of Fantasy and Science Fiction*, 24 (May 1963): 23-27.

NONFICTION
"Day After Tomorrow: Why Science Fiction," *Nation*, 176 (2 May 1953): 364-367;

"Marvels and Miracles–Pass It On!," *New York Times Magazine*, 20 March 1955, pp. 26-27, 56-57;

"The Joy of Writing," *Writer*, 69 (October 1956): 293-295;

"A Serious Search for Weird Worlds," *Life*, 49 (24 October 1960): 116-130;

"How to Keep and Feed a Muse," *Writer*, 71 (July 1961): 7-12;

"Cry the Cosmos," *Life*, 53 (14 September 1962): 86-94;

"Remembrances of Things Future," *Playboy*, 12 (January 1965): 99, 102, 191;

"The Secret Mind," *Writer*, 78 (November 1965): 13-16;

"How, Instead of Being Educated in College, I was Graduated from Libraries or Thoughts from a Chap Who Landed on the Moon in 1932," *Wilson Library Bulletin*, 45 (May 1971): 843-851;

"From Stonehenge to Tranquility Base," *Playboy*, 19 (December 1972): 149, 322-324.

Although Ray Bradbury remains perhaps the best known of all science-fiction writers, and although his stories and themes have permeated all areas of American culture as have those of no other science-fiction writer–through more than five hundred stories, poems, essays, plays, films, television plays, radio, music, and even comic books–Bradbury is still something of an anomaly in the genre. In a field that thrives on the fantastic and the marvelous, Bradbury's best stories celebrate the mundane; in a field preoccupied with the future, Bradbury's vision is firmly rooted in the past–both his past and the past of America. In a popular genre where reputations, until recently, have been made through ingenious plotting and the exposition of scientific and technological ideas, Bradbury built an enormous reputation virtually on style alone–and then, when the rest of the writers in the genre began to discover the uses of stylistic experimentation, turned ever more toward self-imitation and the recapitulation of earlier themes. When science fiction seemed almost exclusively a literature of technophiles, Bradbury became a lone symbol of the dangers of technology, even to the point of refusing to drive an automobile or fly in an airplane. But when science fiction came increasingly to adopt an ambivalent attitude toward unchecked technological progress, Bradbury became an international spokesman for the virtues of spaceflight and technological achievement. Clearly Bradbury cannot be accused of following trends. He is his own most important referent, and despite his widely avowed love of earlier writers from Poe to Thomas Wolfe to Hemingway, it is in Bradbury's own midwestern background that one finds the most important sources for his fiction.

Bradbury is perhaps the most autobiographical of science-fiction writers, and this, too, seems anomalous: how, after all, can one construct meaningful future worlds from so much reference to the past and so little to the present? One answer, of course, is that Bradbury's science fiction is, in fact, seldom extrapolative, for the values Bradbury seeks to express are the values he associates with his own past. Bradbury was born and spent most of his childhood in Waukegan, Illinois, a small community north of Chicago, which was to become the "Green Town" of many later stories. Early in life he was introduced to the world of fantasy and the supernatural. By the time he was six, he had seen many horror movies–notably *The Cat and the Canary,* Lon Chaney's *The Hunchback of Notre Dame* and *The Phantom of the Opera*– and had developed a morbid fear of the dark. (His 1955 children's book, *Switch on the Night,* was based on these memories and designed to allay the fear of darkness for his own children.) His Aunt Neva, whose name was given to a character in a few stories and who received the dedication of the 1953 collection, *The Golden Apples of the Sun,* introduced him to fairy tales and to the Oz

books of L. Frank Baum, whom Bradbury later counted among his chief influences. Bradbury's father, Leonard Spaulding Bradbury, worked as a lineman for the Waukegan Bureau of Power and Light. Not only did "Leonard Spaulding" later become a Bradbury pseudonym, but even his father's mundane occupation was transformed into romance in the 1948 story "Powerhouse," collected in *The Golden Apples of the Sun.*

Numerous Bradbury stories, including several in his 1947 collection, *Dark Carnival,* can be traced back to specific events in his childhood. Even his earliest memories would later become raw material for his fiction: "The Small Assassin" (1946; collected in *Dark Carnival*), about a newborn infant who murders his parents, was supposedly drawn from the author's memories of his first two years of life. "The Lake" (1944; collected in *Dark Carnival*) is based on the experience of a cousin's near drowning in Lake Michigan when Bradbury was seven. The shadowy character called the "Lonely One" who is said to inhabit a ravine in *Dandelion Wine* (1957) is drawn from the author's own fears of such a character when he was eight. The preoccupation with libraries, most evident in *Something Wicked This Way Comes* (1962), is certainly related to the ten-year-old Bradbury's spending each Monday evening with his brother at the Waukegan Public Library. His fascination with circuses and carnivals may be related to the traveling shows of his youth and in particular to a day in 1931 when he appeared onstage as an audience volunteer with Blackstone the Magician. The stories "Uncle Einar" (1947) and "Homecoming" (1946), also collected in *Dark Carnival,* feature a character based on a favorite uncle named Einar, who moved away when Bradbury was fourteen. An early interest in science fiction and the future is indicated by Bradbury's discovery of the pulp magazine *Amazing Stories* in 1928, his discovery of Edgar Rice Burroughs's Martian stories in 1929 and of Jules Verne in 1932, and by his visit with his Aunt Neva to the Century of Progress exposition at the 1933 Chicago World's Fair.

Twice during his childhood, in 1926-1927 and again in 1932-1933, Bradbury lived with his family in Arizona, where his father hoped to find work after being laid off during the Depression. It is possible that these early impressions of the desert affected his later visions of Mars and, perhaps, his sensitive views of Mexican-Americans as well. But both moves were abortive, and in both cases the family returned to Waukegan.

The Bradburys did not move west permanently until their 1934 move to Los Angeles. Bradbury dates his career choice from about this time: at the age of fifteen, he began submitting short stories to major national magazines, hoping ultimately for a sale to the *Saturday Evening Post* but receiving no acceptance. Encouraged by sympathetic high-school literature teachers, however, he became active in his school's drama classes and wrote for school publications.

In 1937 Bradbury's first real connection with the world of science fiction began when he joined the Los Angeles Science Fiction League. There he met Henry Kuttner, a budding professional writer whose first story was published that same year and who would become something of a mentor to the younger writer. The league's fanzine, *Imagination!*, printed Bradbury's first published short story, "Hollerbochen's Dilemma," in 1938, and his increasing involvement as a science-fiction fan led him, in 1939, to begin his own mimeographed publication, *Futuria Fantasia*. That same year he attended the World Science Fiction convention in New York and visited the New York World's Fair.

At the age of twenty Bradbury was still living with his family and selling newspapers for income, but by this time a career as a writer seemed a real possibility. Bradbury had been listed in a national directory of fans of science fiction, and his letters were becoming familiar features of the letter columns in the professional pulp magazines. *Futuria Fantasia* lasted for only four issues, but in the last issue in 1940 Bradbury published a story called "The Piper," which gave early evidence of the central themes of *The Martian Chronicles* (1950). Aided by such professional writers as Robert Heinlein, Leigh Brackett, Jack Williamson, Edmond Hamilton, Ross Rocklynne, and Henry Hasse, he was finally able to break into professional markets in 1941 with "Pendulum," a story written in collaboration with Hasse that appeared in the November *Super Science Stories*. The following year he began selling stories to *Weird Tales*, which, though not a science-fiction pulp in the strictest sense, would prove during the next few years to be the most natural home for the fantasy and horror stories that would make up Bradbury's first collection, *Dark Carnival*. During this time Bradbury was living in Venice, California, which would indirectly provide imagery for much of his later fiction, including his Martian stories and stories of Mexican-Americans. Bradbury soon discovered that his dis-

tinctive poetic style would be more readily welcomed by *Weird Tales*, a few detective magazines, and eventually the "slicks" such as *American Mercury*, *Charm*, and *Mademoiselle*, than by the science-fiction magazines he had so avidly read as a teenager.

By 1944 Bradbury, exempt from the draft because of his poor vision, seemed aware that style was his strong point and became more conscious of developing it. As a teenager he had been briefly infatuated with Thomas Wolfe; now he began to read writers whose work was more spare, more controlled, such as Jessamyn West, Sherwood Anderson, Eudora Welty, and Katherine Anne Porter. He was at the same time discovering new sources of material for his fiction. While selling newspapers in 1940, Bradbury had kept an office in a tenement inhabited largely by Mexican-Americans (whom he would feature prominently in several later stories). In 1945 his interest in Mexican culture deepened during a two-month-long automobile trip to Mexico, when Bradbury accompanied an artist friend to collect masks for the Los Angeles County Museum. Bradbury was increasingly impressed with the growing sense of an alien culture whose values were different from those of the United States, a sense of alienation later captured in stories such as "The Highway" (1950; collected in *The Illustrated Man*, 1951) and "And the Rock Cried Out" (1953; collected in *A Medicine for Melancholy*, 1959), both of which concern the plight of North Americans trapped in Mexican villages while nuclear war devastates the United States. Bradbury would draw more optimistic portraits of Mexican culture in other stories. "En La Noche" (1952) and the award-winning "Sun and Shadow" (1953), two of the stories collected in *The Golden Apples of the Sun*, emphasize what he took to be the uninhibited sensuality of Mexicans. In "Sun and Shadow," for example, a poor Mexican, tired of being treated as a "local," deliberately exposes himself to foil a North American fashion photographer on location; whenever the photographer attempts to take a picture, the Mexican appears and drops his pants.

What most impressed Bradbury about this trip to Mexico was the preoccupation with death that seemed to permeate much of the culture. The trip eventually led to Guanajuato, northwest of Mexico City, where Bradbury was horrified and fascinated by the underground catacombs with their upright rows of mummified remains. In 1978 Bradbury provided the text for a photographic essay on these mummies. This text was "The Next in Line" (1947), another of the stories in *Dark Carnival*. The longest of Bradbury's Mexican stories, it portrays the profound, immobilizing horror a young North American wife feels at the idea of being placed in such a crypt or dying in such a country. Besides the mummies, the most affecting of Bradbury's experiences in Mexico was probably the Day of the Dead celebration, which also figures prominently in "The Next in Line" and is the focus of "El Dia De Muerte" (1947). Whether or not this first real experience with an alien culture influenced other aspects of Bradbury's writing, such as his portrayal of aliens in his many Martian stories, is a matter of conjecture; much of what Bradbury seemed to find attractive about the Mexicans–their respect for the past and their uncomfortably easy union of religion, sensuality, and death–is reflected in his rather sketchy portrayal of the ancient Martian civilization in *The Martian Chronicles*.

Bradbury's reputation as a short-story writer had by the mid 1940s reached the point where book publication began to seem a logical next step. August Derleth, the Wisconsin author who had established the small fantasy press Arkham House primarily to publish in book form the fiction of H. P. Lovecraft and his circle, accepted "The Lake" for his 1945 anthology, *Who Knocks?*, and suggested that Bradbury might prepare a whole volume of fantasy and horror stories for Arkham House. Don Congdon, a New York editor and agent who in 1947 became Bradbury's agent, also began to explore the idea of a collection. His career clearly on the upswing, Bradbury was so confident of his own future output that on the eve of his wedding to Marguerite Mc-Clure in 1947, he claimed he burned more than a million words of his earlier writing that he felt did not meet his current standards.

Bradbury's career also seemed to be moving rapidly in several other directions. His first book, *Dark Carnival*, published by Arkham House in 1947, would bolster his reputation as a writer of weird fiction, but that was a kind of fiction that Bradbury was coming to write less and less frequently. From *Weird Tales* he had moved increasingly into such markets as *American Mercury, Mademoiselle, Charm, Harper's,* and the *New Yorker,* and his fiction was beginning to appear with some regularity in such mainstream collections as *The Best American Short Stories* and *Prize Stories: O. Henry Awards.* Even though many of his stories were fantasy and science fiction, Bradbury was gaining a

reputation as a sensitive stylist who tackled the contemporary social issues of racism and illegal immigration of Mexicans into this country. At the same time, the first of *The Martian Chronicles* stories, "The Million-Year Picnic," appeared in *Planet Stories* in 1946, and by 1949 Bradbury had won such wide acceptance among the legions of science-fiction fans from whom he had sprung that he was voted best science-fiction author of the year by the National Fantasy Fan Federation. With the assistance of shrewd editors and careful packaging of his stories in book form, Bradbury was able to exploit his varied range as a writer during the next twenty years.

One of Bradbury's most consistent themes in this early fiction is that of alienation–from technology, from a culture, even from the body itself–and while this theme is most readily apparent in the stories dealing with Mexicans in America and Americans in Mexico, it permeates other stories in *Dark Carnival* on an even more fundamental level. "The Next in Line" concerns not only the young wife's fear of the strange Mexican society she finds herself in, but also her growing rejection of her own body as she comes to realize that it, too, could become like the mummies of Guanajuato. The story is replete with sensual images of the wife's body, and as she begins to withdraw, she ceases eating, begins to sleep in the nude, and finally seems to abandon any possibility of physical action at all. Other stories in the collection reflect even more directly this discomfort with a fragile physical frame. "Skeleton" (1945) concerns a man so disgusted with his aching bones that he is persuaded by a mysterious little man to have his skeleton removed entirely. "There Was an Old Woman" (1944) portrays a reclusive old woman, literally separated from her body at death, whose passion for life is such that, in a reversal of the usual pattern in these stories of rejecting the body, she visits the mortuary and reclaims her corpse by melding back into it. In "The Crowd" (1943) a man finds that the same crowds seem to gather at all accidents–victims of earlier accidents, again separated from their too fragile bodies. "The Lake" concerns a little girl, drowned in Lake Michigan, whose body is washed up on the shore ten years later, just when her childhood boyfriend, now grown, revisits the site: she is preserved in death, while he has grown older. In "The Man Upstairs" (1947) a young boy becomes fascinated with the anatomy of a mysterious boarder, to the point of dissecting him and revealing him to be some sort of alien or vampire: it is the vampire's body, not his actions, that betrays him. Two stories that deal with a supernatural family, "Uncle Einar" and "Homecoming," focus on characters whose physical bodies alienate them from their surroundings. Uncle Einar is a friendly vampire, but he must stay hidden until he discovers that he can fly disguised as a kite. In a clever reversal on the same theme "Homecoming" depicts a boy who is out of place at his vampire family reunion simply because he is ordinary and has no supernatural powers or physical abnormalities. "The Small Assassin" initially focuses on the fear and alienation a mother feels for her newborn infant, but the infant's own homicidal impulses are later explained in terms of the fierce sense of rejection and hostility a newborn baby must feel at being thrust from the womb at birth. Alienation from children is also the theme of "Let's Play 'Poison'" (1946), which concerns a teacher ultimately murdered by his pupils.

Other stories in *Dark Carnival* concern different kinds of outcasts. "The Handler" (1947) is about a maladjusted mortician, disliked by his community, who wreaks vengeance on the citizens by playing practical jokes on them after they are dead (such as embalming a racist with black ink). In "The Jar" (1944) a hillbilly gains the respect of his community by purchasing from a traveling circus a jar containing the preserved remains of some mysterious creature, which are actually parts of a dismembered animal. When his unfaithful wife threatens to tell everyone what the jar really contains, he kills her and places her piecemeal into the jar. Still other stories touch upon mythical themes and suggest the hostility of elemental nature. In "The Scythe" (1943) a man takes over an abandoned wheat farm in the Midwest, only to find he has also taken on the task of the Grim Reaper. A character in "The Wind" (1943) discovers a hidden valley said to be the source of the world's winds and is pursued and eventually killed by winds.

While many of these tales are firmly connected to the *Weird Tales* tradition by their grotesque imagery and morbid preoccupation with decay and disintegration (many, in fact, would later be adapted with remarkable faithfulness by the horror comic books of Albert Feldstein), many are also compelling prose poems on themes of nature and mortality, slightly plotted and stripped of all but essentials of character and setting. Printed in an edition of only three thousand copies, *Dark Carnival* quickly became a collec-

tor's item among science-fiction and fantasy aficionados. It established clearly the curious mix of stories that was to become a trademark of later Bradbury collections, and it may have the distinction of having been the first book by a popular fantasy author to include stories from sources as diverse as *Harper's*, *Mademoiselle*, and *Weird Tales*.

Although it was significant in demarcating the first stage of Bradbury's professional career, *Dark Carnival*, available in such a limited edition from a specialty press, could not give Bradbury the wide public he eventually achieved. As always, the book market for fantastic literature was more receptive to novels than to short-story collections. When Walter Bradbury, a Doubleday editor, suggested in 1949 that Bradbury put together a book with at least a semblance of narrative continuity, the author's response was almost immediate; he had already published nearly a dozen stories depicting episodes in the colonization of Mars by Earthmen. He quickly produced an outline and began arranging stories and writing connective passages to give the book unity.

Not all of the Martian stories Bradbury had written lent themselves easily to a common narrative. "The Naming of Names" (1949), for example, presents the Martian landscape as exerting such a powerful influence on the colonists from Earth that they are eventually physically transformed into Martians. "The One Who Waits" (1949) depicts a Martian as a troll-like creature living at the bottom of a well, waiting to absorb the personalities of the Earthmen who visit. Stories such as these, which could not easily be made consistent with the larger group of Martian stories that portrayed the colonization of Mars in terms of the colonization of North America in the nineteenth century, were omitted from *The Martian Chronicles* to appear in later Bradbury collections. (Though the title "The Naming of Names" appeared as a bridge passage in *The Martian Chronicles*, the story itself was not collected until *A Medicine for Melancholy*, where it was retitled "Dark They Were, and Golden-Eyed"; "The One Who Waits" appeared in the 1964 collection, *The Machineries of Joy*.) Inappropriate though they may have been in terms of narrative consistency, these stories neatly encapsulate one of the most important themes of *The Martian Chronicles*: the theme that the environment transforms and finally absorbs the settler. While this theme was evident even in some of the stories in *Dark Carnival*, *The Martian Chronicles* gave full range to this and other Bradbury themes. The book was the first opportunity for readers to explore Bradbury's vision in a sustained narrative.

Published in May 1950, *The Martian Chronicles* was a seminal event in the history of science fiction's growing respectability. The book was widely reviewed by a critical community that extended well beyond the science-fiction subculture, most notably by Christopher Isherwood, who praised it lavishly in the journal *Tomorrow*. Impressed by Bradbury's poetic language and unconcerned by his lack of even a semblance of scientific verisimilitude, many readers found in the book a profound exploration of the state of America in 1950 with its fears of nuclear war, its problems with racism and growing book censorship, its confused values, and its yearning for a simpler life. By November 1952 the book had gone through six printings and had appeared in England as *The Silver Locusts;* during the next several years it would remain constantly in print in paperback and be translated into more than thirty foreign language editions, one of which (1955) featured an introduction by Jorge Luis Borges.

Science-fiction readers have criticized *The Martian Chronicles* on the grounds that the Martian colonies of the book are little more than transplanted small towns from the American Midwest of the 1920s. But Bradbury was certainly conscious of this and has repeatedly maintained that his Mars is not a projection of the future but rather a mirror of American life. Indeed the subject matter of the book is more history than science, and what technology the book features is largely technology in the service of exploring new frontiers. Bradbury does not dwell on making machines believable any more than he dwells on making his Mars astronomically accurate; his real concern, it may be argued, is to explore some of the key issues in American history—capitalism, technology, the family, the role of imagination—in a context free of historical constraints. The central myth of the book is the myth of the frontier, and the chronology that Bradbury has imposed upon his stories and bridge passages makes this clear.

After a brief prologue that presents the rocket ship as a harbinger of summer to a midwestern community locked in winter, the narrative begins with the story "Ylla" (1950), which establishes the purely fanciful Martian setting of crystal houses and wine trees and introduces the Martians, who telepathically sense the impending arrival of Earthmen and react with both wonder and fear. Ylla, a Martian wife, is romantically transported by her dream-images of the tall, strange aliens, but her husband senses danger and participates in the murder of these first arrivals. A second expedition from Earth, in the story "The Earth Men" (1948), is also quickly dispatched in a tale that deliberately parodies the notion of triumphant explorers arriving in a new world. In this case the explorers are regarded as hallucinations by the Martians, who attempt a cure by destroying them. "The Third Expedition" (1948), originally titled "Mars Is Heaven," which recalls Bradbury's earlier horror stories, makes full use of the Martians' telepathic abilities to introduce one of the major themes of the book: that of the past as a trap. This time the Earthmen find on Mars what appears to be a community made up of their own memories of childhood and family. Seduced by this telepathic hallucination, they, too, are destroyed, unable until it is too late to overcome the powerful pull of their own past lives. To survive in the new environment, one must be willing to forgo the past entirely.

Unwittingly, however, the Earthmen have already begun the conquest of Mars. By the time of the fourth expedition, in "—And the Moon Be Still as Bright" (1948), virtually all the Martians have died from chicken pox brought by the earlier explorers. Suddenly the perspective on the Martians shifts. No longer are they viewed as the monsters of "The Third Expedition" or the middle-class burghers of "Ylla"; instead, they are seen as the last scions of a civilization that had united art and technology and religion into the kind of stable society that Earthmen seem unable to maintain. In this story the focus is on the different kinds of Earthmen who come to Mars: Spender, sensitive to the fragile Martian environment and cynical about the inevitable destruction of it by future immigrants, who becomes the first American to be transformed by the new environment and comes to think of himself as the last Martian, even to the point of plotting to kill all future arrivals; Parkhill, the small-minded exploiter who seeks to make the planet over in the image of Earth; and Captain Wilder, the man of reason who shares Spender's fears but also realizes the inevitability of men such as Parkhill and the futility of trying to preserve Mars as it is.

A short bridge passage titled "The Settlers" (1950) introduces the second major section of the book, which deals with the colonization of Mars by a wide variety of Americans. (Except for the in-

Bradbury shortly after the release of the film Fahrenheit 451 *in 1966 (Wide World Photos)*

volvement of one or two Mexicans, Bradbury sees the expansion to Mars as a peculiarly American project. He offers the excuse that other nations were too preoccupied with warmongering to devote energy to settling new planets.) The following story, "The Green Morning," clarifies the merging parallel with American history. Little more than a vignette, it tells of Benjamin Driscoll, who goes about seeding Mars with trees in the fashion of Johnny Appleseed. By the time of "Night Meeting" (1950) the settlement of Mars is well underway. This story, which comes as something of an interlude in the ongoing narrative of Martian colonization, reemphasizes the theme of "The Third Expedition": that one must live in the present. But "the present," the reader learns, is subjective: on a lonely road at night Tomás Gomez encounters a Martian, only to find that the Martian sees the world differently. For the Martian, the ancient civilization of Mars thrives, while for Tomás, it lies in ruins, and the new Earth society thrives. Though this apparent time warp is not explained, the story serves as a reminder that the new society on Mars is built in the shadow of an earlier civilization, just as America was built in the shadow of Indian civilizations. This story, which proclaims the integrity of the vanished Martian society, is ironically contrasted later in the volume by "The Martian" (1949), in which a surviving Martian seeks to win acceptance among Earthmen by transforming himself into whatever human form is more acceptable to them. By now the Americans are firmly in control, and it is the Martians who must conform.

This section of the book also explores some of the reasons why people go to Mars. In "Way in the Middle of the Air" (1950) blacks emigrate to escape the oppression of the American South. In "Usher II" (1950) a character named Stendahl builds a mechanized monument to Edgar Allan Poe in defiance of a growing trend toward censorship of all forms of imaginative literature on Earth. (An earlier story, "The Exiles" [1949] in the 1951 collection, *The Illustrated Man*, had even depicted Mars as a haven for the ghosts of imaginative writers whose books were banned on Earth.) The father in "The Million-Year Picnic" flees the hectic rat race of American life and the impending nuclear war. For these characters, Mars represents less an opportunity for exploitation than freedom from an oppressive past and from a society which is rapidly moving toward self-destruction.

The final section of *The Martian Chronicles* concerns the effect of a massive nuclear war on Earth upon the Martian settlers. As with his stories that deal with Americans trapped in Mexico during the nuclear war, Bradbury's premise is that Americans will flock home at the first sign of war. The exploitation of Mars thus comes to an abrupt halt, and in "The Off Season" (1948) those who had greedily sought to acquire land and wealth, such as Sam Parkhill from "–And the Moon Be Still as Bright," find their wealth meaningless. "The Silent Towns" (1949) depicts the loneliness and alienation felt by the few who remain on Mars; the loneliness is so great that in "The Long Years" (1948) a man builds a whole family of robots to keep him company. The robots outlive the man and continue the meaningless charade of family life long after he has died. This idea of technology surviving its makers is also the subject of "There Will Come Soft Rains" (1950), which details the disintegration of a mechanized house on Earth which continues to function long after the family that had lived in it dies in the atomic war.

"The Million-Year Picnic," the final story in the book, synthesizes many of the themes of the earlier stories into what remains one of Bradbury's most memorable short stories. A family escapes the nuclear devastation on Earth by migrating to Mars in a family rocket, which the father promptly destroys upon their arrival. The rocket is only the first of many reminders of the old civilization to be abandoned. As soon as Earth civilization dies, the radio becomes useless, and as the family explores the dead Martian cities in search of a place in which to settle, the father ceremoniously buries stocks, bonds, and other documents

symbolic of the way of life he has chosen to reject (in clear contrast to earlier, unsuccessful settlers who sought to transfer that way of life to Mars). Throughout the story Bradbury gradually builds a pattern of imagery in which the family–particularly the father–is described in terms of features of the Martian landscape, and this invites the reader to come more and more to think of them as somehow native to this environment. Without the dramatic physical transformation of "Dark They Were, and Golden-Eyed" or the pathological rejection of humanity by Spender in "–And the Moon Be Still as Bright," Bradbury presents a convincing parable of the need to adapt to the new environment. When the father promises to show his children some real Martians, it comes as little surprise that what he shows them are their own reflections in the still waters of a canal.

Less than a year after the publication of *The Martian Chronicles* Bradbury brought out a second Doubleday collection, *The Illustrated Man*. Again Bradbury tried to connect the stories by means of a framing device. In this case each story acts out one of myriad illustrations on the skin of an ominous character whom a young man meets on a country road in Wisconsin, but here the frame is much slighter, and there is no attempt to connect the various stories into any kind of an overall narrative. Four of the stories are set on Mars, and two of these have clear connections to *The Martian Chronicles* stories. "The Other Foot" (1951), perhaps a sequel to "Way in the Middle of the Air," concerns a Mars settled mostly by blacks, who see the coming of white men in the wake of a devastating atomic war as an opportunity to reverse the pattern of racism they had suffered on Earth; in the end their compassion gets the better of them. "The Exiles" reiterates the theme of "Usher II" by depicting ghosts of imaginative writers surviving on Mars until the last copies of their books are burned. Thematically, this fantasy also anticipates the growing concerns with book burning that would be a central feature of *Fahrenheit 451* (1953). A third Martian story, "The Fire Balloons" (1951), seems unconnected with *The Martian Chronicles* except in setting, but this thoughtful parable on whether a benign alien life-form can be said to have achieved Christian salvation represents an unusual early treatment of a serious religious theme in science fiction. A second religious story in this collection, "The Man" (1949), is considerably less successful with its portrait of an obsessed rocket captain who travels around the galaxy in search of the Messiah after narrowly missing his advent on an alien planet.

"The Concrete Mixer" (1949), though not set on Mars, manages successfully to capture the social criticism implicit in *The Martian Chronicles* in a much more direct and satirical way: a planned Martian invasion of Earth is foiled not by military might but by the corruption of the Martians themselves in the face of America's relentlessly materialistic culture. Other stories in *The Illustrated Man* return to familiar Bradbury subjects. In "The Veldt" (1950) children murder their parents in an automated playroom, and in "Zero Hour" (1947) children spearhead an alien invasion. "The Highway" concerns a Mexican peasant whose way of life is undisturbed by the atomic war to the north, while in "The Fox and the Forest" (1950) time-travelers escape a dystopian future by hiding in the Mexico of 1938. "The City" (1950) is about an automated monstrosity that waits twenty thousand years for the opportunity to chop up some representatives of humanity who had abandoned it so long ago.

Several of the stories dwell on various aspects of Bradbury's continuing fascination with the romance of space travel. In the simplest of these, "The Rocket" (1950), a poor Italian manages to save enough to buy a rocket simply to give his children a view of outer space. "The Rocket Man" (1951) clearly views the rocket pilot as a romantic hero who dies a romantic death by falling into the sun. Bradbury undercuts the glamour of this by telling the story from the point of view of the son of the rocket man and dealing with the anguish of the wife, for whom the sun will always be a reminder of her husband's death. "No Particular Night or Morning" (1951) is a kind of epistemological fable of a spaceman who, freed of all referents of time and space, comes to doubt the reality of his own past and finally his own surroundings. "Kaleidoscope" (1949), which Bradbury later dramatized, describes the radio conversations of survivors of an exploded spaceship as they drift apart, toward certain death. In the most romantic of these deaths, one of the spacemen falls to earth as a flaming meteor.

By 1952 Bradbury's reputation was firmly established, and *The Ray Bradbury Review*, a fanzine, was devoted exclusively to his work. Bradbury began his involvement with Hollywood by providing an original screen story for a film that would eventually be released as *It Came From Outer Space*

(1953). For Bantam Books he edited an anthology of fantasy fiction, *Timeless Stories for Today and Tomorrow* (1952), that clearly revealed his predilection for psychological symbolism over scientific extrapolation as a basis for fantastic fiction. His early horror fiction began to reappear in comic books. In August 1953 film director John Huston invited him to Ireland to work on the screenplay for *Moby Dick* (1956), and Bradbury's experiences with the Irish later proved a rich mine of material for stories and plays, just as his experiences with Mexicans had been eight years earlier.

In 1953 Bradbury's fourth collection of short stories was also published. Drawing on stories originally published between 1945 and 1953, *The Golden Apples of the Sun* abandoned the frame narrative linking the stories of his two previous collections and freely mixed stories of all genres—fantasy, crime, science fiction, humor, and realism. It was the first of Bradbury's collections to be clearly addressed to a nonspecialty market; fewer than half the stories could be labeled fantasy or science fiction, and only two of them came from the science-fiction magazines (a market Bradbury had understandably moved away from as he began regularly selling to more prestigious markets, but which he never abandoned entirely).

Of the handful of science-fiction stories in the book, one, "The Wilderness," almost serves as a gloss on *The Martian Chronicles*. First published in 1952, the story is little more than a plotless sketch of the anxieties of women preparing to join their husbands on Mars. But the rocket is leaving from Independence, Missouri, and the obvious parallels with the westward movement of the nineteenth century give Bradbury a chance to make this frontier aspect of his Martian stories more explicit than in any of his previous stories. The other science fiction in the book shows Bradbury moving in other directions. Both "The Fog Horn" (1951), which became the barely recognizable basis of the 1953 film *The Beast from 20,000 Fathoms*, and "A Sound of Thunder" (1952) reveal an emerging interest in dinosaurs, and "A Sound of Thunder" reiterates the favorite Bradbury theme of the profound effect of the past on the present, depicting a time-travel safari that inadvertently changes the modern world when a hunter steps on a prehistoric butterfly. The title story, written apparently to illustrate a line from Yeats's "Song of Wandering Aengus," achieves some poetic power at the expense of the outlandish premise that a rocket might deliberately fly into the sun to scoop up "solar matter" for use as an energy source on Earth. But the most effective of Bradbury's science fiction in this collection is thematically related to *Fahrenheit 451* and is indirectly alluded to in that novel. "The Pedestrian" (1951) is a chilling satire of a future society when addiction to television has become such a norm that a man can be arrested for antisocial behavior merely for taking a walk. This growing fear of the impact of technology on daily life is also expressed in "The Murderer" (1953), which concerns a rebellious technophobe who "murders" the automatic appliances and gadgets in his house and is promptly arrested, and in "The Flying Machine" (1953), in which a wise emperor in ancient China executes a man who invents a flying machine when the emperor realizes the device's potential use as a weapon.

The collection also contains some of Bradbury's more sensitive nonfantastic portrayals of Mexicans and Mexican-Americans in "I See You Never" (1947), "En La Noche" (1952), and "Sun and Shadow"; and it reprints for the first time some of his stories concerning the loneliness and isolation of small towns and rural areas, including "The April Witch" (1952), "Invisible Boy" (1945), "The Great Fire" (1949), and "The Great Wide World Over There" (1952). It also includes Bradbury's story of racism in a small town, "The Big Black and White Game" (1945). "The Meadow" (1953), about a night watchman who persuades a movie producer not to destroy the sets of old movies, reveals Bradbury's growing fascination with the details of movie making. While *The Golden Apples of the Sun* may be of limited interest to the reader concerned with Bradbury's contributions to science fiction, it nevertheless was the first of his books to reveal his breadth and variety as a writer of short stories.

Later in 1953 Bradbury published what would become his only work to approach *The Martian Chronicles* in popularity and influence. *Fahrenheit 451* had been germinating as early as 1947 when Bradbury wrote a short story, "Bright Phoenix," about a small town whose residents foil government book burnings by each memorizing one of the censored texts. (Bradbury eventually published this, in a slightly revised form, in the May 1963 issue of the *Magazine of Fantasy and Science Fiction*.) In 1951 this basic premise involving government book banners was expanded to novella length as *The Fireman*, which appeared in the February issue of *Galaxy*. Expanded again to twice the length of *The Fireman*, *Fahrenheit 451* became Bradbury's first and best novel.

Although hindsight invites the reader to view *Fahrenheit 451* as a passionate attack on censorship and perhaps on the McCarthyism of the early 1950s as well, the book is equally an attack on the growing power of mass culture, particularly television, whose dynamics disallow complexity of thought and which consistently falls prey to the demands of special interest groups. Above all, the book-burning firemen of the novel are concerned that culture be made inoffensive, non-threatening, and universally accessible. Books, they feel, confuse citizens with contradictory values and ambivalent portrayals of human behavior. Beatty, the fireman supervisor who explains this to the protagonist, Montag (who has begun to exhibit an unhealthy interest in the books he is burning), traces this tradition of book burning throughout American history; Benjamin Franklin, according to the history of the firemen, became America's first "fireman" in this new sense when he sought to limit the distribution of Royalist pamphlets in the colonies. The history is not as distorted as it may seem: one of the strengths of Bradbury's argument in the novel is that he sees book burning as not simply a totalitarian phenomenon but one that has at least some roots in the process of democratization that led to the rise of American mass culture in the first place.

As with his other science-fiction settings, Bradbury makes little effort to paint a convincing portrait of a possible future society; instead, he strips the story of all but essential details, characters, and images that are needed to make his point. The novel takes place in what appears to be a totalitarian state, but the only feature of this totalitarianism that the reader sees is the book burning, and even that does not seem to be in the service of any particular political philosophy. In fact, it is suggested that the totalitarianism of this state is simply mass culture enforced by law. Nor is there much evidence of technological advancement in this future society; the chief image of technology is the Mechanical Hound, a rather baroque robot version of the traditional firemen's mascot, which is programmed to detect anomalous variations in body chemistry–presumably this is a hint of possible antisocial behavior–and to track down criminals like a real hound. Why a society given to the abolition of imagination would choose to cast its technology in such a bizarrely imaginative form as this is not explained, but as an image of the replacement by an ominous piece of machinery of a tradition of middle-class society, the Hound is effective.

The novel ends when Montag, who has finally come to reject his role as a book burner and has murdered Beatty, escapes a massive manhunt and joins a rural community of individuals who seek to preserve books by memorizing them. Whereas the society from which Montag has escaped is associated with the image of the salamander—the destructive fire-lizard—this new society associates itself instead with the image of the phoenix, rising from the ashes of the burning books. Culture, Bradbury says, periodically undergoes such self-destructive convulsions as the book burning represents and can only be preserved by the self-sacrificing efforts of a few individuals. The individuals in this communal society literally give up their identities to become the books they have memorized: ironically, this new culture seems to care as little for the individual as the mass culture from which Montag has escaped. The difference is that the new society allows for a multiplicity of viewpoints and hence holds out some hope for the eventual revival of the human imagination.

Throughout the first part of 1954 Bradbury remained in Ireland working on the screenplay for *Moby Dick*, toured Europe, and met such luminaries as Bernard Berenson and Bertrand Russell. In 1955, after returning to the United States, he became involved in television writing (primarily for "Alfred Hitchock Presents," later for Rod Serling's "The Twilight Zone") and collected many of the stories from *Dark Carnival* in a new anthology, *The October Country* (1955). Of the four new stories included in the collection, "The Dwarf" (1954) is closest to the earlier *Dark Carnival* stories in spirit, and "Touched with Fire" (1954) is clearly in the tradition of the crime stories that Bradbury had earlier sold to detective magazines. The other two indicate an emerging interest, perhaps sparked by the European trip, in literary and artistic culture. "The Watchful Poker Chip of H. Matisse" (1954) parodies bohemian artists and is surprisingly prescient in its delineation of what would later become known as "camp." In the story a man becomes an artist's hero by virtue simply of his appalling middle-class dullness, until he begins to replace parts of his body with works of art produced by masters. (Matisse's poker chip, for example, becomes a monocle.) "The Wonderful Death of Dudley Stone" (1954) concerns a brilliant writer who, under a murder threat from a jealous competitor, abandons his ca-

reer on the eve of his greatest success, destroying his new novel, only to reveal later that he felt he had lost his talent and needed a graceful way to retire anyway.

A second collection edited by Bradbury for Bantam, *The Circus of Dr. Lao and Other Improbable Stories*, appeared in 1956 and is notable chiefly for the title story by Charles G. Finney—a tale of a bizarre carnival that visits a small town and a clear influence on Bradbury's later novel on a similar theme, *Something Wicked This Way Comes*. The following year Bradbury's first book with no pretensions to being either science fiction or fantasy, *Dandelion Wine*, appeared. Essentially a series of sketches based on Bradbury's childhood in Waukegan, *Dandelion Wine* is distinguished primarily for its evocative style; its only real theme is that, through a series of experiences in a single summer, young Douglas Spaulding (a name compounded from Bradbury's own middle name and that of his father) comes to realize that he is alive. Although most of the contents of *Dandelion Wine* had been published previously as individual short stories and sketches, Bradbury made his greatest effort so far to create the impression of a unified book, revising the stories, writing bridge passages, and dropping individual titles and the table of contents. The result is a highly impressionistic, often moving, but essentially plotless series of episodes valueable not only for their collective portrait of budding adolescence and small-town life but also for the ways in which they reveal the sources of much of Bradbury's other fiction. While none of the new episodes are quite fantastic, many of them capture the fear and wonder of childhood that, transmogrified into the grotesque and the marvelous, provide the basis of Bradbury's science fiction and fantasy. The roots of his horror fiction, for example, can be seen in the episode originally titled "The Night" (1946), which concerns the fears of a family when a young boy is late returning at the end of a day (and which is based on Bradbury's own childhood fears of the neighborhood ravine and the "Lonely One" who reputedly lurked there). Another episode, "The Happiness Machine" (1957), presents a telling childhood view of technology in which machines can magically influence human behavior in ways not to be fully understood. The machine turns out to be more of a wish-fulfillment fantasy than a real invention, as are most of Bradbury's machines. More than any other single book, perhaps, *Dandelion Wine* consolidated Bradbury's reputation as a poet of small-town nostalgia and provided the clearest perspective to date on the essential sources of his overall vision.

By 1958 Bradbury had become one of the most financially successful of American writers and moved his family (now with four daughters) to the Cheviot Hills address in West Los Angeles where he now lives. Deeply involved in various film projects (most of which were never produced), he began to take an increasing interest in the adaptation of his works to other media, particularly the stage. But his reputation remained essentially that of a short-story writer, and another collection, *A Medicine for Melancholy*, including stories originally published between 1948 and 1959, appeared in February 1959. With half of the twenty-two stories either fantasy or science fiction, the collection represented the largest sampling of Bradbury's fantastic writing to appear in print (except for *The October Country*) since *The Illustrated Man* in 1951. But while the collection included samples of the now familiar Martian stories ("Dark They Were, and Golden-Eyed," "The Strawberry Window," 1954), horror stories ("Fever Dream," 1948), Mexican and Mexican-American stories ("The Wonderful Ice Cream Suit," 1958; "The Little Mice," 1955), and romantic views of space travel ("The End of the Beginning," 1956; "The Gift," 1952), it revealed few new directions in Bradbury's fiction. Most notable was the first appearance in book form of two stories based on Bradbury's experiences in Ireland, "The First Night of Lent" (1956) and "The Great Collision of Monday Last" (1958). Both are built around specific aspects of what he took to be the Irish character, such as their legendary drinking and their bicycle-riding habits. Two other stories in the collection later provided the basis for films: "Icarus Montgolfier Wright" (1956) for the animated short of the same title that was nominated for an Academy Award in 1963 and "In a Season of Calm Weather" (1957) for the feature *Picasso Summer* (1972). Perhaps the most notable story in the collection, "All Summer in a Day" (1954), concerns a group of school children on a rain-soaked Venus who get their first view of the sun, which emerges once every seven years when the clouds part.

Except for *Fahrenheit 451* Bradbury had not yet produced a truly unified, sustained work of fiction, and readers and publishers alike looked forward to a major novel, not made up of previously published stories, that would realize the narrative promise so long held out by Bradbury's short fiction. This novel turned out to be *Something Wicked This Way Comes*. A highly self-conscious work, full of allusions to such early Bradbury stories as "The Dwarf" and "The Skeleton," the novel suffers from an artificially inflated style and a barely controlled wealth of imagery and incident. Its theme–the struggle between the power of love and the power of evil–is handled in such a way that the main characters are reduced to symbolic archetypes. The strong point of the novel is the character of Charles Halloway–perhaps Bradbury's first true hero–whose melancholy and isolation are presented as foreshadowings of his final, lonely confrontation with the forces of evil represented by a traveling carnival.

Halloway's thirteen-year-old son, Will, is essentially Douglas Spaulding from *Dandelion Wine*–innocent, open, and optimistic. But Will's close friend Jim Nightshade is, as his name suggests, Will's antithesis. Warned by a traveling lightning-rod salesman of an impending storm, the boys find that, instead of the storm, a mysterious carnival arrives in town in the dead of night–"Cooger and Dark's Pandemonium Shadow Show"–which features a playerless calliope that screams perverted versions of hymns and funeral marches. As in much of Bradbury's earlier fiction, the carnival represents not only present evil, but also the vulnerability of the human form and the seductive dangers of the past. Two of its main attractions, the mirror maze and the carousel, involve returning to a past self (the mirror maze shows reflections of a younger self; the carousel runs backward and actually makes a person younger), and its featured performers are grotesque transformations of familiar characters. (The dwarf, for example, turns out to be the lightning rod salesman from the opening scene, shrunken and deformed.) Characters undergo endless transformations: one of the show's proprietors, Mr. Dark, turns out to be the Illustrated Man; the other, Mr. Cooger, becomes a twelve-year-old boy and later a wizened old man named "Mr. Electrico" (a name taken from an actual circus performer of Bradbury's youth). Miss Foley, the local schoolteacher, becomes a wailing little girl, and both Will and Jim are threatened with being transformed into wax dummies.

Charles Halloway, who works in a library, discovers that this carnival is a continuing source of evil in the world, returning every thirty or forty years to wreak havoc on a local population, and perhaps dating back to medieval Europe or before. Cooger and Dark, aided by a balloon-riding

DEATH IS A LONELY BUSINESS

A NOVEL BY

RAY BRADBURY

Dust jacket for Bradbury's 1985 detective novel that draws upon his memories of Venice, California

witch, engage Halloway in a struggle for the souls of the two boys, particularly Jim's, whose dark personality naturally attracts him to this evil. In a final showdown during a performance in which the witch is to catch a bullet in her teeth, Halloway wins his victory, his ultimate weapon nothing more than the power of laughter. The carnival is vanquished, but in the closing scene Halloway explains that it will return, that it ultimately resides in each individual, and that the struggle never really ends.

Despite the occasional power generated by the sheer wealth of invention in *Something Wicked This Way Comes*, the work failed to establish Bradbury as a significant novelist, and Bradbury began to focus more and more on dramatic writing. His first collection of published plays, *The Anthem Sprinters and Other Antics*, appeared in 1963. These four comic one-act plays all draw upon Bradbury's experiences as an American innocent in Ireland and somewhat make up in language what they lack in dramatic form. All set in a mythi-

cal pub called Heeber Finn's (and with Finn a continuing character), three of the plays–"The Great Collision of Monday Last," "The First Night of Lent," and "The Anthem Sprinters"–are adaptations of previously published short stories, and all deal with the comic recalcitrance and imagination of the Irish as displayed in relatively trivial episodes such as bicycle collisions and attempts to escape movie theaters before the national anthem is played.

The Machineries of Joy appeared in 1964, containing the now predictable mix of stories dealing with Mars, Mexico, Ireland, childhood, and show business, but with little that was new or different. "The Vacation" (1963) offers an earthbound variant on "The Million-Year Picnic," with its family abroad on an endless vacation in a depopulated United States; and "Almost the End of the World" (1957) provides a neat counter to the television-addicted world of "The Pedestrian" and *Fahrenheit 451* in a tale of sunspots wiping out all television and radio signals and forcing people to rediscover each other. With "The Drummer Boy of Shiloh" (1960) and "Perhaps We Are Going Away" (1962) Bradbury turns to historical fiction to depict worlds on the verge of imminent change, and "A Flight of Ravens" (1952) offers a more cynical view of the sophisticated literary life than the author had essayed thus far. "To the Chicago Abyss" (1963) provided the basis for one of Bradbury's more successful science-fiction plays with its depiction of a character in a post-nuclear-war age who goes about reminding people of life before the war.

By the mid 1960s Bradbury was devoting much of his time to drama. *The World of Ray Bradbury* opened in Los Angeles in 1964 and New York in 1965, and *The Wonderful Ice Cream Suit* opened as a musical in 1965. During this time publishers began repackaging much of Bradbury's earlier material in various forms. *R is for Rocket* (1962) and *S is for Space* (1966) consist mostly of previously anthologized stories repackaged for a teenage market, though *S is for Space* is significant for the appearance in a Bradbury anthology of "Pillar of Fire," a 1948 story concerning a man resurrected in a future world where he finds he is the last remnant of literary culture and imagination. *Twice 22* (1966) combined in one omnibus volume *The Golden Apples of the Sun* and *A Medicine for Melancholy;* and *The Autumn People* (1965) and *Tomorrow Midnight* (1966) are collections of comic-book adaptations of Bradbury stories from the early 1950s. *The Vintage Bradbury*

(1965), a representative selection by Bradbury of his own best works, established the author for the first time in a quality paperback format.

The next new collection of Bradbury's fiction did not appear until 1969, with *I Sing the Body Electric!*, which followed the almost formulaic mix of stories of his previous collections. The dangers of the past are again made apparent in many ways. "Night Call, Collect" (1949) concerns a man alone on the deserted post-*Chronicles* Mars, who is haunted by prerecorded phone calls planted by himself decades earlier. The only other Martian story in the book, "The Lost City of Mars" (1967), portrays a hidden, automated Martian city that seduces all who visit it with images drawn from their memories and fantasies; both stories are variations on stories published earlier in *The Martian Chronicles*. Two other stories deal with robots and how they can be used to preserve the past. In "Downwind from Gettysburg" (1969) the assassination of Lincoln is reenacted by a demented man named Booth who shoots a robot Lincoln obviously modeled on the Disneyland exhibit. "I Sing the Body Electric!" (1969) is a sentimental tale of a robot grandmother who raises a motherless family. "The Haunting of the New" (1969) is about a sumptuous mansion destroyed by fire and meticulously reconstructed—only to be haunted by memories of its previous reality. The book memorizers who preserve the past in earlier Bradbury stories are transformed into a failed writer who assumes the identity of Dickens by memorizing his works in "Any Friend of Nicholas Nickleby's is a Friend of Mine" (1966).

I Sing the Body Electric! also included the first appearance in a Bradbury anthology of one of his poems, "Christus Apollo," a Christmas cantata celebrating the Apollo space program in Christian terms. Bradbury's poetry, often characterized by an inflated diction that calls to mind an uncomfortable blend of Whitman and Genesis, came to constitute an increasing amount of his creative output. His first volume of poetry, *When Elephants Last in the Dooryard Bloomed* (an obvious homage to Whitman), appeared in 1973.

During the 1970s Bradbury continued to concentrate on drama and poetry, producing relatively little new fiction. His 1976 collection, *Long After Midnight*, drew heavily on his earlier stories. Nearly half of the twenty-two stories collected dated from before 1955, the earliest from 1946. While the collection had the virtue of bringing back into print some of Bradbury's more unusual

stories, such as the effective horror piece "The October Game" (1948) and his homage to Thomas Wolfe, "Forever and the Earth" (1950), its chief value may lie in the focus it places on a kind of Bradbury story that had long been characteristic, but infrequently collected: the story that depicts an epiphanal discovery of love between two people. "One Timeless Spring" (1946), perhaps the simplest of these stories, is a short evocation of the onset of puberty in a young boy as he first realizes the love he feels for a girl. A more complex story is "Interval in Sunlight" (1954), which portrays a bickering couple on vacation in Mexico who gradually come to appreciate their dependence on one another. "A Story of Love" (1976) concerns the growing mutual love of a teenage boy and his youthful teacher; "The Wish" (1973) deals with the realization a boy comes to of his love for his father. Deeply felt and sensitively written, albeit with occasional overtones of melodrama, it is in these stories that the most basic theme of all of Bradbury's fiction becomes apparent: the power of love to make permanent a valued moment from the past, to overcome evil, or simply to provide the communicative link that draws people together in trying circumstances.

The Stories of Ray Bradbury (1980) is a generous selection of Bradbury's shorter work which helped even further to cement Bradbury's reputation as a category unto himself, as dissimilar from other modern short-story writers as he is from the mainstream of modern science-fiction writers. More than just another recycling of earlier material, this collection provides an overview of Bradbury's career in a way that no earlier collection had, and the number of excellent stories in it is striking. Stories such as these assure Bradbury a permanent place in the history of the American short story, just as his introduction of stylistic sophistication and metaphorical use of science-fiction concepts in the late 1940s earned him a significant place in the history of science fiction. It does not seem at this time that he will attain a comparable stature as a poet or playwright, although his return to the novel form in 1985 with *Death is a Lonely Business* surprised many readers with its frankly autobiographical aspects and its exploration of a form new to Bradbury: the hard-boiled detective novel. Although dedicated to the memory of such masters of this form as Raymond Chandler and Dashiell Hammett, and despite the presence of a detective, Elmo Crumley, whose name seems derived from the contemporary hard-boiled writers Elmore Leonard and James Crumley, the novel is actually more soft-boiled than hard-boiled. Set in Venice, California, in 1949, the novel features an unnamed narrator trying to make a living selling to pulp magazines stories, which clearly are the early stories of Ray Bradbury. Although the characters seem soft-edged and sentimental in comparison to the characters of Hammett and Chandler, and although the resolution of the mystery may prove unsatisfactory to aficionados of the genre, the novel is particularly revealing to students of Bradbury's work. The Venice that Bradbury portrays is a decaying resort community, its canals untended, its oceanfront tourist attractions (including a roller coaster described as a "dinosaur") being dismantled. Despite a style that sometimes verges on affectation and self-parody, Bradbury gradually develops a moving portrait of a place and time in his life that he had seldom previously written about. The novel is thus most interesting as a gloss on his earlier work, suggesting, among other things, that the imagery of *The Martian Chronicles* is as much drawn from Bradbury's years in Venice in the 1940s as from his years in Waukegan in the 1920s. Flawed as it may be, *Death is a Lonely Business* is the most significant work of fiction Bradbury has published in more than a quarter century.

While much of the early criticism of Bradbury's science fiction for its scientific naïveté has abated as the genre has broadened its scope to make room for metaphor and poetry, it is ironic that in recent years the evocative style which led to Bradbury's reputation in the first place has become his greatest curse as a writer. Many readers feel that, while this highly intuitive style served a much-needed purpose in the popular fiction of the 1940s and 1950s, it later evolved into a pattern of self-imitation and style for its own sake. By these terms, Bradbury's most important work remains his earlier stories, and his experimentation with different forms (such as poetry, drama, or detective novels) represents a turning away from his areas of greatest strength in favor of forms which are less disciplined and demanding. At the same time, it would be unfair to expect Bradbury either to return to these earlier forms or, as his own character Dudley Stone did in "The Wonderful Death of Dudley Stone," suddenly abandon writing altogether in the face of the too-great expectations of his public. Bradbury has always been a resourceful artist, and any final conclusions about the value or direction of his later work would be premature. Of his ear-

lier work, however, there can be little doubt: for all its eclecticism and occasional stylistic excesses—perhaps even because of these—it stands as one of the most interesting and significant bodies of short fiction in modern American literature.

Interviews:

R. Walton Willems, "The Market is Not the Story," *Writers' Markets and Methods* (March 1948).

Harvey Breit, "A Talk with Mr. Bradbury," *New York Times Book Review,* 5 August 1951, p. 11.

Everett T. Moore, "A Rationale for Bookburners: A Further Word from Ray Bradbury," *American Library Association Bulletin,* May 1961, pp. 403-404.

F. A. Rockwell, "Ray Bradbury Speaks of Writing as Self-Discovery," *Author and Journalist,* 47 (February 1962).

Frank Roberts, "An Exclusive Interview with Ray Bradbury," *Writer's Digest,* 47 (February 1967): 40-44, 94-96; 47 (March 1967): 41-44, 87.

Pierre Berton, "Ray Bradbury: Cassandra on a Bicycle," in *Voices from the Sixties* (Garden City, N.Y.: Doubleday, 1967), pp. 1-10.

Paul Turner and Dorothy Simon, "Interview with Ray Bradbury," *Vertex* (April 1973): 24-27, 92-94.

Arnold Kunert, "Ray Bradbury: On Hitchcock and Other Magic of the Screen," *Journal of Popular Culture,* 7 (Summer 1973): 227-248.

Robert Jacobs, "The Writer's Digest Interview: Bradbury," *Writer's Digest,* 56 (February 1976): 18-25.

Bibliography:

William F. Nolan, *The Ray Bradbury Companion* (Detroit: Gale Research, 1975).
Elaborate, illustrated biographical and bibliographical compendium of all aspects of Bradbury's work through the mid 1970s.

References:

Kingsley Amis, *New Maps of Hell* (New York: Ballantine, 1960), pp. 90-97.

Classic study of science fiction as satire that discusses *Fahrenheit 451*.

Martin H. Greenberg and Joseph D. Olander, eds., *Ray Bradbury, Writers of the 21st Century Series* (New York: Taplinger, 1980).
Excellent collection of ten critical essays plus an extensive primary bibliography.

David Ketterer, *New Worlds for Old: The Apocalyptic Imagination, Science Fiction, and American Literature* (Bloomington: Indiana University Press, 1974), pp. 31-34.
Includes a brief discussion of Bradbury important for the manner in which it places him in the context of American apocalyptic literature.

Damon Knight, *In Search of Wonder: Essays on Modern Science Fiction*, second edition (Chicago: Advent, 1967), pp. 108-113.
Noted science-fiction writer's critique of Bradbury's use of the theme of childhood.

Sam Moskowitz, *Seekers of Tomorrow: Masters of Modern Science Fiction* (New York: Ballantine, 1967), pp. 351-370.
Traces Bradbury's life and career as a science-fiction writer.

William F. Nolan, "Ray Bradbury: Prose Poet in the Age of Space," *Magazine of Fantasy and Science Fiction*, 24 (May 1963): 7-22.
General appreciation of Bradbury as part of an entire issue of the magazine devoted to his work (also includes bibliography).

Robert Reilly, "The Artistry of Ray Bradbury," *Extrapolation*, 13 (December 1971): 64-74.
Defends Bradbury as a short-story writer and stylist.

Peter Sisario, "A Study of Allusions in Bradbury's *Fahrenheit 451*," *English Journal*, 59 (February 1970): 201-205.
Considers the novel in terms of its relation to other authors and to the climate of the times.

George Edgar Slusser, *The Bradbury Chronicles* (San Bernardino, Cal.: Borgo Press, 1977).
Analysis of Bradbury's major works from the point of view of a traditional literary critic.

William F. Touponce, *Ray Bradbury and the Poetics of Reverie: Fantasy, Science Fiction, and the Reader* (Ann Arbor, Mich.: UMI Research Press, 1984).
Unusual treatment of several Bradbury works in the context of the theories of French philosopher Gaston Bachelard.

Papers:
A collection of Bradbury's manuscripts is located at the University Library of the University of California, Los Angeles.

Robert Cormier

Sylvia Patterson Iskander
University of Southwestern Louisiana

Places	New England		
Influences and Relationships	Ernest Hemingway William Saroyan Graham Greene	John le Carré Ellery Queen	Ed McBain Thomas Wolfe
Literary Movements and Forms	Young Adult Literature	Journalism	The Short Story

Major Themes	Abuse of Power
	Individuality
	Search for
	  Identity
		Peer Pressure
		Alienation
		Family Bonds
		Moral Responsibility
			The Development
			  of the Writer
			Betrayal

Cultural and Artistic Influences	Catholic Schools	Small-Town Life	The Supernatural
Social and Economic Influences	Terroism Censorship	Corruption in Government	The Depression Race Relations

BIRTH: Leominster, Massachusetts, 17 January 1925 to Lucien Joseph and Irma Margaret Collins Cormier.

EDUCATION: Fitchburg State Teachers College, 1943-1944.

MARRIAGE: 6 November 1948, to Constance Senay; children: Roberta ("Bobbie") Susan, Peter Jude, Christine Judith, and Renee Elizabeth.

AWARDS: Associated Press Award for Best News Story in New England, 1959 and 1973; K. R. Thomson Newspapers, Inc. Award for a Human Interest column, 1974; Maxi Award for *The Chocolate War*, 1976; honorary Doctor of Letters degree, Fitchburg State College, 1977; finalist in California Young Reader Medal Award for *I Am the Cheese*, 1981; National Council of Teachers of English Adolescent Literature Assembly (ALAN) Award, 1983, for "significant contribution to the field of adolescent literature."

Robert Cormier (photo by Finkle Photography)

BOOKS: *Now and at the Hour* (New York: Coward-McCann, 1960);
A Little Raw on Monday Mornings (New York: Sheed & Ward, 1963);
Take Me Where the Good Times Are (New York: Macmillan, 1965);
The Chocolate War (New York: Pantheon, 1974; London: Gollancz, 1975);
I Am the Cheese (New York: Pantheon, 1977; London: Gollancz, 1977);
After the First Death (New York: Pantheon, 1979; London: Gollancz, 1979);
Eight Plus One (New York: Pantheon, 1980; London: Lions, 1988);
The Bumblebee Flies Anyway (New York: Pantheon, 1983; London: Gollancz, 1983);
Beyond the Chocolate War (New York: Knopf, 1985; London: Gollancz, 1985);
Fade (New York: Delacorte, 1988; London: Gollancz, 1988).

OTHER: "Forever Pedaling on the Road to Realism," in *Celebrating Children's Books: Essays in Honor of Zena Sutherland*, edited by Betsy Hearne and Marilyn Kay (New York: Lothrop, Lee & Shepard, 1981), pp. 45-53.

PERIODICAL PUBLICATIONS:
FICTION
"The Eye of the Beholder," *Sign Magazine*, 36 (March 1957): 40-43;

"My Father's Gamble," *Sign Magazine* (April 1961);
"Pretend, a Verb: To Make Believe," *St. Anthony Messenger*, 73 (April 1967): 32-40;
"No Time to Be Far from Embraces," *Extension*, 62 (November 1967): 36-41;
"The Day of the Fire Engines," *St. Anthony Messenger*, 78 (January 1971): 32-34, 58-61.

NONFICTION
"Creating *Fade*," *Horn Book*, 65 (March / April 1989): 166-173.

"Teen-agers' Laureate," the title conferred upon Robert Cormier by Tony Schwartz in *Newsweek* (16 July 1979), is fittingly bestowed upon this widely read and critically acclaimed author in the relatively new and somewhat amorphous genre referred to as young-adult literature. For many years a journalist, newspaper editor, and author of fiction, Robert Cormier never wrote for a young-adult audience until first his agent, then his publisher, suggested that *The Chocolate War* (1974) would be a fine young-adult book. Although Cormier did not change any aspect of his writing–perhaps a key to his success–he became known as a young-adult writer. Treating subjects such as terrorism, fear, power, betrayal, death, and courage, Cormier creates unforgettable stories that are suspenseful, psychologically thrilling, and bleak in outlook. While

Cormier's subject matter and pessimism sometimes give rise to controversy, there is no controversy about the clarity of his style, with its vivid figures of speech, lack of sentimentality, and refusal to patronize, or the wholehearted acceptance of his novels by teenagers.

The question arising most often among adult readers is: What kind of person could write such harshly realistic and pessimistic books for young people? Young adults appear to understand Cormier better; they are able to perceive that his novels are not entirely without hope. They ask other types of questions, offer praise, and accept the inevitable conclusions of the stories. Uncompromising in his pursuit of truth, Cormier has explained that he sees his novels as an antidote to the artificial realism of television, where one is always aware that the hero will survive to appear next week.

In addition to these books for young adults, Cormier also wrote three early novels and some fifty short stories. One of his more recent publications, a short-story collection entitled *Eight Plus One* (1980), written for adults but marketed for a young-adult audience, reveals a side of Cormier which is sensitive and compassionate. Any meeting with this slim man with graying hair and eyeglasses confirms the portrait of perceptive, friendly, unpretentious author whose goal is to entertain his audience and involve them emotionally in his stories.

Although his four children are now grown, Cormier continues to maintain the close rapport with his children that he established when they still lived at home. By listening to their problems, often in the wee hours of the morning, and by recalling his own turbulent teenage years, Cormier attunes himself to young people today. He also listens to his readers, saying he wished he had thought to call or write the authors he admired when he aspired to be a writer. He answers all mail with a return address and is gratified that his replies often provoke classroom discussions.

Born in the French Hill section of Leominster, Massachusetts, on 17 January 1925, Robert Edmund Cormier was one of eight children. However, when he was five, his three-year-old brother died. His father, Lucien Joseph Cormier, whose family was originally from Quebec, had moved to Leominster in 1910. Lucien Cormier, like many other French-Canadian Catholic settlers in the area, supported his family by working in factories in or near Leominster, a typical New England town about fifty miles west of Boston.

Cormier's mother, Irma Margaret Collins, who was Irish, created a home which the author describes as "warm, happy, and loving." In his short stories and in his early novels, which often contain autobiographical elements, he frequently depicts caring, dedicated family members.

In an interview with this writer at the Cormier home on 3 July 1980, Cormier recalled his adolescent years outside the home in quite a different fashion. He described himself as an introvert who felt like an outsider in school. His ambition to become an author apparently stemmed from the pronouncement of his seventh-grade teacher, Sister Catherine, who told him that he was a writer after reading a poem he had written. Cormier revealed to William A. Davis (*Boston Globe Magazine*, 16 November 1980) that he considered himself thereafter "a writer in my soul." This conviction enabled him to become more extroverted in high school when he began to write for the yearbook, to act in plays, and to sing in the chorus. In the ninth grade he read Thomas Wolfe's *The Web and the Rock* (1939). Wolfe's story of a young boy living in a small town, hungry for love and fame, struck a responsive chord in Cormier.

After his graduation from high school in 1942, Cormier took a job in a Leominster comb factory, working the night shift so that he could attend Fitchburg State College during the day. There he met Prof. Florence Conlon, who encouraged him to write a short story. "The Little Things That Count," a story about an American soldier wounded in World War II, was the result. Professor Conlon submitted Cormier's story to the *Sign*, a Catholic magazine, which accepted it and paid seventy-five dollars to the elated nineteen-year-old writer. Meanwhile, Cormier realized that the education he was receiving at Fitchburg State College, which was designed to educate primary-school teachers, was not what he wanted, so he dropped out. Years later, in 1977, Fitchburg State College conferred upon him an honorary Doctor of Letters degree. In 1981 Cormier presented his manuscripts to the college for a permanent collection.

Shortly after leaving college, Cormier accepted a series of writing jobs. The first, in 1946, was writing commercials for radio station WTAG in Worcester, Massachusetts. No doubt the discipline of compressing ideas and information into a hundred words or less contributed to Cormier's terse, fast-paced style of writing. Those stylistic elements are traceable as well to the influence of

Ernest Hemingway and William Saroyan, both writers whom Cormier greatly admires.

In 1948, Cormier married Constance Senay and began working as a night bureau man for the *Worcester Telegram and Gazette*. After five years there he accepted an offer from the *Fitchburg Sentinel* to work days. His job required him to cover all aspects of small-town life. A good reporter and wire editor, Cormier excelled when it came to human interest stories.

The Associated Press Award for Best News Story in New England in 1959 went to Cormier for his story about a child severely burned in an automobile accident. The story resulted in a fund being established to help defray the child's medical expenses. In 1973 Cormier was again the recipient of the Associated Press Award, this time for a story written from the perspective of mentally retarded people. The next year, Cormier received still another award for journalism; K. R. Thomson Newspapers, Inc., an international chain, honored the writer for a human interest column written for the *Fitchburg Sentinel* under the pseudonym of John Fitch IV.

While Cormier worked days for the newspaper, he wrote fiction on weekends and at night. Many of his stories were accepted by such magazines as *Redbook*, *Saturday Evening Post*, *Woman's Day*, and *McCall's*, and some of these were later collected in *Eight Plus One*. He also wrote three novels for adults, which were published between 1960 and 1965. At the same time he did some public relations writing to help support his growing family. He was associate editor of the *Fitchburg-Leominster Sentinel and Enterprise* when he resigned on 14 January 1978 to devote all his time to writing fiction.

All of Cormier's works are set in the fictitious town of Monument, Massachusetts, a composite of Leominster and Fitchburg. The models or prototypes for many scenes from Cormier's works can be found in or near these two typical New England towns. The Cormier family has lived in a two-storied shingled house midway between them for some thirty years.

Cormier works every morning in a book-lined alcove off his dining room, where he says most of his ideas come to him. He thinks in terms of what is going to happen to a certain character that day, not in terms of writing so many words or pages a day, and he thinks in terms of scenes, not segments or chapters. A superb craftsman and stylist, Cormier rewrites continuously, sharpening phrases and metaphors and deleting passages that do not advance the plot. He usually does not know the entire plot in advance. A great lover of mystery stories and suspense novels, an admirer of Graham Greene, John le Carré, Ellery Queen, and Ed McBain, Cormier recognizes the reader's desire for straightforward action, not lengthy description. Thus he uses vivid similes and metaphors that evoke images or emotions without long descriptive passages, a writing technique compatible with the taste of young people geared to the action-packed age of television.

This style is evident even in Cormier's first novel, *Now and at the Hour* (1960), written for adults and inspired by Cormier's grief over the death of his father, whom he admired and loved. Cormier describes himself as an emotional writer who seeks to arouse emotion in his readers and relies upon his own emotional involvement to complete a work. *Now and at the Hour*, a work in which Cormier's emotional involvement is still strong after so many years, effectively transmits his feelings to the reader.

Alphege LeBlanc, an ordinary man dying of cancer, has to learn to cope with increasing pain and the fear that his life has been a failure. A man who worked for forty-two years in the Monument Comb Factory, Alph is a devoted father and husband. Possessed of an inner strength, he refuses to ask for pity or to let his family know that he is aware that he is dying. The title, taken from the Catholic prayer "Hail Mary" ("Pray for us sinners now and at the hour of our death") is apt because the novel is concerned with the present—there are few flashbacks—and with the days and hours preceding death. Cormier set a precedent in this novel that he continues to observe: he does not take the easy way out; there are no sentimental endings; nobody rides happily off into the sunset. The reviews of *Now and at the Hour* were complimentary, and *Time* magazine kept it on their "Recommended Reading" list for six weeks. Nonetheless, the book sold only about five thousand copies.

Two more adult novels followed *Now and at the Hour*: *A Little Raw on Monday Mornings* (1963), the story of thirty-eight-year-old Gracie, a widowed Catholic factory worker who finds herself pregnant and considers abortion; and *Take Me Where the Good Times Are* (1965), the story of seventy-year-old Tommy Bartin, resident of a poorhouse. Tommy is one of those characters most difficult to portray convincingly: a good man.

Cormier's fourth novel, however, changed his life and his audience. His agent read the first forty pages of *The Chocolate War* (1974) and told him that he had a young-adult novel. Cormier worried about bad language and sex scenes, but his agent recommended that he write as he ordinarily did. He followed this advice, refusing to change the downbeat ending, which caused several publishers to reject the book before it was accepted by Pantheon.

The story of Jerry Renault's courageous stand against peer pressure and against his high school's corrupt headmaster is not pessimistic, but the fact that Jerry stands alone and is physically and mentally beaten at the novel's close seems to break an unstated requirement of young-adult fiction that there must be some hope, something positive for teenagers to assimilate. No doubt Jerry's parting advice to his friend Goober—to go with the crowd and not to "dare disturb the universe"—is grimly pessimistic, yet most of the novel depicts courage and bravery in the face of overwhelming odds. Jerry does not win, but his fight provides an inspiration or a warning that more people need to take a stand, to support what they believe in, to "dare disturb the universe."

Since the issue of the hero's defeat is central to Cormier's reputation, it is worth noting that in some cases Cormier's message did reach the appropriate audience. Several years ago, when *The Chocolate War* was assigned to an eighth-grade class in a New England school, upset parents objected to the book. A student proposed the unanimous signing of a petition to keep the book. Another student, thirteen years old, argued against the unanimity, for he felt—just as Jerry did—that peer pressure should not be used to force individuals to join the majority. The second student's argument was compelling; the book remained on the reading list.

Cormier seems especially talented at recognizing everyday events as possible topics for his fiction. He has revealed that the impetus for *The Chocolate War* was an incident involving his son, Peter, who came home one day with a bag of chocolates to sell for his high school. Peter did not want to sell them, and Cormier supported his decision; however, the next day as he watched Peter walk up to the door of the school with the unsold candy, he wondered what he had done to his son. Luckily there were no repercussions for Peter; instead, the incident set off a spark in

Cormier's imagination: What if there had been opposition?

The Chocolate War is Jerry Renault's story; however, Cormier introduces a host of other Trinity High School students whose reactions to selling chocolates differ from Jerry's. The abuse of power is prominent in both the students and the teachers at Trinity. Archie Costello, leader of the secret society known as the Vigils, is a manipulator of the worst sort, and Brother Leon, Trinity's headmaster, is a match for him on the adult level. The novel has broader implications, however, as the metaphorical language suggests: Trinity is a microcosm of the world.

Many of the characters in the novel are, of necessity, two dimensional, their primary function being to serve as foils to the main characters. Goober is a foil to Jerry because he is also a good boy, but he lacks Jerry's courage to be a nonconformist. Carter is a foil to Archie in that both are leaders, but Carter prefers to lead by physical force and Archie by mental prowess.

Obie is both Archie's friend and his foe. Often an errand boy for Archie, Obie is, nevertheless, the one who presents Archie with the box of marbles. If Archie draws the black marble, he will have to carry out the assignments which he, as "The Assigner" of the Vigils, forces others to do. Obie sees Archie for the manipulator he is; he notices that Archie "asks" Jerry to sell the chocolates instead of demanding that he do so. Obie believes, and the reader hopes, that Jerry will be Archie's nemesis. When the entire school is assembled to watch Jerry's downfall, an event arranged by Archie, Obie is the one who remembers to bring the box of marbles. Thus Obie does not actually "dare to disturb the universe," but he is not a J. Alfred Prufrock either.

Some of Cormier's readers have concluded that the authority figures in this novel are either ineffectual, like Brother Eugene and Jerry's father, or vicious, like Brother Leon. Although it is true that many of Cormier's authority figures are not admirable, his main emphasis is on other themes, such as the search for identity and the initiation into manhood. Jerry experiences the search for identity as he questions the recent death of his mother and his father's resulting bleak outlook on life. Jerry, Goober, and Obie all experience initiation rites, but only Jerry becomes truly independent.

This novel is many-faceted in its examination of tyranny and peer pressure. Gregory Bailey is one case in point. When attacked viciously by Brother Leon and called a cheat and a liar, Bailey maintains his integrity in the face of the unprovoked attack. Only one voice from the back of the room speaks out in protest–"Aw, let the kid alone"–a protest which Brother Leon calls, "a feeble protest, too little and too late." Brother Leon draws a parallel between those who allowed him to proceed in his unwarranted attack on Bailey and those who allowed the Nazis to take over Germany. This brief scene, occurring early in the novel, foreshadows the attack on Jerry at the novel's end and the failure of Jerry's friend Goober to help Jerry when he is attacked.

The Chocolate War has been well received by the reading public, who have purchased about twenty-five thousand copies in hardback and approximately four hundred thousand paperback copies. For the most part critics praised it. Peter Hunt, writing for the *Times Literary Supplement* (4 April 1975), called it a "tour de force, and a tour de force of realism"; Theodore Weesner, in the *New York Times Book Review* (5 May 1974), thought it "masterfully structured and rich in theme" with action that is "well crafted, well timed, suspenseful." Because of its violence and downbeat ending, *The Chocolate War* also received some unfavorable criticism, such as Norma Bagnall's objection that only the harsh and ugly side of life is being presented under the guise of realism. She notes the absence of positive adult role models for readers to emulate and sees the novel as completely without hope.

Much of the adverse criticism stems from a desire to protect younger readers who may not be capable of recognizing irony or understanding that the novel is not entirely without hope, but rather demonstrates a conflict between good and evil with good, for the present at least, on the losing side. Many teenagers can grasp Cormier's point that the forces of good have to work harder to win. Goodness does not inevitably win, and poetic justice does not always prevail, either in the fictive world of Cormier's novels or in the real world.

As Cormier demands of himself the right image, word, comparison, so he requires of the reader the ability to perceive and comprehend more than the most obvious surface meaning. In this book Cormier shows that tyranny is ugly; one cannot resist it alone. Valuable insights can be gained here; some aspects of reality are entirely bleak, but to elucidate them, to make the reader ponder, is not grim or hopeless, for only then can young adults realize the necessity of

standing up for their beliefs. Cormier has said that the bleak reality which he presents in his novels is an antidote to the happy endings of most young-adult novels and many television shows.

Some critics have compared *The Chocolate War* to J. D. Salinger's *The Catcher in the Rye* (1951) or William Golding's *Lord of the Flies* (1955). Despite its controversial subject matter, its literary qualities are indisputable. Included in the American Library Association's Best Books for Young Adults for 1974, and more recently in their Best of the Best for 1970-1982, it was also a *New York Times* Notable Book for the Year. It was awarded starred reviews in *Kirkus* and *School Library Journal*, and it received the Maxi Award. Foreign editions have been published in England, Italy, France, Germany, Spain, Denmark, Holland, and Sweden. In 1988, *The Chocolate War* was made into a movie, now available on videocassette, which follows the novel closely in the early and middle scenes but drastically changes the ending.

Cormier's second young-adult novel is also powerful and provocative. The full impact of *I Am the Cheese* (1977) does not hit the reader until the final pages as two seemingly separate stories merge, and the reader perceives the illusory nature of reality presented here. Adam Farmer, the fourteen-year-old protagonist, is a sensitive youth who recognizes that there are some strange happenings in his home: his mother calls someone every Thursday evening; his father has periodic visits by the mysterious Mr. Grey; Adam even discovers two birth certificates in his name, each with a different birthdate. Thus, problems of identity are obviously central to this novel. Adam learns that his real name is Paul Delmonte and that his mother calls her sister once a week (Adam had thought that he had no living relatives). His father tells him that Mr. Grey is with the Department of Re-Identification, and that the Delmontes had to take on a new identity because Mr. Delmonte had testified on behalf of the government about connections between organized crime and certain government agencies.

I Am the Cheese has a two-part structure consisting of "boy-on-a-bike" sections (Adam riding from Monument, Massachusetts, to visit his father in a hospital seventy miles away in Ruttenburg, Vermont) and taped interrogation sections (Brint, a psychiatrist or a government spy, using a code initial "T," questions subject "A," who the reader later realizes is Adam). The first-person narrator point of view, used for the boy-on-a-bike sections, makes those sections quite believable. The second sequence alternates in point of view between the dramatic or objective (the interrogation) and a third-person omniscient narrator who fills in the information that "T" is unable to elicit from "A"; that is, information that Adam cannot recall.

The two sequences are skillfully interwoven by having an image in the first section relate to one in the second section. For example, the "boy-on-a-bike" chapter concerning Adam trying to pedal past a ferocious dog is followed by Tape 4, in which Adam recalls the day that he and his father were fleeing from someone or something and how, on entering the woods, they were confronted by a vicious dog. Many of the various motifs which wind in and out of the two plot sequences are taken from Cormier's own youth—the love of Thomas Wolfe's novels, the fear of dogs, the smell of lilacs, the claustrophobia. These, along with the oft-repeated "Farmer in the Dell" song, awaken the reader to the similarities between the sequences while their differences are emphasized by two different types of language. The ordinary language of a fourteen-year-old boy is contrasted vividly with the cold, official, statistical jargon of Tapes 0ZK001-16 with Subject A. The language of the penultimate chapter is thematically perfect, for it requires several readings in order for most readers to comprehend fully the government jargon and then the impact of the statement that Subject A is confined until Policy 979 on termination is revised or Subject A obliterates.

The powerlessness of the individual to stand alone against a corrupt society is another theme of this emotionally riveting novel. Cormier goes a step beyond *The Chocolate War*, for here Anthony Delmonte, an adult, is able to withstand the destructive forces moving against him only for a period of ten years or so. How then is it possible for a fourteen-year-old boy to succeed in standing alone against overwhelming corruption and evil? Yet Adam is brave, his instincts are valid; he senses the evil in Brint, but can do nothing, for he is kept drugged in an institution and allowed to return to reality only once a year, on the anniversary of the death of his parents. His failure to recall what happened to his family is the only reason that he is allowed to live. If he ever does remember, he will be "terminated."

Another reason this novel makes such a powerful impact on the reader is Cormier's effective use of time sequence: the first-person narrator sec-

tions seem to be taking place in the present, and the taped interrogations seem to be recalling the past. The revelation that for Adam (who is kept drugged) there is no true present in the real world (there is only his fantasy world) makes the conclusion of the novel stunning.

No discussion of *I Am the Cheese* would be complete without mention of Amy Hertz, Adam's delightful friend. She and her "numbers" (as she calls her pranks) help relieve the tension that mounts for Adam and for the reader. She helps Adam to accept himself and to become a more well-rounded person when the serious-minded, self-conscious young boy becomes her co-conspirator in "numbers." Very much aware of the value of comic relief in a dramatically tense situation, Cormier created Amy for just that purpose much in the same way that Shakespeare's comic characters appear in each of his tragedies. Actually Amy is delightful and humorous until the reader realizes that she and her father may have participated in the plot to terminate the Farmers. Cormier has said that he deliberately left that question open as he did the question of whether the syndicate put the bomb in the Farmers' car or whether Mr. Grey did.

Indeed, the novel is bleak, but it is also thought provoking. *I Am the Cheese* questions long-held assumptions about the nature of patriotism and governmental agencies and about truth and identity. With foreign editions published in England, Germany, Yugoslavia, Brazil, and Japan, this book has justifiably been the recipient of starred reviews in *Booklist* and *School Library Journal* and high praises by being included in the American Library Association's Notable Children's Books, 1977, in their Best Books for Young Adults for 1977, and in their Best of the Best for 1970-1982. The *New York Times* listed it as a Notable Book of the Year; *Horn Book* included it in their "Fanfare"; *School Library Journal* named it to their list of Best Books, 1977. A movie starring Robert MacNaughton, Robert Wagner, and Hope Lange, with Robert Cormier playing a bit part as Amy's father, premiered on 27 April 1983, in Leominster, Massachusetts. Because it was not well received by the critics, however, it was withdrawn from commercial theaters but can still be seen on cable television and is available on videocassette.

Another carefully structured novel, *After the First Death* (1979), also shatters the reader's complacency. It interweaves the story of three teenagers. First is Ben Marchand, a general's son, a sensitive young student at Castleton Academy, who longs to know and understand his father but ultimately cannot live with the knowledge that his father's patriotism is more important to him than is Ben himself. Second is Miro Shantas, a refugee, orphaned at an early age and trained as a terrorist. He is scheduled to go on his first assignment, to kill for the first time; his target is the driver of a hijacked busload of first graders. And third is Kate Forrester, a beautiful blond eighteen-year-old who, as the substitute bus driver the day of the hijacking, learns much about herself.

After the First Death opens at Castleton, where Ben is writing about his life, about the bullet wound in his chest. The time is two weeks before Christmas, but there are flashbacks to the preceding August when four terrorists hijacked the busload of sixteen children. Ben acts as a go-between for Inner Delta–the special secret agency stationed at Fort Delta, a local army base–and the hijackers, whose unnamed homeland is perhaps in the Middle East. The book alternates between chapters involving Ben and his father and chapters involving the hijacking. Though the novel is twelve chapters long, the climactic meeting of Ben and the terrorists does not occur until chapter 10. In what has become typical Cormier form, chapters 11 and 12 are not just dénouement; they hold, each in their own way, additional surprises for the reader.

The Ben / General Marchand chapters frequently employ the use of flashbacks, while the Miro / Kate chapters move at a steady pace in the present tense with only occasional brief flashbacks. The handling of the time sequence with its relevance to plot is perhaps unique, for the novel continually shocks the reader. By carefully distinguishing both in time and style between the Ben / General Marchand and the Miro / Kate chapters, Cormier expands his point of view and avoids repetition when the same event is described twice.

Richly varied in thematic development, *After the First Death* explores such subjects as the search for identity, patriotism, alienation, betrayal, and sanity. Ben is the most provocative character, for there are two possible interpretations of his role in the novel. Either he is dead throughout the novel, and his schizophrenic father acts out his role; or Ben commits suicide midway through the novel, and his father's inability to handle his guilt causes the general to become schizophrenic. Either interpretation suggests an identity crisis. Ben knows his name, but his repetition of his name, and even his parents' names and his ad-

dress, suggests that he is unsure of his identity as many adolescents are, or that perhaps he actually is the general. Ben does not really know his father. He has never been to the general's office; he has been shut out of his father's highly secretive work; he can only surmise that one of his father's aliases is Gen. Rufus Briggs.

On the other hand, Kate never questions her identity, but she questions her abilities and her innermost qualities. Is she anything more than a cheerleader with honey-colored hair? Is she capable of bravery and courage? She never fully realizes that she passes the test. She acts and she thinks for herself, realizing one of the most important messages revealed in the novel: "the possibility that hope comes out of hopelessness and that the opposite of things carry the seeds of birth–love out of hate; good out of evil. Didn't flowers grow out of dirt?"

Miro has a more serious identity crisis; he does not remember his parents and has never seen his homeland, uses a fictitious name and plans to create an identity by his first killing. The suspicion that Artkin, the leader of the terrorists, could be his father–an idea that Kate suggests after Artkin's death–is more than Miro can bear. He will be a masked terrorist, a shell of a person, a murderer, but he will never allow himself to discover his true identity.

Patriotism carried to extremes is also unbearable. General Marchand is willing to sacrifice his own son, knowing that the boy will break under torture. Ironically, the general's vow to his friend who was killed at Iwo Jima that his death would not be in vain makes the general a superpatriot. There are echoes here of Anthony Delmonte, whose patriotism caused him to testify on behalf of the government at what would prove to be a terrible expense to his family, yet both men act honorably and in accord with their beliefs. Both have high standards, but the general, unlike Delmonte, is incapable of a loving relationship with his son because of his own inadequacies. He pays for these inadequacies when Ben's death precipitates his own mental collapse.

Extreme patriotism is also evident in both Miro and Artkin, who, denied loving relationships and family ties, place the cause of regaining their homeland ahead of everything, including the lives of young children. Both Artkin and Miro are foreigners in America; Miro has been a foreigner his entire life. Their alienation from people and from comfortable surroundings where they feel they belong enables them to carry out their terrorism with a ruthless disregard for the lives of innocent people.

A variation on the theme of alienation occurs in the Miro-Kate relationship and in the Ben-Nettie Halversham one. Sexual attraction is a factor in both relationships, but in neither case does the girl reciprocate. Kate tries to arouse Miro's interest in her as a last resort to save her life and the lives of the children, but Nettie seems to be totally insensitive to a painfully shy Ben.

The novel also examines betrayal on various levels. On a physical level, Kate's body betrays her, causing her to wet her pants at tense moments. Miro's body betrays him by the great sob that emerges involuntarily when he learns of the death of his brother Aniel, by his quivering when Kate touches his arm, by his falling asleep when he is on guard duty, and by his anguished cry when Kate suggests that the now-dead Artkin was his father. Also, according to one interpretation, Ben betrays himself and his father by committing suicide. On the emotional level, Ben cannot live with the knowledge that he has betrayed his country under torture or the fact that his father knew that he would crack under pressure and reveal the time of the attack. Thus Ben's suicide is a result of his betrayal and of his being betrayed by his father. Kate feels that she has betrayed the children who were placed in her care when her attempt to escape by driving the bus off the bridge fails. Miro, likewise, feels that he has betrayed Artkin when he tried to protect his own life rather than warn Artkin in the split second that he had to make a decision. Miro betrays himself when he resolves to keep himself empty, void of any emotional attachments.

The idea of betrayal is closely linked with madness in the case of General Marchand, who loses his sanity as a result of his betrayal of Ben and Ben's subsequent suicide. One can also link Ben's suicide to temporary insanity, the result of betrayal. Betrayal is also evident in the case of Miro, who shoots Kate after comprehending her suggestion that Artkin is his father. The reader never knows whether the shooting is deliberate or accidental, or whether Miro is temporarily or permanently insane. Kate has called him a monster, an innocent monster, for he knows nothing of family, love, children, or even toys. With no knowledge of what most people cherish, Miro can destroy without conscience.

The impetus for *After the First Death* was a series of events and ideas. Cormier said in a recent interview with this writer that he has long felt the

somewhat menacing presence of Fort Devens, an army base near Leominster. Intrigued by what occurs inside its fenced grounds, he also described what happens above–paratroopers bailing out of airplanes as looking "like vultures" or "like evil flowers."

Another seed that germinated in Cormier's mind was a bomb set off in a post office where any number of innocent people might have been killed but luckily were not. Contrary to the expectations of many, the California prank of kidnapping a busload of children, which occurred about the same time that Cormier was writing the novel, did not consciously influence him; the hijackings and bombings, which were frequently making front-page news then, did.

Refugee camps were another topic of interest to Cormier, who shies away from making a direct identification with any specific terrorized organization. Cormier asked what happens when young men are reared in extreme poverty, without parents and love, without a place to call home. For Cormier, the answer was that they become monsters who have a terrible innocence about them: Aniel, who is killed at seventeen; Miro, who did not understand what a toy was; and Artkin, who teaches the brothers terrorist tactics as a means of survival.

Innocent monsters are but one example of the irony in the novel. Ironically, Kate drives the bus, substituting for her uncle, on the very day that Miro is to be initiated into manhood by killing his first victim. Ironically, the one child, Raymond, who refuses to eat the doped candy offered by the hijackers because his mother has told him that candy is not good for his teeth, is the one chosen to be sacrificed. Cormier had a difficult time writing the scene involving the death of the child. In fact, he originally wrote it without a child's name and tried to mitigate the horror by having the death take place offstage, so to speak; only a shot is heard. A terrible irony occurs when General Marchand volunteers his son, Ben, to save the lives of other children, an irony recognized by Artkin when he describes the general as "a great patriot or a great fool." Ironically, General Marchand is both.

After the First Death is not only ironic; it is tense, powerful, "a Dantean Inferno without any hint of Purgatorio or Paradiso," to use Stanley Ellin's description in the *New York Times Book Review* (29 April 1979). It received starred reviews in *Booklist*, *School Library Journal*, and *Kirkus*. It was chosen as an American Library Association's

Best Book for Young Adults in 1979 and was included in their Best of the Best for 1970-1982. The reviews have been almost unanimously favorable for *After the First Death*, which has now appeared in England, Holland, and Sweden.

In rather dramatic contrast to *After the First Death* is Cormier's *Eight Plus One*, a collection of short stories originally published between 1965 and 1975 in magazines such as *Redbook*, *Woman's Day*, *McCall's*, and the *Saturday Evening Post*. The reviews of *Eight Plus One* in general have been favorable, although one critic, Benjamin DeMott, in the *New York Times Book Review* (9 November 1980), criticized it harshly. Other critics have used such words as "poignant" and "perceptive" to describe it. It presents a departure for Cormier from his three previous young-adult novels as, indeed, he meant it to. He added to this collection a series of brief introductions to each story, which a few reviewers have found disruptive. Cormier deliberately included them to answer the questions most often asked him by his teenage audience and to teach certain writing techniques to would-be writers. He says it is the type of book that he would have liked to have read when he was a teenager just discovering that he wanted to be a writer. For teachers and students these introductions provide valuable insights into Cormier's writing and the writing process as he understands it. Cormier envisioned *Eight Plus One* as a textbook for a writing class. He discusses such topics as the genesis of his stories, the transformation of a real-life occurrence into a fictionalized story, multiple levels of meaning in fiction, the importance of figures of speech, especially metaphor and simile, for descriptive purposes, and the significance of titles, tone, and point of view.

Cormier explains the title for this collection: Eight stories have teenagers as the central figures and involve the strengthening of family bonds; in the final story–the "one" of the title–the children are only in the background of the life of a man who plans to leave his wife of many years and their children for a much younger woman. A story which Cormier wrote without needing to polish it, he felt it belonged in this collection. "Bunny Berigan–Wasn't He a Musician or Something?" echoes the other stories in several ways. Walt Crane, a middle-aged, fairly happily married man and devoted father, has fallen in love with a beautiful young model, Jennifer West, who returns his love. Walt invites his long-time friend Jerry for a drink in order to announce his

plans for divorce and to introduce Jennifer to Jerry. The situation is common in real life, but the story is unusual in its choice of point of view. The narrator is Jerry, who experiences a wide fluctuation of emotions, including disbelief, admiration, envy, and sadness. The choice of a middle-aged narrator links this story with some of the others in the collection. All nine reveal Cormier as a creator of compassionate characters and loving families who bridge generation gaps and learn respect for others, and manage to do so without being overly sentimental.

Three stories are written from the point of view of a young boy during the Depression. "President Cleveland, Where Are You?" is on one level the story of a twelve-year-old boy, Jerry, trying desperately to win a baseball glove by being the first person to collect the entire set of cards depicting U.S. presidents. Included in packages of gum, most of the presidential cards are in abundance, but not the one of Grover Cleveland. The story on another level involves Jerry's recognition of the love between himself and his older brother, Armand, and the nature of sacrifice. Some aspects of Armand's character were inspired by Cormier's older brother Norman. "President Cleveland, Where Are You?" is an important story in terms of Cormier's development as a writer, for it was in searching for the way that a twelve-year-old might describe a large white house that he thought of "a big white birthday cake of a house." Cormier says in the story's introduction that in writing it he discovered the importance of "simile and metaphor" and "learned that words were truly tools, that figures of speech were not just something fancy to dress up a piece of prose but words that could evoke scene and event and emotion." This story recently received a Reader's Choice award, especially pleasing to Cormier because the award is determined by young readers in schools all over the country.

A second Depression-era story, "Protestants Cry, Too," takes place just prior to World War II. Jerry and Armand are again the central characters with the action revolving around Armand, from a staunchly Catholic family, who announces his desire to marry a Protestant girl. Jerry watches the reactions within the family, especially his father's, as he learns about the nature of prejudice and the nature of love.

Another story set during the Depression and employing a theme of prejudice is "My First Negro." A young white boy is saved from a beating by Jefferson Johnson Stone, a black boy

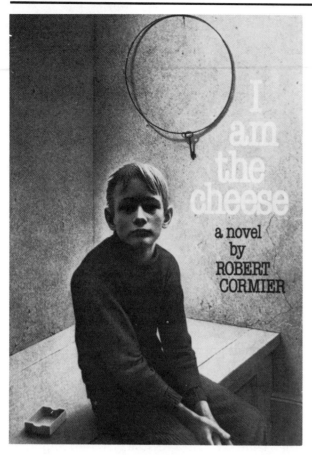

Dust jacket for Cormier's psychological novel about a boy whose family takes part in the government's witness relocation program

about the same age. The two become friends, but the white boy, the narrator, betrays Jeff. The betrayal theme is handled differently here, however, from the way it is in the novels. The story has no nicely resolved ending either, but the reader feels that the narrator has learned a valuable lesson as part of his initiation into a knowledge of people of other races, into the nature of friendship and prejudice, and into maturity.

The three Depression-era stories paint for the teenager of today a realistic picture of the difficulties of life at that time: of the lengths to which a young boy had to go to acquire a baseball glove when his family had no money to buy one, of a hardworking father laid off from his job and his feelings of inadequacy as breadwinner, of the plight of a black man who never had a job from which to be laid off. Cormier vividly describes levels of poverty in "My First Negro" when he classifies them as "comfortable poor," "regular poor," "relief poor," and "destitute poor."

"My First Negro," as well as other stories in this collection, depicts boyhood activities, certain

to evoke a sense of recognition in many readers. A gang of boys–the Midnight Raiders–decides to enact the old Robin Hood theme. In some ways the Midnight Raiders are a forerunner of the Vigils in *The Chocolate War*. The leader, Jean-Paul, who conceives the idea of robbing from the rich to help the poor, is certainly not as vicious as Archie, but he too believes in assigning roles to the underlings and evokes enough fear from the gang members that they are afraid to object to his idea of raiding the Toussaints' garden and taking the vegetables to Alphabet Soup, the poorest section of town.

Two other stories in the collection have a similar theme in that the youthful protagonist recognizes relatives of his for the first time as people, separate and apart from their familial roles. In "The Moustache" seventeen-year-old Mike, visiting his aged grandmother in a nursing home, sees her as a person filled with love for her long-dead husband, and as a person who still suffers because she accused her husband of infidelity shortly before the accident which took his life. A variation of this theme occurs in "Guess What? I Almost Kissed My Father Goodnight," where sixteen-year-old Mike suddenly sees his father as a person who sits on a park bench one afternoon, who continues to read a book of poems received years ago from a young girl, who meets a lovely blonde in the library, and who even feels lonely on occasion. The knowledge that his father is human gives Mike an epiphany, accompanied by feelings of sympathy and love.

Both stories involving Mike also treat the subjects of young love and the relationships between parents and children. "Another of Mike's Girls" also deals with an awakening, but this time Mike's father, not Mike, realizes that while he has been looking at all of his son's girlfriends as cast from the same mold, one of those young ladies has been looking at him as just Mike's father. This story also vividly captures the feelings of rejection by a member of the opposite sex.

The pains and problems of parenthood are evident in "Another of Mike's Girls," just as they are in "A Bad Time for Fathers" and "Mine on Thursdays." The latter two stories involve father-daughter relationships; the first when the daughter, Jane, leaves for college, and her cast-off boyfriend Sam and her father both have to adjust to the change, the second when Holly, whose parents are divorced, spends a Thursday with her father. "Mine on Thursdays" is a poignant story of betrayal and recognition. Holly and her dad spend the day at an amusement park where, forced by her father's reluctance to accompany her, she rides a wild and frightening rocket alone; her father's failure to recognize her need represents the last betrayal she can accept from a person who has betrayed her many times in the past. No comforting thought concludes the story, only the father's realization at last of what he has done to his child. Although he cannot say these words aloud, he thinks them: "I'm sorry for playing Santa Claus when I should have been a father. I'm sorry for wanting the whole world when I should have wanted only those who loved me. I'm sorry for the Rocket Ride–and all the Rocket Rides of your life that I didn't share." Holly's father plans to leave Monument; he knows that he has lost his daughter.

Eight Plus One can be grimly realistic and bleak, although not all the stories could be so described, but in this collection, as in the novels, Cormier refuses to take the popular, sentimental, easy way out. This book has received less critical acclaim than the novels, but the American Library Association has included *Eight Plus One* on its list of Notable Books in the Field of Social Studies.

Cormier's next novel, *The Bumblebee Flies Anyway*, published in 1983, is set in Section 12 of the Complex, the wing for terminally ill youths in an experimental hospital. The author has revealed that the catalysts for this novel were a poster of a bumblebee that he has had for many years in his writing room and his reading about experimental hospitals.

Barney Snow, sixteen, whose surname connotes his innocence, is the narrator. Barney's role is to unite the others: Ronson, a Golden Gloves winner; Allie Roon, with an old man's face, spastic and stammering; Billy the Kidney, wheelchair bound but desirous of adventure; and Alberto "Mazzo" Mazzofono, rich, handsome, athletic, but plugged into a machine. This unlikely cast of characters is brought together by their volunteering to spend their last days as subjects for a study of experimental drugs and techniques which will not save them but will perhaps help someone, someday.

The Bumblebee is a life-size model of a red MG, made of wood, symbolizing the dreams of the others that Barney strives to help them achieve. They will "fly" in the Bumblebee, so named by Mazzo's twin sister, Cassie, after the heavy-bodied, short-winged bee who, aerodynamically speaking, should not be able to lift itself off the ground, but who, blissfully unaware of any such concept, flies anyway. At the heart of this pessimistic, depressing scene of dying teenagers stands Cormier's message to follow one's dreams, to dare to fly.

A central conflict arises in the novel because Barney believes that he is in the Complex to serve as a norm for testing various medicines and treatments. The irony becomes evident when the reader learns that Barney is not a norm but is terminally ill, with his disease temporarily in remission. Barney's refusal to face the unpleasant or to use medical terms indicates his lack of acceptance of his disease. He uses such terms as "Complex" for hospital, "Handyman" for doctor, "merchandise" for drugs, and "invader" for disease. Most readers accept Barney's explanations, since they have little knowledge of the world of an experimental hospital, and thus when they learn that Barney is also dying, some feel tricked or manipulated by the author.

Barney also feels deceived, and he has been, for the experiments to which he is being subjected involve long- and short-term memory. Screens, both visual and auditory, are superimposed over those events and facts of Barney's life that he would most like to forget. Being able to obliterate the fact that he is a terminal patient probably enables Barney to keep his disease in remission: Cormier suggests the role that emotions play in sickness. Clearly, as soon as Barney learns about the "screen" covering his knowledge of his illness, his remission ends.

Cormier relieves the tension of the hospital setting somewhat by introducing a girlfriend for Barney. Cassie, Mazzo's twin, is a beautiful girl who becomes an alter ego, and more, for her brother. She experiences pain whenever her brother does. Although they are fraternal twins, they are reminiscent of the Corsican brothers, identical twins who were bound together by this same sensitivity, which Cassie refers to as "The Thing." "The Thing" is a kind of supernatural phenomenon, going beyond the rules of the natural world. Cassie is a somewhat perplexing character. She engages Barney to "spy" on her brother and report back to her because Mazzo refuses to see his family. This arrangement allows Barney and Cassie to meet frequently, and Barney's love for her blossoms. Cassie enters the novitiate and finds solace in the convent, but what ultimately happens to her is not specified. The reader assumes that Cassie survives the death of her twin but does not know whether or not she becomes a nun.

Thematically, the entire book is a commentary on appearance versus reality; for example, the recurring nightmare that Barney has of an apparently real car accident is actually artificial, yet his disease is real; the nurse who appears healthy is on the terminal wing because she too is in remission; Mazzo, who appears very weak and is actually dying, is nevertheless able to push the Bumblebee up to the roof of the Complex from which it will "fly."

The search for identity is also a major goal for Barney, whose experimentally induced amnesia has previously prevented him from learning that he is Bernard Jason Snow, that his parents were killed years ago in an auto accident, and that he has been reared in foster homes. His search to find the meaning of the nightmare car accident, to recall his mother's face, and to remember other facts about his life before his entry into the Complex proves unfruitful.

Barney's longing for acceptance in spite of the Handyman's recommendation that each patient should keep to his separate compartment and not become too involved with the others, causes him to be especially kind and perform small services for those less able than he. Yet Barney never feels that he belongs to the group because at first he thinks that he is not terminally ill like the others; when he learns that he too is dying, he still feels that he is different, for he refuses to accept his approaching death. Billy the Kidney also desires to belong. He has had so little opportunity to make friends in the past that he used to telephone people he did not know and public services, like Dial-a-Prayer, so that he could talk to someone. Starved as he is for friendship, he is willing to go to his death to accompany Mazzo and Barney when the Bumblebee flies.

Cormier has admitted that this book was difficult to write, but most critics praised his achievement. The few who were negative thought it not quite up to his previous novels. The review in *Booklist* (1 September 1983) criticizes Cassie, "who is convincing as Barney's love idol, but less so as her twin's empathetic alter ego." The reviewer in *Horn Book* (December 1983) sums up his criticism by noting: "the narrative events are less ambiguous, the feelings less subtle and the symbolism less obvious [than in *I Am the Cheese*] . . . [and Cassie is] less convincing [but] Barney and the others do come alive. And their ability to triumph in some measure over the depersonalizing situation represents a marked change from the author's previous work." *Publishers Weekly*, the *Times Literary Supplement*, and the *Bulletin for the Center of Children's Books* gave the novel favorable reviews. The reviewer for *School Library Journal* (September 1983) called it Cormier's "most affirmative novel." The American Library Association listed it among their Notable Children's Books and also as a Best Book for Young Adults for 1983. *School Library Journal* included it in their Best Books, 1983. It was nominated for, but did not win, the Carnegie Medal in England, an unusual honor for an American book.

Also well received was *Beyond the Chocolate War*, Cormier's sequel to the earlier novel. Published in 1985, eleven years after *The Chocolate War*, this novel moves at the same relentless pace as its predecessor. Indeed, Cormier rewrites and revises constantly to achieve his pacing with its gradual disclosure. Cormier has said that questions from readers about Archie or Jerry or even Tubs Casper, which kept the characters alive for him, and his own curiosity about Obie, whom he sees as a tragic but terrific character, were the impetuses for the writing of this novel.

Beyond the Chocolate War has received mostly favorable reviews; any unfavorable commentary apparently stems from a comparison with Cormier's earlier novel as the standard. For example, Hazel Rochman in the *New York Times Book Review* (5 May 1985) describes it as "not as starkly dramatic as its predecessor," and Roger Sutton in *School Library Journal* (April 1985) believes that "as a whole this is less compelling as fiction than it is as a commentary on *The Chocolate War*–Cormier here intensifies and explicates what was powerfully implicit in the first book." Awards include *Horn Book*'s listing it in "Fanfare," *Parents' Choice* (Autumn 1985) including it among their remarkable books, and the *New York Times* naming it a Notable Book of the Year for 1985.

Beyond the Chocolate War takes place in the spring following the fall sale of the chocolates at Trinity High. Cormier introduces several new characters. The first is Ray Bannister, who serves two functions. By using Ray's ability with magic to trick the students at Trinity High, Cormier surprises his readers as well; and by having Obie provide Ray with information necessary to his survival at Trinity, Cormier reveals the background information for the reader unfamiliar with *The Chocolate War*. Cormier does not disappoint his readers. Archie is still the clever, manipulative "Assigner" of the Vigils, and Obie is still obedient.

which meant he was now 65 pounds overweight. Found it hard
to breath going up the stairs, ~~XXXXXXX~~ sweated all the time,
perpetually moist, oozing. And ~~top~~ on top of all that, the
Vigils.

He was bubbling with sweat now as he stood in the
small storage room in the ~~XXX~~ gym. He had to blink to get rid
of the ~~moisture~~ perspiration gathering in his eyes, ~~from the perspiration~~
~~coming from his forehead.~~ He knew that he looked as if he was
crying. But he wasn't. He didn't want anybody to think he
was a weeper. Underneath this terrible fat that he couldn't ~~XXX~~
get rid of, on disguise, he was brave and strong and durable. As he stood
before the members of the Vigils, ~~XXX~~ he was determined to put
up a good front, despite the fat and the sweat. He ~~XXX~~ recognized
some of the guys who sat in the ~~XXX~~ room's dimness, knew their
names but had never ~~XXXXX~~ talked to any of them. Freshmen like Tubs
kept out of the way of upperclassmen. He looked around for
the kid called ~~XXX~~ Obie but did not see him here. Obie was the
only Vigil member he ~~knew~~ had talked with and he preferred ~~XXX~~ not to think about
their association, the ~~only time they'd talked,~~ because it had
to do with Rita ~~and~~ the chocolate.

There was an attitude of waiting in the room, as the
guys talked together in low tones. They ~~XXXXXXXXXXXXXXXX~~ acted as if
~~XXX~~ Tubs didn't exist. Tubs knew ~~XXXXXXX~~ who ~~XXX~~ they were waiting
for. ~~XXX~~ Archie Costello. He dreaded Archie Costello's arrival.
He knew all about him, his power and his assignments. ~~First Rita,~~
~~now XXX this.~~

Page from the penultimate draft of Beyond the Chocolate War, *the sequel to Cormier's earlier novel about the Vigils, a gang
which seeks to dominate the student body of Trinity High School (by permission of the author)*

But Obie falls in love, an action entirely independent of Archie and one that opens his eyes to certain facts about Archie's behavior and about his own. Laurie Gundarson, Obie's girlfriend, is horrified to learn that he belongs to the Vigils. Her reaction, the unpleasant memory of Jerry Renault, and the attack on the young couple by some members of the Vigils, are enough to make Obie realize that he had free choice all along. He did not have to follow Archie; he should have said "no" when his conscience told him to do so. To atone for his own inexcusable behavior, Obie decides to rid the school of Archie forever. Cormier is particularly convincing when Obie's plan fails and when Obie, as well as the reader, learns that there will always be evil. When Archie graduates, Bunting will take his place. It is up to the Obies and the Jerry Renaults of the world to take a stand against evil. Cormier drives his point home more forcibly here than he did in the earlier novel.

Bunting, along with his two stooges, Harley and Cornacchio, are the other new characters. Bunting, lacking the cleverness of Archie, is more heavy-handed. He initiates the near rape of Laurie, thus ruining Obie's chances with her and prompting Obie to seek his revenge by means of the guillotine, constructed by Ray Bannister and described dramatically in the novel's opening sentence.

Although Obie does not succeed in his revenge, Jerry Renault, the crushed hero of *The Chocolate War*, wins a victory at last. Jerry again confronts Emile Janza, his opponent in the dramatic fight on the football field at the close of the earlier novel. This time Jerry is able to deflate and defeat Emile. His refusal to fight on Emile's terms serves as a quiet victory and a positive message for the reader. His nonviolence is a result of his contemplative life in Canada where he sought and found comfort in the church. Cormier intimates that Jerry may become a priest. Jerry becomes a positive role model as a friend to Goober, sensing Goober's problems and responding to them. Goober, on the other hand, is unable to understand Jerry's problems and worries about betraying Jerry.

The theme of betrayal, accompanied by revenge, appears on many levels and in many instances. Obie thinks that Archie ordered the attack on Laurie and him; thus he betrays Archie. Carter notifies Brother Leon of the Vigils' plan to boycott the assembly when the bishop visits Trinity. Archie seeks revenge and Carter suffers, but

Carter was true to his ideals. David Caroni feels betrayed by Brother Leon, who gave him an *F* when he was a straight-*A* student; Caroni's revenge takes the form of an attack on Brother Leon, followed by suicide.

Several characters mature in the course of the novel; and with that maturity, Cormier includes more explicit sexual scenes. Obie's relationship with Laurie is a loving one, in contrast to Archie's relationship with Jill Morton. The inclusion of the near rape of Laurie, the sex scenes with Archie and Jill, and the sexual gratification of Emile Janza from fighting, along with the language Cormier uses in this novel, are more likely to provoke censorship from those who have not recently heard worse in their local high schools.

Maturity also appears in the form of the responsibilities of friendship between Goober and Jerry, the social responsibility that Corter displays, and the moral responsibility that Cornacchio exhibits in his refusal to follow Bunting after the near rape. Perhaps Obie matures the most, however, for he learns that he has always had a choice about following the Archies of the world. Archie's mottoes of "outfox, outwit, outdeal everybody else" and "do unto others, then split" will no longer be accepted by Obie. Obie has grown up, a particularly satisfying conclusion to this provocative novel.

In November 1988, *Fade*, Cormier's most sophisticated book to date, appeared. Spanning three generations and set primarily in Frenchtown, the French Canadian section of Monument, the novel centers on Paul Moreaux, who has inherited the ability to fade or become invisible, a characteristic occurring in the Moreaux family once a generation and passed from uncle to nephew. A fader can recognize another fader and is able to sense the presence of another; as well, he is able to intuit the proper time to seek out the young one in adolescence and educate him about his "power." Uncle Adelard, the fader of the previous generation, cautions Paul about the misuse of power just as Paul will later try to warn his nephew, Ozzie Slater, about the power.

The fade has been interpreted in various ways—as evil, or even as original sin. At first a blessing, it becomes a curse. Its power enables Paul to escape from danger of attack by a Ku Klux Klan member and later by a bully, but it also enables him to observe some sexual acts, shocking to him and perhaps to the teenage reader as well. The fade or lust for power or evil gradually assumes control over the fader until acts of violence and several murders are perpetrated and the fader's life changed irrevocably. Paul vows after an act of revenge not to use the fade again, and he does not until he feels he must to prove to his nephew that he possesses the ability.

Structurally, the novel is complex even though divided into only five sections because of the various settings (Monument; New York; Ramsey, Maine; Boston) and the changes in protagonist (Paul, Susan, Paul, Ozzie, Susan); however, even more important is Cormier's breaking the world of the novel's first section by inquiring in the second whether or not the first is believable. Thus the first and third sections, narrated in first person, focus on Paul Moreaux in 1938 and 1963, respectively. The second and fifth center on Susan Roget, a distant cousin of Paul Roget, the noted author who wrote the Paul Moreaux manuscript. These sections are set in 1988, twenty-one years after Paul Roget's death. Susan has obtained a job working for Paul Roget's former editor, Meredith Martin; she and Meredith question the credibility of the manuscript. Is it Paul Roget's thinly veiled autobiography, or is it a fantasy? The fourth section, narrated in third person, belongs to Ozzie Slater, Paul Moreaux's nephew, also a fader. Ozzie becomes a monster, creating havoc and seeking revenge for his mistreatment and abuse by an adoptive father.

In the concluding section Susan reads a newspaper account of two incidents involving the type of destruction Ozzie perpetrated, although Ozzie is now dead. The article suggests that only an invisible culprit would have been able to penetrate the security systems. Could this vandal be the next generation fader after Ozzie? Is his appearance the reason for Paul's strange request to his lawyer just before he died that the lawyer not submit the manuscript to Paul's editor until twenty-one years later? Cormier, in typical fashion, leaves these questions and others unanswered.

In *Fade* Cormier has employed many of the devices he used in previous novels. Paul Moreaux, the possibly unreliable narrator, echoes Barney Snow from *The Bumblebee Flies Anyway*. Ozzie follows in the tradition of Archie from *The Chocolate War* as a character who lives by no rules. Although *Fade* is told mostly from Paul's point of view, it develops further the narrative patterns of *I Am the Cheese* and *After the First Death* through the device of varying points of view. The ambiguity of certain sections of *Fade*—the "coincidence" that Paul's brother dies young as did Adelard's—echoes unanswered questions in other novels,

such as whether or not the Hertz family was involved in the betrayal of the Farmers in *I Am the Cheese*. Cormier's use here of his characteristic open ending—was there ever a fader and does one still exist?—parallels the ambiguous conclusions in the earlier novels, such as will Jerry Renault survive, did the CIA kill the Farmers, and will Miro continue to kill before he is caught? Even though the alert reader perceives that Cormier employs these devices more than once, the author still surprises, teases, and even tricks his readers, but, above all, he entertains them.

Thematically, *Fade* incorporates a maturation theme, but not the usual one. All recipients of the power of the fade are teenagers; they must learn to weigh good and evil, to make decisions for themselves, and to be responsible for the misuse of power. The terrible secret causes each one to become more isolated from his family and friends. Uncle Adelard becomes a wanderer, afraid his ability will be discovered if he remains in one place too long; Paul becomes a recluse, for fear of discovery. Ozzie, already a loner because he had been given away by his unwed mother at birth and adopted by a woman, now dead, and her two husbands—the second of whom was a wife and child abuser—becomes a wild, reckless, vicious youth who uses his ability to fade to seek revenge by murder. Other themes include gifts that become curses, other types of fading that occur in real life, revenge, abuse, betrayal, incest, as well as family love, sacrifice, and young love.

One topic new to the Cormier canon in this novel is the development of a writer. Not only do readers gain insight about Paul Roget as the author of *Bruises in Paradise*, *Come Home, Come Home*, and *Dialogue at Midnight*, as well as the Paul Moreaux manuscript, but they also become intimately involved with Susan Roget as she struggles to become a writer, quoting a professor's directions on how to begin, on being oneself, and on being willing to take risks. Even the problems of editors are presented, such as Meredith quoting Paul Roget that a novelist is permitted "one major coincidence" in a book, and the pains and difficulties confronting editors in verifying details.

Fade contains many autobiographical elements, and Paul, by Cormier's own admission, is his most autobiographical character. In an article in *Horn Book* (March / April 1989) entitled "Creating *Fade*," Cormier describes the photograph of his father's family, complete with missing uncle, which provided one impetus for the novel. Another was the need to look back, to recapture a time in the past during which he spent two and a half years writing the novel which would later be revised to half its original length. In the 1963 section of Paul's manuscript the scenes between Paul and his father are reminiscent of those between Cormier and his father; he found them especially painful to cut, but they were greatly shortened. Some other autobiographical elements are Paul's desire to be a writer, his attitude toward Catholicism, his paper route, his conflict with a bully, and his crushes on females. Paul's cousin Susan is modeled somewhat after Cormier's youngest child, Renee.

Virtually all critics agree that *Fade* is an exciting book. The American Library Association has included it in its Best Books for Young Adults for 1988. The *Bulletin for the Center of Children's Books* (November 1988) calls *Fade* "brilliant in conception, intricate in structure." The *Voice of Youth Advocates* (December 1988) and *Horn Book* (January / February 1989) reviewers both use the term "thought-provoking"; *Publishers Weekly* (30 September 1988) calls it "gripping" and suggests it "works better as allegory than as fantasy." The *Book Report* (November / December 1988) critic labels it "spellbinding" and "fast-paced . . . sure to enthrall senior high students and adults." The book was marketed, as most of Cormier's books were, both as an adult and young-adult novel. The starred review of *Kirkus* (1 August 1988) calls *Fade* "a profoundly disturbing, finely crafted gem that's hard, cold, and brilliant." The reviewer for *Booklist* (1 September 1988) presents some criticism of the "high-blown language ('the awful anguish of pain') and portentous rhetorical questions ('But then, isn't all of life a kind of fading?') and [of the] plot (the last section focusing on Paul's nephew is predictable and overextended)"; but even that criticism is tempered with the conclusion that "Cormier is a masterful story teller."

Although Cormier claims that he gets his plots from serendipity, he works hard writing and rewriting, often discarding hundreds of pages as he did from *Beyond the Chocolate War* and *Fade*. His work proves his versatility. Avid fans in many countries have purchased millions of copies of his books. He has traveled extensively speaking to and listening to young adults in most of the fifty states, as well as in Australia, England, and Scotland. He said in a recent letter to this au-

thor (23 May 1989) that "teenagers are teenagers all over the world and sitting on school steps in Melbourne with thirteen and fourteen year olds, I could have been in Boston, Massachusetts, or Edinburgh, Scotland." Cormier has acquired these fans because of his sensitive awareness about what actually occurs in the lives of teenagers today and his abundant talent for conveying that awareness through fiction. He has brought controversy and, simultaneously, a new dimension to the field of young-adult literature. He has earned the respect of his readers, regardless of their age, because of his refusal to compromise the truth as he sees it. His superb craftsmanship, his ability to create suspense and to shock the reader repeatedly, and his forcing the reader to think are all qualities which make Cormier's works entertaining, unique, and, indeed, unforgettable.

Interviews:

Paul Janeczko, "In Their Own Words: An Interview with Robert Cormier," *English Journal*, 66 (September 1977): 10-11.
     A discussion of Cormier as a journalist and his transition to a novelist.

George Christian, "Conversations: Novelist Robert Cormier and Reporter Nora Ephron," *Houston Chronicle*, 14 May 1978, p.12.
     An early interview revealing the impetus for Cormier's writing *The Chocolate War* and how Cormier became a young-adult author.

Geraldine DeLuca and Roni Natov, "An Interview with Robert Cormier," *The Lion and the Unicorn*, 2 (Fall 1978): 109-135.
     An excellent discussion of *The Chocolate War* and some discussion of Cormier's earlier adult novels, as well as *After the First Death*.

Laurel Graeber, "PW Interviews Robert Cormier," *Publishers Weekly*, 224 (7 October 1983): 98-99.
     An analysis of *The Bumblelee Flies Anyway* and some commentary on the movie version of *I Am the Cheese*.

Anita Silvey, "An Interview with Robert Cormier," *Horn Book*, 61, Part I (March / April 1985): 145-155; Part II (May / June 1985): 289-296.
     A comprehensive interview including the reasons why Cormier wrote the sequel to *The*

Chocolate War, the effects of serendipity, and the influence of other authors on Cormier's writing.

References:

Norma Bagnall, "Realism: How Realistic Is It? A Look at *The Chocolate War*," *Top of the News*, 36 (Winter 1980): 214-217.
An article voicing mostly negative criticism of *The Chocolate War*.

Patricia J. Campbell, *Presenting Robert Cormier* (Boston: G. K. Hall, 1985).
A well-researched, readable full-length study with a much needed bibliography.

Betty Carter and Karen Harris, "Realism in Adolescent Fiction: In Defense of *The Chocolate War*," *Top of the News*, 36 (Spring 1980): 283-285.
An effective answer to Bagnall's article criticizing *The Chocolate War*.

William A. Davis, "Tough Tales for Teenagers," *Boston Globe Magazine*, 16 November 1980, pp. 17, 22, 24, 26, 30, 32-37.
An analysis of Cormier's career through the publication of *Eight Plus One*.

Helen Dudar, "Books: What Johnny Can't Read," *The Soho News*, 4 June 1980, pp.15-16.
A five-paragraph essay containing the oft-published anecdote about a student successfully defending *The Chocolate War* against censorship.

Lee Grove, "Robert Cormier Comes of Age," *Boston Magazine* (December 1980): 78, 81, 82, 84, 86-90, 92, 94.
A sensitive account of Cormier's career through the publication of *I Am the Cheese*.

Sylvia Patterson Iskander, "Readers, Realism, and Robert Cormier," *Children's Literature Journal*, 15 (1987): 7-18.
An in-depth analysis of Cormier's works using Todorov's levels of realism, some of which elude certain readers, thus providing various interpretations of the same work.

Millicent Lenz, "A Romantic Ironist's Vision of Evil: Robert Cormier's *After the First Death*," *Proceedings of the Eighth Annual Conference of The Children's Literature Association, Minneapolis, Minnesota* (March 1981), pp. 50-56.
A perceptive study of Cormier as a romanticist (beginning with an emotion which leads to character which in turn suggests plot) and as a writer of irony.

Anne Scott MacLeod, "Robert Cormier and the Adolescent Novel," *Children's Literature in Education*, 12 (Summer 1981): 74-81.
The first in-depth article to treat the theme of the power struggle between the individual and various systems (schools, government agencies, military).

Frank Myszor, "The See-Saw and the Bridge in Robert Cormier's *After the First Death*," *Children's Literature Journal*, 16 (1988): 77-90.
A detailed metaphorical, semantic, and structural analysis of *After the First Death*.

Tony Schwartz, "Teen-agers' Laureate," *Newsweek*, 94 (16 July 1979): 87, 88, 92.
A favorable review which brought Cormier's name and novels to the attention of a larger reading public.

Nancy Veglahn, "The Bland Face of Evil in the Novels of Robert Cormier," *The Lion and the Unicorn*, 12 (1988): 12-18.
A provocative analysis of Cormier's creation of evil characters, often adults masquerading as harmless or even benevolent teachers, doctors, fathers.

Papers:
Cormier donated his manuscripts and all his working papers to Fitchburg State College, Fitchburg, Massachusetts, in 1981.

James Dickey

This entry was updated by Ronald Baughman (University of South Carolina) from the entry by Robert Hill (Clemson University) in DLB 5, American Poets Since World War II and the entry by Donald J. Greiner (University of South Carolina) in DLB Yearbook 1982.

Places	Atlanta
	Northern Georgia
	  Wilderness
		The South Pacific
		Vanderbilt
			University of
			  South Carolina

Influences and Relationships	Theodore Roethke Robert Penn Warren James Agee	Gerard Manley Hopkins D. H. Lawrence	Malcolm Lowry Ezra Pound Randall Jarrell
Literary Movements and Forms	Emphasis on Narrative	Platonism Neo-Romanticism	French Symbolists Speech Rhythms

Major Themes	Predator-Prey
	  Relationship
	Intensification of
	  Reality by
	  Poetry
	Renewal of Life
	  as a Result of
	  Survivor's Guilt
		Mystical Exchange
		  between Self and
		  Another Creature
		  or Object
		Emphasis on
		  Writer's
		  Personality
			Life of Consequence
			  as a Result of
			  Energized Living
			Participation of the
			  Dead with the
			  Living

Cultural and Artistic Influences	Ancient Greek
	  Philosophers (Py-
	  thagoras, Heraclitus,
	  Anaximander)
		Astronomy
		Athletics
			Appalachian Music

Social and Economic Influences	World War II	The Depression	Advertising / Business

BIRTH: Atlanta, Georgia, 2 February 1923, to Eugene and Maibelle Swift Dickey.

EDUCATION: Clemson College, 1942; A.B., M.A., Vanderbilt University, 1949, 1950.

MARRIAGE: 4 November 1948 to Maxine Syerson, died 28 October 1976; children: Christopher Swift, Kevin Webster. 30 December 1976 to Deborah Elizabeth Dodson; child: Bronwen.

AWARDS AND HONORS: *Sewanee Review* Fellowship, 1954-1955; Union League Civic and Arts Foundation Prize (*Poetry* magazine), 1958; Longview Foundation, 1959; Vachel Lindsay Prize, 1959; Guggenheim Fellowship, 1961; National Book Award for *Buckdancer's Choice,* 1966; Melville Cane Award (Poetry Society of America) for *Buckdancer's Choice,* 1966; National Institute of Arts and Letters Award, 1966; Consultant in Poetry in English for the Library of Congress, 1966-1968; Prix Medicis, 1971; *New York Quarterly* Poetry Day Award, 1977; Levinson Prize (*Poetry* magazine) for five poems in *Puella,* 1981; elected to American Academy and Institute of Arts and Letters, 1988.

BOOKS: *Into the Stone and Other Poems,* in *Poets of Today VII,* edited by John Hall Wheelock (New York: Scribners, 1960);
Drowning with Others (Middletown, Conn.: Wesleyan University Press, 1962);
Helmets (Middletown, Conn.: Wesleyan University Press, 1964; London: Longmans, Green, 1964);
Two Poems of the Air (Portland, Oreg.: Centicore Press, 1964);
The Suspect in Poetry (Madison, Minn.: Sixties Press, 1964);
Buckdancer's Choice (Middletown, Conn.: Wesleyan University Press, 1965);
A Private Brinksmanship (Claremont, Cal.: Pilzer College, 1965);
Poems 1957-1967 (Middletown, Conn.: Wesleyan University Press, 1967; London: Rapp & Carroll, 1967);
Spinning the Crystal Ball (Washington, D.C.: Library of Congress, 1967);
Babel to Byzantium: Poets & Poetry Now (New York: Farrar, Straus & Giroux, 1968);
Metaphor as Pure Adventure (Washington, D.C.: Library of Congress, 1968);
Poems (1967) (Melbourne: Sun Books, 1968);
Deliverance (Boston: Houghton Mifflin, 1970; London: Hamish Hamilton, 1970);

James Dickey with his daughter, Bronwen, around 1983 (photo by Leonhard Copeland)

The Eye-Beaters, Blood, Victory, Madness, Buckhead and Mercy (Garden City, N.Y.: Doubleday, 1970; London: Hamish Hamilton, 1971);
Self-Interviews, edited by Barbara and James Reiss (Garden City, N.Y.: Doubleday, 1970);
Sorties: Journal and New Essays (Garden City, N.Y.: Doubleday, 1971);
Exchanges (Bloomfield Hills, Mich.: Bruccoli Clark, 1971);
Jericho: The South Beheld, with paintings by Hubert Shuptrine (Birmingham, Ala.: Oxmoor House, 1974);
The Zodiac (Garden City, N.Y.: Doubleday, 1976);
God's Images, with etchings by Marvin Hayes (Birmingham, Ala.: Oxmoor House, 1977);
Tucky the Hunter (New York: Crown, 1978; London: Macmillan, 1979);
In Pursuit of the Grey Soul (Columbia, S.C. & Bloomfield Hills, Mich.: Bruccoli Clark, 1978);
The Enemy from Eden (Northridge, Cal.: Lord John Press, 1978);

Head-Deep in Strange Sounds (Winston-Salem, N.C.: Palaemon, 1979);

The Strength of Fields (Garden City, N.Y.: Doubleday, 1979);

The Waterbug's Mittens / Ezra Pound: What We Can Use (Columbia, S.C. & Bloomfield Hills, Mich.: Bruccoli Clark, 1980)–350 numbered copies, signed;

Scion (Deerfield, Mass.: Deerfield Press, 1980) –300 copies, signed;

The Eagle's Mile (Columbia, S.C. & Bloomfield Hills, Mich.: Bruccoli Clark, 1981)–trade edition and 250 numbered copies, signed;

The Early Motion: Drowning with Others and Helmets (Middletown, Conn.: Wesleyan University Press, 1981);

Falling, May Day Sermon, and Other Poems (Middletown, Conn.: Wesleyan University Press, 1981);

The Starry Place Between the Antlers: Why I Live in South Carolina (Columbia, S.C. & Bloomfield Hills, Mich.: Bruccoli Clark, 1981)–trade edition and 500 numbered copies, signed;

How to Enjoy Poetry (New York: International Paper Company, 1982);

Puella (Garden City, N.Y.: Doubleday, 1982);

Night Hurdling: Poems, Essays, Conversations, Commencements, and Afterwards (Columbia, S.C. & Bloomfield Hills, Mich.: Bruccoli Clark, 1983);

Four Seasons: False Youth (Dallas: Pressworks, 1983);

Bronwen, the Traw, and the Shape-Shifter, illustrated by Richard Jesse Watson (San Diego, New York & London: Bruccoli Clark Layman / Harcourt Brace Jovanovich, 1986);

Alnilam (Garden City, N.Y.: Doubleday, 1987);

Wayfarer: A Voice from the Southern Mountains, with photographs by William A. Bake (Birmingham, Ala.: Oxmoor House, 1988).

Glory came early in James Dickey's career: six years after his first collection appeared in *Poets of Today VII* (1960), he won the 1966 National Book Award for *Buckdancer's Choice* (1965); five years after that, his novel *Deliverance* (1970) and its movie version in 1972 made him famous almost beyond the hopes of any American poet. Despite the glory and fortune proceeding from bestselling novels and movies, Dickey has persisted in his claims that "Poetry is . . . the center of the creative wheel: everything else is actually just a spinoff from that: literary criticism, screenplays, novels, even advertising copy." But Dickey objects to the idea of poetry as only a linguistic exercise: "I dislike the hell out of the notion of poetry or the poem as a kind of a lab subject laid up on the seminar table like a dead cat in a biology lab to be dissected all with a great steaming-up of glasses." Dickey also refuses to be bound strictly to what others might construe to be The Truth: "The poet is not trying to tell the truth; he's trying to make it, and he tries to make a different version of it from the official version that God made or the world made."

For Dickey, as he recounts in the autobiographical *Self-Interviews* (1970), to be an artist is also to be entrenched in the active life. Echoing Wordsworth's theory of poetry, he calls the poet "the intensified man," believing strongly in the pursuit of "wholeness." With that aggressive hold on reality, Dickey has been a football player in high school and at Clemson College, a track-record holder at Vanderbilt, a hunter with bow and arrow, a guitarist (both twelve- and six-string) with a flair for bluegrass music, a World War II air man, and a training officer in the Korean War. Other than poetry and fiction, his occupations have included teaching, lecturing, acting (the redneck sheriff in *Deliverance*), and a six-year stint with advertising firms in Atlanta and New York. In 1961, having received a Guggenheim Fellowship, Dickey went to Europe, leaving advertising behind forever. Since deciding on a literary career, Dickey has held teaching and writer-in-residence positions at Rice University, Reed College, San Fernando State College, the University of Wisconsin, George Mason University, and is presently Poet-in-residence and Carolina Professor of English at the University of South Carolina. He has been broadly honored by critics and the public press, and his national recognition reached honorific peaks with his two-year appointment as Poetry Consultant to the Library of Congress, 1966-1968, his televised reading of "The Strength of Fields" at the Inauguration celebration for Jimmy Carter in 1977, and his 1988 induction into the fifty-member American Academy and Institute of Arts and Letters.

Dickey's early poetry begins with reasonably familiar themes, so it is accessible even as it leads to new ground. The first volume, *Into the Stone* (1960), contains poems about nature, with special attention to the infusion of natural feelings, skills, instincts, and energies into people. In these poems, the human being often acts acquisitively toward nature to gain nonhuman powers; thus, mystery and ritual abide with ghostly presences, often the poet's brother Eugene, without whose death at six of spinal meningitis, Dickey speculates, he himself might never have been conceived by his mother, whose angina pectoris greatly darkened any prospects of childbirth.

Oddly, despite many allusions to the poet's own family, the typical voices of *Into the Stone* are remote and detached, often employing austere, elegant diction. In "The Underground Stream," for example, the speaker lies at the edge of a well, seeking how his spirit could fall deep into the earth through the stream and then come to some reconciliation with his dead brother, who seems to want to "claim his grave face / That mine might live in its place." This activity is inward, mystical and personal; eerily and fearsomely the dead brother in "The Underground Stream" merges with the speaker, and the mystical-natural fusion extends itself in another poem, "The String," to include the speaker's son: "Except when he enters my son, / The same age as he at his death, / I cannot bring my brother to myself." For Dickey, the whole spirit of a person is always to include the spirits of the whole family.

Precise, well-focused war poems such as "The Jewel" and "The Enclosure" recapitulate Dickey's sense of survival and reiterate his apprehension of *otherness* in human experience, that intuition of connectedness and of spiritual immanence which later flowers in "Drinking from a Helmet," "The Being," "Encounter in the Cage Country," "May Day Sermon," and "Madness." "Walking on Water" and other poems in *Into the Stone* flirt with physical experiences that are illusory but imperative to Dickey's convictions about the human potential for mystical, energized realizations. Men and women, universally, are imprisoned, whether actually, as in the case of Airman Donald Armstrong, captured by the Japanese in "The Performance," who must therefore set himself a redeeming task (his gymnastic tricks), which will require the utmost in physical concentration and expertise for a moment, however brief; or, as in "Near Darien," imprisoned simply by the strict limitations of flesh and senses, perhaps to escape in part through transcendent acts of the mind, often represented in natural terms—flight, light, song. As the poem "Into the Stone" implies by its title, the seeking of the self and communion with others by going into the soul as it is caught in paradoxical ecstasy is crucial to the mode of Dickey's first collection:

> The dead have their chance in my body.
> The stars are drawn into their myths.

> I bear nothing but moonlight upon me.
> I am known; I know my love.

Drowning with Others (1962) is more openly social than *Into the Stone*. The speaker of "The Lifeguard," for example, in his failing efforts to save a drowning child, tries to affirm his identity through service to others, rather than through an act of individual self-affirmation like that achieved by Donald Armstrong in "The Performance." *Drowning with Others* is notable, too, for the movement in the nature poems away from plant life to animate creatures: "A Dog Sleeping on My Feet," "Listening to Foxhounds," "The Movement of Fish," and "The Heaven of Animals."

In this second volume, Dickey also experiments with complex, multivoiced narration, especially in the three-part work, "The Owl King." The first part, included in *Into the Stone* as "The Call," is about a father looking for his lost son. The second part is the voice of the owl king, and the third, that of the blind child who is physically and metaphysically lost in the forest. Throughout his work, Dickey has commonly used multiple voices.

Ten years after "The Owl King," in "The Eye-Beaters," his voices remonstrate, comment, and turn himself back upon himself: the reader is told, *His Reason argues with his invention.* In *The Zodiac* (1976), the third-person omniscient narrator frequently merges or alternates with the voice of the drunken poet whose sometimes chaotic but ultimately resolved state of mind is itself the subject of the poem.

In section 2 of *Drowning with Others*, Dickey tries to deal more fully with the prisoner theme as a speaker finds himself literally "Between Two Prisoners" and thus is able to assimilate and report the experiences of others and himself, coming to that fusion of selves so powerfully worked later in "Drinking from a Helmet," "Slave Quarters," and "The Firebombing." This aesthetic viewpoint, with the speaker self-consciously observing, knowing that he has a perspective that is momentary and unique, emphasizes Dickey's exploration of the creative process, especially with regard to the use of narrative voice under special, extreme conditions.

Non-American history is rarely treated in Dickey's poetry prior to *The Zodiac*. Nonetheless, "Dover: Believing in Kings" employs a complex, symphonic structure to touch and to assimilate the history of England for this American Georgian:

> From a child's tall book, I knew this place
> The child must believe, with the king:
> Where, doubtless, now, lay lovers
> Restrained by a cloud, and the moon
> Into force coming justly, above.
> *In a movement you cannot imagine*
> *Of love, the gulls fall, mating.*

Dickey seeks the historical South in "Hunting Civil War Relics at Nimblewill Creek," but the speaker is less intimately fused with the objects of his search, the "other" subjectivity he pursues, than in "Dover: Believing in Kings," since the Civil War relics are so many, disparate, and impersonal (spotted by a mechanical, electronic metal-detector rather than the natural senses). The connection he feels with the participants in that war is faint and generalized, only tenuously like the spiritual trauma seen in the later "Drinking from a Helmet." And so the speaker of the poem is able to speculate even in the negative as to what meaning shall be put at the end: kneeling

> Like a man who renounces war,
> Or one who shall lift up the past,
> Not breathing "Father,"
> At Nimblewill,
> But saying, "Fathers! Fathers!"

Dickey's newfound historical explicitness in *Drowning with Others* goes hand in hand with a growing objectivity about his family themes and images. In such works as "The Hospital Window," Dickey's speakers seem more dispassionate, more fully removed observers than the narrators of *Into the Stone*. A movement beyond the family is also evident in part 4 of *Drowning with Others*, as "The Magus," "Facing Africa," and other poems explore experiences in the larger world.

Certain poems in Dickey's third volume, *Helmets* (1964), are explicitly aesthetic in their execution and theme, forcing the reader to recognize particular artistic effects which might otherwise be artfully concealed: poems about art, poems about the formal imaginative act. In "A Folk Singer of the Thirties," a Christ-like artist is nailed to a boxcar and sent on archetypal missions by a cretinous world of RR agents and local police. The poem is an exercise in the manipulation of authorial point of view, stepping out into a vision of the whole world. "The Beholders" is

also explicitly aesthetic; the two lovers together are the first-person plural voice of the poem:

> From above, we watch over them like gods,
> Our chins on our hands,
> Our great eyes staring, our throats dry
> And aching to cry down on their heads
> Some curse or blessing. . . .

But unlike the speaker of the later poem "The Firebombing" (1964), who decries his own "detachment, / The honored aesthetic evil," the "we" of "The Beholders" act with "the power to speak / With deadly intent of love." However serious Dickey is about aesthetic principles (and his excellent essays in *The Suspect in Poetry* [1964], *Babel to Byzantium* [1968], *Self-Interviews* and *Sorties* [1971], and elsewhere attest to his insight), he knows that "artsiness" is never adequate to the forces of experience.

Two poems in *Helmets*, "The Being" and "The Ice Skin," suggest works to come later, like "Pursuit from Under" (1964) and "The Shark's Parlor" (1965). In these poems the energy of unknown natural creatures elicits spiritual insight possible to human beings from blood-encounters with god-in-nature, which is always frightening and truly dangerous. "Kudzu" is about "something under"–the snakes–the seemingly malicious world. Dickey's speaker is to some extent threatened by the vines tapping on his window and the possibility that his cattle might be bitten by the snakes concealed in the kudzu. But when neighbors come for the ritualistic rooting out of vines and serpents, they seem as fierce as the natural problems; and the allies–the pigs, turned loose into the foliage for their ferocious hunt–are entirely horrifying, the flung snakes falling like so much confetti, far less terrible now than the unstoppable swine.

Helmets ends with three war poems: "The Driver," very like "The Jewel" except that the tread of death is heavy upon the speaker; "Horses and Prisoners," which recalls both "Trees and Cattle" *(Into the Stone)* and "Between Two Prisoners" *(Drowning with Others);* and "Drinking from a Helmet," a poem of mystical communion, with an object at hand capable of mediating between the seeker and some spirit-person who has heretofore never known the narrator. In this poem Dickey deals freshly with the spiritual union of hard-pressed survivors. It is important that this poem concludes *Helmets*, but almost equally important is that it leads directly to the first poem of Dickey's next book, *Buckdancer's*

Dickey in the early 1940s, as a football player at Clemson

Choice: "The Firebombing."

While "Drinking from a Helmet" shows Dickey's mysticism beginning to pull away from the set of images drawn from his immediate family, "The Firebombing" reveals the social breadth of his work—a dimension that has been denied by critics such as Robert Bly. In "The Firebombing" and in the concluding poem of *Buckdancer's Choice*, "Slave Quarters," Dickey makes genuine efforts to confront moral issues: in "The Firebombing" the questions of personal and societal guilt over acts of war along with, perhaps more appallingly, the feelings of guiltlessness familiar to patriotic warriors; and in "Slave Quarters," the questions of guilt over slavery compounded by sexual abuse.

"The Firebombing" is a poem of empathy, realization, ineffectual goodwill, and regret. It in part results from Dickey's own experiences in the

air force and his poetically restrained revulsion at those experiences. The mechanics of war stress objectivity, but such objectivity comes to appall the civilian codes of Dickey's narrator, who opens his eyes in a pantry and suddenly knows about napalm jellies crawling over the things of everyday America. The "aesthetic" distance between the pilot and the "target area" raises questions about the similar distancing power of art, but the poem's chief impact still comes from the immediate inhumanity of war:

> It is this detachment,
> The honored aesthetic evil,
> ....
> That must be shed in bars, or by whatever
> Means. . . .

Dickey's various images fuse the sensitivity and callousness inherent in his experience. He draws upon simple personification so that inanimate objects are caught up in the introspection that has traumatized the narrator: "the engines . . . ponder their sound"; "Japan / Dilates . . . like a thought"; "the lawn mower rests on its laurels"; "My hat should crawl on my head / In streetcars, thinking of it, / The fat on my body should pale."

Probably the richest technical rewards of "The Firebombing" result from Dickey's merging of past and present through years of memories. "Starve and take off / Twenty years in the suburbs," he says, suggesting "take off pounds" and "take off in a plane." The poem's force is redoubled by the blindness of people whose morality is softened by material comfort. The evocative parallels of "sitting in a glass treasure-hole of blue light" and "eating figs in the pantry / Blinded by each and all / Of the eye-catching cans" suggest the fatal seclusion of the mind within the very atmospheres that condition it, the blue fantasy-glory of war and the glittering satiety of American consumerism. The poem strives for resolution, but it achieves only the painful acceptance of expediency. Transcending the "dull narcotics" of "sad mechanic exercise," this poem becomes its own apology and partial expiation: "Absolution? Sentence? No matter; / The thing itself is in that."

Part 2 of *Buckdancer's Choice* begins with the title poem, about the poet's mother and her final illness, a time in which it is appropriate to reminisce and to envision aesthetic pleasures, the scenes of song and dance, the whistling of the breath that now seems so precious; but the mother is other than the speaker's self, one who is separate, though kin. The section continues with poems that deal in other "others," persons and glimpses, suggesting that the speaker is the perceiver and therefore the creator. "Faces Seen Once," "Them, Crying," and even "The Celebration," all deal with *parts* of persons, with eyes, or cries, or accoutrements, to represent the fragmentary quality of human perception and at the same time the fusing of disparate elements accomplished by the human imagination. The poem about parents in this section, "The Celebration," is an exclamation of joy at the discovery of images and memories. The time of wondering and self-seeking, of pursuit of the identity in terms of the family past, is essentially over in Dickey's work.

In the two poems composing "Fathers and Sons," Dickey turns his attention from his esoteric experience, his own personal family, to situations and characters who are purposely not Dickey himself or who stand as surrogates, as aesthetic "others" instead of mystical spirits lingering in the transcendent world. Similarly, the poet treats rather straightforwardly such characters as "Mangham," his former teacher, and in "Angina," his mother again, whose image in *Buckdancer's Choice* is in soft focus (as parents are never entirely accessible to their children). Part 3 of *Buckdancer's Choice* closes with "The Fiend," in which a voyeur climbs into a tree to peer into a tempting window. He merges with the natural objects, the tree particularly, the keys in his pocket sexually rising, the whole scene a nightmarish reverie of the man who cannot have the woman he lusts after, but whose visual pursuit of her is so real to him that the threats in his own mind are close to murder. At different stages, he momentarily gains physical/spiritual identity with nature–he is birdlike, animal-like, treelike. Though there exists the serious threat that the man might one day in his great need actually commit murder, he also, ironically, elevates to goddesslike stature the object of his love-lust.

The last poem in *Buckdancer's Choice*, "Slave Quarters," is about great sexual need in a society which at least implicitly condones the activity, even the eventuality of progeny. A slave master may, with proper discretion and consideration for his wife's knowledge and feelings, bear his sex upon his woman slaves and cause them to bear his children. The effect Dickey accomplishes in juxtaposing "The Fiend" and "Slave Quarters" is quite stunning; society would brand one man as perverse and dangerous; society would once

have frowned or snickered at the other even though his exploitation and degradation are equally heinous, perhaps even more so because the master's child is one whom he may not acknowledge.

Dickey's overtly aesthetic sense persists in the *"Falling"* section of *Poems 1957-1967* (1967). Part 1 is Dickey's second "Reincarnation" poem, but rather than the creature's being the deadly snake of "Reincarnation (I)" in *Buckdancer's Choice*, this one is a sea bird, a momentarily ungainly figure, wallowing in its unease at having found its formerly human spirit in a feathered body. The bird's state of mind modulates from the human until, in long and often hesitant lines, Dickey conveys natural joy in flight and instinctual purpose. Certain of his earlier poems prefigure pieces in this volume, but in *"Falling"* the clarity and intensity of "The Sheep Child," "Power and Light," "Adultery," and "Encounter in the Cage Country" represent an achievement rarely matched.

"Falling," with its adjunct piece, "May Day Sermon to the Women of Gilmer County, Georgia, by a Woman Preacher Leaving the Baptist Church," at the beginning of the book, has been disparaged by some critics for looseness of diction, rambling syntax, and sensationalistic imagery. In fact, however, poems like "Falling" and "The Sheep Child" stand among the finest of Dickey's career. The familiar topics are here, especially the interfusion of man and nature in Dickey's two major nature poems–"May Day Sermon," which uses fairly conventional biblical and archetypal images to portray springtime life forces and their drive through the bodied sensibilities of a dissident woman preacher with her female congregation in Gilmer County; and "The Sheep Child," which is the most radical expression of Dickey's sense of transcendence in fusing man and nature to achieve, if not "some imperishable bliss," as Wallace Stevens longs for in "Sunday Morning," at least, for Dickey, "imperishable vision."

The airline stewardess in "Falling," who accidentally falls from a plane to her death in a field in Kansas, is enormously alive as she hurtles through space, removing her clothes and imagining that she makes love in furious, death-defying motion toward fertile farms and sensuous farm people, who must in their blood understand even such a strange, naked ritual. Hers is a dance all the way to death; she makes a poem of her last life and a fertility prayer of her last breath: "AH,

GOD–." In "Falling" Dickey provides a profusion of imagery drawn from " 'the big basic forms'– rivers, mountains, woods, clouds, oceans, and the creatures that live naturally among them" *(Babel to Byzantium)*. Fertility imagery abounds: the moon; virgin sacrifice; Asherah; planting festivals; the "whores / Of Wichita"; farmers' wives; daughters urgent and sons erect in the night; "Widowed farmers whose hands float under light covers to find themselves / Arisen at sunrise"–all of these are in the figure of the stewardess who accomplishes

> Her last superhuman act   the last slow careful
>   passing of her hands
>
> All over her unharmed body   desired by every sleeper
>   in his dream. . . .

She is no longer a maiden stewardess, but a woman sacrifice, a goddess come to bring fertility to the soil.

The poem is primarily about the artificial trappings, both mental and physical, that tend to separate man from his natural self. Approximately three-fifths of the way through the narrative, the stewardess begins to remove her uniform. Dickey skillfully prefigures and postpones the girl's remembering that "she still has time to die / Beyond explanation." A hint of this ritual disrobing comes earlier with

>   the arms of her jacket slipping
> Air up her sleeves to go   all over her?What final
>   things can be said
> Of one who starts out sheerly in her body in the high
>   middle of night
>
> Air . . . ?

And the poem is an attempt to suggest "what final things can be said." The stewardess, whose thoughts are filled with uniforms, labels, and TV, has "her eyes opened wide" as the world diminishes to one state, and finally to "a little sight left in the corner / Of one eye." And the reader stands with the astonished farmers to see trim technology "driven well into the image of her body / The furrows for miles around flowing in upon her." From Dickey's point of view, the stewardess transcends the mundane and finds a new sense of life in her mortal descent.

The emphasis on sexuality in "Falling" and many of Dickey's other poems reiterates his theme that procreative and pleasurable urges of sex *are* the motion of life and of art. The story of the young lovers in "May Day Sermon to the Women of Gilmer County, Georgia, by a Woman Preacher Leaving the Baptist Church" lives because it is inseparable from the burgeoning spring of Gilmer County. Every year the lovers are resurrected, their sexuality implied again in sermons to new young lovers. Ostensibly the woman preacher speaks on May Day against the sexual sins of the young, but the poet acts through her to show the vital eroticism that underlies much of backwoods religious ecstasy. This major theme of the poem is substantiated by the woman preacher's ambiguous stance as she supposedly levels the lightning of the Word at these amorous young people. Her earnestness in the sermon, the purity of her personal past, and her motives for "leaving the Baptist Church" all come under suspicion. Even as she claims to aid in stifling the springtime mating urges of the local virgins, she never actually condemns the girls, except through her vivid projections of an outraged father, whose sadistic sexual morality is itself in question. In her sermon's chief illustration, she displays an intriguingly specific knowledge of the sexually delinquent girl's punishment:

>   Listen: often a girl in the country,
> Mostly   sweating mostly in spring, deep enough in the
>   holy Bible
> Belt, will feel her hair rise up   arms rise, and this
>   not any wish
>
> Of hers, and clothes like lint shredding off
>   her   abominations
>   In the sight of the Lord; will hear the Book speak like a
>   father
> Gone mad. . . .

With the incantatory lines he has established early in the poem, Dickey heightens emotions until the girl's retributive slaying of her father prevents simple moralizing. The passions' dam has broken, as it does each year when this story is told, and warm floods sweep aside the fundamentalist morality; it is clear that the violence comes simply because of violent attempts to stop the fertile world from being itself each spring. The preacher has no choice but to stand somewhat dazed by her own sermon, perhaps unwittingly reconciled to the same passionate forces she has tried to oppose. The poem-sermon is built and spent in a manner remarkably like that of sexual passion, and the preacher is the author of it.

While it preaches no sermon, "The Sheep Child" attains very nearly the power of mythic utterance. The sheep child itself speaks at the end of the poem, and it shows its magnified view of the truth of two worlds:

> I saw for a blazing moment
> The great grassy world from both sides,
> Man and beast in the round of their need,
> And the hill wind stirred in my wool,
> My hoof and my hand clasped each other,
> I ate my one meal
> Of milk, and died
> Staring. From dark grass I came straight
>
> To my father's house, whose dust
> Whirls up in the halls for no reason
> When no one comes   piling deep in a hellish mild
> corner,
>
> And, through my immortal waters,
> I met the sun's grains eye
> To eye, and they fail at my closet of glass.
> Dead, I am most surely living
> In the minds of farm boys. . . .

At the most elementary level, this poem deals with the frustration of restraining the natural impulses to sex, and the fantasies that make such restraint possible. These fantasies have their Freudian revenge, for a time: "*Dreaming of me, / They groan they wait they suffer / Themselves, they marry, they raise their kind.*" So the farm boys' needs–precipitous in their motion toward sexual fulfillment ("wild to couple / With anything")–are tempered "by legends," the replacement of abstract morality with concrete narrative "truth." Even the sheep child itself is immortalized–"Pickled in alcohol"–in a museum, in "*my immortal waters.*" Classical and Christian mythology associated with this legend abound, with the god-lover coming to serve his procreative blessings upon some mortal female. In *Self-Interviews*, Dickey recalls, "I intended no blasphemy or obscenity by this poem at all. I tried to the best of my ability to write a poem about the universal need for contact between living creatures that runs through all of sentient nature and recognizes no boundaries of species or anything else." It is also important to remember that, although the figure of the sheep child is monstrous, it does demonstrate the fusion of man and nature and that, with "*eyes / Far more than human,*" the sheep child has eternal, unyielding vision.

The Eye-Beaters, Blood, Victory, Madness, Buckhead and Mercy (1970) includes several of Dickey's most familiar poems, among them "Looking for the Buckhead Boys," his poignant exploration of efforts to recapture the past; "Messages," two poems, treating father-son relationships; and "Apollo," his two-poem meditation on the first manned moon landing. In one of the title poems, "The Eye-Beaters," Dickey presents a compendium of many of his ideas about aesthetics and religion; to convey these ideas he has rendered three major physical actions in the poem: eye-beating by blind children, cave-painting, and hunting. The poem ends with the persona, enlightened by his experience from (and to) the depths of his racial memory, going out into the modern world to "hunt":

> The tribal children lie
> On their rocks in their animal skins   seeing in spurts
> of eye-beating
> Dream, the deer, still wet with creation, open its image
> to the heart's
> Blood, as I step forward, as I move through the beast-
> paint of the stone,
> Taken over, submitting, brain-weeping. Light me a
> torch with what we have preserved
> Of lightning. Cloud bellows in my hand. Good man
> hunter artist father
> Be with me. My prey is rock-trembling, calling. Beast,
> get in
> My way. Your body opens onto the plain. Deer, take me
> into your life-
> lined form. I merge, I pass beyond in secret   in
> perversity and the sheer
> Despair of invention   my double-clear bifocals
> off   my reason gone
> Like eyes. Therapist, farewell at the living end. Give
> me my spear.

To hunt–or to render hunting poetically–is to confront nature on its own terms. To hunt is to be able, within some limits of natural animals' instincts, to impose human ritual, human order, upon the nonhuman, animate world. It is in this not-fully-human-controlled / not-purely-instinctual quality that hunting *is* life and *is* art. It is the recognition of this quality that "The Eye-Beaters" offers.

As Dickey progressed through *Helmets* and *Buckdancer's Choice* to *Poems 1957-1967* (1967), he moved more into the tradition of the southern storyteller, so that the point of view of the narrator became almost as interesting in itself as the putative subject matter of the work. This shift in Dickey's self-conscious poetic voice may correlate to his allegation that he became a poet when he "learned the creative possibilities of the lie," that is, the taking on of masks and voices not his own in real life. It may also be tied, at least in part, to Dickey's story that his early poems emerged from precognitive rhythms to which he afterwards fastened words, and then to his later emphasis on narrative as the basis for his most satisfying writing. In "The Poet Turns on Himself" (1966), Dickey wrote, "now and then I began to hear lines of verse, lines without words to them, that had what was to me a very compelling sound: an unusual sound of urgency and passion, of grave conviction, or inevitability, of the same kind of drive and excitement that one hears in a good passage of slow jazz." By the time *Self-Interviews* appeared in 1970, Dickey was declaring how important narrative was to him: "I liked narrative, I liked something that moved from an event or an action through something else, and resolved into something else, so that there was a constant sense of change in the poem. . . . "

Dickey's interest in narrative suffused not only his poetry during the late 1960s but also stunningly manifested itself in his first novel, *Deliverance* (1970), which quickly became a best-seller and an equally successful movie (1972). *Deliverance* focuses on the transformation that occurs in four Atlanta suburbanites who take a weekend excursion down the Cahulawassee River in the North Georgia mountains. Divided into five sections–Before, September 14th, September 15th, September 16th, and After–the novel's structure carefully outlines what the men are before they enter the wilderness and what they become through and after their experience.

Before launching them on their canoe trip, Dickey defines the four characters and their histories: Bobby Trippie is dependent upon the city and its comforts; Drew Ballinger is an idealist and devoted family man; Lewis Medlock is independent and undomesticated, choosing to hone his skills as an outdoorsman, a survivalist. Protagonist Ed Gentry bridges the disparities among these men, sharing a bit of all three, yet dissatisfied with his life as a man who slides through world and experience as a practiced "get-through-the-day man." He is an eager pupil of Lewis's archery, hunting, and canoeing skills, yet also shares the others' wishes to accept life with as little resistance as possible.

Once they enter the world of nature, leaving family and business behind in Atlanta, Ed particularly responds to the challenges of the outdoors. Clearly, he is a novice, but he works hard at improving his hunting and canoeing skills. On the second day of their outing, however, Bobby and Ed are attacked by two mountain men who sodomize Bobby and threaten to sexually abuse Ed. Lewis rescues his friends by killing one of the mountain men with an arrow and scaring

away the other. The central moral crisis of the novel occurs as the men consider what to do with the body. Drew argues that they should turn themselves over to the authorities, asserting that man is much more than a primitive animal. The others, however, override him, proclaiming that man's laws do not apply in the heart of nature; rather, the dictates of nature, not man, must prevail.

As they travel down the river, Drew is either shot from above or is killed falling into the rapids-filled river. At the same point, Lewis falls out of the canoe and breaks his leg, leaving only Bobby and Ed to insure their safety for the rest of the journey. Ed realizes that he is now in command of the expedition and that he must operate as if a killer has shot Drew and is now stalking them. Ed has gained as much as he can from Lewis, and now turns to the river and the mountains to complete his transformation from city dweller to creature of nature. He must think in terms of a predator pursuing its prey.

In one of the novel's most compelling scenes, Ed climbs a sheer mountain cliff to gain an advantage over the other man. His climb, which begins with Ed in a fetal position and ends with his standing fully erect, demonstrates how he has gained a new life in nature. Successfully hunting and killing the man who is presumably attempting to kill the rest of the group, Ed saves Bobby and Lewis's lives. In a much deeper sense he saves himself by changing his own life forever. Although he must confront the troubling moral implications of his act, Ed realizes that it has also transformed him into a man who will now seek consequentiality in all dimensions of his life as he returns to civilization. He has achieved his own deliverance from an empty, routine life by gaining a difficult but significant new life of purpose and commitment.

During the period from 1974 to 1977, Dickey published three books which many people considered disappointments, but to confront these books' subject matter, their themes, and their issuance is to perceive important developments in Dickey's career. These books include *Jericho: The South Beheld* (1974), a heavy, expensive coffee-table book illustrated with color prints of paintings by Hubert Shuptrine; *The Zodiac* (1976), a sixty-two-page poem; and *God's Images* (1977), with black-and-white etchings by Marvin Hayes.

The most striking effect of these three books published in quick succession is that they

Dickey as an airman in World War II

served to consolidate at the half-century of his life Dickey's major cultural influences: southern America, Western Europe, and the Judeo-Christian tradition. *Jericho: The South Beheld* explores the rich prose language and sensual impressions of the American South, which Dickey has publicly championed, especially during and after the election of Jimmy Carter to the presidency. *The Zodiac*, as Dickey says, is a poem "based on another of the same title . . . [which] was written by Hendrik Marsman, who was killed by a torpedo in the North Atlantic in 1940 . . . . Its twelve sections are the story of a drunken and perhaps dying Dutch poet who returns to his home in Amsterdam after years of travel and tries desperately to relate himself, by means of stars, to the universe." The work is studded with references to Western European culture, with the narrator associatively exploring its philosophical and artistic influences. (When he spends several lines on Pythagoras, whose speculations about the Ideal led him into mathematical and musical demonstrations, at least for a moment, Dickey actually transforms

the Grecian lyre into a guitar.) The third book, *God's Images*, is Dickey's prose-poem gesture toward the influence of the Bible on him, his southernness made specifically religious. But the religious images are intended not to be entirely orthodox. For, as Dickey indicates in the foreword, the images are men's and are as subject to men's alterations as to God's: "The Bible is the greatest treasure-house of powerful, disturbing, life-enhancing images in the whole of humanity's long history. They are the images of what generations of men have taken to be those projected on the human race by God Himself, or God as He resides in the souls of men. To an artist such as Marvin Hayes, or to a poet, such as I hold myself to be, these images have unfolded in us by means of the arts we practice. These are *our* images of *God's Images*."

The Zodiac, the most ambitious of the three books, begins with a narrator palpably more in control of things than the main character he is describing: "The man I'm telling you about brought himself back alive / A couple of years ago. / He's here, / Making no trouble. . . . " At one point, the Dutch protagonist moans in self-pity: "No flower could get up these steps, / It'd wither at the hollowness / Of these foot-stomping / failed creative-man's boards / There's nothing to bring love or death / Or creative boredom through the walls." But by the end, the voices of the narrator and the drunken poet have merged by finding some partially satisfying answer (one might argue that the clearer-headed omniscient narrator is actually the recovered protagonist, Marsman's version of Ishmael, "escaped alone to tell thee"):

> So long as the hand can hold its island
> > Of blazing paper, and bleed for its images:
> > Make what it can of what is:
>
> > So long as the spirit hurls on space
> The star-beasts of intellect and madness.

Dickey's work ranges from poems which are introspective and pressurized to those which seem unable to keep their boundaries, displaying energy in a kind of explosion of the poetic personality. He affects no generalized modern voice, no angst-ridden vagueness, until perhaps *The Zodiac*, and it must be remembered that here he essentially rewrote a modernist northern European poem. And yet, with its subject of a bedraggled poet struggling to raise himself to new creations, the poem seems to suit perfectly Dickey's career in the late 1970s, not so much taking a new turn as trying to sustain a deliberate new beginning, willfully to exercise the sophisticated intelligence of James Dickey in his excursions into imitations and translations of non-English poets. There is solid affirmation and impatience with self-pity in Dickey. There is sorrow at what is truly sad and resistance against the cleverly poised paradoxes which came to obsess the poetry of modernism. Dickey has always resisted "schools."

The Strength of Fields (1979) is a Dickey sampler. Drawing its title from the poem written for President Jimmy Carter's inaugural ceremonies, the volume is divided into two sections, the first collecting poems written entirely by Dickey and the second compiling his adaptations or imitations of foreign-language poets. Although few of these poems are as memorable as the best works in *Buckdancer's Choice* and the *"Falling"* section of *Poems 1957-1967*, they do reaffirm favorite Dickey subjects and themes: the vitalizing power of sexuality ("Root light, or the Lawyer's Daughter"), the impact of combat experience upon the memory ("Two Poems of the Military," "Two Poems of Flight-Sleep"), the nature of art and artistic communication ("Exchanges," "The Rain Guitar").

As Dickey says, "it is a fatal flaw among American writers that they tend to repeat what's been successful for them and what people expect of them. I don't want to do the same things. I've written all of the poems in the vein of 'The Heaven of Animals' and 'Falling' that I'm ever going to write; now must come something else . . . . I want to open up poetry more, open up vast new areas of experience. But it won't be like anything I've ever done before." Dickey's 1982 volume, *Puella*, fulfills his promise of a dramatic change in subject matter and technique. Reflection and meditation set the tone, and the volume suggests a delicate stretching toward beauty through the mists of the real. Dickey's fascination with risk is still an issue, but in *Puella* the risk is not only in the technique but also in the exchange of subject matter from masculine energy to female sensibility. The distinctively charged Dickey style is softened. Beauty rather than force abides.

Still, his muse is both dramatic and metaphysical. Dedicated to his wife Deborah as *her girlhood male-imagined*," *Puella* (Latin for *girl*) explores another realm of otherness just as strange to a man as a heaven of animals or a shark's parlor. Adjusting his sights from the alluring invitations of nature, Dickey focuses on a mystery equally enticing: femaleness. The unfamiliar voyage to femininity is, he suggest, a journey that all men must take. Like every voyage that matters, this one begins with the imagination. Dickey raises questions about what woman is–and more specifically, about the lives Deborah has lived in the past. He mixes myth and reality to envision his spouse encountering her adolescence, beginning her relationship with nature, and accepting her initiation into fantasy.

An epigraph from Rainer Maria Rilke suggests the blessing of fate in their meeting: "I know, I know it was necessary for us to have things of this kind, which acquiesced in everything." Have them they do, as the imagination's strength introduces the real poet to the mythical girl in such a way as to make their subsequent marriage inevitable: "A woman's live playing of the universe / As inner light, stands clear, / And is, where I last was" ("Deborah, Moon, Mirror, Right Hand Rising").

These poems extend the dramatic monologue as Dickey encourages his visionary women to speak about dollhouses, horses, and rain–especially rain, as when she describes "gravity's slow / Secretional slashes on this house." The silent listener to these monologues is, of course, the poet, but it is also the reader who peers over the poet's shoulder and through his special lens to see and hear the woman respond to her world. The ultimate listener is finally life itself in the many guises that are the triumph of the Dickey canon. Describing a cycle of experience that carries the girl from childhood concerns into nature's energies and beyond, Dickey ends this voyage of the male imagination with a summons from the all-encompassing other. Life has heard the woman. Now it beckons her from the far side of "the flexing swamp" with "primal instructions" and "invention unending" ("Summons"). But the poet knows that the instructions and invention are also the girl's. Primal energy swirls through all women. The poet can only listen–and imagine–as nonhuman otherness in the guise of the swamp embraces the otherness of womanhood in the form of the wife to guarantee renewal and the affirmation of tomorrow.

Puella is the change of pace in the Dickey canon promised by the transitional collection *The Strength of Fields*. Years will pass before one can say with certainty that individual poems in *Puella* equal the accomplishment of "The Performance," "The Fiend," and "Falling." But comparison of selected titles is not the point. *Puella* is a volume of interlocking poems meant to be read together. Indeed, the entire collection is one poem. What matters, then, is not the excellence or lack thereof of individual poems but the achievement of the whole.

Night Hurdling (1983) is a miscellany composed of four poems and forty-two prose pieces: interviews; commencement addresses; essays on such diverse writers as Robert Penn Warren, Jack London, Ezra Pound, and Vachel Lindsay; considerations of the art of poetry itself; and personal reminiscences. Collecting, as it does, many of Dickey's best but previously inaccessible short nonfiction works (including the poignant title essay and the brilliant "The Enemy from Eden"), *Night Hurdling* reveals Dickey's interests, insights, and unfaltering imaginative / critical energies.

In 1987, seventeen years after the publication of *Deliverance*, Dickey's long-awaited second novel appeared. *Alnilam* focuses on forms and uses of power: an individual's charismatic leadership that inspires followers; the military's official hierarchy that governs masses of men; man's attempt to control nature's forces for his own purposes. Set in the early days of World War II at an Army Air Corps training base in Peckover, North Carolina, the novel's main dramatic focus involves a father's quest to learn about the quality of his son's character and about the facts surrounding his son's presumed death in a fiery training accident. The technical complications of the novel result directly from the father's first-person point of view.

Frank Cahill has been a man removed from life. Separated from his wife when his son, Joel, was born, Frank has distanced himself further from people by constructing an Atlanta amusement park, complete with a wooden tower from which he has watched park visitors without personal involvement. His life is dramatically altered when he is blinded by diabetes and when he learns of his son's plane crash and possible death. Frank becomes an Oedipus-like figure, a blind man seeking the truth, and in the process inverts the traditional literary motif of the son's search for the father. Guided by an unleashed, near-mythic wolf-dog, Zack, Frank is both attracted to and repulsed by the secret society his son has created. He is also intent on experiencing what his son went through as a pilot.

Frank assumes the controls of a light training plane while returning to base at night with Joel's former flight instructor. He believes that through the assertion of his own will and imagination that he can control the airplane, that he can

Dickey on the grounds of the University of South Carolina, where he has served as poet-in-residence since 1969 (photo by Terry Parke)

take command of the air. Throughout the novel, Frank insists on being self-reliant, trusting in his internal vision to see the truth about people and events. The novel records his heightened senses—of smell, touch, taste, and sound—and emphasizes his blend of memory, dreams, and imagination as aids to his inner sight. Dickey graphically records the richness of the blind man's perceptions—and the more mundane vision of the normally sighted—through a split-page technique: a darkly printed column on the left side of the page represents Frank's inner responses to and assessments of his immediate environment, while on the right side are the actual events and people presented in lighter print. Through this means, Dickey is able to dramatize how external, actual events are transformed within Frank's sensual, imaginative apprehension of reality.

Joel Cahill's character pervades the novel even though he does not appear directly. His influence is strongly felt through the secret society of air cadets he has founded, Alnilam, named after the central star in the constellation Orion (the hunter). Like the distant celestial namesake, Joel rises above the ordinary; his followers elevate him to a godlike stature, quoting ceremoniously at meetings from his notebook entries–many of which are drawn from the poetry of the romantic rebel Percy Bysshe Shelley. The group's purpose is evidently to subvert the official military chain of command by establishing their own control of the training facility.

Alnilam's theme of the various manifestations of power is dramatized through the individual characters' story in the context of the large military machinery of the war effort. Ultimately, *Alnilam* combines individual quest with history and myth to achieve a unique artistic and technical accomplishment.

Wayfarer: A Voice from the Southern Mountains (1988), with photographs by William A. Bake and text by Dickey, again pairs a central figure who dominates the narrative with another figure whose presence is felt rather than dramatized. In *Wayfarer*, an Appalachian mountain native explains the lore of mountain ways and mountain people to a young wanderer whose comments are not recorded in the narrative until the final page. This technique allows the protagonist to speak directly to the reader as well as the wayfarer.

Wayfarer's speaker befriends the wandering traveler, becoming as well his guide, instructor, and host. The speaker is both a general representative of the region and a highly individualized character, with his own private conflicts and concerns. He praises his wife, Alma, for her cooking and quilting skills, and the couple appear to be the models of self-sufficiency. Their history contains its dark side, however. Their only child, a boy born with a caul, dies or, as the speaker asserts, has been taken by the devil at the moment of his birth. The mountain man and Alma adopt a parental role toward the wayfarer. To treat the cold and fever their visitor suffers during his first night in their cabin, the narrator applies his knowledge of root medicines, including a combination of "wild cherry bark" tea, "rat's veins" snuff, and a variety of other cures. He feeds him "eggs and ashcakes" for breakfast, tells him of the mountain people's handicrafts in making furniture and stringed instruments, and describes the songs they sing that carry a "natural sadness" reflecting the difficult life people lead in the mountains. He also carries magical stones, giving the wayfarer a "fairy stone" but keeping the "snake

stone" for himself, since it was found a week after they buried their child and "we run the devil off the porch with the caul."

The mountain man's character is kind yet tinged with the region's melancholy. After having the wayfarer drink from a hidden spring, the speaker assures the traveler that he will return to the mountains because now he is part of the region. "You done reached down through the ferns ... You done drink lonesome water. You're bound to the hills ... and you'll come back. ... " William A. Bake's color photographs are warm complements to Dickey's narrative.

The Voiced Connections of James Dickey: Interviews and Conversations (1989) is a compilation of twenty-eight interviews that span the years from 1965 to 1987. In this collection, Dickey discusses his life, defines his major themes and subjects, evaluates other literary figures, and describes his wide range of nonliterary interests. In the process he demonstrates his knowledge of literature in many languages and from many historical periods, quoting with ease from what he has read. This collection, which assembles significant and for the most part previously uncollected interviews, provides a profile of one of America's best literary minds.

Interviews:

The Voiced Connections of James Dickey: Interviews and Conversations, edited by Ronald Baughman (Columbia, S.C.: University of South Carolina Press, 1989).

Bibliographies:

Jim Elledge, *James Dickey: A Bibliography, 1947-1974* (Metuchen, N.J. & London: Scarecrow Press, 1979).

Elledge, "James Dickey: A Supplementary Bibliography, 1975-1980, Part I," *Bulletin of Bibliography*, 38 (April-June 1981): 92-100, 104.

Elledge, "James Dickey: A Supplementary Bibliography, 1975-1980, Part II," *Bulletin of Bibliography*, 38 (July-September 1981): 150-155.

Matthew J. Bruccoli and Judith S. Baughman, *James Dickey: A Descriptive Bibliography* (Pittsburgh: University of Pittsburgh Press, forthcoming 1990).

References:

Ronald Baughman, *Understanding James Dickey* (Columbia: University of South Carolina Press, 1985).
    A reader's companion to Dickey's poetry and prose through *Puella*; examines Dickey's central topics–war, family, society, love, and nature–in terms of the writer's self-description as a poet of survival.

Ross Bennett, " 'The Firebombing' : A Reappraisal," *American Literature*, 52 (November 1980): 430-448.
    Argues that the poem treats self-discovery through multiple points of view.

David C. Berry, "Harmony with the Dead: James Dickey's Descent into the Underworld," *Southern Quarterly*, 12 (April 1974): 233-244.
    Analyzes Dickey's poetic use of the Orpheus motif, through which his speakers attempt but fail to gain union with the dead.

Harold Bloom, "James Dickey: From 'The Other' through *The Early Motion*," *Southern Review*, 21 (Winter 1985): 63-78.
    Argues that Dickey is an "heroic celebrator" whose guilt results from his sense of betrayal by his family; this guilt leads to a schism between mind and body that results in his mystical vision.

Neal Bowers, *James Dickey: The Poet as Pitchman* (Columbia: University of Missouri Press, 1985).
    An assessment of Dickey's popularity as the result of careful self-promotion of his poetry and himself.

Richard J. Calhoun and Robert W. Hill, *James Dickey* (Boston: Twayne, 1983).
    An overview of Dickey's work through *The Strength of Fields*; emphasizes Dickey's neoromanticism, particularly in his relationship with nature.

Paul Carroll, "The Smell of Blood in Paradise," in *The Poem in Its Skin* (Chicago: Follett, 1968), pp. 43-49.
    Defines Dickey's view of nature's heaven as an eternal cycle of violence in predator-prey relationships.

Peter Davison, "The Difficulties of Being Major: The Poetry of Robert Lowell and James Dickey," *Atlantic Monthly*, 220 (October 1967): 116-121.
    Perceives Dickey as an exponent of the archetypes of the American wilderness, both actual and psychological.

Donald J. Greiner, "The Harmony of Bestiality in James Dickey's *Deliverance*," *South Carolina Review*, 5 (December 1972): 43-49.
    Asserts that Ed Gentry is forced into a bestial figure to save himself; undercuts the concept of nature as a benevolent tutor of man.

Daniel L. Guillory, "Water Magic in the Poetry of James Dickey," *English Language Notes*, 8 (December 1970): 131-137.
    Demonstrates that water imagery is both a source of renewal in life and a conduit to the world of the dead.

Linda Tarte Holley, "Design and Focus in James Dickey's *Deliverance*," *South Carolina Review*, 10 (April 1978): 90-98.
    Posits that Ed Gentry's training as graphic artist is his means of saving himself: he achieves deliverance through use of artistic imagination.

Richard Howard, "On James Dickey," *Partisan Review*, 33 (Summer 1966): 414-428, 479-486.
    Asserts that history is Dickey's nightmare and that madness, obsession, and excess are means to confront death.

James Dickey Newsletter, edited by Joyce M. Pair (Dunwoody, Ga.: Dekalb College, Fall 1984-).
    Contains essays, reviews, interviews, poems, and other material treating Dickey, including a continuing primary and secondary bibliography by Robert C. Covel.

John Jolly, "Drew Ballinger as 'Sacrificial God' in James Dickey's *Deliverance*," *South Carolina Review*, 17 (Spring 1985): 102-107.
    Examines Ballinger's character through his connections with the Greek sacrificial figure Orpheus.

Robert Kirschten, *James Dickey and the Gentle Ecstasy of Earth: A Reading of the Poems* (Baton Rouge: Louisiana State University Press, 1988).

An exploration of the philosophical implications of the term *romantic primitivism* through ritual, magic, and myth.

Laurence Lieberman, "The Expansional Poet: A Return to Personality," *Yale Review*, 57 (Winter 1968): 258-271.
Examines Dickey as one who encompasses joy and terror in the creation of the Self and ultimately emerges as a poet of celebration.

Ralph J. Mills, Jr., *Creation's Very Self: On the Personal Element in Recent American Poetry* (Fort Worth: Texas Christian University Press, 1969), pp. 3-4, 9, 18-19.
Emphasizes how Dickey's Self becomes the "informing principle" of all that he writes; determines that such a perspective is part of a new aesthetic in American poetry since World War II.

Joyce Carol Oates, "Out of Stone, Into Flesh: The Imagination of James Dickey," *Modern Poetry Studies*, 5 (Autumn 1974): 97-144.
Identifies Dickey's aesthetic of "entropy," or systematic breakdown in contemporary life; asserts that imagination and creativity are his defense.

Monroe K. Spears, "James Dickey as a Southern Visionary," *Virginia Quarterly Review*, 63 (Winter 1987): 110-123.
Asserts that Dickey is a visionary poet with a highly religious view of nature's and life's wild grandeur.

H. L. Weatherby, "The Way of Exchange in James Dickey's Poetry," *Sewanee Review*, 74 (July-September 1966): 669-680.
Identifies Dickey's central thematic method of the Self's exchange of identities with inanimate objects, animals, and humans to achieve a renewed perspective on the world; remains single most important essay written about Dickey.

Papers:
Holdings of Dickey's manuscript material are located at the South Caroliniana Library, the University of South Carolina, and the Washington University Library, St. Louis.

Joan Didion

This entry was updated by Virginia Dumont (Francis Marion College) from the entries by Paula R. Feldman (University of South Carolina) in DLB 2, American Novelists Since World War II, *Margaret A. Van Antwerp in* DLB Yearbook 1981, *and Mary Doll in* DLB Yearbook 1986.

Places	Hollywood Los Angeles	Las Vegas Miami	Central America Hawaii
Influences and ∘Relationships	Gabriel García Márquez John Gregory Dunne	F. Scott Fitzgerald Ernest Hemingway	Henry James Joseph Conrad William Faulkner
Literary Movements and Forms	New Journalism Literary Nonfiction	Minimalism	Verbal Collage
Major Themes	Marriage / Family Relationships	Alienation	Cultural Decay
Cultural and Artistic Influences	California Lifestyle 1960s Culture	The Women's Movement	Drug Use
Social and Economic Influences	Central American Politics	Cuban Exiles in Miami	California Politics

BIRTH: Sacramento, California, 5 December 1934, to Frank Reese and Eduene Jerrett Didion.

EDUCATION: B.A., University of California at Berkeley, 1956.

MARRIAGE: 30 January 1964 to John Gregory Dunne; child: Quintana Roo.

AWARDS AND HONORS: Prix de Paris (*Vogue* magazine), 1956; Bread Loaf Fellowship in fiction, 1963; *Los Angeles Times* Woman of the Year, 1968.

BOOKS: *Run River* (New York: Obolensky, 1963; London: Cape, 1964);
Slouching Towards Bethlehem (New York: Farrar, Straus & Giroux, 1968; London: Deutsch, 1969);
Play It As It Lays (New York: Farrar, Straus & Giroux, 1970; London: Weidenfeld & Nicolson, 1971);
A Book of Common Prayer (New York: Simon & Schuster, 1977);
Telling Stories (Berkeley, Cal.: Bancroft Library, 1978);
The White Album (New York: Simon & Schuster, 1979; London: Weidenfeld & Nicolson, 1979);
Salvador (New York: Simon & Schuster, 1983);
Democracy (New York: Simon & Schuster, 1984; London: Chatto & Windus, 1984);
Miami (New York: Simon & Schuster, 1987).

MOTION PICTURES: *Panic in Needle Park*, by Didion and John Gregory Dunne, 20th Century-Fox, 1971;
Play It As It Lays, by Didion and Dunne, Universal, 1972;
True Confessions, by Didion and Dunne, United Artists, 1981.

PERIODICAL PUBLICATIONS: "Meditation on a Life," review of Elizabeth Hardwick's *Sleepless Nights*, *New York Times Book Review*, 29 April 1979, pp. 1, 60;
"Letter from Manhattan," *New York Review of Books* (16 August 1979): 18-19;
"I Want to Go Ahead and Do It," review of Norman Mailer's *The Executioner's Song*, *New York Times Book Review*, 7 October 1979, pp. 1, 26, 27;
"Nuclear Blue," *New West*, 4 (5 November 1979);

Joan Didion

"Mothers and Daughters," *New West*, 4 (12 December 1979);
"Boat People," *New West*, 5 (25 February 1980);
"The Need to Know," by Didion and John Gregory Dunne, *New West*, 5 (5 May 1980);
"Without Regret or Hope," review of V. S. Naipaul's *The Return of Eva Perón with the Killings in Trinidad*, *New York Review of Books*, (12 June 1980): 20-21;
"Honolulu Days," *New West*, 5 (14 July 1980);
"In El Salvador," *New York Review of Books* (4 November 1982);
"A Nation of Malls," *Esquire* (June 1983): 329;
"Miami," *New York Review of Books* (28 May 1987): 43;
"Miami: 'La Lucha,'" *New York Review of Books* (11 June 1987): 15;
"Miami: Exiles," *New York Review of Books* (25 June 1987): 35;
"Washington in Miami," *New York Review of Books* (16 July 1987): 22;

"Letter from Los Angeles," *New Yorker* (24 April 1989): 88;

"Insider Baseball," *New York Review of Books* (27 October 1989): 19.

"Things fall apart; the center cannot hold; / Mere anarchy is loosed upon the world." These lines and the William Butler Yeats poem from which they come hold a special fascination for Joan Didion which is reflected in her fictional work. Her protagonists are women whose interior worlds resemble nothing so much as the arid, tortured landscapes which surround them. They feel anguish, yet they do not know why. What has fallen apart is meaning and moral responsibility. Like Nathanael West, Didion pictures the emptiness of the American dream, the cultural sickness, the uncomprehending despair. Her characters are so traumatized by experience they float through life as in a dream, or, more accurately, a nightmare, conscious only of stray, apparently unrelated details. Unable to achieve anything approaching self-respect, they exist within a private hell, albeit in sunny California or South America, numbed or indifferent to the pain of others. Marriage is for them as much a void as love and sex. In the everyday world there is a pervasive sense of impending peril. Dams may break, rattlesnakes may bite, fires and revolutions may break out, the plumbing may begin to take on a menacing life of its own. Yet personal despair in Didion's universe has wider moral implications. In one place she defines evil as the absence of seriousness, and she is a cultural critic in whose fiction every gesture in an unserious world is morally revealing. These gestures, full of fright, show something is profoundly wrong. The past has been forgotten. Humanity is corrupt, fallen, and doomed. What has been lost is forever irretrievable. It is no wonder, then, that pain and disappointment prevail.

Joan Didion was born on 5 December 1934 to Frank Reese and Eduene Jerrett Didion, a family whose roots in California's Central Valley go back five generations. She was raised in Sacramento as an Episcopalian and attended the University of California at Berkeley, where she took her undergraduate degree in 1956 and later taught as a visiting lecturer. Winning *Vogue* magazine's Prix de Paris that same year brought her to New York. There she became associate feature editor of *Vogue* until 1963, the year she won the Bread Loaf Fellowship in fiction. She has written articles and stories for *Mademoiselle*, the *American*

Scholar, the *New York Times Magazine*, *Harper's Bazaar*, *Holiday*, and the *National Review*, where she became a contributing editor.

In 1958 she met John Gregory Dunne, a Princeton graduate from Hartford, Connecticut, and an editor at *Time* magazine. They were married 30 January 1964. Didion's first novel, *Run River*, had been published the previous year. Her collection of essays, *Slouching Towards Bethlehem*, appeared in 1968, followed in 1970 by the novel *Play It As It Lays*, her first large commercial success, and another best-selling novel, *A Book of Common Prayer*, in 1977. Her husband, the author of four books, *Delano* (1967), *The Studio* (1969), *Vegas* (1974), and *True Confessions* (1977), as well as numerous magazine articles, collaborated with her on several projects, including a column in the *Saturday Evening Post*, the screenplays for three films–*Panic in Needle Park* (1971), *Play It As It Lays* (1972), and *True Confessions* (1981)–and the early drafts of the script for *A Star Is Born* (1976). Dunne and Didion moved to Los Angeles in 1964 and now reside in a home on the beach at Trancas, California, with their daughter, Quintana Dunne, born in 1966.

Didion's novels reverberate with a sense of loss, disorder, anxiety, and destruction on both a personal and cultural scale. Her unsentimental style reflects the absurdity and alienation she sees everywhere as she re-creates the nonsense and illogic of everyday conversation. She was influenced early in life by Ernest Hemingway, Henry James, and Joseph Conrad. Her own sentences are precise, spare, and tight. She avoids melodrama by withholding emotion through understatement and indirection and achieves a surprising impact by sustaining a detachment that almost imperceptibly changes into an emotional intensity. It is this technique which provides the emotional rhythm of her prose. Her vision is as tragic, grotesque, and chilling as William Faulkner's, her style as allusive and brief as West's. Sardonic and elliptical, her language is full of bitter wit and pregnant silences. The characters who populate Didion novels are sharply etched, often perfectly crystallized in a mere phrase or sentence. Her women tend to be more fully rounded than her men. But her characterizations are all carefully honed, swiftly and economically achieved. Her technique is often cinematic. Scenes and chapters end suddenly. The influence of television and popular culture is everywhere in evidence. Her irreverent humor is unnerving. Her carefully controlled prose is exact and shapely, full of symbols and recurring detail. Her rhythmic repetition of phrases brings to mind the world of dreams; her eye for the ominous detail suggests the evil lurking; her ear for social cattiness recalls the all-pervasive desolation.

Didion's first novel, *Run River* (1963), was noticed by a small coterie and a few reviewers. Guy Davenport, writing in the *National Review*, praised her superb writing and her uncommon grasp of place and character in a book he deemed reasonable and true. Yet he pronounced it "*too* even, *too* smooth. It sticks to its business with the determined regularity of minor art. All humor, all irony have been pared away. And where is invention? Must realism with all its sincerity be so flat? . . . Miss Didion has polished her prose too well for her own good." In the *New York Herald Tribune*, Robert Maurer admired her coolness and her impressive skill. He noted that "there seems to be nothing technically that she cannot do." Yet, he added, "Her reader suspects that the author, with all of her power . . . might herself not know what she wants, or might not see life, as Philip Roth does, as possessing a tang." However, Alfred Kazin, looking back in 1971 after the publication of Didion's next two books, would declare his preference for *Run River* because of its emotional depth.

The novel opens in August 1959 with a distant pistol shot which the protagonist, thirty-six-year-old Lily McClellan, hears and understands. But before she looks in the empty drawer where her husband, Everett, had kept his .38, she studies her diamond wristwatch, splashes on some *Joy* perfume, and lingers until "all the *Joy* had evaporated." She finds Everett on the dock behind their seventeen-room house standing over the dead body of Ryder Channing, one of Lily's lovers. Everett "had been loading the gun to shoot the nameless fury which pursued him ten, twenty, a good many years before. All that had happened now was that the wraith had taken a name, and the name was Ryder Channing." Lily tells Everett, "We can make it all right," yet it is all beyond repair. The remainder of the novel is the chronicle of how the confusion and chaos of their lives during nineteen years of marriage has ended in murder.

"You say what you want and strike out for it," Walter Knight tells his daughter Lily. But Lily does not know what she wants, and besides, she is not at all sure that getting what you ask for is much of a prize. At the age of seventeen Lily does not know if she wants to marry Everett, but

somehow, like most things in her life, she does it almost unconsciously, not realizing she has done it until after the fact and then vaguely hoping her father will rescue her from her decision or that someone will have the marriage annulled.

After three years of marriage and two children, Lily, whose wealth has shielded her from domestic responsibility, makes some attempt to figure out what the role of a young wife and mother is but gives up. Lily always fails, even as she tries, with pathetic concentration, to apprehend what is expected of her. Early in their marriage Lily thinks of her life with Everett as "an improvisation dependent upon cues she might one day fail to hear." Except in times of crisis, like the death of her father, she can think of little to say to Everett, pretending when she is in bed with him that she is someone else. Yet she looks to him to take care of her. She is, in all senses of the word, his baby. Her first extramarital affair takes place after Everett has enlisted, with some relief, during the war, yet Lily and her lover Joe, like she and Everett, do not talk much, and Lily is never certain that either derives much pleasure from the other. They inhabit a world where each person cons the other, where "everyone had his own shell game."

In the absence of Everett, whose most notable characteristic is his desire for order above all else, the McClellan ranch falls apart. Though Lily begs him to come home for Christmas, he views her letters and calls as the only disturbance in an otherwise content existence. "He missed her and the babies, but not as much as he told her he did, and then only in an abstract way." After Everett's return the narrative follows Lily through an abortion and the events leading up to the suicide of Martha, Everett's sister and Lily's double. Martha drowns herself in the river that is a backdrop to the novel, a symbol of unbridled freedom and destruction.

Lily tries, even while failing, to fill Martha's place for Everett and takes Martha's boyfriend, Ryder Channing, as a lover. Now Everett and Lily have the same argument over and over, so that "it seemed . . . that they were condemned to play it out together all the days of their lives, raking their memories for fresh grievances, cherishing familiar ones, nourishing the already indestructible shoots of their resentment with alcohol and with the inexhaustible adrenalin generated by what she supposed was (at least she did not know any other name for it) love." When Lily finds Everett standing with a pistol over Ryder

Channing's body, the implicit question is what had it all been about, "all the manque promises, the failures of love and faith and honor," Martha's death, Lily's mother addressing invitations and watching *American Bandstand*, the whole long history of Lily's family and of Everett's. It had been, Didion points out, a history of accidents, of aimlessness, of no one knowing what he wanted–that is, until this evening when Everett refuses Lily's plea that they lie to the police and "make it all right." Instead he asks to be left alone. And it is at this point that Didion strikes the only really false note in the novel, preaches with a sledgehammer that "maybe once you realized you had to do it alone, you were on your way home. Maybe the most difficult, most important thing anyone could do for anyone else was to leave him alone; it was perhaps the only gratuitous act, the act of love."

After Lily hears the second shot, the one with which Everett takes his own life, she wonders what she can say of him to her children. She cannot decide on much except the cliché that he was a good man, though she is not certain that he was. But in the fairy-tale world in which she would wander, it is what she would wish for "if they gave her one wish."

When *Slouching Towards Bethlehem* (1968), Didion's collection of essays, was published, it was reviewed favorably by *Commonweal* and the *National Review*. The *Saturday Evening Post* would later recommend her "brilliant" articles over her "depressing" fiction. When her next novel came out, another review complained that "the world is already full of Morbid Female Novelists. But there is a dearth of good reporter-essayists. Skip the novel, buy *Slouching Towards Bethlehem*." As well as inspiring critical enthusiasm, this book gained for Didion a small but devoted following of readers.

It is a skeptical, wary book about cultural and spiritual malaise in America in which its author shows herself to be a perceptive, at times poetic, observer. She writes in the title essay of San Francisco hippies. "Has anyone ever written a better treatment of that overexposed topic of the year . . . ?" Melvin Maddocks asked. Other essays concern themselves with California life-styles, Las Vegas weddings and their vulgarity, Joan Baez, Howard Hughes, and John Wayne. "The future always looks good in the golden land," Didion notes, "because no one remembers the past." There is a section titled "Personals" where Didion's subject is her own private vision, life,

and philosophy. Some of these essays, such as "On Self-Respect," though not exceptional in themselves, are important for an understanding of her fiction. There she says, for instance, "character–the willingness to accept responsibility for one's own life–is the source from which self-respect springs." She insists in "On Morality" that we have no way of knowing what is right and wrong, good and evil, beyond our loyalty to the social code. In "On Keeping a Notebook" Didion paints herself in a way startlingly reminiscent of her protagonists when she observes, "[I] did not like to look in the mirror, and my eyes would skim the newspapers and pick out only the deaths, the cancer victims, the premature coronaries, the suicides, and I stopped riding the Lexington Avenue IRT because I noticed for the first time that all the strangers I had seen for years . . . looked older than they once had." In a third section, "Seven Places of the Mind," Didion includes a splendid essay about Alcatraz, another about living in New York, and one about living in California. Her essay entitled "Los Angeles Notebook" concludes in a way suspiciously similar to the ending of her next novel.

Play It As It Lays (1970) was a best-seller which made Didion a six-figure sum and which catapulted her before the eye of the general public. Yet the critical reception of this book was decidedly mixed. Phoebe-Lou Adams wrote in the *Atlantic*, "The form of Miss Didion's novel is admirably lucid, vivid, and fast-paced. The context is the decline of a self-centered pseudo-actress with a crack in her head. This woman, endowed by the author with the spunk of a jelly fish and the brain of a flea, snivels her way into a mental hospital via a string of disasters that would outsuds any soap opera." In the *Midwest Quarterly*, David C. Stineback pointed to *Play It As It Lays* as a novel which "reveals precisely what a novel cannot afford to do . . . fail to make its characters . . . *worthy of being cared about* by its readers," and a reviewer for *Harper's* complained that "perhaps because of her fashionably fragmented narrative style, perhaps because she never moves beyond cliche (or is it archetype?) in inventing actions and histories for her characters, the book remains a rather cold and calculated fiction–more a problem in human geometry (to which a neat QED can be applied at the end) than a novel that truly lives." Lore Segal, writing in the *New York Times Book Review*, observed that the novel "feels as if it were written out of an insufficient impulse by a writer who doesn't know what else to do with all that talent and skill." She termed it "a bad novel by a very good writer." But David J. Geherin in *Critique* called it "a remarkable novel which never misses in its portrayal of a modern woman caught in a mid-twentieth-century crisis. She has cast anew, in her unique idiom, one of the prevailing concerns of modern literature: confrontation with the void. Despite its preoccupation with death, suffering, boredom, and despair, *Play It As It Lays* is always fresh and alive." *Newsweek* called Didion's "honesty, intelligence, skill . . . wonders to behold"; John Leonard, in the *New York Times*, said, "There is nothing superfluous, not a word, not an incident"; and Guy Davenport, in the *National Review*, remarked, "If her vision of the world is terrifying, it is also accurate."

Maria Wyeth, the tortured protagonist of *Play It As It Lays*, learned, at the age of ten from her gambler father who could never seem to win, that life itself is a crap game, an observation which becomes the central metaphor of the novel. Thirty-one-year-old Maria, institutionalized for a mental disorder but understanding more than anyone else in the book, resents the efforts of psychiatrists to find reasons for the way she is. On tests she prints "Nothing applies" with her magnetized IBM pencil. "What does apply?" the doctors ask "as if the word 'nothing' were ambiguous, open to interpretation." They miss the point that it is nothing which *does* apply. Maria, we learn, is an expert on nothingness. She knows "what 'nothing' means, and keep[s] on playing" the game of life, unlike her homosexual friend BZ who, before he commits suicide in Maria's arms, assures her, "Some day you'll wake up and you just won't feel like playing any more." But Maria plays for Kate, her four-year-old daughter whom she futilely hopes to rescue from the place where "they put electrodes on her head and needles in her spine and try to figure out what went wrong." It is Maria's opinion that looking for answers to anything is beside the point. "What makes Iago evil? some people ask. I never ask," she says.

She is a woman who has difficulty with what she terms "as it was." Her past includes a childhood in Silver Wells, Nevada, a town now literally nowhere, blasted off the map, then later a career as a model and actress in New York where she "knew a lot of Southerners and faggots and rich boys and that was how I spent my days and nights." As she is a woman who allows men to direct her life, it is appropriate that she marries Carter Lang, her director in two films. One film,

which she likes, is a motorcycle movie in which she does not recognize herself as the woman on the screen who, unlike herself, seems to have the ability to control her own destiny. Because she cannot confront herself, she is nauseated by the other movie, titled *Maria*, in which the camera follows her through her own everyday existence.

This novel traces the degeneration of her relationship with Carter through mutual adultery, resentment, and bickering; it pictures the plastic, empty people around her who inhabit the sterile desert world of California, a microcosm of all America; but mostly it chronicles through third-person narration the subjective experience of Maria's breakdown as it progresses from one stage to another. Didion's concern is not with constructing a psychological case study (she intentionally keeps the prognosis vague) but in presenting a metaphysical reality–a spiritual and mental breakdown caused by the awareness of nothingness at the center of the world.

There is so much desolation inside and outside of Maria that she finally cannot differentiate between "where her body stopped and the air began, about the exact point in space and time that was the difference between *Maria* and *other*." She experiences, in other words, the objectification of her inability to have a sense of personal identity. Two specific events haunt Maria: the sudden violence of her mother's death in an auto accident on the desert ("the coyotes tore her up before anybody found her") and an abortion Carter blackmails her into having. A dream in which she whispers words of comfort to children being herded into a gas chamber because it was a "humane operation" demonstrates her sense of guilt associated with her own "humane operation." Despite her attempt to pretend nothing has really happened, she is plagued by thoughts of the fetus in the garbage. This novel is, in many ways, about uniquely feminine experience. One of the most vivid scenes is one in which Maria puts her head down on the steering wheel and cries for the first time since her childhood. "She cried because she was humiliated and she cried for her mother and she cried for Kate and she cried because something had just come through to her, there in the sun on the Western street: she had deliberately not counted the months but she must have been counting them unawares, must have been keeping a relentless count somewhere, because this was the day, the day the baby would have been born."

Dust jacket for Didion's 1970 best-seller about the exploits of "a self-centered pseudo-actress with a crack in her head"

Maria's world is one with no goals, no directions, no moral standards, no meaning in life, no real human contact. All of Maria's attempts to escape her dread fail. She can find no comfort in love or drugs or sex or religion or hypnosis, though she does find temporary relief in driving the freeways. It imposes some sense of order in an otherwise chaotic life. Her father once taught her that "overturning a rock was apt to reveal a rattlesnake," but rattlesnakes pursue her everywhere, on the highway, in her dreams, in her food. Maria does not believe in rewards, "only in punishments, swift and personal," and it occurs to her that "whatever arrangements were made, they worked less well for women." Maria is suffocating. The emotional landscape (characterized by ennui, moral exhaustion, suicide, homosexuality, brain damage) reflects the physical landscape (gambling casinos, drive-in churches, freeways, motorcycle gangs, reconstituted lemon juice). In this fragmented world of chance where she can-

not make the connection between cause and effect, where the will and the emotions are paralyzed, where the natural world provides no beauty and no comfort, where there are no heroes, only victims, where life is only one more grade-B picture with all its obligatory scenes involving other people only as props, BZ asks why one should go on living. Maria asks, "Why not?"

The effectiveness of this novel owes much to the restrained and matter-of-fact tone and to the staccato rhythm of the language, with chapters often just one brief scene long. Didion's technique is highly cinematic, using sharp visual images and often a series of rapid close-ups. The structure of the book itself, with juxtapositions of present and past, important and trivial events, first- and third-person narration along with the absence of continuity between chapters, suggests the disorder in Maria's world.

Didion's next novel, *A Book of Common Prayer* (1977), was a best-seller with even greater

74

commercial success than her previous book. Its critical reception was favorable. Bruce M. Firestone, in the *Library Journal*, observed, "Didion overindulges her passion for sentence fragments, which she often uses as refrains. But the novel comes off anyway. Despite occasional excesses, *A Book of Common Prayer* ranks as Didion's best novel yet." Joyce Carol Oates wrote in the *New York Times Book Review*, "Has the novel any significant flaws? I would have wished it longer, fuller.... [Didion] has been an articulate witness to the most stubborn and intractable truths of our time, a memorable voice, partly eulogistic, partly despairing; always in control."

Didion claims that the source of the novel was a trip to Cartagena, Colombia, in 1973, but *A Book of Common Prayer* is as much about South America as *Moby-Dick* is about whales. It is instead concerned with the misunderstandings, misperceptions, and downright delusions that parents and children have about each other and which keep them apart. It is about the meaninglessness of revolutionary rhetoric and insurrection and the hopelessness of political solutions to human problems. It is about the life of Charlotte Douglas, a woman who "made not enough distinctions ... dreamed her life ... [and] died hopeful."

The narrator is Grace Strasser-Mendana, a former anthropologist from Denver dying of cancer who "lost faith in her own method, who stopped believing that observable activity defined anthropos," and who retired to marry a wealthy Boca Grande coconut planter. At his death she inherited 58.9% of the arable land and the same percentage of the decision-making process in an equatorial country distinguished only by its lack of anything distinctive and its obliviousness to any sense of history. Grace, unlike Charlotte, maintains that she does not dream her life and tries to make enough distinctions. She is interested in Charlotte's story because its meaning eludes her.

Charlotte is a forty-year-old woman from San Francisco, the slight disrepair of whose expensive clothes reflects an "equivalent disrepair of the morale, some vulnerability, or abandon." As a North American, Charlotte is one "immaculate of history, innocent of politics" who believes the rest of the world to be peopled by others just like herself and who lives the unexamined life. When Charlotte is confronted by an unpleasant event, she merely revises it in her mind to coincide with her notion of the way things should have been. She makes up stories, which she herself seems to believe, about her eighteen-year-old daughter Marin, their inseparability, their romantic adventures together traveling all over the globe. She stubbornly assures the FBI that Marin is away skiing, though they say she disappeared after participating in the bombing of a building and the hijacking and burning of a plane.

But Marin understands as little about her mother as Charlotte understands about her only child. Charlotte refuses to see how Marin can contemptuously call her great-grandmother's wedding bracelet "dead metal" (a bracelet the FBI finds attached like a charm to the firing pin of a bomb), just as Marin, who spouts revolutionary rhetoric, refuses to believe her mother spent much of her time in Boca Grande giving malaria inoculations and working in a birth control clinic. She prefers to picture Charlotte in a tennis dress, just as Charlotte pictures Marin in a straw hat for Easter.

Ironically, Marin is indirectly linked to her mother's death. Like Maria Wyeth, Charlotte loves her daughter extravagantly, and her battle to fight the realization that her love is not reciprocated causes Charlotte to remain in Boca Grande during a meaningless "revolution," a coup of which Marin later approves. Charlotte loses her life, an outsider caught in the crossfire. She is senselessly killed by the same kind of gun Marin carries. But, as Didion has said in a *New York Times* interview, Charlotte "finds her life by leaving it." She says she will not leave Boca Grande because, "I walked away from places all my life and I'm not going to walk away from here." Finally, Grace, the narrator, who had seemed so different from Charlotte, recognizes in the telling of her story how closely she and Charlotte are connected, how similar they are in their delusions. If the book is, as Didion maintains, Grace's prayer for Charlotte's soul, it is also, finally, Grace's prayer for her own soul and Didion's prayer for all America.

Telling Stories (1978), a limited-edition keepsake volume prepared for contributors to the Bancroft Library of the University of California at Berkeley, contains the only three short stories Didion ever wrote: "Coming Home," "The Welfare Island Ferry," and "When Did Music Come This Way? Children Dear, Was It Yesterday?" All of them were written in 1964, a crucial year in Didion's literary career, the year after her first novel, *Run River*, was published. Didion recalls 1964 as a time of fear that she might never write another novel: "I sat in front of my typewriter, and believed that another subject would never present itself. I believed that I would be forever dry. I believed that I would 'forget how.'" For this reason Didion wrote the three stories collected in *Telling Stories*, as what she has called "a kind of desperate finger exercise."

The stories, because of their limited printing, received very little critical attention. They are interesting, however, because in them Didion rehearses themes that have now become hallmarks of her prose: the loss of one's home and one's past and entrapment in an alien and often debilitating present.

The White Album (1979) is a collection of twenty journalistic pieces written between 1968 and 1978. Many of them appeared originally in the *Esquire* column "The Coast," written alternately by Didion and Dunne from February 1976 through December 1977. Some are based on Didion and Dunne's experiences as screenwriters in Hollywood, where in recent years they have worked together on a screenplay entitled "Water" and completed the screenplay for *True Confessions* (1981), from Dunne's 1977 novel of the same name. Most notably, all of the essays of *The White Album* are intimate memoirs of Didion's personal and professional life during the last years of the 1960s and the first of the next decade.

Despite her prominent place in the most fashionable literary circles of New York and social circles of Hollywood, Didion is by her own admission an introvert, an outsider. Dunne screens all Didion's telephone calls and often sits in on the interviews she gives, while Didion manages all of the couple's business dealings like the "fragile little stainless-steel machine" one friend has called her. "I'm really too shy," Didion once told an interviewer for *Ms.* magazine. "I don't talk much. I am not articulate. I don't make judgments. . . . I'm only myself in front of my typewriter."

This feeling of ease in front of the typewriter is perhaps Didion's most remarkable feature. As one of her former editors, Ralph Graves, observes: "Joan gives everyone the impression of being very private. Then she'll turn around and write the inside-of-the-stomach stuff that you'd think you'd need to know her five years to find out." For Didion, however, "inside-of-the-stomach stuff" is an essential part of the writer's contract with readers: "If you want to write about yourself," Didion has remarked, "you have to give them something." And this, precisely, is what Didion has done in the most forceful of the essays collected in *The White Album*, a work which

is in many ways a sequel to her 1968 collection, *Slouching Towards Bethlehem*.

The White Album takes its title from the 1968 Beatles album (which has no name but only a plain white jacket). Didion found the record "ominous and disturbing, an album inextricably connected to the Manson murders and the dissonance of the 60s." The Beatles album was one of the last collaborations of the rock group before its fragmentation. The record was also a kind of "catechism" for Charles Manson and his followers: after the brutal murder of actress Sharon Tate Polanski and six others, the title of a song from it, "Helter Skelter," was found written in blood on the refrigerator. All of these facts related to the record seemed somehow symbolic to Didion, corollaries of her own physical and psychic disintegration at the time. The title essay, "The White Album," is a bold and often moving working out of those corollaries.

In the essay Didion uses what she terms the cinematographic technique of the "flashcut" to alternate between evocations of her personal crisis and the national crises of the late 1960s. Of Didion, one learns that she suffered a breakdown during the summer of 1968, around the time that she was named a *Los Angeles Times* Woman of the Year, during the summer of Robert Kennedy's assassination and of the violence at the Democratic convention in Chicago. Didion's experience was characterized by "an attack of vertigo, nausea, and a feeling that she was going to pass out"–facts which Didion claims to record verbatim from the psychiatric report filed on her by a private clinic in Los Angeles. "By way of comment," she writes, "I offer only that an attack of vertigo and nausea does not now seem to me an inappropriate response to the summer of 1968."

Throughout "The White Album" Didion is able to maintain a perfect balance between her personal anguish and her account of the social and political upheaval of the 1960s. As one reviewer notes, "there are many reasons for the effectiveness of 'The White Album,' [but] the most striking has to do with the use to which personal neurosis has been put. Joan Didion . . . gives the impression of having refined it to the point where it vibrates in exquisite attunement to the larger craziness of the world she inhabits and observes." In the essay the "maniacal desire" for order and control that Didion describes elsewhere comes into contact with the chaos of the student strikes that rent San Francisco State University in 1968–strikes in which, Didion observes, "disorder was its own point." She recalls interviewing Black Panther Eldridge Cleaver and speaking with him about the commercial prospects of his book *Soul on Ice*—"not an unusual discussion between writers, with the difference that one of the writers had his parole officer there and the other had stood out on Oak Street and been visually frisked before coming inside." And, along with many other of her experiences as a reporter that seemed to suggest the nature of the breakdown she was about to suffer, she remembers buying the dress for Linda Kasabian, one of Manson's followers, to wear to court to testify against her one-time leader.

Didion's house at the time figures importantly in the essay as a tangible symbol of the disintegration she senses both around and within her: "This house on Franklin Avenue was rented, and paint peeled inside and out, and pipes broke and window sashes crumbled and the tennis court had not been rolled since 1933, but ... during the five years that I lived there, even the rather sinistral inertia of the neighborhood tended to suggest that I should live in the house indefinitely." Didion's interest in the symbolism of house and home is one that runs not only through the title essay but through the entire collection as well. It surfaces in "Many Mansions," suggestive of America's political and moral decline. Here Didion compares the ostentatious, never-inhabited California governor's mansion that Ronald Reagan built with the modest apartment of his successor, Jerry Brown, and the old, "extremely individual house" in Sacramento that belonged to the forerunners of both. It surfaces again in "The Getty," Didion's account of her visit to the "seventeen-million-dollar villa built by the late J. Paul Getty to house his antiquities and paintings," and makes a final appearance in the concluding essay of the book, "Quiet Days in Malibu." In this essay Didion writes of the house to which she moved after her breakdown as if to suggest quiet acceptance of that experience and all that it implied: "When I first moved in 1971 from Hollywood to a house on the Pacific Coast highway I had accepted the conventional notion that Malibu meant the easy life.... By the time we left Malibu, seven years later, I had come to see the spirit of the place as one of shared isolation and adversity, and I think now that I never loved the house ... more than on those many days when it was impossible to leave it when fire or flood had in fact closed the highway."

Another preoccupation that recurs in the essays of *The White Album* is Didion's suggestion that the boundaries between literature and life are indistinct: fictional characters possess the same authenticity as those of flesh and blood. She cites Cecelia Brady, a character in F. Scott Fitzgerald's *The Last Tycoon* (1941), as an authority in the essay "In Hollywood" and says that Evelyn Waugh might have created the students at San Francisco State. James Pike, the controversial Episcopal bishop featured in "James Pike, American," seems "the shadow of a great literary character, a literary character in the sense that Howard Hughes and Whittaker Chambers were literary characters."

In the essay "In the Islands" Didion suggests that places become real only when they become a part of literature: "Certain places seem to exist mainly because someone has written about them. Kilimanjaro belongs to Ernest Hemingway. Oxford, Mississippi, belongs to William Faulkner.... A place belongs forever to whoever claims it hardest, remembers it most obsessively, wrenches it from itself, shapes it, renders it, loves it so radically that he remakes it in his own image."

To interviewer Linda Kuehl, Didion admitted that this sense of confusion and even the dependence of life upon art has been for her a constant concern: "I was one of those children who tended to perceive the world in terms of things read about it. I began with a literary idea of experience, and I still don't know where all the lies are." She further revealed that her penchant for living "life on the edge" is a "literary idea," one that "derives from what engaged me imaginatively as a child." It is this life on the edge that is evident on nearly every page of *The White Album*.

Interestingly, reviewers of the collection paid little attention to Didion's preoccupation with the reality of literary ideas. Most agreed that *The White Album* represented a more mellow, more widely ranging collection than *Slouching Towards Bethlehem*, which Didion herself terms a much less "tentative" work. Praise was nearly unanimous for Didion's style—"a fine steel framework that gives these ... pieces a unity"—and for her incisive and demanding eye for detail. In these regards, the comments of reviewer Robert Towers are typical: "All of the essays—even the slightest—manifest not only her intelligence, but an instinct for details that continue to emit pulsations in the reader's memory and a style that is spare, subtly musical in its phrasing and exact.

Add to these her highly vulnerable sense of herself, and the result is a voice like no other in contemporary journalism."

Most of the critical complaint that surfaced in reviews of *The White Album* has to do with the highly personal, confessional tone of many essays, especially those in which Didion describes her breakdown ("The White Album"), her bouts with migraine headaches ("In Bed"), and the threatened disintegration of her marriage to Dunne ("In the Islands"). Didion's comment, as she announces the possibility of divorce from Dunne, is typical of those that aroused protest: "I tell you this not as aimless revelation but because I want you to know, as you read me, precisely who I am and what is on my mind. I want you to understand exactly what you are getting: you are getting a woman who for some time now has felt radically separated from most of the ideas that seem to interest other people. You are getting a woman who somewhere along the line misplaced whatever slight faith she ever had in the social contract, . . . in the whole grand pattern of human endeavor."

Reporter Hillary Johnson summarizes negative critical reaction to such unburdenings with a revealing anecdote. Johnson met Didion at a 1977 publisher's party to celebrate the appearance of *A Book of Common Prayer*: "Though the space was filled with small groups of New Yorkers chatting loudly and amiably, Didion stood alone, near the iced shrimp and crudites, her face bearing an expression of dread lest anyone approach her. Few did approach her, possibly because they had read some of her magazine essays and articles, which have now resurfaced in a collection called 'The White Album.' " Despite an awareness that it is "Didion's ultrasensitivity that has made her such a unique, perceptive reporter" in *The White Album*, Johnson concludes that "One just wishes the woman wasn't in so much pain." Lance Morrow, reviewing for *Time*, laments especially Didion's inclusion in the collection of thoughts on her own divorce, previously published as "a disagreeably calculated column she wrote for *Life* in 1969." Rosemary Dinnage for the *Times Literary Supplement* focuses upon the "*Despair*" of Didion's insistent message, "*It doesn't matter*," while Ann Hulbert for the *New Republic* feels that "we . . . want to know *why* Didion wants to expose such raw, private experience, to feel that we are walking around with her bad dreams for some other reason than that she's self-indulgent and we're morbidly curious."

A small group of critics demonstrated concern over Didion's sincerity in the essays. In an article for the *Nation* Barbara Grizzuti Harrison spoke of the author's "covertly political messages" in *The White Album* and elsewhere called her style "a bag of tricks . . . (I don't know why they have evoked so much wonder)," and declared that most episodes of *The White Album* "put me more in mind of a neurasthenic Cher than of a writer who has been called America's finest woman prose stylist." "Entrepreneurs of Anxiety" John Lahr titled his article on Didion and Dunne for a recent issue of *Horizon*. She is the "Princess of angst"; he is unable to "see the hellishness behind the vulgarity he enjoys"; together they are "the Lunts of the Los Angeles literary scene," "pretenders to the throne of high culture; and only a society indifferent to literature could tolerate their pretensions to excellence." Critics sharing a strong inclination toward feminism similarly found fault with Didion's essay "The Woman's Movement," which describes the movement as a "curious historical anomaly" based on a Marxist vision of women as the proletarian class. As Martha Duffy (*Time*, 10 August 1970) summarized it from a feminist point of view, the essay errs in its examination of "only threadbare documents of the movement." Of Didion, Duffy writes, "One can almost hear Hemingway cheering her on."

The most academic of the discussions among critics of *The White Album* centered on the question of where Didion's greatest talents lay, in the writing of fiction or nonfiction. Ironically, for Didion "never wanted to be a journalist or reporter," it is for her nonfiction that the critical accolades are more willingly given. It is Morrow who best summarizes the current case for the superiority of Didion's reportorial work: "Didion's novels," he writes, "are less interesting than her collections of magazine pieces; paradoxically, the novels do not exert the dramatic force of her journalistic essays."

In *Salvador* (1983), an example of reportage or new journalism, and *Democracy* (1984), a novel "that tries to tell the truth," she has maintained her stance as a writer in both the fiction and nonfiction modes, blending the two into new forms. A first collection of writings about Didion, *Essays and Conversations* (1984), contains scholarly criticism of her work culled from such journals as *Modern Fiction Studies, Contemporary Literature, Critique: Studies in Modern Fiction, Commentary,* and the *New York Times Book Review*. That she should be the subject of serious scholarship is a credit not only to her technique but to her vision. With her latest work Didion raises basic questions about the concepts of democracy, narration, motherhood, and memory.

It is not Didion's intention to provide solutions for the problems she sees in modern life. Solutions, and the salve they bring to a reader's mind, are, in Didion's view, the province of the narrative tradition. According to her, narration has historical significance and "makes" sense. It assumes that time contains recognizable segments of the past, present, and future which, because they connect, can provide coherence. It has enabled writers to write about heroes who move through plot, accomplishing goals and solutions. But as Didion's work reveals, often with biting nostalgia, the narrative tradition is no longer adequate to the stories of today.

Nevertheless, Didion is firmly rooted in the very tradition she challenges. Her reportorial drive for "getting it right" and her novelist's ear for the way conversation fleshes scene reflect her deep appreciation for such literary predecessors as Hawthorne, Orwell, Hemingway, and Conrad. Being rooted in a culture that gives one despair is among the many fascinating contradictions she feels between romantic yearning and existential angst, detachment and intimacy, desire for fiction in a world of fact, despair in fact's truth power. But perhaps because of these and other tensions, because she has made her private questions public, Didion compels attention.

Salvador was originally published serially in the *New York Review of Books* in November and December 1982. The essays are an account of a two-week trip taken by Didion and Dunne to El Salvador in June 1982. On a fact-finding mission to the revolution-torn republic of El Salvador, Didion finds that there are no facts sufficient to describe the place; there are only details. Salvador is to reality what Boca Grande was, in *A Book of Common Prayer*, to fiction: a landscape of the equatorial zone "suited for its irrationality, meanness, disease, and unrest." As the final political frontier, it is the logical place where Didion's sensibility could go to work. There the writer cannot make sense; she can only evoke it.

In the *New York Times Book Review*, Warren Hoge remarked: "No one in El Salvador has interpreted the place better. 'Salvador' shines with enlightening observation.... [Didion's] novelist's eye examines policy on a plane seldom reached in Congressional hearings or State Department briefings." Paul Stuewe in *Quill Quire* said it was

"overwhelmingly effective ... a timely and timeless work of creation." And Frederick Kiley, in a scholarly essay entitled "Beyond Words: Narrative Art in Joan Didion's *Salvador*," compared it to Picasso's *Guérnica* for the way both shape observations as metaphors.

Other critics tended to dismiss *Salvador* for what Mark Falcoff described in *Commentary* as the book's "two big problems. One has to do with the facts, the other with Joan Didion. There are some serious inaccuracies in the text, and many, many more half-truths.... What is even more disturbing about 'Salvador' ... is the way in which she makes the tiny republic of El Salvador into a mirror reflecting her own basic contempt for liberal democracy and–why not say it?–the American way of life." As Gene Lyons commented in *Newsweek*, "Most readers will not get very far in this short book without wondering whether she visited that sad and tortured place less to report than to validate the Didion world view."

Clearly, with her rejection of the narrative tradition's assumptions about history, Didion has tapped a deep emotional core. She does so ironically, acknowledging her indebtedness to Joseph Conrad, master narrator. The epigraph in *Salvador*, taken from Conrad's novella "Heart of Darkness" (1899), contrasts the naive political observations of Marlow with hidden political realities. Marlow is so taken by the "burning noble words" written by Kurtz for the historical record that he hardly notices a postscript. Scrawled in pencil at the end of the report is the phrase "Exterminate all the brutes!" Conrad's point is Didion's: good language distorts bad truth.

Didion expresses a simmering rage in *Salvador* at the rhetorical tricks of the history makers. Her tone represents a shift from the detachment she showed (with the exception of "Bureaucrats") in *The White Album*. Now she views linguistic distortion as nothing short of obscene. Killing, she observes, is made into an abstraction by the phrase "to be disappeared." Numbers, as in body counts, can be obscured to hide the fact that they relate to human beings. Corpses and mutilated bodies are reported and counted by the Salvadoran government "in a kind of tortured code." As reporter, Didion must attempt the impossible task of penetrating the code in a climate where, because words do not signify, facts do not apply.

She catalogs documents, speeches, reports, and communiqués, as well as firsthand observable accounts by herself and others, in this decoding attempt. Code is pervasive on "both sides of the imperialist mirror," used as if "a linguistic deal had been cut." On the side of the Salvadorans are such terms as improvement, perfection, and pacification, which express not reality but wish. She cites the work of Gabriel García Márquez, whose fiction illuminates a prevailing social realism of "wishful thinking," but which in the present situation has become a perverted habit of mind. "Language as it is now used in El Salvador is the language of advertising, of persuasion, the product of being one or another of the *soluciones* crafted in Washington or Panama or Mexico, which is part of the place's obscenity."

Those on the other side–the American president, the ambassadors, the State Department–use code words as well. Phrases like "democratic turbulence," to describe political disaster, and "birth pangs of nascent democratic institutions," to describe nighttime killing raids, illustrate an absurd connection between language and truth. Didion juxtaposes rhetoric with coincidental detail to undercut the seriousness of the policymakers. The effect is always ironic, often appalling, sometimes hilarious. An example of the latter is a juxtaposition of President Reagan, political actor, with Ronald Reagan, movie actor. She cites a description from his 1982 speech before both houses of the British Parliament: "brave freedom fighters battling oppressive government forces on behalf of the silent, suffering people of that tortured country." Next to this in her text she places a description of a movie she happened to be watching while reviewing the speech, a 1952 film with Doris Day called *The Winning Team*. Its phrase "Play ball!" acts as the hidden metaphoric connector between the two media. Burning, noble words, she indicates, are just showmanship to be tossed around, to keep the ball rolling.

Didion is serious about games. For her, evil is the lack of seriousness. Tawdry ritual, frivolous rhetoric, banal expressions are all surface beneath which lies bad truth. Not being able to find facts on the surface, she writes to uncover them in metaphor. Government spokesmen are "players" who take part in "performances"; local events have the feel of "opera" with even extras like herself seeming to live "onstage"; a local general is a "main player" perceived by some as "a wild card"; and symbolic action is a pretense for "playing the game," "playing ball." By exposing the metaphor of gaming, mirroring it in her own sentences, she turns language against itself; she cracks the code.

Didion's thesis is problematic. "That we had been drawn, both by a misapprehension of the local rhetoric and by the manipulation of our own rhetorical weakness, into a game we did not understand, a play of power in a political tropic alien to us, seemed apparent, and yet there we remained." Seeing the appearances of things does not mean finding solutions. But she does discover this: in a place of "cultural zero" language is debased, human life is worthless, rituals are only "moves." And so, in a telling passage, she comments on a new way to read the signs of landscape. The place is Puerta del Diablo, where bodies are dumped, "or what is left of the bodies, pecked and maggoty masses of flesh, bone, hair." It is a place that–in "an older and distinctly literary tradition"–would have been described in words of pathos: "the sky 'broods,' the stones 'weep,' a constant seepage of water weighting the ferns and moss." Without a depth dimension, however, and in the absence of meaning, one is forced to reapply the old words, literalizing them. Indeed, the only kind of truth available to her reporter's eyes are the truths of a convention turned upside down, metaphors becoming real and reality metaphorical.

Democracy (1984) continues Didion's critique of language and society. Its title alludes to Henry Adams's paean on the idea of democracy in his 1880 work of the same title. What Adams envisioned as promise–democracy, Christianity, moral victory–is seen a century later darkly, through the glass of Didion's mirror. Speaking in fiction through the voice of Inez Christian Victor, she also intrudes her own voice onto the text, showing that she unites her identity with her female character, not with Adams.

The novel describes one post-Vietnam year (1975) as it affects the private life of the main character Inez and the public lives of her senator husband Harry and her businessman lover Jack Lovett. The husband is a member of the Alliance for Democratic Institution, funded to keep a particular framework of "democratic" ideals operative. His public image is undermined, however, by the women in his family. Inez carries on an adulterous relationship with Jack Lovett and eventually flees the country; Jessie, his daughter, runs away to find a job in Saigon at the exact time of massive troop evacuation; and Janet, his sister-in-law, is murdered by his demented father-in-law. That the plot is the stuff of which soap opera is made is deliberate. Didion's point is that public scandal of the magnitude of Vietnam has a convulsive effect, infiltrating and making scandalous the lives of private citizens. *Democracy* thus continues the critique in *Salvador* of the inappropriateness of abstract ideals in a world gone crazy. But here her critique is specifically feminist. She implies that America's democratic heritage was founded by men whose patriarchal ideals excluded women.

Reviews of the novel were mixed. Phoebe-Lou Adams in the *Atlantic* called it "striking, provocative, and brilliantly written." Walter Clemons commented in *Newsweek*, "Didion's latest novel is very chic, knowing and romantic. Reading 'Democracy' is like spending a privileged weekend with the great. . . . I had a swell time." And Francis Marnell, writing for the *National Review*, called it "an intelligent and engaging work well worth reading." In a longer review in *Commentary* Joseph Epstein compared Didion with Renata Adler. Epstein wrote that *Democracy* is "her richest novel since *Run River*," with "lively details, sharp observations, risky but always interesting generalizations, real information." He argued, however, that Didion's vision offers only "plain" pessimism, unrelieved by heroism.

Negative criticism focused partly on tone, partly on style. It was felt she was either too feminist or too pessimistic, and the critics were further bothered by the intrusion of author Joan Didion into the novelistic form, as when Didion would complain, "This is a hard story to tell" or "I am resisting narrative here." Janet Wiehe in *Library Journal* said, "As ever-present narrator and minor character in her own novel, Didion achieves the immediacy of journalism at the expense of emotional depth." And Paul Stuewe of *Quill Quire* remarked that the book was more like a "glittering mosaic than a coherent novel."

These criticisms ignore Didion's challenge to story telling as a way of presenting truth. Her concern is like that of Susan Sontag: to raise basic questions about interpretation and evaluation; to avoid the sense of "final" meaning imposed by an omniscient author. Commenting on the shape the novel was taking in her mind, she said in an interview: "I was going to Honolulu because I wanted to see life expanded to a novel. . . . I wanted room for flowers, and reef fish, and people who may or may not be driving one another to murder but in any case are not impelled, by the demands of narrative convention, to say so out loud." What she has in fact done is write a novel that challenges narrative convention. By not assuming an all-knowing pose of the

author's authority, she presents a different perspective on telling stories.

The seeds of *Democracy* were sown in "Angel Visits," the working title of a novel never completed. What Didion had in mind was to write about a dark journey, explored beneath the glamorous surface of an extended dinner party in the glittering setting of Hawaii. Throughout *Democracy* reference is made to the aborted work. Didion writes, " 'Imagine my mother dancing' that novel began in the first person. The first person was Inez, and was later abandoned in favor of the third. 'Inez imagined her mother dancing.' " Here Didion's challenge is to the authority of the *I*. The switch from first- to third-person narration exchanges the omniscient *I* narrator for a more limited third-person viewpoint. In *Democracy* the first person becomes Joan Didion, who writes in chapter 3, "You see the shards of the novel I am no longer writing, the island, the family, the situation. I lost patience with it. I lost nerve." These disclaimers serve several functions. One is to unsettle the reader; another is to imply a certain instability on the part of the author. A third and most important function of these intrusions into form is to suggest that abandonment and aborted effort are female rites. The dark journey beneath the glittering surface is ritually undertaken by women, even by authors, in a male-dominated world.

The men in *Democracy* are thrivers and survivors. They have survived the Vietnam War unwounded and can thrive on its aftermath. Jack Lovett is typical of male heroics in the post-Vietnam age. As a successful "actor" in the field of international business, Jack is "less interested in laser mirrors than in M-16s, AK-47s, FN-FALs, the everyday implements of short-view power." Jack's sense of reality is shaped according to the "information" he receives. Didion writes about him, "It would be accurate only to say that he regarded the country on whose passport he travelled as an abstraction, a state actor, one of several to be factored into any given play." Dwight Christian, the uncle of Inez, is also a successful image maker, who builds himself up as a culturally astute person by quoting philosophy from the pages of *Forbes*. And Billy Dillon, whose last name evokes the essence of Western heroics, is Harry Victor's PR man who understands, absolutely, the "moves" of "the game." He is to *Democracy* what the State Department briefings are to *Salvador*: knowing "the moves," he calls the shots.

These male caricatures are part of the reason that *Democracy* is Didion's most devastating feminist work to date. The other reason is the women. They become refugees inside their own country, their own homes, their own beds. Didion shows that women, the targets of sexual and international schemes, are deluded by old ideals and new promises. Inez is the latest in a series of Didion women—Maria in *Play It As It Lays*, Lily in *Run River*, Charlotte in *A Book of Common Prayer*—all of whom are white, Anglo-Saxon socialites: unstable, sexually compelling, enmeshed in a web of violence spun by men. The battleground becomes the female psyche, which turns mothers and daughters against each other. Inez tries to salvage her relationship with her heroin-addicted daughter Jessie. But the strands of that relationship were woven by Inez's relationship with *her* mother, a woman who left home to find a more attractive career in modeling.

Such misapprehension reverberates on the feminine consciousness, making women the victims, not the victors, in their world. Didion's point is that women have been molded by men. Inez, for example, carries the names of the two men in her life: Christian and Victor. To pretend that she embodies either Christianity or Victory is to place her on a too-abstract plane. Whatever Christian or heroic motives she displays are confused substitutes for her roles as mother and wife. In bringing female darkness to light, Didion exposes a gulf between public and private, high and low, male and female images.

Didion's theme in *Democracy*, physical and spiritual abandonment of the homeland, applies a feminist response to the forefathers. It seems that women are refugees in the foreign land of their homes, and so they flee to establish their otherness. Inez's mother abandons her children for a more glamorous life in San Francisco. Inez abandons her children to do good works in Kuala Lumpur. Jessie abandons her mother to get a job in Saigon. These women are all cut off from mothering and so from the real source of nourishment within themselves. In citing a Wallace Stevens poem, Didion makes a statement about the artificiality of the female soul, "without human feeling, a foreign song." Even Didion feels this disconnectedness, able, she says, only to tell (not to write) her story.

Two metaphors establish a sense of the disintegrating female world. One is the metaphor of dance. Women dance, and so give romantic images of themselves—as in the recurrent film clip of Inez dancing on the St. Regis roof. Jack Lovett's first image of Inez is of her at a ballet. These romantic images stand in sharp contrast to the events which surround them. Didion makes a similar point in *Salvador* with a dance ceremony performed by a local Indian tribe. Their costumes of crinkled foil and their downcast eyes are potent metaphors for the impotence of culture. Dance, as celebration of life and grace, has lost meaning.

A second metaphor is that of memory. To be able to say "I remember" is to establish one's self in a particular place at a particular time, to remove one's self from history. When Inez confesses to a loss of memory, she is suggesting that female connectedness to the deep past, to myth, to the roots of culture, has all gone. In a stunning scene Inez is interviewed. It is the height of her husband's political career; public image is at stake. Inez is asked what she believes to be the major cost of her husband's political success: " 'Memory, mainly,' Inez said . . . 'something like shock treatment . . . I mean you lose track. *As if* you'd had shock treatment.' "

Didion's women are detached, cut off even from memory, the ground of being. In *A Book of Common Prayer*, Charlotte "forgets" the details of her daughter's revolutionary activities, leading her to sustain certain fictions about her daughter. Here Inez presents herself as such a fragmented person that "even the most straightforward details of place and date were intrinsically unknowable, open to various readings." Cut off from self, cut off from country, cut into by abortion or by sex or by flash-cut images, what are women left with?

"Colors, moisture, enough blue in the air." This phrase explains why Inez seeks refuge in India. Women must reclaim their senses of sight, sound, and touch in new settings. Removed from the old paradise, from the great American male myth of the frontier, women have to regenerate *themselves*. They have to find another time sense, until the phrase "Every day is all there is" contains ritualistic meaning.

Perhaps this phrase is the closest Didion comes to finding *la verdad*. The meaning of truth is deeper than fact or history or narration. It lies deep within culture—in dance—and within nature. A recent study of Didion by Katherine Usher Henderson concludes that despite her pessimism, Didion is convinced that truth exists and can be approached. Her vision contains the shards of broken dreams, but it also contains the redemption of style. Style is character, revealed in a rhythm of sentences spoken and written, in metaphor, and in the rituals of the day.

The *New York Times Magazine* featured Didion and Dunne on the cover of its 8 February 1987 issue. In the accompanying feature, "The Rewards of a Literary Marriage," interviewer Leslie Garis reveals how Didion and Dunne continue to work together on many projects, noting that both writers are "fueled as artists by their investigations into current events." Although much of the article centers on the couple's work as screenwriters and on a book Dunne was working on, two telling comments regarding Didion emerged.

First, Garis describes Didion as "a stranger whose nose is pressed up against the window of life," and her works as frequently evoking "a world in disintegration. Her vision is dark, even apocolyptic." Such views of Didion and her work appear as constant threads throughout her literary career. Further, Garis quotes Didion as saying, "I think writers to some extent consider themselves people who walk through life picking up vibrations of what's going on around them. I've thought of myself that way since I was a little girl." In Didion's next major work to appear, though, the nonfiction book *Miami*, there were those critics and readers who felt Didion's ability "to pick up the vibrations" had been somewhat blunted.

Miami, published in 1987, some sections of which initially appeared as a series of excerpts in the *New York Review of Books*, examines the increasing Cuban domination of Miami. Ignoring the glitz of the drug trade usually associated with Miami, the book looks at the ways in which the minority Anglo community often avoids the presence of the Cuban exiles and the manner in which official Washington has continually exploited those who fled Castro's terrorism in the early sixties.

Use of language is one of the prevailing themes in the book. Didion demonstrates the distance between the city's Anglo population and the Cuban community in the use–or non-use–of Spanish. She says that "(t)his question of language was curious." In one chapter Didion describes how a *Miami Herald* reporter was sent to do a story on a course offered by Florida International University in the fall of 1986 called "Cuban Miami: A Guide for Non-Cubans." She notes that only thirteen people signed up for the course and that at the second meeting of the

class, two students appeared with a security guard because of telephone threats. Didion sees the development of "parallel cultures" as problematic for the city. Didion further explores language used by official Washington to describe the political situation in Cuba (past and present); terms like "disposal problem," used in reference to the Bay of Pigs invasion, greatly disturb Didion. Reviewer James Chace in the *New York Times Book Review* comments on the political climate achieved by use of such official, evasive language.

Other reviews of *Miami* were decidedly mixed. Christopher Lehmann-Haupt in the *New York Times* described the book in terms of style, stating that "the repetition of syntactical construction," for example, contributes to the effect of Didion's prose being "finely tuned to paranoia." He compares *Miami* to several other books about Miami published at about the same time, including *Miami: City of the Future* and *Going to Miami: Exiles, Tourists and Refugees in the New America.* Lehmann-Haupt calls Didion's *Miami* "brief and impressionistic, a pointillist nightmare from which the author never even tries to awaken."

In *The New Republic* Nicholas Lemann also compares Didion's *Miami* with the same books mentioned in the Lehmann-Haupt review and states that "Didion presents herself as a case-hardened foreign correspondant with no time for cute details" but complains that she gives the reader "no new facts about Cuban terrorists." *Publishers Weekly* calls Didion "a very personal sort of stylist and here, too, her style, while it suffers overload, will delight her readers." In the same review of *Miami*, though, reviewer Stuttaford Genevieve points to the book's "rather narrow deliberate focus." Jeffery C. Cohen in *National Review* and Robert Wilson of *USA Today* are harsher: Cohen says the book is a "thoroughly muddled picture, a swarm of insinuated accusations, and precious little enlightenment," while Wilson rates *Miami* as one of the worst nonfiction books of 1987. Mark Winchell, author of the most complete study on Didion, rightly points out that one reads Didion for "her amazing facility with language," yet even he calls *Miami* (as well as *Salvador*) "embarrassingly modest failures."

Since *Miami*, however, Didion continues to write nonfiction, most notably "Insider Baseball" (*New York Review of Books*, 27 October 1989) and "Letter from Los Angeles" (the *New Yorker*, 24

April 1989), two incisive journalistic pieces concerned with politics. "Letter from Los Angeles" discusses the re-election of Tom Bradley as mayor of Los Angeles in April 1989, and Didion captures the pulses of the mayoral race as a seasoned insider regarding California politics. "Insider Baseball" analyzes the 1988 Presidential election process with telling detail. Both of these pieces demonstrate what Didion does best—use precise language to reflect specific aspects of American culture of particular times and places. Mark Royden Winchell and others cite the importance of place in Didion's work and she has been termed a "chronicler of a society in transition" and a "regional writer akin to Faulkner and Steinbeck." Her use of language has intrigued rhetoricians as well as literary critics, and in *Style as Argument* (1987), Chris Anderson discusses Didion's rhetorical techniques and notes that Didion, like Capote, Mailer, and Tom Wolfe, "pushes language to its limits."

Didion has already secured a place for herself in literary history as one of the most perceptive observers, both in fiction and nonfiction, of the American consciousness and culture in the last twenty years. Since she has continued to experiment with form and style, there is no reason to believe that her forthcoming productions will not surpass what she has already achieved. Didion's work will continue to excite comment as she continues to write about contemporary frontiers, whether they be cultural, psychological, political, or geographical.

Interviews:

Susan Braudy, "A Day in the Life of Joan Didion," *Ms.*, 5 (February 1977): 65-68, 108-109.

Digby Diehl, "A Myth of Fragility Concealing a Tough Core," *Saturday Review*, 4 (5 March 1977): 24.

Sara Davidson, "A Visit With Joan Didion," *New York Times Book Review*, 3 April 1977, pp. 1, 35-38.

Linda Kuehl, "Joan Didion," in *Writers at Work: The Paris Review Interviews*, fifth series, edited by George Plimpton (New York: Viking, 1981), pp. 339-357.

James Atlas, "Slouching Towards Miami," *Vanity Fair* (October 1987): 48, 52, 56.

Bibliographies:

Fred Rue Jacobs, *Joan Didion—A Bibliography* (Keene, Cal.: Loop Press, 1977).
Useful, but flawed.

Donna Olendorf, "Joan Didion: A Checklist, 1955-1980," *Bulletin of Bibliography*, 32 (January-March 1981): 32-44.

References:

Chris Anderson, *Style as Argument* (Carbondale: Southern Illinois University Press, 1987).
Rhetorical study of Capote, Mailer, Tom Wolfe, and Didion; excellent rhetorical analysis of Didion's stylistic devices.

Samuel Coale, "Didion's Disorder: An American Romancer's Art," *Critique*, 25 (Spring 1984): 160-170.
Discussion of Didion's first three novels.

Joseph Epstein, "The Sunshine Girls," *Commentary*, 77 (June 1984): 62-67.
Ironic article.

Ellen Friedman, ed., *Essays and Conversations* (Princeton, N.J.: Ontario Review Press, 1984).
Contains "Why I Write," three "conversations with the author," and fourteen essays; useful.

Leslie Garis, "Didion and Dunne; The Rewards of a Literary Marriage," *New York Times Magazine*, 8 February 1987, p. 18.
Useful inside look at the personal life and work habits of Didion and Dunne.

Lynne T. Hanley, "To El Salvador," *Massachusetts Review*, 24 (Spring 1983): 13-29.
Discusses *A Book of Common Prayer* and *Salvador*.

Barbara Grizzuti Harrison, "Joan Didion: The Courage of Her Afflictions," *Nation*, 229 (26 September 1979): 277-286.
Interesting and useful article, though quite negative in places.

Katherine Usher Henderson, *Joan Didion* (New York: Ungar, 1981).
Brief but useful study.

Alfred Kazin, *Bright Book of Life: American Novelists and Storytellers from Hemingway to Mailer* (Boston: Little, Brown, 1973), pp. 189-198.
Short critical account covering Didion's works through *Play It As It Lays*.

Kazin, "Joan Didion: Portrait of a Professional," *Harper's*, 243 (December 1971): 112-122.
Critical essay with some biographical information; portions appear in *Bright Book of Life*.

John Lahr, "Entrepreneurs of Anxiety," *Horizon*, 24 (January 1981): 36-39.
Critical attack on Didion and Dunne.

Mark Schorer, "Novels and Nothingness," *American Scholar*, 40 (Winter 1970-1971): 168-174.
Discusses Didion's style.

David C. Stineback, "On the Limits of Fiction," *Midwest Quarterly*, 14 (July 1973): 339-348.
Somewhat useful discussion of Didion's techniques.

C. L. Westerbeck, Jr., "Coppola Now," *Commonweal*, 106 (28 September 1979): 531-532.
Discussion of the film world and Didion.

Mark Royden Winchell, *Joan Didion*, revised edition (Boston: Twayne, 1989).
Excellent analysis and discussion of Didion, her work, and her overall literary career.

E. L. Doctorow

This entry was updated by Beverly Spears Blackmon (Francis Marion College) from the entry by Mildred Louise Culp in DLB 28, Twentieth-Century American-Jewish Fiction Writers, *and from the entry by Carol MacCurdy (University of Southwestern Louisiana) in* DLB Yearbook 1980.

Places	New York		
Influences and Relationships	Miguel de Cervantes Philip Roth	Daniel Defoe William Faulkner James Joyce	John Dos Passos Theodore Dreiser Saul Bellow
Literary Movements and Forms	"Nonfiction as Fiction as Nonfiction"	Naturalism Experimental Fiction	Postmodernism Historical Novels
Major Themes	Manipulation of History Marital and Family Conflict	Jews as Historic Victims Reality and Imagination	The Government as Enemy
Cultural and Artistic Influences	Radical Jewish Humanism	Movies	Celebrities
Social and Economic Influences	Socialism The Depression	The Extended Family Labor Unions	American "Robber Barons"

BIRTH: New York, New York, 6 January 1931, to David Richard and Rose Levine Doctorow.

EDUCATION: A.B., Kenyon College, 1952; Columbia University, 1952-1953.

MARRIAGE: 20 August 1954 to Helen Setzer; children: Jenny, Caroline, Richard.

AWARDS AND HONORS: National Book Critics Circle Award for *Ragtime*, 1976; Arts and Letters Award from the American Academy and National Institute of Arts for *Ragtime*, 1976; L.H.D., Kenyon College, 1976.

BOOKS: *Welcome to Hard Times* (New York: Simon & Schuster, 1960); republished as *Bad Man from Bodie* (London: Deutsch, 1961);
Big As Life (New York: Simon & Schuster, 1966);
The Book of Daniel (New York: Random House, 1971; London: Macmillan, 1971);
Ragtime (New York: Random House, 1975; London: Macmillan, 1976);
Drinks Before Dinner (New York: Random House, 1979);
Loon Lake (New York: Random House, 1980; London: Macmillan, 1980);
Lives of the Poets: Six Stories and a Novella (New York: Random House, 1984);
World's Fair (New York: Random House, 1985).

PLAY PRODUCTION: *Drinks Before Dinner*, New York Shakespeare Festival, Estelle R. Newman Theatre, 22 November 1978.

PERIODICAL PUBLICATIONS: "The Bomb Lives!," *Playboy*, 21 (March 1974): 114-116, 208-216;
"After the Nightmare," *Sports Illustrated*, 44 (28 June 1976): 72-82;
"False Documents," *American Review*, 231 (November 1977): 215-232;
"Living in the House of Fiction," *Nation*, 226 (22 April 1978): 459-462;
"Dream Candidate: The Rise of Ronald Reagan," *Nation*, 1 (19-26 July 1980): 65, 82-84.

One of the most celebrated and controversial novelists of the past two decades, E. L. Doctorow has an uncanny ability to reach both the general audience (*The Book of Daniel, Welcome to Hard Times*, and *Ragtime* have been made into movies) and the literary scholar, with works that challenge and expand accepted definitions of the art

E. L. Doctorow (photo copyright © by Jerry Bauer)

of the novel. He has distinguished himself among American-Jewish writers by the diversity of his work: an allegorical Western, a science-fiction satire, three novels (one with a large component of poetry), and a play. Doctorow is discussed primarily as an innovator in narrative technique. Yet he is also a distinctly Jewish writer, his replication of characters and events throughout his work reflecting his concern for the persistence of moral crises in history and calling into question modern responses to the problems of evil and individual responsibility.

Born in New York City on 6 January 1931 to David Richard and Rose Levine Doctorow, Doctorow attended the Bronx High School of Science before enrolling at Kenyon College, where he studied with John Crowe Ransom. He received his A.B. with honors in 1952 and was awarded an L.H.D. in 1976. Senior editor of the New American Library from 1959 to 1964 and editor in chief at Dial Press from 1964 to 1969, Doctorow was writer in residence at the University of California at Irvine (1969-1970) and later served on the faculty at Sarah Lawrence College and Yale University. In 1972 Doctorow received a

National Book Award nomination for *The Book of Daniel;* in 1976 he won the National Book Critics Circle Award and an Arts and Letters Award from the American Academy and National Institute of Arts for *Ragtime.* He lives in New Rochelle, New York, with his wife, Helen Setzer.

Doctorow's novels are demanding reading. His heroes, while not always Jewish, are, with one possible exception, intellectuals trying to make sense of a chaotic world infused with violence and evil. And his plots, simple and absorbing but seldom linear, serve as vehicles to analyze the composing process as a parallel to life itself. *Welcome to Hard Times* (1960), Doctorow's Western, has been described by Victor S. Navasky as "a play against the genre." An allegory, it belongs essentially to a Jewish literary tradition, focusing on the radicality of evil and the inexplicable cruelty of the alien aggressor toward an insulated community. Set in the Dakota Territory, *Welcome to Hard Times* is narrated by Mayor Blue, the first in Doctorow's series of characters who speak about the act of writing. The plot is a unified, seemingly simple one, beginning with the brutal ravaging of a small town by Turner, the "Bad Man from Bodie," and ending with Turner's bloody retribution. Through the tale Doctorow explores the awesome force of rampant evil, the impotence of reason without will, and the morbid predictability of both. Turner is evil incarnate, and the Old West of *Welcome to Hard Times* prefigures the Holocaust. When the town becomes a conflagration in Turner's hands, its inhabitants' passivity is terrifying. Molly Riordan, the town's conscience, urges the mayor to confront Turner, and she herself tries to stop Turner with a stiletto–a reminder of the impotence of weapons in the face of intractable evil. Molly's attraction to Turner symbolizes a universal fascination with the demonic. And Blue, the self-styled "promoter" of the town whose compulsive record-keeping–"it was something that had to be done"–represents the inability of the intellectual to control evil, fails to recognize the strength of Turner's power and allows it to become superhuman.

In *Welcome to Hard Times,* despite what David Emblidge has called "a spirited hopefulness," there is little cause for hope, and the radical evil is not confined to a single cowboy. *Welcome to Hard Times* is, as Marilyn Arnold has observed, "a testimony to human stories that keep repeating themselves," an early indication of Doctorow's theme of replication. The death of the Bad Man is not the end of the evil that moti-

vated him. Wirt Williams has remarked that Doctorow, like Conrad, suggests our ability to resist evil psychically. Yet when Blue concludes the narrative, no progress has been made. "Nothing is ever buried," he says, "the earth rolls in its tracks, it never goes anywhere, it never changes."

While *Welcome to Hard Times* explores the nineteenth-century West, *Big As Life* (1966) is set in the New York of the future. Intended as satire, *Big As Life* is Doctorow's most neglected work, partly, perhaps, because the satire itself is uneven and diffused. A pair of giant creatures, "big as life," position themselves over the Pan-American Building and refuse to budge, sending the city into panic and prompting the president to send in the army and blockade Manhattan. Posited against the government's overreaction is the empty response of Wallace Creighton, the satirized intellectual who reacts like the historian he is: like Mayor Blue, he will keep records. But the satire breaks down, apparently, as the creatures become more predictable, less monstrous. Their oblivion to the panic around them, and their show of affection for each other, is mirrored in the private sweetness of a human couple, Red Bloom and Sugarbush. As Creighton comes to realize, the parallel is no accident. The creatures are monstrous products of our world; "we're joined to them, they are in our world, they *are* our world and if we destroy them we destroy ourselves." That observation, however, makes the satire less pointed. Which response is the appropriate one–the ineffective intellectualizing of Creighton, the simplemindedness of the military, or the oblivion of the lovers? If, as Barbara L. Estrin has suggested, *Big As Life* is a vision of Armageddon, Doctorow is indicting man's inability to respond at all. Creighton reacts to disaster by the single-minded pursuit of his record keeping, and Red returns to hearth and home.

While satire may not be Doctorow's forte, *Big As Life* does prefigure his next work, artistically and ideologically iconoclastic, filled with grotesque minor characters, and challenging in its questions about the human condition. Published in 1971, *The Book of Daniel* was Doctorow's most compelling novel up to that time. Narrated by Daniel Isaacson Lewin, a graduate student at Columbia who is trying to piece his life together, *The Book of Daniel* addresses, on one level, events of the McCarthy era, specifically the case of Julius and Ethel Rosenberg, who were electrocuted in 1953 after their conviction for espionage. Enigmatic like his Old Testament namesake, Daniel is

*Dust jacket for Doctorow's 1975 novel about three families
in pre-World War I America*

writing in the late 1960s. His quest is agonizing and ends, as Richard Schickel has pointed out, without a shred of certainty "about the meaning of anything." The ambiguity is at once irritating and arresting. But Doctorow's failure to provide answers is evidence of a maturing of his craft. Doctorow himself admitted, in his 1977 essay "False Documents," that he had become "more interested in discovering what may be wrong with us than in expressing pieties."

Much of Doctorow's effect results from the way he approaches the art of composition in the novel. In Daniel's scrambled, episodic narration, the act of writing becomes itself part of the story; Daniel the narrator becomes linked with Mayor Blue of *Welcome to Hard Times* and anticipates the Little Boy of *Ragtime* and the poet in *Loon Lake*. The experiments with voice and point of view in *The Book of Daniel* suggest Doctorow's impatience with fictional forms, his attempts to reform the novel by reconstructing it. Moreover, as he has

hinted in "Living in the House of Fiction" (1978), those experiments may be a metaphorical statement on "our need to transform our lives and remake ourselves."

On several levels, *The Book of Daniel* is Doctorow's most overtly Jewish work. It draws upon Jewish history and culture–the biblical Daniel, for instance, figures prominently in the narrative– and like its Old Testament namesake, it is filled with dreams and visions that remain unexplained. Daniel's sprawling ruminations call up the pogroms of czarist Russia, the great wave of Eastern European migration at the turn of the century, the sweatshop existence of first-generation immigrants, and, in Daniel's obsession with the electrocution of his parents, the horror of the Holocaust and the world that could permit such horror to occur. Politically, too, the novel is self-consciously Jewish, concerned as it is with class struggle and the oppression of political outcasts. When Paul and Rochelle Isaacson are imprisoned for their Communist sympathies, their incarceration suggests a wider imprisonment, that of America during the McCarthy Era. If Doctorow's Daniel discovers anything, it is that for Jews there will be more questions than answers. Juxtaposed to references to the Old Testament God of justice, Daniel's story is painfully ironic. And Daniel himself becomes a prophetic figure, delivering truths that we do not want to hear, castigating us for political complacency in a nuclear age. In *The Book of Daniel*, and in his essay "The Bomb Lives!" (1974), Doctorow explores humanity's responses to the technology it has created.

Ragtime, written while the author was a Guggenheim fellow, took the literary world by storm when it appeared in 1975. An antinostalgic novel of replication set in the decade prior to World War I, *Ragtime* "rags" an array of historical figures, including Houdini, William Howard Taft, J. P. Morgan, John D. Rockefeller, Jung, Freud, Henry Ford, Big Bill Haywood, Scott Joplin, Emma Goldman, Thomas Edison, and Archduke Ferdinand. So carefully does Doctorow weave history with events of the imagination that by the end of the novel the nature of historical truth is called into question.

The main fictional figures are part of a triptych of families through which Doctorow delineates the American experience at the turn of the century. The first is headed by Father, the quintessential American who earns his living by manufacturing flags, bunting, and fireworks and for whom America is most properly WASPish: "no Negroes . . . no immigrants." Mother reinforces the vestiges of Victorian prudery; Mother's Younger Brother defies those standards in some of Doctorow's most graphic sex scenes; and the Little Boy in the sailor blouse records the scene. Cultural counterparts of this family are the Jewish Mameh, Tateh, and Daughter and the black family grouping of Coalhouse Walker, Jr., Sarah, and her infant.

Through the experiences of these families Doctorow reveals a world in flux, modern culture at its birth–an era of frustration and violent change. Immigrant life on the Lower East Side and Coalhouse Walker's extended rampage both give the lie to Father's pristine vision of America. Younger Brother's sexual experience with Goldman and Evelyn Nesbitt ends in a shower of sperm "like falling ticker tape," a symbolic outpouring of frustration over the satisfactions of post-Victorian morality.

Finally, *Ragtime* is another reminder that for Doctorow, writing is performance. Through the Little Boy, for whom the world, like statues in the park, seems constantly to be composing and recomposing itself "in an endless process of dissatisfaction," Doctorow creates a self-reflexive novel, one that questions not only the nature of historical truth but also the authority of the narrative voice. Critical reception of the novel has been generally favorable, though varied. Daniel Zins contends that ethnicity and racial unrest are the key issues for Doctorow; for Cobbett Steinberg the novel is a tribute to the oppressed. And, as Jonathan Raban observes, the book is Jewish, evoking the fiction of Abraham Cahan, Henry Roth, and Bernard Malamud.

Doctorow's one foray into drama, *Drinks Before Dinner* (1979), is an almost plotless two-act play. The vision of *Drinks Before Dinner* is of a disturbingly postexistentialist world. At a gathering of friends, the main character, Edgar, whips out a pistol and harangues the others at gunpoint. Despairing about life in our time, Edgar articulates the theme that Doctorow pursues in his other works: if our civilization is to continue, we must overhaul it, while doing something about ourselves. For the distraught Edgar, automobiles become symbols for the senseless enslavement of humanity by technology; we create them, he says, then they entrap us in an automotive existence. Edgar laments that cars "suggest the dreariness of biology, the predictability of the plan of mindless excess by which we reproduce ourselves." Suicidal and out of control, Edgar presents an apoca-

lyptic scenario that concludes with a vision of nuclear destruction.

Edgar's despair contrasts with the resigned optimism of Joel, a physician who works with "disgusting and degrading means of dying" and, almost ritualistically, performs the same operation five or six times a day. In the face of this dull existence, Joel endures. What sets him apart from the other characters is his ability to accept life for what it is, and to keep going. Joel's response to Edgar may well be the most memorable lines in the play: "So it is clear, then, that those who do best in life are those who get on with it. Life is surely merciful to those who get on with it." A play of ideas and words, *Drinks Before Dinner* rests– as Doctorow himself admits in his introduction– on "a sense of heightened language." The barrage of words reflects Doctorow's genius as a writer, but most of his critics and his audience were unprepared for it. Judging by reviews of its 1978 production, *Drinks Before Dinner* is less effective on stage than on paper.

As a result of the critical controversy surrounding *Ragtime*, the publication of *Loon Lake* in the fall of 1980 marked an important point in Doctorow's career. In this fifth novel the author pushes his experiments with technique further. As he explained to John F. Baker in a *Publishers Weekly* interview (30 June 1975), in *Ragtime* he deliberately concentrated on "the narrative element" and "wanted a really relentless narrative, full of ongoing energy . . . the sense of motion." And indeed the novel's vigorous prose style with its rhythmic "ragtime" effect accounted for much of its success–proving it to be both accessible and entertaining. However, in *Loon Lake* Doctorow is more formally ambitious, again focusing on narration. In a *New York Times Book Review* interview with Navasky, Doctorow notes that in *Loon Lake* "the narrator throws his voice, and the reader has to figure out who and what he is. The convention of the consistent, identifiable narrative is one of the last conventions that can be assaulted, and I think it has now been torpedoed. For the first time, I've made something work without the basic compact between narrator and reader, and technically I'm pleased at being able to maintain a conventional story despite giving up that security."

In *Loon Lake* Doctorow intentionally provides no conventional narrative exposition. Time sequences are not only juggled, but shifts in narrative viewpoint occur so frequently that the reader does not always know who is talking. At times the

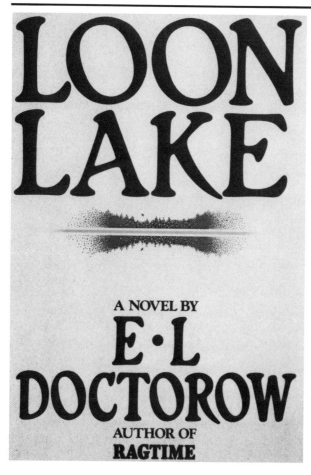

Dust jacket for Doctorow's 1980 novel about a young drifter's involvement with an eccentric industrial tycoon and his entourage during the Depression

point of view switches suddenly from first to third person or vice versa. In his interview with Navasky, Doctorow explains his purpose: "Here you don't know who's talking so that's one more convention out the window. That gives me pleasure, and I think it might give pleasure to readers, too. Don't underestimate them. People are smart, and they are not strangers to discontinuity. There's an immense amount of energy attached to breaking up your narrative and leaping into different voices, times, skins, and making the book happen and then letting the reader take care of himself. It's a kind of narrative akin to television—discontinuous and mind-blowing."

As in *Ragtime*, Doctorow evokes a period in American history, in this case the 1930s. Although the novel glances back to the 1920s and looks to the 1970s, the present action takes place in 1936, during the Great Depression. The action is narrated mainly by Joe Korzeniowski of Paterson, New Jersey, who has left his impoverished home and is on the road. Having toured hobo

camps and worked as a carnival roustabout, he finds himself lost in the woods one night near a single-track railroad in the Adirondack Mountains. A private train goes by, and through the window, he catches a glimpse of a naked girl reflected in a mirror. As if propelled by a vision, he follows the tracks until he comes to Loon Lake, a hidden wilderness estate of thirty thousand acres owned by one of the country's richest men, F. W. Bennett. An industrial tycoon of the robber-baron variety, Bennett plays host at his grand retreat to gatherings of celebrated people. Rather eccentric, Bennett takes a liking to Joe, who stays on as one of the estate's workers.

Also present at Loon Lake are Bennett's wife Lucinda, a world-famous aviatrix who occasionally flies in on her hydroplane, and Warren Penfield, a great-hearted poet and drunkard in residence, who narrates some of the action in a poetic form that resembles blank verse. The girl whose image on the train captivated Joe turns out to be a guest also. A tough blond beauty, Clara Lukács is the moll of the gangster Tommy Crapo, who works for Bennett as a strikebreaker. While visiting Loon Lake on business, Crapo gives Clara to Bennett, who in turn leaves her to Penfield's care.

Eventually Joe helps Clara escape from Loon Lake with Penfield's aid and a Mercedes stolen from Bennett. Their destination is California, and on their cross-country tour they witness the nightmare of the Depression. Afraid that Bennett is pursuing them, they hide out most of the time until Joe decides he must take a job to earn some cash. He decides that one of the last places Bennett would look for him is on the assembly line at one of his own auto plants. For a while he and Clara live a domesticated life in an Indiana factory town. However, violent union disputes soon erupt. A neighbor and friend, Red James, who is an active union member, turns out to be a fink, a company operative under the employ of Tommy Crapo. When his role as a double agent is discovered, Red is killed—not by union members but by Crapo's thugs. Joe, who is implicated by his friendship with Red, is badly beaten by these thugs at the same time and is later accused of Red's murder. Crapo arrives at the police station and spirits Clara away while Joe pleads innocence and professes to be Bennett's true son.

The hoax works, and Joe eventually struggles back to Loon Lake, stripped of everything and feeling "dispossessed." Although desiring revenge, Joe declares that "no simple motive could

-50-

I could hear the engine clearly now and knew it was moving
at a slow speed. The first I saw of it was a diffuse
paling of the darkness along the curve of the embankment.
Suddenly I was blinded by a powerful light, as if I had
looked into the sun. I dropped to my knees. The beam
swung away from me in a transverse arc and a long conical
ray of light illuminated the entire rock outcropping, every
silvery vein of shist glittering as bright as a mirror,
every fern and evergreen flaring for a moment as if torched.
I rubbed my eyes and looked for the train behind the glare.
It was passing from my left to my right. The locomotive and
tender were blacker than the night, a massive movement forward of shadow, but there was a passenger car behind them
and it was all lit up inside. I saw a porter in a white
jacket serving drinks to three men sitting at a table. I
saw dark wood panelling, a lamp with a fringed shade, and
shelves of books in leather bindings. Then two women sitting
talking at a group of wing arm chairs that looked textured,
as if needlepointed. Then a bright bedroom with frost glass
wall lamps and a canopied bed and standing naked in front
of a mirror was a blonde girl and she was holding up for her
examination a white dress on a hangar.

Oh my lords and ladies and then the train had passed
through the clearing and I was watching the red light
disappear around the bend. I hadn't moved from the moment
the light had dazzled my eyes. I'd heard of private

Typescript page from Loon Lake, *which Doctorow described as "a kind of narrative akin to television—
discontinuous and mind-blowing" (courtesy of the author)*

fill the totality of my return." At Loon Lake he discovers Bennett wasting away, grieving over the plane-crash death of his wife and Penfield. Rather than satisfying his urge for revenge, Joe marks his return by a baptismal plunge into Loon Lake and emerges with a new identity. The novel concludes with a biographical sketch outlining the remainder of Joe's career–as soldier (an officer in strategic services), deputy assistant director of the Central Intelligence Agency, ambassador, and chairman of the board of the steel corporation and the Bennett Foundation. These accomplishments are catalogued in the best Horatio Alger tradition. Joe Korzeniowski of Paterson becomes Joseph Paterson Bennett, not only the adoptive son of F. W. Bennett but now the "Master of Loon Lake."

Loon Lake presents Doctorow's ironic comment on the traditional American dream, for Joe pays his dues to the system and becomes a material success as well as a moral failure. Clearly, what Joe earlier ran away from–the corruptibility of wealth's impersonal force–he epitomizes at the end. As George Stade analyzes the novel's ending, Joe "triumphs over his adoptive father by becoming him, only worse–" for his is "revenge through usurpation." Stade concludes: "In America, . . . the sons win; they destroy the past only to preserve the worst of it in themselves, and thereby destroy the future. Such is Doctorow's variation on the conventional American success story."

Doctorow underscores the violent contrast between the American dream and the reality of the American experience through his stylistic manipulation of structure, narration, and symbol. The title of the novel itself holds the novel's prevailing symbols. The lake with its shimmering reflections suggests the use of corresponding images in the novel as well as what Robert Towers refers to as the "concentrically expanding ripples of implication." In his review in the *New York Times Book Review*, Towers calls *Loon Lake* "a world of mirrors, a fascinating, tantalizing novel in which nearly every image or episode has its counterpart somewhere else in the book." Likewise functioning as a symbol, the loon is a bird which hunts fish by diving into the lake, shattering its surface, and then rising with its catch. Doctorow certainly suggests the process of diving and rising with the novel's fragmented structure, the radical alternations in time sequence and narrative viewpoint, and especially with the two extremes of Joe's life.

In the *New Statesman*, Nicholas Shrimpton argues that Doctorow's stylistic methods of "vertiginous alternations" serve to intensify the novel rather than complicate it. On the other hand, Towers "felt trapped in a Barthian funhouse of mirrors" and suggests that the "loon-lake symbol" is not enough to give the novel shape. However, he concludes on a positive note: "Yet the novel is so rich in its disorder that I can regret only to a point the lack of a final coherence. The experience of reading *Loon Lake* . . . was exhilarating."

Although many reviewers noted the structural flaws in *Loon Lake*, most praised Doctorow's formal ambitions. As Paul Gray says in *Time* magazine, "Doctorow may try to do too much in *Loon Lake*. . . . But the author's skill at historical reconstruction, so evident in *Ragtime*, remains impressive here; the novel's fragments and edgy, nervous rhythms call up an age of clashing anxiety. *Loon Lake* tantalizes long after it is ended." In the *New York Review of Books*, Diane Johnson likewise gives a positive assessment: "Doctorow's faith in his version of American history, and his willingness to run the large artistic risks involved in asserting it, make him one of the bravest and most interesting of modern American novelists. . . ."

Although *Loon Lake* has not generated the same enthusiastic acclaim as initially greeted *Ragtime*, it has nevertheless been a critical and commercial success. Like *Ragtime*, it, too, had a large first printing, was a best-seller, and a Book-of-the-Month Club selection. Thus Doctorow seems to have maintained his popular support while continuing to pursue his formal experiments, perhaps proving his faith in his reader's willingness to explore with him. Anthony Burgess may best explain Doctorow's accomplishment in *Loon Lake* when he says that "the serious novelist's problem is to be uncompromising and yet to find an audience. Doctorow has found an audience and nothing could be less of a fictional compromise than *Loon Lake*." In this respect, *Loon Lake* is something of a milestone for Doctorow. Because this fifth novel confirms Doctorow as a serious contemporary novelist and a commercial success, it stands as an important addition to his literary accomplishments.

Doctorow's 1984 collection of short fiction, *Lives of the Poets: Six Stories and a Novella*, shows more than any of his other works the range of his writing. Some of the stories are straightforward in narrative technique; others are as experimental and demanding as *Loon Lake*. Doctorow's "smart" reader will appreciate "The Leather

Man," an example of Doctorow's shifting narration as well as his way of centering upon political and social messages. The title story, "Lives of the Poets," is less demanding in technique and more ordinary in content: the characters are middle-aged, creative (or formerly creative) people, most of whose private relationships are unsatisfying. Any reader who has ever suspected that writers and other artists are unpleasant people may find these suspicions justified by "Lives of the Poets." Most clearly autobiographical is the initial story, "The Writer in the Family," a well-put-together exploration of the effect of extended-family attitudes upon sensitive boys. All in all, this collection offers an accurate sampling of its author's content, the results of his attitudes toward authorship and toward readers, and the variety of his experiments with narrative.

World's Fair (1985) is so clearly autobiographical that the *New York Review of Books* said that the term "novel" is inappropriate to describe it. Phoebe-Lou Adams of the *Atlantic* showed sharp disappointment in her December 1985 review: "In all, the novel induces a weary sense of deja vu, which is the last thing a reader expects from the work of this normally stimulating and original author." Robert Towers, reviewing for *New York Review of Books* (19 December 1985) wrote: "The characters, while convincingly reproduced and analyzed, are not really memorable, and the book as a whole lacks the movement and suspense of good fiction." Others were more appreciative but all agreed that Doctorow was writing a memoir of his own childhood.

This book may nevertheless be Doctorow's best. It has imperfections which are like those in earlier novels, perhaps the most lamentable of which is his weakness in depicting women–or, in *World's Fair*, in having a female character fail to make herself believable through narration. His by-now-well-known use of multiple points of view appears to make such an attempt necessary, but Doctorow has not so far proved able to meet the challenge. But *World's Fair* shows no falling off in Doctorow's abilities nor in execution, and it exemplifies a tighter hold (to use a wrestling image) in his determined struggle toward a meaningful view of human existence. In *World's Fair* he comes closer to looking at events with eyes unclouded by doctrine and self-righteousness. After more than two decades as a public figure, the rebel has not succumbed. E. L. Doctorow is still writing how and what he chooses.

Like most novelists, Doctorow respects the boundaries of tradition. In *Loon Lake* he has created a romance in the manner of Hawthorne and social realism after Cahan and Michael Gold. Yet he will be remembered for his experiments with those boundaries: overlapping genres in *Welcome to Hard Times* and *Big As Life*, integrating fiction and history in *Ragtime*, toying with narrative voice in *The Book of Daniel* and *Loon Lake*. The first-hand material with which Doctorow works in *World's Fair*, unlike the second-hand views he espoused and preached in *Ragtime* and other earlier works, may prove the background he needs to go on to become (like Nathaniel Hawthorne, whom he admires and claims as an influence) a writer for the ages, rather than for the age. His concern for the pluralism of American society is mirrored in the variety of his experiments with fictive conventions; his continual grappling with the problems of the permanence of evil and the responsibilities of modern mankind are themes as time-honored as the novelistic tradition he respects. For Doctorow, writing is an act of recovery and discovery, the process of composition akin to the moral need to create and re-create. In Doctorow's hands the novel becomes a distinctly American document that looks backward in criticism and forward in nervous anticipation, that indicts our inequities yet celebrates our diversity, that shows a distressing sameness while holding out the promise of change.

Interviews:

John F. Baker, "E. L. Doctorow," *Publishers Weekly*, 207 (30 June 1975): 6-7.

Victor S. Navasky, "E. L. Doctorow: 'I Saw a Sign,'" *New York Times Book Review*, 28 September 1980, pp. 44-45.

Hilary Mills, "E. L. Doctorow," *Saturday Review*, 7 (October 1980): 44-48.

References:

Marilyn Arnold, "History as Fate in E. L. Doctorow's Tale of a Western Town," *South Dakota Review*, 18 (Spring 1980): 53-63.
Discusses the nature of evil in Doctorow's imagined Old West.

Mildred L. Culp, "Women and Tragic Destiny in Doctorow's *The Book of Daniel*," *Studies in American Jewish Literature*, 2 (1982): 155-166.

One of the few discussions of Doctorow's female characters.

David Emblidge, "Marching Backward into the Future: Progress as Illusion in Doctorow's Novels," *Southwest Review*, 62 (Autumn 1977): 397-408.
Presents Doctorow's negative view of social progress.

Barbara L. Estrin, "Surviving McCarthyism: E. L. Doctorow's *The Book of Daniel*," *Massachusetts Review*, 16 (Summer 1975): 577-587.
Clarifies Doctorow's political views.

Nicholas Shrimpton, "New Jersey Joe," review of *Loon Lake*, *New Statesman*, 100 (31 October 1980): 27.
Analyzes the character of the protagonist in *Loon Lake*.

Cobbett Steinberg, "History and the Novel: Doctorow's *Ragtime*," *University of Denver Quarterly*, 10 (Winter 1976): 125-130.
Discusses the interaction of fiction and non-fiction in the novel.

Robert Towers, "A Brilliant World of Mirrors," review of *Loon Lake*, *New York Times Book Review*, 28 September 1980, pp. 1, 45-47.
Discusses imagism and symbolism in *Loon Lake*.

Richard Trenner, "Politics and the Mode of Fiction," *Ontario Review*, 16 (Spring-Summer 1982): 5-16.
Discusses the role of political beliefs in Doctorow's novels.

Trenner, ed., *E. L. Doctorow: Essays and Conversations* (Princeton, N.J.: Ontario Review Press, 1983).
Includes essays by Larry McCaffrey, Paul Levine, Arthur Saltzman, John Clayton, and others.

Daniel Zins, "E. L. Doctorow: The Novelist as Historian," *Hollins Critic*, 16 (December 1979): 1-14.
A good discussion of Doctorow's blurring of the distinction between fact and fiction.

Ernest J. Gaines

This entry was updated by Keith E. Byerman (University of Texas) from his entry in DLB 33, Afro-American Fiction Writers After 1955.

Places	Rural Louisiana	California	
Influences and Relationships	William Faulkner Eudora Welty	Ernest Hemingway Leo Tolstoy	Ivan Turgenev Nikolai Gogol
Literary Movements and Forms	Nineteenth-Century Russian Literature	Southern Literature	Local Color
Major Themes	The Land Manhood History	Afro-American Freedom and Dignity	Father / Son Relationships
Cultural and Artistic Influences	Black Folk Life	Cajun and Creole Cultures	Black Music Oral Tradition
Social and Economic Influences	The New South Agricultural Systems	Civil Rights Movement	Slavery

See also the Gaines entries in DLB 2, American Novelists Since World War II *and* DLB Yearbook 1980.

BIRTH: Oscar, Louisiana, 15 January 1933, to Manuel and Adrienne Gaines.

EDUCATION: B.A., San Francisco State College, 1957; Stanford University, 1958-1959.

AWARDS AND HONORS: Joseph Henry Jackson Award for "Comeback," 1959; National Endowment for the Arts Grant, 1967-1968; Guggenheim Fellowship, 1972; California Literature Medal Award, Fiction Gold Medal for *The Autobiography of Miss Jane Pittman*, 1972; Louisiana Literature Award for *The Autobiography of Miss Jane Pittman*, 1972.

BOOKS: *Catherine Carmier* (New York: Atheneum, 1964; London: Secker & Warburg, 1966);

Of Love and Dust (New York: Dial, 1967; London: Secker & Warburg, 1968);

Bloodline (New York: Dial, 1968);

The Autobiography of Miss Jane Pittman (New York: Dial, 1971; London: Joseph, 1973);

In My Father's House (New York: Knopf, 1978; London: Prior, 1978);

A Gathering of Old Men (New York: Knopf, 1983).

Ernest J. Gaines is one of the best known of contemporary black writers. He received popular and critical recognition for the publication and subsequent television production of *The Autobiography of Miss Jane Pittman*. His importance in this and other works is his ability to capture the experiences of the common black people of the rural South. Through dialect, setting, and characterization, he has brought to life both a region and a group of people that have been previously ignored.

Gaines was born on a plantation in Oscar, Louisiana, to Manuel and Adrienne Gaines. He grew up in rural Louisiana and at nine years old was already digging potatoes for fifty cents a day. One of his earliest influences was his Aunt Augusteen Jefferson, who, though she had no legs, was able to provide for the young child. Rather than feel self-pity for her condition, she adapted to it and found ways to do all that was necessary to see that he was fed and clothed. These two factors have influenced all of his published work. The world of the plantation, both before and after slavery, is the setting of his novels and sto-

Ernest J. Gaines (photo by Jim Santana)

ries. And Augusteen is the model for the recurrent figure of the aunt, a woman of strong character and religious faith whose self-sacrifice makes possible a better life for the next generation. Such characters appear in virtually all his books.

In 1948, when he was fifteen, Gaines went with his mother and stepfather to Vallejo, California, where he received a more thorough education than had been previously possible, and he began reading extensively, especially about the South. He has said that the trouble with what he read was that it did not include the people he had known, especially blacks. Coming from a story-telling family, he began writing around 1950 to fill in those gaps. He found that reading Russian novelists such as Turgenev, Tolstoy, and Gogol gave him a sense of how to write about rural people. This apprenticeship period of reading and writing continued while he attended Vallejo Junior College and served for two years in the army. His first published short stories appeared in 1956 in *Transfer*, a little San Francisco magazine, while he was a student at San Francisco State College, from which he graduated in 1957. He took advantage of a Wallace Stegner award to study in the creative writing program at Stanford University during the 1958-1959 academic year, and his serious professional writing efforts began.

His novels and short stories focus on the folkways of rural Louisiana. They capture the languages and mores of the blacks, Cajuns, and Creoles who make up the population of mythical Bayonne and the surrounding plantation country. The tales are centrally populated by the aunt figures, older, usually religious women who have seen and endured much. In the process, they have accommodated themselves to existing conditions, and they are distrustful of those who advocate change, even if that change is intended to improve conditions for blacks. Gaines's attitude toward these women is ambivalent: he admires their endurance, their strength of character, and their accumulated folk wisdom, but he also recognizes the need for change in society.

He makes it clear that reform is essential through his depictions of whites and the racist social order they have created. That order is deteriorating in most of his works, but that does not necessarily make life easier for blacks, since the way of life they found under that order is also threatened by changing economic and political conditions. Moreover, during the early and middle twentieth-century setting of the books, whites are still capable of using force to resist social change.

The challenge is issued by black men who, unlike the aunts, refuse to accept the longstanding racial relationships. Though these men come from the folk community, they reject its conservative approach and demand radical change. In some cases, their resistance is private and ineffectual, but often it is public and ultimately responsible for gains in black civil rights and education. While members of this latter group frequently die for their beliefs, they die heroes.

Catherine Carmier (1964), Gaines's first published novel, was patterned after Turgenev's *Fathers and Sons* and has as its protagonist Jackson Bradley, a young man who is returning to the plantation after several years of education. This training has alienated him from the values of the rural black community and especially his Aunt Charlotte, a very religious woman who had hoped that he would return to teach in the local school. Jackson wishes to leave but finds himself imprisoned by his inability to tell Charlotte the truth and by the rekindling of his love for Catherine. The title character is the daughter of a black Creole farmer, Raoul, who believes himself racially and socially superior to blacks and who has forbidden his daughters to have anything to do with

them, including Jackson. This isolates Catherine, who nonetheless feels a deep love for her father, a man she sees as courageously resisting the Cajun takeover of all the good farmland. Though she loves Jackson, she cannot leave Raoul. Thus, both Catherine and Jackson are immobilized by the pressures of this rural community.

These twin themes of isolation and paralysis give the novel an existential quality. Characters must face an unfriendly world without guidance and must make crucial choices about their lives. Raoul, an embittered, lonely man, works his land and restricts his daughters, not out of hope for a better future, but because he defines his manhood in terms of his resistance to both Cajun greed and to what he sees as black acquiescence to that greed. He takes pride in both his family history and in his own ability to work hard and productively. His increasing age and lack of a son cause him despair over the future; though doomed to ultimate failure, he continues to struggle because it is the struggle that has given his life meaning.

Aunt Charlotte seems in many ways the opposite of Raoul. She has had two sources of hope in her life: her religion and Jackson. Her religion has given her the strength to endure the difficulties of her life because she believes that there is an underlying spiritual meaning to everything that has happened. Unlike Raoul, she puts her faith in something outside herself. Her initial crisis comes when Jackson refuses to attend church services with her; she sees this as a possible judgment on her own faith and on the efficacy of her prayers. But because Jackson has returned, she has confidence that he will eventually completely reenter the community, including the church. The greater crisis occurs when he finally announces to her that he will not remain. We discover that Charlotte, like Raoul, has staked all of her hopes on a son. Her frustration is in some ways even greater because she has the son (psychologically if not biologically), and he fails to live up to her expectations. She feels so deeply betrayed that not even her religious faith can give her real relief from despair. She becomes physically ill, and even after she recovers, she cannot fully accept the meaning of the experience.

Jackson, though he intends no harm to Aunt Charlotte, cannot help but hurt her because of his own lack of faith. His experience of the outside world has led him away from what he considers the parochial values of his aunt and her community. He cannot accept an unquestioning faith in a divine order when he has both learned the value of reason and has used the reason to gain an understanding of human behavior. And though not politically active, he rejects the idea that the existing racial order is either natural or unchangeable. His problem is that he has no new values with which to replace the old ones. His reason has left him with skepticism and not with hope. The source of his despair is thus the very opposite of that of Raoul and Charlotte. The future seems closed to them because there is no one to whom they can pass on their values; to Jackson, the future is far too open because he is young but has no direction. The story is in one sense Jackson's search for a home, a place he can have faith in and still be true to his reason.

He tries to create this place through his love for Catherine, but this effort is made extremely difficult by her attachment to her father. At first, she rejects the idea that she even cares for Jackson, even though they had loved each other before he left. That separation was caused in part by Raoul's refusal to allow his daughter to have anything to do with any of the young black men. While Jackson was gone for several years, the relationship between father and daughter deepened, to the extent that her mother, Della, claimed that Catherine was more of a wife than she herself was. While no incest is implied, Raoul's attitude toward his daughter is very much that of a jealous husband. He watches over her constantly and will not allow her to develop any close ties to any other people in the community. When she falls in love with a young Creole man and bears his child, Raoul drives off the baby's father and isolates Catherine even more completely. Despite his fanatical behavior, Catherine accepts Raoul and even sees in him a kind of heroism for showing so much devotion to the land and to his family. She gladly becomes a substitute son for him, even though his actions virtually guarantee that his land will be lost to the Cajuns after his death.

Jackson disturbs this unnatural equilibrium by seeking and getting Catherine's love. But in place of Raoul's imprisoning devotion to land and family, the young man can offer escape to nowhere and nothing in particular. Catherine is torn between the desire for freedom and her love of her father and the soil. Much of the book is devoted to an analysis of her fluctuating loyalties and to Jackson's uncertainties about the meaning and future of the relationship. Meanwhile the two of them continue to meet in secret, fearful of Raoul's anger. In a final confrontation, Jack-

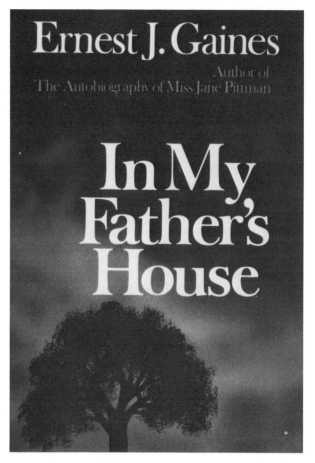

Dust jacket for Gaines's 1978 novel about a civil rights leader and his illegitimate son

son defeats Raoul in a fistfight and believes himself to have literally won Catherine. To his surprise, however, she insists that she must nurse her father back to health and that the conqueror must wait to gain his prize. Jackson's bitterness at this ironic turn is neutralized somewhat by Della's observation that he has in fact won; Catherine no longer sees her father as heroic, and her admiration has turned to pity. If the victor will be patient, he will have what he sought. Crucial to Della's understanding is the revelation that Raoul deliberately killed their son, Marky, the product of Della's extramarital liaison with a black man. In effect, what all the family now understands is that Jackson has exacted Marky's revenge, has in effect become the son that Raoul destroyed. Consistent with the naturalistic tone that dominates the work, the father acquires the son only by being beaten and supplanted, and the son can acquire a father and a family only by allowing himself to be imprisoned in the very life he wishes to escape. The end of the novel has Jackson waiting in the yard, "hoping that Catherine would come back outside. But she never did." The reader is left in a state of uncertainty, having to choose between Della's optimistic reading of events and Jackson's own despair. Neither possibility will bring him comfort. Either he has lost Catherine or, the deepest irony, he has succeeded in his quest, but at the price of his freedom.

Perhaps because of this ambiguity and pessimism, the book did not receive much attention when it was first published. Even with Gaines's increasing reputation, *Catherine Carmier* has been largely neglected. Those who have commented on it tend to see its pessimism as reflective of the influence of Hemingway, an influence which Gaines himself has conceded. It is considered the most despairing of his works and, perhaps for that reason, the least characteristic. While this latter point can be debated, given the tone of some later works, it is clear that *Catherine Carmier* is not entirely successful in presenting its major characters and their motivations. It is hard to understand, for example, what draws Catherine and Jackson together, given the experiences and values they have accumulated over the time of separation. Moreover, the revelation of the cause of Marky's death is unnecessarily melodramatic. On the other hand, Gaines does begin here to create a sense of the black community and its perceptions of the world around it. Shared ways of speaking, thinking, and relating to the dominant white society are shown through a number of minor characters. This element of Gaines's fiction continues to develop throughout his career; it is the very richness of this social fabric that calls into question the frustration and sterility of the major characters in this first novel.

Though *Catherine Carmier* was not a critical or financial success, Gaines steadfastly worked on his writing. Though he does not consider himself prolific, he wrote four novels (of which only *Catherine Carmier* was published) and a dozen short stories before *Of Love and Dust* brought him recognition in 1967. Some of the success of the book can be explained by certain differences between it and his first novel. This newer book deals much more directly with the black-white relationship, including miscegenation, and thus could be considered more accessible than the earlier work, which focused almost exclusively on black life. In addition, *Of Love and Dust* more clearly condemns the economic, social, and racial system of the South for the problems faced by its characters. While Gaines is not a protest novelist in the tradition of

Richard Wright, his questioning of the Southern political structure certainly would strike a chord at the socially tumultuous time it was published. Finally, hope, if not optimism, is apparent at the end of this work, which clearly was not the case with *Catherine Carmier*.

Of Love and Dust is narrated by Jim Kelly, a middle-aged black man who has gained a degree of respect on the plantation where he works. He is trusted by both the owner and the overseer to do his job well. Part of that job becomes the supervising of Marcus, a young man charged with stabbing another and released into the custody of Marshall Hebert, the plantation owner. Jim is asked by Miss Julie Rand, another of Gaines's "aunt" figures and Marcus's godmother, to take care of Marcus while he is at the plantation. She believes Marcus to be good despite his obvious bitterness, hostility, and insensitivity.

Sidney Bonbon, the white overseer on the farm, expects Jim to help break Marcus of his rebelliousness and arrogance by forcing him to labor in the fields under intolerable conditions. As a result Marcus considers Jim a traitor to his race for cooperating with the white bosses and contemplates ways of getting even with the whites. While Jim tries to keep his promise to Miss Julie, he finds it difficult to deal with a man so unwilling to adapt to his conditions. The entire black community becomes alarmed when Marcus starts paying attention to Bonbon's black mistress, Pauline, with whom the overseer is very much in love. In fact, he cares more for her than he does for his white wife. One of the accomplishments of the novel is Gaines's presentation of the nuances of such a relationship. Everyone on the plantation, including Bonbon's wife, knows of this love, yet no one can in any way acknowledge it, not even the two children who are its products. A very careful social etiquette is followed by which everybody ignores what they all in fact know.

When Marcus is rejected by Pauline, he turns his attentions to Bonbon's wife, Louise, who desires revenge on her husband for his infidelity. The black community, represented in this instance by Aunt Margaret, is horrified by this development, not merely because of Marcus's motives, but more important because his action threatens the security of the whole community. If it is discovered that a black man is violating this most sacred of Southern taboos, then every black man is a potential target of white violence. But even though he is repeatedly warned by Jim against such behavior, Marcus's desire for self-gratification overwhelms the need for community safety.

What in fact happens is that Marcus and Louise transcend their exploitative motives and begin to love each other, much like Pauline and Bonbon. They then plot an escape with the aid of Marshall Hebert, the owner, who has his own reasons for getting back at his overseer. Hebert then betrays the lovers by arranging Bonbon's presence at the moment of their leaving. Marcus is killed; Louise goes insane; and Bonbon and Pauline flee the plantation. Jim also must leave, because Hebert realizes that he knows too much to be fully trustworthy.

In the process of telling the story, Jim comes to understand two things. One is Bonbon's statement to him that they are all victims. Race is ultimately less important than one's position in the social and economic hierarchy. Hebert and the system he has created and maintained are vastly more powerful than any of the petty manipulations of Marcus and Bonbon. The second insight Jim gains comes from observing Marcus. While Marcus's motives are primarily selfish, he still displays a courage and spirit that deserve respect if not emulation. Jim learns that he himself has been too willing to accept his victimization. Throughout the story he has been a blues performer, singing and talking of lost loves and opportunities. He has chosen to be self-pitying and self-protective, but Marcus has taught him that risk is necessary if one is going to live in dignity. Jim acknowledges this lesson when he refuses to accept Hebert's offer of a recommendation. Though it will make his life more difficult, he realizes that his integrity requires cutting all ties to such a man. Unlike Jackson of *Catherine Carmier*, Jim has hope at the end of the novel because he has found something to believe in—himself.

By moving to a first-person narrative in *Of Love and Dust*, Gaines renders life in rural Louisiana much more effectively. Jim both speaks in the idiom of the place and time and instinctively asserts the values of the black community. Thus, a much greater immediacy is apparent here than in *Catherine Carmier*. But beyond these benefits, the first-person narration also comes closer to the ideal of the folk storyteller and thus is more appropriate than omniscient narration to the folk materials Gaines uses in his fiction. He has said that the novel was inspired by a Lightning Hopkins blues song, "Mr. Tim Moore's Farm," and clearly Gaines's method of presenting the story comes closer than his first novel to resembling black folk stories of love and trouble.

Some of Gaines's best use of folk material comes in the stories collected in *Bloodline*. Although this book came out in 1968, some of the stories were among the first of his work to be published. Three of the five, "A Long Day in November" (1958), "Just Like a Tree" (1962), and "The Sky Is Gray" (1963), preceded *Catherine Carmier*. Nonetheless, a number of factors unify the collection. The sequence is determined in part by the age of the narrator or central figure: beginning with a six-year-old in the first story, these characters get progressively older until Aunt Fe, in the last story, is on the verge of death. Further, the action of each story is confined to a single day in the area around Bayonne, Louisiana. Thematically, the stories in *Bloodline* are about the relationships between younger and older generations; more specifically, they usually deal with a son's heritage from his father. Stylistically, they are presented in the folk idiom of rural Southern blacks. Gaines displays in these stories a mastery of these speech patterns, giving them an authenticity that is seldom present in dialect writing.

The first of these folk voices, Sonny, the child narrator of "A Long Day in November," tells the story of a day of conflict between his father and his mother. At the heart of the conflict is Amy's feeling that Eddie cares more for his car than he does for his family. She leaves him, taking along Sonny, and returns to her mother's home. Unable to understand the significance of his parents' behavior, the child becomes so nervous and confused that he cannot recite his school lesson. Because of this disorientation, he replicates his father's public embarrassment by urinating on himself in front of the class.

Father and son then join in a quest for manhood. Eddie seeks advice from a variety of sources, but the only one who truly understands is the local conjure woman. He resists her demand that he burn his car, but when nothing else works, he ceremoniously drives the vehicle into a field and sets it afire. After this ritual sacrifice, he takes his place as the head of his family. Amy, comprehending the social importance of his role, insists that he beat her for her disrespectful actions. Though both Sonny and Eddie frown upon such mistreatment, the beating does take place and the family roles are firmly established. The happy resolution is reflected in Sonny's naive yet specific final words: "I hear the spring on Mama and Daddy's bed. I get 'way under the cover. I go to sleep little bit, but I wake up. I go to sleep some more. I hear the spring on Mama and Daddy's bed. I hear it plenty now. It's some dark under here. It's warm. I feel good 'way under here."

Gaines's selection of point of view makes it possible to see the operation of human relationships at their most basic. Sonny's innocence forces the reader out of conventional adult assumptions about what men and women expect of each other. At the same time, the concreteness of his description makes it possible to see how social rules structure private, sexual behavior.

In "The Sky Is Gray" the eight-year-old narrator also learns about social rules, in this case the rules about race relations and personal integrity. Gaines has said that this story is patterned after Eudora Welty's "A Worn Path," and the connection is clear in the journey motif and in the need for certain rituals. The difference is in the level of experience of the central character: while Welty's Phoenix Jackson has taken her journey many times, this is the initial and thus most important journey for James.

He has already had several painful episodes in his young life when his mother sought to teach him crucial lessons in survival. Because his father is in the army, she is the only one who can provide for the family. Fearing that something might also happen to her, she wants James to be able to take care of the others. Out of this necessity, she one day forces him to kill two small redbirds he has caught in a trap. When he cries that they should be set free, she beats him until he stabs them. Since the birds make very little food, James fails to understand her actions until an aunt explains that the mother wants him to learn that survival is more important than sentiment.

When he develops a toothache, an opportunity develops for him to learn another lesson in survival, this time black survival in a white-dominated, racist society. What James must become aware of is the system of rules that dictates black-white relations. His grasp of the rules is evident when he gets on the bus and immediately moves to the back, past the "White-Colored" sign, before looking for a seat. What he will acquire in Bayonne is a sense of the complexity of the system and of the means of maintaining one's dignity under such conditions.

In the dentist's office he is presented with two different perspectives on social adaptation in a confrontation between an alienated, educated young man, much like Jackson of *Catherine*

Carmier, and a black preacher who defends the principles of faith and humility. The young man rejects those principles in the name of reason and the harsh view of reality reason has given him. In frustration over this attack on his way of life, the preacher strikes the young man. The preacher acts this way not only in order to protect what is for him a relatively successful compromise with the powers that be but also because the refusal to compromise could be a threat to the entire black community. This same fear was expressed in *Of Love and Dust*. The community would be doubly threatened if its children began to admire the spokesmen of such a view, as James does here: "When I grow up I want to be just like him. I want clothes like that and I want to keep a book with me, too."

When the dentist closes for lunch without attending to James, he and his mother must walk the streets in the bitterly cold weather. Not permitted to enter any of the white-owned restaurants, they have no way of keeping warm. James now receives another lesson in survival and racial etiquette. His mother takes him into a hardware store and positions him by a hot stove. She then asks to examine an axe handle. While she looks over several, she keeps glancing at James; when she sees that he is warm, they leave without buying anything. In this way, she provides him an example of how to get the necessities of life without giving whites the satisfaction of seeing her beg.

A third lesson that is social in nature comes in an encounter between mother and son and a white couple who sincerely desires to help them. The white woman wishes to give them food, but James's mother refuses to accept it as charity. They agree that the boy must work for the food by carrying around the garbage cans. Though he believes the cans to be empty, James is prevented by the women from opening them. After the meal, James's mother wishes to buy a small amount of salt pork in the couple's tiny grocery and is offended when the owner attempts to give her a piece much larger than the quarter will buy. James's mother refuses to accept more meat than she can pay for.

This scene is important in showing the nuances of race relations. Even those people who wish to transcend racial hostilities must do so in the context of the social rules. These two women cannot face each other candidly; they must play their socially assigned roles despite their personal desires. Moreover, in the charade of the garbage cans, they conspire to teach James that the main-

Dust jacket for Gaines's 1983 novel about the murder of a Cajun work boss

taining of dignity in human contacts is a fragile process. That James may have started learning this and the other lessons is indicated in the mother's last words: " 'You not a bum,' she says. 'You a man.' "

"Three Men" is much more explicit in the lessons it teaches. The narrator, Proctor Lewis, a nineteen-year-old in jail and accused of stabbing another black man, is told the nature and meaning of his violent life by Mumford Bazille, a jailmate who has been through virtually identical experiences. At the end Proctor must choose whether he will accept the advice of this man who has become a father figure to him. Initially, the young man seems doomed to a lifelong cycle of work-violence-imprisonment-work release, much like that of Bazille himself. Proctor has turned himself in to the sheriff because he knows that Roger Medlow, a wealthy white man, will pay to have him released in exchange for his labor in the fields. He is thus like Marcus in *Of Love and Dust* at an earlier, more malleable state of development.

But the narrator of "Three Men" must con-

front an issue that never came up in the novel. As Bazille explains to Proctor, he is doing exactly what the whites want by resigning himself to the cycle. By accepting work rather than imprisonment, he is in fact refusing responsibility for his actions and thus collaborating in his own emasculation. As long as black men make themselves dependent on whites by such evasions, they serve as justification for the continued oppression of the race. But to choose prison is to choose a long period of insults and beatings, perhaps even death. Thus, the choice is not an easy one.

While the narrator is mulling over Bazille's comments and tending to reject them, a fourteen-year-old black boy is thrown into the cell after being beaten. Proctor sees in this boy a young image of himself, just as in Bazille and Hattie, the homosexual, he sees alternative older images. In the process of nursing the boy's wounds, he becomes a father figure and feels compelled to assert his manhood. At the end of the story he is passing on Bazille's advice with his own added sense of uncertainty about the outcome of his choice. But for the meaning of the story, the choice is more important than the result.

An existential theme that runs through most of Gaines's work is perhaps most clear in this story. In a world where there are no good choices and where the end cannot be known, the good man is the one who accepts responsibility and who chooses according to his deepest and truest nature. The choice becomes the key self-defining act when others control one's behavior so completely. Unlike Hemingway, whom he often takes as a model, Gaines is interested less in bold, forceful actions than in honorable, dangerous choices.

In the title story of *Bloodline* this attitude is tested against the realities of the white world. Felix, the seventy-year-old narrator, recounts the experiences of Copper Laurent, a black ex-soldier who has returned to the plantation to claim his birthright. As the son of Walter Laurent, he is the only direct descendant of the white family which owns the land. The action of the story comprises his efforts to force his dying white uncle Frank to recognize him as a rightful heir. Frank, though he accepts the rightness of Copper's assertions, refuses to violate the rules of white supremacy that nullify his nephew's claims.

The irony of the story is that Copper is more truly a Laurent than his uncle. In comparison to Frank's weak, dissipated condition, Copper is forceful, commanding, and proud. He refuses to enter the main house through the back door; he physically overwhelms the men sent to get him; and he calls himself General. Finally, Frank must come to him if they are to talk. Such behavior indicates some madness, but that, too, is consistent with the reckless arrogance that is his Laurent heritage.

He does not get back the land, for Frank insists that it will be kept just the way it is, in part to take care of the blacks who have been loyal. Copper does, however, achieve recognition of his claim to a bloodline. He leaves after threatening to return with his army—all those blacks who have been disinherited from the land they earned through their work and suffering.

"Just Like a Tree" tells the story of a woman who is deeply rooted in the soil Copper wants to reclaim. The central character, Aunt Fe, has always lived on the land, but her family fears for her safety and wants to move her to the city. The move seems necessary because Emmanuel, her grandnephew, has been active in the civil rights movement; as a result, whites have started bomb-

ing black homes. The setting of the story is Fe's home the night before she is to leave. Family and friends have come for a final celebration of her life. The story is narrated by these visitors, following, as Gaines has noted, the structure of William Faulkner's *As I Lay Dying*. Significantly, the only characters we do not hear from directly are Emmanuel and Fe herself. The effect is to give us a broadly based sense of both the public and private meanings of one of Gaines's aunts. The voices of the old and the young, male and female, black and white offer a broad and deep sense of the quality of life for which the characters in the other stories have been searching. At the end of "Just Like a Tree" we see why that quest is so crucial. In an ironic play on the spiritual from which the title is derived, Aunt Fe "will not be moved": she dies after a nightlong conversation with Aunt Lou, her lifelong friend. Her death, which seems willed, signifies that life for her is sustained by a time, place, and community that contain the richness of her experience. To leave all that is to die spiritually, and, for her, physical life is nothing without the spirit.

Critics have seen *Bloodline* as a series of portraits of Southern black rural life in which the characters search for manhood. While Gaines is praised for the effectiveness of his characterizations and settings, doubts are raised about his way of defining manhood as primarily aggressive, head-oriented behavior and about the apparent lack of resolution in the stories. The latter assessment is somewhat off the mark since Gaines deliberately leaves his characters facing the future, trying to apply the lessons they have learned.

The time after the publication of *Bloodline* was devoted to the writing of what turned out to be Gaines's most effective and most popular work, *The Autobiography of Miss Jane Pittman* (1971). The novel started out as a communal biography, a fuller version of "Just Like a Tree." In writing, Gaines made the brilliant discovery of Jane's own voice, which radically changed the nature of the book. Through this point of view came both a fully rounded character and a folk history of the black experience in America from the Civil War to civil rights. One hundred eight years old when she tells the story, Jane captures the experiences of those millions of illiterate blacks who never had a chance to tell their own stories. By focusing on the particular yet typical events of a small part of Louisiana, those lives are given a concreteness and specificity not possible in more general histories. Gaines accomplishes this by showing the impact of the larger events of those one hundred years–the war, Reconstruction, segregation, the civil rights movement–on individual blacks. But the work is not simply another historical novel, for the narrator enriches the story with elements of popular culture and folk experiences. Boxing and baseball on the radio, comic strips, sermons, voodoo, and superstitions all make their way into Jane's story. What we have, in effect, is the totality of life as lived by Jane; in the process, the author reveals what it is that gives his aunt figures, including Jane, Fe, and Charlotte, their stability and dignity.

The journey motif so evident in Gaines's other works is also significant here in a variety of ways. Early in the book, a group of recently emancipated blacks set off from Southern Louisiana to find Ohio. When they stop after a day's journey, they set about renaming themselves. By doing so, they destroy the vestiges of white domination and create new, self-determining identities. That white supremacy cannot be so easily escaped is made fatally clear when the group is attacked and massacred by a band of former Confederate soldiers. The only survivors are Jane and Ned, the son of Big Laura, who led the group and died fighting. The two children continue their journey, even though they have no idea where Ohio might be. Repeatedly they meet people, both black and white, who try to dissuade them from their quest. Only when an old man shows them on a map how small a distance they have traveled and how many years it will take to get to Ohio do they decide to make their lives in Louisiana.

But the end of this trek does not mark the end of the quest for those things Ohio symbolized–equality, security, dignity. Jane becomes a steady center point from which a series of men move toward those ideals. Ned, after being threatened for his political activity, goes off to Kansas to get an education. After several years he returns, renamed Ned Douglass, after Frederick Douglass. He opens a school, where he teaches the children both academic subjects and the principles of political democracy and equality. The white community is so disturbed that they finally have him assassinated.

During part of this period, Jane is married to Joe Pittman, a man who seeks economic rather than political equality. Despite the owner's duplicitous efforts to keep him, Joe leaves the plantation on which he works in order to provide a better life for his family. He works as a horse breaker and is willing to ride any animal, though Jane fears for his safety. Symbolically, he challenges nature out of the same impulse that leads Ned to challenge the social-political order. And, like Ned, he dies in pursuit of his ideals.

In both cases Jane for the most part resigns herself to the deaths of those she loved. Such resignation culminates in her own religious "travels," her experience of Christian salvation. She describes the experience as a dangerous journey across a river: "I looked where He was pointing, and yes, there was a river. I turned back to Him, but He was gone. I started toward the river with the sack of bricks on my back. And briars sprung up in front of me where snakes had not been, and wide ditches and bayous with green water stood before me where they was not before."

Jane's devotion is so strong that she becomes the church mother, one of the spiritual guides for the community. This role does not make her self-righteous, however, for, she explains, the position is soon taken away from her when she skips Sunday services to listen to baseball games on the radio.

The spirituality of the community is important to the development of the third strong male character, Jimmy Aaron. Out of their allegorical reading of the world, the old people see Jimmy virtually from birth as the One, a religious leader who will guide them in the future. He is to be a new Moses, reviving what they feel is a dying way of life. Because of this perception, they treat him differently by seeking to keep him pure and to prepare him for his life's special work. He tries but finds it difficult to share their religious faith.

He goes off to New Orleans for an education and later returns, now a civil rights activist. He has in fact become the One, but he seeks to lead the people into a secular rather than religious Promised Land. Consequently, he is regarded with distrust by the faithful, who see in his efforts a threat to their deeply engrained way of life and thought. Just as the community in *Of Love and Dust* feared Marcus's action, so these blacks fear that Jimmy's activities will bring the wrath of the whites down on them.

The one who does not hold this view is Jane. When Jimmy asks her to participate in his march, she questions not the rightness of his action but the effectiveness of her own: "What can I do but get in the way?" Throughout the book, she has been passive, saying repeatedly that it is not her time. But when Jimmy is killed in Ba-

177

Lou Dimes

Remembering that I was still on the job, I took out
my pen and pad and jotted down a few notes:

"Fifteen old black men with shotguns--guns probably
old as they. Five or six women old as the men. Two of the
women wear faded head rags; couple other wear aprons of
gingham that has been washed so many times the cloth has
lost all its color, too. Two or three nappy headed barefoot
children sit with the men and women. A stubborn silence
prevails.

"Framed house--your typical plantation quarters's
house--gray from sun, rain, wind, dust, sits on leaning xxxxx
cement blocks half sunkend into the ground. House probably
fifty, maybe sixty, possibly seventy five-years old. Has
not seen an ounce of paint during half that time.(Note: must
ask Candy exactly age of house, also when last time painted.)
Tin roof. No loft between roof and porch, and in Summer porch
becomes an oven. Large cracks between the boards in the wall.
Originally chucked with mud; now paper and pieces of torn
cloth keep out cold in Winter, mosquitoes in Summer. Two of
the four steps leading from ground to porch missing. Weeds,
weeds, weeds. A small garden right of porch. Mustards,
turnips, cabbages, collards. Hog in backyard. Chickens

Page from the typescript of A Gathering of Old Men, *in which Gaines uses multiple narrators to depict the many forms of racial injustice endured by the black workers on a Louisiana plantation (courtesy of the author)*

yonne, it becomes her time. At the end of the novel, she confronts Robert Samson, the owner of the plantation and symbol of the white power she has had to accommodate herself to for decades. This time is different: "Me and Robert looked at each other there a long time, then I went by him."

Though this work, like the earlier ones, leaves the character at the beginning rather than at the end of some experience, Gaines gives a much stronger sense of the character's probable success in whatever must be endured. This optimism is doubtless one reason why the book was both critically and financially successful. Consistently the work has been praised not only for its effective use of folk materials but also for its integration of political and artistic concerns.

The popularity of the book was such that a television movie was made of it. Though Stacy Keach, Jr., wrote the screenplay, Gaines was actively involved as a consultant. The production received high ratings and won praise from television critics. Because of key changes from the novel, however, the movie did stir some controversy in academic journals. The shift from a black to a white frame figure who interviews Jane, the revision of certain historical elements, and the revised ending, where Jane actually goes to Bayonne to drink from a segregated fountain, all have been cited as evidence that the producers of the film undercut the novel's message in order to make it more palatable to a largely white audience.

Gaines remained out of the controversy, preferring to return to his writing. He received a Guggenheim Fellowship in 1973-1974 to continue his work. He began a novel, "The House and the Field," which he later put aside in order to write *In My Father's House*, which was published in 1978.

This novel returns to the father-and-son theme of the earlier works. As in *Catherine Carmier*, a key character is a young man whose life is rootless and who seeks some meaning for his existence. But *In My Father's House* differs from the earlier works in its urban setting and the noncentrality of rural folk materials. The transition from rural to urban life has largely cut away such connections. Reflecting this change, the novel is set several years after the conclusion of *The Autobiography of Miss Jane Pittman*. Though the central character, Philip Martin, is a civil rights leader, the movement, like the black community, is in transition. Throughout, characters

question the utility of protest and of white participation in the movement. The idealism that inspired Ned Douglass and Jimmy Aaron has dissipated.

The plot of the novel involves Martin's recognition of his illegitimate son and then his quest to find out the truth and consequences of his past. In the beginning he is a highly respected, now rather conservative leader in the community whose reputation has been made in earlier nonviolent activism. His efforts for equality have necessarily shifted from social and political protests to less dramatic economic protests. In the process, many people, including the black middle class represented here by schoolteachers, have become indifferent and cynical. In the midst of arousing enthusiasm for a new demonstration, Martin is confronted with the return of his son, who calls himself Robert X. The father is so shocked by this ghost from his past that he faints when he first sees the young man. Martin's inability to justify having abandoned Robert and his mother and Robert's hostility toward his father make communication between the two impossible. Nonetheless, Martin becomes obsessed with this aspect of his past, to the neglect of his civil rights activity. He returns to the plantation where he grew up, where he loved and lived with Johanna many years before. He then goes to Baton Rouge and encounters friends of his youth, including Chippo Simon, his alter ego, who has become as dissipated as Martin would have been if he had not found religion and civil rights. In a final dramatic scene Martin learns that his son has committed suicide. He fights with Chippo over the question of responsibility for the past and achieves a tentative reconciliation with his wife.

In some ways, *In My Father's House* is one of the most pessimistic of Gaines's books. All of the son figures are somehow misguided. Robert has been destroyed by his own hate and frustration; Billy, a young man Martin meets in Baton Rouge, has lost all contact with his father and has turned to suicidal revolutionary violence; and Jonathan, the young minister in Martin's church, refuses, in his arrogance and inexperience, to be guided by the wisdom of the past in his role as new leader. Given such characters, the future holds little promise. Moreover, the circumstances of Martin's tragedy suggest a rather strong destructive and deterministic aspect to human experience. Martin's final perception that nothing can be done about the past, and that it does not necessarily bring life or enlightenment, contradicts

Jane Pittman's implicit assertion that history is full of meaning and that it gives vitality to the present.

This nihilistic undertone is perhaps responsible for some of the weaknesses of the book. Inadequate motivation is provided for Martin's immediate acceptance of Robert as his son and the resultant obsession with private responsibility to the neglect of social responsibility. He suddenly wants to be a father after abandoning Johanna and her children twenty years earlier. The son Martin sacrifices himself for is a flat, burned-out character whose psychological deadness is inadequately accounted for. The deterministic element gives the book a mechanical quality, with characters functioning more as opportunities for Martin to talk about fathers and sons than for effective dramatic action to take place. The resolution and hopefulness at the end seem imposed and not the natural product of the story's development.

A Gathering of Old Men (1983) returns to the rural world of Gaines's earlier fiction, but its time is closer to the present. On the Marshall plantation, the only ones left are the old blacks who have worked the land all their lives, the white Marshalls, and the Cajuns, who are gradually displacing the blacks. In one sense the novel is a detective story. A Cajun work boss, Beau Boutan, has been killed in front of the cabin of Mathu, one of the blacks. Since the latter has a history of confrontations with the Boutan family, the case seems open-and-shut. But when Sheriff Mapes arrives on the scene, several black men are present with their recently fired shotguns. Moreover, Candy Marshall, in order to protect the old man who essentially raised her, claims that she is the guilty one. With an excess of suspects and the possibility of racial violence, Mapes is compelled to listen to all of their stories. Complicating the situation is the fact that the sheriff believes that, of the men, only Mathu has enough courage to commit murder, and so he is baffled by this group compulsion to confess.

The emotional center of the novel is the collection of stories. Each man tells of the accumulated frustrations and injustices of his life–raped daughters, jailed sons, public insults, economic exploitation–that serve as sufficient motive for murder. Though Beau Boutan is seldom the immediate cause of their anger, he clearly represents the entire white world that has deprived them of their dignity and adulthood. The confessions serve as ritual purgings of all the hostility

and self-hatred built up over the years. If they did not literally kill Boutan, they symbolically did so many times, and thus their confessions are psychologically true. What makes their narratives especially poignant is their previous submissiveness and even impotence; in addition to Mapes, the Cajuns, Candy, and, most important, Mathu have always assumed that they are weak and insignificant. Through their stories they face their self-hatred and enter, at least metaphorically, their adulthood. The actual murderer turns out not to be Mathu, as everyone, including all the "confessors," believed, but Charlie, who for fifty years has been the weakest of them all. He has always absorbed abuse and run away from trouble, even though he is the biggest and hardest working of the blacks. When he can absorb no more, he responds to Boutan's physical abuse by striking back in self-defense. He then tries to run, but Mathu threatens to beat him if he does. So he takes the old man's shotgun and kills the Cajun, who has come after him with his own gun. Then he runs again after begging Mathu to take the blame, which he does. But Charlie finds that something–his nascent manhood–prevents him from escaping. So he returns to accept responsibility and thus fully becomes a man, a change which is acknowledged by everyone, including the sheriff, when they call him Mr. Biggs.

Meanwhile, change is also being experienced in the Cajun community. The Boutans are planning their usual revenge on the blacks, but they come up against certain modern realities. Gil, Beau's brother, plays football at Louisiana State alongside a black running back. They are known throughout the region as Salt and Pepper. Their success as a combination has made race largely irrelevant; working together, they have the possibility of becoming All-Americans. The possibility will be destroyed for Gil if he is linked to racial violence. In other words, he has begun to measure his life by values different from those of his father and brother. His reluctance offends his father, Fix, who refuses to accept change, but at the same time the father will not act without the son. Both are frustrated, but the effect creates a new order.

Neither father nor son can prevent the final explosion of racist violence, led by a family associate, Luke Will. He and others arrive at Marshall just as Mapes is taking Charlie away. The whites open fire, and the old black men, who have in a sense been frustrated because their confessions had so little effect, get their chance to do what they have only dreamed of. The ensuing battle blends the absurd with the heroic. Some of the blacks accidentally fire their guns through Mathu's roof, and all of them miss their targets. In the end only Charlie and Luke Will are killed. Charlie dies because he refuses to use the protection of the darkness; instead he stands at his full height and openly challenges the whites to shoot him. He kills Luke Will while being shot himself.

One of the most effective devices of the book is the variety of narrators. Developing the technique he used in "Just Like a Tree," Gaines employs white, Cajun, and black voices. He achieves thereby a range of social values as well as different perspectives on the action. Significantly, as in the earlier story, the central characters do not narrate; the words and actions of Candy, Mathu, and Charlie are reported by others. The author creates in this way a communal rather than an individual story. The narrative works best when focused on the black community; the Cajun scenes lack the same rich texture, and the killing off of Charlie and Luke Will seems more related to the author's moral imperatives than to narrative necessity.

With *A Gathering of Old Men* Ernest J. Gaines moved back from the urban setting to what seems his natural fictional world. With the emphasis on folk culture, he regained the hopefulness and sense of wholeness missing from *In My Father's House*. He has continued to find new possibilities in that culture, even though he has from the beginning suggested that it is dying out. What he brings out through the representation of it is not nostalgia for something gone, but rather a sense that even in its passing and with its limitations, it signifies certain enduring human values. Whether he has more tales to tell of this world remains to be seen. But whatever direction he takes in the future, Ernest J. Gaines has secured a permanent place for himself in black literature through his writing about the strong black identity that comes with an understanding of the folk past.

Interviews:

"An Interview: Ernest Gaines," *New Orleans Review*, 1 (1969): 331-335.

Forrest Ingram and Barbara Steinberg, "On the Verge: An Interview with Ernest J. Gaines," *New Orleans Review*, 3 (1972): 339-344.

Ruth Laney, "A Conversation with Ernest Gaines," *Southern Review*, 10 (1974): 1-14.

References:

William L. Andrews, "'We Ain't Going Back There': The Idea of Progress in *The Autobiography of Miss Jane Pittman*," *Black American Literature Forum*, 11 (1977): 146-149.
Excellent examination of Gaines's use of history in his best-known novel.

Keith E. Byerman, *Fingering the Jagged Grain: Tradition and Form in Recent Black Fiction* (Athens: University of Georgia Press, 1985), pp. 67-103.
Detailed discussion of all of Gaines's published fiction, with emphasis on folk materials.

Callaloo, special Gaines issue, 1, no. 3 (1978).
Several critical essays on Gaines, as well as some original material by him.

Jack Hicks, *In the Singer's Temple: Prose Fictions of Barthelme, Gaines, Brautigan, Piercy, Kesey, and Kosinski* (Chapel Hill: University of North Carolina Press, 1981).
Analysis of Gaines as an experimental writer.

William Peden, *The American Short Story: Continuity and Change, 1940-1975* (Boston: Houghton Mifflin, 1975).
Explication of some of Gaines's short stories.

Noel Schraufnagel, *From Apology to Protest: The Black American Novel* (DeLand, Fla.: Everett / Edwards, 1973).
Discussion of the civil rights movement as an influence on Gaines's early writing.

Ken Kesey

This entry was updated by Laura Zaidman (University of South Carolina at Sumter) from the entry by Stephen L. Tanner (University of Idaho) in DLB 2, American Novelists Since World War II *and from the entry by Ann Charters (University of Connecticut) in* DLB 16, The Beats: Literary Bohemians in Postwar America.

Places	Eugene, Oreg.	California	
Influences and Relationships	Neal Cassady Jack Kerouac William Faulkner	Allen Ginsberg Malcolm Cowley John Clellon Holmes	William S. Burroughs
Literary Movements and Forms	Literary Bohemianism	Romanticism	Transcendentalism
Major Themes	Freedom vs. Control Revolt Against the Establishment	Evolving Consciousness Humor as a Source of Sanity	Nature vs. Technology Self-Reliance
Cultural and Artistic Influences	Back-to-Nature Movement Psychedelic Drugs	1960s Culture Comic Strips Eastern Religion	West Coast Pop Psychology The Merry Pranksters
Social and Economic Influences	The Penal System Mental Institutions	The Logging Industry	Labor Unions

BIRTH: La Junta, Colorado, 17 September 1935 to Fred and Geneva Smith Kesey.

EDUCATION: B.A., University of Oregon, 1957.

MARRIAGE: 20 May 1956 to Faye Haxby; children: Shannon, Zane, Jed, Sunshine.

BOOKS: *One Flew Over the Cuckoo's Nest* (New York: Viking, 1962; London: Methuen, 1963);
Sometimes a Great Notion (New York: Viking, 1964; London: Methuen, 1966);
Kesey's Garage Sale, by Kesey and others (New York: Viking / Intrepid Trips, 1973);
Kesey, edited by Michael Strelow (Eugene, Oreg.: Northwest Review, 1977);
The Day After Superman Died (Northridge, Cal.: Lord John Press, 1980);
Demon Box (New York: Viking, 1986).

OTHER: *Whole Earth Catalog, March 1971 Supplement*, edited by Kesey and Paul Krassner.

A writer who came of age on the West Coast during the late 1950s, Ken Kesey has been profoundly influenced by the Beats both in his life and in his work. Strictly speaking, he is not a Beat writer in his early books, although he admired Jack Kerouac and claims the influence of Kerouac, John Clellon Holmes, and William S. Burroughs on his prose style. Kesey is a pivotal figure between the Beats and the Hippies, the leader and chief chronicler of the activities of his associates, the Merry Pranksters, a group of friends including Neal Cassady who helped Kesey originate the "acid tests" that popularized the use of the drug LSD in psychedelic mixed-media "happenings" in California in the 1960s. As the leader of the Merry Pranksters, described by one newspaperman as a "day-glo guerrilla squad for the LSD revolution in California," he turned from writing to search for new forms of expression induced by drugs—forms of expression in which there would be no separation between himself and the audience; it would be all one experience, with the senses opened wide. Tom Wolfe's *The Electric Kool-Aid Acid Test* (1968) chronicles this search and the escapades of the Merry Pranksters.

Kesey was born on 17 September 1935 in La Junta, Colorado, to Fred and Geneva Smith Kesey. He attended public schools in Springfield, Oregon, where his father had moved to establish

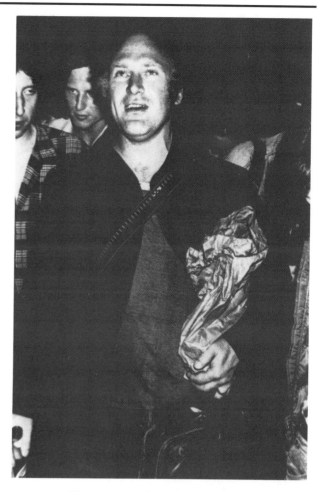

Ken Kesey (photo by Gerard Malanga)

a dairy cooperative. In 1957 he graduated with a B.A. from the University of Oregon, where he was involved in fraternities, drama, and athletics—as a champion wrestler he barely missed qualifying for the Olympics. On 20 May 1956 he married his high-school sweetheart, Faye Haxby; they now have four children: Shannon, Zane, Jed, and Sunshine. After graduating from the University of Oregon, he worked for a year, toyed with the idea of being a movie actor, wrote an unpublished novel about college athletics entitled "End of Autumn," and then in 1958 began graduate work in creative writing at Stanford as a Woodrow Wilson fellow studying with Wallace Stegner, Malcolm Cowley, Richard Scowcraft, and Frank O'Connor.

Kesey completed another unpublished novel, "Zoo," which dealt with San Francisco's North Beach, before he began writing *One Flew Over the Cuckoo's Nest* in the summer of 1960. About this time he was introduced to drugs, specifically LSD, as a paid volunteer for government drug experiments conducted at the Veterans Administration Hospital in Menlo Park, California. Soon afterward he took a job as an aide in that hospital. Both the experience with drugs and the hospital work provided material for his novel, some of which he wrote during his night shifts, and, according to Kesey, some of it under the influence of peyote.

One Flew Over the Cuckoo's Nest (1962) was a critical success from the beginning. Its popularity, particularly among college students, has grown steadily, with paperback sales soaring into the millions. The 1975 film adaptation starred Jack Nicholson and Louise Fletcher. Its apparent message of contemporary man's need to get in touch with his world, to open the doors of perception, to enjoy spontaneous sensuous experience, and resist the manipulative forces of a technological society has had wide appeal.

One Flew Over the Cuckoo's Nest describes how a section of a mental hospital, controlled efficiently by Miss Ratched, known as Big Nurse, is disrupted by the arrival of Randle Patrick McMurphy, an exuberant, fast-talking hustler fresh from a prison work farm. The story is told from the point of view of a large, schizophrenic Indian named Bromden, an inmate pretending to be deaf and mute as a defense against a society to which he cannot adapt. In the course of the novel McMurphy, through his irrepressible energy and laughter, helps the patients, particularly Bromden, find the self-confidence and courage to rebel against the sterile, mechanistic, manipulative forces represented by Big Nurse. McMurphy is sacrificed in the process. Allusions and motifs from the Gospels, blended with those from comic books and popular culture, lend a mythic quality to the conflict. It is a struggle between good and evil with McMurphy as hero. More specifically, the forces of nature, spontaneity, motion, and freedom are pitted against those of static, technological control—contemporary American society's "Combine."

One Flew Over the Cuckoo's Nest is tightly organized, consisting of four symmetrical parts linked by consistent patterns of imagery associated with the opposition of nature and the machine. A central theme is the power of laughter as a source of vitality and sanity. Bromden, the narrator, acknowledges that McMurphy taught him "you have to laugh at the things that hurt you just to keep yourself in balance, just to keep the world from running you plumb crazy." When McMurphy has finally produced spontaneous and unin-

hibited laughter among his fellow inmates, his purpose as hero or savior is essentially complete. The kind of salvation he brings about is most clearly seen in Bromden's recovering his ability to sense with pleasure the natural world once again. Before McMurphy came, he lived in a numbing, hallucinated fog that he imagined was produced by machines in the hospital.

Some readers see antifeminism as an important theme in the novel. Big Nurse is certainly a personification of some negative aspects of our society, and she is just the principal figure among several domineering and manipulating females in the novel. One of the characters complains specifically about "the juggernaut of modern matriarchy." It can reasonably be argued, however, that Kesey's attack is not directed against women but against the perversion of the feminine. Big Nurse's ample breasts, tightly bound within a starched uniform, symbolically suggest human warmth, tenderness, and generosity stifled by cold, sterile, technological efficiency. And the suppression or perversion of the natural in Big Nurse corresponds to a similar situation in American society: nature and the personal perverted by misguided technology and the impersonal. From this point of view, Kesey's attitude toward the feminine is as positive as his attitude toward nature.

McMurphy's refreshing vitality has been much admired, and his flamboyant rebellion against repressive, depersonalizing forces in modern life is appealing, but some critics believe Kesey's treatment of moral problems is somewhat sentimentalized and oversimplified. One critic suggests that he enters the comic-strip world of super heroes and arch villains too uncritically in defense of the Good. Another points out that self-assertion and freedom are good, but they cannot be attained in any meaningful way simply by casting off inhibitions.

After finishing *One Flew Over the Cuckoo's Nest* in June 1961, Kesey returned to Oregon's logging country and began gathering material for *Sometimes a Great Notion* (1964). On mornings and evenings he rode in pickup trucks taking loggers to and from camps. At nights he visited bars where loggers went. After about four months, he returned to Stanford to write. In the summer of 1963 he moved to a mountain home in La Honda, fifteen miles from Palo Alto, which became the headquarters for the Merry Pranksters. There he completed the novel.

In *Sometimes a Great Notion* a logging family defies a labor union, and thereby the whole community they live in, by continuing their logging operations during a strike. There is also conflict within the family: Hank Stamper is in conflict with his half brother, Lee, a bookish college student who has been living in the East. As a child, Lee witnessed his mother engaged in sexual intercourse with Hank, and this has disturbed him emotionally. He returns to avenge himself by seducing Hank's wife. In the end both brothers come to understand themselves better through their conflict. Kesey once said about the novel that in writing it he wanted to find out "which side of me really is: the woodsy, logger side–complete with homespun homilies and crackerbarrel corniness, a valid side of me that I like–or its opposition. The two Stamper brothers in the novel are each one of the ways I think I am."

Despite its stylistic and psychological complexity, this novel treats an essentially simple theme: the ability of the self-reliant individual to prevail over awesome antagonistic forces. Hank Stamper, like Randle McMurphy, is big, lusty, and physically and personally vibrant. He, too, has a quarrel with civilization. Each is a version of a heroic type associated with the American frontier: the man who cherishes the freedom of life close to nature, responsible to no one but himself, considering social cooperation a weakness, possessing an indomitable will to maintain his independence. Hank resembles the classic western hero, and the oral tales sprinkled through the novel reinforce this nineteenth-century western link. Ostensibly Hank acts as a strikebreaker to save the family business, but obviously it is not the business but the independence it represents that is important to him. In order to protect his independence and the natural existence that is its source, he will defy all the usual assumptions of contemporary society. Getting the logs down the river to the company is his consuming passion, and to succeed he must overcome such obstacles as union opposition, growing hostility in the community, bad weather, death in the family, and a half brother intent on settling a grudge against him. Although Hank succeeds, the cost of his victory is high.

Sometimes a Great Notion, a large and ambitious novel, has some of the flavor of William Faulkner, whose fiction Kesey greatly admired. In a way reminiscent of Faulkner's *Light in August*, Kesey's novel begins near the moment of climax, then shifts to the past, gradually revealing through childhood experiences and family relationships the psychological makeup of the main characters. Abandoning conventional narrative chronology, he moves forward and backward in time, giving the reader, piece by piece, the information necessary for understanding characters, plot, and theme. Point of view is handled with similar freedom. Both Hank and Lee narrate in the first person in sections throughout the novel. From the third-person point of view, family history going back to 1898 is related, and the thoughts of such characters as the union leaders are revealed. Often shifts in point of view are abrupt, sometimes occurring more than once in a single paragraph. Frequently Kesey uses the device of presenting several incidents widely separated in space as simultaneous action. These techniques are interesting and often effective, but they make considerable demands upon the reader. Despite remarkable triumphs in language, the novel is somewhat strained and meandering, its experimental style at times difficult. Although it has sold well, it has achieved neither the enthusiastic praise nor the wide attention given to *One Flew Over the Cuckoo's Nest*.

In the summer of 1964 Kesey and the Merry Pranksters, dressed in outrageous costumes and transported in a bus painted fantastically with day-glo paint, traveled to New York for the publication of *Sometimes a Great Notion*. They shot more than forty hours of film of themselves during this trip. This film came to be known as "The Movie" and was later used frequently at Prankster-sponsored drug and music presentations–the so-called "acid tests."

In 1965 Kesey was arrested for possession of marijuana. A year of hearings and court appearances followed, resulting in his conviction. Early in 1966 he fled to Mexico to avoid prosecution, but he returned after about six months and was arrested. Eventually he served sentences totaling about five months in the San Mateo County Jail and Honor Camp, and he was released in November 1967.

In 1968 he moved to a farm in Pleasant Hill, Oregon, where he has remained. At the time of his arrest he expressed the intention of giving up writing for more "electrical forms." "I'd rather be a lightning rod than a seismograph," he explained. But later his interests returned once again to writing. When asked in 1971 if he had once believed writing to be an old-fashioned and artificial occupation, he replied, "I was count-

Caricature of Gregory Corso, Allen Ginsberg, Neal Cassady, Jack Kerouac, and William S. Burroughs from the Cassady issue of Spit In The Ocean, *published by Kesey*

ing on the millenium. Now I guess I'm tired of waiting."

Kesey's personal revolt during the 1960s with the Pranksters is most vividly documented in the book *Kesey's Garage Sale*, published in 1973 as a joint production of the Viking Press and Intrepid Trips, an informal association of Kesey and his friends Ken Babbs, Paul Foster, and Kenneth Barnes. The book is a collage of some of the material still in the Prankster Archives at Kesey's farm in Oregon. Five large cardboard boxes of material (including the holograph notes and various drafts of *One Flew Over the Cuckoo's Nest* and *Sometimes a Great Notion*) were deposited at the University of Oregon, but articles and interviews dating from Kesey's later involvement with the Pranksters were gathered into *Kesey's Garage Sale* and presented with mock-seriousness in the book as an attempt to clear the clutter of the archives. As Barnes states in the preface to the volume, "Every jeweled fragment of penultimate worth must be isolated from its mass of surrounding effluvia and made available to the inquisitive

ponderings of a curious and exceedingly penetrating audience."

The tone of the book is given as much by the "acidophilic artisticizing" of its illustrator, Paul Foster, as it is by the satiric texts. Words are less important, in fact, than images in *Kesey's Garage Sale:* the table of contents is lettered and drawn in comic-book style, and the subsequent pages are filled with illustrations, photomontages, and typographic design in the tradition of the layout of the earliest Beat literary magazines like *Beatitude*, later developed more completely in the visual effects of Stewart Brand's *Whole Earth Catalog*. Kesey had edited a supplement issue of the *Catalog* in 1971 with Paul Krassner of the *Realist* magazine, and their collaborative efforts were also reprinted in *Kesey's Garage Sale*. In this section of the book, Kesey gives tribute to books and people who influenced his life: the Bible, the I Ching, Martin Buber, Malcolm X, Hemingway, Faulkner, Burroughs, Timothy Leary, the Beatles, Woody Guthrie, and Joan Baez, among others. *Kesey's Garage Sale* could, in fact, be deposited in a time capsule as a record of the chaotic influences that shaped the "revolutionary consciousness" of the 1960s. It also contains the screenplay *Over the Border*, in which Kesey sought to immortalize the heroic character of Neal Cassady, who had died in 1968.

Kesey opens the prologue in *Over the Border* with "the dramatic narrative of an Orson Wellesian Voice in the Sky" announcing the theme that will be explored in the work: "Once upon a time a young man of American background thought he had discovered the Great Secret, the Skeleton Key to the Cosmos, the Absolute Answer to the Age-Old Question asked by every Wizard and Alchemist and Mystic that ever peered curiously into the Perplexing Heavens, by every Doctor and Scientist and Explorer that ever wondered about the Winding Ways of this world, by every Philosopher and Holyman and Politician that ever listened for the Mysterious Song beneath the beat of the Human Heart . . . the answer to 'What Makes It All Go?' "

In burlesqued comic-book style *Over the Border* dramatizes Kesey's search for the answer to the same question. After experiences with LSD and marijuana, his autobiographical hero Devlin Deboree (rhymes with "debris") believes he is in contact with the primeval energy source of creation, but he realizes that there is a question beyond "What Makes It All Go?"–"How Do I Drive It?" In the answer lies nothing less than the means to a "Full Revolution," and the screenplay is the story of Deboree's quest to gain control of, or "drive," the elemental energy fields like lightning surrounding the planet earth. The unexpected appearance in his life of the San Francisco police, however, who want to send Deboree to jail for smoking marijuana on the roof of an apartment building, makes necessary the quick trip to Mexico, where he is joined by his Prankster friends. After several comic adventures–and close calls with Mexican police and jail–they participate in an LSD session that almost ends in tragedy when Deboree's small son nearly drowns. This brush with death brings the hero to a realization that he is a victim of his own pride, when he understands that there is a "third inevitable question" beyond the first two: "How do I get off ?" The end of the screenplay a short time later brings back the "Voice in the Sky" with the didactic announcement that "this troupe's departure doesn't end our course. This was only a demonstration of ways not to fly. . . ."

Over the Border can be read as a morality play conceived in the modern form of a psyche-

delic comic-book film scenario, with line drawings on every page representing the action dramatized in the text. The characters are based on "real life people" given comical names like "Sir Speed" Houlihan (Cassady) and transformed into cartoon figures by Kesey's exaggeration of personal characteristics and idiosyncratic speech patterns. Just beneath the surface, under the high-camp fun and games, however, there is an unmistakably serious investigation proceeding, as if Kesey were evaluating his life with the Pranksters and his involvement with hallucinogenic drugs. At the end of the screenplay, when Deboree is ready to leave Mexico and turn north to face his responsibilities in America, he is a changed man. As one of the characters describes him, "He amped out on too much something; I don't know whether it was psychedelics, electronics or heroics."

Kesey decided that the answer to the riddle was that Cassady's life "was the yoga of a man driven to the cliff-edge by the grassfire of an entire nation's burning material madness. Rather than be consumed by this burn he jumped, choosing to sort things out in the fast-flying but smog-free moments of a life with no retreat. In this commitment he placed himself irrevocably beyond category. Once, when asked why he wouldn't at least *try* to be cool, he said, 'Me trying to be cool would be like James Joyce trying to write like Herb Gold.' "

Kesey's renewed interest in writing has been accompanied by a turning away from drugs. He once believed that drugs like LSD could open wonderful, mind-expanding experiences. Though he might not have given up that belief entirely, he has lost interest in deliberate experimenting. "There are dues," he has said, and "even if it were safe and sanctioned we just don't have the right." "The biggest thing I've learned on dope," he said in 1970, "is that there are forces beyond human understanding that are influencing our lives." His hope and fascination now seem to be the mystique of the land, the cycles of nature, and farming for awareness, not money. He has been active in arousing public interest and participation in planning for the next twenty-five years of Oregon's growth.

Since 1974 Kesey has edited a magazine called *Spit in the Ocean*, based in Eugene, Oregon. Portions of a novel in progress, "Seven Prayers by Grandma Whittier," appeared both in this magazine and in a collection, *Kesey* (1977). The central character of *Over the Border*, Devlin Deboree,

Notes for One Flew Over the Cuckoo's Nest, *Kesey's 1962 novel inspired by his night job on a psychiatric ward (courtesy of the author)* appears here in a secondary role. The point of view is that of an eighty-six-year-old grandmother, a spry, self-reliant Christian woman whose compassion and understanding are brought to bear upon some unusual aspects of contemporary American society.

Demon Box (1986), somewhat like *Kesey's Garage Sale*, is a disorganized miscellany of previously published essays, short stories, and articles, with a few new pieces. Instead of being the "long rambling novel about cattle raising" that Kesey described in *Esquire* (March 1976), it is a rambling anthology of works about the legacy of the 1960s. Again using the thinly disguised autobiographical narrator Devlin Deboree, Kesey reflects on past experiences, still searching for the Merry Pranksters' vitality and freedom. His writing style has been compared to the free-association prose of the New Journalism.

Essays on Egypt and China explore the complex relationships between Americans and foreigners, but the focus remains primarily on West Coast counterculture life-style. He pays tribute to Cassady ("The Day After Superman Died") and homage to John Lennon ("Now We Know How Many Holes It Takes to Fill the Albert Hall"), and he recounts his own downfall after being arrested for marijuana and staying at the San Mateo County Jail and Honor Camp. "The Last Time the Angels Came Up" recalls a visit to Kesey's farm by bikers, complete with obscenities. The title essay, "The Demon Box," epitomizes the changes endured by the "tarnished Galahad" on his quest for life's meaning. Alter-ego Deboree believes in the hot-tub Gestalt Realization ("the hottest therapy in the Bay Area") of German psychiatrist Dr. Klaus Woofner and his theory that modern civilization's angst is a fear of "running empty" like a demon in a box, governed by physics' laws of thermodynamics. Ten years later Deboree (like Kesey) is running dry, unable to write an acceptable movie script for *One Flew Over the Cuckoo's Nest*. He attends a convention of psychiatric superintendents at Walt Disney World and hears Woofner, this time attacking psychedelic drugs as means to control the demons of modern life. Deboree's two-day drunken stupor in Fantasyland is his way of avoiding reality, perhaps, as he battles the demon entropy. Kesey suggests that the superego accepts pleasant thoughts and dismisses the unpleasant, resulting in the entropic decline of modern consciousness. *Demon Box* testifies to Kesey's quest for that energy of madness that catapulted him to fame in

the 1960s. The Book of the Month Club and Quality Paperback Book Club selected *Demon Box* as an alternate selection in August 1986.

Kesey has called himself a "parabolist," which means, he says, "that I am not a reporter. I don't ask my reader to believe characters or situations exist anyplace other than in our minds–and there's a *possibility* for such existence in his mind and in my mind." He believes that "passing off what-might-be-true as fiction" is a better vocation than "passing off what-is-quite-possibly fiction as truth." "A single *Batman* comic book is more honest than a whole volume of *Time* magazines." He does not discount the value of reporting reality but suggests: "A writer must practice lying for a long time before he can trust himself with anything so delicate as the truth." But he is a parabolist in another sense also. His writing and interviews are filled with little anecdotes or parables. Narrative is for him the natural and spontaneous vehicle for concepts. His insights come not as abstract ideas but radiate from story and anecdote. Similarly, he loves a tale, the type of down-home tale characteristic of the American frontier in its various phases.

At the center of his imaginative vision is fascination with the American cultural hero, particularly as he is revealed in popular art forms. Patterns in the novels suggest the patterns of popular myths in folktales, westerns, and comic strips. Explicit allusions are made to heroes such as Paul Bunyan, the Lone Ranger, and Captain Marvel. This fascination is perhaps at bottom a manifestation of Kesey's preoccupation with transcendence. His experimentation with drugs, his interest in psychic phenomena, his use of the I Ching, his dabbling in Eastern religions, his focus on the Bible, his 1975 trip to Egypt in search of the occult Hidden Pyramid–all such characteristically Kesian behavior suggests a transcendental quest, an inveterate faith in infinite possibility for the individual. His tendency toward mysticism, his distrust of political movements and revolution, and his attraction to nature, simplicity, self-reliance, and freedom link his vision to that of the New England Transcendentalists. Kesey well deserves recognition for his strongly individualist works portraying this distinctly American counterculture.

References:

William C. Baurecht, "Separation, Initiation, and Return: Schizophrenic Episode in *One Flew*

Over the Cuckoo's Nest," Midwest Quarterly, 23 (Spring 1982): 279-293.
A mythic approach to the quest theme in the novel.

Bruce Carnes, *Ken Kesey* (Boise, Idaho: Boise State University Press, 1974).
Brief introduction to the life and works of Kesey.

Leslie A. Fiedler, *The Return of the Vanishing American* (New York: Stein & Day, 1968).
A brief analysis of *One Flew Over the Cuckoo's Nest* as pop art rather than belles lettres, influenced by the comic-book form and defining the "West of Madness."

Robert Forrey, "Ken Kesey's Psychopathic Savior: A Rejoinder," *Modern Fiction Studies*, 21 (Summer 1975): 222-230.
Attack on *One Flew Over the Cuckoo's Nest* as conservative, reactionary, sexist, psychopathological, and very lowbrow; claims that repressed homosexuality is evident in the novel.

John Gatto, *Monarch Notes on Kesey's One Flew Over the Cuckoo's Nest* (New York: Monarch Press, 1975).
Summary and notes as a study guide to the novel.

James O. Hoge, "Psychedelic Stimulation and the Creative Imagination: The Case of Ken Kesey," *Southern Humanities Review*, 6 (Fall 1972): 381-391.
View of Kesey, "erstwhile novelist and psychedelic superhero," as a reactionary against rational intellect in favor of sensorial experience.

Janet Larson, "Stories Sacred and Profane: Narrative in *One Flew Over the Cuckoo's Nest*," *Religion and Literature*, 16 (Summer 1984): 25-42.
Myth and Christian imagery explored as themes in the novel.

Barry H. Leeds, *Ken Kesey* (New York: Ungar, 1981).
Brief biography followed by a critical study of Kesey's works to date, concluding that charges of sexism, racism, and oversim-

plicity in his first novel are indefensible in view of his later work.

Martin Levin, review of *One Flew Over the Cuckoo's Nest*, *New York Times Book Review*, 4 February 1962), p. 32.
Labels the novel a "work of genuine literary merit," a parable of good and evil.

Fred Madden, "Sanity and Responsibility: Big Chief as Narrator and Executioner," *Modern Fiction Studies*, 32 (Summer 1986): 203-217.
Analysis of madness and manipulation in *One Flew Over the Cuckoo's Nest*.

Irving Malin, "Ken Kesey: *One Flew Over the Cuckoo's Nest*," *Critique*, 5 (Fall 1962): 81-84.
Overview of the novel, focusing on Kesey's brand of realism (Gothicism and comedy) and the theme of "the compulsive design" to exert power over others.

Terence Martin, "*One Flew Over the Cuckoo's Nest* and the High Cost of Living," *Modern Fiction Studies*, 19 (Spring 1973): 43-55.
A positive assessment of the novel's values: interdependence, a sense of self, and freedom (see Forrey's "rejoinder").

Nicolaus Mills, "Ken Kesey and the Politics of Laughter," *Centennial Review*, 16 (Winter 1972): 82-90.
Argument that Kesey's 1960s admirers focused more on his life-style than his literary work, and that even Tom Wolfe's book obscures his literary accomplishments.

Julian Moynahan, review of *Sometimes a Great Notion*, *New York Times Book Review*, 10 September 1964 , pp. 14-15.
Criticizes the novel as "deeply perplexed and ambiguous" in its treatment of men and women in Oregon's coastal logging region.

Raymond Michael Olderman, "The Grail Knight Arrives," in his *Beyond the Waste Land: A Study of the American Novel in the Nineteen-Sixties* (New Haven: Yale University Press, 1972), pp. 35-51.
Discussion of *One Flew Over the Cuckoo's Nest* as it reflects the wasteland motif and the Grail Knight's quest.

Donald Palumbo, "Kesey's and Forman's *One Flew Over the Cuckoo's Nest*: The Metamorphosis of Metamorphoses as Novel Becomes Film," *CEA Critic*, 45 (January 1983): 25-32.
Study of the film adaptation by Miloš Forman.

M. Gilbert Porter, *The Art of Grit: Ken Kesey's Fiction* (Columbia: University of Missouri Press, 1982).
Criticism and interpretation of Kesey's works.

John Clark Pratt, ed., *One Flew Over the Cuckoo's Nest: Text and Criticism* (New York: Viking, 1973).
Critical essays attacking and defending the perceived values of the novel, its author, and the literary worth of both.

Mordecai Richler, review of *Kesey's Garage Sale*, *New York Times Book Review*, 7 October 1973 , pp. 6-7.
Dismisses the book as a catch-all collection of previously published work, "no more than a trifle."

John Riley, "Bio: Novelist Ken Kesey Has Flown the 'Cuckoo's Nest' and Given Up Tripping for Farming," *People*, 5 (22 March 1976): 25-28.
Portrait of Kesey and his family, interviewed and photographed on their farm a decade after his arrest for drugs.

Elaine B. Safer, "The Absurd Quest and Black Humor in Kesey's *Sometimes a Great Notion*," *Critique*, 24 (Summer 1983): 228-240.
A treatment of the archetypal quest, the absurd, and black humor.

Terry G. Sherwood, "*One Flew Over the Cuckoo's Nest* and the Comic Strip," *Critique*, 13 (1970): 96-109.
Analysis of the novel as somewhat sentimentalized oversimplification of moral problems with an unclear victory over Evil, for the comic-strip world is not reality–but an escape from it.

Janet R. Sutherland, "A Defense of Ken Kesey's *One Flew Over the Cuckoo's Nest*," *English Journal*, 61 (January 1972): 28-31.
Argument that the novel condemns rather than espouses blatant sexism.

Stephen L. Tanner, *Ken Kesey* (Boston: Twayne, 1983).
Biographical and critical study in the Twayne U.S. Authors Series.

Tanner, "Labor Union versus Frontier Values in Kesey's *Sometimes a Great Notion*," *Rendezvous*, 19 (Fall 1983): 16-21.
Analysis of the conflict between labor unions and individualism.

Tanner, "Salvation through Laughter: Ken Kesey and the Cuckoo's Nest," *Southwest Review*, 58 (Spring 1973): 125-137.
Discussion of Kesey's theme that the power of laughter and humor is the source of life's vitality.

Joseph J. Waldmeir, "Two Novelists of the Absurd: Heller and Kesey," *Wisconsin Studies in Contemporary Literature*, 5 (Autumn 1964): 192-204.
Comparison of the style of Kesey and Joseph Heller (*Catch-22*) and their knack for twisting realism into the absurd, forming searching parables of government and the governed.

Kingsley Widmer, "Contemporary American Outcasts," in his *The Literary Rebel* (Carbondale: Southern Illinois University Press, 1965).
Examination of Kesey's allegorical techniques, with satiric parable of good versus evil.

Tom Wolfe, *The Electric Kool-Aid Acid Test* (New York: Farrar, Straus & Giroux, 1968).
Portrait of Kesey and his Merry Pranksters, celebrating their feverish pursuit of the drug experience–the psychedelic life lived as a work of comic fiction.

John Knowles

This entry was updated by Robert M. Nelson (University of Richmond) from his entry
in DLB 6, American Novelists Since World War II, Second Series.

Places	Phillips Exeter Academy West Virginia	New England The French Riviera	The Hamptons, N.Y.
Influences and Relationships	Thornton Wilder	Truman Capote	
Literary Movements and Forms	Travel Narrative	The Novel	Coming of Age Novel
Major Themes	Adolescence War Identity	Individuality vs. Conformity	Cultural Dualism The Doppelgänger
Cultural and Artistic Influences	New England Protestant Ethic "Jet Set" Society	Environment Determinism Drama	Psychoanalysis Architecture Prep School Life
Social and Economic Influences	World War II	The Cold War	

BIRTH: Fairmont, West Virginia, 16 September 1926, to James Myron and Mary Beatrice Shea Knowles.

EDUCATION: B.A., Yale University, 1949.

AWARDS AND HONORS: National Institute of Arts and Letters Rosenthal Award for *A Separate Peace*, 1960; William Faulkner Foundation Award for *A Separate Peace*, 1960.

BOOKS: *A Separate Peace* (London: Secker & Warburg, 1959; New York: Macmillan, 1960);
Morning in Antibes (New York: Macmillan, 1962; London: Secker & Warburg, 1962);
Double Vision: American Thoughts Abroad (New York: Macmillan, 1964; London: Secker & Warburg, 1964);
Indian Summer (New York: Random House, 1966; London: Secker & Warburg, 1966);
Phineas (New York: Random House, 1968);
The Paragon (New York: Random House, 1971);
Spreading Fires (New York: Random House, 1974);
A Vein of Riches (Boston & Toronto: Little, Brown, 1978);
Peace Breaks Out (New York & Canada: Holt, Rinehart & Winston, 1981);
A Stolen Past (New York & Canada: Holt, Rinehart & Winston, 1983; London: Constable, 1984).

John Knowles, the third of four children of James Myron and Mary Beatrice Shea Knowles, was born in Fairmont, West Virginia. He has an older brother and sister who are twins, and a younger sister. Knowles left West Virginia at fifteen to attend the Phillips Exeter Academy in New Hampshire during World War II. After graduating in 1945 he enlisted in the U.S. Army Air Force Aviation Cadet Program, eventually qualifying as pilot. Following his discharge after eight months, Knowles attended Yale University, served briefly after graduating in 1949 as an assistant editor for the *Yale Alumni* magazine, and then worked from 1950 to 1952 as a reporter and occasional drama critic for the *Hartford Courant*. Knowles was a free-lance writer from 1952 to 1956. After a year or so abroad, touring Italy and southern France and writing his first novel, "Descent into Proselito" (which he decided not to publish, partly on the advice of his mentor, Thornton Wilder), Knowles returned to the United States in 1955. He took up residence in New

John Knowles (Gale International Portrait Gallery)

York City's Hell's Kitchen section, where he shared an apartment with actor Bradford Dillman. He wrote occasional drama reviews while his first short stories (including "A Turn with the Sun" in 1953 and "Phineas" in 1956) were being published. During this period he continued to benefit from Wilder's interest in his work and began to write *A Separate Peace*.

After *Holiday* magazine published his article on Phillips Exeter Academy in late 1956, Knowles moved to Philadelphia in 1957 to assume the post of associate editor for *Holiday*. During this time *A Separate Peace* was published, first in England (1959) and then in the United States (1960). When it became clear soon after its American publication that *A Separate Peace* would be highly successful, Knowles, then thirty-four, resigned his editorship in August 1960 to embark on a two-year tour of Europe and the Middle East. His 1964 travelogue, *Double Vision: American Thoughts Abroad*, recounts his sojourn. His second novel, *Morning in Antibes* (1962), was published while Knowles was still abroad. Established as a professional writer, Knowles returned from Europe and moved to New York City, where he lived throughout the 1960s while continuing to travel abroad for short periods. During these years he served as a writer in residence, first at the University of North Carolina for the 1963-1964 session and then at Princeton in 1968-1969. His third novel, *Indian Summer*, which was dedicated to Thornton Wilder, was published in 1966, and a collection of short stories, *Phineas*, appeared in 1968. Two of his essays were published in the *New York Times*, "Where Does a Young Writer Find His Real Friends?" in 1962 and "The Writer-in-Residence" in 1965. In 1970, the year his father died, Knowles took up permanent residence in Southampton, Long Island, where his neighbors in nearby villages have included Truman Capote, Winston Groome, Willie Morris, and Irwin Shaw. His fourth novel, *The Paragon*, appeared in 1971, followed by *Spreading Fires* in 1974 and *A Vein of Riches* in 1978. *Peace Breaks Out*, designed to be a companion piece to *A Separate Peace*, was published in 1981, followed by *A Stolen Past* (which can be read as a companion piece to *The Paragon*) in 1983. A motion picture version of *A Separate Peace* was released in 1972. Outside of commentaries on *A Separate Peace*, there has been very little serious critical attention paid to Knowles's work.

The settings of Knowles's novels reflect those environments he feels most influenced him. *A Vein of Riches*, which traces the fortunes of the Catherwood family from 1909 until 1924, is set in Middleburg, West Virginia, a coal-boom community not unlike Fairmont. The Phillips Exeter Academy takes on fictional form as the Devon school, where Gene Forrester spends most of the World War II years in *A Separate Peace* and where Pete Hallam returns to teach in *Peace Breaks Out;* the academy appears again (though less recognizably) as the Wetherford Country Day School attended by both Cleet Kinsolving and Neil Reardon prior to World War II in *Indian Summer*. Cleet returns to Connecticut after his military discharge in 1945 to see his brother off to Yale; in *The Paragon* Louis Colfax comes to Yale in 1953 following an early discharge from the U.S. Marine Corps; in *A Stolen Past* the narrator returns to Yale, his alma mater, to deliver an address and to review the life he created there thirty years previously. Knowles's own strong affinity during the early 1950s and early 1960s for the French Riviera is reflected in the settings of both *Morning in Antibes* and *Spreading Fires* (which takes place at the villa Mas Tranquilitat, "overlooking Cannes").

Knowles's talent for describing local atmosphere, developed during his years with *Holiday*,

has been frequently admired by his critics and is one of the mainstays of his appeal as a fiction writer. Knowles typically employs local description to forward the thesis that cultures are to a significant degree products of their geographical limitations, so that individual personalities are to be understood as ultimately shaped as much by the characteristics of their native climates and terrains as by heredity. The wanderlust of many of Knowles's protagonists reflects their needs to escape the subtle determinism of such environmental shaping. This thesis plays an especially strong part in the thematic development of his two Mediterranean novels as well as in *Indian Summer*, in which Cleet Kinsolving's desire to "roll out his life full force" is complemented by his "fear of being trapped" into returning to his small hometown. In *The Paragon* the "irascible climate" of Connecticut shapes a people who become "unresting, ever on the alert to what's next, brittle from the fatigue of ever adapting to their commanding climate." A similar line of speculation about how climate and geography determine the characteristic "climates" of various national cultures runs throughout *Double Vision: American Thoughts Abroad*, a collection of impressions gathered during Knowles's junkets to England, southern France, Greece, and the Middle East. In *Double Vision* Knowles tests his own acquired assumptions and expectations against a variety of external milieus; this process of self-testing is a major recurring motif in his novels, and Knowles's work is perhaps best understood as his series of attempts to work out the psychological implications of his crucial observation in *Double Vision* that "the American Character is unintegrated, unresolved, a careful Protestant with a savage stirring in his insides, a germ of native American wildness thickening in his throat."

The idea for Knowles's first published novel, *A Separate Peace*, grew out of his short story "Phineas," which appeared in *Cosmopolitan* in May 1956. Frequently compared critically to J. D. Salinger's *The Catcher in the Rye* (1951) and written despite Wilder's initial skepticism about the feasibility of the project, *A Separate Peace* is today one of the most widely read postwar American novels; it was in it sixty-fourth Bantam paperback run in March 1986, with a total of over seven million copies in print. It won in 1960 the first William Faulkner Foundation Award for a notable first novel as well as the 1960 Rosenthal Award of the National Institute of Arts and Letters.

A Separate Peace represents Knowles's discovery of those psychological forces informing what he came to call in 1964 the prototypically New England "American character." This paradigmatic self is composed of two elements: the "germ of wildness," an essentially libidinal, creative primary element bent on expressing itself upon the world, and the "cautious Protestant," a secondary element committed essentially to defending, protecting, and conserving that primary self. The impulses and urges of the primary self manifest themselves in the form of anarchic human needs and desires and in the emotions of love and hate; the most obvious manifestations of the secondary self in Knowles's work are the institutions—governments, academic curricula, cultural ethos—which evolve out of the impulse of the secondary self but which, once created, take on an independently self-protective character and end up stifling the very spirit they exist ontologically to protect. At their deepest level Knowles's novels are designed to isolate and study these two complementary but conflicting elements in the American character; hence the frequent appearance of doubles and alter ego figures in his work. The novels focus upon the limited variety of adaptive strategies his protagonists invent to reconcile the urges within themselves to the prevailing shaping forces—the characteristic "givens" of culture and climate in which Knowles sets them.

The retrospective first-person point of view of *A Separate Peace* allows Gene Forrester to review his adolescent personality's disintegration and the subsequent process of reintegration through the distance of fifteen years, a distance which enables Knowles's protagonist to analyze as well as evaluate the evolution of his identity. As a prototype of the American character, Gene comes to Devon school controlled by the "cautious Protestant" in his character; various cultural and climatic images of conservatism at the school, including the adamantine First Academy Building, the frozen New Hampshire winterscape, and the "dull, dark green called olive drab" which he identifies as "the prevailing color of life in America" during World War II years, all serve to reinforce this strain of his character. He is drawn to Brinker Hadley, the epitome of the "cautious Protestant." Student leader and class politician, Brinker is New England conservatism personified. At the same time, the repressed "germ of wildness" in Gene's character is attracted to Phineas, an indifferent student but a natural athlete and eccentric individualist who

rules the playing fields of Devon during the summer session with a spirit of spontaneous anarchy. In contrast to the patriotic (and military) olive drab, which is the color of defensive conservatism for Gene, Phineas's emblem is an outrageously bright pink shirt.

Gene's shifts of allegiance between these two projected versions of his own potential identity constitute "a study," according to Knowles, "of how adolescent personality develops, identifying with an admired person, then repudiating that person." Gene's early attempts to identify with Phineas (by reluctantly joining the Super Suicide Society, by accompanying Phineas on an overnight trip to the Atlantic Ocean) activate a conflict between the "cautious Protestant" and the "germ of wildness" within Gene's character, a conflict won by the cautious Protestant. When Gene causes Phineas to break a leg in a fall from the jumping tree, from which boys have been jumping into the river as a test of courage, Gene is forced to recognize the part of himself that identifies with Phineas. After Phineas has left school to recuperate from his injury, Gene secretly tries on Phineas's pink shirt and finds that it fits. Gene's attempts to cultivate this awakened "germ of wildness" within himself are inhibited, however, by the presence of Brinker Hadley, who moves into the room across the hall from Gene's and immediately forces Gene to confront his disloyalty. Guided by Brinker, Gene decides to enlist in the armed forces, thus reducing the pains of coming to terms with his evolving identity by letting the military design his identity for him. Before Gene enlists, Phineas reappears at school, and Gene once again finds himself unable to repudiate completely either the anarchic forces within himself or his conservative defenses against those forces. Tutored by Phineas, Gene begins to train himself for the chimerical 1944 Olympics. At the same time, Brinker, having lost his direct sway over Gene's allegiances, "had begun a long, decisive sequence of withdrawals from school activity ever since the morning I deserted his enlistment plan"; having changed his uniform from "well-bred clothes" to "khaki pants supported by a garrison belt," Brinker represents Gene's own lessening, but nonetheless active, commitment to the prevailing olive-drab way of life. As attractive as Phineas's "choreography of peace" is to Gene, the part of himself which identifies with Phineas's emotional hedonism once again finds itself at odds with the relentless shaping forces of the outside world, which finally intrude upon

Devon in the form of a telegram from Elwin "Leper" Lepellier, a schoolmate who enlisted and has gone "psycho" in boot camp. Gene sees in Leper's condition a warning against going out into the world unprepared for dealing with hostility, a reminder that the "cautious Protestant" is a necessary element of an identity which hopes to survive in the world. Thus reminded of his dual commitment, but once again unable to reconcile the unintegrated forces within and without himself, Gene becomes a helpless observer of a climactic kangaroo court scene in which Phineas, and by extension, the part of Gene identifying with Phineas, is put on trial by Brinker for refusing to cooperate with the "givens" of a world at war, with Leper serving as chief witness for the prosecution. Phineas rejects the trial, only to stumble blindly down the marble stairs of the First Academy Building, incurring a second and ultimately fatal fracture of his leg. Gene then isolates himself, at least temporarily, from these three characters and, by extension, from their three separate strategies for coming to terms with one's self in the world; thus removed from the shaping forces of his past, he finally succeeds in achieving an integrated "double vision" which fuses, albeit tenuously, the warring parts of his character. The "separate peace" of the title refers to this valuable but temporary act of self-integration, which produces a personality which is a replication of neither of the essential forces which generated it but rather a delicate orchestration of those forces.

Where Gene Forrester seeks peace against the backdrop of World War II, Nick Bodine in *Morning in Antibes* seeks love during the French-Algerian crisis of the late 1950s. The use of a world crisis as a metaphor for an individual struggle is only one of several major motifs which have been transposed from *A Separate Peace* into *Morning in Antibes* and so into the cultural and climatic milieu of the French Riviera, in many ways the antithesis of the frozen New Hampshire setting of the first novel. A grown-up Gene Forrester, Nicholas Petrovich Bodine, the emotionally exhausted narrative voice of the novel, is a congeries of acquired attitudes and institution-oriented habits of thinking (his father a White Russian and his mother French, Nick himself has been raised in New England); his culturally conditioned personality holds, enveloped and stifled for most of the novel, a "seam of value" which however, is in danger of "withering from disuse." The novel traces the process by which Nick's capacity for loving is reactivated and finally liberated,

a process which involves the simultaneous dismantling of his acquired identity. To do so, Nick instinctively seeks out the languid summer climate of Antibes and Juan-les-Pins, as though the climate itself might help to thaw his frozen New England personality and draw out whatever urges and impulses might be lying dormant within him.

A necessary ingredient to the process of Nick's rehabilitation is the figure of Jeannot the Algerian, who serves as a role model for Nick's hidden, redeeming self. Jeannot's personality expresses directly his anarchic heart: "he didn't care about goals . . . ," and his sentiments, which he does care about, "began with himself and arched iridescently over into certain friends . . . they did not include anything so abstract as patriotism, either French or Algerian." For Nick, Jeannot stands as the archetype of a personality formed out of the single drive for authentic self-expression: "the crude battering prow of this drive, with him and with all of us, was engulfing desire, was love." Jeannot's struggle in the novel is to maintain this loving personality, unencumbered by forced commitments to the causes of others; when finally he is forced by circumstances arising out of the French-Algerian conflict to become a warrior, he predictably aligns himself with the National Liberation Front against the colonialist French establishment.

Counterbalancing the figure of Jeannot in the novel is Marc de la Croie, an older and more intractable version of Brinker Hadley. M. Marc, still desperately committed to the Pétainist mentality he adopted in 1940 and currently a ringleader of the Ultraist conspiracy to suppress the Algerian revolt (and thus the liberation-seeking spirit of Jeannot), is as bent on drawing Nick into the witheringly civilized spirit of the de la Croie villa as Jeannot is on drawing Nick's other self out into the warming circle of his loving spirit.

Poised like Nick between the forces represented by Jeannot and M. Marc is Liliane, Nick's estranged wife, whom Nick married because he was strongly attracted to "not herself but the uncontainable excitement I saw in her." Though Nick desires to possess the giving, outgoing self he sees in Liliane, their marriage "came apart" because Nick has held back from expressing the corresponding streak of giving within himself. Nick's divided self becomes at least tentatively consolidated at the end of the novel when he affirms the "hidden seam of value" he detects within himself and identifies in Liliane. Though his own capacity for love has diminished, he exercises what is left of it first by recklessly denying M. Marc possession of Liliane and then by reconciling himself maritally with Liliane.

Morning in Antibes is a flawed novel. Though Knowles's talent for rendering atmosphere does justice to the setting, his hastily sketched characters seem underdeveloped and "perfunctory." Offered as a paragon of individualism, Jeannot seems rather a paradigm of those cultural characteristics attributable to Algerian Arabs. The heavy-handed use of the French-Algerian crisis as a metaphor for Nick's internal struggle of liberation is an unconvincing version of the more successful analogy Knowles creates in *A Separate Peace* between the progress of World War II and the progress of Gene's evolving vision of peace. General critical consensus holds *Morning in Antibes* to be an unfinished book which was, "unhappily," rushed into publication, perhaps to capitalize upon the prior success of *A Separate Peace*.

Following publication of his travelogue, *Double Vision*, in 1964, Knowles turned his concerns back to a more familiar Connecticut landscape. The dominant themes of *Indian Summer* are familiar: the totalitarian forces of culture and climate tend to overwhelm the people who must coexist with them, and personal adaptations to these forces in turn give rise to dual and usually imperfectly integrated identities. The vehicles Knowles chooses for presenting these themes, however, are new. A shift to a relatively detached third-person point of view allows Knowles to supply motivational insights into his characters which, as he acknowledges in a 1962 essay for the *New York Times*, are unfortunately missing in *Morning in Antibes;* this narrative device also creates new opportunities for both dramatic irony and for occasional corrective satire, both of which appear in *Indian Summer* and, even more inventively, in *The Paragon*. A second major shift involves Knowles's choice of protagonists; whereas in his earlier two novels the focus is on the rediscovery by the careful Protestant in the American character of his more fundamental and unconservative self, in *Indian Summer* and in *The Paragon* the focus is clearly on the process through which the "savage stirring in his insides, a germ of native American wildness" attempts to ensure its continuing viability.

A Phineas figure endowed with a capacity for survival, twenty-three-year-old Harold "Cleet" Kinsolving returns from the Pacific in 1946 to an America trying to demobilize its wartime identity. Cleet, like America, having adapted imperfectly

to the rhythms of military priority for four years, dreams now of staying mobile and unregulated, if only to give himself time to "work the war-induced knots out of his character" in private "and without risk of hurting anybody close to him." Accordingly, he drifts from Texas to St. Joseph, Missouri, where he begins working with a small crop-dusting outfit and dreams of creating a small cargo line running between Seattle and Alaska, a dream which combines his need for the freedom he finds in flying and the creativity he would express in being able to "produce something." Coupled with Cleet's need for freedom is his lifelong "fear of being trapped": a runaway at age twelve from "the feeling of bare survival, an antiquated hollowness and brittleness" which characterizes old houses in Wetherford as well as the town in general, and an escapee from a hasty marriage at seventeen, barely able to tolerate the academic rigors of Wetherford Country Day School, Cleet is by nature a "privateer," and he attributes this nature to the "Indian" strain inherited from his maternal grandmother. Like Phineas and Jeannot before him, Cleet's energy and emotions run close to the surface of his personality, so close that emblematically he cannot wear a wristwatch: excess static electricity in his body renders one inoperable.

Cleet's alter ego is Neil Reardon, heir to High Farms and the history of exploitation it represents, the "formidable and fortress-like" Reardon estate built on coal, oil, iron ore, and most recently on real estate. Conditioned by a life of wealth coupled with an upper-class education at both Wetherford Country Day School and Yale, fresh from a shining military career, Neil has become the spokesman for old-fashioned New England intellectual and economic conservatism masked in Marxist rhetoric, lecturing the nation on the "bankrupt values and flabby laissez-faire anarchy of the pre-World War II generation in economics, politics, and sex." Like his father, Neil has become a paragon of the Wetherford spirit, the symbol of which–the 250-year-old Wetherford elm–has begun to die back, "inevitably." Like Gene Forrester and Nick Bodine before him, Neil is dimly troubled by an inner conflict between his adopted capitalist values and a subconscious resentment against the constraints they impose upon his life's shape; predictably, Neil deals with this germ of an anarchic self first by selecting as his mate Georgia Sommers, whose "proletarian mentality" is "one of the principal reasons he married her," and second by hiring Cleet to do odd jobs for him. Unfortunately, Neil's psychological adaptation to the Reardon way of life compels him to establish a possessive rather than a giving relationship with Georgia, the "unreplaceable part of himself."

Neil's possession of Georgia, in whom Cleet detects the same "something unguarded and aspiring, something brave and a little vulnerable, gaiety and strength" he values in himself, serves in the novel as one model of a relationship between the "cautious Protestant" (actually Neil is a Catholic) and the "savage" in the American character. A second paradigm is represented by "The Heir," the child Georgia is carrying, who represents to both Cleet and Neil some future hybrid of the adaptive individualist in Georgia and the frozen cultural spokesman in Neil. Georgia's father represents to Cleet "what he himself might be someday" should he fail to try to realize his dream of owning an independent airline, a man who has "failed, missed, thrown himself away, not gotten to the priceless core of himself and used it and made something of it, not contributed it to life and so become immortal." Lynn, Georgia's sister, represents a final strategy for relating the "savage" to the "cautious Protestant": Lynn decides to leave the Reardon enclave to strike out on her own while she still can.

Cleet finally chooses to follow Lynn's example, and he flees the various traps which Wetherford and the Reardons pose for him, but not before he wreaks havoc on the Reardon empire. After discovering that Neil's father and Neil, who have become "partners . . . two adult millionaires" during the war years, intend to renege on their promise to finance Cleet's dreamed-of airline, the "ignorant Indian" within Cleet takes "animal revenge" on Neil by venting its sexual energies upon Georgia, "mate of Neil, enemy." Georgia in turn suffers a miscarriage that leaves her sterile, brought on by her "profound emotional shock" at the ease with which Cleet has managed to resurrect the "savage" in her. Having symbolically destroyed any hope for a reconciliation between the savage and the cautious in the American character, Cleet's final act before leaving is an act of "love" in which he draws all Neil's awakened anger and outrage onto himself, thus protecting Georgia and at the same time providing himself as an object upon which Neil can express his otherwise self-destructive emotions.

Most critics view *Indian Summer* as being allegorically overweight, and indeed perhaps too much is made of Cleet's Indian heritage and his "magnetism." Though motivation of character is vastly more discernible in *Indian Summer* than in *Morning in Antibes*, these motivations clearly are designed to fit the demands of Knowles's thesis about the components of the American character, and consequently it is a patently "written" novel in which symbolic implications tend to overwhelm the demands of psychological realism.

Knowles resumes in *The Paragon* the careful third-person exploration of the "germ of native American wildness in the American Character" begun in *Indian Summer*. Again this novel is set in New England, where the "commanding climate" of a Connecticut autumn is clearly analogous to Yale University's architecture, depicted by Knowles as having been designed for "self-defense" and looking like "some long-established and only infrequently attacked permanent military installation." Yale University is adamantly committed to preserving its fixed form at all costs, thus becoming a haven of that "Bastille psychology" associated with the institutionalized past and its human allies characteristic in Knowles's work. As Clement Jonaz, an Afro-Brazilian Marxist misfit at Yale whose antiestablishmentarianism is emblematically genetic as well as political, puts it, "They're brainwashing us here with the dogmas of capitalism with a thin overlay of bourgeois government planning, plus ancestor-worship."

Throughout *Indian Summer* Cleet Kinsolving dreams of escaping the shaping totalitarianism of the New England climate and ethos; in contrast Louis Colfax, designed to become a paragon of American character, tries to make a place for himself within this ethos without being assimilated by it. Lou represents that heir to both strains in the American character who was miscarried in *Indian Summer*, the union of the potentially self-annihilating separation of the "cautious Protestant" and the "germ of wildness" within the individual psyche. Cleet's wildness is part of the personal past Lou brings back to Yale as the novel opens. This past is tied to the image of the "Black House" (located in the wilderness an hour from New Haven), Lou's inheritance from his mad Aunt Alice and representative of some "Colfax madness," in which Lou senses "an overpowering feeling of isolation, of holding fast to some bleak inner fact." Knowles uses the device of frequent flashback to sketch out Lou's earlier attempt to ally his ego's New England heritage with his alter ego, Charlotte Mills, a British drama student who has come to America to es-a 11

Nick Blackburn CHAPTER TWO

Amo mounted the ~~spirl spiri~~ spiral staircase to the small

Readers' Retreat Room, about twenty feet square, ~~with~~ long shelves

crowding the wallspace with ~~wm~~ volumes of every size, shape, and

degree of importance, upward to the ceiling and a ~~big,~~ foggy-looking
                                    TOWARD
~~skylih~~ skylight.

Buckley was slouched in ~~anowm~~ easy chair in t~~ow~~~~er~~ corner,
                                                      the
pouring over a massive volume. He looked up, nodded briefly,

and ~~immersed~~ himself ~~ac~~ again in his book.
    IMMERSED

The word "wayward" popped into Amo's mind as he covertly

studied Buckley's head , hair, hunched shoulders, long hands.
                    h   T   Almost AN Affectation,
The l~~on~~ hair was rather long for Devon, as though he saw himself
                                        It was)
as ~~ac~~ Maestro of ~~an~~ some symphony, reddish brown in color.
                  M
He had a straight nose, slightly sloping hazel X eyes, remnants

of freckles on his rather long face. His shoulders were tense,

despite his slouch. Amo had earlier noticed ~~thex no~~ nicotine stains

on hi~~'~~s long hands.

"I'm glad i~~t~~ you aren't some creep coming up here.

I can't   concentrate with creeps around," ~~ae~~ said Buckley. His

voice was mellif~~j~~lous, urbane, ~~and~~ almost ~~pedxx~~ pedantic;

Amo felt it was an appropriate ~~accompanim no~~ accompaniment

to his somehow singular appearnce, a ~~reif~~ r~~i~~enfocement of it; th~~ere~~

there was a languor to his voice and his ~~x~~ movements and whole

demeanor which, Amo ~~sid suddenly conclud   concluddd,eeeeeeeeee~~

~~concluddeddddddddddddd   concluddddddddddddddddddddddddddddddddddddd~~

~~dddddddddddddddddddddd~~
Suddenly
concluded, was designed to mislead, the steely languor of a cat

creeping up upon an unaware bird.

Revised typescript for one of Knowles's novels about Devon school, which he modeled after Phillips Exeter Academy in New Hampshire (courtesy of the author) cape her upper-middle-class rearing and in whom Lou identifies "some kind of an anarchy" which he needs to nurse within himself. Lou's early attempts to take possession of his own capacity for love by displacing it onto Charlotte and dealing with it externally lead to calamity when Charlotte leaves him and the Black House in pursuit of her drama career. Like Cleet, Lou runs from the place which has become a symbol of hollow possessiveness; unlike Cleet, though, Lou runs to the Marine Corps, where he submits himself to the training designed to "break down previous personality and put in its place a human machine conditioned for combat," only to find himself discharged after eight months for the good of the corps.

Thus having already failed at three different strategies for coming to terms with his divided psyche, Lou returns to Yale. The two prized possessions he brings with him, a carton brimming with two thousand unsent letters and a mammoth Soviet flag, symbolize his need to reconcile rather than divorce the warring impulses within himself. Lou's way of expressing his volcanolike "seam of value" within the constricting framework of a New England mentality is his reckless strategy for coming to terms with the forces that have defeated him three times already: an almost suicidally impulsive expression designed to take these forces by surprise.

Lou's first test is his new roommate, Gordon Durant, scion of the Durant Chemicals empire, which has contributed heavily to the Yale endowment fund for three generations. Gordon's "code of life," a crystallized version of the wealthy New England ethos, has no place in it for the "spooky wraith" of creative but unpredictable individualism he sees in Lou. Gordon, who at one point characterizes Lou as being like certain thoroughbred horses on his family's stud farm, "a mass of nervous impulses barely held together by a desperate will, a being the French would call *fin de race*, the end of his line," ultimately concedes the value of Lou's aggressively proffered friendship after Lou manages to return to its stall the high-spirited polo pony Gordon has drunkenly ridden into their dormitory room one Saturday night. Gordon and Lou reach their separate peace the following morning, when during "the last crisis of their friendship" Gordon uncharacteristically apologizes for being so unlikable, and Lou responds by vowing he loves Yale.

Lou's second and more difficult campaign involves his need to come to terms with the part of himself invested in Charlotte Mills, a need reactivated early in the novel when he finds a photograph of her with her young son (who might be Lou's) hanging on the wall of the Black House. Lou's need to somehow work the figure of Charlotte back into his own reevolving identity is the product of the terror of incompleteness which informs his recurring nightmare about not being allowed to graduate because he has neglected to take a course from each Yale department. Under the patient tutelage of Norma, Gordon's young but delphically wise Greek ex-stepmother, Lou comes to see that the sense of inner emptiness associated with the Black House is a psychological prerequisite for expressing the positive creative impulses which constitute the "seam of value" in his character. After attempting for most of the novel to repossess Charlotte and then, failing that, kidnapping her child, "the image of Charlotte in a distinctly male recasting," Lou finally gives up trying to fulfill his inner emptiness by taking from the world and reconciles himself instead to a future of giving *to* the world–a course of creative effort which may compensate for, but never eliminate, the "devastating sense of nothingness and emptiness and vulnerability" underlying all human desire. As Knowles has Lou put it, "partial people do the great things in this world . . . to make up for the inner knowledge that they were condemned all their lives to be incomplete people."

Spreading Fires, Knowles's fifth novel, is his shortest and perhaps his most unusual work to date. Dedicated to Truman Capote, the novel for the first six of its nine chapters blends themes common to Knowles's earlier works with the spare surface suspense of Capote's best terror stories (the protagonist's sister's name is Miriam, after the character in Capote's short story of the same name); the final three chapters, however, sacrifice this surface tautness in order to examine the underlying psychological terrain Knowles seems more predisposed to working with.

Knowles returns to maritime France in the languid months of July and August, and as in *Morning in Antibes* the benevolent climate draws out whatever suppressed urges and emotions people bring to it. The protagonist, Brendan Lucas, is a twenty-nine-year-old career diplomat–the third generation of Washington, D.C., Lucases to serve in the foreign service–who has rented the villa Mas Tranquilitat both to remove himself for a while from his professional world of "deceptions and lies and betrayals and cynicism" and to host a prenuptial party for his sister Miriam and her fiancé, Xavier Farel de Dornay, who was Brendan's Georgetown University schoolmate and wrestling partner. The season, the setting, and the occasion converge to trigger long-repressed adolescent emotions in all three characters: Brendan and Miriam spent their adolescent vacation years in this region, "thrown together a lot" during the years of their sexual awakenings, and this return to the area strikes Miriam as "weird . . . like having a dream about your childhood." The atmosphere within Mas Tranquilitat, itself "girded for attack on all fronts," becomes supercharged with a network of powerful and thinly displaced sexual desires (Brendan's for his sister and for Xavier, Miriam's for Xavier, Xavier's for both) which constitute some of the "spreading fires" of the title.

The counterbalancing spirit of repression is represented by the villa's resident cook, Neville, whose personality is "satisfactory on the surface" but is ravished at a deeper level by a severe degree of dissociation of the "cautious" from the "savage." Neville has committed himself the past three years to "extreme solitude and ceaseless work." Knowles likens Neville's "arid childhood—and not much of a fertile life since" to the "decadent strain" of deformed orange trees growing in the villa orchard, draped with sour, inedible oranges and with the bags of arsenic Neville has hung there to ward off fertilizing insects. With the occasion of the prenuptial party Neville feels himself attacked from without by the libidinal energies he has imperfectly repressed within, and his latent paranoia surfaces with terrifying force. Clearly, Neville's threatening personality gathers its energy in part from the inhibitions being shed by Brendan and his party, and Neville's increasingly overt threats against the lives of the members of the party (suggested first by his use of words, then by his method of hacking and partially decapitating chickens in the kitchen, and finally by his wielding a butcher knife) correspond in intensity to the degree to which the members of the party become more controlled by their reawakened adolescent passions.

In the final three chapters Neville comes to represent more specifically Brendan's private double, the repressive part of himself with which he has unconsciously been struggling for the past fifteen years. Brendan's earlier ambivalence about his desire for Miriam leaves his dual identity open to the puritanical control of both his mother and Neville, who comes to replace her,

and Brendan himself lives his dual psychological existence only vicariously through Xavier's love for his sister and, finally, Neville's inhibitions against love. From Knowles's point of view Brendan's inner struggle cannot be resolved until he chooses to ally himself either with the "cautious" or with the "savage" in his own character. Not surprisingly, he aligns with the former near the end of the novel, when, interpreting Neville's gesture of embrace as a gesture of attack, Brendan plunges a butcher knife into Neville's stomach. Brendan's identity thus seems designed to confirm Knowles's fundamental thesis about the hold of the past over the shape of the present: in Brendan's genealogy an inescapable part of Brendan still remains "the result of his [predominantly Anglo-Irish] ancestors and who they were and what they believed."

Critical reception of *Spreading Fires* reflects the uneven tonality of the novel's two-part structure. Proponents of Knowles's earlier work find the first part of the novel perhaps too hastily developed, while others feel the descriptive and analytic components of this novel are imperfectly synchronized.

A more ambivalent cultural and geographical climate is presented in *A Vein of Riches*. The West Virginia in this sixth novel is designed to reflect in its composition both of those shaping forces at work on the American, and more generally the human, identity. Knowles emphasizes West Virginia's precarious achievement of statehood during the Civil War, a time of shifting allegiances and ambiguous political affiliations during which West Virginia took on neither Northern nor Southern identity but remained passively resistant to the forces at war on her soil. The unresolved tensions of the state's compound cultural heritage become strained by the discovery of vast reserves of coal throughout West Virginia and her sudden preeminence as a "vein of riches" at the turn of the century. The novel is set during 1909-1924, a period during which the northern part of the state, controlled by exploitative coal barons who in turn are backed by "many millions of eastern dollars," finds itself pitted against the long-repressed forces of anticapitalist sentiment vested in the southern part of the state, which finally surface in the form of the United Mine Workers uprising of the summer of 1921. The conflicting forces are in turn replicated in the social, cultural, and economic composition of Middleburg, West Virginia, founded by pioneers of the coal industry who became within a decade "the great Middleburg coal barons, rulers of the biggest, the best, and the richest coalfield in the world" but surrounded by the shantytowns of the impoverished miners.

The personality of Knowles's protagonist, Lyle Catherwood, is, like West Virginia, determined at birth to be an arena of conflicting allegiances. Lyle is not only the son of Clarkson Catherwood, and thus heir to the sprawling Clarkson Coal Company and the future burdens of ownership, but is also the child of Minnie, a "whimsical" spirit who intuitively mistrusts her husband's self-investment in the vast but finite natural resources of King Coal and who devotes herself instead to the small farm she acquires.

As in Knowles's previous works, the protagonist's struggle is to achieve some coherent identity, a process through which the inherent dualism of his American character becomes resolved by his responding appropriately to externalized images of those forces operating within him. Outside shaping forces, however, conspire from the novel's beginning to make this process difficult. Clarkson and Minnie have had no sexual intercourse since Lyle's birth; to exacerbate their separateness, Minnie's sympathies lie not with her husband's need to defend his coal holdings but rather with the inevitable by-product of his "greed," the squalid living conditions of the miners and their families in nearby Poundville. Lyle's identification with his father is thus offset by the values inculcated by his mother during his preadolescent years. The constant internal strife in Lyle's family prepares him for the economic friction informing the charged political atmosphere of West Virginia, which surfaces as the labor-management showdowns of the early 1920s and especially in the Logan County incident of August 1921.

Lyle's first attempt to come to terms with these warring forces is to remain a neutral party to these conflicts; at eighteen he adopts the pose of a reporter for the *Middleburg Exponent*, changes his name to Lew Jenkins, and fantasizes reportorial coups to be acquired by infiltrating the ranks of the labor union army then marching from Charleston upon Logan County, where the entrenched forces of nonunion mining interests (including Lyle's father) await to repel the invasion. As though to force Lyle to reject his simplistic strategy of dissociation, Lyle's identity as the son of Clarkson Catherwood is exposed during the march, and the subsequent effort to rescue Lyle from the enemy camp brings about the acci-

dental shooting death of Clarkson's aide, Virgil Pence. Lyle's immediate reaction is to deny any personal responsibility for them; this conclusion, however, proves unsatisfactory to that need for a sense of personal value and purpose which, in Knowles's vision, personal identity exists to confirm, a sense Lyle recognizes as "the elemental animal inside his personal self" which refuses to stay "trapped inside" the incoherent pastiche of contrary impulses Lyle currently has for an identity. Attempting to redeem this elemental self, Lyle imitates the strategy his mother used earlier to verify her "salvation" and consults with the Reverend Ramsey Fullylove Roanoke. Lyle's prayer session with the reverend is, however, inconclusive. Lyle's evolving relationship with Doris Lee Pence, widow of the man for whose death Lyle now holds himself responsible, in whom Lyle identifies a quality of "vitality" and "a kind of breeziness which she herself seemed unconscious of"—qualities which significantly go generally unrecognized and unappreciated in the Middleburg community—measures his growing awareness of the value of the corresponding germ of vitality in himself: "I have a lot of deep feelings, he thought. It's something running right through me, very deeply, a vein or seam, . . . it's what I've really got, what I've always really lived for, and I guess always will live for." As in the cases of Nick, Cleet, and Lou, the redemption of Lyle's creative possibilities depends upon his ability to free himself from the psychological bondage to the "cautious Protestant" in his nature. Lyle's discovery of this need coincides in the novel with the sudden collapse of West Virginia's coal industry in the first two weeks of April 1924, a collapse which forces Clarkson and Lyle to draw upon their respective hidden reserves of character. Thus disencumbered of his social status, Lyle experiences, in sympathy with that "germ of wildness" which constitutes his personal "vein of riches," "a weird sense of exhilaration, almost somehow of hope fulfilled, a wildest dream realized."

Despite its epic proportions and its fidelity in acknowledging the socioeconomic forces which may be considered to have shaped Knowles's own family background, *A Vein of Riches* is considered by most of Knowles's critics his weakest novel. The problem lies not with his interpretation of West Virginia history or with the psychological motivation of the characters per se, but rather with the obtrusive and relentlessly methodical presentation of precise correlations between outside force and evolving identity, a technique used in all of Knowles's fictions, but used in *A Vein of Riches*, as before in *Morning in Antibes*, to excess.

Knowles returns to the Devon Academy as the setting for his seventh novel, *Peace Breaks Out*, dedicated to the memory of Thornton Wilder and designed as a sequel to *A Separate Peace*. The same characteristic "givens" of culture and climate which informed *A Separate Peace* animate *Peace Breaks Out* with one significant modification: World War II is suddenly and finally over. "Surprised by peace," the schoolboys of Devon Academy in the year 1945 cast about almost desperately to find new ways to express that "germ of wildness" which for the past four years has been displaced onto the prospect of fighting in a culturally endorsed world war. Locked into a war mentality but no longer having any mutually agreed-upon enemies to fight, they naturally (from Knowles's point of view) tend to turn upon one another: "the victors of the Second World War were commencing to see one another as enemies, the earlier enemies having been vanquished." This statement introduces one of the major motifs of the novel, the analogy between the ontology of the personal war to "save the peace" which develops at Devon and the phylogeny of the cold war which developed in the postwar years–not only the international conflict which the term usually suggests but also the climate of internal suspicion and persecution associated with such postwar phenomena as the McCarthy Era and the Rosenberg Affair.

The story of *Peace Breaks Out* is delivered from a detached, third-person point of view filtered through the sensibilities of Pete Hallam, one-time star hockey player and wounded combat veteran of the Italian Campaign who has returned to Devon Academy, in his memory idealized as a place "untainted and unthreatened" by the war, to teach American history and physical education and to recuperate from the leg wound and the POW internment he has recently suffered. Though maimed physically and psychologically by the war, Hallam has managed a fragile and provisional reconciliation of the Phineas-like athletic optimist in himself with the more worldly–and weary–conscientious adult in his character. It is his lot in the novel to have to witness the evolution of the microcosmic cold war brought on by the postwar American character's internal conflict.

The combatants in this new war are Wexford, Hochschwender, and the Boys of Pembroke

House, represented in the novel mainly by Cotty Donaldson and Tug Blackburn. Collectively, the Boys function in the novel much as does the character of Phineas in *A Separate Peace:* they are excellent athletes but indifferent scholars, and though they occasionally lament the lost opportunity to serve in World War II, their good spirits and generally amenable characters (they are "popular" figures on campus) make them seem a potent but nonbelligerent force in the novel. The battle of Devon, 1945-1946, begins with the confrontation between Wexford, a "precociously jaded" scion of the self-made New England capitalist class, and Hochschwender, a midwesterner of German extraction who arrogantly champions neo-Nazi views of history and American character and thus challenges the supremacy of Wexford's strongly espoused but weakly integrated (capitalist) traditionalism. Pale, nonathletic Wexford (significantly he is attributed no first name throughout the novel) cares what others think of him, a need which perhaps explains why he contrives to align himself with the Boys in his battle with Hochschwender by appealing to their naive patriotism. Hochschwender, on the other hand, is a true loner and is contemptuous of the Boys, American chauvinism, public opinion, and Devon's traditions in general.

Appropriately, the struggle between Wexford and Hochschwender begins in Hallam's American history class. When one of the students characterizes U.S. history as "one long success story" and Hochschwender rejoins with a comment about America's "mongrel" character, Wexford attempts to belittle Hochschwender's nonconformist opinions, only to be turned into the butt of the class's ridicule because of his affiliation with the school newspaper. Stung by this public humiliation, Wexford embarks on his campaign to destroy Hochschwender by identifying him with alien forces "trying to destroy our freedom and our way of life," a strategy calculated to enlist the sympathy of the Boys on the side of what is fundamentally a very private and personal war between Wexford's own shaky ego and the anarchic "germ of wildness" within himself which he has projected onto Hochschwender. Thus when Hochschwender later submits a letter to the Devon school newspaper calling for the abolishment of daily chapel services, Wexford, who is editor of the newspaper, is delighted to print it on the front page: "here, playing into his hands, was just the enemy he had been randomly probing for at Devon, out to destroy Our Traditions and

Our Way of Life." Though Wexford sees no more intrinsic values in the chapel services than Hochschwender does, he gleefully composes a bombastic editorial to accompany Hochschwender's letter, attacking it (and its writer) as "godless," "corrupting," and "blasphemously un-American," a bit of rhetoric designed to appeal to the chauvinistic sentiments of the Boys. For a while Wexford's campaign gains momentum; the Boys attempt to encourage Hochschwender to leave Devon by destroying his bicycle. However at this point the physical climate of New England begins to exercise its shaping power over the temperament of Wexford's unwitting stooges: "The students hibernated as though they were bears. . . . Rage and prejudice and plain orneriness fell asleep for the winter." By the time Wexford can return to the attack after Christmas break (the first winter term issue of the *Devonian* carries a long editorial by Wexford warning of a "conspiracy to destroy America from within since the Nazi-Fascist Axis has failed to destroy it from without"), the fires of animosity in the Boys have been banked for the winter, and they are ready to turn the war between Wexford and Hochschwender into a joke (one boy writes a letter to the newspaper nominating Hochschwender to compose a "class prayer" for this first postwar graduating class). Wexford is thus compelled to bide his time and wait for "the first tumultuous, galvanizing rustles of spring" to reanimate the seasonally dormant libidos of the Boys.

Prior to spring, however, Wexford contrives to enlist the sympathies of the Boys in the ingenious scheme of sponsoring a "permanent memorial to the Devon dead," a stained glass window commemorating World War II, to be installed in the school chapel. Wexford's plan finds allies in the Boys mainly because "they felt too guilty, too subtly, unconsciously guilty" to do other than endorse this "idealistic proposal." In his dedicatory speech early in the spring term, Wexford declares that his class is "ready to dedicate itself to guarding the victory won by their heroic predecessors," thus identifying the stained glass window with the class's collective need for a righteous cause to fight for, even if paradoxically their aggression is to be called making "peace" rather than "war." Wexford shatters the window and blames Hochschwender, the one recognizable "enemy of Our Way of Life" on campus. The Boys self-righteously form a posse and corner Hochschwender while he is out sculling alone on the river; Hochschwender suffers a heart attack

during their rather brutal attempt to extort a confession from him (conducted, as Knowles points out, "ritually, like those messianic unison roars of 'Heil Hitler!' at the monstrously glorious rallies at Nuremberg") and then later dies in the Devon infirmary. Much to the chagrin of Hochschwender's roommate, who haunts the Boys with the charge of murder, the institution whitewashes the incident; the Boys, whose discovery of "their own capacity for violence had stunned them," are appropriately remorseful privately, but publicly disclaim their actions; and Wexford emerges triumphant from a final confrontation with Hallam (when Hallam accuses him directly of having shattered the window, Wexford counters with his possession of evidence proving the culpability of the Boys in the death of Hochschwender, and the confrontation ends in a standoff), Wexford convinced he is "the most powerful member of the class of 1946." The novel concludes with Hallam's prevision, during commencement exercises for the graduating class, of Wexford as an "incipient monster," destined for "perhaps the Senate, or Sing Sing," representative of a breed of post-World War II warmongers.

Speaking of *Peace Breaks Out* prior to its publication, Knowles referred to it as a "companion piece" to *A Separate Peace*, and any reader familiar with the earlier work will recognize immediately the affinities of setting, theme, and psychological motif between the two works. Though it is possible to read *Peace Breaks Out* as an "updating" of *A Separate Peace*, it is also worth noting that a significant shift in authorial perspective differentiates the two works: the first-person perspective of the first novel has been replaced by the relatively more detached and objective third-person point of view of the later book (one reviewer complained that "everything is so remote" in *Peace Breaks Out*).

In much the same way that *Peace Breaks Out* functions as a "companion piece" to *A Separate Peace*, *A Stolen Past* (1983) can be understood as a companion piece to Knowles's earlier novel *The Paragon*. It is not a sequel but rather a significantly revised version of many of those cultural forces and psychological concerns associated with the Yale setting, a revision perhaps best understood as a reflection of the change in Knowles's own perceptions of his role as a writer as well as in his perceptions of his own past during the intervening decade.

As the title suggests, *A Stolen Past* treats the theme of the shaping power of personal history which recurs so frequently in Knowles's work. Knowles uses first-person narration to weave a richly textured, multilayered plot fabric which traces the subtle ways in which disparate lives, shaped by different cultures, become tangled in one another. As the novel opens, Allan Prieston is returning to Yale after a thirty-year absence to deliver a literary lecture; it is October, and the anticipation of the coming New England winter, a force which operates so clearly in three previous Knowles novels (including *The Paragon*), seems to trigger in Prieston a desire to clarify his relationship to his own past here in the autumn of this year and, more figuratively, of his life. Though Prieston is reluctant to visit Yale and the "ghosts" which haunt that place in his mind, another part of him is perhaps detached enough by the intervening years to review that earlier self–though not without trepidation. "The past was a treasure and a fragile one," Prieston declares early in the novel. "Wasn't the past the only thing we truly possessed, irrevocable and unchangeable? It was there, the ballast of our lives, stabilizing us. Should it ever be disturbed, tampered with, even revisited?" The notion that the past is a "possession" is an important one, since it implies that an individual might do otherwise than "own" his past, be it self-created or inherited; for instance, he might attempt to disown it in any of several ways, or it might be somehow stolen from him, or it might be somehow misplaced. Thus, while the past as a shaping force might be per se "irrevocable and unchangeable," people are still obliged to come to their individual terms with that force. This concept, integrated as it is in this novel with the struggle posed in so many of Knowles's earlier works between that part of the individual shaped by the "irrevocable and unchangeable" cultural and climatic conditions of his past (and devoted to preserving its value) and that other part of the individual, that "germ of wildness" committed to freeing itself of any entangling alliances with the past or with other people's values and expectations, accounts for much of the pattern and plot of *A Stolen Past*.

Using flashbacks to connect the events of 1980 with those of 1950-1951, the novel focuses on the developing relationships among three pairs of major characters. The most obvious figures of the past are the Princess Zinaida Petrovna and her husband Prince Alexis Gregorievich Trouvenskoy, the parents of the narrator's college roommate, Greg. The necessity for these members of the Old Russian aristocracy to abandon their shaping culture and country and to try to re-create lives for themselves in America leaves Naida and Alexis with unresolvably dual cultural identities: for all their willed Americanization, the elder Trouvenskoys still perform the samovar ceremony on special occasions. The figures of a gracefully acculturated New England past are Reeves Lockhart, Yale's writer in residence, winner of three Pulitzer Prizes in drama and fiction, and the narrator's adoptive mentor, and his companion Millicent Montcrieff, a small, energetic, and gracious woman still alive in 1980 to serve as a living link between the narrator and his own improperly buried past. Completing the troika of paired lives in this novel are Greg Trouvenskoy, a "study in insouciance" and a veteran of World War II who is attending Yale on the G.I. bill, and his fiancée, Merryfield Carr. All seven of these characters are presented both as heirs–in some ways beneficiaries, in others victims–and as transmitters of their own and one another's pasts.

The most obvious symbol of the past as a "fragile treasure" is the Militsya Diamond, a "complexly cut octagonal bluish" stone worth one hundred thousand dollars, which the Trouvenskoys keep in a wall safe. To Naida, the diamond represents the lost splendor of the Romanoff dynasty as well as the lost (but still recoverable in memory) gift of her own youth. To Alexis, the diamond represents a potential gift of freedom to his son, a possible means of securing for Greg the American dream of the freedom to invent a life which the older Trouvenskoys cannot pursue directly. The theft of the diamond not only violates the small but precious comfort which this concrete emblem of their past provides the Trouvenskoys but also shatters their projections of future redemption of their lives. Much of the tragedy of the Trouvenskoys' lives is that the Militsya Diamond could *be* such an apt image of their lives; very precious, exquisitely multifaceted, but also small and defensively secreted, and terribly susceptible to irretrievable loss.

Compounding the tragedy in the novel, it is Greg Trouvenskoy who steals and sells the Militsya Diamond, ostensibly to obtain enough money to court Merryfield Carr, a debutante attending Vassar, but more generally to underwrite his dream of personal autonomy; as Prieston observes of Greg and Merry in 1950, "Both of them were very downright and unpretentious, he about his *passé* royal blood, she about her money. Those were accidents of birth, and [they] seemed determined to be evaluated for themselves and not for the appurtenances they happened to possess." At least one reviewer has seen echoes of *The Great Gatsby* in this novel (early on, the narrator mentions having regarded it in his college days as a near-perfect work), and no doubt Knowles intends his readers to see something of Gatsby's motives for pursuing Daisy in Greg's quintessentially American pursuit of Merry. For Greg, the Trouvenskoy legacy is an intolerable burden cluttered with ghosts and motives he cannot understand. Forced by circumstances to declare allegiance either to the shaping powers of his parents' White Russian past or to his own internal desire to create a life for himself, free of such a priori restraints, he "impulsively" opts for the latter; and though this strategy gives him greater control of his own future, it also burdens him inevitably with the guilt of having betrayed his own parents.

As Prieston's mentor, Reeves Lockhart, declares at one point in the novel, the diamond theft is part of a "domestic drama," and he subtly advises Prieston to let it remain just that. But it becomes more than that when the narrator willingly involves himself in the affair—partly out of altruistic motives, to be sure, but also partly because as a budding writer he is excited by the dramatic possibilities inherent in the case and by the chance to manipulate those possibilities. Hence he, too, comes to know guilt when he realizes that he was not above capitalizing on the suffering of the Trouvenskoys, in a sense stealing their present agony to add to his own store of experience; and indeed the narrative he presents in 1980 depends on some such capitalization. In this sense, the events of 1950-1951 which inform Prieston's narrative are, by Prieston's own quiet confession, themselves a "stolen past." Prieston's own assessment of his complicity in such thefts is best articulated at the end of the novel when, responding finally to a question posed by Millicent Montcrieff in the first chapter of the novel regarding what he "lost" by involving himself in the Militsya Diamond affair, he allows that as a result of coming to understand his role he is now "tougher, coarser, more impatient [. . . .] I'm no gentleman. I'm dedicated. I'm a mischievous, conniving rascal and a cheat: I'm a writer."

Knowles's reputation, as of this writing, is based almost entirely on his achievement in *A Separate Peace*. Only occasionally have any of his subsequent works received unqualified praise in a major book review, and none has drawn substantial critical attention. At its best, Knowles's work is generally regarded as showing admirably his "understanding of emotion and a sensitivity to the psychological struggles between love and enmity, between loyalty and freedom, between the need to accept guilt and the need to be absolved from it"; the flaws in his later works are generally attributed to a characteristic "mechanical neatness" in Knowles's handling of plot and setting as vehicles for dramatizing these psychological struggles, a handling which strikes many reviewers as being contrived. Critics both pro and con, however, generally concur in their assessment of Knowles as both master craftsman and a serious student of that seemingly irreducible dualism he perceives at the heart of the American character.

References:

Bernard Carragher, "There Really Was a Super Suicide Society," *New York Times*, 8 October 1972, II: 1, 17-18.

Relates the comments of Knowles and John Heyl, who played the role of Phineas in the 1971 film version of *A Separate Peace*, about Phillips Exeter Academy.

James Ellis, " 'A Separate Peace': The Fall from Innocence," *English Journal*, 53 (May 1964): 313-318.

Discusses the themes of loss of innocence, escape, and coming of age; the seasonal imagery; the symbolism of two rivers; and the war/peace dichotomy.

John Gardner, "More Smog from the Dark Satanic Mills," *Southern Review*, 5 (Winter 1969): 224-244.

Sardonic review of *Indian Summer*, calling the novel a "brainless sermon" and criticizes Knowles's inconsistent use of "hoked-up symbols."

Franziska Lynne Greiling, "The Theme of Freedom in 'A Separate Peace,' " *English Journal*, 56 (December 1967): 1269-1272.

Sees the character of Phineas as a personification of the Platonic ideal and discusses the theme of freedom in the tradition of fifth-century Greece.

Jay L. Halio, "John Knowles's Short Novels," *Studies in Short Fiction*, 1 (Winter 1964): 107-112.
Claims that *Morning in Antibes* completes the search for identity begun in the earlier, and superior, novel, *A Separate Peace*.

Wayne J. Henkel, "Pas de Feux," *Washington Post Book World*, 23 June 1974, p. 2.
Criticizes *Spreading Fires* for its "pulp tale tackiness" and classifies the characters as "wet kindling," while briefly praising Knowles's "beautifully rendered" style and "subtle word play."

James L. McDonald, "The Novels of John Knowles," *Arizona Quarterly*, 23 (Winter 1967): 335-342.
Sees Knowles as a novelist of manners in the tradition of Henry James, F. Scott Fitzgerald, and a naturalist in the tradition of Theodore Dreiser.

Ronald Weber, "Narrative Method in 'A Separate Peace,'" *Studies in Short Fiction*, 3 (Fall 1965): 63-72.
Comparing the novel with J. D. Salinger's *The Catcher in the Rye*, discusses the use of narrative devices to further the coming-of-age theme.

Ursula K. Le Guin

This entry was updated by Nancy Barendse (University of South Carolina) from the entry by Brian Attebery (College of Idaho) in DLB 8, Twentieth-Century American Science Fiction Writers *and from the entry by Andrew Gordon (University of Florida) in* DLB 52, American Writers for Children Since 1960: Fiction.

Places	Berkeley, Cal.	Portland, Oreg.	
Influences and Relationships	J. R. R. Tolkien Philip K. Dick Sir James Frazer Leo Tolstoy	Ivan Turgenev Cordwainer Smith Lord Dunsany Italo Calvino	Anton Chekhov Boris Pasternak E. M. Forster
Literary Movements and Forms	Romanticism Science Fiction	Children's Fiction	Fantasy
Major Themes	Archetypes Identity Coming of Age Balance / Wholeness	Journey / Process / Cycles De-Alienation Pacifism	*Wu-wie* (action through stillness) Stereotypes
Cultural and Artistic Influences	Mythology Fairy Tales Cultural Anthropology	Psychoanalysis Ludwig van Beethoven Dream Research	*Tao Te Ching* Jungian Psychology Franz Schubert
Social and Economic Influences	Anarchism Feminism	1960s Peace Movement	Ecology Movement

BIRTH: Berkeley, California, 21 October 1929, to Alfred Louis and Theodora Kracaw Brown Kroeber.

EDUCATION: A.B., Radcliffe College, 1951; A.M., Columbia University, 1952.

MARRIAGE: 22 December 1953 to Charles A. Le Guin; children: Elisabeth, Caroline, Theodore.

AWARDS: Fulbright Fellowship, 1953; Boston Globe-Horn Book Award for *A Wizard of Earthsea*, 1969; Nebula Award for *The Left Hand of Darkness*, 1969; Hugo Award for *The Left Hand of Darkness*, 1970; Newbery Silver Medal Award for *The Tombs of Atuan*, 1972; Hugo Award for "The Word for World Is Forest," 1973; National Book Award for Children's Literature for *The Farthest Shore*, 1973; Hugo Award for "The Ones Who Walk Away from Omelas," 1974; Nebula Award for "The Day Before the Revolution," 1974; Jupiter Award for "The Day Before the Revolution," 1974; Nebula Award for *The Dispossessed*, 1974; Jupiter Award for *The Dispossessed*, 1974; Hugo Award for *The Dispossessed*, 1975; Jupiter Award for "The Diary of the Rose," 1976; Gandalf Award for the writing of fantasy, 1979; Janet Heidinger Kafka Award for *Always Coming Home*, 1986; Prix Lectures-Jainesse for *Very Far Away from Anywhere Else*, 1987.

BOOKS: *Rocannon's World* (New York: Ace, 1966; London: Tandem, 1972);
Planet of Exile (New York: Ace, 1966; London: Tandem, 1972);
City of Illusions (New York: Ace, 1967; London: Gollancz, 1971);
A Wizard of Earthsea (Berkeley: Parnassus, 1968; London: Gollancz, 1971);
The Left Hand of Darkness (New York: Ace, 1969; London: Macdonald, 1969);
The Tombs of Atuan (New York: Atheneum, 1971; London: Gollancz, 1972);
The Lathe of Heaven (New York: Scribners, 1971; London: Gollancz, 1972);
The Farthest Shore (New York: Atheneum, 1972; London: Gollancz, 1973);
From Elfland to Poughkeepsie (Portland, Oreg.: Pendragon, 1973);
The Dispossessed: An Ambiguous Utopia (New York: Harper & Row, 1974; London: Gollancz, 1974);

Ursula K. Le Guin (photo by Lisa Kroeber)

The Wind's Twelve Quarters (New York: Harper & Row, 1975; London: Gollancz, 1976);
Wild Angels (Santa Barbara, Cal.: Capra, 1975);
The Word for World Is Forest (New York: Berkley, 1976; London: Gollancz, 1977);
Very Far Away from Anywhere Else (New York: Atheneum, 1976); republished as *A Very Long Way from Anywhere Else* (London: Gollancz, 1976);
Orsinian Tales (New York: Harper & Row, 1976; London: Gollancz, 1977);
Dreams Must Explain Themselves (New York: Algol, 1979);
The Language of the Night: Essays on Fantasy and Science Fiction, edited by Susan Wood (New York: Berkley/Putnam's, 1979);
Malafrena (New York: Putnam's, 1979);
Leese Webster (New York: Atheneum, 1979);
The Beginning Place (New York: Harper & Row, 1980); republished as *Threshold* (London: Gollancz, 1980);
Hard Words (New York: Harper & Row, 1981);
The Adventure of Cobbler's Rune (New Castle, Va.: Cheap Street, 1982);
The Compass Rose (New York: Harper, 1982);

The Eye of the Heron (New York: Harper & Row, 1983; London: Gollancz, 1983);

Solomon Leviathan's Nine Hundred and Thirty-First Trip Around the World (New Castle, Va.: Cheap Street, 1983);

The Visionary: The Life Story of Flicker of the Serpentine (Santa Barbara, Cal.: Capra, 1983);

Always Coming Home (New York: Harper, 1985);

Buffalo Gals and Other Animal Presences (Santa Barbara, Cal.: Capra, 1987);

Catwings (Shapleigh, Maine: Orchard, 1988);

A Visit from Dr. Katz (New York: Atheneum, 1988);

Wild Oats and Fireweed (New York: Harper & Row, 1988);

Dancing at the Edge of the World: Thoughts on Words, Women, Places (New York: Grove, 1989).

OTHER: *Nebula Award Stories Eleven*, edited by Le Guin (London: Gollancz, 1976; New York: Harper, 1977);

"The Diary of the Rose," in *Future Power*, edited by Jack Dann and Gardner Dozois (New York: Dutton, 1977);

Interfaces: An Anthology of Speculative Fiction, edited by Le Guin and Virginia Kidd (New York: Ace, 1980);

Edges, edited by Le Guin and Kidd (New York: Pocket Books, 1980).

PERIODICAL PUBLICATIONS: "On Norman Spinrad's *The Iron Dream*," *Science-Fiction Studies*, 1 (Spring 1973): 41-44;

"Surveying the Battlefield," *Science-Fiction Studies*, 1 (Fall 1973): 88-90;

"European SF: Rottensteiner's Anthology, the Strugatskys, and Lem," *Science-Fiction Studies*, 1 (Spring 1974): 181-185;

"Ketterer on *The Left Hand of Darkness*," *Science-Fiction Studies*, 2 (July 1975): 137-139;

"A Response to the Le Guin Issue," *Science-Fiction Studies*, 3 (Spring 1976): 43-46;

"The Space Crone," *The CoEvolution Quarterly*, 10 (Summer 1976): 108-111.

Ursula K. Le Guin is a writer of great versatility and power, acclaimed for her science fiction, fantasy, and children's literature. All her fiction is distinguished by careful craftsmanship, a limpid prose style, realistic detail in the creation of imaginary worlds, profound ethical concerns, and mythical reverberations created through the use of symbolic and archetypal patterns. Her typical story involves a hero's quest for maturity and psy-chological integration, and her major theme is the need for balance and wholeness. Her goal in writing is to show her readers themselves and their lives at a distance, the better to create orderly patterns out of random information.

Ursula K. Le Guin was born in Berkeley, California, in 1929, the youngest of four children and the only daughter of Alfred and Theodora Kroeber. Her father was a renowned professor of anthropology, an expert on California Indians; her mother was an author in her own right, with several children's books published by Parnassus Press, but best known for *Ishi in Two Worlds* (1961), the biography of the last "wild" Indian in North America. Le Guin grew up in Berkeley in a secure and intellectually stimulating environment. Her parents were progressive and non-sexist in childrearing. The house was filled with books, and her father was frequently visited by major figures in anthropology and other fields. She claims that her parents' interest in anthropology strongly influenced her writing: "My father studied real cultures and I make them up–in a way, it's the same thing."

As a child, Le Guin wanted to be a biologist and a poet. She read widely as a youngster, preferring Frazer's *Golden Bough*, Norse myths, and science-fiction magazines, though she temporarily lost interest in science fiction as she matured. As she explained in *The Language of the Night* (1979), "it seemed to be all about hardware and soldiers." Lord Dunsany's *A Dreamer's Tales*, which she encountered at age twelve, was a revelation to her, making her realize that grown-ups were still creating myths. It opened up to her "the Inner Lands" which she calls "my native country."

Le Guin wrote her first fantasy story at nine, about a man persecuted by evil elves, and submitted her first science fiction, a story about time travel that she wrote when she was ten or eleven, to *Amazing Stories*. It was rejected, but *Amazing Stories* was to publish her first science fiction more than twenty years later. She received a B.A., Phi Beta Kappa, from Radcliffe in 1951 and an M.A. in French and Italian Renaissance literature from Columbia in 1952. On a Fulbright Fellowship to France in 1953, she met and married a fellow Fulbrighter, history professor Charles A. Le Guin. She abandoned graduate studies to raise a family: the Le Guins have three children and reside in Portland, Oregon.

Le Guin started writing, according to an introductory note in her short-story collection, *The*

Wind's Twelve Quarters (1975), at about age five. She wrote poetry, some of which was published, and stories, which were not. In the note she mentions a science-fiction story written in 1942, when she was twelve. It was rejected by John Campbell, the editor of *Astounding Science-Fiction*. Her next try at the genre was accepted by Cele Goldsmith Lalli for *Fantastic*–twenty years later. That story, "April in Paris" (collected in *The Wind's Twelve Quarters*), was her first published piece of fiction. It is a lightly comic time-travel story using her knowledge of medieval France. Several more stories appeared in the mid 1960s. One of them, "The Dowry of the Angyar" (1965), or, to use the title Le Guin prefers, "Semley's Necklace" (*Amazing*, 1964; collected in *The Wind's Twelve Quarters*), grew into her first published novel, *Rocannon's World* (1966). Another, "Winter's King" (*Orbit 5*, 1969; collected in *The Wind's Twelve Quarters*), established the setting for her first major critical success, *The Left Hand of Darkness* (1969). These stories and novels, along with two intermediate works, *Planet of Exile* (1966) and *City of Illusions* (1967), form a loosely organized future history usually referred to as the Hainish cycle after the original race of humanity who are said to have arisen on the planet Hain and colonized other planets, including Earth, until galactic war isolated the various human settlements. All of Le Guin's Hainish stories take place long after the war and a subsequent dark age and cover about twenty-five hundred years, during which contact is gradually being reestablished with the colony worlds. In the meantime, however, most of these colonies have forgotten their origin, and many of their humanoid inhabitants vary widely from "Hainish normal" biologically as well as culturally, altered by time and independent evolution and perhaps, as it is suspected of the androgynous Gethenians of *The Left Hand of Darkness*, by biological experiments conducted by the ancient Hainish. The Hainish cycle also includes *The Dispossessed: An Ambiguous Utopia* (1974), the novella *The Word for World Is Forest* (1976), and two more of the stories in *The Wind's Twelve Quarters*, "Vaster Than Empires and More Slow" (*New Dimensions 1*, 1971) and "The Day Before the Revolution" (*Galaxy*, 1974). These last four are set centuries before *The Left Hand of Darkness*, which represents the furthest point in time of the cycle so far.

All of her stories are about reciprocal relationships. There is a sort of golden rule in her fictional world, which states that whatever you touch touches you. This golden rule has a scientific backing in ecology; it also has philosophical underpinnings in Taoism and in Zen. Le Guin is uncomfortable when critics claim her as a great and original thinker, for she works best with what she calls "fortune cookie ideas," ideas proposed by someone else and capable of expression in very simple terms. Beginning with such an idea–ecological balance, for example–she can show through her stories how simple terms hide a mass of complexity and contradiction that surfaces only when the idea interacts with human lives.

Gaverel Rocannon, the protagonist of *Rocannon's World*, is an ethnologist specializing in alien cultures. In "Semley's Necklace," which serves as a prologue to the novel, he is a minor character whose primary function is to comment on the action, his wistfully scientific outlook contrasting effectively with the high-flown, legendary quality of the rest of the story. In the novel he is the central figure in a quest that grows increasingly mythlike. Seeking revenge for the destruction of his ethnographic survey team, he sets out with a group of native friends to warn his home world about the rebels who have set up a military base on Fomalhaut II, later known as Rocannon's World. His most important companions are the aristocratic warrior Mogien, the servant Yahan, and the elf Kyo. Each has a different view of Rocannon and his quest: to Mogien, Rocannon is a warrior avenging his honor; to Yahan, Rocannon is a powerful wizard fighting the evil magicians who are laying waste to the world; to Kyo, Rocannon is a man fulfilling a strange and wonderful fate. A series of encounters with thieves, nature, and various alien beings serves to reinforce each view of Rocannon, according to each companion's perspective. Yet at the same time Rocannon's own view remains the central one and the view the reader is most likely to have. Rocannon sees himself as "an ordinary League scientist," middle-aged, physically unprepossessing, and fundamentally peaceable. In the end he plays the traditional mythic hero's role by gaining a great gift at high cost. His treasure is the ability to make contact with other minds telepathically. He uses the gift as a weapon against his enemies and as a consequence must share the experience of their deaths. After the book's climax he seems to fade away, consumed in the legend that is growing around him. One hopes, however, that he will pass on his gift to others, freed of its penalty by his own sacrifice.

Other themes in the novel impress themselves on the reader almost independently of the story's color and adventure: the conflict between rationality and an irrational universe, the responsibilities of a technologically advanced civilization in dealing with a less advanced society, the danger of judging from prejudice, the wonder of establishing ties with someone different from oneself, and the tragedy of having to take up violent means to defend oneself against violent adversaries. Rocannon is the rational being in an irrational world: a scientist in the midst of legend. He learns that truth hangs suspended somewhere between his notions of cause and effect and his friends' belief in spells and talismans. He comes to respect their understanding of the world and their way of life as valid alternatives to his own, the knowledge of which enriches his life. As an anthropologist, he objects to the manipulation of this recently discovered planet by the League of All Worlds and puts a stop to its use as a weapon in a cosmic arms race.

Prejudice takes many forms in the novel. The Centaurans who made the initial contact with Fomalhaut II chose to deal only with the crafty, cave-dwelling, tool-making Gdemiar, or Clayfolk, ignoring the other intelligent races on the planet and thus upsetting carefully balanced interspecies relationships. Rocannon makes a similar mistake in assuming intelligence in the tall, humanoid, winged creatures of the southern plains and in failing to recognize it in the small, furry, furtive beings who live among them. The former turn out to be mindless predators, while the latter are not only intelligent but friendly, saving the lives of Rocannon and his companions. Rocannon's life is saved several times in the novel. These rescues serve not only to advance the plot but also to point out how vulnerable man is alone and how dependent upon the goodwill of friends and strangers. By seeking out individuals unlike himself, meeting them on their own ground, offering them his loyalty and accepting theirs, Rocannon not only completes his quest but also raises its significance beyond a mere exercise in warfare. His passing alters the world he travels through, so it is appropriate that it be given his name.

Le Guin's second novel takes up the same themes: prejudice, technology, clashing worldviews, and communication across barriers of race and culture. In *Planet of Exile* the telepathic skills won by Rocannon have become codified mental disciplines taught throughout the League of All Worlds. The novel deals with a League colony which has, for unknown reasons, been abandoned. Left without a spaceship or ansible (Le Guin's term for an instantaneous message transmitter), the colony on Werel has struggled to preserve its cultural heritage without unduly influencing the native cultures for a period of ten Werelian years—each equivalent to more than sixty Earth or League years. As the book opens, the planet is entering winter, a brutal season lasting a quarter of a lifetime.

As in *Rocannon's World*, there is conflict in this story between two cultures, one technological, the other atechnological and illiterate. There are some interesting reversals in this pair of opposing civilizations, however, that prevent our reading the book as a conventional meeting between civilized explorers and colorful savages. The native Tevarians, who live a life so marginal that they have not invented the wheel or learned to sing, are fair-skinned. The colonists from Earth are dark. The colonists practice a variety of psi skills: the skeptical natives view their neighbors as witches. Both groups are inbred and stagnant. The Earthmen are gradually losing the knowledge and skills their ancestors brought with them. Their numbers are shrinking because of a high incidence of infertility and spontaneous abortion. Their body chemistry is alien to the planet: no microorganisms will attack them, but neither can they eat native foods without special medication. The native population is not decreasing, but they have not furthered their way of life for many generations, and there is no place among them for exceptional individuals like the girl Rolery.

The stalemate between these two cultures is broken by the combined onslaught of winter and the nomadic, plundering Gaal, a rival native culture. Finding a common enemy gives the two groups a common cause. The catalyst bringing them together at last is the Romeo-and-Juliet love between Rolery, the only native born in summer, out of season, and Jakob Agat, a young leader of the colonists. Since the natives are truly aliens, separated long enough by time and perhaps by experiment from their ancient Hainish ancestors to have become almost a separate hominoid species, the love of Jakob and Rolery carries an onus of miscegenation in addition to the division between the two societies.

This star-crossed romance is brought about by a mistake. Jakob warns Rolery by mindspeech, or telepathy, when she is in danger of drowning in the incoming tide, even though telepathic contact with the natives is strictly forbidden. The initial contact establishes a bond between the two. They meet again when Jakob goes to Rolery's ancient father, Wold, to ask his aid in fighting the approaching Gaal hordes. Angry Tevarians see them meeting in a forest hut and attack Jakob, breaking off the uneasy truce he has engineered with Wold.

When the Gaal attack, Wold's village is destroyed, and the survivors seek refuge in the city of the farborn, or colonists, where Rolery is already Jakob's wife. Together, the two groups hold off the Gaal until the first winter storms put an end to fighting and the Gaal move south. During the fighting, the colonists discover themselves to be, for the first time, susceptible to infection. They have begun to adapt to their adopted world and may even prove able to interbreed with natives. Jakob and Rolery are the beginning of a new, vigorous, hybrid race.

Telepathy is again a metaphor for communion between unlike individuals. In the case of Jakob and Rolery it grows into love and the redemption of two societies. But mental powers, as in *Rocannon's World*, can be misused. The old farborn woman, Alla Pasfal, uses her psychic skills to overhear the thoughts of the Gaal. Misunderstanding what she hears, the colonists are unprepared for a last, devastating attack. To make communication into a one-sided thing, in which one ventures nothing oneself but only takes from others, is a major sin in Le Guin's universe, and it is duly punished. But to reach out, to take off one's mental armor before a stranger, is a heroic act that always results in some good. *Planet of Exile* contains a clearer statement than ever before of Le Guin's central theme that the "other" that one fears is really one's most important potential ally, because he or she, being different, has what one lacks. In *Planet of Exile* everything centers on Werel's long, violent year. Trees live a single season, specialized plants bloom between winter snows, birds and animals make long migrations, and people spend years preparing for the oncoming cold. Details are striking and plentiful. The reader finishes the book with a sense of having experienced that immense turning of the seasons.

Cultural details are also more carefully depicted than in the earlier novel. The proud half-empty city of the farborn and the winter camp of the natives are presented with equal care and compassion. The portrayal of both cultures is abetted

by occasional looks from one to the other: one sees the farborn through the eyes of both Rolery and Wold, and one sees the scornful picture of native life held by many of the colonists. A scene such as the rock-pounding council of the natives is seen from the inside as a time-honored mainstay of tribal harmony and from the outside as a comically barbaric rite.

Characters, too, are strong in this work. Agat is much like Rocannon and equally attractive. Rolery is a woman in a culture that pays little attention to women, but it is her act of daring that sets events in motion and her endurance that saves Agat's life. She questions, experiments, adapts, and mediates between her people and the farborn. Wold, the old chieftain, is the most memorable of all. He is earthy, crafty, forgetful, and immensely dignified. A strong and rebellious warrior in youth, he is a wise leader in old age. He shares his people's prejudice against the farborn, but he rises above it in his dealings with individual colonists. Alone among his people he remembers the previous winter, and he is willing to drop pride and mistrust in the interests of survival.

The weaknesses in *Planet of Exile* have to do with conflicts between plot and theme. There is considerable reduplication of adversaries: the Gaal, winter, and the grotesque snowghouls represent the same threat, and it is a threat imposed from outside, not one which grows from the acts and thoughts of the principal characters. Having an outside adversary is not necessarily a flaw, but it lessens the importance of the rapprochement of Earthman and alien. *Planet of Exile* is nevertheless an enjoyable story and might seem more satisfying if Le Guin had not shown in *The Left Hand of Darkness* what more could be done with the same materials.

One learns why the colony in *Planet of Exile* was cut off in Le Guin's next novel, *City of Illusions*. A hostile race called the Shing has conquered the League of All Worlds and has taken Earth for the capital planet. Mankind on Earth exists in isolated pockets kept by their Shing overseers from making any real advancements or joining forces to share what knowledge is left to them. The book begins with a nameless amnesiac who appears mysteriously in the vast forests of occupied Earth. He is found by a young girl named Parth in the clearing near her forest home. Although he knows nothing, not even how to speak, he learns quickly from Parth and the other members of her small community. They name him Falk, meaning yellow, because of his strange golden eyes. When he has learned all that they can teach him, he decides to set out for Es Toch, the legendary city of the Shing, far away in the western mountains, to find out who he is.

Falk's quest is a journey toward his own maturation through a landscape that complements the stages of his growth. His path leads from the simplicity of the forest to the savagery of the prairies to the unexpected sophistication of the desert to the uneasy civilization of the mountains. There is a hidden valley in the forest where animals speak, and where men are brutal because of their fears. Many of the groups and individuals he meets along the way are notable. An old man has isolated himself from other men because he is a powerful empath, one who reads feelings as a telepath reads thoughts, and he cannot stand the presence of so many emotions; he welcomes Falk, however, and gives him important information. A tribe of wandering herdsmen lives rigidly controlled lives of custom and taboo amid the boundless openness of the prairie. A woman, Estrel, is, like Falk, imprisoned by the herdsmen. They escape together, and she becomes his guide and lover. Ultimately she betrays him, as suggested by her unwillingness to return Falk's confidences or his physical passion. She manipulates him by playing the passive sexual object. The Prince of Kansas, an old man with some of the kingly madness of Othello or Lear, reads Falk's fortune on a device called a patterning frame. The picture of him working it strongly suggests fate or some god ordering the movements of the universe: "Turquoise shot to the left and a double link of polished bone set with garnets looped off to the right and down, while a fire-opal blazed for a moment in the dead center of the frame. Black, lean, strong hands flashed over the wires, playing with the jewels of life and death." Falk's fortune is read twice, on different patterning frames, and both times the yellow stone that represents him refuses to conform to any known pattern except the mystical configuration known as Vastness. Falk thus represents the unknown, the outsider who will break the deformed pattern imposed by the Shing upon the Earth.

Falk reaches his goal—the glass city of Es Toch—almost halfway through the book and then discovers that he has an equal mental and moral distance left to traverse. The Shing confuse him: they treat him with alternating roughness and concern; they lie and then refute their own lies;

their city is made of glass, but the glass is murky so that nothing shows clearly through the floors, walls, and ceilings of its towers. They produce a boy who claims to be of Falk's people, like him a traveler from another world. They offer to restore Falk's memories but say the operation will unavoidably destroy his personality, the self he has built up since he first appeared in the forest. They even tell him that there are no Shing: they are men, they say, maintaining a fiction for the benefit of other men, who would otherwise turn to warfare and destruction. Estrel may or may not be one of their agents. Falk must find his way through all these webs of half-truths and outright lies.

He decides to let them restore his former self, to trade his memories for those of Agad Ramarren, descendant of Jakob Agat of *Planet of Exile*, navigator for the first Werelian expedition to Earth. But he also plants a clue by which his old self might discover and incorporate the new. It is a clue so subtle that even the Shing will not detect it, merely a passage from the so-called Old Canon of man: "The way that can be gone / is not the eternal Way. / The name that can be named / is not the eternal Name." Falk meditates on that passage, which is Le Guin's adaptation of the opening of the Taoist book, *Tao Te Ching*, until it becomes so much a part of him, body and soul, that it might become a road for his return from the nothingness into which the Shing wish to cast him. He succeeds—the memory carries across the imposed mental block—and two personalities, Falk and Ramarren, coexist in one brain. The combined knowledge and strengths of his two selves help him outwit the Shing, penetrate their lies, and escape. He sets out for his home planet, presumably to help prepare the way for ultimate victory over the Shing and the eventual establishment of a new and more humanely conceived League of All Worlds.

The great lie of the Shing, which Falk/ Ramarren penetrates, is their one law: "It is wrong to take life." It is a lie because it pretends to be adequate and inflexible, because it denies conscience and moral complexity. The Shing allow themselves to cheat and mistreat mankind in any way short of causing death. As Falk comments, they made a law about killing because it is the only thing they really desire to do. The lie is accompanied by one great secret, hinted at by the old empath in the forest: the Shing are sterile. There are few of them, and they cannot mate with humans. Their position is much like that of the colonists on Werel, except that those colonists finally reached across to their neighbors, mentally and physically, and were able thus to renew their race. The Shing cannot even communicate with mankind. They defeated the worlds of the League by their ability to mind-lie. No one else could tell a lie telepathically, and the League was built on that fact. But the Shing cannot send thoughts directly; they can only project what seem to be true thoughts. This inability, which they use as a weapon, is their tragedy. Lacking truth, they devote themselves to falsehood. Their culture emphasizes perversion; their architecture relies on illusion and disorientation. Falk, who vows as he sets out on his journey never to tell an untruth, is able to confound their lives with his trust.

Running counter to the law of the Shing is a theme that helps unify the novel despite its shifts in locale and its mazes of falsehood. It is the Way, the Tao. Falk is seeking his own Way, the path to his true nature, which cannot be guided by arbitrary rules like the Shing law. He carries with him a copy of the Old Canon when he begins his journey: it is stolen by the fearful men who capture him in the forest. The old empath is a Thurro-dowist—he lives his life according to Taoist teachings augmented with Thoreau's *Walden*, the Younger Canon. The Prince of Kansas gives Falk another copy of the *Tao Te Ching* to replace the one he lost, and it is that copy which enables him to retain his personality.

Earlier sections of the book reveal Le Guin's growing authority over her material. The forest is deftly, quickly built up with relatively few images. It already carries the connotations of sleep, dream, and the origins of things, which will become important in later stories about forests. The physical setting throughout seems solid and alive, as if Le Guin were taking real pleasure in exploring an unspoiled America. Emotional relationships take on new complexity in this novel. The Prince of Kansas is a minor character but an impressive one: his section is as packed with implication as a poem. Language is generally used more tellingly than in earlier works with less feeling of ornamentation, more of conviction. Symbols develop unobtrusively and are picked up later for further investigation in such a way that one would never suspect them of having been purposefully planted. As Falk journeys down the Ohio River, for instance, he encounters an illusion of a boating party from a long-vanished city. He is in-

vited to return with the members but fears some trap; the illusion may have been produced by the Shing. But the promise in his mind, the image of a thriving human city, helps him later to reject Es Toch because it is not a true, living city. The image expands beyond its original context in an unexpected direction and enriches the story without ever seeming to impose itself upon the reader.

Each of these first three novels holds out the promise of better work to come. In *The Left Hand of Darkness* their individual strengths—*Rocannon's World*'s interplay of legend and science, *Planet of Exile*'s clash of cultures, *City of Illusions*'s controlled use of symbolism and its ethical base—are combined and the promise fulfilled. Le Guin's previous books were all narrated anonymously by someone outside the story. The narrator of *The Left Hand of Darkness* is also its protagonist, Genly Ai, a native of Earth sent to a planet called Winter or Gethen. Ai is the lone envoy of a post-League organization, the Ekumen, which is not so much a political body as an idea and a hope of free commerce and communication among far-flung worlds. The Ekumen has mystical overtones reminiscent of the Instrumentality of Man in the novels and stories of Cordwainer Smith, who is one of the few science-fiction writers Le Guin acknowledges as an influence. Genly Ai comes alone to Gethen bearing the message to its natives that they are not alone in the universe, that there is a family of similar worlds which they are invited to join. He is alone because a lone alien will generate curiosity without triggering fear, but behind him stands a wise and benevolent organization that has learned from the mistakes of its predecessor and from the conflict with the Shing. He is an apostle of the gospel of peaceful interdependence.

Genly Ai is not old, wise, and experienced. He is young, fervent, and often mistaken in his judgments of people and events. He is telling a story that is still very close to him and still painful, and he resorts to a rich variety of methods to tell it. Into his narrative he pulls reports by previous Ekumenical observers, recorded myths and legends from different parts of Gethen, and the diaries of his principal ally, Therem Harth rem ir Estraven, who he does not even know is an ally until late in the story.

The story is Ai's own report to the Ekumen, but it is no impersonal listing of contacts and treaties. The Ekumen would not be satisfied by that sort of thing, nor would Ai consider it sufficient.

He says, at the outset, "I'll make my report as if I told a story, for I was taught as a child on my homeworld that Truth is a matter of the imagination. The soundest fact may fail or prevail in the style of its telling: like that singular organic jewel of our seas, which grows brighter as one woman wears it and, worn by another, dulls and goes to dust." Le Guin makes good use of her narrator and of his complex relationship with the events he is recounting. He is sensitive enough to allow her to display her gifts for description and metaphoric analysis; he is fallible enough to generate considerable tension through gaps in understanding; and he is deeply enough involved in the story to lend it tremendous emotional weight.

An important aspect of the book is the culture in which it is set. The story begins with a parade, an exotic, colorful ritual surviving from Gethen's distant past. There is no military aspect to this parade; instead of soldiers there are merchants, lords, and entertainers. The cars in the parade are electric, one discovers later. This is no backward world to be conquered or raised up by civilized invaders, nor is it a mechanistic wonderland. Instead of either of these clichés, it is a culture approximately on a level with our own, a rarity in science fiction. Gethen, or this particular part of it, Karhide, is a monarchy, and the purpose of the parade is to accompany the king to the dedication of a new bridge. Ai's talk with his neighbors at the ceremony contains little details that begin to fix Karhide in the reader's mind. More of the capital city of Erhenrang is seen as Ai returns to his home, and more is learned about its climate, history, and social organization. An unfamiliar word appears in passing–"kemmer"–and then a related form, "kemmering." Ai goes to dinner at Estraven's home, and only then is the important fact about Gethen revealed: its people are neither men nor women. They are androgynes, sexless except for their periods of sexual potency–kemmer–during which they may take on the characteristics of either sex. This is further explained by a Karhidish tale about two "brothers," one of whom bears the other's child. The Gethenian sexual arrangement does not become the central issue of the story but develops into an effective vehicle for exploring the implications of sexual differentiation. It is a part, though not usually the commanding element, of every institution in Karhide.

The dominant influence upon Gethen is its climate. The physical environment becomes a third noticeable feature, after narrator and culture. Gethen is cold, even in the tropics; elsewhere there is nothing but ice fields and volcanoes. Life is marginal, and because of the cold, change is slow. Time-tested traditions survive into the machine age virtually intact. People dress in furs, travel cautiously, gather together in great communal dwellings, eat much and often, conserve every resource. They have innumerable words for ice, fog, and snow. Feuds are common, but full-scale warfare is unknown–though the novel suggests that this may be due to a lack of masculine aggressiveness. As the story progresses, its background of cold and ice intensifies until at the climax there is nothing in sight but two people and a sled on an immense field of ice. Le Guin says she conceived the book starting with that image. It is a mark of her virtuosity that the wealth of detail in the first half of the book gives way smoothly and naturally to the starkness of the second.

Two themes carry over from *Planet of Exile*. One is winter as a commanding force in men's lives and a symbol of all that is implacable in nature. The other is the companionship that can spring up between strangers in the face of such a mindless enemy as cold. Like the earlier book, *The Left Hand of Darkness* is in large part a love story. This, however, is a love born in mistrust, crossed not by the stars but by the protagonists' prior loyalties and preconceptions. The love between Genly Ai and Estraven, prime minister of Karhide, is subtler, more mature, and less easily fulfilled than that of Jakob Agat and Rolery. For Estraven, it grows out of a recognition, in the Ekumen, of the values he has spent his political career fostering: from this recognition evolves a personal attachment to the Ekumen's envoy. For Ai, Estraven represents everything he finds most disturbing about Karhide. Estraven is a master at the intricacies of prestige that dominate Karhidish society. He is powerful and proud, yet through the eyes of Ai, who insists on trying to view Gethenians as men, he is womanish. Only when these two are isolated on the great ice field are they able to reconcile Ai's blunt hastiness and the ambiguities that underlie Estraven's character. Even so, their love stops short of the sexual contact that is theoretically possible between them, although Ai comes to terms with Estraven's androgyny when the latter enters kemmer in the female phase, responding to Ai's permanent masculinity. Their true consummation is through mindspeech, which is previously unknown on Gethen. Even that pure form of communication is troubled between them, because Estraven "hears" Ai's telepathic speech in the voice of his long-dead brother and lover.

Le Guin's customary story-telling format, the journey of discovery, takes two forms corresponding to the two parts of the book. In the first half of the book Envoy travels around Karhide and into the other large region of the Gethenian Great Continent, Orgoreyn. His discoveries are primarily cultural ones, as Le Guin explores the ramifications of her major postulates, androgyny and an ice age. The first half of the book exposes a wealth of supportive detail that brings the world of Gethen to life. Slow, silent electric cars that crawl over mountain ranges; a plump, chatty "landlady" who shows strangers into the Envoy's room for a small fee; a glimpse of a sort of monastery perched on seemingly inaccessible cliffs; an ancient city whose streets are tunnels because of the ever-present snow; a religion that praises all things incomplete and uncertain; a ritual that seems to foretell the future accurately but also shows how useless it is to mankind to know the future; tragic tales; icy myths; and blood-colored palaces—all these contribute to the atmosphere of Karhide and its way of life. Orgoreyn has a different set of cultural clues: great, smelly fish warehouses; enormous banquets of bland food and fierce liquor; luxuries unknown in Karhide, like hot showers; secret police and endless piles of paperwork; and prison camps out in the vast western forest of the country. Orgoreyn is clearly modeled on Stalinist Russia, which leads many critics to assume Karhide to be America. However, Karhide retains values that American and Soviet societies tend to push aside: harmony with nature, unlimited hospitality, continuity with the past, social grace, and inner tranquility. These are Oriental values, and the primary religion of Karhide, Handdara, blends aspects of Taoism and Zen. The rival religion of Orgoreyn, Yomesh, is more like Christianity or Islam, that is, an activist faith based on revelation.

The second half of the book recounts Genly Ai's rescue by Estraven from an Orgota prison camp and their flight over the glaciers back to Karhide. During this time Ai begins to absorb everything that he has observed on Gethen and to relate it to himself. Against the blank background of ice and snow, Gethen and the Ekumen meet and merge in the persons of Ai and Estraven, thus demonstrating what the Ekumen

is: a meeting face to face or mind to mind of unlike individuals, like a marriage on a grand scale.

From this elevated conception of human interaction, Le Guin jumps, in her next sciencefiction stories, back down the scale of social evolution to the troublesome near future. *The Lathe of Heaven* (1971) takes place on Earth in the twentyfirst century and concerns a man, George Orr, who changes the Earth without the knowledge of anyone except the other two main characters. He does so by dreaming. For reasons unknown and unimaginable, certain of George's dreams change the fabric of existence; furthermore, they do so retroactively, so that unless one is aware of the dream as it occurs, one's memory is changed along with everything else. The dream, as George says, hides its traces.

This capacity to change things disturbs George. He is content with the world as it is, with adapting himself to reality rather than wrenching reality to fit his expectations. In an effort to suppress his dreams he resorts to sedatives, and that results in his being assigned to a governmentaffiliated psychologist, Dr. Haber. Dr. Haber is also a researcher, a specialist in dreams, and he is excited by the strange wave patterns generated by George's sleeping brain. He does not admit to himself that he believes George's story, but he begins using the dreams to bring about specific changes, giving George hypnotic suggestions about their content. He has George reduce population, alter weather patterns, and give him, Haber, the directorship of a large dream-study institute. George is alarmed; he is now upsetting things more than he had been on his own. Haber will neither acknowledge his power nor stop taking advantage of it. George enlists the aid of a lawyer, a skeptical young woman named Heather Lelache. She observes a dream session with Haber and feels the change as it occurs, though Haber half convinces her that nothing has happened. In the end it takes George, Heather, and some improbable turtlelike aliens dreamed up by George to overcome Haber and let the Earth return to its own course.

The Lathe of Heaven is rare among Le Guin stories in that it is not cast in the form of a journey. Instead it revolves around the interactions of three main characters, George, Heather, and Dr. Haber. It almost seems, for a while, like a tug-of-war between Heather and Haber, with George as the rope, but the reader realizes eventually that George, passive as he seems, is the strongest of the three. He is more like the fulcrum on which the other two rock back and forth. The power Dr. Haber seems to have is only what George lends him, and Heather, under a mask of cold efficiency, is frightened and insecure and needs George's quiet confidence.

Each character has a role to play, and each role is matched by the character's name. George Orr is the dreamer and the adjudicator. He lives among possibilities; he poises on the either-or's. He is the Tao personified: one who accepts and loves, who welcomes whatever occurs and is never overwhelmed. Both of the other characters see him as weak at first, but Heather later finds in him integrity. His power is somehow related to his inner peace: he is so sure of himself that the world accommodates itself to his dreams.

Haber is the manipulator. His name (English "haver," one who has; Latin "havere," to have) suggests possessiveness, the will to have or control. He is a caricature of the Judeo-Christian tradition of striving toward progress. He wishes to move forward without knowing where he stands. Whereas Orr is a solid block of wood, Haber is compared to an onion–all slippery layers, with no core. He is so out of touch with his motivations that he never realizes he is lying to George or to himself. In the end, when he has learned to duplicate George's gift, his hidden self breaks through and nearly plunges the world into a permanent nightmare.

Heather Lelache is the coward. (That is what *le lâche* means in French.) Coward, however, is more her self-assessment than fact. The mask she has built up for herself, that of a hard-edged, ambitious, calculating spiderwoman (she also calls herself the Black Widow), does enable her to take action, to help George when he needs help. She has the courage to believe George, to stand beside him, and, when necessary, to let herself draw on his strength.

The book follows the shifting relationships among these three people, which are further complicated by the successive reality shifts caused by George's dreams. These changes are never exactly what Haber intends them to be: George's unconscious mind always throws in unexpected elements without disobeying instructions. Like wishes in many traditional fairy tales, George's dreams have their own logic and proportion that defy control by an outsider. They cannot be dictated to: there is always an unexpected penalty with every boon. Population is reduced, but at the expense of a devastating worldwide plague. War ends on Earth, but only because aliens at-

tack from outer space. Racial strife stops, but at the loss of all variation among mankind. Everyone is gray. During this sequence Heather, who is black, disappears briefly, then reappears with much of her personality gone along with her color. George, the arbitrator, assigns the cost of every change, and as the designs get more grandiose the penalties grow more severe.

A summary of *The Lathe of Heaven* does not reveal the wry humor running through it. Much of what happens is rather grim: people are crowded and unhappy before Haber takes command and oppressed and unhappy afterward, but Orr's cheerfulness saves the book from too much darkness. Some of the humor consists of inside jokes about its setting, and some of it comes from the characters' self-appraisals. The aliens that appear either from the depths of space or from the equally obscure depths of George's unconscious are indubitably comical. They look like giant sea turtles and talk in mangled English peppered with quotations and platitudes. They are also connected with one of the most beautiful images developed in the book, one associating sleep with the ocean: the waking mind is compared in the opening passage to a jellyfish drifting onto a rocky shore. The aliens are creatures who live in a state closer to dream than to waking life; the universe of dream is their native habitat. And in that universe they are no longer comical and awkward. George dreams of them, near the end of the book: "His dreams, like waves of the deep sea far from any shore, came and went, rose and fell, profound and harmless, breaking nowhere, changing nothing. Through his sleep the great, green sea turtles dived, swimming with heavy inexhaustible grace through the depths, in their element."

Le Guin's "discovery" of Earthsea began with her story about a wizard, "The Word of Unbinding." A later story, "The Rule of Names," developed both the islands of Earthsea and the rules of its magic and introduced a dragon. Both stories were published in *Fantastic* in 1964 and were later collected in *The Wind's Twelve Quarters.* In 1967 Herman Schein, publisher of Parnassus Press in Berkeley, California, wanted to branch out from the young juvenile market and asked Le Guin to write a book for older children. Schein gave her complete freedom of subject and approach. Le Guin returned to the imaginary islands of Earthsea she had discovered and wrote *A Wizard of Earthsea,* which was published in 1968. The second volume of the Earthsea trilogy,

UKL

If they are hermaphroditic –
Who raises the kids?
     People who choose to do so, in government-supervised creches – about ⅓ of the people between 25 + 50 are engaged thus. In early times & in villages now, it is simply an essential job like any other, farming soldiering tailoring etc – In the modern cities it is well paid + pensioned, + rather over-volunteered-for. Primitively, rearing was communal.
     Who nurses them?
     The one who bears them – for about 6 mos – 2 yrs.
     There is no marriage, + fidelity is not legalised in any way, tho' there are moral + religious semi-institutions + arrangements. Essentially, however, they do not pair, + love is, institutionally, par with earth-friendship.
     During a period of about 3 days out of 26, a Gethenian is sexually receptive/active, but only (except in perversities) with another person in 'oestrus' (Kemmer). During court-ship + sexual play one (normally) begins to be dominated by m. or f. hormones, + his/her behavior rapidly triggers the opposite reaction in the partner; the respective organs engorge + dominate, + consummation is possible within ½ hour to 24 hours. It is not a notably efficient arrangement as so much depends on place + timing; but conception is equivalently frequent. The partner who played female conceives at least 85% of the time. There are contraceptive drugs. There are also cycle-inducing + postponing drugs, often used by repetitive partners. Hormone derivatives are taken by those who prefer one à the other sex-role.
     The other 23 days of the month, the whole sexual complex, physical-emotional, is 'checked' by inhibitors. it is not absent, but suppressed by these secretions, genetically implanted by the colonisers of Hain in this one colony-stock – As an experiment? who knows? – The sexual energy typical of humans is not lessened, but

Working notes for The Left Hand of Darkness, *in which an envoy visits a frigid planet whose inhabitants are androgynous (courtesy of the author)*

The Tombs of Atuan, followed three years later. *The Farthest Shore* completed the series in 1972. Although each novel can be read independently, the same themes and images reverberate through all three, and they form a unit which is greater than the mere sum of the parts.

The trilogy covers the youth, young manhood, and old age of the Wizard Ged, who rises from goatherd to become Archmage of all Earthsea. We are told at the beginning of *A Wizard of Earthsea* that the hero will become famous in song and legend. He is a mythic hero, and the trilogy follows many of the traditional patterns of myth: the orphan hero of obscure origins, the early evidence of his great powers, the wizard who guides him, his struggle with inner demons, the quest, and the initiation whereby he is made whole and comes into full possession of his powers. Aside from the borrowings from standard myth, the trilogy shows a decided Jungian influence, which many critics have noted, though the author denies having read Jung at that time. Le Guin's father was, for a while, a practicing psychoanalyst, and Jung's name was *the* four-letter word in the Kroeber household.

Other critics have mentioned the possible influences on the trilogy of Tolkien, George MacDonald, M. R. James, and C. S. Lewis's fantasies. Le Guin creates a world without a deity, although magic exists, along with tremendous powers for good and evil. Hers is a modern, existential, humanistic universe where the weight of responsibility rests on the individual to act wisely, for by acting otherwise he can imperil the balance of the world. As Ged is taught at the school for wizards on Roke Island, " 'you must not change one thing, one pebble, one grain of sand, until you know what good and evil will follow on that act.... To light a candle is to cast a shadow....' " In the emphasis in the trilogy on balance–of good and evil, light and dark, life and death–many critics have seen the influence of Taoist notions of dynamic equilibrium, of the necessity for a balance of yin and yang.

The plot of *A Wizard of Earthsea* concerns the disastrous consequences of power used unwisely, disturbing the Equilibrium. Like the classic "sorcerer's apprentice," young Ged overreaches himself through pride and anger. While summoning up the spirits of the dead, he unleashes his own formless "shadow" and nearly dies from the encounter. Chastened, he completes his training; but once he leaves the protection of Roke, he is pursued across the world by the evil shadow until his old mentor, the wizard Ogion, advises him to turn from hunted to hunter and seek out the shadow. After many adventures, he finally confronts the shadow on the open sea and calls it by its name: *Ged*, his own name. By accepting and embracing his dark side as part of himself, Ged is made whole and becomes a man.

What the child needs to grow up, Le Guin asserted in *The Language of the Night*, "is reality, the wholeness which exceeds all our virtue and all our vice. He needs knowledge; he needs self-knowledge. He needs to see himself and the shadow he casts. That is something he can face, his own shadow, and he can learn to control it and to be guided by it." Le Guin sees fantasy as a psychic and a moral journey "to self-knowledge, to adulthood, to the light." The goal of that journey is psychic wholeness. *A Wizard of Earthsea* succeeds as myth, as moral allegory, and as vivid adventure story. It received the Boston Globe-Horn Book Award and was named an American Library Association Notable Book.

The Tombs of Atuan concerns a feminine coming of age to match the masculine one of *A Wizard of Earthsea;* it focuses on the rite of passage of the adolescent Tenar. Tenar had the misfortune to be born the same day the old Priestess of the Tombs of Atuan died and so was hailed as her reincarnation. She is taken away from her parents, given the new name of "Arha," or "The Eaten One," and raised to become the next Priestess. The place of the Tombs is an unchanging, sterile, desert environment where no men are allowed, only females and eunuchs. Everything is consecrated to the perverse worship of death and the "Nameless Ones," the dark powers who inhabit the Tombs and the immense underground Labyrinth. The first third of the novel deals with the childhood apprenticeship of Tenar in this gloomy place, where her natural humanity is suppressed.

The adventure begins when Tenar, now an adolescent Priestess, discovers a light in the Labyrinth. It is Ged, seeking the lost half of the ancient Ring of the wizard Erreth-Akbe. The Ring contained a lost Rune of Wholeness; once the two halves of the broken Ring are brought together, wholeness and good government can be restored to Earthsea, and the wars may cease. But Ged has defiled the holy place. As Priestess, it is Tenar's duty to have him put to death. Nevertheless, she becomes fascinated by this man and keeps him imprisoned instead, thereby earn-ing the enmity of Kossil, the Priestess of the Godking, who has the power to destroy Tenar. Eventually, Ged wins Tenar over. He tells her her original name, so that she can be reborn as a whole human being, and entrusts her with the restored Ring (which serves as a symbolic wedding ring for the two). Finally they escape from the Labyrinth with the Ring. An earthquake swallows the Tombs and the Labyrinth, and the worship of death and evil is ended.

The novel resonates with image patterns of silence versus sound, dark versus light, and death versus life. For example, Ged tells Tenar, "You were never made for cruelty and darkness; you were made to hold light, as a lamp burning holds and gives its light." Once again, Le Guin emphasizes the need for balance: darkness must be recognized and accepted as a part of the whole, but it must not be allowed to overwhelm the balance. The dark powers "should not be denied nor forgotten, but neither should they be worshipped. The Earth is beautiful, and bright, and dark, and cruel. . . . There are sharks in the sea, and there is cruelty in men's eyes. And where men worship these things and abase themselves before them, there evil breeds. . . . They exist. But they are not your Masters." *The Tombs of Atuan* was a Newbery Honor Book and was nominated for the National Book Award for Children's Literature.

The Farthest Shore, a novel of epic scope, brings the trilogy to an exciting conclusion. It won the National Book Award for Children's Literature. If *A Wizard of Earthsea* concerns balance and wholeness on the individual level and *The Tombs of Atuan* concerns the union of two people, then *The Farthest Shore* extends the concern with Equilibrium to the entire cosmos. *The Tombs of Atuan* deals with the imbalance caused by worshiping death over life; *The Farthest Shore* shows the imbalance created by worshiping life over death.

As the novel opens, there is trouble in Earthsea, signified by ominous signs such as wizards forgetting their craft. Prince Arren of Enlad is sent by his father as a messenger to the Archmage Ged on Roke Island to inform him of the trouble in their region. Ged decides to go on a quest to find the source of the rapidly spreading decline, and he invites young Arren to accompany him. They sail first to Hort, a town with no laws or rulers. There Arren is sold into slavery and rescued by Ged. Next they travel to Lorbanery, an island of weavers who no longer weave. After Ged is wounded in a savage attack by the islanders of Obehol, he and Arren drift in

their boat until they are saved by "the children of the open sea," a tribe of gentle raft people. Yet the decline reaches even there; the singers forget the words to their songs.

Finally, the dragon Orm Embar leads Ged and Arren to the deserted island of Selidor, "the westernmost cape of all the lands, the end of the earth." There Ged meets the anti-King, the Unmaker, the cause of all the trouble: the renegade wizard Cob. Cob made a spell to open the gate between life and death, so that no one will ever die. But in defeating death, he destroyed the Equilibrium and also defeated life, causing it to lose its savor and reality, lack a center, and become a hollow void. To defeat Cob, Ged and Arren must descend into the kingdom of death itself. There Ged shuts the door between the worlds of life and death. Arren guides and carries the exhausted Ged over the Mountains of Pain back into life. A dragon returns them to Roke. Ged then disappears on the dragon's back, his great task of restoring the Equilibrium done and his wizardry ended. Arren is acclaimed King of all Earthsea, having fulfilled the prophecies about a ruler who would return from the land of death.

The relationship between Arren and Ged is reminiscent of that between young Arthur and Merlin; and Arren, like Arthur, wields a magic sword, fulfills the prophecies, and unites the land. Ged has come full circle in the trilogy, from the young apprentice to the master who must pass his wisdom on to the next generation. In Ged's training of Arren, Le Guin gives us the fullest exposition of the necessity to learn to keep the balance of contraries and to do only what is necessary: " 'On every act the balance of the whole depends. . . . we must *learn* to do what the leaf and the whale and the wind do of their own nature. We must learn to keep the balance. Having intelligence, we must not act in ignorance. Having choice, we must not act without responsibility.' " Only man, of all creatures on earth, is capable of evil. But " 'in our shame is our glory. Only our spirit, which is capable of evil, is capable of overcoming it.' "

The *Earthsea* trilogy is the sort of fantasy which teaches about reality and is appropriate for all ages. Because it draws on the powerful, archetypal patterns of myth, the stories have an inevitability and an ethical and psychological truth. Le Guin's only failing is an occasional preachiness; not content to let the action speak for itself, she must elucidate the moral. Nevertheless, the trilogy works both as high fantasy and realistic epic adventure. It establishes the patterns of initiation, fine style, and ethical concern that can be seen in all of Le Guin's books for children, which, while not on the scale of the trilogy, are nonetheless worthy achievements.

When Le Guin returns to the Hainish universe in *The Dispossessed*, it is markedly different. The difference is reflected in the novel's setting, both time and place. The time is early, long before the events of even *Rocannon's World*. There is no "ansible," no mindspeech. Technology is not much advanced from what we know today, although the people of Hain have interstellar spaceships. The place is a pair of planets known as the Cetian worlds. We have not heard much about these twin worlds before, only that they produced an advanced mathematical system which will subsequently be adopted by all other worlds, even the home planet of Hain. The Cetian worlds share a single orbit, and each circles the other. They are like the Earth and the moon, only more equal; each is the other's moon. One world is lush and watery and is the home planet for the Cetians. The other is dry and spare and was colonized many years before the story begins by a group of anarchists who hoped to create utopia.

The story has no alien beings, only men of various persuasions. It has no disguised magic, such as telepathy or precognition. Everything is slow, sober, down-to-earth. The writing verges on pure naturalistic reporting, except that the places being written about do not exist on Earth. When Le Guin wrote *The Dispossessed*, she was in the middle of her fantasy trilogy of Earthsea; all of her impulse toward magic seems to have gone into the latter and none into this story. But it is fuller than any other of her stories in character and in social and political interplay.

At the beginning of the book Shevek, the hero, is getting ready to leave his home planet, the colony world Anarres. It is the exact middle of his story. The second chapter returns to Shevek's childhood on Anarres. From there the chapters alternate, one on Anarres, taking Shevek toward the point of his departure, and then one on Urras, following his exploration of a new world and his eventual return home. Anarres is a harsh and ugly world. Most of it is barely habitable desert with no margin for elegance or much comfort. Everyone is occupied with survival. People work hard. For vacations from their regular work they work at something else. The code of behavior is very strict. Sexual

standards are loose, but in other ways it is an almost puritanical place. The reforming fervor that launched the colony has settled down into moralistic conformity. Custom, as is often the case, proves more binding than law. But there is a certain joyfulness among the people of Anarres that grows out of a spirit of cooperation. Men and women are treated equally: even their names are interchangeable, being randomly assigned at birth by a computer. All occupations carry equal dignity. There still remains from the old revolutionary impulse a sense of common cause. In addition, the fact that no one on Anarres owns anything begins to seem wonderfully liberating. There is a certain gypsy feeling that comes of having no "hostages to fortune." Le Guin captures the excitement of living in an ongoing experiment in freedom.

The experiment is based on the theories of a philosopher named Odo, whose life and ideas are modeled on such figures as Karl Marx and anarchists Emma Goldman and Peter Kropotkin. Odo proposed a society without laws or institutions, a society based on personal responsibility, on each member's recognition of his own needs and the needs of others. Odo's theories inspired a number of people on Urras to reject every governmental and economic system offered to them. Soon after her death, a large group of her followers took up an offer by the State to be transported to the moon, that is, to Anarres. This move was designed to get those troublesome followers off the hands of the various Urrasti governments.

The Dispossessed is subtitled "An Ambiguous Utopia" because Anarres is both utopia and dystopia. However, Urras is also a mixture of the flawed and the ideal. Urras is a place of great beauty, vivid colors, and luxuriant life. There is inequality, but the poorest people are not much worse off than the people of Anarres. It is a world of variety. There are three main countries, corresponding approximately to our own capitalist, communist, and Third World nations. The reader discovers most about the capitalist state. It has much elegance and beauty, but sharp social and sexual divisions. Shevek finds intolerable the fact that everything and everyone there is essentially owned by someone else. He is treated as a commodity, with all the respect given to a valuable object and none of the sensitivity owed to fellowmen. The pampered, artificial women of Urras both fascinate and repel him. He sees little difference between the capitalist and socialist states. To an Odonian, as long as there is property it does not matter whether individuals or the state own it, and as long as there is a state, it does not matter how firm or lenient it is. Odonians consider socialism to be a betrayal of their own movement, a halfway gesture.

But, as Shevek discovers, there are freedoms on Urras which cannot be found on Anarres, values which Anarres has sacrificed along with property and government. Urras is rich not only in material things. It has a history from which Anarres has cut itself off. It allows a free play of ideas that is limited by the utilitarianism of a collective society. It is in communication with the rest of the universe, whereas Anarres has closed itself off for fear of contamination. On Urras, Shevek discovers the work of the Terran mathematician Ainsetain (Einstein). It provides him with the clues he needs to finish his theory of Simultaneity. With his completed theory and the technology of Urras, the ansible can be built. Instantaneous communication between worlds will allow for a League of All Worlds, just as mindspeech later offers the possibility of a greater union, the Ekumen.

On Anarres, in the alternate chapters, Shevek acts as the conscience of the Odonian revolution. He and his friends start an organization which they call the Syndicate of Initiative. Its main purposes are to publish the work of Shevek and other original thinkers who have not been able to convince the majority of its value, and to open communication with Urras after generations of isolation. On Urras, Shevek is the messenger of freedom. In spite of the efforts of his official hosts to isolate him from the lower classes, who still hold some Odonian sentiments, he meets some rebels and partakes in a spontaneous rally against the government, or, more precisely, against Government. He is shot at, goes into hiding, and takes refuge at the Terran embassy. Neither world is comfortable with his presence, which indicates that both have need of him. When he makes his breakthrough and discovers the equations for Simultaneity, he also comes to a decision. He refuses to let Urras buy his ideas, and he refuses to let Anarres suppress them. The alternative is to give his equations away to all groups, all worlds, so that none can either keep them hidden or profit from them. He dispossesses himself. Then, with nothing to burden him, he goes home.

The political, economic, and mathematical aspects of *The Dispossessed* have occupied the attention of most readers of the book. But its thematic core is about a man throwing a rock over a wall. In the opening scene both rock and wall are physically present, but we do not know yet what they signify. More often they are there only as terms in analogies: Shevek is a rock, Anarres is a rock hanging in space, Shevek finds himself locked in or out of a room, his syndic breaches the wall of distance to open radio contact with Urras, and his theory of Simultaneity formulates in his mind as a picture of a rock perpetually approaching but never reaching its goal. The act of throwing a rock is a sign in the book for a refusal to accept boundaries. Even on Anarres walls are constantly springing up, and even an Odonian finds it difficult to pick up the rock and throw it. Shevek, who is to some degree based on Le Guin's childhood memories of the physicist J. Robert Oppenheimer, is the sort of individual every society tolerates most grudgingly and needs most desperately; he is a free and creative man. He cannot help picking up the rock: scientific curiosity will leave nothing unexamined. But to throw it is to call attention to oneself, to be labeled uncooperative, dangerous, a traitor. Le Guin says that even in utopia there are rocks to be thrown, social or mental boundaries to be crossed. That is a further refinement of her concept of heroism, and Shevek is the most fully realized and developed of her heroes.

Between *The Dispossessed* and *The Eye of the Heron* (1983), Le Guin concentrated her science-fiction efforts in short stories. *The Wind's Twelve Quarters* contains a few post-*Dispossessed* pieces, including a lovely, elegiac portrait of Odo called "The Day Before the Revolution" (1974). Some earlier stories provide starting points for novels: "Semley's Necklace" begins *Rocannon's World*, "The Word for Unbinding" and "The Rule of Names" belong to Earthsea, and "Winter's King" is a prologue to *The Left Hand of Darkness*.

Le Guin is fond of forms that fall between the short story and the novel. One of her most widely reprinted short pieces, a story called "Nine Lives" (1969), was nominated for a Nebula Award in the novelette category. Another piece, included along with "Nine Lives" in *The Wind's Twelve Quarters*, is slightly longer: Le Guin jokes in her introduction about its deserving all too well the title "Vaster Than Empires and More Slow." "The Word for World Is Forest," which first appeared in Harlan Ellison's anthology *Again, Dangerous Visions* in 1972, came out in a volume by itself four years later. In these middle-length fictions Le Guin tends to come out more strongly on issues that concern her than in short stories, which do not allow for sufficient development, or in novels, which require a fuller and therefore more equivocal treatment of theme.

Aside from "Nine Lives," a fairly straightforward story on cloning, these novelettes and novellas are a disturbing group. "Vaster Than Empires and More Slow" is troubling because of its characters, who are all psychological misfits. The story concerns an expedition, very early in League history, to the far reaches of the galaxy. The trip is to be long and quite possibly fruitless. If the members return at all they will be faced with a time gap of hundreds of years due to the speed of their ship. Only maladjusted people volunteer for such an expedition: people seeking escape from the complexities of normal society.

The cast of the story is not only an odd one, it is singularly unattractive, or at least seems so at first. One expedition member who particularly irritates his fellow travelers and the reader is Osden. He is defensive, egotistical, and sarcastic. He is also sensitive not only to human emotions but to those of any sentient being. He feels the hostility of those around him and feeds it with his offensive behavior, bringing out the worst in everyone else. Even the most sympathetic character, the commander Haito Tomiko, is angry and destructive around Osden. The least engaging character, Porlock, is a quivering slob, a blend, as the name suggests, of Philip Roth's Portnoy and H. G. Wells's Morlock. The atmosphere aboard ship is one of profound unease, and the tension increases when they land on the first planet on their path.

The world they encounter is an all-vegetable one: trees, grasses, shrubs in profusion, but nothing mobile, no foragers or grazers or predators. The explorers see furtive shapes in the shadows, though there should be none; their fear intensifies when Osden is mysteriously attacked (by Porlock, it turns out). Osden finally realizes that the planet's biosphere is one sentient organism, connected by nervelike roots just below the surface. The fear they feel is the forest's fear of them, the invaders. He breaks through the fear and enters into communication with the great green being. While the others depart, he remains behind, having found a companion who does not fear or pity him.

Most of the story is disconcerting and the descriptions harsh. The early League years seem to be, for Le Guin, a time of trouble and misunderstanding. But the forest world encountered by the explorers, much as they fear it, is a thing of great beauty. It grows in the reader's mind until it finally overpowers the rest of the story. At the end there is a vision of timeless peace, as Osden shares the forest's perception of light, growth, and wholeness.

The Word for World Is Forest carries over the same picture of a world of unbroken greenery, the Garden of Eden before the Fall. This time inhabitants share the forest's peace: small greenish men of Hainish stock, hunters and food gatherers living in harmony with the forest. These people are dreamers, able to induce a dream state while they are awake and to control it. They live among visions, and the visions keep them sane and whole. The story could have been a charming study of these people who live amid shadows–forest shadows and dream shadows. But into this setting comes an echo of the author's times: war in Vietnam, exploitation of resources, dominance of one racial or cultural group by another more powerful. The clash between peaceful natives and brutal Terran colonists results in a story that seems, in contrast with Le Guin's usual elegance, raw, fierce, and ungoverned.

The apexes of this story are Lyubov, a Terran scientist; Davidson, a military leader; and Selver, a native. Lyubov is a typical Le Guin hero, with a twist. He respects the natives, is intrigued by their culture, and tries to protect them against the abuses of the colonists, but he is weak. Davidson, on the other hand, is strong, but, in Le Guin's view, quite mad. He represents Le Guin's attempt to get inside the masculine-dominant mind. He views this world the way he views women, as a conquest. Natives are work animals, their women a temporary substitute for women of his own species. He and most of the other men in the colony call them Creechies, evidently a corruption of "creatures." Selver is a leader among the natives, Athsheans, as they call themselves. Bullied and humiliated by the Terrans, neither he nor any other Athshean has put up resistance until his wife is raped by Davidson and dies. Then the deep pacifism of his culture gives way to the realization that Terrans will not treat Athsheans as fellow men and therefore cannot be treated as such. Selver becomes possessed of a new vision, the possibility of violence. He becomes, in Athshean terms, a god: one who translates a heretofore unknown dream or vision into action. In leading an Athshean uprising, Selver loses the balance of dream and waking that keeps his people sane. He is

Dust jacket for Le Guin's 1982 collection of short stories, which she claims "take place all over the map, including the margins"

nearly overcome by the vision of murder that fills him but escapes it in the end, aided by the dream self of his murdered friend Lyubov.

Davidson finds no such escape. His private war with the Creechies escalates even after his people have surrendered to them. He had made the wrong decision long before to treat all Others as if they did not matter. Everything unlike himself—and that ultimately comes to include everything—is a thing to be utilized for his benefit. This decision leads him on a course with no retreat. He can only respond to gentleness with scorn and to resistance with savagery. He must "teach them a lesson" and "save his honor." There is no compromise. Selver is wiser. He twice decides not to kill Davidson when he has the opportunity. Davidson is ultimately exiled to an island which he and his exploiters have made into a desert. The Terrans abandon their colony. Unlike most Le Guin stories, this one ends with no meeting of strangers,

only a bitter lesson learned on both sides and the hope of reconciliation between the two peoples in some distant future.

Very Far Away from Anywhere Else (1976) is a rare Le Guin try at straight realism. It was named an American Library Association Notable Book for Young Adults. This contemporary love story about two adolescents is Le Guin's first attempt to deal in fiction with the problems of adolescent sexuality. Central characters Owen Griffin and Natalie Field are teenagers in their senior year of high school, both extremely bright—he wants to be a scientist, she a composer—and consequently both misfits and loners in the local school, although Natalie is more self-confident and better adjusted than Owen. They are drawn together out of loneliness. Natalie has the confident assertiveness Owen lacks, and Owen has a sense of humor that brightens Natalie's severe, disciplined existence. They become best friends because they can understand and talk to each other. Problems arise when sex intrudes on their relationship, because neither is ready for it yet. Natalie kindly but firmly rejects Owen's blunt sexual aggression. Distraught, Owen drives recklessly, and his car turns over on a curve. After he recovers from the accident, he finally stops being childishly angry at Natalie, and they are reunited. In the end, as they go off to separate colleges, it seems likely they will remain friends and may one day mature into lovers. Meanwhile, both have grown and learned about life and themselves from the relationship. Owen learns to stop being scared of life, to accept himself as he is and thereby to accept others. Like all Le Guin's fiction, *Very Far Away from Anywhere Else* concerns the painful effort involved in becoming a whole human being.

Orsinian Tales (1976), eleven stories set in an imaginary Eastern European country, shows Le Guin venturing into mainstream fiction. Composed before and during her work on the Hainish novels and the Earthsea trilogy, they retain techniques from her other works, such as the circular journey, the blending of fantasy and realism. James W. Bittner (*Science-Fiction Studies*, November 1978) identifies their theme as the certainty of human relationships amid the fluidity of everything else–politics, geography, psychology, morality. As such, they are "acts of the imagination that transform the calamity of history that is central Europe into a celebration of the individual's ability to survive bad times." "Imaginary Countries," the last story, forms the collection's chronological center. This distinctly autobiographical tale includes a young girl who tries to trap unicorns and pretends to be various mythological characters. The other stories range in time from 1150 to 1965, yet each, says critic Charlotte Spivack, "presents a moral turning point in the lives of its principal characters. . . . Love for another often proves to be the road to freedom." Concluding in typical Le Guin fashion, most end at a beginning place, "essentially a prologue to an unknown future."

Malafrena (1979), an historical romance, is also set in Orsinia, between 1820 and 1830. Itale Sorde, a young political revolutionary, leaves his country estate for the city to fight for freedom. After establishing himself in work (editing a liberal journal), friendship (with a long-admired writer), and love (with the baroness Luisa), he is imprisoned for two years. Between the accounts of Itale's successes and trials in the city, Le Guin tells the stories of his friends and family in the country. Eventually freed with Luisa's help, Itale goes back to Malafrena a broken man, only to find a beginning place in his return. Using the circular journey to explore her coming-of-age theme, Le Guin shows again that it is the certainties in relationships–friendship, integrity, love, fidelity–that are important.

Leese Webster (1979), a fiction for young juveniles, is a charming, wise little story about a spider. The delicate line drawings by illustrator James Brunsman, in black against a gold background, are appropriate for the intricate spiderwebs Leese weaves. Le Guin uses images of spiders, webs, and weaving throughout her works, with both positive and negative connotations, so this story is a logical extension of the concerns of the rest of her fiction. Moreover, little children can often identify with spiders, who are like children in certain positive ways: small, persistent, industrious, creative, and beneficial.

Leese Webster is a spider born in a deserted palace. She grows up alone, in the bedroom of a princess. At first, Leese spins her family's traditional webs, but then she begins to experiment with new patterns. Not all her experiments succeed, but she tries copying the patterns she sees around her in the paintings and carpets. The other spiders either ignore her webs or dismiss them as a waste of time. Nevertheless, Leese persists and begins creating successful original designs. But no matter how hard she tries, her webs are grey and cannot approach the beauty she remembers of the jewels on the throne, which had light inside them.

When the palace is cleaned to be made into a museum, Leese's webs amaze the authorities, who preserve them behind glass. Leese is saved by a cleaning lady, who says, " 'Never kill a spider. . . . It's bad luck,' " and drops Leese out the window. Leese's long plunge into the garden outside is traumatic, and she imagines herself to be dead. But it proves instead to be a rebirth into a marvelous new world. The stars appear to her like the jewels in the throne room. Flies are plentiful, so Leese no longer goes hungry. Best of all, Leese achieves her highest goal as an artist, for the light of sunrise on the dewdrops clinging to her webs makes them shine "brighter than the jewels of the throne, brighter even than the stars." While the tourists admire her weavings inside the palace, Leese is happy with her "wild webs" outdoors, "shining with the jewels of the sun."

The story shows Le Guin's style, with its clarity and natural patterns of imagery, at its best. And though Le Guin omits the usual moralizing, the message of the story is nevertheless clear: it is a parable about the artist and her craft. It implies that the artist may suffer loneliness, neglect, and even ridicule, but it is worth persevering. The artist must constantly experiment to grow, even if those experiments do not always work. Leese triumphs through talent, hard work, and persistence. The final message of the story is that nature itself is the greatest work of art and that our own creations will shine brightest not as they copy other man-made things but as they approach the status of natural artifacts. Though children may not register all these messages consciously, they will be encouraged by the story of Leese to persist in their own creative efforts, knowing that, although the rewards may be slow in coming, the effort is worthwhile in terms of self-fulfillment.

Le Guin's other books for young children include *The Adventure of Cobbler's Rune* (1982), *Solomon Leviathan's Nine Hundred and Thirty-First Trip Around the World* (1983), *A Visit from Dr. Katz* (1988), and *Catwings* (1988).

The Beginning Place (1980) is another story of adolescent maturation and love, almost a companion piece (although far superior) to *Very Far Away from Anywhere Else*. Once again, male and female adolescent misfits find companionship, love, and maturity together. Here, however, Le Guin creates a unique blending of realism and romantic fantasy. Her teenage hero and heroine escape from homes which are not real homes and families which are not real families into a fantasy world, "a good place." She returns to the mythic quest mode of the Earthsea trilogy but goes further in showing the complementary relationship between the fantasy world and our so-called real world.

The central characters of *The Beginning Place* are Hugh Rogers and Irene Pannis. Hugh wants to attend college and become a librarian, but he has stayed at home because of his possessive mother and worked as a supermarket checker. He lives in a development named Kensington Heights. "To get to Oak Valley Road, he crossed Loma Linda Drive, Raleigh Drive, Pine View Place, turned onto Kensington Avenue, crossed Chelsea Oaks Road. There were no heights, no valleys, no Raleighs, no oaks." Finally, Hugh runs away from home and discovers in the woods at the outskirts of the city a gateway into a land of perpetual twilight. In that land he finds a town called Tembreabrezi, which exemplifies a pastoral, ordered, medieval form of existence.

Irene has left home because of a stepfather who makes sexual advances toward her and has been living with a couple who are in the process of breaking up. She has vowed never to fall in love, associating it only with the power to inflict pain. Years before Hugh does, she has discovered Tembreabrezi and made an alternate home there with a tranquil, totally accepting substitute family. She idolizes the master of the town; he is both father and lover to her, for he seems to offer "desire without terror . . . love without effect, without penalty or pain. The only price was silence." But as she grows up, she finds it increasingly difficult to pass through the gateway.

When Irene discovers Hugh in Tembreabrezi, she resents him as an intruder on her secret land. However, the villagers hail Hugh as their long-awaited savior. The town has fallen under a curse: no one visits, and the roads are closed. It all seems to be caused by some unnamed menace in the mountains. The Master tries to leave with Irene but cannot pass the borders of the town. Seeing his fear, Irene loses faith in him. Hugh accepts the sword of the Lord of the region and agrees to slay the menace because he wants to help the people, and he has fallen in love–ironically, not with Irene, but with Allia, the Lord's daughter.

Hugh and Irene go into the mountains together to face the menace, just as Ged and Tenar threaded the Labyrinth hand in hand to restore wholeness to Earthsea. When Hugh finally slays the dragon, the act is vividly described in terms that suggest sexual intercourse and matricide. In a symbolic rebirth, the wounded Hugh is dragged out from under the dead creature by Irene. Together they find their way back to the city, where Hugh recovers from his wounds in a hospital. In a rather abrupt ending, Hugh's mother refuses to let him come home, so Hugh and Irene take an apartment and decide to make a life together. As she does in all her fiction, Le Guin emphasizes in *The Beginning Place* the need to accept the pain and suffering involved in growing up and falling in love.

The achievement of *The Beginning Place* is its vivid, detailed realism, which brings alive both the plastic suburb and the haunting twilight land and makes us believe in the possibility of crossing the threshold between the two. The "real" world and the "fantastic" one are coexisting and complementary: the people of Tembreabrezi need Hugh and Irene to save them, and the young couple in turn need Tembreabrezi so that they may find themselves and grow up. Le Guin's writing in *The Beginning Place* has her characteristic purity and clarity and is frequently lyrical. She shows an admirable new restraint in not spelling out her moral for the reader but allowing the story to speak for itself.

The Compass Rose (1982) is a collection of twenty short stories, some previously published separately. In her preface, Le Guin says of the collection, "This is the compass in four dimensions, spatial, temporal, material, and spiritual, the Rose of the New World . . . the stories it contains tend to go off each in its own direction. . . . Within it, various circling motions may be seen. . . . It gives rise to apparent excursions outward which are in fact incursions inward." She includes one more Orsinian tale and several humorous stories, such as "SQ"–in which a secretary is left running the world after almost everyone else has failed the sanity quotient test–and "Intracom"–a satire of *Star Trek*.

Others take for their theme miscommunication, such as "Mazes," in which a behavioral scientist fails to understand the sophisticated physical language of the animal under study, and "The Eye Altering," in which colonists on a new world mistake adaptive mutations for illness. "The Author of the Acacia Seeds and Other Extracts from the *Journal of Therolinguistics*," "The Wife's Story," and "Mazes," are quirky experiments in point of view. The frequently anthologized "New Atlantis" and critically acclaimed "Diary of the Rose" both speak against oppressive, authoritarian government. "The Water Is Wide" ends with Gideon's arrival at a beginning place, a theme more and more prominent in Le Guin's current fiction.

"The New Atlantis," a dark, sardonic picture of life in a future America, is an illustration of the fact that oppression can come from any quarter, from free enterprise and the American Way as surely as from any "ism." The heroine of this novella is a violist in Portland not too far– maybe twenty years, maybe a hundred–in the future. Her husband, a physicist, has just been released from a Rehabilitation Camp, really a concentration camp for radicals, intellectuals, and other groups deemed dangerous to the state. "The New Atlantis" shows the love between the musician, Belle, and the scientist, Simon, in a society where marriage is illegal and even fidelity is suspect. They survive illness, shortages of food and resources, and FBI surveillance, but when Simon and his friends discover a method of tapping solar energy directly, without expensive equipment, the government moves in and takes him away again.

Running throughout the story is a series of counterpoint passages, perhaps Belle's dreams, about a drowned continent and the beings who have begun to awaken as it starts to rise again. The reader is given no explanation of these passages, only the sensations of pressure and darkness giving way gradually to light and life. Other clues suggest that Belle may be in tune with the unknown Atlanteans. For instance, a man on a bus with her starts talking about rising and sinking continents, and although he tells her that it is all in the pamphlet he is reading, the pamphlet proves to be completely unrelated. Later, when she improvises on her viola, listeners in the next room have a vision of white towers rising from the sea. The underwater speakers tell of music that they hear as they rise: "the voices of the great souls, the great lives, the lonely ones, the voyagers."

Nothing is explained: who or what is in the New Atlantis, why the sea beds are rising and the continents sinking, what those have to do with Belle and Simon. The lack of clear connections is frustrating. It is not that the story seems meaningless: one gets a sense of purpose beyond human comprehension. The Atlanteans are waiting for some consummation, but it never comes. The story ends with their questions, "Where are you? We are here. Where have you gone?" People on the surface have failed to keep the appointment. Because Simon's discovery is suppressed or lost, civilization ends before the white towers break into the air. As in *The Word for World Is Forest*, there is no meeting. It is a sad and puzzling story, a story of squandered opportunity.

The Eye of the Heron first appeared in *Millenial Women*, a collection of feminist science fiction, before being published separately. What makes it unusual for a Le Guin story is that the main character, Luz, is a woman. The daughter of Boss Falco, Luz lives in Victoria City on the planet Victoria, a dumping ground for undesirables from Earth. Begun as a penal colony, the society in Victoria City has developed as authoritarian, violent, and male-dominated. Outside the city is the town of Shantih, where the People of Peace, who were exiled from Earth for being pacifists, live. Inevitably, the two clash. The story describes Luz's development of self-identity, which she achieves at the cost of her family, her city, and the man she loves. But her story, too, ends at a beginning place.

Familiar images and ideas abound–cycles, journeys, coming of age. The heron, Spivack notes, is a sacred image in Taoism, signifying vigilance, quietness, and the ability to enter higher states of consciousness. Showing what happens when pacifists fight back, thematically the novel comes between *The Dispossessed*, with its pacifists who refuse to fight, and the psychology of war Le Guin presents in *The Word for World Is Forest* and *Always Coming Home*. Spivack finds other similarities to *The Word For World Is Forest:* both contain effective nature symbols, yet in both worlds the good characters are unambiguously good and the bad have no redeeming qualities.

Le Guin's most recent novel, *Always Coming Home* (1985), is set in a post-nuclear-holocaust future but is more cultural anthropology than science fiction. It is the story of the peaceful Kesh or Valley people and the warrior Condor people who, as she says in her "First Note," "might be going to have lived a long, long time from now in Northern California." The narrator, Stone Telling, looks back over her life caught between the two cultures. Growing up with her Kesh mother, Stone Telling knows from the inside the Valley culture: pacifist, anarchist, matrilineal, free, with all members participating in decision making, where wealth is measured by how much one gives. As a young woman, she goes to live with her Condor father and discovers how different Condor culture is: patrilineal, highly structured and authoritarian with strict divisions of labor and gender, violent–against man and nature, where wealth is measured by how much one has. Although she marries a Condor man and bears him a child, she never fits into Condor life, and with her father's help she returns with her daughter to the Kesh. Because she has family ties to both groups, no matter where she goes Stone Telling is always coming home. Because she feels different from those who are wholly Kesh or wholly Condor, she never fully arrives at home, remaining in the process of coming.

Le Guin fills *Always Coming Home* with familiar themes and images: circular journey, coming of age, definition of humanity (to the Condor, Kesh are animals), and identity through naming. Taoism informs the sets of opposing forces: male/female, authoritarian/anarchist, violent/pacifist,

public/private, foreign/familiar, dystopia/utopia. Stone Telling's story is her lifelong attempt to achieve wholeness. Le Guin also seeks wholeness for her novel by blurring the line between fact and fiction: in addition to the samples of Kesh poetry, stories, drama, myths, legends, recipes, and alphabet, and essays on dances, clothing, and time, the book comes with an audio tape of Kesh music.

The critic Peter Nicholls has praised Le Guin for bringing to the field of science fiction "an intelligent and feeling use of image structures, in the manner of a poet" and "the interest of the traditional novelist in questions of character and moral growth." She brings these same talents to the fields of fantasy and children's literature. Le Guin has great gifts as a writer; she has been lauded by many critics for her style, her adaptation of mythic structures, her psychological insight, and her moral wisdom. Having mastered high fantasy, Le Guin has moved on to straight realism, fantasy for juveniles, and a unique blend of realism and romantic fantasy.

Interviews:
"Ursula K. Le Guin Interviewed by Jonathan Ward," *Algol*, 12 (Summer 1975): 6-10.
    Discusses *Left Hand of Darkness*, *The Dispossessed*, publishing science fiction, and anarchism.

George Wickes and Louise Westling, "Dialogue with Ursula Le Guin," *Northwest Review*, 20, nos. 2 and 3 (1982): 147-159.
    Interview covering childhood influences, writing process, preferred topics, location of Malafrena, and screenplay for Earthsea trilogy.

References:
John Algeo, "Magic Names: Onomastics in the Fantasies of Ursula Le Guin," *Names*, 30 (June 1982): 59-67.
    Looks at charactonyms, or trait-names, in *The Lathe of Heaven* and *A Wizard of Earthsea*.

Brian Attebery, "*The Beginning Place:* Le Guin's Metafantasy," *Children's Literature*, 10 (1982): 113-123.
    Explains the novel as exploring the relation between fantasy and reality and the use of fantasy "to evade or to achieve psychological growth," such as Irene and Hugh seeing in the monster a reflection of what each sees

as "his worst, hidden self" and both falling in love with reflections of themselves.

Søren Baggesen, "Utopian and Dystopian Pessimism: Le Guin's *The Word for World Is Forest* and Tiptree's 'We Who Stole the Dream,'" *Science-Fiction Studies*, 14 (March 1987): 34-43.
Using ideas of Ernst Bloch, posits two kinds of pessimism in these stories of victorious slave-rebellions: dystopian, found in Tiptree's story, expressing resignation to "the already decided," and utopian, found in Le Guin, a militant pessimism against "the not yet decided."

Douglas Barbour, "Wholeness and Balance in the Hainish Novels of Ursula K. Le Guin," *Science-Fiction Studies*, 1 (Spring 1974): 164-173.
After an introductory discussion of imagery in several novels, focuses on balance in *The Left Hand of Darkness* and *The Word for World Is Forest*, concluding that "Le Guin's artistic vision is multiplex, dualistic, and holistic" and that she recognizes the cultural relativity of truth.

Marlene S. Barr, ed., *Future Females: A Critical Anthology* (Bowling Green, Ohio: Bowling Green University Popular Press, 1981).
Fifteen essays about women in science fiction as characters and writers; essays by Barr and Norman Holland concern Le Guin specifically, both being transactive responses to *The Left Hand of Darkness;* these personally revealing essays yield surprising analyses of interest for critical approach as much as for content.

Barr and Nicholas D. Smith, eds., *Women and Utopia: Critical Interpretations* (Lanham, Md.: University Press of America, 1983).
Ten essays on utopian fiction by women; of particular interest is J. P. Rhodes's essay on androgyny in *The Left Hand of Darkness* and L. T. Sargent's essay defining anarchism, a concept central to the understanding of Le Guin's fiction.

Craig Barrow and Diana Barrow, "*The Left Hand of Darkness:* Feminism for Men," *Mosaic*, 20 (Winter 1987): 83-92.

Claims that the key to Le Guin's feminism and the feminist misunderstanding of her works is that she writes for an audience of biased, heterosexual males; Genly Ai's role is to expose male attitudes so that readers can recognize and come to terms with them.

James W. Bittner, "Chronosophy, Aesthetics, and Ethics in Le Guin's *The Dispossessed: An Ambiguous Utopia*," in *No Place Else: Explorations in Utopian and Dystopian Fiction*, edited by Eric S. Rabkin, Martin H. Greenberg, and Joseph D. Olander (Carbondale: Southern Illinois University Press, 1983), pp. 244-270.
Argues that Le Guin's theme is process—as demonstrated in a linguistic explication of *odo*, the building and unbuilding of walls, circular journey, Shevek's General Field Theory of the linear/cyclic relations in time, the structure of the chapters—comparing the mythical with the mathematical with the musical.

Bittner, "Persuading Us to Rejoice and Teaching Us How to Praise: Le Guin's *Orsinian Tales*," *Science-Fiction Studies*, 5 (November 1978): 215-242.
Identifies typical Le Guin concerns—circular journey, blending of fantasy and realism—and argues that her theme is the certainty of human relations (fidelity, constancy, love) in contrast with the fluidity of politics, geography, psychology, morality, concluding with close readings of "Imaginary Countries" and "An Die Musik."

Barbara J. Bucknall, *Ursula K. Le Guin* (New York: Ungar, 1981).
Traces development of Le Guin's career through a close reading of novels and selected stories through *The Eye of the Heron*, emphasizing her use of myths, themes of balance and utopia/dystopia, and the *Tao Te Ching*.

Thomas D. Clareson, ed., *Extrapolation*, special Ursula K. Le Guin issue, 21 (Fall 1980).
Includes ten articles on Le Guin and a review of *The Beginning Place*, covers themes of androgyny, balance, utopia, cyclical renewal, feminism, and influences of *Tao Te Ching*, myths, Jungian archetypes in Earthsea trilogy, *The Left Hand of Darkness*, *The Dispossessed*, *The Word for World Is Forest*,

City of Illusion, "The Day Before the Revolution," and one poem.

Anna Valdine Clemens, "Art, Myth and Ritual in Le Guin's *Left Hand of Darkness," Canadian Review of American Studies,* 17 (Winter 1986): 423-436.
Identifies Le Guin's themes as fidelity and betrayal, guilt and responsibility (with accompanying theme of sacrifice) and examines archetypal feminine images in the novel and draws parallels to several Greek myths.

Robert Collins, "Fantasy and 'Forestructures': The Effect of Philosophical Climate upon Perceptions of the Fantastic," in *Bridges to Fantasy,* edited by Rabkin, George E. Slusser, and Robert Scholes (Carbondale: Southern Illinois University Press, 1982), pp. 108-120.
Using a phenomenological model, argues that what is fantastic is relative; includes brief discussion of *The Farthest Shore* as illustration of Heidegger's "Abyss."

Richard D. Erlich, "Ursula K. Le Guin and Arthur C. Clarke on Immanence, Transcendence, and Massacres," *Extrapolation,* 28 (Summer 1987): 105-129.
Shows how both work for peace and the global family against the "Ramboesque ideal of good Alien as *dead* Alien," personally and through their fiction, focusing the discussion of Le Guin on *The Left Hand of Darkness, The Lathe of Heaven,* and *The Word for World Is Forest.*

James P. Farrelly, "The Promised Land: Moses, Nearing, Skinner, Le Guin," *Journal of General Education,* 33 (Spring 1981): 15-23.
In discussing *The Dispossessed,* likens Shevek to Moses, only Le Guin's character is more prophet than leader; Shevek learns that paradise is a relative term.

Donald M. Hassler, "The Touching of Love and Death in Ursula Le Guin with Comparisons to Jane Austen," *University of Mississippi Studies in English,* 4 (1983): 168-177.
Draws comparisons between Austen and Le Guin (*The Left Hand of Darkness, The Dispossessed)* in their use of love, courtship, and marriage as "a hedge against death."

Keith N. Hull, "What Is Human? Ursula Le Guin and Science Fiction's Great Theme," *Modern Fiction Studies,* 32 (Spring 1986): 65-74.
Argues that Le Guin's dominant theme is defining what is human, emphasizing culture in her writing and just enough hard science to establish the alien situation.

David Ketterer, *New Worlds for Old: The Apocalyptic Imagination, Science Fiction and American Literature* (Bloomington: Indiana University Press, 1974).
Includes chapter on *The Left Hand of Darkness* as an archetypal "winter-journey" emphasizing the "mythic pattern of death and rebirth [that] underlies the action of the novel," reinforced by images, Gethenian myths, Estraven's family history of "bringing unity out of discord through 'treachery,'" cycle of seasons, cyclic journey.

Karl Kroeber, "Sisters and Science Fiction," *The Little Magazine,* 10 (Spring-Summer 1976): 87-90.
Claims that his sister is an imaginative writer, not a science-fiction writer, and states that by imaginatively experiencing a novel or play readers learn "useful truths of human existence" and become, as a result, "more competent human (e.g., moral) organisms."

David J. Lake, "Le Guin's Twofold Vision: Contrary Image Sets in *Left Hand of Darkness," Science-Fiction Studies,* 8 (July 1981): 156-164.
Interprets the novel by means of William Blake's theory of Contraries and Negations, setting up a cold team of images and ideas to go with Orgoreyn and a warm team for Karhide.

Susan McLean, "*The Beginning Place:* An Interpretation," *Extrapolation,* 24 (Summer 1983): 130-142.
Identifies the recurring Le Guin theme of incest, focusing on *The Beginning Place,* her "most Oedipal book to date," in a Jungian (but readable) interpretation, with some discussion of names and Minotaur myth.

Walter E. Meyers, *Aliens and Linguistics: Language Study and Science Fiction* (Athens: University of Georgia Press, 1980).

Surveys "the uses, whether sound or unsound, to which [science fiction] writers . . . put linguistics," including scattered but insightful references to Le Guin, with a fairly thorough discussion of language control in *The Dispossessed.*

R. D. Mullen and Darko Suvin, eds., *Science Fiction Studies: Selected Articles on Science Fiction 1973-1975* (Boston: Gregg, 1976), pp. 146-155, 223-231, 233-304.
Articles from volumes 1 and 2 of *Science-Fiction Studies,* including articles by Le Guin and those from the special issue (*Extrapolation*) on her concerning structure of the Hainish novels, utopian narrative in *The Dispossessed* and *The Left Hand of Darkness,* forest metaphor in *The Word for World Is Forest* and "Vaster Than Empires and More Slow," public and private conflict in *The Left Hand of Darkness,* ambiguity in *The Dispossessed, The Left Hand of Darkness* and *The Dispossessed* as social-science fiction, theme of de-alienation.

Victoria Myers, "Conversational Technique in Ursula Le Guin: A Speech-Act Analysis," *Science-Fiction Studies,* 10 (November 1983): 306-316.
Using speech-act theories of Austen and Searle, focuses on two conversations in *The Left Hand of Darkness* to show how Le Guin makes the reader aware of language barriers between Genly Ai and the "aliens," why he misunderstands them, and how he reduces those barriers; somewhat difficult.

Joseph D. Olander and Martin Harry Greenberg, eds., *Writers of the 21st Century Series: Ursula K. Le Guin* (New York: Taplinger, 1979).
Nine essays covering topics such as Jungian reading of Earthsea trilogy, journey pattern as physical action reflecting psychic action, elements of the Romantic tradition in the vegetable-world stories, influence of Kropotkin (anarchism) on *The Dispossessed,* androgyny and structural unity in *The Left Hand of Darkness,* anarchism and utopian tradition, touch as theme and metaphor in all the novels, evolution of Le Guin's shadow motif, and patterns of integration in the Earthsea trilogy; includes bibliography through 1978.

Donald Palumbo, *Erotic Universe: Sexuality and Fantastic Literature* (New York: Greenwood Press, 1986).
Fifteen essays with extensive annotated bibliography; three essays focus on Le Guin's *The Left Hand of Darkness* and *The Dispossessed.*

Robert Scholes, *Structural Fabulation: An Essay on the Future of Fiction* (Notre Dame: University of Notre Dame Press, 1975).
Four lectures advocating serious treatment of science fiction with emphasis on *The Left Hand of Darkness* and brief mention of *A Wizard of Earthsea;* the fourth lecture argues for Le Guin's place among all contemporary writers because she shows "how speculative fabulation can deal with the social dimensions of existence as adequately as the most 'realistic' of traditional models."

Bernard Selinger, *Le Guin and Identity in Contemporary Fiction* (Ann Arbor: UMI Research Press, 1988).
Applying psychoanalytic theory (to counterbalance the numerous Jungian interpretations of her works), argues through close readings of her major novels that Le Guin's central theme is the "puzzle of identity."

Charlotte Spivack, "Only in dying, life: the Dynamics of Old Age in the Fiction of Ursula Le Guin," *Modern Language Studies,* 14 (Summer 1984): 43-53.
Focusing on Wold from *Planet of Exile,* Odo from "The Day Before the Revolution," and Ged in *The Farthest Shore,* shows Le Guin's concern for breaking stereotypes through her dialectic of age: characters at once both strong and weak, participants and antagonists, capable of action and contemplation, for whom death is a positive experience.

Spivack, *Ursula K. Le Guin* (Boston: Twayne, 1984).
Traces Le Guin's career through *The Beginning Place* through close readings of all novels and stories, discussing themes, language, structure, images, use of myths, especially cyclical elements; includes chapters of Le Guin's poetry and critical works.

Ian Watson, "Le Guin's *Lathe of Heaven* and the Role of Dick: The False Reality as Media-

tor," *Science-Fiction Studies*, 2 (March 1975): 67-75.
Argues that *The Lathe of Heaven* is a pivotal work between early Hainish novels and the direction taken in *The Word for World Is Forest* and *The Dispossessed* toward the paranormal, comparing her use of false reality to the model found in works by Philip K. Dick; of more general interest is the timeline in footnote 4 in which Watson works out a chronology for the novels in AD, League, and Ekumenical Years.

Kingsley Widmer, "The Dialectic of Utopianism: Le Guin's *The Dispossessed*," *Liberal and Fine Arts Review*, 3 (January-July 1983): 1-11.
Describes this novel as presenting "utopian-dystopian concepts and the permanent call to revolution," stating that she establishes then evaluates "a thoughtfully elaborated anarchist utopia" rooted in a "projection of contemporary American society."

Susan Wood, "Discovering Worlds: The Fiction of Ursula K. Le Guin," in *Voices for the Future*, volume 2, edited by Clareson (Bowling Green, Ohio: Bowling Green University Popular Press, 1979), pp. 154-179.
Summarizes Le Guin's career through *The Wind's Twelve Quarters* and *The Dispossessed*, briefly touching on recurrent themes, images, philosophy, with fuller discussions of the novels.

J. R. Wytenbroek, "*Always Coming Home*: Pacifism and Anarchy in Le Guin's Latest Utopia," *Extrapolation*, 28 (Winter 1987): 330-339.
Contrasts the Valley people with the Condor people through a psychology and anatomy of war, calling this novel "a powerful and timely anti-war statement."

Marilyn Yalom, ed., *Women Writers of the West Coast: Speaking of Their Lives and Careers* (Santa Barbara: Capra Press, 1983).
Collection of ten dialogues with women writers from the West Coast; Le Guin speaks of family influences, her early writing, other science fiction writers, feminist 'problems' with her works.

Norman Mailer

This entry was updated by J. Michael Lennon (Sangamon State University) from the entries by Philip M. Bufithis (Shepherd College) in DLB 2, American Novelists Since World War II *and* DLB Yearbook 1983; *Joseph Wenke (University of Connecticut) in* DLB 16, The Beats: Literary Bohemians in Postwar America; *and Alden Whitman in* DLB Yearbook 1980.

Places	Brooklyn Provincetown, Mass.	Alaska Egypt	Mexico Paris
Influences and Relationships	Leo Tolstoy Ernest Hemingway James T. Farrell	John Dos Passos Henry Miller André Malraux	Herman Melville Henry James

Literary Movements and Forms	Literary
	   Existentialism
	American Neo-
	   Romanticism
		The Beat Movement
		Naturalism
		Novel of Ideas
		Surrealism
			New Journalism /
			   The Nonfiction
			   Novel

Major Themes	Cosmic War
	   Between God
	   and the Devil
	Growth and
	   Courage
		Alienation
		Sex
		Violence
		Primitivism and
		   the Sensual
			Father-Son
			   Relationships
			The Artist
			   and Society

Cultural and Artistic Influences	Jazz The Theater Movies	Modern Architecture Sports Modern Art	Science and Technology
Social and Economic Influences	Socialism World War II The Holocaust	American Political Parties	The Bureaucracy The Vietnam War

See also the Mailer entries in DLB 28, Twentieth-Century American-Jewish Fiction Writers *and* DLB Documentary Series 3.

BIRTH: Long Branch, New Jersey, 31 January 1923, to Isaac Barnett and Fanny Schneider Mailer.

EDUCATION: S.B., Harvard University, 1943.

MARRIAGES: 1944 to Beatrice Silverman (divorced); child: Susan. 1954 to Adele Morales (divorced); children: Danielle, Elizabeth Anne. 1962 to Lady Jeanne Campbell (divorced); child: Kate. 1963 to Beverly Bentley; children: Michael Burks, Stephen McLeod. Common-law marriage to Carol Stevens (separated 1976); child: Maggie Alexandra.

AWARDS AND HONORS: First prize, *Story* magazine's annual college fiction contest for "The Greatest Thing in the World," 1941; National Institute of Arts and Letters grant, 1960; elected, National Institute of Arts and Letters, 1967; National Book Award, Pulitzer Prize, and Polk Award for *The Armies of the Night*, 1969; MacDowell Medal, 1973; Pulitzer Prize for *The Executioner's Song*, 1980.

SELECTED BOOKS: *The Naked and the Dead* (New York: Rinehart, 1948; London: Wingate, 1949);

Barbary Shore (New York: Rinehart, 1951; London: Cape, 1952);

The Deer Park (New York: Putnam's, 1955; London: Wingate, 1957);

The White Negro: Superficial Reflections on the Hipster (San Francisco: City Lights Books, 1957);

Advertisements for Myself (New York: Putnam's, 1959; London: Deutsch, 1961);

Deaths for the Ladies (and other disasters) (New York: Putnam's, 1962; London: Deutsch, 1962);

The Presidential Papers (New York: Putnam's, 1963; London: Deutsch, 1964);

An American Dream (New York: Dial, 1965; London: Deutsch, 1965);

Cannibals and Christians (New York: Dial, 1966; London: Deutsch, 1967);

The Bull Fight: A Photographic Narrative With Text by Norman Mailer (New York: Macmillan, 1967);

The Deer Park: A Play (New York: Dial, 1967; London: Weidenfeld & Nicolson, 1970);

Norman Mailer (photo copyright © Jerry Bauer)

Why Are We in Vietnam? (New York: Putnam's, 1967; London: Weidenfeld & Nicolson, 1969);

The Short Fiction of Norman Mailer (New York: Dell, 1967); republished in *The Essential Mailer* (Sevenoaks, Kent, U.K.: New English Library, 1982);

The Idol and the Octopus: Political Writings on the Kennedy and Johnson Administrations (New York: Dell, 1968);

The Armies of the Night: History as a Novel, The Novel as History (New York: New American Library, 1968; London: Weidenfeld & Nicolson, 1968);

Miami and the Siege of Chicago (New York: World, 1968; London: Weidenfeld & Nicolson, 1968);

A Fire on the Moon (London: Weidenfeld & Nicolson, 1970); republished as *Of a Fire on the Moon* (Boston: Little, Brown, 1971);

Maidstone: A Mystery (New York: New American Library, 1971);

King of the Hill: On the Fight of the Century (New York: New American Library, 1971);

The Prisoner of Sex (Boston: Little, Brown, 1971; London: Weidenfeld & Nicolson, 1971);

The Long Patrol (New York: World, 1971);

Existential Errands (Boston: Little, Brown, 1972); republished in *The Essential Mailer*;

St. George and the Godfather (New York: New American Library, 1972);

Marilyn: A Biography (New York: Grosset & Dunlap, 1973; London: Hodder & Stoughton, 1973);

The Faith of Graffiti (New York: Praeger, 1974); republished as *Watching My Name Go By* (London: Mathews, Miller, Dunbar, 1974);

The Fight (Boston: Little, Brown, 1975; London: Hart-Davis, 1976);

Genius and Lust: A Journey Through the Major Writings of Henry Miller (New York: Grove, 1976);

Some Honorable Men: Political Conventions, 1960-1972 (Boston: Little, Brown, 1976);

A Transit to Narcissus (New York: Howard Fertig, 1978);

The Executioner's Song (Boston: Little, Brown, 1979; London: Hutchinson, 1979);

Of Women and Their Elegance (New York: Simon & Schuster, 1980; Sevenoaks, Kent, U.K.: Hodder & Stoughton, 1980);

Pieces and Pontifications (Boston: Little, Brown, 1982; Sevenoaks, Kent, U.K.: New English Library, 1983);

Ancient Evenings (Boston: Little, Brown, 1983; London: Macmillan, 1983);

Tough Guys Don't Dance (New York: Random House, 1984; London: Michael Joseph, 1984).

PLAY PRODUCTION: *Strawhead*, New York, Actor's Studio, 1986.

SCREENPLAYS: *Wild 90*, Supreme Mix, 1968;

Beyond the Law, Supreme Mix / Evergreen Films, 1968;

Maidstone, Supreme Mix, 1971;

The Executioner's Song, Film Communications Inc. Productions, 1982;

Tough Guys Don't Dance, Cannon Films, Inc., 1986.

Norman Mailer's achievement lies primarily in his treatment of the conflict between man's search for self-actualization and the strictures society places upon him. Mailer has rendered this theme with an energy of style, an ideational power, and a vivid drama that have earned him an international reputation. His books have been translated into more than twenty languages. They stir foreign audiences because, notes Anthony Burgess, they are "political, which is a great recommendation to all Europeans, and British fiction is just about unexportable manners. I mean 'political,' of course, in the widest sense—the sense of protest or counterprotest."

Mailer presents a special problem to anyone trying to arrive at a clear understanding of his work, for he has gained notoriety as a public figure as well as a writer. His extraliterary activities—acts of civil disobedience, running for mayor of New York, tempestuous marriages, contentious remarks on television talk shows, belligerent behavior at parties—have caused him in many quarters to be more read about than read. It might appear that his public role has been a self-aggrandizing one, that since the publication of *Advertisements for Myself* (1959), he has been huckstering himself into fame, but this view is predicated on the false assumption that his public performances are strategies designed to promote his books. Actually, Mailer's escapades are crucial to the creation of his work, not to its promotion. He behaves as he does the better to write. He tries to realize in his life the beliefs, hopes, and imaginings that he expresses in his work. "Till people see where their ideas lead, they know nothing," he has said. As one would expect, the process becomes cyclical, for what Mailer discovers by testing his fictional ideas in the world is the need to modify or enlarge upon those ideas by writing more books. The important point is this: there exists in the case of Norman Mailer a symbiotic relationship between life and art. To do in one's life what one has said in one's art is an assertion of creative individuality.

By involving himself in the major crises of our time, Mailer has endeavored to reanimate for modern man a belief in the struggle between God and the Devil. Man's courage—or lack of it—against the encroachment of technology, authoritarianism, and mass values will contribute, Mailer believes, to the outcome of that struggle. His engagements in national events represent his attempts to oppose such encroachments. In 1948, at the age of twenty-five, he campaigned for Henry Wallace, the Progressive party's candidate for president. He gave over twenty-five speeches as a member of the Progressive Citizens of America, wrote articles for the *New York Post*, and spoke on the subject of academic freedom at the convention for the National Council of Arts, Sciences, and Professions. But he soon became disillusioned with progressivism's alliances with communism and announced at the Waldorf Peace Conference in New York that the Russian and American governments were equally imperialistic, equally bent on securing new markets for themselves by dominating backward countries. In 1962, to demonstrate against the desperate logic of nuclear bomb shelters, he stood in City Hall Park in New York and refused to take shelter during a civil defense drill. In 1967, while participating in the antiwar march in Washington, he crossed the United States Marshals' line and headed alone for the Pentagon. Mailer was arrested. In 1969 he announced his candidacy for mayor of New York. Running on a secessionist platform, he advocated that New York City be made into the fifty-first state and that its neighborhoods effect self-governance. He came in a distant fourth in a field of five. In 1974 he founded the Fifth Estate, a citizens' organization established to investigate the activities of the Central Intelligence Agency and the Federal Bureau of Investigation. These actions by Mailer may be put under one ideological rubric or another, but they all go beyond politics to the individual's ambition to do battle with whatever fate society has designed for him and thereby gain for himself a larger life.

The pattern of Norman Mailer's early life, however, does not prefigure with any certainty the defiant eccentricities that would come later. The first child and only son (he has a sister, Barbara) of Isaac Barnett Mailer and Fanny Schneider Mailer, he was born on 31 January 1923 in Long Branch, a resort town on New Jersey's north shore, where his mother's family was in the hotel business. Isaac Mailer, of Russian-Jewish extraction, served in the British army as a supply officer and immigrated to America from South Africa via London shortly after World War I. When his son was four years old, he moved his family to the Eastern Parkway section of Brooklyn, "the most secure Jewish environment in America," Mailer recalls. Isaac (Barney) worked as an accountant in Brooklyn until his death in 1972. Mrs. Mailer ran a nursing and housekeeping service there until a few years before her death in 1985. Barbara has worked from time to time as her brother's secretary.

Mailer and his sister both graduated with honors—he from Harvard and she from Radcliffe. Norman "always had the highest marks," his mother recalled. He was a confident youngster who played the clarinet and spent untold hours building model airplanes. Aeronautics was his first love, but it is noteworthy that as early as the age of nine he expressed this love in a literary way. He filled 250 notebook pages with a fantastical story called "An Invasion from Mars." At Boys' High School in Brooklyn, Mailer published his first work, an article on how to build model airplanes. Upon graduation he set his sights on the Massachusetts Institute of Technology and the study of aeronautical engineering. Because he was only sixteen, M.I.T. wanted him to go to prep school for an additional year, so he chose Harvard instead.

In his first semester at Harvard Mailer discovered the modern American novel—*Studs Lonigan, U.S.A.* and *The Grapes of Wrath* were particularly influential. He devoted himself to writing, read Wolfe, Hemingway, and Faulkner, and vowed that he would become a major American novelist. His first short story, "The Greatest Thing in the World," was published in the *Harvard Advocate*. Derivative in conception, it was clearly written under the influence of his first masters: James T. Farrell, John Dos Passos, and John Steinbeck. Encouraged by his writing professor Robert Gorham Davis, he submitted the story to *Story* magazine's annual college contest and won first prize. Like all literary prizes, though, this one brought its weight of worry. Eighteen-year-old Truman Capote was already creating stories of consummate artistic beauty while Mailer feared that he was merely writing prose that, as he put it, "reads like the early work of a young man who is going to make a fortune writing first rate action, western, gangster, and suspense pictures."

After graduating from Harvard in 1943, Mailer set out to allay his natural feelings of callowness and garner some experiences on his own. He was inducted into the army in March 1944. That same month he married Beatrice Silverman of Chelsea, Massachusetts, who became a lieutenant in the WAVES. Sent to the Pacific, Private Mailer became by his own admission "the third lousiest GI in a platoon of twelve." Actually he was not much interested in becoming a good soldier. Rather, he was obsessed with satisfying what he called that "cold maniacal thing in my heart, sharp as a shiv"—the desire to write the definitive American novel of World War II. He went ashore with the United States infantry forces in the invasion of Luzon. Then, with his appointment to a desk job as a clerk-typist, the excitement came to a stop. Eager to get the experience necessary to write his novel, he volunteered as a rifleman with a reconnaissance platoon fighting in the Philippine mountains. After his discharge in April 1946, he settled down to fifteen months of writing. *The Naked and the Dead* achieved a remarkable critical and popular success. By 1948, the year of its publication, Norman Mailer found himself the most celebrated young writer in America.

The Naked and the Dead tells the story of a fourteen-man infantry platoon that lands on the barren beach of a small Japanese-held island in the South Pacific. The platoon is part of a six-thousand-man force charged with the task of seizing control of the island in order to clear the way for a larger American advance into the Philippines. Mailer carefully delineates the differences—emotional, geographic, social, economic—of each man in the platoon, for he intends it to represent a microcosm of the American populace. The platoon includes a God-fearing Mississippi dirt farmer; a sensitive Jew from Brooklyn; a socially oppressed Mexican-American; an embittered, itinerant laborer from the coal mines of Montana; a reactionary Irishman from South Boston's working class; a dull, middle-class Kansas salesman; a cynical Chicago hoodlum; and a dissipated hedonist from Georgia.

Over the perspective of both officers and enlisted men prevails the narrative voice of Mailer, who remains a detached, omniscient observer. He conveys the tribulations of war objectively. Though his prose recalls the clarity and precision of Steinbeck's *The Grapes of Wrath*, the stance he takes toward his characters resembles that of Dos Passos in his *U.S.A.* trilogy. Mailer refuses to allow the reader to get involved with a character or to imagine that any man has control over the historical moment in which he finds himself. Mailer discourages sympathy for his characters by shifting the narrative to another character or scene. In the case of Lieutenant Hearn, for example, the reader draws near only to be cut off from him with a sudden notice of his death: "A half hour later, Hearn was killed by a machine-gun bullet which passed through his chest." It seems that only the grimmest of interpretations can be drawn. In a dumb, wanton universe man labors to die. He does not really fit into the universe; he is an outlaw on an earth not designed for him. In a profoundly anti-Christian vein, Mailer concludes that God does not take any interest in man.

Front cover for Mailer's 1957 exploration of the "existentialist synapses of the Negro" as a psychic model for the adventure-seeking "hipster" or "white Negro"

The compelling dramatic tension of this novel derives from Mailer's fascination with the lives of three men—General Cummings, Sergeant Croft, and Lieutenant Hearn—who press their wills upon necessity. Their efforts to define themselves in opposition to a deterministic universe present all that Mailer held to be of moral value at this stage in his career. These three men, without losing their individuality, are modern incarnations of the great mythic figures of western civilization. Cummings, in his overweening urge to shape reality to his own needs and make the world answerable to them, represents Faustian man. Hearn, in his dispassionate rejection of everything that would impose conditions on the autonomy of his thought, is Socratic man. And Croft, in his irrepressible desire to climb Mount Anaka (the mountain in the center of the island), resembles the Satanic hero. The mythic heroism of these three men and the naturalistic universe they oppose constitute the primary conflict in *The*

Naked and the Dead. In thematic terms, the conflict is between romance and idealism. The interplay between these two elements gives this novel its identifying form as a work of art.

The action of the novel is both foreshadowed by and centered on Mount Anaka. When Croft undertakes to lead the reconnaissance platoon over the mountain, his rebellion attains archetypal proportions. For in climbing Mount Anaka, Croft intends to confirm that he is not what the mountain, in its aloof splendor, seems to say he is: mere flesh, a weak, transitory creature. The mountain symbolizes to Croft the deific qualities which mock man's mortality. To scale Mount Anaka would mean to him that man is more than mere flesh, that he possesses the mystical strength of the mountain. But when Croft fails to reach the summit, he despairs in the knowledge that he was wrong. Man may be *in* nature—for Mailer he is entrapped in it, embroiled in it—but he is not *of* it. No intimate kinship exists between man and nature.

Mailer chose war as the subject of his first novel because he was convinced that only in a crisis could man's real nature be revealed. In *The Naked and the Dead* Mailer dealt with two age-old human tensions—the struggle between animal desire and spiritual aspiration and the struggle between individualism and authority—in their essential pattern, with power, gravity, and veracity. A hammering scrutiny of life's damage leaves an earnest respect for the people who must sustain it.

The success of *The Naked and the Dead* allowed Mailer to cut loose from his old identity of nice-Jewish-boy-from-Brooklyn and to seek a new one. Always sympathetic to socialism, he entered first the realm of politics, but his espousal of Henry Wallace's bid for the presidency had made him realize that the end result of all governmental systems is oligarchic dominance. He traveled next to Hollywood, where he wrote an original screenplay for M-G-M, but it was rejected, and Mailer, concluding that fiction was his proper medium after all, left Hollywood. He returned East, where he wrote the greater part of his second novel, *Barbary Shore*.

Deeply influenced by Jean Malaquais—the left-wing French intellectual who became Mailer's friend and guided him through the tortuous roadways of Marxist philosophy—*Barbary Shore* (1951) is an odd, febrile story of five desiccated lives caught between American and Soviet authoritarianism. Mailer wrote the book at an anguished pitch and came up with some starkly illuminating insights into the psyche of the Fascist, the Trotskyite, the secret agent, the psychotic, the existentialist, and mass man. The critics were not impressed. Those intent on upholding the puritanism of Eisenhower-era America called the book solid; others called it ponderous.

A divorce from Beatrice Silverman followed the publication of *Barbary Shore*. For some time Mailer had been wanting to free himself and move to Greenwich Village, where he imagined he could live a life of adventurous pleasure. When a friend introduced him to the beautiful Adele Morales, a Spanish-Peruvian painter, he found the world of lavish excitement he had been missing. They were married in 1954. In the next year Mailer founded, with Daniel Wolf and Edwin Fancher, the *Village Voice*, a pioneering weekly newspaper on politics and the arts. (Mailer came up with the name.) His use of more and more potent stimulants—liquor, marijuana, Benzedrine, Seconal—took its physical toll—appendicitis and a damaged liver. But it seemed as though Mailer was willing to rush death rather than return to normalcy, for he was convinced that experimentation with drugs had brought him Dionysian knowledge.

In the midst of his delusion, his recklessness, and what he thought of as his sloth, Mailer set out to write a novel that he hoped would regain for him the distinction he had lost with the publication of *Barbary Shore*. He committed himself fully to the writing of *The Deer Park* (1955), a novel about the symbolic hell of a Hollywood resort and the venal people in it. The novel's *raisonneur* is a movie director, Charles Eitel. Eitel directed brilliant films of honest social consciousness in the 1930s; but after World War II, when a congressional investigative committee accuses him of Communist involvements, he refuses to become a "friendly witness" and thereby sacrifices a successful career as one of Hollywood's top box-office directors. Blacklisted by every studio, Eitel tries to revive his dormant creative powers and write a screenplay that will atone for all the slick, gaudy movies he has made since his fine early work. His inability to do so constitutes the central drama of the novel.

Despite personal defeat, Eitel harbors an inviolate vision of what it is to grow—a vision that is the guiding light of the novel. He realizes his sterile condition and reflects that "there was a law of life so cruel and so just which demanded that one must grow or else pay more for remaining the same." He imparts the lessons of his self-judgments to Sergius O'Shaugnessy, the novel's narrator. The Eitel-Sergius relationship is a tutor-tyro one. Eitel frankly assesses Sergius and encourages "self-analysis." What Eitel means by self-analysis is the creation of an "art work." For he believes that only in an art work can man discover his inner self and give form to his strivings. For all the concentration on the mores of stars, starlets, producers, sensualists, and panderers in *The Deer Park*, its ethical imperative is rather outdated: only sacrifice and hard work will transcend "the mummery of what happens, passes, and is gone." The reader is led to believe that in a conformist society the creation of art is the only strategy against anonymity. An art work, Sergius eventually realizes through Eitel's sad example, will give him "dignity" and enable him to "keep in some permanent form those parts of myself which are better than me." Art teaches Sergius that only through identification with impersonal beauty can human suffering and human limitation be transcended. In Sergius's terms, the world embodied in an art work is the "real world" because it is the honest and permanent distillate of one's selfhood. Desert D'Or (the Hollywood resort of the story) is the "imaginary world" because it is devoted to that which is corporeal and therefore wholly perishable–physical beauty and material success.

Yet the problem with *The Deer Park* is that Sergius, for all his talk, is really an underdeveloped character. One does not have a sense of involvement with him because he is undersensitive and nearly devoid of tenderness; at least that is how he presents himself. Things happen to him without things happening inside him. What more than compensates for the flaws in the characterization of Sergius is the delineation of the affair between Eitel and the woman he loves–Elena Esposito, sometime actress and castoff of other men. With scrupulous honesty Mailer renders the relationship with its dynamic of sensual rapture and love, its attendant disillusionment, its deterioration, and its final stale disablement. Mailer's two characterizations are charged with life: Eitel, the suave but tortured gentleman whose perverse will compels him, despite his intelligence, to debase his artistic talents; Elena, the desperate, graceless beauty, humiliated by men and simple in her understanding of life, but valiantly in possession of self-dignity. Sergius talks about himself with a phony tartness, but he narrates the Eitel-Elena affair with dispassionate wisdom.

The novel's setting, Desert D'Or, reinforces the doomed, airless quality of the love affair. It is the center of the book which gives form to the "prisons of pain, the wading pools of pleasure, and the public and professional voices of our sentimental land." This for Mailer constitutes American culture at large. Desert D'Or is an infernal arena of "middle aged desperados of corporation land and the suburb" locked into a perpetual round of greed and lust. The desert that surrounds the resort symbolizes the spiritual wasteland within. Windowless facades and walled-in patios give sanctuary to people who have relinquished their souls to Mammon and Eros. The town possesses no tradition or heritage or recognizable past. It is a "no-man's land of the perpetual present." Sergius remarks on the "air cooled midnight" of the town's bars: "Drinking in that atmosphere, I never knew whether it was night or day. . . . afternoon was always passing into night, and drunken nights into the dawn of a desert morning. One seemed to leave the theatrical darkness of afternoon for the illumination of night, and the sun of Desert D'Or became like the stranger who the drunk imagines to be following him." Man has been divorced from the diurnal cycle. Symbolically, his connection with organic life has been severed. Mailer's purgatorial vision of Desert D'Or intensifies the novel's theme enunciated by Eitel: " 'One cannot look for a good time, Sergius, for pleasure must end as love or cruelty'–and almost as an afterthought, he added–'or obligation.' " *The Deer Park* is an ironic prose elegy about people seeking pleasure as though it were happiness.

When *The Deer Park* appeared, it met with mixed reviews. It was only a partial success, which, on Mailer's competitive scale of all or nothing, meant a failure. Because the world had not, he believed, tried to understand him, he resolved that he would no longer try to understand the world. Rather, he would turn inward to explore his own psyche in such a way that one would come to believe it was America's psyche itself that was being explored. He succeeded. *Advertisements for Myself* established Mailer as a writer of searing candor and oracular brilliance. He became *philosophe maudit* to the nation.

Advertisements for Myself (1959) is a compendium of Mailer's writings, almost all previously published, from the first eighteen years of his career. It is a multigeneric display of short stories, poems, plays, essays, articles, interviews, letters, excerpts from novels, and columns from the *Village*

Voice. This assemblage is interlinked with commentary, what Mailer calls "Advertisements," in which he chronicles his fervent efforts–through honor and dishonor, security and paranoia, aspiration and disillusion, recklessness and remorse–to realize the best in himself through art. In writing openly and movingly about these struggles, Mailer came out from behind his fiction and established himself as a national personality, an undeniable literary presence whose admissions recalled the self-promoting strategies of Walt Whitman. An undertone of vehemence, however, balances the book's narcissism: "I have not gotten nicer as I have grown older, and I suspect that what has been true for me may be true for a good many of you."

Mailer may rather enjoy being embittered; he certainly must have gotten satisfaction from his "Advertisements" because they are written with a color, a freedom, and a brio never before found in his work:

> The shits are killing us, even as they kill themselves–each day a few more lies eat into the seed with which we are born, little institutional lies from the print of newspapers, the shock waves of television, and the sentimental cheats of the movie screen. Little lies, but they pipe us toward insanity as they starve our sense of the real. We have grown up in a world more in decay than the worst of the Roman Empire, a cowardly world chasing after a good time (of which last one can approve) but chasing it without the courage to pay the price of full consciousness, and so losing pleasure in pips and squeaks of anxiety.

"The White Negro" lies at the heart of *Advertisements for Myself.* Published originally in *Dissent,* a literary-intellectual journal of the New Left, it has gained enormous popularity and is frequently anthologized. It represents a shift in Mailer's focus, because here for the first time he concentrates on psychic rather than social reality. He takes as his province the instinctual consciousness of the urban American Negro, who operates in accordance with subliminal needs. By replacing the imperatives of society with the imperatives of the self, the urban black makes it impossible for institutions of social control to account for him in their own terms. This demonic rebel is for Mailer the essence of "hip" and the model for "a new breed of adventurers, urban adventurers who drifted out at night looking for action with a black man's code to fit their facts. The hipster had absorbed the existentialist synapses of the Negro, and for practical purposes could be considered a white Negro."

The hipster's response to experience is intuitive, sensuous, and violent. Mailer's radical assumption is that each act of individual violence, no matter how heinous it may be, subtracts from the collective violence of the state (such as the liquidation of European Jews or the nuclear bombings of Japan). He was later to suggest, in his writings of the late 1960s for example, that the war in Vietnam was partly the result of our inhibitive lives. Mass private constraint, a population "starved into the attrition of conformity," can precipitate mass catastrophe. Unlike individual violence, no one supposedly is responsible for war; so, says Mailer, war becomes a socially acceptable means of expressing violence. It is in defiance of the "collective murders of the State" that the hipster develops into a psychopath. "The strength of the psychopath is that he knows (where most of us can only guess) what is good for him and what is bad for him at exactly those instants when . . . the potentiality exists to change [or] replace a negative and empty fear with an outward action. . . ." Mailer is saying that if violence alone will overcome fear, let violence be. Man is better off close to death than hag-ridden by the dictates of a conformist society or emasculated by an anesthetic modular world.

This hipster psychopath is an authentic existentialist because his philosophy is felt, not conceptualized. Informed by the writings of Jean-Paul Sartre, Mailer contends that the only value is that value which answers one's own psychological needs. "There are no truths other than the isolated truths of what each observer feels at each instance of his existence. . . ." To judge or view man "from a set of standards conceived a priori to . . . experience, standards from the past," is to preclude his right to grow according to whatever measure he sets for himself. The energy with which the hipster psychopath spurs himself on to growth is derived from a continual search for "an orgasm more apocalyptic than the one which preceded it. Orgasm is his therapy–he knows at the seed of his being that good orgasm opens his possibilities and bad orgasm imprisons him." Mailer reverses the spirit/flesh dichotomy. It is the flesh that gives sanction and value to the spirit, not vice versa. In the orgasmic moment the hipster believes he can become identical with God Who is "located in the senses of the body."

Ultimately, "The White Negro" goes beyond social psychology and sexology and turns out to be Mailer's portrait of his own psyche and of his own creative processes. Each of Mailer's subsequent protagonists in his novels is emotionally (though not factually) autobiographical and modeled on the hipster delineated in this essay. The vitalizing madness and compulsive energy that underlie *The Naked and the Dead* and *Barbary Shore* surface here.

The turbulence which expressed itself exuberantly in *Advertisements for Myself* fearsomely rocked Mailer's personal life. In 1960, after an all-night party at their new Manhattan apartment, he stabbed his wife Adele with a penknife, seriously wounding her, and entered Bellevue hospital for seventeen days of psychiatric observation. His wife did not press charges; she recovered and they were soon reconciled. But in 1962 he and Adele were divorced. That same year he married Lady Jeanne Campbell, daughter of the Duke of Argyll and granddaughter of Lord Beaverbrook. His marriage with Lady Jeanne was calamitous and short. After a year, in which a daughter, Kate, was born, they were divorced, and Mailer promptly married actress Beverly Bentley. What an astonishing departure all this is from the soft-voiced man who said in 1948, "Actually, I've got all the average middle-class fears." Now Mailer had become the terrible ruffian of American letters.

For sensation-seeking journalists Mailer became little more than material for racy copy. He was arrested in Provincetown for taunting and fighting with police officers; in a televised interview with Mike Wallace, he suggested that juvenile delinquency in New York could be decreased by holding once-a-year medieval jousting tournaments in Central Park between members of rival gangs; he was arrested at Birdland, a New York nightclub, in a bellicose argument over his liquor bill; at a poetry reading he had the curtain brought down on him for alleged obscenity; after Sonny Liston knocked out Floyd Patterson, he confronted the bearish Liston and told him to wise up and let him promote his next fight; he financed Jose Torres's bid for the world light-heavyweight championship and later donned a pair of boxing gloves himself to go four rounds with Torres on Dick Cavett's television show. These acts may seem exhibitionistic or absurd, but by Mailer's logic they help him to write well and therefore are not foolish.

Just how objectionable Mailer's behavior is depends then, in large part, on one's estimation of his writing, which has become more compelling since his emergence as a public personality. With the miscellanies–*The Presidential Papers* (1963) and *Cannibals and Christians* (1966)–he developed a reputation as an astute critic of politics and society in America. With *The Armies of the Night* and *Miami and the Siege of Chicago*, he gained an international reputation for a dramatic rendering of the same subjects. His two novels *An American Dream* and *Why Are We in Vietnam?* project the daydreams and subliminal compulsions of the American character with tonal colorations never before seen in American fiction.

An American Dream, which first appeared in installments in *Esquire* in 1964, was published separately in revised form the following year. In the novel the protagonist, Stephen Richards Rojack, affirms many of the ideas contained in Mailer's philosophy of Hip. Like the hipster, Rojack believes that death is "a creation more dangerous than life." Rojack came to this conviction during combat in World War II while staring into the eyes of a German soldier whom he had mortally wounded. The experience also led Rojack to the conclusion that "magic, dread, and the perception of death" are "the roots of motivation." By "magic" Rojack means the involvement of the supernatural–that is to say, God and the Devil–in human affairs. By "dread" he refers generally to an abject fear of the consequences of taking risks. Specifically, Rojack fears for the extinction of his soul as the result of a life in which he has wasted his talent and betrayed his ideals for the opportunities to acquire money, prestige, and social power. Over the years Stephen Rojack, Phi Beta Kappa, winner of the Distinguished Service Cross, and congressman, has successively become Stephen Rojack, author, professor, TV talk-show host, and husband of Deborah Caughlin Mangaravidi Kelly, who is the daughter of Barney Kelly, a man who personifies demonic social, economic, and political power. The roles change, but the problem remains the same. Whoever Rojack may really be beneath the accretion of social roles, that person has never been given a chance to live. Thus, the Stephen Rojack that one sees at the beginning of the novel is a self-proclaimed failure, believing in suicide as the last chance for his soul's survival and fearing that he feels the first stirrings in himself of cancer, the disease that both Mailer and Rojack believe is a cultural symptom of spiritual extinction–the body's

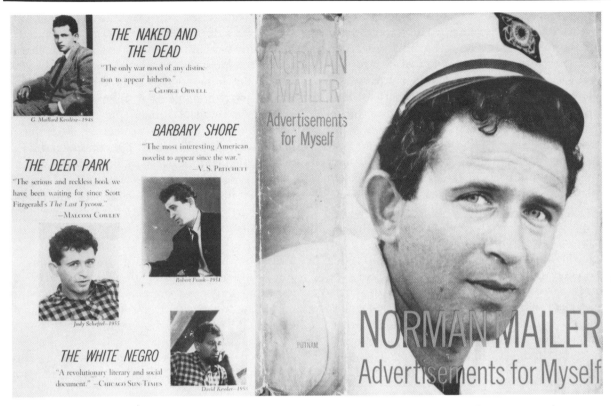

Dust jacket for Mailer's 1959 volume of miscellaneous writings interspersed with personal statements tracing his struggles as an artist

judgment on itself in the insane multiplication of cancerous cells.

More than anything else, it has been marriage with Deborah that has brought Rojack to such a wretched defeat. He originally thought that marriage to her might somehow lead to the presidency. Unfortunately, the relationship has become nothing more or less than the "war" of his life, and, as he admits, it has been "a losing war." In fact, marriage with Deborah has caught Rojack in a polarity of destructive emotions. Living with her, Rojack is murderous; trying to separate from her, he is suicidal. He can extricate himself from this trap only by fully engaging in the war with Deborah and winning it. In order to save himself, he decides that he must kill Deborah. In choosing to do so, he severs his most significant relations with the society that has seduced his soul. He renounces all of the compromising roles that for so many years have been counterfeiting his real identity, and he gives himself the chance to find out what that real identity is. Thus, like the hipster, Rojack is willing to commit an act of individual violence in order to liberate himself from the collective violence of society. Yet in committing such an act, Rojack is taking

only the first step in extricating himself from spiritually debilitating social relationships. Indeed, killing Deborah is merely a symbolic renunciation of compromise. Complete renunciation will require that Rojack do battle with society on every level of his relationship with it and emerge victorious.

Thus, after killing Deborah, Rojack goes through a series of confrontations with the police, the Mob, and Barney Kelly, meeting also in the course of his existential adventures Cherry, the blonde nightclub singer who represents Rojack's chance for physical and spiritual fulfillment. Rojack's courage throughout most of these confrontations gives him a personal victory over the collective powers of society. Nevertheless, that victory is undercut by Cherry's death. She is murdered by a friend of her former lover, Shago Martin, who mistakenly believes that she was involved in Martin's murder earlier that evening. But the novel insists, as one of a series of irrational implications, that Cherry might have been removed from danger if only Rojack had had the courage to risk spending the night in Harlem rather than confronting Barney Kelly. Rojack's personal victory over society is also undercut by the fact that while the society that he has extricated himself from remains substantially the same, the new life that he has won is necessarily a life of isolation, for he has lost everything but his knowledge of the truth of his "private vision." Thus in this novel one is left with a sense of both the moral complexity of existential risk and the demonic resilience of the conspiratorial powers of modern American society.

In his fifth novel, *Why Are We in Vietnam?* (1967), a hunting party of Dallas corporate executives goes to Alaska to kill grizzly bear. They hire a helicopter to flush out of the wilderness not only grizzlies but wolf, Dall ram, and caribou. Laden with guns powerful enough to drop an elephant, the huntsmen engage in a grotesque sporting holiday of blood. The parable is clear: the hunting party is the American military in miniature, replete with commanders and their GI subordinates. The crazed animals being annihilated by aerial machines are the people of Vietnam napalmed by the air force, but such pat equations do little to help one understand the art of this book.

It is the character of young D.J.'s voice that carries all of the novel's thematic, symbolic, and structural weight. "Grassed out" on marijuana at his parents' Dallas mansion and enjoying his farewell party–he will be inducted into the army the next day–D.J. narrates the events of this Alaskan odyssey in a punning prose that is a dazzling collage of speech from almost every arena of American life. In rapid-fire shifts, he speaks the language of an urban black, a pedantic psychoanalyst, a corporate bureaucrat, a southern redneck, a revivalist preacher, an academic philosopher, a physicist, and a McLuhanite media critic. The impression is of a jammed radio receiver picking up from multiple wavelengths all the ideologies, buried fantasies, fears, and desires of the collective American psyche and transmitting them across the land. D.J. calls himself "Disc jockey to the world." He is telepathically tuned into the rumblings, the groanings, the screams, and the palpitations of our subterranean selves; and his voice, he imagines, is a "tape being made for the private ear of the Lord, Who will register it in His Univac-like celestial archives." D.J. is the recording secretary of repressed compulsions–dreams of power, ecstatic sexual hopes, hatreds, and bigotries.

D.J.'s consciousness is in the throes of trying to rid itself of that which has glutted it–namely "mixed shit," Mailer's collective symbol for all the slogans, categories, and presumptions of popular American culture. The novel is not intended to be a study of character, because it assumes that individual character cannot survive in a world where the mind-control techniques of the mass media have homogenized human thought and where the value of human productivity is measured by impersonal forces such as government, business, and industry. D.J.'s consciousness has been made manic by excessive input. What particularly engorges his mind are thoughts of the violence that historically has been so large and pervasive a part of our national character that it was eventually exported to Southeast Asia. The energetic onrush of the tale D.J. tells may be interpreted as his attempt to purge himself of his psychic overload. But even after fleeing from the hunting party and immersing himself in the pure, raw wilderness, D.J. eagerly declares at the novel's end: "Vietnam, hot damn."

What is to be made of such grotesquerie? It is Mailer's means of exploding the whole Adamic tradition of American literature. *Why Are We in Vietnam?* is a deliberate rebuttal of the revered notion that if man removes himself from the corruptness of civilization and enters the realm of unspoiled nature, he can revive within himself something of the purity of heart and nobility of spirit that Adam must have felt in that first world that God set specially before him. While Mailer believes that man does indeed divorce himself from the mystical harmonies of nature, greedily ravage it, build war machines, and decimate his own kind, he clearly suggests, by way of D.J.'s Arctic experience, that the origin of man's barbarity is nature itself. Evil was in nature before it was in man. Such is Mailer's premise, and he shares it with William Burroughs, whose novel *Naked Lunch* inspired this one. "America," Burroughs writes, "is not a young land: it is old and dirty and evil before the settlers, before the Indians. The evil is there waiting." Traditional notions of a serene pastoralism, of a virgin land, are for Mailer–tough-minded urbanite that he is–nostalgic inventions of a primitive past that never was. I will be savage, D.J. seems to be saying, because I recognize that civilization is but another of savagery's masks, not an enlightened journey out of darkness.

The cultural conflicts of *Why Are We in Vietnam?*–the individual versus the corporation, independent thought versus the electronic media–are left unresolved because Mailer is inspired in this book by the impulse to escape from culture itself into a realm where nature is terrible, yet beautiful. Finally, however, the real achievement of this novel has more to do with the re-creation of cultural contradictions than with escape from them; D.J.'s narrative presents the dire divisions within American society. How he renders such divisions can be seen in a passage early in the novel when, speaking in urban black vernacular, he describes the menacing interrogation of a country Negro: "Whitey the Green Eye" has a nose "red as lobster . . . a-hovering and a-plunging like a Claw, man. . . ." The narrative then modulates to the patter of a white, drug-ridden hipster: "ex-acid is my head, Love Is Death . . . it's square to be frantic. . . ." Then it shifts to the voice of an ingratiating "true-blue Wasp-ass" Texan extending a down-home southern hospitality invitation to Jesus to "come visit." Here is capitalism trying to make its peace with Christianity. Interwoven in the passage are two threads. One is a brief excerpt from "In the Cool, Cool, Cool of the Evening," a popular song about the idyllic amicability of provincial American life. Another is a pun, "sick with the tick," which refers to time and to the parasitic insect, both destroyers of life–thus D.J.'s query, "oh blood how rot is thy sting?" Encapsulated here on half a page are the hatreds and fears, delusions and dreams, weltering within American society. This novel is an oratorio for many voices, each one of which infuriates, stupefies, or calls up dark laughter. By re-creating the duplicities and tensions that infect the American character, Mailer explains why we were in Vietnam.

Furthermore, just as the value of the book is that it enlarges perceptions rather than offers solutions, so the moral of the book is artistic, not ideological. Style, the very act of writing itself–of release in the form of expressive invention–is the one strategy Mailer invokes against the numbing effects of the mass media and the "communication engineers" of a programmed society. By mimicking the languages of the land, he sees through them and their beguilements and coercions. Verbal play is restorative, a spiritual tonic. Mailer suggests it is the last psychic liberty. The book's style is complex. "I say create complexities," says Mailer in *The Presidential Papers*, "let art deepen sophistication, let complexities be demonstrated to our leaders, let us try to make *them* more complex. That is a manly activity." It is an activity which can, he asserts, diminish the totalitarian forces of government, business, and mass communication that simplify life and brutalize man's

mind by expunging ambiguity and diversity. A style crackling with disparate images–a style like D.J.'s–may be, Mailer hopes, the force to fight the progressive collectivism of human life. *Why Are We in Vietnam?* is a book that will not be categorized, for its intention is to subvert all category.

In its inventive prose style and in its indictment of big business and the electronic media, *Why Are We in Vietnam?* is a novelist's novel. But the general reader did not know what to make of it. To some people it was obscure, to others it was obscene, to most it was both. *The Armies of the Night* (1968), however, reestablished Mailer with a wide audience and won him high critical acclaim as well. It received the National Book Award and a Pulitzer Prize. Subtitled *History as a Novel, The Novel as History*, the book is an on-the-spot account of the antiwar march on the Pentagon in October 1967. It is novelistic because it sensitively describes the effects of the march on a participant-protagonist, Mailer himself, and historical because it scrupulously describes the facts of the march.

The book's unity of time and its strict enclosure within the limits of a particular time and place give it a classical sharpness of design. Mailer was compelled to record reality rather than invent it. His previous novels shaped events; now events shape the book–events, moreover, that people know about and can therefore relate to. Tom Wolfe comments on the winning qualities of this "new journalism": it "consumes devices that happen to have originated with the novel and mixes them with every other device known to prose. And all the while, quite beyond matters of technique, it enjoys an advantage so obvious, so built-in, one almost forgets what power it has: the simple fact that the reader knows *all this actually happened*. The disclaimers have been erased. The screen is gone. The writer is one step closer to the absolute involvement of the reader that Henry James and James Joyce dreamed of and never achieved."

What makes *The Armies of the Night* so extraordinarily engaging is the characterization of the protagonist, Norman Mailer. Usually he refers to himself simply as "Mailer" or "he," but his occasional use of other names as well–the Ruminant, the Beast, the Existentialist, the Historian, the Participant, the Novelist, the General, the Protagonist, Norman–attests to the diversity of his behavior, to the fact that all along he is at will improvising identities the better to accommodate himself to the multifariousness of American society. An assumption guides him: in an extremely pluralistic nation, the self, to operate effectively, must also be pluralistic. Generally, though, Mailer is a self-preserving rogue in this book, a character of exorbitant disproportions, for always offsetting every sacrificial act of civil disobedience is some ludicrous vanity. He daringly instigates his arrest at the hands of a federal marshal, but he has engaged a filmmaker to follow him closely and take movies of his arrest. Herded into an army truck with the other prisoners, he finds it a "touch awkward" climbing over the tailgate, "for he did not wish to dirty his dark blue pinstripe suit." When he is finally put behind bars, a single thought keeps recurring to him: Can he be released in time to attend a Saturday-night party in New York "which has every promise of being wicked, tasty, and rich?" Mailer may not be convincing as an earnest radical or a "Left Conservative" (his own term for himself) hero—but as a comic hero he is a marvel.

His self-satire is due largely to his "command of a detachment, classic in severity (for he was a novelist and so in need of studying every last lineament of the fine, the noble, the frantic, and the foolish in others and in himself)." And therein lies the power of *The Armies of the Night*—in its novelistic attributes, its evocations of character and milieu and situation. When Mailer departs from his novelistic rendering of material, the book loses its thrust. The narrative-descriptive style, in which explicit details cohere with implicit moral moments, gives way to the oracular-ruminative style which dotes on abstractions and cultural *cum* philosophical questions. The last paragraph of the book is a case in point. Mailer imagines "America, once a beauty of magnificence unparalleled," now horribly diseased because of her involvement in the Southeast Asian war. "She will probably give birth, and to what?—the most fearsome totalitarianism the world has ever known? Or can she, poor giant, tormented lovely girl, deliver a babe of a new world brave and tender, artful and wild? Rush to the locks. Deliver us from our curse. For we must end on the road to that mystery where courage, death, and the dream of love give promise of sleep." Such writing borders on cant and obscurity. How unduly apocalyptic this passage seems now that American society has settled back into relative normality. One may find Mailer, the self-styled Jeremiah, rather tiresome, but when he goes about the business of "studying" every "lineament" and exploring human behavior—his own, the demon-

strators', the soldiers'—with the old-fashioned tools of the novelist, his writing incandesces.

Living and reporting the historic stresses of the 1960s, Mailer began to suspect that our national reality had become more fantastical than any fiction. His suspicion was confirmed by the National Aeronautics and Space Administration's announcement that it was ready to rocket man to the moon. Commissioned by *Life* magazine, he flew to Houston and Cape Kennedy to cover the flight of Apollo 11. As spectacular as Mailer believes the moon shot is in *A Fire on the Moon* (1970), he holds that the cosmic forces of existence are present just as provocatively, just as sublimely, in the relationship between man and woman as in the infinite reaches of space. Mailer contends that the interplay between the sexes is a process that God has ordained to bring symmetry and balance to creation. The heterosexual relationship "is one of the prime symbols of the connection between all things."

The chief experiences of Mailer's life have always concerned women. In 1970 he separated from Beverly Bentley and their two sons, Michael Burks and Stephen McLeod. That same year, leading exponents of the new feminists denounced him as the principal voice of male chauvinism on the American literary scene. He counterattacked with *The Prisoner of Sex* (1971). In this comically trenchant treatise he reexplores his relationship with women by examining the nature of his love for them and sets forth his own ideas on the sex game and his own sexuality. The further Mailer ponders the new feminism the more he comes to realize that it is a subject rich in possibilities. After all, he says, "the themes of his life had gathered here. Revolution, tradition, sex and the homosexual, the orgasm, the family, the child and the political shape of the future, technology and human conception, waste and abortion, the ethics of the critic and the male mystique, black rights and new thoughts on women's rights."

He first argues his position against Kate Millett. The freedom that she envisions for women once technology delivers them from the bondage of the womb, Mailer can only perceive as a deeper bondage for the whole human race. Semen banks, genetic engineering, artificial wombs, human birth by parthenogenesis—all such schemes for a scientifically immaculate conception he regards as totalitarian stratagems leading to worldwide homogeneity. On the question of the sex act itself, he scorns those feminists who applaud Masters and Johnson, the experimental sexologists who rescued their patients from frigidity and impotence by encouraging them, in comfortable laboratory conditions, to use those stimulative techniques most conducive to orgasm. All this, complains Mailer, is so clinical, so vapid, so very much beside the point. Sexuality is not genitality. Rather, he insists that it has to do–and he quotes William Blake–with "comminglings from the Head to the Feet." He implies that only a man of imagination, a novelist, can decipher the message of human orgasm.

At this juncture Mailer argues in support of two brother artists, Henry Miller and D. H. Lawrence. For Millett, Miller is America's vile pasha of depersonalized sex. She cites passages from his early novels, *Tropic of Cancer* (1934) and *Tropic of Capricorn* (1939), in which, she contends, men use women as mere carnal fodder. But Mailer accuses Millett of hypocrisy and is at his comic and mischievous best defending Miller and lampooning Millett for her dogged, tractarian approach, her insensitivity to Miller's humor and metaphoric power. As for Lawrence, Mailer refutes Millett's charge that the sexual act in Lawrence's work is a matter of male will and female submission. *Both* sexes must deliver themselves, in Lawrence's words, "over to the unknown," a mystical power far greater than themselves.

Mailer goes on to poeticize the womb as woman's alliance with eternity, her inner cosmos into which man, the striver, must make his way. Sexual intercourse becomes an apocalyptically grave engagement in which the sperm, a writhing "limb of the soul seeking to be born," takes a leap toward "every call of the woman for what was magnificent or large as her idea of future life." Mailer ecstatically visualizes the ovum as an expectant priestess choosing to receive only the most valiant of wriggling voyagers that enter through her door. The more poetically he treats sexuality the more meaning he attaches to it, until he becomes "The Prisoner." "No thought was so painful as the idea that sex had meaning: for give meaning to sex and one was the prisoner of sex–the more meaning one gave it, the more it assumed, until every failure and misery, every evil of your life, spoke their lines in its light, and every fear of mediocre death."

A year after *The Prisoner of Sex* was published Mailer again braced himself to take the plunge into the female psyche. He was offered a large sum of money to write a preface to a photographic retrospect of Marilyn Monroe. Long fasci-

nated with persons who, like himself, have been intimate with the prizes and perils of playing to a national audience, he could not resist expanding his twenty-five-thousand-word preface to a "novel biography" almost four times that length. He felt this was a chance to explore a spiritual twin. His basic contention is that if the real Monroe is to be discovered, a novelist must do it. To conceive of her novelistically, his premise goes, is to come closer than any pure biographical reportage can to the truth of what her "unspoken impulses" were. "Exceptional people have a way of living with opposites in themselves" that puts them beyond the pale of logical inquiry and renders traditional "biographical tools" insufficient. Yet his writing suffers when it moves from concrete description to abstraction. For example, what sense can be made of his explanation of how Ingmar Bergman puts his personal imprint on film: "all the hoarded haunted sorrows of Scandinavia drift in to imbibe the vampires of his psyche– he is like a spirit vapor risen out of the sinister character of film itself." Such writing generates more heat than light. Another example occurs in *Gentlemen Prefer Blondes*, when Monroe proves herself a "great comedian," "which is to say she bears an exquisitely light relation to the dramatic thunders of triumph, woe, greed, and calculation"–hardly a clarifying definition of a great comedian. Long priding himself on being one of the fastest writers alive–he has entitled one piece in *The Presidential Papers* "Ten Thousand Words a Minute"–Mailer wrote *Marilyn: A Biography* (1973) in two months in order to get it published for the summer-fall book season. It seems that the power and precision of his language have been sacrificed to the requirements of time.

And it is a pity, for the thesis of *Marilyn* is profound. Monroe's selfhood, the identity she desperately groped for all her life, was a mirage. Not able to find it by her own efforts, she sought out other people–her husbands, agents, directors– to help her find it. Unsatisfied with the results of the impossible task she set them, she sought solace in pills. Her search for an identity beneath or beyond her multiple roles was necessarily futile because, Mailer believes, identity exists *within* roles. The mask is the face. Here, then, is a clue to Mailer's own behavior. His identity is self-created and deliberately prismatic. In *The Armies of the Night*, for instance, he is master of ceremonies, actor, director, ambassador, general, banker, historian, and novelist. Since *Advertisements for Myself* the assumption of his books has been that if identity is diversified, it is more diffi-cult for internal and external suppressors–the su-perego, the corporation, the state–to retard indi-vidual growth. Marilyn Monroe's problem was that, like Charles Eitel, she was caught in the cor-porate web, in this case Hollywood, and com-pelled to play the role it forced upon her, that of vibrant sex goddess. In the process–to recall an image from *The Deer Park*–the life of the "cave," of the creative mind, atrophied.

If the 1960s were Mailer's autobiographical decade, the 1970s were his biographical period. His next book after *Marilyn* was *The Faith of Graffi-ti* (1974), a celebration of New York's ghetto art-ists. But he followed this with examinations of two of America's greatest egotists of the twenti-eth century, Muhammad Ali and Henry Miller. In *The Fight* (1975) Mailer almost disappears as a character ("He was no longer pleased with his pres-ence. His daily reactions bored him"), but in com-pensation he provides a sharply etched portrait of Ali, "the embodiment of loquacious defiance," as Philip M. Bufithis describes him in his study of Mailer's work. The narrative is ostensibly an ac-count of the Ali-George Foreman heavyweight title fight in Kinshasa, Zaire, but it is really struc-tured around Ali, who, Bufithis notes, "seems a version of Mailer himself."

Henry Miller, it could also be argued, is a ver-sion of Mailer, or perhaps a prototype. Mailer has acknowledged Miller's influence and paid trib-ute to him in *Genius and Lust: A Journey Through the Major Writings of Henry Miller* (1976). The edi-tion contains selections from ten of Miller's books and eighty pages of commentary–some of Mailer's finest literary criticism–on Miller as well as Ernest Hemingway and D. H. Lawrence.

Mailer's most important work of the 1970s, however, was *The Executioner's Song* (1979), for which he received the 1980 Pulitzer Prize for fic-tion. This 1,056-page "true life novel," as Mailer chose to call it, was widely reviewed, receiving an eight-to-one majority of favorable notices. Many of the book's negative critics questioned the moral-ity of devoting so much dispassionate attention to a murderer with no apparent redeeming social merits. Positive critics, on the other hand, argued that Mailer's nonjudgmental treatment of a proba-ble psychopath gained force from its reportorial accuracy. All the reviews agreed that *The Execution-er's Song* was a substantial book produced by a liter-ary master. The more laudatory notices accented what they called Mailer's artistry.

Virtually every review, including that in the *Times Literary Supplement*, noted that Mailer had been hired to write the book by Lawrence Schil-ler, a free-lance journalist who had purchased the rights to the stories of the book's principals for a large sum, and disclosed that Schiller paid him $250,000. In interviews and in the book Mailer acknowledged Schiller's paramount role in the genesis of the book.

The unusual arrangement between Schiller and Mailer raised questions in the literary commu-nity. Schiller's purchase of exclusive rights to the principals' stories was generally criticized as "checkbook journalism," and his hiring of Mailer was scored as further evidence of his eagerness to exploit the principals' "sordid" stories for pri-vate gain. Mailer's willingness to write for Schil-ler also stirred some controversy, but this died down when he explained that he had complete freedom to handle Schiller's material in any fash-ion he chose.

"This book does its best to be a factual ac-count of the activities of Gary Gilmore and the men and women associated with him from April 9, 1976, when he was released from the United States Penitentiary at Marion, Illinois, until his exe-cution a little more than nine months later in the Utah State Prison," Mailer writes in the book's af-terword. After stating that his book is based on in-terviews, documents, court records, and other original material, Mailer adds: "Out of such revela-tions was this book built and the story is as accu-rate as one can make it. This does not mean it has come a great deal closer to the truth than the recollections of the witnesses. While important events were corroborated by other accounts wher-ever possible, that could not, given the nature of the story, always be done, and, of course, two ac-counts of the same episode would sometimes di-verge. In such conflict of evidence, the author chose the version that seemed most likely. It would be vanity to assume he was always right."

Recited by a masterly reporter and an en-thralling storyteller whose own point of view is no-tably absent, *The Executioner's Song* is a stark and so-cially realistic chronicle of the last nine months in the life of Gary Gilmore, one of the outcasts of American society who spent eighteen of his thirty-five years in various prisons for a variety of crimes. Many involved ill-conceived thefts. Aso-cial and strongly given to fantasy, he was re-leased on parole to his Mormon cousins in Provo, Utah, in April 1976. Motivated by good-heart-edness, the cousins accepted Gilmore into their home and introduced him to their circle of friends. They found him work, and they probed gently for ways to fit him into the routines of their lives.

But Gilmore's basic violence often broke through. To the dismay of his relatives and their friends, he engaged in fights and contests of physical strength with violent overtones. He also stole six-packs of beer and once proposed stealing a two-ton truck and repainting it for sale. In Mailer's telling, Gilmore seems pathetic as he alternated between conforming to community values and flouting them; at times he expressed repentance for his behavior and pledged not to repeat it. He won a certain sympathy for himself as "a guy [who] has been locked up a long time [and] takes a while to get used to being out."

At the same time, he caused uneasiness by cadging loans, overindulging in beer, and buying a secondhand car with only flimsy means. The car, a Mustang, made him feel like somebody as he raced it around the countryside.

His attitude toward the law also disturbed his acquaintances. Irked by the complications of getting a driver's license, he nonetheless declined to sign up for a required training course. "I'm a grown man and it's beneath me," he said. A friend attempted to reason with him. "The law is for everybody. They're not singling you out," the friend argued. "Do you think you're better than I am?" "Excuse me," Gary said at last. . . . As he walked off, he said, "Real good advice." He was quick to get away, adds Mailer.

The contradictions of Gilmore's life amount to a social statement in the Theodore Dreiser or Frank Norris mode. A sense of inevitable tragedy hovers over Gilmore; events portray him as a loser, one who has been buffeted and whose perhaps creative nature has been stunted from childhood. Although it is possible to perceive Gilmore as a hardened criminal, psychotic, misshapen by his parents and thus meriting little compassion, it can also be argued that he is largely the product of uncaring prison regimes–that his antisocial tendencies and easy acceptance of violence were reinforced in jail. There is no evidence that Gilmore benefited from rehabilitation, if indeed he was significantly exposed to it.

The first section of the book, "Western Voices," carries Gilmore from his parole and introduction to Provo through a crude sexual liaison with Nicole to two cold-blooded killings. The first was of a gas-station attendant and the second, the following night, was of a motel clerk. Both were exhibitions of Gilmore's rage.

Almost immediately captured, he was back in prison after three and a half months of freedom. What stands out in this period is Gilmore's striving for quick and easy gratification of animalistic desires: food, drink, and sex. His tempestuous affair with Nicole was made possible in large measure because both partners were sexually voracious. Both also liked the excitement of violent actions.

"Western Voices" is written with great tautness and suspense. Paragraphs are seldom more than one sentence long, as if Mailer were a busy newspaper rewrite man working against a deadline and turning out copy one "take" at a time. The literary artistry in sustaining this style without making the narrative seem jerky is of a very high level. The power and the realism of the prose are remarkable.

By deft description and telling use of quotation, Mailer evokes both the goodwill and the banality inherent in lower-middle-class life in Provo. The American scene is painted without enhancement; its dependence on television for stimulation and diversion is starkly reported, as is the vacuity of its conversations, which are limited to concepts gleaned from television or the movies. Equally though, Mailer is at pains to represent Provo's (and America's) human kindness. Although members of Gilmore's circle repeatedly suffer from him, they are reluctant to send him back to jail; they are baffled and hurt by his erratic conduct. Even Nicole, slapped and knocked about, "could feel a lot of ugliness beginning to collect in her" only after repeated instances of abuse.

The second portion of *The Executioner's Song*, called "Eastern Voices," deals with the events from November 1976, after Gilmore's conviction, to his execution by a firing squad on 17 January 1977. There is a marked shift in tone as Mailer takes the reader into the criminal justice bureaucracy and into the world of the news media. Once Gilmore enters the Utah criminal justice system and once he declares his determination to die for his killings, he becomes the focus of a "story" for the electronic and the pencil press, both of which symbolize the East. The East is also the headquarters of those groups and organizations that oppose capital punishment and intervene in vain to save Gilmore.

By quoting extensively from police and court documents, Mailer demonstrates the impersonality of the criminal justice system; the drama of the otherwise bleak legal proceedings is transformed by the media. "The Gilmore case" is brought into being, particularly as Gilmore's final days tick off. In depicting members of the press as hawks and vultures, seekers after sensation, Mailer includes Schiller among them. Once initiated, "the Gilmore case" creates its own momentum; it accumulates a bureaucracy, assessments from the psychiatric profession, a legal corps, and recorders of the phenomenon from the national and world press. Indeed, as the firing squad's guns bark, reporters are within a couple of feet of the action.

Mailer's detachment, his role as a panoptic observer after the case was closed, was confirmed in an interview for this article. Noting that the book relied heavily on research materials supplied by others, he said the novel was "probably the least personal of my books." He continued:

> There is an irony in this, and it is that *The Executioner's Song* is my most intense work since *The Naked and the Dead*. And there is a further irony: All my personal books–and they were terribly personal–repelled as many critics as they attracted. With this book, however, the criticism has been that it is impersonal. I think this demonstrates that critics cut their cloth to fit their biases. When I sat down to write this book, I decided to skip experimentation and to follow well-charted paths. In this sense the book displays my skills, but not necessarily my talents as a writer. Since the Gary Gilmore story was not my own experience, I could not feel as near to it as if it had been something that had arisen out of my life.

There is an argument to be made that the book's impressive strength derives from the absence of a clear authorial voice. By letting the Gilmore story speak for itself, the unappealing and seedy side of American life is presented without palliatives. Mailer leaves it up to the reader to decide whether Gilmore is representational of criminal conduct, or whether his conduct reflects the failure of our prison system, or whether the criminal justice system functions with compassion, or whether the press distorts and sensationalizes such cases as his. Descriptive, but not prescriptive, *The Executioner's Song* raises a host of social questions. In doing so, it adds luster to Mailer's standing as one of our foremost writers.

Mailer followed *The Executioner's Song* with *Of Women and Their Elegance* (1980), a fictional au-

Dust jacket for Mailer's 1983 novel chronicling the four incarnations of the Egyptian, Menenhetet

tobiography of Marilyn Monroe that in 1986 he adapted into a play, "Strawhead." Several versions of this dramatic adaptation have been staged at the Actor's Studio in New York with Mailer's daughter Kate in the title role.

Every three or four years beginning in 1959 Mailer has collected the bulk of his accumulated periodical writings into miscellanies. His fifth such collection, *Pieces and Pontifications*, appeared in 1982. The first part of the collection contains a dozen of his best essays from the 1970s, and the second, edited by J. Michael Lennon, contains twenty interviews from 1958 to 1981. In several of these interviews Mailer discusses his huge work in progress, generally referred to before publication as "the Egyptian novel." Begun in 1971 and worked on in between the several other works he wrote in the 1970s, *Ancient Evenings* was published with much fanfare in 1983.

Set in Egypt during the nineteenth and twentieth dynasties (1290-1100 B.C.), the novel traces, in 709 large pages, the complex fate of one man, Menenhetet, who has been reincarnated three times. Murdered in his first life while copulating with a queen of Ramses II, Menenhetet reincarnates himself in her womb. He effects his next two reincarnations by self-inducing his death while copulating.

Menenhetet narrates the story of his four lives at a dinner party in the palace of Ramses IX. The occasion is the Night of the Pig, a time of lambent wildness when irregularities and iconoclastic talk are permitted. As thousands of caged fireflies illumine the pharaoh's pillared patio against the surrounding dark, Menenhetet imparts his autobiography to four listeners–Ramses IX, the pharaoh's Overseer of the Cosmetic Box, the Overseer's beautiful wife, and their six-year-old son, who is Menenhetet Two, the great-grandson of Menenhetet. Intensified by the social drama that frames it, Menenhetet's story extends to the threshold of the dawn, and so nearly to the end of the novel.

Menenhetet's four lives form an arc. In his first life he ascends from peasant beginnings to his apex as First Charioteer to His Majesty, Ramses II. Later he becomes overseer of Ramses II's harem of queens. In his second life he is a formidable high priest whose occult practices, people say, risk profanity. In his third life he is a shrewd brothel keeper who becomes a vastly rich papyrus manufacturer. In his fourth life he is a respected nobleman–astute, corrupt, and thwarted in his ambition to be vizier to Ramses IX and eventually pharaoh himself. He dies a grave robber.

The other major narrative voice is that of the departed soul–the Ka or ghost–of Menenhetet Two, who was murdered at the age of twenty-one and now describes the dinner party from his memory of it. The desolate Ka of Menenhetet Two opens the novel with its most fascinating section, the thirty-eight-page "Book of One Man Dead." The Ka vividly describes its agonizing struggle to wrest itself free from entombment in the Great Pyramid of Khufu; quaking with fear, it recollects how two embalmers, step by horrific step, prepared its body for mummification. There is a consciousness here not met with in any other fiction. The reader is pulled into the Ka's strange cares and yearnings as it painfully orients itself to the shock of its nonmortal existence and meets the grim, awesome Ka of Menenhetet. The evocation of the Great Pyramid–its enclosed spaces and furnishings, the view from it of the immense starry night over the land–

imparts a felt sense of mystery, wonder, and dread. The last scene of the novel is also striking. After six hundred pages, Mailer's prose soars as the Ka of Menenhetet Two resumes its narration in the Great Pyramid and continues its talk with the Ka of Menenhetet, who guides the young Ka through the Land of the Dead. *Ancient Evenings* constitutes, then, two mountains between which lies the vast plain of Menenhetet's dinner-party narrative.

No novel resembles it. One may well ask, then, just what Mailer has done. The answer, no less true for its simplicity, is that he has written a novel about magic. Mailer is telling us–there is always that rabbinical teaching streak in him–that a life lived according to a belief in magic can be deeply vitalizing and creative, for when the gods dwell in the things of this world, energy and powerfully sustaining meaning can be found everywhere. Mailer wants us to believe that magic can make as much sense out of the world as science and its handmaiden, technology. The novel's title is meant to suggest that an evening spent in Egypt three thousand years ago could well have been as fully interesting–though not the same–as an evening spent anywhere in the world today.

In an interview for the *Washington Post* (20 April 1983) Mailer informatively discussed some of the thinking that went into *Ancient Evenings:*

"This is one of the few books I know," Mailer says, "that treats magic with respect. See, magic bears the same relation to the Egyptians that technology does to us. One of the things I wanted to shock and startle the reader with is: Look what a comprehensive world view magic gives you. When it works, it's marvelous and it fortifies their view of the universe. When it doesn't work, it's that something went wrong with the *process.* It's never the fundamental belief that's shaken." Similarly, "our belief in science is, if not tragically misplaced, certainly megalomaniacal." In fact, "it could be said by future generations, if there are any, that we're much sillier than the Egyptians," because we use technology "to slowly but systematically deaden and debase our way of life. Each year there's more real poverty in the synapses than there was the year before." The chief (and predictable) offender: television.

"I feel as if we've all gone completely in the wrong direction. When God first conceived the world, I don't think it was His or Her notion– that much effect the women's movement has had on me!–that we would have television. I don't think all those worlds came out of the cosmos in order to have people sitting around like sheep looking at a livid luminescent screen."

But this animism he finds so appealing in the Egyptians–has he experienced it himself? "Well, let's say I find it philosophically congenial. For instance, listen to this–are you ready?" And he rips a piece out of the sandwich bag with a noisy flourish. "Now the Egyptians would doubtless have said that sound is what the god of this bag uttered when wounded. And that makes absolutely as much sense to me as some incredibly difficult and incomprehensible discussion on the collision of sine waves. I believe there are all sorts of forces in the universe, some more tangible than others, nearly all of them invisible, that sort of aid us or f--- us up. One of the ways you can spot that is that you can be engaged in something that you're dead serious about. It can turn out badly or well, but you feel considerably more or less elation or despondency than you should. One knows instinctively that there were bad spirits or good ones around affecting the result."

Far better that one seek help from magic than from science, for magic, Mailer believes, speaks to the soul–to the transcendent–in man. The novel's fundamental theme forcefully addresses Western postindustrial life: man has insulated himself within rationality, shrunken himself into it, yet it can never explain what or who he is or where he has come from or where he is going.

Mailer's religious vitalism resembles that of the American transcendentalists; though, of course, he does not share their characteristic quietism. Over the past forty years Mailer's combined works have constituted an epic satire based on his observations of what the transcendentalists were always noting–the spiritual puniness man has reduced himself to. "Man is the dwarf of himself," wrote Emerson. And so, Mailer would add, he has come to allow lifelessness–television and plastic–to surround him and stultify his nerve endings. Absorbed in television, he lives vicariously. And every time he uses a plastic object instead of a natural one, he chooses a bit of death over a bit of life. Plastic does not resonate. It is separate from nature. It is the waste material of oil–the excrement of oil. Mailer sounds like Menenhetet.

Mailer's outsized intention in *Ancient Evenings* is to rejuvenate the human species by showing it how life can be lived on the edge of dread and thereby intensified. Menenhetet propels himself toward physically and morally brave acts in war and in love and so builds new synapses, counteracting the perpetual forces of atrophy. He continually exchanges comfort for life and more life.

When he stops doing so, he slides into convention and begins to die. There is no such thing, Mailer wants us to know, as stasis. One is either in a state of growth or death, and the gods have a stake in which it will be.

The gods in *Ancient Evenings* are most unchurchly, for they are not benign or omniscient or omnipotent. Like man himself, they are struggling for completion in the existential sense of making themselves. And man, far from having a bit part in the cosmic drama, is the embodiment or instrument of their endeavor to grow. They enlist man to help them and thereby impel him beyond his natural limits. Mailer refutes, then, the modern literary image of man as a sadly laughable creature caught up in a network of circumstances beyond his power to know or control. Menenhetet trembles. He falters. But he never believes that his being alive is mere happenstance. He has been launched into the cosmos by powers greater than himself, and it is his purpose to actualize those powers through the exertions of his own creative will.

Missing the metaphysics and focusing on the literal plot of *Ancient Evenings*, some reviewers have labored under two serious misapprehensions: (1) the novel takes as its subject human decadence; (2) it is historically inauthentic. When Ramses II buggers Menenhetet, who recalls at the dinner party that the pharaoh's semen flowed forth as prodigiously as the waters of the Nile, the act is not decadent. Nor is the imagery ridiculous or sensational. On the contrary, it accurately expresses how such an act was viewed by a pagan. The point is that Ramses II strengthens himself by the act. Egypt and he prosper by it. When Menenhetet eats the flesh of dead Hittite soldiers, the act is not vile. Nor are the frequent scenes of incest. The reviewers' imputations of decadence reveal their own dispositions, not the world of *Ancient Evenings*. Actually, Mailer is daring the reviewers into such a reaction to prove his point of how provincial and presumptuous the contemporary American mind can be–how immured in its own very finite time. The novel portrays a pre-Judeo-Christian world. The two narrators are pre-Judeo-Christian. Their morality is not ours. *Ancient Evenings* is an invitation to the reader to get out of himself.

The novel's so-called noxiousness is not only Mailer's way of inveighing against American parochialism. It is his way of assailing America's ongoing obsession with sanitizing nature out of more and more areas of life. Thus *Ancient Eve-*

nings could be the most olfactory novel ever written, profusely evoking, as it does, the odors of excrement, sweat, human and animal breath, putrefying plants and animals. Mailer is not driving readers through ancient Egypt on a sightseeing bus–he is rubbing their noses in it.

The second erroneous assumption about the novel is that it inauthentically portrays the ancient Egypt of history. Real Egyptians, the argument goes, did not believe in mental telepathy or physical reincarnation, and *Ancient Evenings* contains a considerable measure of both. If Mailer had wanted to write a factual, entirely accurate historical novel about ancient Egypt he would have or would have tried to. He has done neither because neither was his intention. He has tried, however, to evoke the spirit, the atmosphere, the feel of ancient Egypt. David B. O'Connor, curator of the Egyptian section of the University of Pennsylvania Museum, has said in the *Pennsylvania Gazette* (May 1983) that though he found minor errors in *Ancient Evenings*, Mailer had grasped well the cultural and historical thrust of ancient Egypt.

Mailer returned to the shores of America with his next novel, which he wrote in two months, a thriller titled *Tough Guys Don't Dance* (1984). This was his first book with Random House, with whom he signed a multi-book contract after fourteen years with Little, Brown. Set in Provincetown, Massachusetts, where Mailer has summered for more than thirty years, and other parts of Cape Cod, the novel is a reassertion of old prerogatives in its exploration of courage and dread, and an advance in its rich delineation of a father-son relationship, one much different than those in earlier novels such as *Why Are We in Vietnam?* Like almost all of Mailer's books, *Tough Guys Don't Dance* received mixed reviews (the most notable exceptions are *The Naked and the Dead*, *The Armies of the Night*, and *The Executioner's Song*, which received reviews almost entirely favorable, and *Barbary Shore*, the opposite), largely because of its overly complicated plot.

Besides continuing to work on "Strawhead" in the period after *Tough Guys Don't Dance*, Mailer traveled to Russia and wrote an essay on his visit for *Parade* (19 August 1984) which, considering recent events there, confirmed his reputation for political prescience. He also wrote a long essay on *Huckleberry Finn* (*New York Times Book Review*, 9 December 1984) and then began work on several screenplays, including one for *Tough Guys Don't Dance*. The movie, directed by Mailer and pro-

duced by Cannon Films, was released in 1986. Like the book, it was highly praised and roundly criticized. It is currently undergoing a revival on videocassette.

In 1987 Mailer began a novel about the CIA. The title, adapted from his 1976 essay on the CIA (reprinted in *Pieces and Pontifications*), is "Harlot's Ghost." Set in the 1950s in Maine, Washington, D.C., and elsewhere, this spy novel will examine WASP influence and culture, among other things. Excerpts have appeared in *Esquire* (July 1988) and *Playboy* (December 1988). "Harlot's Ghost" will be published by Random House, probably in 1991.

Interviews:

Charles Ruas, "Norman Mailer," in his *Conversations with American Writers* (New York: Random House, 1985), pp. 18-36.
Contains a long discussion of Mailer's involvement with murderer Jack Abbott.

J. Michael Lennon, ed., *Conversations with Norman Mailer* (Jackson: University Press of Mississippi, 1988).
Thirty-four interviews, 1948-1987, including three self-interviews and a chronology. Note: See also Mailer's *Pieces and Pontifications*, edited by J. Michael Lennon (Boston: Little, Brown, 1982), a collection of twenty interviews, 1958-1981.

Bibliography:

Laura Adams, *Norman Mailer: A Comprehensive Bibliography* (Metuchen, N.J.: Scarecrow Press, 1974).
Besides primary and secondary items, this indispensable bibliography contains lists of unpublished manuscripts, dissertations, reviews of books about Mailer, and interviews.

Biography:

Hilary Mills, *Norman Mailer: A Biography* (New York: Empire Books, 1982).
The first major biography, flawed by lack of documentation and research, but containing many interviews with Mailer's friends.

References:

Laura Adams, *Existential Battles: The Growth of Norman Mailer* (Athens: Ohio University Press, 1976).
Good introductory discussion of themes and narrative technique in Mailer's work, includ-

ing excellent coverage of his early narrators; includes descriptions of his extra-literary activities.

Adams, ed., *Will the Real Norman Mailer Please Stand Up* (Port Washington, N.Y.: Kennikat Press, 1974).
Fifteen essays examining Mailer as playwright, filmmaker, politician, performer, etc., and including Tony Tanner's brilliant essay on *An American Dream*.

Robert J. Begiebing, *Acts of Regeneration: Allegory and Archetype in the Works of Norman Mailer* (Columbia: University of Missouri Press, 1980).
Close reading of major works from *Barbary Shore* on, from a Jungian perspective; excellent discussion of Mailer's "heroic consciousness."

Harold Bloom, ed., *Norman Mailer: Modern Critical Views* (New York: Chelsea House, 1988).
Sixteen reviews and essays covering Mailer's major work; several appear in earlier collections on Mailer.

Leo Braudy, ed., *Norman Mailer: A Collection of Critical Essays* (Englewood Cliffs, N.J.: Prentice-Hall, 1972).
Thirteen essays on important Mailer works, especially *An American Dream*, by leading critics: Diana Trilling, John W. Aldridge, Michael Cowan, and Richard Poirier.

Philip M. Bufithis, *Norman Mailer* (New York: Ungar, 1978).
Perhaps the most readable and reliable study of Mailer's work.

Robert Ehrlich, *Norman Mailer: The Radical as Hipster* (Metuchen, N.J.: Scarecrow Press, 1978).
Examination of Mailer's work through *Marilyn* as an expression of the hipster philosophy of "The White Negro."

Joe Flaherty, *Managing Mailer* (New York: Coward-McCann, 1970).
Vivid account of Mailer's 1969 New York mayoral race by his campaign manager.

Richard Foster, *Norman Mailer* (Minneapolis: University of Minnesota Press, 1968).

This monograph is the first extended treatment of Mailer's work, and still one of the best.

Andrew Gordon, *An American Dreamer: A Psychoanalytic Study of the Fiction of Norman Mailer* (Cranbury, N.J.: Associated University Presses, 1980).
Freudian study of Mailer's books through *The Armies of the Night;* notable for its cataloging of imagery patterns.

Stanley T. Gutman, *Mankind in Barbary: The Individual and Society in the Novels of Norman Mailer* (Hanover, N.H.: University Press of New England, 1975).
Able discussions of all of Mailer's major novelistic themes.

Donald L. Kaufman, *Norman Mailer: The Countdown (The First Twenty Years)* (Carbondale: Southern Illinois University Press, 1969).
Despite a confusing organizational scheme, this pioneering study contains useful material on morality in the early novels.

Barry Leeds, *The Structured Vision of Norman Mailer* (New York: New York University Press, 1969).
Another pioneering work, this clearly written study has an excellent chapter on *An American Dream* and others on Mailer's poetry and drama.

J. Michael Lennon, ed., *Critical Essays on Norman Mailer* (Boston: G. K. Hall, 1986).
Ten reviews and ten essays on Mailer's major works; includes Robert F. Lucid's provocative overview of his projected biography and Michael Cowan's essay on Mailer's literary roots.

Robert F. Lucid, ed., *Norman Mailer: The Man and His Work* (Boston: Little, Brown, 1971).
Thirteen essays and reviews on Mailer's work through the 1960s and four biographical essays.

Peter Manso, *Mailer: His Life and Times* (New York: Simon & Schuster, 1985).
Massive oral biography consisting of interviews with over two hundred individuals but lacking any thesis or framework except chronology.

Manso, ed., *Running Against the Machine: The Mailer-Breslin Campaign* (Garden City, N.Y.: Doubleday, 1969).
Collection of position papers, speeches, etc., relating to Mailer's unsuccessful 1969 campaign for mayor of New York.

Robert Merrill, *Norman Mailer*, revised edition (Boston: Twayne, 1990).
Thoughtful examination of the formal structure of both Mailer's novels and nonfiction narratives; includes biographical chapter.

Jonathan Middlebrook, *Mailer and the Times of His Time* (San Francisco: Bay Books, 1976).
Impressionistic essay on Mailer's similarities to other writers, especially to American Romantics.

Modern Fiction Studies, special issue on Mailer, 17 (Autumn 1971): 347-463.
Contains nine essays centering on Mailer's early work and a checklist of criticism.

Richard Poirier, *Norman Mailer* (New York: Viking, 1972).
Considered by many to be the finest study of Mailer published to date, focusing on Mailer's dialectical style.

Jean Radford, *Norman Mailer: A Critical Study* (New York: Harper & Row, 1975).
General survey of Mailer's work from a feminist perspective.

Robert Solotaroff, *Down Mailer's Way* (Urbana: University of Illinois Press, 1974).
Another general survey containing a comprehensive and penetrating examination of Mailer's existentialism.

Robert Wenke, *Mailer's America* (Hanover, N.H.: University Press of New England, 1987).
Thematic study limited by omission of consideration of narrative technique. Contains first extended treatment of *Ancient Evenings*.

Larry McMurtry

This entry was updated by Sarah English (Meredith College) from the entries by John Gerlach (Cleveland State University) in DLB 2, American Novelists Since World War II, *Brooks Landon (University of Iowa) in* DLB Yearbook 1981, *and English in* DLB Yearbook 1987.

Places	Texas Houston San Francisco	Hollywood Washington, D.C.	Las Vegas New York
Influences and Relationships	Thomas Berger Leo Tolstoy Emily Brontë	Walter Prescott Webb Homer	J. Frank Dobie Billy Lee Brammer Ken Kesey
Literary Movements and Forms	Satire Pulp Fiction	The Beat Movement	Southwestern Literature
Major Themes	Unmaking of Myths Nostalgia & Anti-nostalgia	Mythmaking Coming of Age Sexual Love	Marriage Friendship Loneliness
Cultural and Artistic Influences	Country and Western Music	Movies (Westerns)	Rare-book Dealing
Social and Economic Influences	The Vanishing Frontier	The Sexual Revolution	The Women's Movement

BIRTH: Wichita Falls, Texas, 3 June 1936, to William Jefferson and Hazel Ruth McIver McMurtry.

EDUCATION: B.A., North Texas State University, 1958; M.A., Rice University, 1960.

MARRIAGE: 15 July 1959 to Josephine Ballard (divorced); child: James Lawrence.

AWARDS AND HONORS: *Aresta* awards for essay and poem, 1957; Wallace Stegner Fellowship, Stanford University, 1960; Texas Institute of Letters Jesse H. Jones Award for *Horseman, Pass By*, 1963; Guggenheim Award for creative writing, 1964; Academy of Motion Pictures Arts and Sciences Award (Oscar) for best screenplay based on material from another medium for *The Last Picture Show*, 1972; Pulitzer Prize for *Lonesome Dove*, 1986.

BOOKS: *Horseman, Pass By* (New York: Harper, 1961); republished as *Hud* (London: Sphere, 1971);
Leaving Cheyenne (New York: Harper & Row, 1963; London: Sphere, 1972);
The Last Picture Show (New York: Dial, 1966; London: Sphere, 1972);
In a Narrow Grave (Austin: Encino Press, 1968);
Moving On (New York: Simon & Schuster, 1970; London: Weidenfeld & Nicolson, 1971);
All My Friends Are Going to Be Strangers (New York: Simon & Schuster, 1972; London: Secker & Warburg, 1972);
Terms of Endearment (New York: Simon & Schuster, 1975);
Somebody's Darling (New York: Simon & Schuster, 1978);
Cadillac Jack (New York: Simon & Schuster, 1982; London: Allen, 1986);
The Desert Rose (New York: Simon & Schuster, 1983; London: Allen, 1985);
Lonesome Dove (New York: Simon & Schuster, 1985; London: Pan, 1986);
Texasville (New York: Simon & Schuster, 1987);
Film Flam: Essays on Hollywood (New York: Simon & Schuster, 1987);
Anything for Billy (New York: Simon & Schuster, 1988).

PERIODICAL PUBLICATIONS: "The Texas Moon, And Elsewhere," *Atlantic Monthly* (March 1975): 29-36;

"Learning to Relax With an Uzi Man," *Atlanta Constitution*, 12 June 1988, C1: 8.

Although Larry McMurtry has moved beyond the status of a minor regional writer, he is still closely identified with Texas. His first six novels and a collection of essays (*In a Narrow Grave*, 1968) reflect life in his native state, and he has returned to Texas as a setting in his three more recent books. The son of William Jefferson McMurtry, a rancher, and Hazel Ruth McIver McMurtry, he was born on 3 June 1936 in Wichita Falls. He was educated in Texas, receiving a B.A. from North Texas State University in 1958 and an M.A. from Rice University in 1960. A Stegner Fellowship enabled him to do further graduate work at Stanford, but he returned to Texas to teach creative writing at Rice from 1963 to 1969. In those days he was friends with Ken Kesey and wrote about the Beats. Since then he has left the academic world and Texas to live in Washington, D.C., where he owns a rare-book store called Booked-Up.

Houston and the fictional town of Thalia recur frequently as settings in McMurtry's first six novels, and some of the same characters, Emma Horton, Patsy Carpenter, and Danny Deck, reappear in several books. He has developed his stories in a number of different modes, sometimes striving for a tightly controlled single action, at times aiming for a looser, open-ended flow; sometimes seeing the action through the eyes of a sober, serious youngster, at times withdrawing to a more elevated, omniscient, and ultimately comic perspective. His first novel, *Horseman, Pass By* (1961), is carefully controlled and economical: the central event, the discovery of hoof-and-mouth disease among cattle on Homer Bannon's ranch, develops inexorably toward the eventual destruction of the cattle, and with them Homer's will to live. The story is narrated by Homer's grandson Lonnie, who is clearly in the tradition of Huck Finn, discerning much of the falseness around him, unwilling to corrupt himself. Lonnie's voice as a narrator can be heard in his comments on Homer Bannon's funeral: "They had put paint on him, like a woman wears, red paint. I could see it on his cheeks, and caked around his mouth. I could see slick oil on his hair, and some sticky stuff like honey around his eyes. I wished I could have buried him like he died; he was better that way."

In the course of living through his grandfather's ordeal, Lonnie rejects his earlier desire to

Larry McMurtry (photo by Diana Walker)

leave the ranch, rejects Hud, a cynical, brutal son of Homer's second wife, and rejects Jesse, a floating forty-year-old cowboy who has seen everything and missed everything. Ultimately he elects to stay on the land, "looking at the green grass on the ground and watching the white clouds ease into the sky from the South," in acceptance of his responsibilities to the land and his friends. Beneath these affirmations there is his unsettling attraction to Halmea, the black helper on the Bannon ranch. He desires her partly as lover, partly as mother. The tenderness, lack of fulfillment, and separation due here to differences in age and race trace out the beginning of what becomes an essential theme in later works—people's needs do not match their circumstances.

Leaving Cheyenne (1963) also explores this theme of mismatching and the isolation it ultimately brings. Two friends, Gideon and Johnny, are attracted to Molly, but Molly eventually marries a third fellow, Eddie. Instead of having children by Eddie, she has one son by Gideon and one by Johnny, and both the sons of her two lovers die in World War II. The story is told by three narrators—first by Gideon, who tells of the group as young adults, then by Molly, who narrates the middle period during which she raises the children and attends to all three of the men, and finally by Johnny, who as an old man tells of

Gideon's death. The expanded time scheme and number of narrators enrich the themes of the novel.

Both *Leaving Cheyenne* and *Horseman, Pass By* are set near the mythical town of Thalia; *The Last Picture Show* (1966) deals with Thalia itself. The effect of several levels of experience is retained but this time is transformed by the use of an omniscient narrator. The central focus is on three teenagers: Sonny, his friend Duane, and a girl they both desire, Jacy Farrow. As in *Leaving Cheyenne*, neither boy can keep the girl for himself, and the girl seems always about to slip into the hands of a third rival. The characters in *The Last Picture Show* are amusingly diminished by their comic sexual-initiation rituals, Jacy by her activities at a swimming party and later in a motel with Duane, and Duane and Sonny by their frustrating visit to a whorehouse in Mexico. Their stumbling ascent to maturity runs parallel to the revelation of the past relationship between Jacy's mother and Sam the Lion, who is a father figure for Sonny and Duane. Her affair with Sam is now only a memory. After Sam dies, Thalia seems to rush to extinction: the movie house closes, Duane goes off to Korea, and Billy, a retard, in despair at the closing of the movie house, puts on two eye patches and is run over by a truck. The relation of Lonnie to the older black woman, Halmea, in

Horseman, Pass By, resembles Sonny's affair with Ruth Popper, the wife of the high-school coach. Temporarily leaving her for Jacy, Sonny returns after a brief experience with Jacy's mother. In Mrs. Farrow's words, "Your mother and I sat next to one another in the first grade. . . . We graduated together. I sure didn't expect to sleep with her son. That's small town life for you." As Sonny is reconciled to Ruth, who is also old enough to be his mother, it is clear that love is sad, impossible, and sweet in its contrasts and absurdities.

In *Moving On* (1970) McMurtry expanded his material much further. The marriage of Jim and Patsy Carpenter is about to end, but not before it is tested by and compared to the relationship of Pete and Boots, a January-May couple; the relationship of rich Eleanor Guthrie and world champion cowboy Sonny Shanks, who has his girls in the converted hearse he lives in; the relationship of Bill Duffin, the cynical professor of modern literature who has published eight books, and his wife, Lee, the campus Cassandra; and the relationship of Clara Clark, the California Girl playing at being a graduate student, and her graduate-student boyfriend, Hank Malory. The setting moves through the same kind of random sequence; after several hundreds of pages of rodeo locations, the setting shifts to graduate school at Rice. McMurtry further risks losing the reader's attention by presenting very ordinary people: Patsy speaks at times with a sharp tongue, as does her friend Emma Horton, but then none of them consistently speaks with distinction over 794 pages. The character of Jim, Patsy's husband, is portrayed through his hobbies–photography, linguistics, and then graduate school. There are countless sexual arousals, a somewhat smaller number of consummations, fragments of popular songs, dozens of book titles and authors (Lumiansky, Fiedler, Tolstoy, and Ian Watt), and meals with comments on the freshness of the salad or the gristle in the steak. In his review in the *New York Times*, titled "*Moving On*, and On . . . and On," John Leonard commented, "it's a little like turning on the radio and leaving it on for years."

And yet, by the final quarter of the book, "Summer's Lease," the very size of the book and accumulation of material do begin to work. Jim finds out about Patsy's affair with Hank; she wishes to break it off but does so in a most jagged, continuously backsliding way. In time, she breaks from Jim as well, with an equally pro-

longed assortment of vague reconciliations and indirections. Flap, Emma's husband, tries to commit suicide and fails. Emma's comment, "I knew the minute I started going with him years ago that I'd never get rid of him and I just couldn't believe he would die," gives some indication of McMurtry's purpose. This is a world of unshakable banality, one that could not be represented with the normal economies of fiction. The publication of this book would seem to be coordinated with McMurtry's own break with the academic world, which *Moving On* describes in particularly dreary terms.

All My Friends Are Going to Be Strangers (1972) returns to more normal fictional dimensions, and to a wandering feast of humor wilder than that of *The Last Picture Show*. Danny Deck, who has published one novel, is working on a second book and a hopeless marriage. During pregnancy his wife turns from him to a blind man downstairs. Danny moves from one adventure to another, trying to live with a kindly and talented cartoonist named Jill, who is not interested in sex. He visits his Uncle L, who sleeps in a bedroll behind his luxurious ranch house, digs postholes indiscriminately, keeps a menagerie, including a camel, instead of cattle, and has three Mexican helpers, each named Pierre. Danny drowns the manuscript of his second novel in the Rio Grande. Early in the book there is a curious image of a janitor in the Rice University Library: "Petey was not important enough to merit a giant waxer, but he didn't care. He had a middle-sized waxer and spent his evenings smoking marijuana while he followed his waxer in and out of the fifth floor stacks. He loved to get high and follow his waxer around." If the reader wishes to enjoy himself, he must assume Petey's role and follow this middle-sized plot without concern for its direction.

In *Terms of Endearment* (1975) McMurtry returns to a tighter structure by concentrating primarily on a single character, Aurora Greenwood, a widow. Aurora, who is Emma Horton's mother, ought to be intolerable: she corrects the grammar of her friends, exploits her suitors, and calls her daughter to say, "I was thinking you might want to wish me good night." But Aurora is lovable because she loves life and because she can turn a phrase. As she says of two of her suitors, "The brutal fact is that they're both old, short, and afraid of me. If I stacked them one on top of the other they might be tall enough, but they'd still be afraid of me." Her story has endless permutations but no motions; she is timeless. The last quarter of the book deals with Emma, dying of cancer, and peacefully terminates that long-suffering victim of this and two previous novels.

At this point in his career, McMurtry was still considered a Texas novelist. Some critics, such as Alan F. Crooks, argued that he needed a sense of place to do his best work, and Charles D. Peavy maintained that McMurtry wrote better of the country than of the city.

In a biting 1975 essay in the *Atlantic Monthly*, "The Texas Moon, And Elsewhere," McMurtry bade a not-so-fond farewell to the region his novels had so richly mined. "I was halfway through my sixth Texas novel," he explained, "when I suddenly began to notice that where place was concerned, I was sucking air." Pinning his fatigue on "the kind of mental and emotive inarticulateness" he found in Texas, McMurtry concluded: "The one basic subject it offers us now is loneliness, and one can only ring the changes on that so many times." In 1978 McMurtry put away his "Minor Regional Novelist" T-shirt (actually, he reports he lost it in a Laundromat) and published his seventh novel, *Somebody's Darling*—leaping from the frying pan of Texas literature into the well-stoked fire of novels about Hollywood.

Somebody's Darling, a comedy of manners and of vulgarity, is about movie people and moviemaking and has all the earmarks of the Hollywood novel: hopeless dreamers, bitchy stars, cynical writers, artless directors, colorful has-beens, and sad hangers-on. McMurtry's Hollywood is all about "frippery, pretense, indulgence, overconspicuous overconsumption." It is a place where gofers hold elevators for their bosses and a dalmatian can, unnoticed, eat eight hundred dollars worth of caviar at a director's party. It is a place where *whatever* is the word to end all conversations and equivocation is the order of the day.

As early as 1968 McMurtry was indicating in his essays that California and Texas had much in common, going so far as to predict that "the new Texas is probably going to be a sort of kid brother to California, with a kid brother's tendency to imitation." And he was quick to acknowledge the challenge this "big brother" posed: "California, whether as a subject or a place to live, is almost too taxing. There the confusion is greater, the rivalries of manners more intense: the question is whether anyone can live in California and comprehend it clearly now. Nathanael West would have a harder time with the state today than he had in 1939."

Certainly, McMurtry's knowledge of Hollywood is extensive. Peavy, author of the most systematic study of McMurtry's work, notes that "few contemporary American novelists have been as intimately associated with motion pictures" as has McMurtry. By the time he wrote *Somebody's Darling* three of his novels had been made into movies (*Horseman, Pass By* as *Hud*, 1963, starring Paul Newman; *The Last Picture Show*, 1971, on which McMurtry collaborated with Peter Bogdanovich; and *Leaving Cheyenne* as *Lovin' Molly*, 1973); two others sent Texas characters to Hollywood, and McMurtry—an avowed aficionado of "bad movies"—was a contributing editor of *American Film* magazine. One critic claimed that his involvement with Hollywood made him "a pivotal figure who demonstrates how an exchange between film and fiction can each enrich the other."

Against such a background, the surprising thing about *Somebody's Darling* is that it never really tries to be much of a Hollywood novel: Hollywood provides its context but not its subject. While Jonathan Yardley contended in the *New York Times Book Review* that the novel's "principal concern is the ambiguous relationship between craft and art as it manifests itself in Hollywood," *Somebody's Darling* seems much more concerned with familiar McMurtry themes, ringing one more change on the subject of loneliness. Indeed, everything about the book is familiar: its three-narrator structure is very similar to that of *Leaving Cheyenne*; two of the three narrators—Joe Percy and Jill Peel—and a couple of minor characters reappear from *Moving On* and from *All My Friends Are Going to Be Strangers*; and the third narrator—Owen Oarson—is a Texan, a slightly more urbane and complicated version of Paul Newman's Hud. Two of the most memorable characters in *Somebody's Darling*, Elmo Buckle and Winfield Gohagen, are good ol' boy screenwriters from Austin, Texas, and that native Texas delicacy, chicken-fried steak, even makes a guest appearance. In one humorously self-conscious moment one of McMurtry's narrators laments: "There's no getting away from cowboys, no place I've ever been." In another such moment one of the two puckish Texan screenwriters counsels that "Texas is the ultimate last resort. . . . It's always a good idea to go to Texas, if you can't think of anything else to do."

Somebody's Darling tells the story of thirty-seven-year-old Jill Peel, Hollywood's first female director, a woman somewhat randomly catapulted by her directorial debut into success and out of her long-standing and deep friendship with Joe Percy, a sixty-three-year-old contract screenwriter. Joe, the first of the novel's three narrators and easily its most endearing character, has been reduced to writing plots for a television series based on the song "Wichita Lineman." He is a dapper widower, a self-styled "pseudo-sage," who manages to be both avuncular and sybaritic. One of Hollywood's last gentlemen, Joe is a man whose consideration and simple kindness prove irresistible to a string of young Hollywood wives. Joe feels himself to be the last of an old breed, but unlike so many of McMurtry's earlier patriarchal dinosaurs, he can accept change: he misses the old days of Hollywood but does not delude himself that they were idyllic. Joe lives his life knowing that at any moment, in any relationship, "the bottom could always drop out." And, when Jill begins an affair with Owen Oarson, an opportunistic ex-football star now determined to become a Hollywood producer by bedding the right women, the bottom does drop out of their long friendship. "Friendship, too, is ruinable," Joe sadly notes, "and can be destroyed as quickly and as absolutely as love."

Owen detests Jill's respect for old-timers such as Joe and, in fact, detests most of her characteristics. She is as principled as he is not, as sentimental as he is callous. However, Jill has an intellectual toughness that Owen grudgingly admires, a kind of integrity he cannot understand since "a woman like her destroys all the simple appetites." For all his unpleasantness and cruelty, Owen remains the book's most pathetic figure: his hustling never slows, but his own recalcitrant complexity keeps betraying him. "I've always aspired to pure opportunism," he complains, "but I never make it."

Jill Peel is the momentary darling of the movie industry, the recipient of "more general love than anybody." But specific love has always been her special problem, a chronic victim of her complicated principles and pride. She recognizes all of Owen's flaws, but his crude attraction to her counters her debilitating need for over-intellectualizing relationships. Jill is one of McMurtry's most complex characters, paradoxically strong and weak at the same time. McMurtry told interviewer Patrick Bennett that his women characters give him the problem of "finding men worth having in the same book with my women." McMurtry elaborates: "Women are always the most admirable characters in my novels. . . . I feel I write about them well, but that's not necessarily to say that I understand them. My writing frequently convinces women that I understand them, but I don't know whether that means I really do, or whether it means they are easily persuaded, or that my writing is especially persuasive when it comes to descriptions of women."

Although she is torn by her conflicting feelings for Owen, Jill's greatest concern is for her old friend Joe Percy. Even more than she had disapproved of Joe's affairs with young wives, Joe had disapproved of her involvement with Owen, and Joe and Jill had quietly grown apart. Jill worries: "We're such old friends we've forgotten how to be friends. Maybe we really aren't friends any more and just don't want to admit it." The most compelling scenes in *Somebody's Darling* deal with Jill's and Joe's fumbling attempts to make sense once more of "the little roads that lead people up to and then away from one another." The great poignancy of their final scene together probably stems, at least in part, from the pivotal role his endings play in McMurtry's writing. He explained to Bennett: "I consider it a process of discovery, writing a novel. But I always start with an ending. My novels begin with a scene that forms itself in my consciousness, which I recognize as a culminating scene. . . . and the writing of the novel is a process in which I discover how these people got themselves to this scene."

While reviewers variously grumbled that *Somebody's Darling* failed to answer "important questions" or that it set its sights too low, the novel's critical reception was by and large genial, as critics acknowledged the appeal of both McMurtry's characters and his prose. McMurtry uses the device of multiple narrations to refract his characteristic concerns with kinds of initiation, with loneliness, and with the passing of old orders through the prism of Jill's relationships with Joe and Owen. In Joe Percy and Jill Peel, McMurtry has created two of his most mature and most fully realized characters. In Elmo and Winfield ("neither of them quite trusted a woman until she'd slept with them both") McMurtry has created two screamingly funny characters–crazy but endearing Texans. Yet McMurtry was not satisfied with *Somebody's Darling*, seeing it as "an enjoyable read," but as no more than an interesting failure.

In the 1980s Larry McMurtry has produced five novels, including a Pulitzer Prize-winner, *Lonesome Dove* (1985). *Terms of Endearment* was made into a successful film in 1983, and *Lonesome Dove* has been adapted for television as a widely popular and critically acclaimed miniseries. He continues to run his Washington, D.C., rare-book store. As he describes his life, it is hard to see when he finds time to write: "I have a little track that I follow about once a month. I start in Washington and go to Texas, Arizona, and California in easy stages. I check on my stores and see family and friends." But though McMurtry is dazzlingly prolific, he is not repeating himself. In every novel he takes some kind of risk, enters some new territory. And although not all of his ventures have been uniformly well received, he is at long last beginning to be recognized as a serious writer.

Cadillac Jack (1982), McMurtry's first novel of the decade, is his only one set in Washington, D.C., where McMurtry has lived since the early 1970s. The hero, Cadillac Jack–named for his pearl-colored Cadillac–is a one-time rodeo cowboy, now a roving antique dealer, who has arrived in Washington for the first time. The novel follows him closely for a week of his life, during which time he attends three dotty Washington parties, goes to Texas to acquire fifty pairs of cowboy boots, turns down a chance to buy eleven thousand bird's nests, and commences love affairs with three women while keeping in touch with his three ex-wives (primarily through the phone in the Cadillac) and also taking time out to visit two teenagers who give Jacuzzi massages (one version is called the Double Bubble Brunch). The novel moves a bit uneasily through two worlds: that of Washington's social / political elite and Jack's world of antique auctions, collectors, and swap meets. What holds it together is the presence and voice of Jack, who tells his own story.

McMurtry's picture of Washington is satire of the broadest kind. In fact, his penchant for satire has been somewhat underrated; in *Film Flam: Essays on Hollywood* (1987) he notes that he had intended *The Last Picture Show* to be a satire and was surprised by director Peter Bogdanovich's view of the book: "My task, for a while, was to keep the balloon of Bogdanovichian romanticism from lifting us clear off the earth. In rereading the book I realized that, despite my efforts at savage satire, I had still somewhat romanticized the place and the people." It is impossible to miss the satire on Washington in *Cadillac Jack*. To start with, McMurtry has given his Washington charac-

ters totally outlandish names, such as Dunscombe Cotswinkle, an aged statesman; his wife Cunard (nicknamed Cunny); Pencil Penrose, a Georgetown hostess; Lilah and Andy Landry, socialites; Oblivia Brown, hostess with the mostest; and Harris Harisse, an heir.

McMurtry had been reading Alexander Pope and Evelyn Waugh when he wrote the book, but his satire is broader than Pope's, more on the order of Samuel Butler's. There is a CIA plot to sell off everything in the Smithsonian, and Jack cannot even find a journalist interested in investigating the story. At the first Georgetown dinner party Jack attends, a couple of pugs named Wog-ers and Gog-ers are invited onto the table, where they eat one guest's coq au vin and crawl into the bosom of another. At the second dinner party he attends, the guests are served a tablespoon of soup and "the breasts of some very small bird." The book seems to suggest that life in Washington, D.C., is insufficiently nourishing: the guests at an embassy reception descend on the hors d'oeuvres like locusts, and the bureaucrats look pallid and underfed.

The novel's reviewers in general were not amused by the satire on Washington. Eden Wash Lipson found it "cartoonist" (*New York Times Book Review*, 21 November 1982), and Peter Prince commented in the *Nation* (20 November 1982) that McMurtry's "wild fantasies about Washington high life . . . give the impression of society observed purely through a keyhole." McMurtry himself, in the preface, suggests a link between his picture of Washington and Jack's activities as a collector: "The city, as the old nest collector observed, is a graveyard of styles. It is also a city of museums, and its defining attitudes are curatorial. Indeed, its ponderous social life is not unlike a museum exhibit, in which a good many of the major canvases have long needed dusting. The book became a kind of exhibit of capitol portraits."

The reviewers were more pleased with the novel's antique dealers and collectors. McMurtry, of course, knows their world from his career as a book scout and dealer. They are a gallery of eccentrics, most of whom finally seem a bit sad, like Beulah Mahoney, Rudolph Valentino's former secretary, who sold Jack the hubcaps from Valentino's car and died within six months of parting with them. Some collectors end up snowed under by their growing collections. Others, like Jean Arbor, Jack's most interesting lover, who is beginning a new life as a single mother and antique dealer, so love the objects in their stores that they take little pleasure in making a sale.

Jack, traveling scout and dealer in objects, who refuses to be tied down to a store, seems to have his relationships to objects licked: "One of my firmest principles is that those who sell should not keep. The minute a scout starts keeping his best finds he becomes a collector. All scouts have love affairs with objects, but true scouts have brief intense passions, not marriages. I didn't want to own something I loved so much I wouldn't sell it." His problem, of course–and one that he is aware of–is that he relates to women just as he relates to objects. He wants a number of them at the same time and is unable to make a commitment to any of them. In the preface McMurtry calls Jack "a very detached man." A couple of reviewers found that detachment a flaw, Peter Prince called it "apathy, depression, and world weariness." Jack's detachment is leavened, though, by genuine if sometimes bewildered kindness: he is willing to make love to a woman out of pure kindness if he thinks that the act will wipe out her unhappiness for a little while. He is like other McMurtry characters–and like McMurtry himself–in his love of travel for its own sake. In bad moods, Jack says, "I usually hit the road . . . trusting that the long roads and blue skies of America will restore me to lucidity and a simple sense of purpose."

Sometimes McMurtry seems to lose control of *Cadillac Jack*. There are more characters than can be easily sorted out and a number of incidents that do not lead to much of anything. These "flaws," though, may be part of McMurtry's satiric vision of contemporary life.

McMurtry's next novel, *The Desert Rose* (1983), was written in three weeks as a vacation from working on *Lonesome Dove*. McMurtry was asked to write a screenplay about the life of a Las Vegas show girl; he did some research and began writing, and, he says in the preface to the paperback edition, "before I had written a paragraph I knew I was writing a novel."

The Desert Rose alternates between the points of view of Harmony, a show girl approaching middle age, and her teenage daughter, Pepper, a rising star as a dancer. Both women are beautiful, and that is about all they have in common. In the preface McMurtry explains that the theme attracted him because show girls are "a dying breed": "I have always been attracted to dying crafts–cowboying is one such. It became clear that the showgirls were the cowboys of Las Vegas; there were fewer and fewer jobs and they faced bleak futures, some with grace, and some without it."

Harmony faces her bleak future with optimism. During the week or so of her life that the novel portrays, she suffers setbacks; a boyfriend who has left her after totaling her car steals the insurance check out of her mailbox; a fellow show girl falls on stage and shatters an ankle; Harmony herself turns thirty-nine and is fired from the Stardust on the same day. At the same time, her daughter Pepper drops out of high school, gets a job as a dancer at the Stardust, and accepts a marriage proposal from a wealthy older man– all without consulting her mother, whom Pepper resents for no good reason. Through it all, Harmony continues to tend to her pet peacocks and sympathize with her friends. Harmony's resilience is admirable, but the optimism of her narrative voice gets somewhat predictable.

Although *The Desert Rose* was not widely reviewed, critical comment was generally favorable, with the exception of D. Keith Mano's comment in the *National Review* (25 November 1983) that the novel was a dull and overly sentimental picture of "women who get used up by the Male System." In the *New Leader* of 14 November 1983 Emily Benedek found *The Desert Rose* to be a breakthrough book, the first in which McMurtry proved himself "capable of writing about the modern West without being derailed by ghosts or stylistic artifice."

However, it was McMurtry's next novel that proved to be his real breakthrough into popular and critical success. In *Lonesome Dove*, which won the Pulitzer Prize for Fiction in 1986, McMurtry moves back in time to the post-Civil War West, the West of cattle drives, Indian fighting, saloons, and outlaws, the West that has been turned into myth in thousands of American novels and movies. In the grittiness of its details McMurtry's picture of the old West is realistic and antiromantic (or low mimetic, as Northrop Frye would say), in the manner of Thomas Berger's *Little Big Man* (1964). *Lonesome Dove* lets the reader know that buffalo hunters and their hides smelled awful. One of the two heroines, Lorena, is a whore–of course–but the Dry Bean saloon where she works is no glamorous dance hall but a grubby bar with a hot and dusty bedroom upstairs. The other heroine, Clara, raises horses in Nebraska; she has spent much of her life in a sod house and is realistic about its hardships: "Clara had always hated the sod house–hated the dirt that seeped down

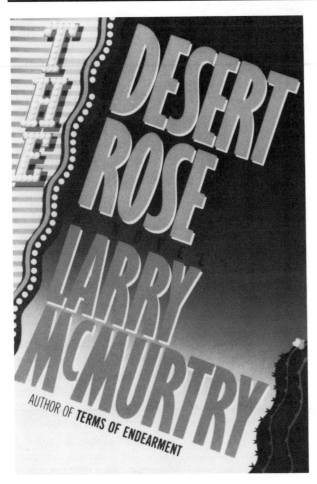

Dust jacket for McMurtry's novel about the trials of an aging but optimistic Las Vegas show girl

on her bedclothes, year after year. It was dust that caused her firstborn, Jim, to cough virtually from his birth until he died a year later. In the morning Clara would walk down and wash her hair in the icy waters of the Platte, and yet by supper time, if she happened to scratch her head, her fingernail would fill with dirt that had seeped down during the day. For some reason, no matter where she moved her bed, the roof would trickle dirt right onto it. She tacked muslin, and finally canvas, on the ceiling over the bed but nothing stopped the dirt for long."

The novel is also realistic about the hardships of a cattle drive. In the main action the heroes drive a herd of cattle (most stolen from below the Mexican border) from Lonesome Dove in south Texas to the northern border of Montana to start a ranch. They endure thunderstorms (where the lightning sometimes glitters on the horns of the cattle), a cloud of grasshoppers, quicksand, a desert, a sandstorm, and, by the end, snow. Some of the most appealing characters die, killed by savage accidents like being struck by lightning or bumping into a nest of moccasins in a river or being ambushed by the occasional bunch of starving Indians who have enough energy left to fight. It takes courage and endurance–and luck–to survive in McMurtry's old West.

McMurtry's main characters emerge as authentic heroes without becoming stereotypes. The leaders of the cattle drive are Captains Woodrow Call and Gus McCrae, former Texas Rangers who are fine fighters, little disposed to tolerate insolence from anyone. Woodrow Call is a worker and a planner, tense behind his silences, so embarrassed by his only love affair that he refuses to acknowledge his illegitimate son. Gus McCrae is Call's opposite: a native of Tennessee, a University of Virginia graduate (although he has forgotten his Latin), a constant talker whose voice carries for a hundred yards over the plains. What he has to say is often surprising and funny. It was Gus who composed the sign that advertises their livery stable in Lonesome Dove; it says, among other things:

FOR RENT: HORSES AND RIGS
FOR SALE: CATTLE AND HORSES
GOATS AND DONKEYS NEITHER
    BOUGHT NOR SOLD
WE DON'T RENT PIGS.

Gus also articulates some of the novel's major themes. He recognizes that he and Call and the Texas Rangers, in bringing order to Texas, have helped to create a civilization where they are no longer needed. He also recognizes that there is a certain pointlessness in the cattle drive, since he and Call have little desire to be ranchers. The point of the trip, for Gus, is the fun of discovering unsettled country. Like the classic western hero, Gus chooses the pleasure of discovery over the love of women, but unlike that hero, Gus likes and even understands women; he has experienced love and knows its value.

The other characters are also more than stereotypes. Newt, Call's unacknowledged son, comes of age during the cattle drive (hardships like storms are often narrated from his point of view, making them especially vivid). Newt's growth into manhood is acknowledged by the classic gifts–horses, saddles, guns–but the gifts usually make him feel sad and guilty, and he spends much of his journey in tears over his lost friends. A small-town sheriff and his deputy are generally ineffectual, incapable of fighting outlaws or even of finding their way to Texas without help. The sheriff's wife, Elmira, is going mad from boredom, missing the old days when she was an outlaw's mistress. The most important outlaw, Jake, a former Texas Ranger turned horse thief and killer, is no black-mustached villain but a handsome drifter, a gambler who cannot make strong commitments to other people. Lorena is no stock whore-with-a-heart-of-gold: she is young, beautiful, and vulnerable, yet she knows exactly what the adoration-from-afar of the cowboys means and how little good their affection would do her.

McMurtry also shows an amazing fertility of imagination in creating secondary characters. Po Campo, the Mexican cook who gathers wild birds' eggs for breakfast and fries grasshoppers for dessert, lets it be known rather casually that he killed his wife (and still misses her biscuits). Some of the most vivid characters are animals: the Hell Bitch, Call's aptly named mare; a Texas bull that picks a fight with a bear; the pigs Gus would not rent, who follow the cattle drive all the way to Montana on their own initiative, only to be eaten during the winter.

By and large the novel won over the reviewers. Whitney Balliett of the *New Yorker* (11 November 1985) found the adventures of the cattle drive facile, but called Clara a "Jamesian heroine," one of the "few full-scale female protagonists" in American fiction. *Newsweek*'s Walter Clemons called *Lonesome Dove* "a marvelous novel," "amply imagined and crisply, lovingly written" and having "just about every symptom of American Epic except pretentiousness" (3 June 1985). In *Time* (10 June 1985) R. Z. Sheppard wrote: "The book's great length and leisurely pace convey the sense of a bygone era, while the author's attachment to misfits and backwaters never goes out of style."

Perhaps the most perceptive comment came from Nicholas Lemann in the *New York Times Book Review* of 9 June 1985. He argued that *Lonesome Dove* begins as a realistic "antiwestern" but that the action transforms Gus and Call "from burnt-out cases into–there is no other word– heroes . . . absolutely courageous, tough, strong, loyal, fabulously good fighters." Lemann continued: "All of Mr. McMurtry's antimythic groundwork–his refusal to glorify the West– works to reinforce the strength of the tradition-

ally mythic parts of 'Lonesome Dove' by making it far more credible than the old familiar horse operas. These are real people, and they are still larger than life. The aspects of cowboying that we have found stirring for so long are, inevitably, the aspects that are stirring when given full-dress treatment by a first-rate novelist."

Nostalgia and realism have been jostling each other in McMurtry's work for some time now. Both attitudes are present in many of his characters, and nostalgia is often an issue in McMurtry's own comments about his fiction. He has said in print, more than once (*In a Narrow Grave*, *Film Flam*), that he prefers the film *Hud* (1963) to his first novel, *Horseman, Pass By*, because he believes that the novel over-idealized Homer Bannon, the aging rancher who adheres to the code of the old West, at the expense of his wild stepson Hud, a more modern character who is perfectly willing to lease the family ranch to oilmen. McMurtry's comments about the 1971 adaptation of *The Last Picture Show* as a film reveal that he had somehow made that novel more romantic and nostalgic than he intended. In 1981 McMurtry called on other Texas writers to stop dwelling on the past and to write about the realities of modern, urban Texas. During the same year, in a *Rolling Stone* article entitled "Bedtime for America," he criticized Ronald Reagan for capitalizing on "the politics of nostalgia." McMurtry seems to mistrust his own nostalgia. His novel *Texasville* (1987) declares all-out war on that emotion.

Paradoxically, McMurtry breaks into new territory in *Texasville* by returning to Thalia, Texas, the fictional version of his own hometown, Wichita Falls, that was the setting of *The Last Picture Show*. *Texasville* is primarily a novel about the middle-aged. It features some of the central characters from *The Last Picture Show* now in their forties. Moreover, there is a significant change in point of view from *The Last Picture Show*. The earlier novel was written in third person but most often seen through the eyes of Sonny Crawford. At the end of the novel Sam the Lion, that grand old man of the West, has died and left Sonny his pool hall, along with his memories of an older and more heroic Texas. In *Texasville* Sonny still owns the pool hall (now a video arcade), and he has acquired a hotel, a Laundromat, a convenience store, a car wash, and several other downtown properties; he has also become the mayor. He still has his memories–and they are driving him crazy. More and more frequently, Sonny thinks he is in the 1950s; he wanders into the ruins of the picture show to watch nonexistent movies and drives his car into what once was Ruth Popper's garage and now is another family's television room. At one point he considers suing the whole town for the alienation of his intellect. Once sensitive and nostalgic, Sonny now seems merely pathetic. Ruth says that what is wrong with him is resignation. Jacy (now a sympathetic character, though she was vain and self-centered in *The Last Picture Show*) elaborates: "I just don't want to see him. Something about him makes my skin crawl. It happened the day I married him, too. My skin started crawling. . . . It's his willingness to be unhappy, or something. It gave me the creeps then, and it gives me the creeps now." Sonny himself explains his problem to his friend Duane Moore: "You don't care about the past. But I care about it. I started thinking about it and now I can't stop." Nostalgia has clearly gotten Sonny nowhere, and in *Texasville* the point of view has shifted from him to his tougher friend Duane.

Duane has come home from Korea and become an oil millionaire, only to see his wealth evaporate in the oil glut of the 1980s. (The whole town is affected by the oil situation: at one point an oilman suggests bombing OPEC, and when Sonny disappears into the picture show the crowd at the Kwik-Sack becomes convinced he has been kidnapped by Libyan terrorists and rounds up a posse.) Duane owns four deep oil rigs that cost almost three million dollars each and are now worthless, a twelve-thousand-square-foot mansion that he mostly finds irritating (he has moments when he can barely make it across the waterbed), a swimming pool and a Jacuzzi, and a two-story log doghouse built like "a replica of a frontier fort"–and none of it is paid for. One motif of his quietly desperate life is that he is being smothered by the things he owns; once, in a fit of hostility, he runs his pickup truck over some eighty-five Willie Nelson tapes. His beautiful wife, Karla, who is given to wearing T-shirts with slogans like "WOMAN'S PLACE IS IN THE MALL," cannot give up her compulsive shopping now that she and Duane are poor: on the same day when they install a satellite dish she goes to Dallas and buys "a Betamax, a VHS, and four thousand dollars worth of movies."

Duane's family life is as ragged as his financial state. He has four children: Dickie and Nellie, who are more or less grown, and eleven-year-old twins who were born ten years after Karla had her tubes tied. All are problems. Twenty-one-year-old Dickie is the local drug dealer. Engaged to an unstable girl who threatens to shoot him, he nonetheless commences an affair with a married woman in her forties, with whom Duane is also having an affair (the woman ultimately prefers Dickie; in the meanwhile her estranged husband moves into Duane's house). At nineteen Nellie has been married three times and is living at home and neglecting her two babies. The twins have spent most of their childhood in the emergency room because of the wounds they inflict on each other; Karla "learned never to take the twins to the hospital at the same time: there were too many weapons in the hospitals." Duane feels helplessly responsible for all of them: "He couldn't tell that he had made any impression on any of his children. It was a haunting feeling, because in many respects he knew he had been a fairly effective man." Despite his problems, Duane is in better shape than most people in Thalia: he and Karla have remained genuine, if argumentative, friends, and he has kept his interest in life and his sense of his humor.

Other characters from the earlier novel have also undergone changes. Jacy, now famous for her role as a jungle queen in Italian movies, has come home to pull herself together after losing a son in a freak accident on a movie set. Ruth Popper, now Duane's secretary and a passionate jogger, is being rewarded for an unhappy youth by a happy old age. Lester Marlow, Jacy's old boyfriend, is now the president of the local bank and soon to face trial for seventy-three counts of fraud. His wife leaves him during the course of the novel; she takes up with Dickie and shows more than a passing interest in Duane. Joe Bob Blanton, who returns for his class reunion, has become a spokesperson for the pedophiliac community in Syracuse, New York. There are a number of new characters, most of them a bit sketchy, and everyone is sleeping with everyone else. Sex is still the main recreational activity in Thalia, and affairs are commenced with fewer romantic illusions than in *The Last Picture Show*. The marriages are generally joyless: as Duane says, "It's hard to stay exciting for a whole lifetime."

Texasville gets such structure as it has from the preparation for and celebration of Thalia's centennial, which also allows McMurtry to poke fun at nostalgia. The planned events of the centennial celebration include a replica of Texasville, a

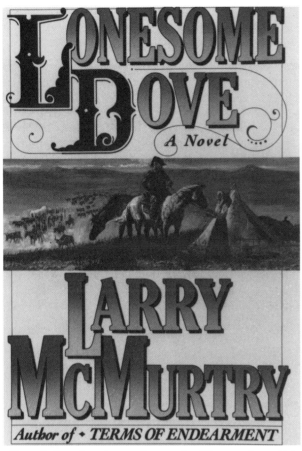

Dust jacket for the anti-romantic Western for which McMurtry won a Pulitzer Prize in 1986

wagon train (it gets lost), a marathon (Ruth wins), souvenirs (too few are sold), dances, floats, parades, and a pageant that begins the town's history with Adam and Eve (played by Duane and Jacy). The unplanned events include a tumbleweed stampede and the arrival in town of a long-distance trucker hauling sixty thousand eggs. When he leaves the truck for a nap, the children find the eggs and throw all sixty thousand of them, beginning hostilities against the Byelo-Baptists, teetotalers who have spent the centennial knocking beer out of people's hands with brooms. Their preacher reacts: "It's punishment time! The Lord's raining down egg bombs on this haven of sots."

Texasville is a funny book. Its undertone of melancholy notwithstanding, it is full of satiric comedy. There is nothing romantic / mythic / nostalgic about McMurtry's vision of Texas here. Instead, the novel confirms what McMurtry said as a panelist in a symposium commemorating Texas's sesquicentennial in 1986: "Texas does have to come to grips with the psychological fact

that societies are not necessarily and inevitably progressive–that things don't always get better and better." In *Texasville* Duane comes to the same grim realization, musing about himself and his friends: "What *would* they do with the rest of their lives? He had no idea, but whatever it was, it seemed all too likely that they would do it less well than what they had done so far–a depressing prospect."

Texasville received generally good reviews. John Skow of *Time* admired McMurtry's "wonderfully loose-jointed narrative style" and "the Jamesian restraint of the language" (20 April 1987). Michiko Kakutani of the *New York Times* also praised the sureness of McMurtry's voice and his "feeling for people and place" (8 April 1987). In the *New York Times Book Review* Louise Erdrich compared *Texasville* to *The Last Picture Show* with some reservations about the newer book: "The leisurely, lyrical character development, description and complexity that distinguished the first book are absent from the sequel. . . . 'Texasville' often reads like a movie script, all dialogue and situation. The individual scenes are sharp, spare, full of longhorn humor and color, but motivation is sketchy, rarely described, clued by action rather than reflection" (19 April 1987). Too often it seems to be McMurtry's fate to be accused of sentimentality when he is lyrical, and lack of feeling when he is satiric.

McMurtry's next book, *Film Flam: Essays on Hollywood* (1987), is a collection of essays on the movies, most of which originally appeared in *American Film*. Most of the essays are either meditations on being a screenwriter or discussions of specific movies–in the voice of a man who calls them movies, not films. A self-confessed fan of silly movies, McMurtry can find little to admire in the Hollywood product these days: "With rare exceptions the pictures coming out of Hollywood today are the last resorts of the gutless. In my opinion, a little film flam is all such an industry deserves." Generally skeptical about European "art" films since he walked out on *L'Avventura*, McMurtry writes penetratingly about movies as audiences experience them in settings like drive-ins and the "fringe theaters" of Times Square; such audiences, he argues, are not seeking "pedestrian realism"–their own lives offer plenty of that–but the illusion of "the heroic–the triumph over circumstance."

McMurtry's comments about movies are direct and unpretentious, most interesting when they illuminate his own work, as does his contention that the "fragmented contexts of modern life" have made love an impossible subject for movies. McMurtry's comments about the film adaptations of his novels are singularly modest. He explains the success of *The Last Picture Show*: "The Last Picture Show* was exactly the kind of novel from which good pictures are made–that is, a flatly written book with strong characterizations and a sense of period and place. Films like *The Blue Angel*, *Jules and Jim*, and *The Treasure of the Sierra Madre* were made from just such books– books that offer a director no stylistic resistance whatever. Towering classics always have a style, and adapting them is like attempting to translate poetry, only more difficult.... True equivalents simply don't exist, and the book that best lends itself to filming, in my view, is the book from which one can abstract a place, a period, and a story for which the director can feel free to develop a style of his own." Thus McMurtry is also modest in his discussion of the screenwriter's craft. He insists that in itself a screenplay is only a "blueprint," useful for budgeting and casting but less a self-sufficient work of art even than an architect's plan or a musical score. And McMurtry is engagingly ready to admit that what has drawn him into screen writing is the money.

Anything for Billy (1988), McMurtry's most recent novel, about a character no less a legend than Billy the Kid, departs from what little is "known" about this infamous gunslinger. His Kid is named Billy Bone, not William H. Bonney; the Lincoln County War becomes Billy's vendetta against a rancher named Isinglass; Pat Garrett never appears. McMurtry creates a new cast of characters: the immensely wealthy and ruthless Isinglass; his chief hit man Mesty-Woolah, a seven-foot-tall African who rides a camel; Joe Lovelady, a perfect, gentle cowboy; Katie Varga, Isinglass's half-Mexican daughter–a crack shot and the leader of her own gang–who becomes Billy's lover; Cecily Snow, an English botanist, who is Isinglass's mistress and also becomes Billy's lover; and, most notable of all, the narrator Ben Sippy, a Philadelphian writer of dime Westerns who comes West to be a train robber– when he rode up to a train waving his gun, the conductor just waved back at him–and falls in with Billy by the merest chance, bumping into him on a foggy morning. In fact, the whole plot of the novel seems random, even fragmented– perhaps because of the shortness of the chapters. Billy rides around the Southwest, in and out of the lives of the two women, from time to time kill-

ing people for little reason, with no remorse. McMurtry's Billy really is just a kid: "I would have guessed him to be no more than seventeen at the time, and short for his age at that. In fact, he was almost a runt, and ugly as Sunday. His dirty black coat was about three sizes too big for him." Moreover, he can barely shoot straight: "he never killed a man who stood more than twenty feet from him. Billy was a blaster, not a marksman." Billy emerges as a sad kid, with all capacity for empathy just somehow missing from his makeup. Why people in the novel like him so well is something of a mystery, one that points to the greater mystery of why Americans turned him into a legend. *Anything for Billy* is a thoroughly antiromantic treatment of the myth of the gunfighter. In an interview McMurtry said that some people had misread *Lonesome Dove* "as a reinforcement of the myth" of the cowboy: "People need to believe that cowboys are simple, strong and free, and not twisted, fascistic and dumb, as many cowboys I've known have been.... The idea that men are men and women are women and horses are best of all is not a myth that makes for the best sort of domestic life, the best of cultural life." It is impossible to so misread *Anything for Billy*.

Some aspects of McMurtry's realism here will be familiar to readers of *Lonesome Dove*. Once again the physical and social landscape of the Southwest is disheartening: Ben Sippy is troubled less by banditos than by bugs–"lice, chiggers, mosquitoes, nits, ticks, houseflies, horseflies, bedbugs, beetles, ants, spiders, roaches, centipedes, scorpions, and gnats"–and he describes the town of Greasy Corners: "It was said to be a den of whores and cutthroats, but that part didn't worry me. Most of the local settlements were dens of whores and cutthroats." Sippy's ten-day stagecoach ride from Galveston to El Paso is a bumpy unromantic ordeal, made worse by quadruplets with diarrhea and their mother, who farts in her sleep. (" 'You mean she farted right there in the coach?' Billy Bone asked, badly shocked.") Here, as in *Lonesome Dove*, death and violence are random and often accidental. What makes *Anything for Billy* different from *Lonesome Dove* is the absence of structure–there is no cattle drive to Montana to give the protagonists' movements a direction–and the absence of heroes. What makes *Anything for Billy* a fascinating experiment, though, is McMurtry's use of Ben Sippy to explore the roots of myth and legend. A literate Easterner, Sippy has obvious advantages as a narrator. As Jack Butler observed in *The New York Times Book Review*, "American popular culture has always been a rather mute one, and yet any fine writer wants to do more with words than merely master a realistic patois. That's a good trick, but if you love words, it wears thin. How do you write about primarily reticent or illiterate characters and yet give scope to your talent? Through Ben Sippy, Mr. McMurtry can write of the strong, mostly silent characters of the West and yet allude to Edward Bulwer-Lytton or speak of the wind 'keening its disquieting symphony.'" If nothing else, Ben Sippy reminds readers of how formidably well-read McMurtry is: anyone who knows that a literate nineteenth-century American would have been acquainted with the poetry of Mrs. Hemans has read a lot. As a writer of dime novels Sippy offers McMurtry the chance to question how legends are made. Sippy constantly mythologizes his experience by turning it into pulp fiction so embellished and embroidered that its connection to fact is mostly emotional. For example, his most successful book, *The Butler's Sorrow; or, Chittim's Treck*, was triggered by his remorse on the day his butler collapsed and died on the sidewalk in Philadelphia, returning from the newsstand. Out of this experience Sippy wrote:

> the story of a loyal butler who crossed the Sonoran desert on foot in order to deliver an important document to his beloved young mistress, a rich girl soon to be richer, but presently taking the waters at a spa in California. The document informed her that she had just inherited a vast ancestral estate.
>
> The loyal butler, knowing that he could aspire to nothing more, hoped that at least the young lady would take him with her to her new home and keep him as her butler forever, but the heartless vixen, annoyed by his shabby appearance–there had been the usual scrapes with Apaches and Gila monsters–sacked him on the spot. The poor man's despair was such that he lost his way, drifted south, and was eventually eaten by cannibals in Ecuador.

Sippy's profession certainly points to the dime novel as a source of McMurtry's inspiration for *Billy*–perhaps the short chapters are a homage to the genre–and Sippy's compulsion to make fictions may also make readers question his reliability as a narrator and suggests the impossibility of telling anything like the "truth" about Billy the Kid, a historical figure whose legend is so cloudy that encyclopedias do not agree about the num-

ber of people he killed, or even the number of people he was *credited* with killing. Sippy as narrator is an ideal vehicle for McMurtry's avowed purpose with this novel: "I'm not so much demythicizing as remythicizing. I'm reinventing some myths for my own pleasure. In the process, of course, that warps whatever residual myths that were left in the consciousness . . . I suppose you don't remythicize without demolishing the one that was there, or certainly renovating it. Think of it as akin to historical renovation. Some people renovate houses. I'm renovating the cowboy." In academic parlance, perhaps McMurtry is deconstructing the cowboy.

The reviews of *Anything for Billy* were sometimes puzzled, but universally respectful. The tone reviewers took suggests that McMurtry is finally being seen as a major American writer. Jack Butler began his review of *Anything for Billy:* "As much as I hate to say it about somebody who can sell 200,000 copies of just about any novel he writes, I think Larry McMurtry may be a great writer. He's doing something with the American West that is very much like what Faulkner did with Mississippi. He is re- (not de-) mythologizing it. . . . Like Faulkner, Mr. McMurtry is weaving a complete history. In his recent books, he has been alternating the Old Wild West with the West of the present or near-present, connecting time past to time not realized." Michiko Kakutani of the *New York Times* called *Anything for Billy* "a ballad of one outlaw's misspent life as well as a lament for a time and place that once existed in our collective imagination"; R. Z. Sheppard of *Time* called it "a folklore about the making of folklore." *Anything for Billy* made the best-seller lists almost immediately; McMurtry's days of being known only through the film versions of his novels seem to be over.

The popularity and informality of McMurtry's fiction have encouraged critics to place him somewhere below the first rank of American novelists. Again and again reviewers have praised his characters, his readability, his original narrative voice, his mixture of humor and bleakness, and always, when he writes about Texas, his sense of place–only to imply that his novels are popular and somehow not quite serious. In a *New Yorker* review (15 June 1987) of *Texasville* and *The Thanatos Syndrome*, by Walker Percy (a writer who has been taken far more seriously than McMurtry), Terrence Rafferty neatly sums up the relative standing of the two writers: "Covering the same span of history, the two novelists form a nearly perfect dialectical pair: the visionary and the realist, the cosmic and the regional, the major and the minor. Percy has squeezed out six ambitious works of fiction in twenty-six years; McMurtry has knocked off eleven of his readable, character-dominated novels in that time. Percy's books rate front-page reviews and all manner of awards and honors; McMurtry's get made into movies. . . . 'The Thanatos Syndrome' is dedicated to Harvard psychiatrist Robert Coles, 'Texasville' to Cybill Shepherd, who played the beautiful tease Jacy in the film of 'The Last Picture Show.' Both writers are trying to portray what it's been like to live in America for the past two and a half decades, yet the work of each reads almost like a science fiction version of the other's, as if they were describing alternative universes. (And Louisiana isn't even that *far* from Texas.)"

However, there are three recent signs of serious critical regard for McMurtry's work. The first, chronologically, is a short discussion of all of McMurtry's novels through *Lonesome Dove*, published in the December 1986 *English Journal*. Within the confines of two pages, Don Melichar can do little more than tell what each book is about and recommend the novels to other readers; nonetheless, the essay's appearance in an academic journal is encouraging. The second sign of encouragement is Rafferty's above-quoted review. Having acknowledged McMurtry's place as a "minor regional writer," Rafferty argues that in some ways McMurtry is superior to Walker Percy, less inclined to repeat himself and cannibalize from his own earlier work, gifted with more "comic precision," better able to create a novel that "really *is* about history, at least as Americans live it." Most recently, in the *New York Review of Books* (13 August 1987), no less a scholar/critic than Robert M. Adams made a case for the depth and originality of McMurtry's vision. Confining his discussion to three of the novels, *The Last Picture Show*, *Lonesome Dove*, and *Texasville*, Adams argues that McMurtry has been underrated: "As a serious novelist he hasn't received much consideration, probably because his western settings have led eastern critics to confuse him with writers of cowboy melodramas. He can do cowboy melodrama, and do it very well, but even as he does it, there are overtones and nuances of feeling that transcend the formulas."

Interview:
Patrick Bennett, "Larry McMurtry: Thalia, Hous-

ton, & Hollywood," in *Talking With Texas Writers: Twelve Interviews* (College Station: Texas A & M University Press, 1980), pp. 15-36. McMurtry discusses his writing techniques.

Bibliography:
Charles D. Peavy, "A Larry McMurtry Bibliography," *Western American Literature*, 3 (Fall 1968): 235-248.
A definitive bibliography of McMurtry's work up until 1968, including letters and unpublished writing.

References:
Robert M. Adams, "The Bard of Wichita Falls," *New York Review of Books* (13 August 1987): 39-41.
An important and favorable reassessment of McMurtry's fiction through *Texasville*, written by a major critic.

Kerry Ahearn, "Larry McMurtry," in *Fifty Western Writers: A Bio-Bibliographical Sourcebook*, edited by Fred Erisman and Richard W. Etulain (Westport, Conn.: Greenwood Press, 1982), pp. 280-290.
Assesses McMurtry's work through *Somebody's Darling*, seeing initiation, loss, and marriage as major themes. Includes a survey of criticism and a bibliography.

David Braun, "Is *Lonesome Dove* a Turkey?" *Washington Post*, 5 February 1989, D5.
A widely syndicated article, published when *Lonesome Dove* was aired as a miniseries, that asserts that there are historical inaccuracies in the novel.

Alan F. Crooks, "Larry McMurtry–A Writer in Transition: An Essay-Review," *Western American Literature*, 7 (Summer 1972): 151-155.
Argues that McMurtry needs a sense of place to do his best work. Based partly on interviews.

Kenneth W. Davis, "The Themes of Initiation in the Works of Larry McMurtry and Tom Mayer," *Arlington Quarterly*, 2 (Winter 1969-1970): 29-43.
Discusses how region shapes the experiences that lead McMurtry's young protagonists toward manhood.

E. Pauline Degenfelder, "McMurtry and the Movies: *Hud* and *The Last Picture Show*," *Western Humanities Review*, 29 (Winter 1975): 81-91.
Argues that McMurtry's style was deliberately more cinematic in the later novel.

James K. Folsom, "*Shane* and *Hud*: Two Stories in Search of a Medium," *Western Humanities Review*, 24 (Autumn 1970): 359-372.
Discusses the film adaptation of *Horseman, Pass By*.

John Gerlach, "*The Last Picture Show* and One More Adaptation," *Literature/Film Quarterly*, 1 (April 1973): 161-166.
Discusses the film adaptation of *The Last Picture Show*.

Don Graham, "Regionalism on the Ramparts: The Texas Literary Tradition," *USA TODAY*, 115 (July 1986), pp. 74-76.
Compares McMurtry to other Texas writers.

Thomas Landess, *Larry McMurtry* (Austin, Tex.: Steck-Vaughan, 1969).
Discusses McMurtry's work through *In a Narrow Grave*, arguing that McMurtry is a fine craftsman and a provocative social critic.

Don Melichar, "Recommended: Larry McMurtry," *English Journal*, 75 (December 1986): 49-50.
A brief overview of McMurtry's fiction through *Lonesome Dove*.

Jane Nelson, "Larry McMurtry," in *A Literary History of the American West* (Fort Worth, Tex.: Texas Christian University Press, 1987), pp. 612-619.
Argues that the new West in McMurtry's fiction "becomes a woman's place."

Charles D. Peavy, "Coming of Age in Texas: The Novels of Larry McMurtry," *Western American Literature*, 4 (Fall 1969): 171-188.
Discusses the theme of initiation into sexuality in *Horseman, Pass By; Leaving Cheyenne;* and *The Last Picture Show*.

Peavy, *Larry McMurtry* (Boston: Twayne, 1977).
Peavy consulted with McMurtry to get biographical data; this book is the best single source of information about the author. It sees McMurtry's major themes as initiation, loneliness, ephemerality or the sense of loss, and marriage. The book contains a chronology and a very full bibliography; it discusses McMurtry's work through *Terms of Endearment*.

Peavy, "Larry McMurtry and Black Humor: A Note on *The Last Picture Show*," *Western American Literature*, 2 (Fall 1967): 223-227.
Examines the black humor in *The Last Picture Show*.

Raymond C. Phillips, Jr., "The Ranch as Place and Symbol in the Novels of Larry McMurtry," *South Dakota Review*, 13, no. 2 (1975): 27-47.
Discusses the ranch as symbol in the novels through *All My Friends Are Going to Be Strangers*.

Terrence Rafferty, "The Last Fiction Show," *New Yorker* (15 June 1987): 91-94.
A long and favorable review of *Texasville*.

Clay Reynolds, "Back Trailing to Glory: *Lonesome Dove* and the Novels of Larry McMurtry," *Texas Review*, 8 (Fall / Winter 1987): 22-29.
Discusses *Lonesome Dove* as a reexamination of the western myth, putting it into relationship with McMurtry's earlier fiction.

Mervyn Rothstein, "A Texan Who Likes to Deflate the Legends of the Golden West," *New York Times*, 1 November 1988, C17: 21.
An interview with McMurtry about *Anything for Billy*, in which the author explains that he is trying to "renovate" the myth of the cowboy.

Dorey Schmidt, ed., *Larry McMurtry: Unredeemed Dreams*, Living Author series 1 (Edinburg, Tex.: School of Humanities, Pan American University, 1978).
Contains a bibliography, an interview, and eight essays generated by McMurtry's visit to a university campus.

Calvin Trillin, "US Journal: Washington, D.C.–Scouting Sleepers," *New Yorker*, 54 (14 June 1978): 86-92.
Follows McMurtry through several days of his activity as a book scout.

Toni Morrison

This entry was updated by Elizabeth B. House (Augusta College) from the entry by Susan L. Blake (Lafayette College) in DLB 33, Afro-American Fiction Writers After 1950.

Places	New York City Syracuse, N.Y.	Howard University Lorain, Ohio	Greenville, Ala.
Influences and Relationships	Gayl Jones Jane Austen	Gustave Flaubert Maria Tallchief	William Faulkner Virginia Woolf
Literary Movements and Forms	Afro-American Folktales	The Fairy Tale "Magical Realism"	The Russian Novel
Major Themes	Importance of Community The Family The Power of Memory	Conflicts of Power Black-White Relationships Nature	The Nature of Evil The Quest for Identity
Cultural and Artistic Influences	Afro-American Heritage The Bible	Rejection of White Aesthetics Jazz	West Indian Culture
Social and Economic Influences	Civil Rights Movement	The Depression Slavery	Black Power

See also the Morrison entries in DLB 6, American Novelists Since World War II, Second Series *and* DLB Yearbook 1981.

BIRTH: Lorain, Ohio, 18 February 1931, to George and Ramah Willis Wofford.

EDUCATION: B.A., Howard University, 1953; M.A., Cornell University, 1955.

MARRIAGE: To Harold Morrison (divorced); children: Harold Ford, Slade Kevin.

AWARDS AND HONORS: Ohioana Book Award for *Sula*, 1975; National Book Critics Circle Award for Fiction for *Song of Solomon*, 1978; elected to the American Academy and Institute of Arts and Letters, 1981; Pulitzer Prize for *Beloved*, 1988; Robert F. Kennedy Book Award for *Beloved*, 1988; Common Wealth Award in Literature, 1989.

BOOKS: *The Bluest Eye* (New York: Holt, Rinehart & Winston, 1970; London: Chatto & Windus, 1979);
Sula (New York: Knopf, 1973; London: Allen Lane, 1974);
Song of Solomon (New York: Knopf, 1977; London: Chatto & Windus, 1978);
Tar Baby (New York: Knopf, 1981; London: Chatto & Windus, 1981);
Beloved (New York: Knopf, 1987).

PLAY PRODUCTION: *Dreaming Emmett*, Albany, Market Theater, 1986.

OTHER: *The Black Book*, compiled by Middleton Harris, edited by Morrison (New York: Random House, 1974).

PERIODICAL PUBLICATIONS: "What the Black Woman Thinks About Women's Lib," *New York Times Magazine*, 22 August 1971, pp. 14-15, 63-64, 66;
"Cooking Out," *New York Times Book Review*, 10 June 1973, pp. 4, 16;
"Behind the Making of the Black Book," *Black World*, 23 (February 1974): 86-90;
"Rediscovering Black History," *New York Times Magazine*, 11 August 1974, pp. 14, 16, 18, 20, 22, 24;
"Reading," *Mademoiselle*, 81 (May 1975): 14;
"Slow Walk of Trees (as Grandmother Would Say) Hopeless (as Grandfather Would Say),"

Toni Morrison (photo copyright © 1981 by Layle Silbert)

New York Times Magazine, 4 July 1976, pp. 104, 150, 152, 160, 162, 164.

Toni Morrison is one of America's most important writers of fiction. She has received critical acclaim, most notably the 1988 Pulitzer Prize for *Beloved* (1987), the 1978 National Book Critics Circle Award for *Song of Solomon* (1977), and the eighteen-thousand-dollar 1989 Common Wealth Award in Literature. In addition, she has enjoyed a wide readership, and her books have sold well. Besides writing novels, Morrison has also been a senior editor at Random House, and she is well known as an inspiring teacher. Currently she teaches creative writing at Princeton University, and she has taught at a number of other institutions such as Bard College, Yale University, and the State University of New York at Albany.

Born Chloe Anthony Wofford, Toni Morrison grew up in the Depression in Lorain, Ohio, the second of four children of strong-minded, self-reliant parents. Her father, George Wofford, a shipyard welder, worked three jobs simultaneously for most of seventeen years and was proud enough of his workmanship that he wrote his name in the side of the ship whenever he welded a perfect seam. Her mother, Ramah Willis Wofford, sang in the church choir, reasoned with the bill collectors, and, when the family was on relief and received bug-ridden meal, wrote a long letter to Franklin D. Roosevelt. Her parents disagreed, Morrison recalls, about "whether it was possible for white people to improve." Her father thought not. Thus, "distrusting every word and every gesture of every white man on earth, [he] assumed that the white man who crept up the stairs one afternoon had come to molest his daughters and threw him down the stairs and then our tricycle after him." Her mother, on the other hand, believed in white people's possibilities. But both acted from the assumption that "black people were the humans of the globe," and both "had serious doubts about the quality and existence of white humanity." Thus they believed and taught their children that "all succor and aid came from themselves and their neighborhood."

The neighborhood of the imagination, however, stretched from Jane Austen's Mansfield Park to the supernatural. Her parents told her ghost stories. Her grandmother used a dream book to play the numbers. When she entered the first grade, Chloe was the only child in the class who knew how to read. As an adolescent, she read avidly–the great Russian novels, *Madame Bovary*, Jane Austen. As any gifted writer does, Morrison tells universal truths using whatever materials suit her purpose. Understandably, she is particularly irritated by those who try to pigeonhole writers or their work and thus deny the universal appeal of good literature. For example, in the 30 March 1981 issue of *Newsweek*, which features her picture on its cover, Morrison explains that the Jane Austen novels she read as a youngster "were not written for a little black girl . . . but they were so magnificently done that I got them anyway–they spoke directly to me out of their own specificity." Then, in a *Vogue* interview, Morrison details her annoyance with people who classify her books too rigidly: "People . . . say, 'I know you're writing black novels, but I was really interested.' It used to offend me very deeply. I said, 'Well, I read a little Dickens, I thought it was wonderful.'" And to a person who complained that he had trouble understanding her

books because his experience was so different from the black one her novels portray, Morrison says she retorted, "Boy, you must have had a hell of a time with *Beowulf* !"

After graduating with honors from Lorain High School, Chloe Wofford went to Howard University, where she majored in English and minored in classics and changed her name to Toni– because people had trouble pronouncing Chloe. Howard was a disappointment: "It was about getting married, buying clothes and going to parties. It was also about being cool, loving Sarah Vaughan (who only moved her hand a little when she sang) and MJQ [the Modern Jazz Quartet]." In reaction to this sterility, she immersed herself in the Howard University Players and, in the summers, traveled with a student-faculty repertory troupe that took plays on tour in the South. Traveling in the South was a revelation to her, as she made it to the character Milkman later in *Song of Solomon*. It illustrated the stories of her grandparents, who had migrated north from Greenville, Alabama, in 1912–archetypal stories of lost land, trumped-up debt, the sharecropping trap, and surreptitious flight–and provided a geographical and historical focus for the sense of cultural identity her parents had instilled in her.

Chloe Wofford's early influences and experiences are clearly reflected not only in the texture but also in the themes and forms of Toni Morrison's fiction. Each of Morrison's novels presents a dialectic of values, alternative ways of being human. As her father was an exacting workman, Morrison is an exacting stylist who continues to revise, she says, even after her books are bound. Her deft evocation of place and culture reflects the specificity she admired in the nineteenth-century classics, but she fits it into a mythic or fabulistic context that reflects her education in black folklore and the family habit of story telling. "Quiet as it's kept" begins the narration of *The Bluest Eye* (1970), and the reader senses that what follows is not a slice of life but a story, with all of a story's indifference to distinctions among various kinds of truth.

Morrison began to write after she returned to Howard in 1957 as an instructor in English. She had earned a master's degree in English at Cornell in 1955, taught for two years at Texas Southern University, and, at Howard, met and married Harold Morrison, a Jamaican architect. The marriage was trying and remains a subject of sensitivity; although she has explained its difficulties in part as the result of cultural differences, she refuses to disclose its date. In it, she says, she felt bankrupt: "It was as though I had nothing left but my imagination. I had no will, no judgment, no perspective, no power, no authority, no self–just this brutal sense of irony, melancholy and a trembling respect for words." When she had run out of "old junk" from high school to take to the writers' group she had joined, she dashed off a story about "a little black girl who wanted blue eyes," which became the kernel of her first novel.

She developed the story into a novel several years later in Syracuse. In 1964, after her divorce, she returned with her two small sons–Harold Ford and Slade Kevin–to her parents' home in Lorain. A year and a half later she found an editing job with a textbook subsidiary of Random House in Syracuse. Alone, in a strange place, restricted by small children, she worked on the novel in the evenings after the children were asleep. She sent an unfinished version to an editor, who encouraged her to finish it. In 1970 Holt, Rinehart and Winston published *The Bluest Eye*, the story of three girls at the threshold of maturity in Lorain, Ohio–two who survive the assault of the world, and one who does not.

The Bluest Eye is a novel of initiation, a microscopic examination of that point where sexual experience, racial experience, and self-image intersect. The plot of the novel is simple: Pecola Breedlove, eleven, who considers herself ugly and thinks blue eyes would make her beautiful, is raped by her father, bears a child that dies, and retreats into madness, believing that her eyes are not simply blue but the bluest of all. The point, however, is not *what* happens but *why* it happens. And the interest of the novel lies not in the *why* itself, which is common psychological knowledge, but in how Morrison constructs it.

Pecola is a victim whose story is also the story of her family and her culture. Much of the novel is composed of the stories of other characters who violate Pecola in one way or another as a reaction to ways in which they themselves have been violated: Geraldine, a fastidious black woman to whom Pecola represents the degradation she has been fleeing all her life; Soaphead Church, a West Indian "spiritualist" who feeds Pecola's delusions out of his own disgust at blackness; and most centrally, Pecola's parents. Her mother, Pauline, neglects her family and storefront apartment, devoting herself to her white employers, whose clean, well-stocked house and pretty little daughter are the closest she can come

to the white culture's ideals of beauty and love that she has absorbed from the movies. In one memorable scene she abuses and denies Pecola, who has accidentally spilled a hot berry cobbler on "her" spotless floor, while soothing the little white girl who does not even know who Pecola is. Pauline's ideals of beauty and love have also led her to reject her husband, Cholly, who himself had been abandoned by his mother in infancy and repudiated by his father in adolescence. Cholly cannot provide the money to feed Pauline's illusions and drinks to assuage his frustration at the failure of his own quest for love and freedom. When he rapes Pecola, he is acting out of a combination of revulsion against the accusation he reads in her pathetic posture and tenderness aroused by its suggestion of Pauline when he first met her.

Pecola's madness is the manifestation of her belief that she can attain love only by being someone she is not. The characters who push her to it are, like her mother, acting on or, like her father, reacting against the same belief. Thus the ironically named Breedlove family–which includes symbolically all those in the community who contribute to Pecola's destruction–breeds not love but self-hatred. The novel's individual narratives develop the network of interrelationships inherent in the verb *to breed*.

The narrative structure of *The Bluest Eye* conveys the tension between Morrison's negative and positive themes. Pecola's story is a parody of the general fairy tale in which she and her mother believe. The chapters about the Breedlove family are headed by excerpts from the Dick-and-Jane basic readers, their white-picket-fence complacency emphasizing the grotesqueness of the Breedlove family life. The final scene, in which Pecola demands assurance from her mirror image that she has the bluest eyes of all, casts Pecola, the innocent victim, in the role of the wicked queen. The subverted fairy tale, however, is set within an etiological tale narrated by Pecola's schoolmate Claudia MacTeer which purports to explain how there came to be no marigolds in the fall of 1941 but more significantly explains how Claudia and her sister Frieda have grown up successfully in a perilous world. Present events are seen from Claudia's nine-year-old point of view. Stories of past and distant events are told by an omniscient narrator who seems to be both Claudia grown up and, since she states opinions implicit in the structure of the novel, the author. Thus the novel sets the Breedlove family against, on the one hand, the white "ideal" family of the basic readers and, on the other, the strong, supportive MacTeers (who closely resemble the Woffords).

If the white ideal is destructive to the Breedloves, it is flat in comparison to the MacTeers. Claudia's memories of sagging brown stockings and Black Draught, bronchitis and burnt turnips, her mother's singing and fussing, detail a rich and secure family life, punctuated with pain but suffused in "love, thick and dark as Alaga syrup." In a scene that parallels the one in Pauline Breedlove's white-folks' kitchen, Mrs. MacTeer is firm with her daughters and firm with the white neighbor girl who has come to tattle. In a scene that parallels the rape of Pecola, Mr. MacTeer throws out the roomer who has fondled Frieda and then (like George Wofford) throws the children's tricycle at his head. The MacTeers raise daughters who, "guiltless and without vanity," love themselves and know, at some level, that the popularity of Maureen Peal, the well-dressed and self-satisfied mulatto newcomer at school, is not their fault or even hers: "The *Thing* to fear was the *Thing* that made *her* beautiful, and not us." The difference in character between Claudia and Pecola is illustrated in Claudia's frustration with her friend: "She seemed to fold into herself, like a pleated wing. Her pain antagonized me. I wanted to open her up, crisp her edges, ram a stick down that hunched and curving spine, force her to stand erect and spit the misery out on the streets. But she held it where it could lap up into her eyes."

Frieda and Claudia lose their innocence in the course of the novel, through Pecola's experiences as well as their own. But for them the loss, like their childhood pain, is "productive and fructifying" because they have a firm foundation from which to deal with it. The metaphoric style and fabulistic form of the narrative are themselves evidence of the narrator's ability to control experience and make it productive. In another sense, however, Pecola's pathos is a component of Claudia's strength: "We honed our egos on her, padded our characters with her frailty, and yawned in the fantasy of our strength." The recognition of complicity in the fate of Pecola makes *The Bluest Eye* a complex rather than complacent fable.

The Bluest Eye received moderate though appreciative critical notice. Whether for praise or blame, most reviewers singled out the same characteristics of Morrison's writing–qualities they have continued to remark upon in her subsequent novels: the impact of her vision of black life, her poetic prose, and her construction of a narrative out of discrete scenes and stories. John Leonard, in the *New York Times*, praised "a prose so precise, so faithful to speech and so charged with pain and wonder that the novel becomes poetry." Frankel Haskell, in the *New York Times Book Review*, on the other hand, complained of "fuzziness born of flights of poetic imagery" and lack of focus as "the narratives branch out to assorted portraits and events." Leonard identified the book's subject as "institutionalized waste . . . [of] children [who] suffocate under mountains of merchandised lies." Liz Gant, in *Black World*, identified a more specific theme: "an aspect of the Black experience that many of us would rather forget, our hatred of ourselves." To Ruby Dee, in *Freedomways*, who agreed that the novel was "not . . . a story really, but a series of . . . impressions," the important thing was that they were "painfully accurate impressions" that made the reader "ache for remedy."

By the time *The Bluest Eye* was published, Morrison had moved to an editorial position at Random House in New York. In the early 1970s she began to be sought after, by the *New York Times* especially, as a commentator on black life and books about it. In 1971 and 1972 she reviewed twenty-eight books for the *Times Book Review* and wrote on "What the Black Woman Thinks About Women's Lib" for the *Times Magazine*. Although the novel she had recently published and the one she was then writing, *Sula*, deal with attitudes that govern women's identities and relationships, Morrison concluded that as long as women's lib is concerned with attitudes it is irrelevant to black women; when it focuses on equal pay for equal work it will be of more interest.

Morrison's vision of moral ambiguity is developed further in *Sula*, published in December 1973. Peopled with bizarre characters and punctuated with violent deaths, *Sula* has perplexed many readers. Shadrack, a shell-shocked World War I veteran, founds–and twenty years later the whole community observes–National Suicide Day. Eva Peace, Sula's grandmother, a one-legged woman who reputedly laid her leg across a train track to collect the insurance money to feed her children, sets fire to her junkie son Plum and hurls herself from her third-floor window in a vain effort to save her daughter Hannah, who has caught fire while canning in the yard. Sula herself lets a little boy named Chicken Little slip from her hands into the river, and never tells; takes, and then casually discards, her best friend's husband; and puts her grandmother into a wretched old folks' home. Worse, the reader never knows quite what to think of these characters and events: whether to applaud Eva's self-sacrifice or deplore her tyranny, whether to admire Sula's freedom or condemn her heartlessness.

The neighborhood in which the story is set is called the Bottom, though it is up in the hills. The narrator explains its origin as a "nigger joke": a white farmer who had promised freedom and a piece of bottom land to his slave but did not want to part with rich valley land tricked the slave into believing that "bottom land" was in the hills–"the bottom of heaven." By the narrator's present, however, when the valley farms have been developed into hot, dusty town while the hills remain cool and shady, the white folks have changed their minds. So buildings have been leveled and trees uprooted for the Medallion City Golf Course. The Bottom has become the suburbs, and the multiple ironies of its naming and history signal the shifting relationships of value throughout the novel.

The novel focuses on the relationship between Sula Peace and Nel Wright (both ironically named), childhood friends who grow apart when Nel marries and Sula leaves home. Morrison's original intention in *Sula* "was to do something with good and evil." Nel, a more complex literary descendant of Geraldine in *The Bluest Eye*, is the conventionally good woman. Sula, in Morrison's words, is "a classic type of evil force." But there are ways in which Nel is also wrong and in which Sula is a force for good. Nel is standing by when Chicken Little slips into the river and is the first to think of escaping blame. Like Eva, Nel is possessive of the people she nurtures. Her possessiveness and her husband's immaturity are as much responsible for Jude's desertion as Sula's casual affair with him is. Sula is neither possessive nor competitive; "she simply [helps] others define themselves." "Their conviction of Sula's evil" makes the townspeople their best selves; they begin to "cherish their husbands and wives, protect their children, repair their homes and in general band together against the devil in their midst."

Ultimately, the alternatives embodied in Nel and Sula are not good and evil, but constraint and freedom. Sula and Nel are both trying to forge their own identities as black women. "Because each had discovered . . . that they were neither white nor male, and that all freedom and triumph was forbidden to them, they had set about creating something else to be." Neither is completely successful. At ten, on her return from a trip to New Orleans with her mother for her great-grandmother's funeral, Nel discovers, "I'm me. I'm not their daughter. I'm not Nel. I'm me. Me." The discovery gives her the strength to cultivate a friend as different and disapproved of as Sula. But Nel becomes Jude's wife, her children's mother, and a member of the community who not only follows but endorses the community's conventions. Sula, on the other hand, leaves everything in her quest for freedom: leaves Medallion, repudiates what others consider responsibility, discards what others value. She wanders perpetually in search of something she never finds; she has "no center, no speck around which to grow." Yet when Nel, as responsible church woman, visits senile Eva Peace in an old folks' home twenty-four years after Sula's death, she is shocked into realizing her identity with the girl who let Chicken Little go and the woman who took her husband: " 'All that time, all that time, I thought I was missing Jude. . . . O Lord, Sula,' she cried, 'girl, girl, girlgirlgirl.' " Sula and Nel are in fact parts of one whole character, fragmented by the pressures put on the people of the Bottom by a world of topsy-turvy values.

Sula embodies what Shadrack's Suicide Day commemorates: the unknown and uncontrollable in Nel's life and everyone else's–death, natural disaster, even their own rage at their manipulation by the white world. Her repudiation is evidence that the structures with which people contain these forces are only structures. Like the unfinished tunnel begun in 1927–the deferred dream of commerce with towns across the river and employment for black men–they are subject to collapse on the heads of those who build them (or in the case of the tunnel, ironically, wish to build them). Morrison playfully completes the characterization of Sula as the representative of another world when she follows her into the afterlife: " 'Well, I'll be damned,' she thought, 'it didn't even hurt. Wait'll I tell Nel.' " This comic moment in a fundamentally tragic story attests, too, to the ordinariness, the immanence, of the other world and to the inseparability of what seem to be opposite modes of perception.

Offered as an alternate selection by the Book-of-the-Month Club, excerpted in *Redbook*, and

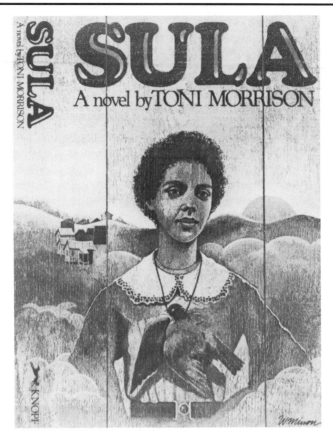

Dust jacket for Morrison's second novel, the story of an amoral woman who embodies "a classic type of evil force"

nominated for the 1975 National Book Award in fiction, *Sula* brought Toni Morrison national recognition as a writer. While its poetic prose drew from reviewers the same kinds of positive and negative responses that *The Bluest Eye* had, *Sula* elicited more commentary, most of it favorable, on the reality of its surreal portrayal of black life. Barbara Smith in *Freedomways* focused on the novel's faithfulness to the felt experience of black women. Although Addison Gayle's "Blueprint for Black Criticism" in *First World* offered *Sula* as an example of negative stereotyping of black characters by black authors, both Jerry Bryant in the *Nation* and Roseann P. Bell in *Obsidian* remarked on the "originality" and "three-dimensional humanity" of the characters. Bryant considered the unsettling implications of this originality: "There is something ominous in the chilling detachment with which [writers like Toni Morrison, Ed Bullins, and Alice Walker] view their characters. It is not that their viewpoint is amoral–we are asked for judgment. It's that the characters we judge lie so far outside the guidelines by which we have always made our judgments." Odette C. Martin in *First World* also acknowledged ambigu-

ity in the novel's value judgments and concluded that *Sula* was a "polemic against the destructiveness [for Blacks] of an unreasonable and unreasoning sense of powerlessness." Sarah Blackburn was virtually alone in her view, expressed in the *New York Times Book Review*, that "in spite of its richness and its thorough originality," *Sula* lacked "the stinging immediacy, the urgency, of [Morrison's] non-fiction." Her review brought letters of protest from Alice Walker and Clarence Major and a sharp response from Morrison herself: "She's talking about my life. It has a stinging immediacy for me."

One of Morrison's foremost concerns is the immediate relevance of black history. In essays for the *New York Times Book Review* on summer pleasures and in the bicentennial issue of the *New York Times Magazine* on the situation of black Americans–"Slow Walk of Trees (as Grandmother Would Say) Hopeless (As Grandfather Would Say)"–Morrison focused on the relationships among black history, her family's history, and her own sense of identity. In February 1974, two months after the publication of *Sula*, Random House published *The Black Book*, which, though her name appears nowhere on it, was Toni Morrison's idea and very much her project. Composed of newspaper clippings, photographs, songs, advertisements, patent office records, recipes, rent-party jingles, and other memorabilia from the collections of Middleton Harris and others, *The Black Book* is a scrapbook, such as we would have, says Bill Cosby in the introduction, if "a three-hundred-year-old black man had decided, oh, say, when he was about ten, to keep a record of what it was like for himself and his people in these United States." As she explained in two articles that served as birth announcements for the book, Morrison conceived it as a way to recognize the history made by "the anonymous men and women who speak in conventional histories only through their leaders" and to rescue it from the faddism of mass culture and the "mysticism" of the Black Power movement. "Being older than a lot of people," she said in *Black World*, "I remember when soul food was called supper." That was a time, she added in the *New York Times Magazine*, "when we knew who we were." For Morrison, black history is the core of black identity: not in "forging new myths" but in "re-discovering the old ones" lies the clue not only to "the way we really were" but to "the way we really are."

This view of history is at the center of Morrison's third novel, *Song of Solomon* (1977), the story of Milkman Dead's quest for identity. Milkman finds himself–discovers his own courage, endurance, and capacity for love and joy; grows up, in short–when he discovers his connection with his ancestors. The reader of Morrison's personal essays realizes that the novel itself acknowledges the author's connection with her ancestors; the names Solomon and Sing and Milkman's grandfather's lost farm are parts of Morrison's family history.

Morrison has said that compiling *The Black Book* (1974) was like living through black history again. This is what Milkman has to do to solve the riddles that lead him to his great-grandfather Solomon. As he travels southward from his Michigan home, he moves back through the generations in his family history. In Danville, Pennsylvania, he discovers his grandfather; in Shalimar, Virginia, his great-grandfather. To make sense of the clues he finds in each location, he must put himself imaginatively into the lives of his forebears, but to find the clues, and even to survive in these strange places, he must first put himself into the minds of the people he meets. It is, of course, the *process* of discovery, the geographical and imaginative journey out of self, that transforms the selfish and immature Milkman: the connection with his ancestors that he discovers is the connection with his contemporaries that he has learned to acknowledge.

Like *Sula* and *The Bluest Eye*, *Song of Solomon* dramatizes dialectical approaches to the challenges of life. The principal character pairs are represented by Milkman's father, Macon, and his aunt, Pilate, and by Milkman himself and his friend Guitar. Macon Dead, the richest black man in a Michigan town, represents material progress achieved at the expense of human beings. He advises his son to follow his own example when he says, "Own things. And let the things you own own other things. Then you'll own yourself and other people, too." His sister Pilate, on the other hand, to whom "progress was a word that meant walking a little farther on down the road," represents folk and family consciousness, which she demonstrates by listening to her father's ghost and befriending Macon's wife and son. Milkman's progress on his quest for identity is progress from his father's values to Pilate's; he sets out looking for gold, ends up looking for family.

A variant of this dichotomy is dramatized in the relationship between Milkman and Guitar, who represent respectively self-centeredness and racial consciousness. But Guitar and Milkman move in opposite directions, and the definitions and values of these terms shift as the novel progresses. At first Guitar's racial consciousness is associated with Pilate and her humane values. Later it is contrasted favorably with Milkman's utter selfishness, illustrated in his callous reaction to the murder of Emmett Till. Eventually, however, his racial consciousness leads Guitar to violate the humane values it first fostered. He joins the Seven Days, a vigilante group that kills whites, any whites, in retaliation for the murder of blacks, just as blacks have historically paid indiscriminately for alleged crimes against whites; by the end of the novel he is the one obsessed with gold, and his ability to kill whites has developed into the determination to kill his "brother" Milkman, whose own development has by this time led him to a healthy and productive self-awareness.

The fabulistic qualities of Morrison's earlier novels are organized in *Song of Solomon* by the general pattern of the fairy-tale quest and the specific structure of an Afro-American folktale (reported in the Georgia Writers' Project book *Drums and Shadows*, to which Morrison has clearly referred) about a group of African-born slaves who rose up from the plantation and flew back home to Africa. Milkman's quest parallels that of the traditional fairy-tale hero, who finds his treasure with the help of magical guides who appear once he learns to share his crust with a dwarf or make love to a crone. It also metaphorically reenacts the legendary flight of his great-grandfather Solomon (or Shalimar) based on that of the Africans in the folktale. Discovery of his ancestor's triumph enables Milkman at the end of the novel to leap toward Guitar and potential death himself, for it has given him his life: "Now he knew what Shalimar knew: If you surrendered to the air, you could *ride* it."

But just as Milkman's discovery of his relationship with his ancestors is actually a result of his acknowledgment of his relationship with his contemporaries, so is his surrender to the air a symbolic repetition of the journey by plane and bus and car that has brought him into the history of his family and his people (indistinguishable terms in the novel) and thus into knowledge of himself as it has carried him southward. Thus Milkman's quest focuses the tension the novel has maintained throughout between fantasy and realism.

Song of Solomon was received favorably on the front page of the *New York Times Book Review* and offered as a main selection of the Book-of-the-Month Club—the first novel by a black writer to be so distinguished since Richard Wright's *Native Son* in 1940. Most reviewers responded to the relationship between realism and fantasy in the novel. Expecting realism, Diane Johnson in the *New York Review of Books* asked, "Are blacks really like this?," and Norma Rogers, in *Freedomways*, called the novel "a mockery of Afro-American life." Recognizing the interpenetration of realism and fantasy, and expressing what has become a theme in Morrison criticism, John Leonard in the *New York Times* compared the novel to Gabriel García Márquez's *One Hundred Years of Solitude*: "It builds out of history and language and myth, to music. . . . The first two-thirds of 'Song of Solomon' are merely wonderful. The last 100 pages is a triumph." Inevitably, *Song of Solomon* was compared with Morrison's earlier novels. Reynolds Price in the *New York Times Book Review* said, "Here the depths of her younger work are still evident, but now they thrust outward, into wider fields, for longer intervals, encompassing many

more lives." Both Claudia Tate in *CLA Journal* and Margo Jefferson in *Newsweek*, however, found *Song of Solomon* less magical and less interesting than the earlier novels. The novel's selection by the Book-of-the-Month Club reminded Jefferson "of an Academy Award denied an actress for her best performance and given several years later for a lesser one. *Song of Solomon* is flashier and more accessible than its predecessors. It is also less striking and less original."

Song of Solomon made Toni Morrison a major American writer. It became a paperback best-seller (the rights having been sold for a reported $315,000), with 570,000 copies in print in 1979. In 1978 the novel won the fiction award of the National Book Critics Circle; Morrison received an American Academy and Institute of Arts and Letters Award and was featured in the PBS series "Writers in America." In 1980 Morrison was appointed by President Carter to the National Council on the Arts, and in 1981 she was elected to the American Academy and Institute of Arts and Letters. The publication of her fourth novel, *Tar Baby*, in March 1981 was heralded by a cover story in *Newsweek*.

Tar Baby is a departure from Morrison's previous work in two important ways. First, the book's setting is more exotic than the American small-town atmosphere found in Morrison's three earlier novels. More significant, though, *Tar Baby* contains this author's first fully realized white characters. In her earlier books Morrison portrays small-town cultures which undoubtedly have been affected by whites, but which are peopled almost solely by blacks. White figures, when they appear, do so only peripherally. In *Tar Baby*, however, while she again uses the myth, magic, and poetic language which figure so largely in her first three novels, Morrison deftly moves her setting from Paris to a Caribbean island to New York.

Tar Baby is dedicated to five women who, Morrison says, always "knew their true and ancient properties," and the book's preface carries a quotation from Corinthians, "For it hath been declared unto me of you, my brethren . . . that there are contentions among you." These two bits of prose aptly introduce the novel's two major themes, the difficulty of settling conflicting claims between one's past and present and the destruction which abuse of power can bring. As Morrison examines these problems in *Tar Baby*, she suggests no easy way to understand what one's link to a heritage should be, nor does she offer infallible methods for dealing with power. Rather, with an astonishing insight and grace, she demonstrates the pervasiveness of such dilemmas and the degree to which they affect human beings, both black and white. Much of the novel's power and clarity come from Morrison's careful craftsmanship, especially her symbolic use of names and precise juxtaposition of characters and settings. *New Republic* reviewer Maureen Howard observed that *Tar Baby* is "as carefully patterned as a . . . poem," and, indeed, the book's themes are integral parts of a finely wrought and artistic design.

The familiar story of Brer Rabbit and the Tar Baby provides a frame for the patterns of Morrison's fourth novel. In a pre-Uncle Remus version of this tale, a farmer (rather than Brer Fox) devises the tar baby to lure and then trap Brer Rabbit, who has been raiding gardens. As the farmer expects, Brer Rabbit is entranced by the tar decoy and tries to engage it in conversation, but when the lure refuses to answer, the rabbit becomes angry, hits the tar baby, and entangles himself in its sticky surface. Eventually, of course, Brer Rabbit outsmarts his captor by begging not to be thrown back into the briar patch, which, in reality, is his only place of safety. The outwitted farmer tosses the wild creature back into the brambles, and the sadder but wiser animal scurries away.

Morrison has said that the tar baby of her fourth novel is the black woman who attracts the black male, and Jadine Childs, the book's protagonist, is indeed enticing. A graduate of the Sorbonne, the young black American is also a sought-after model; she has had a small part in a movie; and as one might expect, she is showered with the attention of suitors. However, in the midst of all her successes, Jadine feels "inauthentic," and she finally leaves Europe to decide whether or not to accept a wealthy white man's offer of marriage.

One of the many orphans in *Tar Baby*, Jadine has been raised by her Aunt Ondine and Uncle Sydney Childs, both longtime servants of Valerian Street and his wife, Margaret. Valerian, now seventy, has retired as head of the family's Philadelphia candy business and moved with his wife and two faithful servants to Isle des Chevaliers, a Caribbean paradise named for mythical black horsemen who are said to roam the island. Before white men invaded the paradise, Isle des Chevaliers had been a lush rain forest, but now its tropical greenery has been tamed and to a large extent destroyed by civilization's "improvements." As his last name suggests, Valerian has helped pave the forest and thus destroy the island's natural beauty, but that offense is perhaps offset by his unusually generous nature. In addition to other philanthropic labors, the candy magnate has sent Jadine through school and financed her European travels. Thus, when the exquisite young woman must decide whether or not to marry, she comes to Isle des Chevaliers to spend Christmas with her foster parents, Ondine and Sydney, and her friends Valerian and Margaret. Unfortunately, Jadine's island holiday only exacerbates her indecision about whom and where she wants to be. Part of the conflict she must resolve is occasioned by her unique position as the servants' relative and the employers' protégée. Another unsettling fact of Jadine's life at Isle des Chevaliers is the older Childses' belief that their adored niece neglects her duties as their foster daughter and thus fails to live up to her last name. The old couple's greatest fear, and the notion to which they have become accustomed, is that Jadine will be too busy to make funeral arrangements for them when they die.

Once Jadine is on the island, she and her hosts await the arrival of the Streets' son, Michael, a twenty-nine-year-old man who is described alternately by his mother as someone who helps others preserve their heritages, and by his father as a "cultural orphan" who seeks societies he can live in without ties and thus without risk of pain. As a youth, Michael had urged Jadine to leave the posh school where she was studying art history and go out into the world with him to "help her people." Jadine demurred, and since that time Michael has apparently drifted from studying poetry and anthropology to working on Indian reservations and aiding migrant workers. In fact, the only people he seems reluctant to associate with are his parents. Valerian was seven when his own father died, and perhaps because of this loss, the candy magnate particularly wants to pass the family business on to Michael. However, unlike the third-century Roman emperor for whom Valerian is named, the candy manufacturer's son will not carry on his work. When Emperor Valerian took the throne, he gave half his land to his son, Gallienus, to rule. But when twentieth-century Valerian tries to give Michael the candy business, the boy refuses to enter into the family endeavor.

Predictably, Michael never appears on Isle des Chevaliers, but the man who does come for

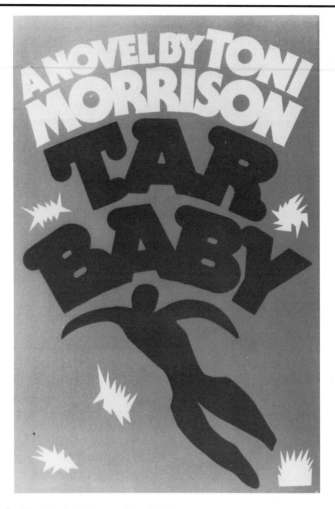

Dust jacket for Morrison's 1981 novel modeled on the tale of Brer Rabbit and the Tar Baby

Christmas dinner, a young black drifter named William "Son" Green, proves to be a catalyst for an explosion of pent-up conflicts. An American, Green has jumped ship and survived on the island by foraging for food and stealing chocolate from the Streets' kitchen, and he is first discovered in Margaret's closet. From there, ever-dutiful Sydney promptly drags his fellow black man before the head of the household. Perhaps saddened by Michael's absence or perhaps only to show his own power, Valerian then shocks both blacks and whites by inviting the intruder to sit down to dinner rather than turning him over to the police. Son accepts the invitation, and eventually, to the group's further amazement, Valerian installs him in the guest bedroom for a visit of indefinite length.

Son's presence upsets the household's equilibrium not only because he enters their lives in a strange manner, but, most clearly, because he observes none of the rules of social hierarchy to which they are accustomed. In fact, Son Green is different in most ways from every other character in *Tar Baby*. Except for him, all of the characters in *Tar Baby*, both black and white, are either in some sense orphans or lonely parent figures who have been deserted by their children. In both cases cultural links between parents and child, between generations, have been broken, and continuity of a life-style is threatened. Also, except for Son, all the people in *Tar Baby* are either agents of or accede to the hierarchy of power and "progress" which controls the modern business world and has helped destroy Isle des Chevaliers's natural beauty. Jadine has been a willing and apt student of Valerian's life-style, itself an exemplum of the imperial ease which money and power can bring. And Sydney's and Ondine's social standing places them well above the Streets' other servants. In contrast, Son Green, as his name suggests, is closely tied to his heritage and to the earth. Rather than despoiling the land as Valerian and his kind have done, Son has an extraordinary talent for making plants bloom, and he sees no value in artificial social barriers which ensure that some people will control others. He shocks Sydney, for example, by cheerfully saying "hi" to the solemn butler as he serves a formal meal. And only Son takes the trouble to learn that Gideon and Thérèse are the real names of two black servants whom Sydney and Ondine, along with the rest of the household, know only as "Yardman" and "Mary," the name given to every baptized black female on the island.

The household's facade of order and tranquillity finally crumbles at Christmas dinner when Valerian casually mentions that he has dismissed Yardman and Mary for stealing apples. At first only Son questions Valerian's right to fire the two, but the young man's audacity sets off a sequence of events which alters each character's life. Following Son's retort, Valerian orders the man to leave his house, but Son quietly refuses to do so. This conflict of wills between host and guest leads to a release of Ondine's and Sydney's long-closeted frustrations, and in the heat of recriminations which follow, Ondine reveals a damning truth–that as a young woman she had seen Margaret obsessively sticking pins into young Michael's flesh. After Ondine details this terrible secret, Margaret explains to Valerian that she tortured their son "because I could . . . and I stopped doing it or wanting to do it when I couldn't. . . . When he was too big, when he could do it back, when he could . . . tell." Although no other person in the novel uses power with malevolent intentions equal to Margaret's, every character except Son does use power over another person simply because it is possible to do so. Objectively, Margaret's aberrations can be seen as merely another embodiment of the power with which Valerian rules his household: Jadine controls her aunt and uncle; Sydney and Ondine direct other servants; and white men impose their wills upon nature.

In the emotional chaos which follows Ondine's revelations, Jadine finds herself torn between her Parisian jet-set life and her almost primeval attraction to Son Green, who, now clean and well fed, proves to be a gorgeous reminder of simpler times. Almost inevitably, Son and Jadine become lovers, but they move in two different worlds even when residing in the same house. The pair first travels to New York, where Jadine thrives but where Son feels kinship only with the concrete lion on the library steps. The situation reverses, however, when Son and Jadine visit his small, rural hometown, Eloe, Florida. There Son is in complete harmony with himself and his heritage, while Jadine is an alien, an intruder from a busier, more worldly, more dominant culture. Jadine attempts to pull Son into her world by having him enroll in college, but he wants no part of lessons in what he sees as the white man's view of life. Conversely, Son tries to show Jadine the heritage that she has thrown away by assimilating Valerian's customs and values, his money, power, and privilege, but she sees no future in returning to life as it is lived in Eloe.

Unable to reconcile their differences, Jadine and Son part. Following the pair's separation, Jadine visits Isle des Chevaliers, and then rumors suggest she has left the Caribbean on Air France, accompanied by a handsome white man. Son still loves Jadine and vows to find her, but at a crucial point in his search Thérèse guides him, not to Valerian's dock as he had asked, but rather to the wild backside of Isle des Chevaliers. When Son questions her, Thérèse replies that Jadine is not worthy of him and that on this beach he can choose either to walk to Valerian's house on the island's opposite side or to join the free black horsemen who, she believes, still inhabit this unspoiled portion of Isle des Chevaliers. After Thérèse's instruction, Son begins to walk away from the shore, and then, in the novel's last words, he is described as running toward the woods, "Lickety-split. Lickety-split. Lickety-lickety-lickety-split."

Morrison does not specify whether Son chooses to join the mythical horsemen or continue his search for Jadine. However, in light of the book's folktale frame and the storybook words with which it ends, she seems to suggest that the rabbit has escaped to the briars, that Son will not attempt to join Jadine's fast-paced life. Whatever choice he makes, though, the novel's ending is not happy. For all his virtues, Son can be part of Jadine's life only if he rejects his true self, his ancient properties. But living in the briar patch is not a perfect choice either, for the past, the world of myth and storybooks, cannot be the sole habitat of a mature person. Similarly, while Jadine is suffocated by Eloe's provincialism, Paris offers only superficial pleasures which will continue to make her feel inauthentic. Ultimately, the tale Morrison weaves is about problems rather than solutions.

Tar Baby has garnered Morrison a good deal of media attention, but the novel itself has received surprisingly mixed reviews. Negative critics' most valid complaints touch upon the book's plot structure and are exemplified by Darryl Pinckney's insistence in the *New York Review of Books* that "picking out what happens in *Tar Baby* is like trying to keep one's balance in a swamp." In contrast, more satisfied reviewers such as Jean Strouse of *Newsweek* argue that the book's merits far outweigh any flaws it may have. Strouse writes that some readers may find the plot of *Tar Baby* "too consciously wrought, but if there are flaws in the novel's construction they don't matter: Morrison's voice, with its precision and musical cadence, is so original, she has so much to say about modern life and she creates such indelible characters that she leaves you affected, astonished, and appalled." In a similar positive vein, Maureen Howard labels *Tar Baby* "a fine new novel," lauds the author's character descriptions as a "series of stunning performances," and adds that "thematically, this novel is much tighter than Morrison's earlier works."

Morrison's Pulitzer Prize-winning fifth novel, *Beloved* (1987), is a ghost story set mainly in post-Civil War America. The book is prefaced by the line, "Sixty Million and more," which, Morrison explained to Walter Clemons, "is the best educated guess at the number of black Africans who never even made it into slavery—those who died either as captives in Africa or on slave ships." Thus *Beloved* is Morrison's holocaust story and her memorial to Africans who died in the slave trade, an endeavor which killed more human beings than were murdered in Hitler's camps.

Morrison got the idea for this novel from an 1855 newspaper clipping about a runaway Kentucky slave named Margaret Garner, who thought she had found a haven for herself and her four children with her freed mother-in-law in Cincinnati. However, Garner's owner found her, and, when he came to take her back to Kentucky, the woman tried to kill her children rather than have them returned to slavery. After her violent acts, she was described as being "serene."

Substitute the name "Sethe" for Margaret Garner and the events described in the newspaper clipping comprise the central plot of *Beloved*. After escaping from the ironically named Kentucky farm, Sweet Home, Sethe joins her husband's mother, Baby Suggs, in Cincinnati. There

she and her four children appear to be safe. However, Schoolteacher, the man who runs Sweet Home, employs slave catchers to find his valuable property. When Sethe sees these white men approaching, she attempts to kill her children and herself so that, as she explains later, in death they can be together on "the other side." Although the distraught woman succeeds only in murdering her toddler daughter, this action is enough to make Schoolteacher retreat to Kentucky, convinced that his "property" is so mentally deranged as to be worthless.

Sethe is taken to prison but later released through the efforts of abolitionists. However, her life is changed by the murder, for she isolates herself and her surviving daughter, Denver, from the rest of the community and believes that the ghost of the dead child haunts her house. This is the setting into which the mysterious stranger, the girl called Beloved, appears. The one word Sethe could afford to have carved on her dead child's tombstone was "Beloved." Thus, the coincidence of the girls' names, the fact that the stranger is about the age the dead child would have been, and Sethe's and Denver's loneliness combine to convince them that Beloved is indeed the flesh-and-blood incarnation of the baby Sethe murdered.

However, supernatural events are not the dominant theme in Morrison's fifth novel. In *Beloved* the author explores the importance of mother-child relationships, the power of memory, the importance of community, and the way in which slavery deprived black parents of child-rearing responsibilities and privileges. In fact, through Beloved's memories, Morrison suggests that the girl is not a supernatural being at all, but rather a young person who has suffered the pains of being brought from Africa to America on a slave ship. Slavery itself, though, has not been the most painful part of Beloved's life. The girl is haunted by the image of her African mother jumping into the ocean, a suicidal act committed, no doubt, to escape the living hell of the slave ship. However, the untutored girl does not realize that the woman's disappearance is final, and she continues to search for her mother.

Beloved has lost a mother; Sethe has lost a child. The two people come together in what seems to be a case of mutual mistaken identity. Thinking that Sethe is her long-lost mother, Beloved constantly berates the woman for having deserted her. Believing that Beloved is the child she murdered, Sethe uses every breath to explain her actions to the girl. Beloved and Sethe become so wrapped up in what each thinks the other to be that they separate themselves from the rest of humanity, even Denver. The pair begins to consume each other's life, and only Denver's going out to become part of the community again saves the family from starvation.

Although most reviewers praised *Beloved*, Stanley Crouch in the *New Republic* (19 October 1987) writes that in the novel "Morrison almost always loses control. She can't resist the temptation of the trite or the sentimental . . . had Toni Morrison the kind of courage, had she the passion necessary to liberate her work from the failure of feeling that is sentimentality, there is much that she could achieve." On a more positive note, Judith Thurman noted in the *New Yorker* (2 November 1987) that *Beloved* is in some respects melodramatic, but she also finds "something great in it: a play of human voices, consciously exalted, perversely stressed, yet holding true."

More typical of the novel's evaluators, Walter Clemons in *Newsweek* (28 September 1987) called *Beloved* "difficult, sometimes lushly overwritten, but profoundly imagined and carried out with burning fervor." Labeling the novel a "triumph," Margaret Atwood in her *New York Times* review of 13 September 1987 concludes that Morrison's "versatility and technical and emotional range appear to know no bounds. If there were any doubts about her stature as a preeminent American novelist, of her own or any other generation, 'Beloved' will put them to rest." In a similar vein Thomas Edwards in the 5 November 1987 issue of the *New York Review* calls *Beloved* an "extraordinary act of imagination" and says that the novel will "convince any thoughtful reader . . . that Toni Morrison is not just an important contemporary novelist but a major figure of our national literature. She has written a work that brings to the darkest corners of American experience the wisdom, and the courage, to know them as they are."

Asked whether whites could adequately respond to *Beloved*, Morrison replied that she had been misunderstood if people think that she writes only for black readers. Continuing, she explained, "When I write, I don't try to translate for white readers. I imagine Sethe in the room. If I read to her what I've written, will she say I'm telling the truth? Dostoevski wrote for a Russian audience, but we're able to read him. If I'm specific, and I don't overexplain, then anybody can overhear me" (*Newsweek*, 28 September 1987).

Morrison is a major figure in American literature, and one reason is the insight with which she describes problems all people face. In his Nobel Prize speech William Faulkner noted that a writer's only true subject is "the human heart in conflict with itself." Morrison, who wrote a master's thesis on Faulkner and Virginia Woolf, seems to agree, for at the core of all her novels is a penetrating view of the unyielding, heartbreaking dilemmas which torment people of all races. Morrison writes out of the specificities of black experience, but reading her novels—"overhearing" her beautiful language, her striking creation of characters, and her masterful use of symbols—is a privilege open to anyone.

Interviews:

Mel Watkins, "Talk with Toni Morrison," *New York Times Book Review*, 11 September 1977, pp. 48, 50.

Robert B. Stepto, " 'Intimate Things in Place': A Conversation with Toni Morrison," *Massachusetts Review*, 18 (Autumn 1977): 473-489.

Jane S. Bakerman, "The Seams Can't Show: An Interview with Toni Morrison," *Black American Literature Forum*, 12 (Summer 1978): 56-60.

Bettye J. Parker, "Complexity: Toni Morrison's Women—An Interview Essay," in *Sturdy Black Bridges: Visions of Black Women in Literature*, edited by Roseann P. Bell et al. (Garden City, N.Y.: Doubleday, 1979), pp. 251-257.

Thomas Le Clair, " 'The Language Must Not Sweat,' " *New Republic*, 184 (21 March 1981): 25-29.

Jean Strouse, "Toni Morrison's Black Magic," *Newsweek*, 97 (30 March 1981): 52-57.

Cathleen Medwick, "Toni Morrison," *Vogue*, 171 (April 1981): 288-289, 330-332.

Nellie McKay, "An Interview with Toni Morrison," *Contemporary Literature*, 24 (1983): 413-429.

Claudia Tate, "Toni Morrison," in *Black Women Writers at Work*, edited by Tate (New York: Continuum, 1983), pp. 117-131.

Gloria Naylor and Toni Morrison, "A Conversation," *Southern Review*, 21 (Summer 1985): 567-593.

Bonnie Angelo, "The Pain of Being Black: Interview with Toni Morrison," *Time* (22 May 1989): 120-122.

References:

Jane S. Bakerman, "Failure of Love: Female Initiation in the Novels of Toni Morrison," *American Literature*, 52 (January 1981): 541-563.
Analyzes the reasons why many young girls in Morrison's fiction do not enter adulthood successfully.

Gerry Brenner, "*Song of Solomon*: Morrison's Rejection of Rank's Monomyth and Feminism," *Studies in American Fiction*, 15 (Spring 1987): 13-24.
Argues that Morrison disdains heroes and hero worship and that she creates bizarre caricatures showing what humans become when they imitate heroes.

Barbara Christian, "Community and Nature: The Novels of Toni Morrison," *Journal of Ethnic Studies*, 7 (Winter 1980): 65-78.
Discusses the effects migration from one community to another has on Morrison's characters.

Cynthia Dubin Edelberg, "Morrison's Voices: Formal Education, the Work Ethic, and the Bible," *American Literature*, 58 (May 1986): 217-237.
Questions what the author sees as Morrison's denigration of education, the work ethic, and religion as ways "out" for black Americans.

Mari Evans, ed., *Black Women Writers: 1950-1980, A Critical Evaluation* (New York: Anchor Books, 1984).
Contains an interview with Morrison as well as two essays, "The Quest for Self: Triumph and Failure in the Works of Toni Morrison" and "Theme, Characterization, and Style in the Works of Toni Morrison."

Elizabeth B. House, "Artists and the Art of Living: Order and Disorder in Toni Morrison's Fiction," *Modern Fiction Studies*, 34 (Spring 1988): 27-44.
Concludes that in order to create purposeful lives, people must balance the form and chaos in their experiences.

House, "The 'Sweet Life' in Toni Morrison's Fiction," *American Literature*, 56 (May 1984): 181-202.
Uses food imagery to contrast people who choose "idyllic values" and those who opt for "competitive success" rules of living.

House, "Toni Morrison's Ghost: the Beloved Who is Not Beloved," *Studies in American Fiction*, forthcoming Autumn 1989.
Argues that Beloved's stream-of-conscious memories show her to be not a ghost but a real person who was captured in Africa and brought to the United States on a slave ship.

Bessie W. Jones and Audrey L. Vinson, *The World of Toni Morrison: Explorations in Literary Criticism* (Dubuque: Kendall / Hunt, 1985).
Contains an interview with Morrison and nine essays by the two authors which explicate the first four novels and treat various motifs in Morrison's fiction.

Joyce Ann Joyce, "Structural and Thematic Unity in Toni Morrison's *Song of Solomon*," *CEA Critic*, 49 (Winter / Summer 1986-1987): 185-198.
Shows how Morrison crafted *Song of Solomon* by connecting threads of various themes and motifs.

Lauren Lepow, "Paradise Lost and Found: Dualism and Edenic Myth in Toni Morrison's *Tar Baby*," *Contemporary Literature*, 28 (Fall 1987): 363-377.
Examines *Tar Baby* in the context of the myth of the Garden of Eden and the relationship of dualism to the creation of the world.

Nellie McKay, ed., *Critical Essays on Toni Morrison* (Boston: G.K. Hall, 1988).
Contains reviews of Morrison's first four novels, interviews with Morrison, and essays on *The Bluest Eye*, *Sula*, *Song of Solomon*, and *Tar Baby*.

Marilyn E. Mobley, "Narrative Dilemma: Jadine as Cultural Orphan in Toni Morrison's *Tar*

Baby," Southern Review, 23 (Autumn 1987): 761-770.
Treats Jadine's relationship to Afro-American culture.

Catherine Rainwater and William J. Scheick, eds., *Contemporary American Women Writers: Narrative Strategies* (Lexington: University Press of Kentucky, 1985).
Contains an essay, "Mastery of Narrative," on Morrison's narrative technique and a bibliography of her writing.

Ruth Rosenberg, "Seeds in Hard Ground: Black Girlhood in *The Bluest Eye*," *Black American Literature Forum*, 21 (Winter 1987): 435-445.
Treats the theme of the childhood of Afro-American women in Morrison's first novel.

Joyce Carol Oates

This entry was updated by Nancy Barendse (University of South Carolina) from the entries by Michael Joslin (University of South Carolina) in DLB 2, American Novelists Since World War II, *Alex Bateman (University of South Carolina) in* DLB 5, American Poets Since World War II, *and Holly Mims Wescott (Francis Marion College) in* DLB Yearbook 1981.

Places	Rural Upstate New York	Detroit	Canada
Influences and Relationships	D. H. Lawrence Henry James Emily Brontë	Franz Kafka Flannery O'Connor Fyodor Dostoyevski	Nathaniel Hawthorne Edgar Allan Poe William Faulkner
Literary Movements and Forms	"Re-Imagining" of Traditional Forms Tales of Suspense	Psychological Realism The Fairy Tale The Short Story	Naturalism Romance Experimental Fiction Poetry
Major Themes	Religion The Outsider Struggle for Order and Control Invisibility of Women	Dissolutions of Relationships Food / Hunger / Gluttony The Inner Lives of Women	Reality vs. Illusion Obsession as a Means of Transcendence Violence
Cultural and Artistic Influences	The Psychology of R. D. Laing	Catholicism	Popular Music
Social and Economic Influences	Academic Life The Depression	Violence of the 1960s	The Women's Movement

BIRTH: Lockport, New York, 16 June 1938, to Frederic James and Caroline Bush Oates.

EDUCATION: B.A., Syracuse University, 1960; M.A., University of Wisconsin, 1961.

MARRIAGE: 23 January 1961 to Raymond Joseph Smith.

AWARDS AND HONORS: *Mademoiselle* college fiction award for "In the Old World," 1959; National Endowment for the Arts Grant, 1966-1967, 1968-1969; Guggenheim Fellowship, 1967; O. Henry Award for "In the Region of Ice," 1967; Richard and Hinda Rosenthal Foundation Award for *A Garden of Earthly Delights*, 1968; National Book Award for *them*, 1970; *Playboy* Editorial Award for "Saul Bird Says," 1971; O. Henry Award for "The Dead," 1973; Pushcart Prize, 1976; O. Henry Award for "My Warszawa," 1983.

BOOKS: *By the North Gate* (New York: Vanguard Press, 1963);

With Shuddering Fall (New York: Vanguard Press, 1964; London: Cape, 1965);

Upon the Sweeping Flood and Other Stories (New York: Vanguard Press, 1966; London: Gollancz, 1973);

A Garden of Earthly Delights (New York: Vanguard Press, 1967; London: Gollancz, 1970);

Expensive People (New York: Vanguard Press, 1968; London: Gollancz, 1969);

them (New York: Vanguard Press, 1969; London: Gollancz, 1971);

Anonymous Sins and Other Poems (Baton Rouge: Louisiana State University Press, 1969);

The Wheel of Love and Other Stories (New York: Vanguard Press, 1970; London: Gollancz, 1971);

Love and Its Derangements (Baton Rouge: Louisiana State University Press, 1970);

Wonderland: A Novel (New York: Vanguard Press, 1971; London: Gollancz, 1972);

The Edge of Impossibility: Tragic Forms in Literature (New York: Vanguard Press, 1972; London: Gollancz, 1976);

Marriages and Infidelities: Short Stories (New York: Vanguard Press, 1972; London: Gollancz, 1974);

Angel Fire (Baton Rouge: Louisiana State University Press, 1973);

The Hostile Sun: The Poetry of D. H. Lawrence (Los Angeles: Black Sparrow Press, 1973);

Do With Me What You Will (New York: Vanguard Press, 1973; London: Gollancz, 1974);

Miracle Play (Los Angeles: Black Sparrow Press, 1974);

The Hungry Ghosts: Seven Allusive Comedies (Los Angeles: Black Sparrow Press, 1974; Solihull, U.K.: Aquila, 1975);

Plagiarized Material, as Fernandes (Los Angeles: Black Sparrow Press, 1974);

The Goddess and Other Women (New York: Vanguard Press, 1974; London: Gollancz, 1975);

New Heaven, New Earth: The Visionary Experience in Literature (New York: Vanguard Press, 1974; London: Gollancz, 1976);

Where Are You Going, Where Have You Been? Stories of Young America (Greenwich, Conn.: Fawcett, 1974);

The Seduction and Other Stories (Los Angeles: Black Sparrow Press, 1975);

The Poisoned Kiss and Other Stories from the Portuguese, as Fernandes (New York: Vanguard Press, 1975; London: Gollancz, 1976);

The Assassins: A Book of Hours (New York: Vanguard Press, 1975);

The Fabulous Beasts (Baton Rouge: Louisiana State University Press, 1975);

The Triumph of the Spider Monkey (Santa Barbara: Black Sparrow Press, 1976);

Childwold (New York: Vanguard Press, 1976; London: Gollancz, 1977);

Crossing the Border: Fifteen Tales (New York: Vanguard Press, 1976; London: Gollancz, 1978);

Night-Side: Eighteen Tales (New York: Vanguard Press, 1977; London: Gollancz, 1979);

Son of the Morning: A Novel (New York: Vanguard Press, 1978; London: Gollancz, 1979);

Women Whose Lives Are Food, Men Whose Lives Are Money (Baton Rouge & London: Louisiana State University Press, 1978);

All the Good People I've Left Behind (Santa Barbara: Black Sparrow Press, 1979);

Cybele (Santa Barbara: Black Sparrow Press, 1979);

Unholy Loves (New York: Vanguard, 1979; London: Gollancz, 1980);

Bellefleur (New York: Dutton, 1980; London: Cape, 1981);

Three Plays (Princeton, N.J.: Ontario Review Press, 1980);

A Sentimental Education (New York: Dutton, 1980; London: Cape, 1981);

Joyce Carol Oates (photo by Graeme Gibson)

Contraries: Essays (New York: Oxford University Press, 1981);

Angel of Light (New York: Dutton, 1981; London: Cape, 1981);

A Bloodsmoor Romance (New York: Dutton, 1982; London: Cape, 1983);

The Invisible Woman: New and Selected Poems 1970-1982 (Princeton, N.J.: Ontario Review Press, 1982);

The Profane Art: Essays and Reviews (New York: Dutton, 1983);

The Mysteries of Winterthurn (New York: Dutton, 1984; London: Cape, 1984);

Last Days: Stories (New York: Dutton, 1984; London: Cape, 1985);

Solstice (New York: Abrahams / Dutton, 1985);

Marya: A Life (New York: Dutton, 1986);

Raven's Wing (New York: Dutton, 1986);

You Must Remember This (New York: Dutton, 1987);

Lives of the Twins, as Rosamond Smith (New York: Simon & Schuster, 1987);

On Boxing (New York: Doubleday, 1987);

The Assignation (New York: Ecco, 1988);

(Woman) Writer: Occasions and Opportunities (New York: Dutton, 1988);

American Appetites (New York: Dutton, 1989).

PLAY PRODUCTIONS: *The Sweet Enemy*, New York, Actors Playhouse, 1965;

Sunday Dinner, New York, St. Clement's Church, 1970;

Ontological Proof of My Existence, New York, Cubiculo Theatre, 1972;

Miracle Play, New York, Playhouse 2 Theatre, 1974;

Triumph of the Spider Monkey, Los Angeles, Los Angeles Theatre Center, 31 October 1985.

OTHER: *Scenes from American Life: Contemporary Short Fiction*, compiled by Oates (New York: Random House, 1973).

Creating fictional worlds has always been an obsession for Joyce Carol Oates. She began as a child–even before she could write she told her tales through pictures. During her elementary school years she wrote stories and constructed two-hundred-page books, which she designed and bound herself. When she was fifteen her first novel was submitted to a publisher but was rejected as too depressing for the market of young readers; the book concerned a dope addict who is rehabilitated by caring for a black stallion.

More frequently known for her fiction than for her poetry, Oates had her first collection of stories, *By the North Gate*, published in 1963. The title is taken from a poem by Rihaku in which the north gate is the boundary between civilization and savagery. The existence of savagery in civilized society is one of the predominant themes of both Oates's poetry and fiction. In all of her works social form becomes merely a disguise for the undercurrents of psychological, and often physical, brutality. Since the publication of these stories (followed in 1964 by her first novel, *With Shuddering Fall*), Oates's critical acclaim has grown steadily.

Joyce Carol Oates was born in the small town of Lockport, New York, on 16 June 1938 and grew up in a rural setting nearby in Erie County. Together with her brother, Frederic, and sister, Lynn Ann, she was raised as a Roman Catholic in a home free from the depressing economic problems which plague so many of her fictional families. Her father, Frederic James Oates, was employed as a tool and die designer, while her mother, Caroline Bush Oates, ran the household. Oates received her early education in a one-room country schoolhouse but attended junior and senior high school in town. In 1956 she graduated from Williamsville Central High School. Seldom does Oates discuss her growing up, and she dismissed this period of her life to a *Newsweek* interviewer as " 'dull, ordinary, nothing people would be interested in,' not because it was really dull and ordinary but because it was terrible to talk about. 'A great deal frightened me,' she said cryptically, but would not elaborate."

Traces of her early environment appear regularly in Oates's short stories and novels. Her most frequently used setting is Eden County, a fictional version of her western New York State milieu. She creates from the area near Buffalo, Lockport, and the Erie Canal a country of poor and wealthy farmers, small hamlets, towns, and growing cities. Lockport and the Erie Canal appear in *Wonderland*, while many of her other works are set in the rural areas of Eden, an allusive name, about which Oates has said, "It's not paradise at all. It's pretty bad as a matter of fact."

At Syracuse University, where she began studying in 1956, Oates turned out a novel a semester while majoring in English and minoring in philosophy. Her writing professor Donald A. Dike introduced her to Faulkner, who she admits became a major influence on her work. Another important literary influence was Kafka: "In college, I was Franz Kafka for a while." The university library magazine provided one forum for her publications, and she was cowinner of the *Mademoiselle* college fiction award in 1959 for her short story "In the Old World," which appeared in that magazine. In addition to her writing, she was an

outstanding student, was elected to Phi Beta Kappa, and served as class valedictorian when she received her B.A. degree in June 1960.

After her graduation Oates entered the University of Wisconsin graduate English program. While working on her master's degree, she met Raymond Joseph Smith, a doctoral candidate, whom she married on 23 January 1961. Oates received her degree in June of the same year and followed her husband to Beaumont, Texas, where he held his first teaching post.

Around that time she discovered that one of her short stories had been cited in the honor roll in the latest volume of Martha Foley's *Best American Short Stories*. "I hadn't known about it until I picked it up and saw it. I thought, maybe I could be a writer. . . ."

Since that time Oates's publishing record has been overwhelming; novels, short stories, poems, plays, essays, and critical studies seem to flow effortlessly from her active mind. She readily confesses to "a laughably Balzacian ambition to get the whole world into a book." She composes her work rapidly and spends little time rewriting. "It's mainly daydreaming, I sit and look out at the river, I daydream about a kind of populated empty space. There's nothing verbal about it. Then there comes a time when it's all set and I just go write it. With a story it's one evening, if I can type that fast." Despite the rate of composition, Oates's strongly individualized writing voice carries her quickly and evenly through her novels and stories.

The presentation of a realistic sensation of life that provides a moral lesson to the reader is the intention behind her work. The concern with capturing the whole experience leads her to pile fact upon fact, to overload her fiction with detail. Often criticized for this superabundance of graphic minutiae, she responds, "One has to be exhaustive and exhausting to really render the world in all its complexities and also in its dullness." She attempts more than a detailed picture, as she has clearly explained in an interview, "What I would like to do, always, in my writing is an obvious and yet perhaps audacious feat; I would like to create the psychological and emotional equivalent of an experience, so completely and in such exhaustive detail, that anyone who reads it sympathetically will have *experienced* that event in his mind (which is where we live anyway)."

Although she is quite certain about the intention of her work, Oates is less exact about her antecedents. A legion of writers has contributed to her development. In addition to Faulkner and Kafka, she includes as other important influences, "Freud, Nietzsche, Mann–they're almost real personalities in my life. And Dostoevsky and Melville . . . and Proust. And Sartre's *Nausea*." Beyond this diverse list, she sees herself as a romantic in the tradition of Stendhal and Flaubert. She also has obvious bonds with the great American naturalists–Dreiser, Farrell, and Steinbeck–but her concern with unusual psychological states and her lyricism and vivid imagery remove her from their company. The result of this wide variety of artistic models is an original synthesis which defies simple labels–realist, naturalist, gothicist, psychologist, satirist, and journalist–that have been pinned on her. Oates has been advised by her critics to cease work for awhile to allow writer and reader alike to digest and properly evaluate what has been produced. Nevertheless, she continues to create and publish at an incredible rate; each month her output grows; each year a new novel, or a volume of short stories or poems, or a critical work appears. She contributes stories and essays across the entire spectrum of periodical publications, from *Playboy* and *Cosmopolitan* to *Southern Humanities Review* and the *Shakespeare Quarterly*.

Oates's first novel, *With Shuddering Fall*, sounds the themes of violence, madness, and lust which have become her trademarks. This story of a country girl, Karen Herz, and of her destructive love affair with a stock-car racer, Shar Rule, demonstrates the immense power of feminine passivity in its battle with masculine violence. From the moment that the thirty-year-old Shar roars into Eden County to bury his hated, dying father until, defeated by Karen, he smashes into the wall of the Cherry River raceway, he attempts to force the eighteen-year-old girl to respond to his violence. Karen, however, acting to avenge her father whom Shar has seriously beaten, is indomitable.

While many reviewers responded favorably to this first novel, most missed the point of the story, which "was conceived as a religious work. Where the father was the father of the Old Testament who gives a command, as God gave a command to Abraham, and everything was parallel–very strictly parallel–and how we can obey or not obey it, and, if we do obey it, we're not going to get rewarded for it anyway," as Oates told Linda Kuehl, an interviewer for *Commonweal*. The parallel is explicit in the novel: Mr. Herz reads from

the Bible the story of Abraham and Isaac on the day before he commands Karen, "Don't come to me until you get him. Kill him. Kill him." Karen fulfills his command, despite her growing love for Shar, filling the story with violence, riots, perverse lust, and death. This religious theme is an important aspect of *With Shuddering Fall* and indicates the religious questioning of the author, who is a lapsed Catholic and was then examining the role of religion in her life. That she was haunted by her Catholic upbringing is evident in much of her early writing, but her Catholic heritage grows less and less important in her later works.

Technically *With Shuddering Fall* is fairly simple and straightforward. The narrative point of view is third person, limited throughout, with Karen the center of consciousness for most of the novel, although Shar and others assume the center for certain sections. The novel is divided into three books, "Spring," "Summer," and "Fall," which coincide with Karen's meeting with, destruction of, and recovery from Shar. The prose style helps maintain control, as John Knowles in his *New York Times* review notes: "This material is not as garish as it sounds because of the clarity, grace, and intelligence of the writing." On the other hand, H. G. Jackson, in *Harper's*, calls it "merely hysterically incoherent," while Dorrie Pagones, in *Saturday Review*, writes, "Miss Oates is often both esoteric and violent, adjectives seldom ascribed to women writers, and her imagination seems to have no limits."

Her second novel, *A Garden of Earthly Delights* (1967), is the opening volume of an informal trilogy which develops the dual themes of problems caused by economic circumstances and of the difficulties of young people striving to free themselves from the oppressive situations of their lives. The chronicle of three generations, *A Garden of Earthly Delights* depicts the sordid world of the migrant laborer, the lonely world of the social outcast, and the sterile world of the comfortable middle class. The novel opens powerfully with the birth of the heroine, Clara, in the back of a decrepit transport truck for migrant workers in the 1920s. "Very much like Dreiser here, Miss Oates's honest grip on reality makes us feel but not flinch," Elizabeth Janeway writes in her *New York Times* review.

Clara's escape from the endless road and her establishment in Tintern, a small town in Eden County, are affected by the enigmatic young man, Lowry, who fathers her son. When Lowry, not knowing that Clara is pregnant, leaves for Mexico, she decides to bring her life into control by seeking out and surrendering to Revere, the local wealthy patrician who has been attracted to her. Taking her from her dime-store saleswoman's existence in the town, he establishes her as his mistress in her own home in the country and, following his wife's death, marries her and brings her and her son, Swan, whom he thinks is his, into his world. To give Swan a strong position in life is Clara's main reason for marriage, but this decision leads to disaster, as he induces a miscarriage for Clara by causing in a hunting accident the violent and bloody death of one of his stepbrothers. Finally, after destroying Revere's original family for Swan's benefit, Clara sees Swan shoot his stepfather and then himself. As a result, she sinks gradually into insanity, as did her migrant mother. Most of the reviewers find this ending melodramatic and contrived.

From the migrant world and farming community of *A Garden of Earthly Delights* Oates moves to the earthly paradise of the sheltered suburbs of wealthy America in *Expensive People* (1968). About this volume she has written, "*Expensive People* is the second of three novels that deal with social and economic facts of life in America, combined with unusually sensitive–but hopefully representative–young men and women who confront the puzzle of American life in different ways and come to different ends." Her "sensitive" but "representative" youth in this work is an eighteen-year-old, 250-pound maniac, Richard Everett, who presents the story in the first person as a memoir he is writing prior to committing suicide.

Expensive People is Richard's tale of his pitiful life. He is the child of a highly successful corporate executive, Elwood Everett, who jumps from position to position, ever bettering his prestige and salary, and of a minor woman writer, Natashya Romanov, who poses as the daughter of émigré Russian nobles but who is really the daughter of poor immigrants. Richard is hopelessly neurotic, perhaps psychotic. Wallowing in self-pity, he describes the promiscuous conduct of his social-climbing mother, whom he hopelessly loves. Her periodic desertions of him and his father drive Richard to murder.

Natashya, or Nada ("nothing") as Richard calls her, provides the plot for her own destruction by leaving behind her notebook in which she has sketched out a psychological novelette about a young man who terrorizes people by sniping at them but missing the first three times, "then the fourth, when you've been conditioned to the others, results in the murder." Interpolated in *Expensive People* is a published Oates story, "The Molesters," which is presented as one Nada contributed to the *Quarterly Review of Literature*. Richard interprets the tale to mean that his parents are knowingly "molesting" him. Richard follows the plot of the novelette, and the next time that Nada packs her bags to leave, he shoots her. Or does he? The psychiatrists say that the experience is a hallucination and that someone else shot Nada. Richard insists that he did kill her; so at eighteen he writes his chronicle of disintegration, after which he begins to commit suicide by eating until he bursts.

This novel is a sharp reversal from Oates's earlier efforts. It is a satire on the moral and artistic bankruptcy of the upper-middle class. This presentation is effective, although she continues to present the details of day-to-day existence. Oates undercuts the realism of the narrative by extending her descriptions to absurd lengths, as when she has Nada telephone more than thirty different services necessary to suburban life. The use of the first-person narration is also a departure for Oates, one she found to be successful. In addition, the subject matter of this eccentric novel gives her a chance to discuss writing technique (Richard explains in great detail his theory about "How to Write a Memoir Like This," using tips from articles in *The Writer* and *Amateur Penman*, *Let's Write a Novel!* by Agnes Sturm, and *Waiting for the End* by Leslie Fiedler). The critical reception of this volume was varied; some reviews were quite enthusiastic, while others were skeptical of the value of this unusual work.

The final volume of Oates's informal trilogy is *them* (1969), winner of the 1970 National Book Award. In this novel she turns to the world of the lower-middle class to chronicle the survival of the Wendall family from 1937 to 1967. "In the years 1962-1967 I taught English at the University of Detroit. . . . It was during this period that I met the 'Maureen Wendall' of this narrative." This young woman was a student and later a correspondent of Oates's, who incorporates in the body of the novel letters purportedly received from "Maureen." Oates describes Detroit with accuracy and a great profusion of detail, which at times encumbers the narrative, although she further states that "the various sordid and shocking events of slum life, detailed in other naturalistic works, have been understated here, mainly because of my fear that too much reality would be unbearable."

Shot through with violence from beginning to end, *them* depicts the lives of Loretta Wendall and her son, Jules, and daughter, Maureen. Early in the novel, sixteen-year-old Loretta is jolted from her sleep by the sound of a bullet crashing through the skull of her first lover. Her brother, the murderer, flees, leaving her to muddle her way through the problem; she finds a policeman, Howard Wendall, whom she knows slightly, and brings him to the sordid apartment, where he, aroused by the thoughts evoked by the body in Loretta's bed, takes her on the kitchen table. He marries her after helping to dispose of the body but is suspended from the police force, and they move to the country. Howard goes off to war, and Loretta moves back to Detroit, where she is arrested for prostitution by the first man she approaches. Ever-resilient Loretta bounces back and survives, lives through several years with Howard until he is killed in an industrial accident, and then passes from man to man, ever hopeful, never truly touched by the horrors surrounding her.

Loretta's daughter, Maureen, is a composite of Oates and the "real" Maureen. One of the tragedies of the fictional girl's youth is the loss of her class minutes book for which she, the class secretary, is responsible. That Oates can make this insignificant event poignant and memorable is a measure of her power. Oates says this of the episode: "This is something that had happened to me too, and both of us responded in a very weak, rather victimized way, by being annihilated almost and reduced to tears and despair by a completely foolish event which is so small and yet, when you're that age, it can sort of run over you." Always the victim, Maureen turns to the library and literature to find peace and order; she reads Jane Austen and feels great sympathy for Emma but cannot feel such sympathy for her own relatives–the horrible reality of her life has become surreal to her. After literature, the only escape route she can envision is wealth.

Money is magic in *them*, and the characters pursue it almost by instinct. Maureen at fourteen begins picking up older men in her craving for money. She hides the money she earns in a book of poetry in her room, but her stepfather finds the money and beats her into a catatonic state, in which she hides from life for more than a year. Her brother, Jules, is similarly enthralled with money. His early years are believably depicted,

but when he reaches manhood, his bizarre adventures make him merely a name acting through a series of unbelievable events. He has a relationship with a beautiful kept woman, who introduces him to the strange Bernard Geffen. A wealthy man trying to become a success through the gangster world, Geffen hires Jules as his chauffeur, pays him hundreds of dollars, gives him ten thousand dollars to buy a new car for them, and finally leaves Jules sitting in the car while he goes into a decaying building and has his throat slit. During his brief career as Geffen's driver, Jules catches sight of his employer's niece, Nadine, the daughter of some wealthy people in Grosse Pointe.

Nadine, who symbolizes the riches of a world he can never enter, becomes the overriding compulsion of Jules's life. He persuades her to run away with him, and while they drive to Texas, Jules commits petty crimes to support them. Nadine, however, refuses to have sex with him, and when he becomes disgustingly ill, she leaves him. Several years later they meet again and finally consummate their relationship. After an afternoon and evening of making love, Nadine shoots her lover and then herself. Jules recovers only to become a caricature of success.

At the conclusion of the novel Jules and Maureen both escape from the horror of their lower-class backgrounds. Jules, after pimping for a young, upper-middle-class student whom he turns to prostitution, becomes involved in the Detroit riots of 1967, during which he kills a policeman and makes friends with one of the organizers of the riots. After the destruction the organizer lands a federal grant to set up an antipoverty program in California. Joining with him, Jules heads west in a parody of the traditional Amèrican hero striking out for new frontiers. Maureen's success is her seduction away from his wife and family of a dumpy, community college, part-time English teacher, who marries her and takes her to the haven of the suburbs. In the world of *them*, these are "success" stories.

The critical reception of this work was generally favorable. Almost all reviewers were impressed by the detailed panorama displayed by Oates. Robert M. Adams, in the *New York Times*, said, "Miss Oates writes a vehement, voluminous, kaleidoscopic novel, more deeply rooted in social observation than current fiction usually tends to be." With this novel, Joyce Carol Oates became a major figure in the literary world.

Dust jacket for Oates's family saga, the first novel in her trilogy of "genre experiments"

Following *them*, she began a series of novels which, in her words, "deal with the complex distribution of power in the United States." The first novel of this group is *Wonderland* (1971), which concerns the medical world and the "phantasmagoria of personality." The "hero" of *Wonderland* is Jesse Harte / Pedersen / Vogel. His story begins in blood with his father's mass murder of the rest of the family and his suicide after wounding Jesse. Jesse Harte is eventually adopted by the famous physician and mystic, Dr. Pedersen, who awakens his slumbering intellect. Living several years in Lockport with the strange Pedersen family, all of whom are grotesquely fat, eccentric geniuses, Jesse develops a drive to emulate Dr. Pedersen. When he helps the alcoholic Mrs. Pedersen attempt to escape from the perverse domination of her husband, Jesse is ejected from the family. Without Pedersen's help, Jesse, now Vogel, struggles through medical school and internship but then marries the daughter of one of his medical professors and becomes the protégé of a brilliant brain surgeon. With an in-

heritance, Jesse establishes a clinic and becomes himself a successful neuro-surgeon. Despite his professional success, Jesse cannot control his life or his children's lives: his marriage is unhappy; his children are alienated from him; his attempt at a love affair fails; the novel ends in despair.

The catalog of violence and perversion in this novel includes mass murder, drug addiction, castration, abortion, homosexuality, self-mutilation, the assassination of President Kennedy, cannibalism (a doctor eats a broiled uterus which he has cut from an attractive cadaver), and the more typical horrors a doctor sees in the emergency room. *Wonderland* is unrelenting in its assault on the reader. Although many of the individual episodes are magnificent accomplishments, the novel as a whole does not reach the level of Oates's other work.

The critical reception of *Wonderland* was mixed. Many reviewers were highly impressed, while others were repelled by the work. The unmitigated pessimism of the novel makes it one of the least attractive of Oates's works, but *Wonderland* has such power and intensity that it cannot be ignored.

Do With Me What You Will (1973), her next novel, presents the world of lawyers and is in Oates's words, "a celebration of love and marriage." Structured to resemble a legal presentation, *Do With Me What You Will* is divided into four parts: "Twenty-eight Years, Two Months, Twenty-six Days," "Miscellaneous Facts, Events, Fantasies, Evidence Admissible and Inadmissible," "Crime," and "The Summing Up." The first two sections are temporally parallel, with each part presenting the story of one of the two main characters; "Part One" is Elena Howe's, and "Part Two" is Jack Morrissey's. The third section documents their love affair, and the fourth neatly concludes the novel by updating all of the main characters' lives and setting them on their ways.

Elena's story is an updated Sleeping Beauty fairy tale. Kidnapped by her crazed, divorced father when she was seven, Elena early withdraws into a protective shell and remains oblivious to the world. When rescued from her father, Elena, ill and confused, cannot even speak, and when she finally does, she stutters. Her mother, a cold-blooded, man-hating opportunist, never understands Elena's problems and drags Elena through childhood and adolescence until she marries her at seventeen to a famous criminal lawyer, Marvin Howe. At the end of "Twenty-eight Years, Two Months, Twenty-six Days" Elena is frozen in a trance, staring at a statue in Detroit, where she and Marvin live.

Jack Morrissey's story commences when his father murders a wealthy man. Marvin Howe defends his father and, by coaching Jack as his star witness, gains an acquittal by reason of temporary insanity. Astounded by the power of the law, Jack decides to become a lawyer himself. He does, but unlike the rich and celebrated Howe, Jack crusades for the poor and downtrodden. While in the South working with the American Civil Liberties Union to help the blacks, Jack meets Rachel, whom he marries. Later they move back to Detroit, where Jack continues to help the impoverished and gains a reputation as a top lawyer for liberal causes. They never have much money because Rachel insists on sharing their money with the oppressed. When he sees Elena Howe and learns who she is, Jack feels compelled to know her. At the end of "Part Two" he is trying to awaken her from the trance which ended "Part One."

The third part of *Do With Me What You Will* depicts the progress of the love affair which develops between Jack and Elena. With her first sexual climax, she begins to awaken to reality, but because she is frightened, as well as exhilarated, by her emergence, she hides from Jack. When he forces her to choose between him and Marvin, she withdraws from him altogether, returns to Marvin, and confesses her sin. Marvin, certain he has gotten her back permanently, burns the files of evidence which his detectives have gathered since the affair began.

"The Summing Up" follows the main characters to a final decision. Elena rejects Marvin and security and pursues Jack, who has returned to his wife and the child they adopted to salvage their marriage. She succeeds. The novel ends affirmatively with Jack and Elena together.

Technically, this volume is one of Oates's most successful efforts. The critical reception of *Do With Me What You Will* was positive; after the extravagances and horrors of *Wonderland*, most readers and reviewers welcomed the restraint and affirmation of this novel. As the second volume of the trilogy which concerns the basis of power in the United States, *Do With Me What You Will* brilliantly reveals the complex fabric of law which envelops all of society.

Leaving the orderly world of law, Oates enters the chaotic world of politics in her next volume, *The Assassins: A Book of Hours* (1975). There is a multiplicity of themes in this novel: politics and political assassination, art and religion, heroes and hero worship; unfortunately, none of these themes is fully developed. Critics of *The Assassins* were baffled and worn out by the narrative. J. D. O'Hara, in the *New York Times*, expressed his frustration: "Joyce Carol Oates has subtitled her novel, 'A Book of Hours.' And painfully exasperating hours they are, every one of them."

The novel chronicles three confused lives, whose center, a powerful political figure, has been destroyed. Divided into three parts, the novel gives these characters—Hugh, Yvonne, and Stephen—an opportunity to demonstrate their relationships with the assassinated ultra-right-wing hero Andrew Petrie and the ways in which the violent death has affected them. Hugh opens the novel with his first-person account of his hatred for his brother Andrew, whose death moves him toward insanity. Hugh is an artist, a caricaturist, whose savage cartoons have earned him respect, but whose disintegration isolates him from all society. The second part of the tale falls to Yvonne, Andrew's young wife, whose story is one of love and hero worship. She tries to carry on Andrew's work, but her limited ability to understand subtle differences confuses her. Third comes Stephen's narrative. He is Andrew's youngest brother, a religious mystic whose tale reveals Andrew to have been the subject of his religious compassion. Hugh ends his account by shooting himself in the head; Yvonne is shot and dismembered by an ax-wielding hunter at the conclusion of her section; and Stephen wanders off on a pilgrimage when his tale is finished.

The narratives are each individually confusing, and although they are mutually illuminating, much remains unclear. The story progresses through flashbacks and dreams whose confusion is compounded by the unreliability of the narrators. Hugh is an unabashed liar, Yvonne is often confused and is bent on protecting her husband's reputation, and Stephen lives in a world not of this earth. The novel is chaotic, but then Oates obviously intends to present as accurately as possible the chaos of modern life.

Childwold (1976) is Oates's most free-flowing novel, the most intentionally Joycean in its structure, language, and narrative technique. Childwold is a rustic hamlet in Eden County whose name has symbolic value: the novel is full of children and childlike adults. Near this small town on a decaying farm lives the Bartlett family, and when Fitz John Kasch, the principal character of the novel, falls in love with fourteen-year-old Laney Bartlett, he muses over the name, composing "a litany, a sacred chant, the words of which were so beautiful I woke weeping–Childwold/ Childwood / Childwide / Childworld / Childmold / Childwould/Childtold." This type of wordplay is an important part of the novel, as demonstrated by a page-length "litany" on the same word later on and by similar expansions of Kasch's name. Many different characters–Kasch, Laney, Grandpa Hurley, Arlene Bartlett, and her two sons, Vale and Brad–tell significant parts of the story, each in a distinctive voice. Throughout the novel Oates's increasing fascination with psychic matters is manifested in the strange experiences of the characters.

Childwold is the story of Kasch and his interaction with the Bartlett family, a colorful menage of Arlene Bartlett, her married daughter Nancy, and their many children, legitimate and illegitimate, who provide the most obvious explanation

of the title. Hovering over the novel, the not-yet-ghost of times past, is Arlene's eighty-three-year-old father, Joseph Hurley, upon whose farm the family lives. The world-traveling Kasch returns to recover his lost innocence in the nearby town of Yewville, where he meets and falls in love with Laney Bartlett, whom he pursues and instructs, lusts after and lends books to. However, when Arlene arrives to ask Kasch about his relationship with her daughter, he transfers his affection to the more mature woman. He marries Arlene and celebrates their homecoming and the consummation of their marriage through a lyric marriage song, which reveals him at the pinnacle of his physical and poetic life. However, bliss is short-lived in Oates's novels; defending his new family, Kasch smashes to pulp the skull of one of Arlene's former suitors. Tried, acquitted, hospitalized in a mental institution, Kasch withdraws from all society, and upon his release he buys the old farm and lives in the crumbling house as a hermit.

As usual with Oates's novels, plot summary leaves out much of importance: Grandpa's extraordinarily rich psychic life; Vale's brutal, degraded existence; Laney's fragile, failing childworld. The novel is full of poetry, the self-conscious rhythms of Kasch, the untutored, natural music of Grandpa. This is an excellent novel by any standard, as most critics recognized. Irene H. Chayes, in *New Republic*, wrote, "This is a novel that at last is comparable to the best of her stories and by an evolutionary leap has already moved beyond them, into the tradition of literature, going back at least as far as the Romantics, in which the philosophical problems of man's existence and his destiny are bound up with the problems of art."

Eden County provides the background for *Son of the Morning* (1978), which Oates describes as "a first person narration by a man addressing himself throughout to God. . . . the whole novel is a prayer." The title of the novel comes from the book of Isaiah, in which Satan is called "son of the morning." In Oates's novel the son of the morning is Nathan Vickery, a charismatic preacher conceived during the gang rape of a virgin. Though, unlike Satan, Nathan does not willfully bring about the downfall of others, his one-sided view of life has evil effects. He has seven visions of God, the first at the age of five, and these become his obsession. The novel presents the various characters who enter and then leave

Nathan's life: his mother, who is too young and too immature to care for him; his grandmother, who nurtures his spirituality; his grandfather, a skeptical intellectual; the various preachers who attempt to act as mentors in his youth; Leonie, a young woman whom he first desires and then rejects; and Japheth, the theology student who becomes his disciple but later attempts to murder him.

One of the most dramatic moments in *Son of the Morning* occurs when Nathan, remorseful over having felt lust for Leonie, puts his eye out before a congregation. Rather than repulsing his followers, this act strengthens his appeal to them. He goes on to lead a group called the Seekers of Christ, attracting hangers-on who hope to profit personally from his powers of leadership. He, however, is detached from their desires for money and power, as he is from all things worldly. After Japheth's attempt to murder him, Nathan is changed. There is a final apocalyptic downfall, but only symbolic death. At novel's end, he returns to Yewville, the town where he was born, having renamed himself William Vickery and divorced himself from his evangelistic past. However, he still searches for God, and his despair in this search permeates the novel.

"I wanted to write about religious experience from the other side, about interior experience," Oates said about *Son of the Morning*. Oates aimed to show in this book "how interior experience becomes modified and can't be controlled as it is taken over by the evangelical church." While writing this novel, Oates devoted hours each day to reading the Bible in an attempt to put herself "in the place of a fundamentalist Protestant who could go to the Bible every day for guidance and would not have any critical or historical preconceptions. . . . Getting into that frame of mind was a very shattering experience. Every day is a battle between good and evil, between God and the devil." *Son of the Morning* was generally well received by critics, who admired both its ambition and what they saw as its varying achievements.

Cybele (1979), named for an ancient bisexual goddess who was celebrated in orgiastic rites by eunuch priests, tells the tale of a man who is sexually powerless but who nevertheless is doomed by his sexual desires. *Cybele* focuses on Edwin Locke, successful and attractive, with a wife, two children, and a good education—all the requisites for a happy life—and the mid-life crisis that leads him to engage in a series of affairs, each more dis-

astrous than the last. First he pulls Cathleen, a married woman from his own social circle, into an affair; she is followed by Risa, a swinging gold digger who takes him for his money and then leaves with a former lover; and finally, after attempting reconciliation with his wife, Cynthia, he becomes involved with Zanche, an artist who has a strange daughter and who introduces him to bohemian life. Edwin is impotent; sex therapy is expensive and offers no help. Everyone seems to want only Edwin's money, and there is the suggestion that money is all he has to give. His sons, with whom he has never spent much time, are estranged from him, and his attempts to win them over fail. By the end of the tale Cynthia has built a new life for herself. Edwin, however, is more miserable than ever.

The final scene of the novel is characteristically Oatesian in its grotesqueness and violence. Edwin attempts to make love to Zanche's nine-year-old daughter, Chrissie, only to discover that the daughter has a penis. He hurts her and begins to tear apart the apartment. Zanche returns with friends, who attack Edwin. He manages to get away from them, but they catch up with him later, and his decaying body is eventually found near the expressway. In the last paragraphs, which flash back to an earlier moment, Rok, one of the killers, is trying to get his lighter to work so he can set fire to Edwin's body. *Cybele* reiterates effectively a favorite theme of Oates's, the moral bankruptcy of the upper-middle class. Edwin's fate is of his own making, and he has no redeeming nobility to earn the reader's respect.

In Oates's next novel, *Unholy Loves* (1979), the setting is Woodslee University in upstate New York, an expensive and prestigious school for Ivy League rejects. Covering faculty politics and personal lives during one school year, the plot focuses on the social occasions that bring the faculty together. The catalytic event of this novel is the arrival of Albert St. Dennis, a distinguished elderly poet, for a year's residence. He is alcoholic, possibly senile at times, and near the novel's end he dies in a fire he has accidentally started after an evening's revelry.

The most important of the novel's many character's is Brigit Stott, who is having a difficult time writing her third novel. A member of the English department, as are many of the characters, she is separated from her husband and feels she is a failure both as an artist and as a woman. At a party to introduce St. Dennis to the faculty she is led into an affair with Alexis Kessler, a brilliant but erratic pianist and composer who is in danger of being fired from Woodslee, largely for his temperamental and bizarre behavior. The affair between Brigit and Alexis is at first idyllic, then stormy, violent. The novel's last scene brings them together briefly, but their relationship is over. The affair, however, has helped to push Brigit beyond the stalemate she has reached; she is considering leaving Woodslee for a job nearer her family, from whom she has previously felt estranged, and she is back at work on a new novel. This conclusion provides a sense of optimistic completion and the implication that one may gain a degree of control over one's own life. Brigit says, "But whatever happens to me for the rest of my life . . . won't be inevitable. I think that's why I feel so optimistic." However, Alexis has the novel's last sentence, introducing an element of doubt: "But surely, my love, that won't last?"

Much of the third-person omniscient narration in *Unholy Loves* presents the insides of the characters' minds. The reader finds himself flitting from character to character and from thought to thought within each character's mind. However, the style is appropriate for the subject matter. Two of the characters keep journals, and in presenting the mental journals of the various characters, the book itself takes on a kind of journal-like quality. (Oates herself keeps a formal journal, which she says "resembles a sort of on-going letter to myself, mainly about literary matters.")

Oates claims that there has been "humor of a sort in my writing from the first, but it's understated or deadpan." *Unholy Loves* is probably a good example of that humor, but in this novel it sometimes seems intentionally catty, the laughter often closer to sneering. Critics recognized the novel's achievement while noting that this was not one of Oates's major efforts.

Bellefleur (1980) is an ambitious novel dealing with six generations of the Bellefleur family. Jean-Pierre Bellefleur has established an empire whose power is made visible by the sixty-four-room castle built by his nephew. The castle, called Bellefleur, provides a suitably Gothic background for the strange beasts, transformations, and prophetic events which provide the fabric of the novel, including such oddities as a half-wit boy who seems to turn into a dog, a captured gnome who becomes a devoted servant, a strange beast that is actually a house cat, and a giant bird that steals a baby. The story jumps back and forth from generation to generation but focuses

on Gideon Bellefleur and his beautiful wife, Leah, who attempts to restore the decaying Bellefleur empire to its former grandeur. In the end her hopes are quite literally crushed when Gideon crashes his airplane into the castle, destroying himself and his family. It is left to Jedediah, the holy man of the family who has made his hermitage on the mountain, to come down from the mountain and found a new Bellefleur line. "The point," John Gardner writes in his review of the novel, "is one made in *Son of the Morning* and elsewhere. Loving God completely, one cares nothing about the world, not even about people whom one sees, rightly, as mere instances; on the other hand, completely loving oneself or the world, one loses one's soul and becomes (as Gideon in the end) a figure of death."

A rich and complex story, *Bellefleur* creates a weirdly Gothic setting against which strange occurrences seem normal. Gardner notes that "what is known in Shakespeare criticism as 'sliding time' becomes a calculated madness" in *Bellefleur*. Though there are realistic details and a genealogical chart, no dates are given and one feels that specific time is deliberately obscured in order to create an other-worldly feeling.

Oates says she attempted to write *Bellefleur* for years: "I would collect images along the way–a clavichord I saw, a snatch of conversation I heard–but I never could find the right voice." She finally began the novel after suddenly envisioning a woman sitting beside a baby in a cradle in a shabby but lushly overgrown walled garden. The novel took possession of her, and she attempted to write a chapter a day. She calls *Bellefleur* her "vampire" novel. "Even talking about it still drains me," she says. "I've had many such psychic vampire experiences in the past." Writing this novel helped her to develop theories about nineteenth-century Gothicism: "Using the werewolf, for instance, is a way of writing about an emotional obsession turning into a kind of animal." Finishing the novel left her with a kind of homesickness, "like loving a place you know you will never go back to."

Critics responded to *Bellefleur* much as they did to *Son of the Morning*, applauding its ambition, seeing much that is good and a little that is not. They were generally enthusiastic but did not find the novel flawless.

Angel of Light (1981) takes its title from the name Thoreau gave to John Brown, some of whose descendants are the central characters of this novel. The book is loosely based on the fall of the House of Atreus, brought about when Orestes, at the urging of his sister Electra, avenged the murder of his father, Agamemnon, by killing his mother, Clytemnestra, and her lover, Aegisthus, who have killed Agamemnon in his bath. In Oates's novel Maurice Halleck, director of the Commission for the Ministry of Justice, apparently commits suicide by driving his car off the road into the deep water of a swamp. He leaves a note, confessing his involvement in a bribery scandal, which clears his old school friend and assistant, Nick Martens, who is the actual lawbreaker. His daughter Kirsten, an anorexic, drug-using boarding-school student, cannot accept her father's guilt. Though she has no hard evidence otherwise, she is too aware of his great integrity to believe that he would accept a bribe. She is convinced that his death was somehow caused by her mother, Isabel, and Nick, who have been in love since shortly after Isabel's engagement to Maurice. Kirsten's monomania eventually draws in her brother Owen, a success-oriented Princeton senior bound for Harvard Law School and a career like his father's. Their determination to kill Isabel and Nick ultimately brings their own downfalls as well, in scenes of Oatesian violence that leave Owen and Isabel dead and Kirsten and Nick, who now confesses his guilt, in self-imposed exiles.

Thomas R. Edwards writes that "In her portrayal of the Halleck children, Miss Oates achieves a fresh and frightening picture of a desire that exceeds any available attainment. Owen and Kirsten . . . strive to reconstruct reality in the image of their dream of justice, as [John Brown] had once also tried to do, with equally shattering effect." Edwards speaks of *Angel of Light* as "another chapter in Joyce Carol Oates's ongoing exercise of the imagination, but . . . also a strong and fascinating novel on its own terms. Coming after her haunting fantasy *Bellefleur*, which in effect levitates above the history and geography of the known world to report that its larger moral contours remain deeply mysterious, *Angel of Light* gravitates back towards the terra firma of a novel like Miss Oates's *them*, where social circumstances and personal fate are closely and realistically linked." He adds, however, that "enough mystery persists in *Angel of Light* to suggest that this prolific and various novelist is staking out new fictional ground." Some other critics were not so generous with their praise, seeing in the novel more soap opera than human drama.

Oates continues her cycle of genre experiments with *A Bloodsmoor Romance* (1982), her version of the family saga in Victorian America. Ostensibly about John Quincy Zinn, it tells the story of the five Zinn daughters through the point of view of an unreliable narrator. Diane Johnson identifies Oates's theme as "the lot of women, especially the customs and attitudes that confined and oppressed them in the 19th century, but also the present-day remnants of those conditions." It is apparent that the narrator is unreliable because "she expresses [her views of feminine conduct] so pointedly that we cannot miss the novelist's intention, which is to emphasize their ridiculousness."

Sometimes referred to as Oates's *Little Women*, *Bloodsmoor* chronicles the lives of Constance Philippa, Malvinia, Octavia, Samantha, and Deirdre Zinn, beginning with Deirdre's abduction in a balloon. On the day of her marriage to a German baron, the tomboy Constance runs away; she returns for the reading of Aunt Edwina's will disguised as a young man, Phillipe Fox. Malvinia runs away with an actor, has an affair with Mark Twain, and ends up as a faculty wife. Octavia, the dutiful daughter, endures a first husband given to sexual perversity (whom she kills) and a vicious son (whom she allows to die) to be rewarded with a loving, ideal second husband. Samantha, inheriting her father's scientific inclinations, elopes with an obscure young man and invents the baby stroller and disposable diapers while her father formulates atomic weapons. Deirdre returns as a famous medium who, when subjected to scientific investigation, loses contact with her spirits but saves the world (for the time being) by allowing her father's nuclear formula to burn in the fire that destroys his laboratory.

In the third novel of her cycle of genre experiments, *The Mysteries of Winterthurn* (1984), Oates "re-imagines" the detective story. She introduces the young consulting detective Xavier Kilgarven and presents three of his most baffling cases, three of his failures. Setting the novel in nineteenth-century upstate New York, Oates also employs such nineteenth-century conventions as the omniscient–although unreliable–narrator, slow pace, and ornate language.

Kilgarven's cases involve crimes against women, underscoring Oates's theme of the invisibility of women. Powerless in nineteenth-century patriarchal society, their intelligence and common sense are ignored by men, and their differences from men are viewed as symptoms of dis-

Dust jacket for Oates's "re-imagining" of the Greek tale of the fall of the House of Atreus

ease. In the first, "The Virgin in the Rose Bower, or The Tragedy of Glen Mawr Manor," Kilgarven, while falling in love with his cousin Perdita, investigates a series of murders at his cousins' home, deaths attributed to angels in a ceiling mural who come to life. In "Devil's Half-Acre, or The Mystery of the 'Cruel Suitor,'" five local factory girls are raped and butchered by Valentine Westergaard, a young man in Kilgarven's social set. And in "The Bloodstained Bridal Gown, or Xavier Kilgarven's Last Case," a minister (Perdita's husband), his mother, and his adulterous lover get axed.

Throughout these stories the unreliable narrator speaks for society in blaming the victims for the crimes, and the reader must infer the true plight of these women. When the narrator reports that Kilgarven's aunts died because his uncle married women of inferior stock, the reader infers that he was a wife beater and they died from abuse. Westergaard is found innocent of murder because the working-class girls "asked" for his upper-class attentions and "deserve" their fate. Perdita's oldest sister, Georgina, is accused of periodic bouts of peculiar behavior and lack of attention to her personal appearance,

when in fact she is being used incestuously by her father and bears him five children.

While one critic calls this "one of Oates's more accessible books," "essentially an entertainment," another sees a loftier aim: rather than being a detective's search for the truth, it is "a philosophical investigation into the nature of 'Mystery.'" Literary allusion abounds in the work: Kilgarven, modeled after Sherlock Holmes, thinks like Emerson; Georgina, a reclusive poet, is patterned after Emily Dickinson and, through her pen name Iphigenia, is connected with the Greek myth; the cousins are like creations of the Brontës; one critic finds similarities between *Winterthurn* and works by Charlotte Perkins Gilman and Djuna Barnes.

When considered with *Bloodsmoor*, Eileen Teper Bender believes that "these two novels demonstrate one of Oates's most interesting literary discoveries"–the similarities between detective fiction and romance. Both "affirm the drive for control," and "Oates reveals a Gothic grimace beneath the mask of ratiocination."

As Rebecca Pepper Sinkler points out, "Almost a half-century ago, Virginia Woolf called for a new kind of fiction, one in which women would be described not 'only in relation to the other sex.' . . . Joyce Carol Oates, never squeamish about looking into the dark places of the soul," has written such a fiction in *Solstice* (1985). The novel tells the story of an improbable friendship between Monica Jensen, the narrator, who is divorced and beginning her life again as a teacher in a private school, and Shelia Trask, an artist and widow of a famous sculptor, "dark, mercurial, driven, reclusive." Their relationship, says Mary Soete (*Library Journal*, 15 November 1984), "turns on a subtle undercurrent of sexuality and on Monica's passivity and ultimate victimization, as [Shelia] . . . leads her into a labyrinth." Through these women Oates looks at the transformation of a friendship into an obsession, described by Michael Harper (*Los Angeles Times Book Review*, 6 January 1985) as "love for another that ultimately becomes a struggle for the survival of self." Sinkler concludes that *Solstice* "should dispel a lot of comforting ideas about the nature of women."

In *Marya: A Life* (1986) Oates returns to upstate New York. She tells a fairy tale in which, Mary Gordon notes, "a deprived child [is] mysteriously transformed not into a princess but a scholarship girl. [The story is] an intensively and compassionately observed account of the lives of dirt-poor but intellectually passionate young women." Oates takes up Marya Knauer's story when she is eight; her father has been bludgeoned to death, and her mother, Vera, takes her to see the body before abandoning Marya and her two younger brothers. Turned over to an uncle's family, Marya is repeatedly sexually abused by her cousin, and she develops a shell of brilliance and sarcasm to keep people at a distance. Pushing herself through college and graduate school, Marya becomes a tenured professor, only to quit for success in the literary world of New York. At mid-life she realizes she must reclaim what Elaine Showalter calls her "matrilineal past," and she returns to her hometown to try to discover her mother. This is only right, says Gordon, since the romance of the novel is not between Marya and her various men but between the abandoned daughter and her mother.

Oates structures the novel in chapters that are almost short stories. Each presents a slice of Marya's life, focusing on an important person in her life–in particular three men, all of whom die–who for a time defines her and gives her "a life." Her return to her mother is her further attempt to solve her identity problem.

You Must Remember This (1987) is also set in upstate New York, beginning in 1953. It is the story of the Stevick family, especially the passion between fifteen-year-old Enid Maria and her thirty-year-old half-uncle Felix, a former boxer. Oates begins with Enid's suicide attempt, establishing what John Updike calls the pattern of Enid's "flirtations" with nothingness, a blending of self-destructive and erotic impulses; masturbation, reckless jumping on a trampoline, swimming to exhaustion, shoplifting, contemplating her wallpaper, her attraction to the canal and to the narrow footbridge below the railroad trestle, her affair with Felix. Updike also describes the novel as a 1950s fairy tale of options for women: Geraldine marries into "a local life of chronic pregnancy and domestic drudgery," Lizzie becomes a singer and possibly a New York hooker, and Enid goes to college.

Robert Phillips believes Oates's theme is love: familial love, romantic love, and lust, with subplots about the love of power, music, and boxing. Calling it her "most blatantly sexual book," he describes it as "a toccata and fugue on the mysterious and unfathomable nature of sexual desire." Noting superficial similarity to Nabokov's *Lolita*, he finds Oates's eroticism to be like that of D. H. Lawrence. The novel was heralded by many critics for the realism and power of Oates's boxing descriptions. Updike commented that, on the strength of her fight scenes, the sport should be outlawed. But Sven Birkerts notes that in this novel Oates relies "much less on the kind of violence that saturated . . . *them* and *Wonderland*. The violence is now carried inward, where it has a chance of being countered by other psychic forces."

Lives of the Twins (1987) was published under the pen name Rosamond Smith, perhaps because the spare style of this book contrasts so drastically with her usual abundance. On one level it is a horror story of psychological suspense; on another it is a metaphysical novel about identity and freedom, and their illusions. Molly Marks falls in love with her therapist, Johnathan McElwain, and learns that he has a twin, James, who is also a therapist. The twins have nothing to do with each other because of a hurt James inflicted on Johnathan in the past. When Molly seeks out James to discover what that hurt was, she becomes a pawn in the brothers' lifelong war for domination. Oates unifies the novel with many sets of doubles–characters, actions, pets, lunches, deceptions. Susan Fromberg

Schaeffer sees the novel as an exploration of the deepest desires of human beings and what happens when people drop the masks they normally wear.

Oates's most recent novel, *American Appetites* (1989), includes familiar elements of her style and some variations. Oates focuses on Ian and Glynnis McCullough, married for twenty-six years, whose relationship comes to an abrupt end rather than the slow deterioration characteristic in many of Oates's novels. Despite the pervasive violence in most of her works, the fight between Ian and Glynnis is the only act of violence in the novel, the bulk of which is Ian's trial for the murder of his wife, whom he has killed in self-defense. In a variation of her hunger theme, Oates shows that Ian and his friends have only appetites—not hunger; they have no imagination or passion.

Novels represent only a part of Oates's literary production. Her short stories are considered by many to be her most polished pieces; she has written and published hundreds of tales and has assembled a number of them in ten volumes. Her style, technique, and subject matter achieve their strongest effects in this concentrated form, for the extended dialogue, minute detail, and violent action, which irritate the reader after hundreds of pages, are wonderfully appropriate in short fiction. The disoriented and disturbed characters whom the reader follows with exasperation and doubt through the novels captivate him when depicted concisely at the moment of crisis. Her short stories present the same violence, perversion, and mental derangement as her novels and are set in similar locations: the rural community of Eden County, the chaotic city of Detroit, and the sprawling malls and developments of modern suburbia. An additional milieu explored in her tales is that of the academic world; many of her pieces concern the shallow nature of her fellow professors and their inability to communicate to their students or among themselves. While experimenting more freely in her stories than in her novels, Oates creates pieces of consistently high quality that the compactness of the genre enables her to maintain. According to Oates, "Each of the story collections is organized around a central theme and is meant to be read as a whole—the arrangement of the stories being a rigorous one, not at all haphazard."

In *By the North Gate* (1963), her first collection of short stories, Oates establishes themes she will explore in many subsequent works. Set in Eden County, these stories show some characters confronting evil and violence beyond their control while others must confront the vacuousness of their lives. In most, the main characters encounter people radically different from themselves, and their perception of the world is shaken. Few can articulate their anxieties and confusion, yet most are longing for another, a lost, "Eden."

Upon the Sweeping Flood and Other Stories (1966), the second collection, introduces characters seeking order through violence, family, and love. Oates continues her inarticulate characters' search for order and explores the emptiness some find within themselves. She emphasizes the interrelationships among people, beginning her focus on family ties and the mysterious emotions of love still under examination in her most recent works. Academic life and religion, institutions she will repeatedly criticize, do not provide the refuge some characters seek; neither does food. In these first two collections Oates establishes the theme for many of her works: the isolation of an individual complicated by an inability to control, or even understand, their experiences.

Oates uses stories in *The Wheel of Love and Other Stories* (1970) to experiment with point of view, narrative structure, and other conventions. Yet the collection finds thematic unity in what Joanne V. Creighton describes as "the mysterious, volatile, and disorienting power of love." Those characters able to feel seek escape from love, often through death. Many, however, have so cut themselves off from experience that they are "emotionally sterile."

Two of her most anthologized stories—"In the Region of Ice" and "Where Are You Going, Where Have You Been?"—show Oates at her best in this collection. Sister Irene has isolated herself from feeling; Connie is too shallow to understand her emotions. Connie is helplessly drawn into experience, but Sister Irene lacks the courage to participate. "How I Contemplated the World from the Detroit House of Correction and Began My Life Over Again" shows Oates's innovations in viewpoint and structure: scattered notes for an essay by an unnamed teenaged narrator. In all the stories Oates demonstrates her mastery of psychological realism.

In *Marriages and Infidelities* (1972), her fourth collection, Oates presents twenty-four stories in which she writes about death, madness, and obsessive relationships in working-class and lower-middle-class lives. These people, Peter Straub observes in *New Statesman* (23 August

1974), are not usually found in fiction written by women, but they are familiar characters from her novels. The most outstanding stories are what Oates calls "re-imagining" of stories by five famous authors: James, Kafka, Thoreau, Joyce, and Chekhov. She borrows plots and atmosphere from the original stories but translates them into contemporary works, with contemporary psychology. Through these, she works with her theme of the individual's relation to community while at the same time establishing her own relation to the community of writers, her literary heritage. Re-imagining becomes for Oates an important technique, as shown in her current cycle of novels which explore the genres of the family saga, the detective story, the Gothic romance, and the horror story.

The Goddess and Other Women (1974) collects twenty-five stories, about unliberated women, in which Oates presents various images of Kali, the Hindu goddess of the dark side of feminine nature. Continuing a theme introduced in *The Wheel of Love*, Oates writes about girls at the point of discovering their sexuality and its power. Other women are passive, frightened, or withdrawn as a result of living in a vacuum, sometimes self-created. Professional women find that success only makes their lives more difficult; Oates sees them as intruders into the male world of professionalism, different from men biologically, emotionally, socially. Through these women who are unable to come to terms with their entire sexuality—being stuck in the dark side, Kali's side—Creighton believes Oates "exposes the sexual roots of female nonliberation."

The Hungry Ghosts: Seven Allusive Comedies, also published in 1974, focuses upon academics, another unliberated group. In these stories she ridicules the character types and situations common to academic life, which may narrow their appeal for some readers. As these characters hunger for degrees, jobs, publications, fame, Oates exposes their accompanying insecurities, vindictiveness, and sexism. Drawing on a world she knows well, Oates sets four stories at a fictional university in Ontario; Oates herself taught in Windsor from 1967 to 1978.

For *The Poisoned Kiss and Other Stories from the Portuguese* (1975) Oates takes credit only as the translator of these works by "Fernandes de Briao." But, as Julian Barnes notes in *New Statesman* (21 May 1976), they take place in "Oates territory of obsession, extremity, solitude, and violence." These stories investigate the mysterious and sometimes unwanted attraction one feels for what is alien. The bond—the "kiss"—between a character and what is alien becomes "poisoned" because the experience is disquieting and brings no happiness with it. And the kiss may cause the character to metamorphose, such as the young man in "Distance" who is transformed into one of the vagrants who so disgust him.

In *The Seduction and Other Stories* (1975) Oates returns to her exploration of working-class lives. Elizabeth Pochoda (*New York Times Book Review*, 31 August 1975) finds this collection to contain "some of her best revelations of the complexity in lives ordinarily thought to be without depth or value," with characters like those in her early novels who are "inarticulate yet highly complex." In the title story Oates develops the theme of the city and how its size is part of its destructive power, causing feelings of anonymity, missed connections, and isolation.

Oates organizes *Crossing the Border: Fifteen Tales* (1976) by spreading the seven stories about the deteriorating marriage of Renee and Evan Maynard throughout the fifteen stories in the collection. The familiar themes of isolation and love run through the episodes about their separation and reunion. By interrupting their narrative with unrelated stories, Oates is able to explore their relationship in detail without a novel's demands for structure and character development.

Night-Side: Eighteen Tales (1977) is Oates's collection of horror stories. As the title indicates, these are tales, not stories, in the vein of Poe and Hawthorne. John Romano describes the characters as a "gallery of people haunted, spooked, driven mad or victimized in general by invasions from outside the sane, rational borders of consciousness." These are not literal ghost stories; in them characters must confront "what they can't deny or suppress" about themselves, and most of them lose.

The same kind of sequencing is evident in *All the Good People I've Left Behind* (1979), in which Oates examines her theme of disintegrating relationships through two series of stories which come together in the final story. The Annie Quirt stories concern a single woman's succession of lovers, all failed relationships. "High" and "Intoxication" concern the estrangement of partners in dissolving couples. The last story, which gives the volume its title, traces the history of two couples from graduate school, when they are good friends, to mid-life, when the ties of neither friendship nor marriage bind them, for each has become alienated from the others. Never really losing their innocence, they move from one wrong idea of life to another. Their happiness at the beginning of the story is destroyed, yet they neither learn nor grow. Knowledge and experience bring only pain; all the stories in the book carry out this essential idea. By and large, the characters are intelligent, neurotic sufferers. Unable to learn from their mistakes, they simply go on to other, more disastrous mistakes. And they are unable to sustain the relationships which might support them in their despair.

A Sentimental Education (1980), a collection of six stories, received mixed reviews. One of the stories, "The Precipice," could easily have given the book its title, for all six stories reflect the statement that Wesley quotes in that story: "We run carelessly to the precipice, after we have put something before us to prevent us seeing it." All the characters shield themselves in some way from truths they prefer not to see; the ultimate revelation of the truth is the climax of each story. The word *education* in the title of the collection is also appropriate, but most of the characters learn too late.

The title novella is about Duncan Sargent's murder of his cousin Antoinette. Duncan, a bright nineteen-year-old who has dropped out of Johns Hopkins because of a nervous breakdown, is spending the summer in Maine with his mother, her widowed sister, and the sister's two daughters, the older of whom is fourteen-year-old Antoinette. A secret affair develops between Duncan, who indulges in alternate fantasies of tender love and sadism, and Antoinette, who is also caught by mercurial sexual impulses which frighten her. During a secret meeting on a rocky area of the beach, Duncan at last penetrates Antoinette. She is scared by the pain, and when she threatens to tell, Duncan pounds her head against the rocks, killing her. Circumstances lead everyone to believe strangers are guilty of the murder; Duncan is not suspected at all, and the family cannot understand why he grieves so much over the death of a cousin he has seemingly ignored. In the past he suppressed his feelings rather than trying to deal with them, and when they were let go, murder resulted. He sees the precipice too late, and there is nothing he can do now to turn time back.

Last Days: Stories (1984), according to Greg Johnson, "suggests the dual focus characteristic of all of [Oates's] fiction: the detailed, compelling presentation of individuals plunged into various kinds of emotional and psychological upheaval, combined with the larger social, political, and philosophical crises for which these individual narratives serve as nightmarish emblems." Through this collection Oates examines the "personal and political barriers to wholeness, health, integrity." The five stories in the first section present people at their moments of crisis, points so extreme that they cannot survive; the characters are experiencing, in fact, their last days. The title story, based on the same actual Detroit case which was the source for "In the Region of Ice," illustrates a phenomenon Oates discusses in *New Heaven, New Earth: The Visionary Experience in Literature* (1974), the "death throes of romanticism." Exploring again another theme from *The Wheel of Love*, in "The Man Whom Women Adored," she presents a character who has deliberately cut herself off from feeling. The stories in the second group place American intellectuals in Eastern Europe in order to examine the philosophical as well as political conflicts between East and West and the relationships between personal and historical tragedy.

In *Raven's Wing* (1986) Oates gathers eighteen stories on the theme of "the improvised nature of human life." All the characters seem caught by the illusion of appearance and fear of desolation. Many of them are undereducated, physically and psychologically flawed, and presented in their gritty reality, with no humor or ironic relief. Yet Oates makes them matter to the reader. Stephen Goodwin of the *Washington Post Book World* (3 November 1986) assesses them as "crackling with rage" and a "charged-up, visceral excitement" and credits Oates with giving "the confused passions of late adolescence an unusual respect and dignity."

Oates's most recent short-story collection, *The Assignation* (1988), has not received as favorable criticism as her previous volumes. The stories are very short, most only seven or eight pages, and contain familiar characters and little action. The relationship she explores in these stories is for the most part physical, described by James Atlas in the *New York Times Book Review* (2 October 1988) as passion "unpleasant in its intensity," desire as "an omen of betrayal"; instead of being liberating, sex imposes bondage. On the whole, critics see this book as a collection of "literary exercises" and "notebooks for the novels," not Oates at her best.

Oates's writings are by no means limited to fictional forms. Her poems, generally held to be

233

her weakest efforts, also appear continually and have been partially collected in six volumes. Her critical essays often reveal an artist's imaginative insight into the classics of other times and into the work of contemporaries; in addition to many essays which have appeared in periodicals, she has published five critical volumes, as well as *On Boxing* (1987).

Oates's first volume of poetry, *Anonymous Sins and Other Poems*, did not attract much attention when it first appeared in 1969, although Robert French remarked that "the volume is charged with a nervous excitement that draws the reader irresistibly into its fictions." The poems owe more to their ability to startle with discord than to any power to captivate. Repeated themes—horror, isolation, love, violence, and suffering—unify what is otherwise a disjointed effort. Most of the poems are indeed anonymous confessions of sins, told by narrators whose transgressions are violent wrenchings of the psyche. Side by side with language that is occasionally flat and abstract are some of the most startling images in contemporary poetry, images that begin in the commonplace and end in horror, as in "A Married Woman's Song":

I need help. Marriage auspiciously
Drapes you in white, and then
          rapes you with hung
Bodies of broken birds.

Her imagery focuses on the human anatomy—skin, bones, eye sockets, the rind and pulp of the human body—as a symbol of a humanity at war with its soul. From this focus comes a surface whose grotesquerie is as likely to alienate as it is to entice.

Her next volume of poetry, *Love and Its Derangements* (1970), was widely received, although the attention was not always favorable. Arthur Oberg (*Southern Review*, Winter 1973) believes that "If Miss Oates wishes to move poetry toward something that is more readable and available, terrible costs to the language are involved." In contrast, Jerome Mazzaro says that the volume "provides an important interesting alternative to what, since Ezra Pound's *Homage to Sextus Propertius*, has become a narrow, near monotonous attack on the misuses of language." The poems of *Love and Its Derangements* are short, intense vehicles for often violent inner perceptions, clearly accessible, but sometimes at the expense of genuine lyricism. The emphasis of *Love and Its Derange-* *ments* is clearly on the derangements, although the work ends positively with a series of poems entitled "A Landscape of Love." From love's passionate beginnings, there is a breaking apart in which the love is repeatedly lost in the trivia of the mundane world–in thoughts of suicide, in violent anger, and in psychological struggle. The lovers continually dive into the pool of their feelings, only to be cast back up by the depths. Always there is a fear of being trapped and typed to the detriment of the self's conception of its own identity. Despite the obstacles, however, there is an even stronger desire to maintain the struggle for love in the face of what seem to be impossible odds.

In *Angel Fire* (1973) Oates offers poetry that demonstrates her true lyrical gifts. The lines are surer, sharper, and less abstract than in her previous poems. They have, in fact, the sensual quality of D. H. Lawrence, from whom she takes the epigraph for the volume: "Ours is the universe of the unfolded rose / the explicit / the candid revelation." The first section, "Lovers' Bodies," moves from the physical features of the human anatomy to its reverberations in the spiritual, psychological, and emotional life. Like the poems of the first section, those of the second, "Domestic Miracles," represent brief moments of epiphany. Common events of everyday life, such as merely moving about the house or driving on a mountain highway, suddenly reveal entire landscapes that have become invested with psychological meaning and new perceptions. The third section, "Revelations," begins with the realization of the ultimate aloneness of human beings. In an impersonal world the self struggles to maintain its separate identity yet tries simultaneously to identify with the external world and to become one with it. The ultimate victory over these forces, which tend to pull the self apart, comes, not through some newfound peace, but through a terror that returns the self to wholeness, as in "The Secret Sweetness of Nightmares":

Yet the nightmare redeems
for it is everything you have accomplished
leading up close behind you
shallow footprints
it is in the finite shape
of your body as it lies, private
sweetened by a terror
no chaos
can interrupt.

The Fabulous Beasts (1975), perhaps Oates's most accomplished work, begins in a winter world of the soul. Images of snow and ice predominate as the attempt to communicate meets with pain and silence. Yet the silence itself becomes a bond between people that draws them closer together than any language. There is in this work a feeling that one must return again and again to the beginnings, back beyond the common language to the common soul.

The isolation, the suffering for an identity, the love, and the pain all culminate in *Women Whose Lives Are Food, Men Whose Lives Are Money* (1978). As the title suggests, women are devoured, and men spend themselves freely to consume women. Of all Oates's works, this is her darkest. The poems move from a preoccupation with social roles through a series of transformations that are accompanied by horror. In "The Resurrection of the Dead," the third section of the volume, the soul angrily demands the things of the earth as well as the things of the spirit. The result is a soulless America crowded with useless consumer objects, an America where "immense with appetite we hurry to devour / cockleshells and periwinkles and tiny moons are shattered / beneath our feet."

In *The Invisible Woman: New and Selected Poems 1970-1982*, published in 1982, Oates collects poems from previous works and contributes new ones, all on the theme of invisibility. In this collection she is considered at her best when writing out of her most personal experiences. Although she continues to receive criticism for focusing too much on abstract concepts and emotions, this volume echoes the themes in her fiction.

On the whole, Oates's poetry is not the strength of her canon. Certainly, she has a flair for lyricism, and her images often startle the reader into sensibility, but the subject matter is often too conventional and the language flat and abstract.

Three Plays (1980) includes three plays which were produced Off Broadway during the 1970s: *Ontological Proof of My Existence* (1972); *Miracle Play* (1974); *Triumph of the Spider Monkey* (1979). Violent to the point of surrealism, the plays explore what Oates calls "rites of sacrifice" and "the inexpressible coherence of 'fate': the disharmonic music that is torn from us at certain moments in our lives and in history." Although they have merit on their own, they also make interesting thematic footnotes to her prose fiction.

As one would expect, the critical writing of Oates is imaginative and revealing. She has written on a wide variety of subjects ranging from Shakespeare to Beckett, and each of her essays elucidates both the work under discussion and her own novels, short stories, and poems. While Oates's critical pieces are not examples of careful, exhaustive scholarship, they are the products of a widely read, creative mind that considers deeply the forms and values of literature and renders erudite and fresh discussions of the works she approaches.

The Edge of Impossibility: Tragic Forms in Literature (1972) is her first collection of critical essays. Including some work written as a graduate student, she discusses Shakespeare, Melville, Dostoyevski, Chekhov, Yeats, Mann, and Ionesco. In these early works she establishes her critical approach: to subject rarely questioned assumptions about an author to close scrutiny. One problem she finds for modern writers is difficulty in creating tragedy out of characters whose lives are more or less equal and whose God is dead. Oates herself rejects nihilism; death is not a means for transcendence. Instead, her characters resist despair through dreaming.

New Heaven, New Earth: The Visionary Experience in Literature is another collection of essays on famous writers: James and Woolf, Lawrence (previously published separately as *The Hostile Sun*, 1973), Beckett, Plath, O'Connor, Mailer, Dickey, and Kafka. In them Oates elaborates on the relationship between the artist and the receiver of the art, a sacred relationship for which the artist must take responsibility. The artist's mission, Oates says, is "to force up into consciousness the most perverse and terrifying possibilities of the epoch, so that they can be dealt with and not simply feared" even if, as a result, the artist is denounced.

Contraries: Essays (1981), a collection of seven essays written over a period of about twenty years and intermittently revised, were originally stimulated, Oates tells the reader, "by feelings of opposition and, in two or three cases, a deep and passionate revulsion." Her initial responses to such varied works as Oscar Wilde's *The Picture of Dorian Gray*, Dostoyevski's *The Possessed*, and Lawrence's *Women in Love* provoked questions to which she responds with close attention to specific texts.

The Profane Art: Essays and Reviews (1983) puts together another group of Oates's critical works. In these her evaluations seem clearly biased by her own philosophy of writing, views at times self-vindicating, but that is not necessarily a problem. As Robert Dawidoff observes in the *Los Angeles Times Book Review* (29 May 1983), "She is evangelical rather than scholarly and a lucid advocate of making people want to read good books . . . [The conversation about books she envisions is] among friends, with whom the formalities of argument are not so important."

On Boxing grew out of Oates's research for *You Must Remember This*, in which a main character, Felix, is a former boxer. She assesses boxing historically, from ancient Greece and Rome to today, concluding that the introduction of the referee in the nineteenth century is what "makes boxing possible" because he frees the boxer's conscience. Although her father used to take her to the fights, she admits to starting out with a feminist preconception: "I was interested in the sociology of masculine violence, and then I got more sympathetic with it, and saw it as really inevitable and quite natural." Criticized for overlooking the vulgarity of boxing dominated by television and promoters, she finds even in today's version of the sport that it has merit as tragic theater.

In a 1988 collection of essays, *(Woman) Writer: Occasions and Opportunities*, Oates gathers thirty-five pieces, all previously published, covering a wide range of topics. Some of the more academic include philosophic discussions of art, of writing in particular, and of the works of Dickinson, Kafka, Hemingway, Charlotte Brontë, and Thoreau, among others. There are prefaces to her novels and an account of the screen adaption of "Where Are You Going, Where Have You Been?" as *Smooth Talk* (1986). She covers topics as diverse as Mikhail Gorbachev, Winslow Homer, a hundred-thousand-dollar Ferrari, and Mike Tyson. In all, one critic says, her opinions are "marred–or enlightened," depending on the reader's bias, by a feminist sensibility.

With each succeeding work Oates demonstrates her growing ability to write highly artistic, yet socially relevant, fiction: her potential is limited only by her energy and her control. Of her energy there is no question; already her output resembles the prodigious collections of the prolific novelists of the nineteenth century. Of her control, however, many still entertain doubts; careful rewriting and precise editing are not often evident in her published novels. That Oates is today a major American novelist is an established fact, for her powerful imagination presents compelling visions of contemporary society which cannot

be ignored; yet her continuing success and her position in the future depend upon her ability to impose a rigorous artistic restraint upon her compositions.

Interview:

Leif Sjöberg, "An Interview with Joyce Carol Oates," *Contemporary Literature*, 23 (Summer 1982): 267-284.

Conducted during composition of *Bellefleur*, briefly touches on many topics.

Bibliography:

Francine Lercangee and Bruce F. Michelson, *Joyce Carol Oates: An Annotated Bibliography* (New York: Garland, 1986).

Lists Oates's literary works (through 1986) and annotates her critical essays and reviews (through 1985); for secondary sources, annotates critical books (through 1984) and articles (through 1983) and lists interviews, bibliographies, reviews, and dissertations. Note: some short critical articles are listed in the reviews.

References:

Katherine Bastian, *Joyce Carol Oates's Short Stories Between Tradition and Innovation* (Frankfurt am Main: Lang, 1983).

Limited to the stories in eight collections, includes discussions of Oates's "re-imagining" of stories by James, Kafka, Thoreau, Joyce, and Chekhov; transformation of story genres such as encounters with the extraordinary, recognition, and initiation; and her grouping of stories in cycles.

Eileen Teper Bender, *Joyce Carol Oates, Artist in Residence* (Bloomington: Indiana University Press, 1987).

Focusing almost exclusively on the novels (through *Marya: A Life*, 1986), argues Oates's predominant theme as an individual's struggle for order and control in a chaotic world, and her predominant technique as revision of genres, connecting Oates with many other writers and literary schools.

Sven Birkerts, Review of Oates's *You Must Remember This*, New York Times Book Review, 16 August 1987, p. 3.

Emphasizes the intensity and pace of the novel and the change in the kind of violence Oates employs–from outward to inward.

Rose Marie Burwell, "Joyce Carol Oates and an Old Master," *Critique,* 15, no. 1 (1973): 48-58.
Claiming the novel is moral allegory, not realism, looks at "those instances in which the imagery and plot of [*A Garden of Earthly Delights*] touch most closely the iconography and intention of" the painting by Hieronymous Bosch, using them to explain the novel's climax.

Cara Chell, "Un-tricking the Eye: Joyce Carol Oates and the Feminist Ghost Story," *Arizona Quarterly,* 41 (Spring 1985): 5-23.
Citing influences on this novel by several other women writers, claims that Oates "has matured into writing feminist fiction," in this case a detective novel about the invisibility of women, relying on the techniques of the unreliable narrator and the supernatural.

Walter Clemons, "Joyce Carol Oates: Love and Violence," *Newsweek,* 80 (11 December 1972): 72-77.
Discusses biographical influences, writing process, themes, and relation to other writers, for the most part in Oates's own words.

Joanne V. Creighton, *Joyce Carol Oates* (Boston: Twayne, 1979).
After placing Oates in biographical and critical context, discusses only fiction works through 1976, focusing on characteristic style and themes; includes annotated bibliography.

Sharon Dean, "Faith and Art: Joyce Carol Oates's *Son of the Morning,*" *Critique,* 28 (Spring 1987): 135-147.
Examines the relationship between religious faith and the artistic process, the dilemma between love of God and love of humanity, the tension between humility and pride, emphasizing the motif of casting off and renaming.

Constance Ayers Denne, "Joyce Carol Oates's Women," *Nation,* 219 (7 December 1974): 597- 599.
Cataloging the women in most of Oates's works but emphasizing *Do With Me What You Will,* argues that Oates is concerned with bringing artistic traditions back to life as well as bringing them to life and that through her women characters, liberated and unliberated, Oates shows the way to freedom through awakened human consciousness.

John Ditsky, "The Man on the Quaker Oats Box: Characteristics of Recent Experimental Fiction," *Georgia Review,* 26 (Fall 1972): 297-313.
In an article covering several writers, posits that Oates (in particular in *Wonderland*) is "superficially similar to realistic fiction, yet tonally aligned with the experimentalists" because "her fiction shares the latter group's concern with inner states," sharing with them "the shattered vision" of contemporary life.

Thomas R. Edwards, "The House of Atreus Now," *New York Times Book Review,* 16 August 1981, pp. 1, 18.
In updating Agamemnon's story to encompass American government, business, finance, ideology, and organized crime, Oates presents a "thriller, a romance of desire and betrayal in high society, psychological examination of alienated youth, a study of marital failure in a declining aristocracy, an uncovering of the personal roots of public violence," as well as a philosophical look at the impossibility of justice.

Dean Flower, "Fables of Identity," *Hudson Review,* 39 (Summer 1986): 309-321.
Discusses structure of *Marya: A Life* and theme of Marya's search for her own identity.

Robert H. Fossum, "Only Control: The Novels of Joyce Carol Oates," *Studies in the Novel,* 7 (Summer 1975): 285-297.
Considering only the first five novels, claims they portray the psychological conflict of characters "bewildered by American experience" who are caught between "desire for the order, permanence, and communion of the Home" and "desire for the excitement, movement, and autonomy of the Road."

Doreen A. Fowler, "Oates's 'At the Seminary,' " *Explicator*, 41 (Fall 1982): 62-64.
Discusses theme as nature vs. religion (denial of nature), focusing on symbols.

Robert French, "The Novelist-Poet," *Prairie Schooner*, 44 (Summer 1970): 177-178.
In a positive review of *Anonymous Sins*, finds these poems—or "free verse meditations"—"difficult to grasp" because "they deal with delicate shades of mood, feeling, and perception" while charged with tension, not meditative calm, focusing on the themes of pain, dark, dream, and love.

Ellen G. Friedman, *Joyce Carol Oates* (New York: Ungar, 1980).
Covering only novels through 1976, concludes that Oates's fiction "affirms that man is located in a universe that he can neither transcend nor control and from which there is no separation or redemption."

John Gardner, "The Strange Real World," *New York Times Book Review*, 20 July 1980, pp. 1, 21.
Review of *Bellefleur* as "medieval allegory of . . . love and selflessness versus pride and selfishness" in the characters' struggle for order, concludes the novel is an "heroic attempt to transmute the almost inherently goofy tradition of the gothic . . . into serious art."

Christina Marsden Gillis, " 'Where Are You Going, Where Have You Been?': Seduction, Space, and a Fictional Mode," *Studies in Short Fiction*, 18 (Winter 1981): 65-70.
Discusses Oates's narrative technique as that of transforming fairy tale and dream into seduction story (an eighteenth-century genre), focusing on the violation of one's space, whether literal (screen door marks the line between innocence and experience) or interior (Arnold knows too much, violating Connie's consciousness).

Victoria Glendinning, "In Touch with God," *New York Times Book Review*, 13 August 1978, p. 10.
Review of *Son of the Morning*, focusing on theme of hunger.

Mary Gordon, "The Life and Hard Times of Cinderella," *New York Times Book Review*, 2 March 1986, p. 7.
Favorable review of *Marya: A Life*, claims the story is a fairy tale about a poor but bright young girl, a romance between a daughter and the mother who abandons her.

Mary Kathryn Grant, R.S.M., *The Tragic Vision of Joyce Carol Oates* (Durham: Duke University Press, 1978).
Discussing selected works from all genres through 1975, explores Oates's violent language and three themes—woman, city, community—as they merge violently into "an all-too-real nightmare."

David K. Gratz, "Oates' 'Where Are You Going, Where Have You Been,' " *Explicator*, 45 (Spring 1987): 55-56.
Expands on Larry Rubin's article (*Explicator*, Summer 1984), explaining the story as a dream about all of Connie's fears, not just of sex but of growing up in general—the traumas of adolescence.

C. Harold Hurley, "Cracking the Secret Code in Oates' 'Where Are You Going, Where Have You Been,' " *Studies in Short Fiction*, 24 (Winter 1987): 62-66.
Rebuts Mark Robson's analysis (*Explicator*, Summer 1982), interpreting the code as signifying sexual deviation, not referring to scriptures.

Diane Johnson, "Balloons and Abductions," *New York Times Book Review*, 5 September 1982, pp. 1, 15-16.
Review of *A Bloodsmoor Romance*, identifies the theme as "the lot of women" as they were restrained by nineteenth-century social attitudes and Oates's use of an unreliable narrator to ridicule those conventions.

Greg Johnson, *Understanding Joyce Carol Oates* (Columbia: University of South Carolina Press, 1987).
Focusing on eight of Oates's forty volumes, gives excellent overview of major themes and progress of her career, with an annotated bibliography.

William T. Liston, "Her Brother's Keeper," *Southern Humanities Review*, 11 (Spring 1977): 195-203.
Detailed comparison of "In the Region of Ice" as a re-imagining of Shakespeare's *Measure for Measure*, the point of both being that a Christian cannot practice her religion by withdrawing from the world.

Carol A. Martin, "Art and Myth in Joyce Carol Oates's 'The Sacred Marriage,'" *Midwest Quarterly*, 28 (Summer 1987): 540-552.
Argues that re-imagining (from *Marriages and Infidelities*) of ancient myth and Dionysian rite can be understood in terms of Oates's theory of the transforming power of art.

Jerome Mazzaro, "Feeling One's Oates," *Modern Poetry Studies*, 2, no. 3 (1971): 133-137.
In reviewing *Love and Its Derangements*, presents its theme as the difficulty "of getting others to accept an individual as he conceives of himself," especially the subjugation of women by men, and connects Oates with Sartre, Albee, Lawrence, Pound, and Ginsberg.

Torborg Norman, *Isolation and Contact: A Study of Character Relationships in Joyce Carol Oates's Short Stories 1963-1980* (Goteburg: Acta Universitatis Gothoburgensis, 1984).
Basing her interpretation on pragmatic speech act theory, emphasizes the verbal interaction between characters as the means of their creation, covering (some in close detail) one hundred of Oates's stories.

Sue Simpson Park, "A Study in Counterpoint: Joyce Carol Oates's 'How I Contemplated the World from the Detroit House of Correction and Began My Life Over Again,'" *Modern Fiction Studies*, 22 (Summer 1976): 213-224.
States that the story's unity comes not from the form, the twelve divisions, but from interwoven motifs (e.g., animal and religious imagery), verbal echoes, and patterns of contrast.

Robert Phillips, Review of Oates's *You Must Remember This*, *America*, 157 (14 November 1987): 360-361.

Discusses the theme of various kinds of love, the integral part sex plays in the story, and comparisons with Dreiser, Nabokov, and Lawrence.

Samuel F. Pickering, Jr., "The Short Stories of Joyce Carol Oates," *Georgia Review*, 28 (Summer 1974): 218-226.
Although conceding some stories are "well-written and provocative," in general finds her work flat or melodramatic or too subjective–even on the level of sentence structures and individual words–to project meaning to a large audience.

Sanford Pinsker, "Suburban Molesters: Joyce Carol Oates' *Expensive People*," *Midwest Quarterly*, 19 (Autumn 1977): 89-103.
Emphasizes elements of parody and humor in the novel.

Mark Robson, "Oates's 'Where Are You Going, Where Have You Been?'" *Explicator*, 40 (Summer 1982): 59-60.
Explains the secret code of numbers on Arnold's car as references to Genesis and Judges.

John Romano, "A Way with Madness," *New York Times Book Review*, 23 October 1977, pp. 15, 18.
Review of *Night-Side*, notes Oates's connections with Poe and Hawthorne in these psychological horror stories.

Larry Rubin, "Oates's 'Where Are You Going, Where Have You Been?,'" *Explicator*, 42 (Summer 1984).
Interprets story as a daydream concerning Connie's fear of sex.

Susan Fromberg Schaeffer, "The Lover Had a Brother," *New York Times Book Review*, 3 January 1988, p. 5.
Review of *Lives of the Twins*, sees the novel as not just a suspense thriller but as a metaphysical exploration of freedom, identity, and their illusions, emphasizing Oates's use of many sets of doubles.

Allen G. Shepherd III, "Faulknerian Antecedents to Joyce Carol Oates's *Mysteries of Winterthurn*," *Notes on Contemporary Literature*, 17 (November 1987): 8-10.

Proposes sources for *Winterthurn* in Faulkner's "A Rose for Emily."

Elaine Showalter, "My Friend, Joyce Carol Oates: An Intimate Portrait," *Ms.* (March 1986): 44-50.
Including much biographical information, shows Oates evolving into a feminist writer, especially in her trilogy of feminine genres–*Bellefleur, Bloodsmoor, Winterthurn*–and *Solstice* and *Marya*.

Rebecca Pepper Sinkler, Review of Oates's *Solstice*, *New York Times Book Review*, 20 January 1985, p. 4.
Believes Oates has fulfilled Woolf's call for a new kind of fiction about women.

Janis P. Stout, "Catatonia and Femininity in Oates's *Do With Me What You Will*," *International Journal of Women's Studies*, 6 (May-June 1983): 208-215.
Calling Oates a feminist in spite of herself, explains that through extreme stereotyping of her main character (passivity, physical beauty) Oates shows feminine perfection to be disease and deformity.

Gordon O. Taylor, "Joyce 'after' Joyce: Oates's 'The Dead,'" *Southern Review*, 19 (Summer 1983): 596-605.
Detailed comparison of James Joyce's "The Dead" with Joyce Carol Oates's "The Dead."

Taylor, "Joyce Carol Oates: Artist in *Wonderland*," *Southern Review*, 10 (Spring 1974): 490-503.
Presents the major theme of the novel as metamorphosis, the main character's only means of survival, as reflected in the "inwardly spiraling, shell-like" structure of the novel.

Mike Tierce and John Michael Crafton, "Connie's Tambourine Man: A New Reading of Arnold Friend," *Studies in Short Fiction*, 22 (Spring 1985): 219-224.
Argues that Arnold in "Where Are You Going, Where Have You Been?" is not just a satanic figure but also can be seen as a creative figure and savior or a shadowy version of Connie herself; explains a number of associations between Arnold and Bob Dylan.

John Updike, "What You Deserve Is What You Get," *New Yorker*, 63 (28 December 1987): 119-123.
Review of *You Must Remember This*, calls the novel a 1950s fairy tale for women's options in life and emphasizes Enid's "flirtations" with death and nothingness–Oates's blending of the self-destructive and erotic impulses.

Marie Mitchell Olesen Urbanski, "Existential Allegory: Joyce Carol Oates's 'Where Are You Going, Where Have You Been?,'" *Studies in Short Fiction*, 15 (Spring 1978): 200-203.
Argues that in addition to being realistic the story is also allegorical–the seduction of Eve–and existential–the forces confronting Connie are beyond her control; an understandable article in spite of some technical language.

Linda W. Wagner, "Oates' *Cybele*," *Notes on Contemporary Literature*, 11 (November 1981): 2-8.
Describes novel as account of male mid-life crisis, in a mythic pattern but using a documentary, realistic tone.

Wagner, ed., *Critical Essays on Joyce Carol Oates* (Boston: G. K. Hall, 1979).
Collection of reviews and critical essays, some available only in this volume, gives an overview of Oates's career and concerns and her critical reception.

Carolyn Walker, "Fear, Love, and Art in Oates's 'Plot,'" *Critique*, 15, no. 1 (1973): 59-70.
Citing this story (from *Marriages and Infidelities*) as another example of the Outsider who turns to art (writing) as a means of creating order in life, argues that to understand "Plot," one must consider how the form of the story and the narrator's rhetoric reflect the theme, in this case art's failure to save the narrator.

G. F. Waller, *Dreaming America: Obsession and Transcendence in the Fiction of Joyce Carol Oates* (Baton Rouge: Louisiana State University Press, 1979).
Mentioning all genres but concentrating on the novels, discusses Oates's relation to many other writers, especially Lawrence, and argues that obsession is the means for transcendence; assumes a reader familiar

with the vocabulary and ideas of contemporary literary criticism.

Joyce M. Wegs, " 'Don't You Know Who I Am?': The Grotesque in Oates's 'Where Are You Going, Where Have You Been?,' " *Journal of Narrative Technique,* 5 (January 1975): 66-72.
Showing how the grotesque arises from debased religious imagery, the characters' moral poverty and superficiality, presents Arnold as more than a psychopathic killer— he is also the devil and the incarnation of Connie's erotic dreams and desires.

William R. White, "Place Names in *Childwold,*" *Notes on Contemporary Literature,* 15 (January 1985): 2.
Citing Oates's use of actual names of places in New York along with fictitious ones, discusses the implications of the names for fertility and riotous growth.

Paul D. Zimmerman, "Hunger for Dreams," *Newsweek,* 75 (23 March 1970): 108, 110.
Written in response to *them* receiving the National Book Award, emphasizes dream as Oates's impulse for writing.

Philip Roth

This entry was updated by Jeffrey Helterman (University of South Carolina) from his entries in DLB 2, American Novelists Since World War II *and* DLB Yearbook 1982.

Places			
	Central Europe	London	Jerusalem
	New Jersey	Connecticut	New York
	Chicago	Prague	Iowa

Influences and Relationships			
	Nicolay Gogol	Saul Bellow	Arthur Miller
	Franz Kafka	Milan Kundera	William Styron
	Henry James	Gustave Flaubert	Norman Mailer
	Bernard Malamud		

Literary Movements and Forms			
	Postmodernism	Literature of Iron	Jewish-American
	Deconstruction	Curtain Nations	Fiction
	Narrative		

Major Themes			
	Art for Art's Sake	Oedipal Conflict	Family Conflict
		The Diaspora	Alienation

Cultural and Artistic Influences			
	Ballet	Zionism	Judaism
	Baseball	Freudianism	Academia
	Rembrandt		

Social and Economic Influences			
	Jewish Assimilation	Suburbia	The Depression
	The Military	The Inner City	Nixonian Politics

See also the Roth entry in DLB 28, Twentieth-Century American-Jewish Fiction Writers.

BIRTH: Newark, New Jersey, 19 March 1933 to Beth Finkel and Herman Roth.

EDUCATION: A.B., Bucknell University, 1954; M.A., University of Chicago, 1955.

MARRIAGE: 22 February 1958 to Margaret Martinson Williams, divorced, 1966.

AWARDS: Houghton Mifflin Literary Fellowship for *Goodbye, Columbus,* 1959; National Institute of Arts and Letters grant, 1959; Guggenheim Fellowship, 1959; Daroff Award for *Goodbye, Columbus,* 1959; *Paris Review* Aga Khan Award for "Epstein," 1959; William and Janice Epstein Fiction Award for *Goodbye, Columbus,* 1960; National Book Award for *Goodbye, Columbus,* 1960; Ford Foundation grant, 1965; elected, National Institute of Arts and Letters, 1970; National Book Critics Award for *The Counterlife.*

BOOKS: *Goodbye, Columbus and Five Short Stories* (Boston: Houghton Mifflin, 1959; London: Deutsch, 1959);
Letting Go (New York: Random House, 1962; London: Deutsch, 1962);
When She Was Good (New York: Random House, 1967; London: Cape, 1967);
Portnoy's Complaint (New York: Random House, 1969; London: Cape, 1970);
Our Gang (New York: Random House, 1971; London: Cape, 1971);
The Breast (New York: Holt, Rinehart & Winston, 1972; London: Cape, 1973);
The Great American Novel (New York: Holt, Rinehart & Winston, 1973; London: Cape, 1973);
My Life as a Man (New York: Holt, Rinehart & Winston, 1974; London: Cape, 1974);
Reading Myself and Others (New York: Farrar, Straus & Giroux, 1975; London: Cape, 1975);
The Professor of Desire (New York: Farrar, Straus & Giroux, 1977; London: Cape, 1977);
The Ghost Writer (New York: Farrar, Straus & Giroux, 1979; London: Cape, 1979);
A Philip Roth Reader (New York: Farrar, Straus & Giroux, 1981; London: Cape, 1981);
Zuckerman Unbound (New York: Farrar, Straus & Giroux, 1981; London: Cape, 1981);

Philip Roth (photo copyright © by Jerry Bauer)

The Anatomy Lesson (New York: Farrar, Straus & Giroux, 1983; London: Cape, 1983);
Zuckerman Bound: A Trilogy and Epilogue (New York: Farrar, Straus & Giroux, 1985);
The Counterlife (New York: Farrar, Straus & Giroux, 1986; London: Cape, 1987).

TELEPLAY: *The Ghost Writer, American Playhouse,* PBS, 17 January 1984.

PERIODICAL PUBLICATIONS:
FICTION
"The Day It Snowed," *Chicago Review,* 8 (Fall 1954): 34-45;
"The Contest for Aaron Gold," *Epoch,* 5-6 (Fall 1955): 37-50;
"Heard Melodies Are Sweeter," *Esquire,* 50 (August 1958): 58;
"Expect the Vandals," *Esquire,* 50 (December 1958): 208-228;
"The Love Vessel," *Dial,* 1 (Fall 1959): 41-68;
"Good Girl," *Cosmopolitan,* 148 (May 1960): 98-103;
"Novotny's Pain," *New Yorker,* 38 (27 October 1962): 46-56;

"On the Air," *New American Review*, 10 (10 August 1970): 7-49;

" 'I Always Wanted You to Admire My Fasting'; or Looking at Kafka," *American Review*, 17 (May 1973): 103-126.

NONFICTION

"Mrs. Lindbergh, Mr. Ciardi, and the Teeth and Claws of the Civilized World," *Chicago Review*, 11 (Summer 1957): 72-76;

"The Kind of Person I Am," *New Yorker*, 34 (29 November 1958): 173-178;

"Writing American Fiction," *Commentary*, 31 (March 1961): 223-233;

"Writing About Jews," *Commentary*, 36 (December 1963): 446-452;

"Reading Myself," *Partisan Review*, 40, no. 3 (1973): 404-417.

In 1973, Philip Roth wrote a satirical novel about baseball which he entitled *The Great American Novel*. The title refers to the parodies of a number of classic American novels in the book, but it also may be an answer to critics who keep waiting for him to write the great American novel and keep castigating him when he doesn't. From the time of the publication of his second novel, *Letting Go*, critics have been wondering aloud when Roth is going to stop squandering his enormous gifts and create the legitimate American masterpiece. This is not to say that Roth's large and varied output has been unappreciated. *Letting Go* has been seen as one of the finest achievements in the novel of manners since James; *Our Gang* has been called Swiftian and Orwellian; *Portnoy's Complaint* has been regarded as a brilliant exploitation of the new freedom in language granted to the novelist in the 1960s. Yet through more than half of the reviews of everything written after *Goodbye, Columbus*, there remains the complaint– the complaint in fact of many of Roth's heroes who have more than enough to keep them contented and yet are always asking for more.

Philip Roth was born into a lower-middle-class Jewish family in Newark, New Jersey, on 19 March 1933 to Beth Finkel and Herman Roth, an insurance salesman. Although he was born during the heart of the Depression, Roth grew up in the slightly more prosperous times of World War II. His memories of Newark and the social stratification in the nearby suburbs are evident particularly in *Goodbye, Columbus* and in *Portnoy's Complaint*. After two years at the Newark branch of Rutgers University, Roth earned an A.B. at Bucknell University, where he was elected to Phi

Beta Kappa and edited the school's literary magazine. After receiving an M.A. in English from the University of Chicago, Roth joined the army in 1955 but was discharged after being injured in basic training. He returned to the University of Chicago in 1956, pursuing a Ph.D. and working as an instructor in English. His experiences at the University of Chicago play a large part in the background of his second novel, *Letting Go*. Roth dropped out of the Ph.D. program in 1957 and began reviewing films and television for the *New Republic*. In 1959, his career was launched auspiciously when his first book, the novella *Goodbye, Columbus* and five stories, won the National Book Award. The following two years Roth was on the faculty of the Writers' Workshop of the University of Iowa, and in 1962 he became writer in residence at Princeton, where he remained until 1964. Since then he has taught, first at the State University of New York at Stony Brook and then sporadically at the University of Pennsylvania. The financial turning point of Roth's career was in 1969 when *Portnoy's Complaint* became the number one best-seller and the enormously successful movie version of *Goodbye, Columbus* was released.

The title novella and the stories of *Goodbye, Columbus* (1959) all involve the attempt of the hero to invade and make sense of a culture alien to his own. In each case, both the invader and the alien culture are Jewish, but aside from this they have little in common. In some cases the invasion is unsuccessful, and the hero beats a somewhat hesitant retreat to his own milieu; in others the hero wins at least the admiration of the reader if not that of his contemporaries. In an interview accompanying a review of the book, Roth noted that he had already earned the distinction of being that most renegade of renegades, the anti-Semitic Jew, a charge which was to blossom with new fervor after the publication of *Portnoy's Complaint*.

In *Goodbye, Columbus*, Neil Klugman sets out from the lower-class confines of his Newark home and invades the upper-middle-class environs of Short Hills, New Jersey. He has fallen for Brenda Patimkin, the archetypal Jewish American Princess, the pampered girl who has been given everything. The Patimkin household is the gross fulfillment of the American dream of financial success, conspicuous consumption, and endless active leisure. Nevertheless, despite his awareness of the crassness of Brenda and everything she stands for, Neil does not transcend or reject the Patimkin world. Instead, he and Brenda break up in a silly argument, self-righteous on both sides. Neil creates a haven for himself in his job at the library, where he befriends a young Negro boy who comes to look at the lush tropical paintings of Paul Gauguin. Despite his sincerity, Neil is somewhat condescending to the boy but never realizes that the Patimkin's refrigerator is as much a false paradise for him as is Gauguin's Pacific island for the boy.

A more complete invasion of the opposing culture occurs in "Eli the Fanatic," in which the hero, a Jewish lawyer named Eli Peck, is asked by his middle-class, suburban community to get rid of the Yeshiva (a school for Orthodox Old World Jews) that is becoming a source of irritation for its assimilated neighbors. Peck finds that his legal background is no match for the unswerving belief of the Yeshiva's rabbi and eventually tries to gain some leverage by bribing the rabbi's messenger with a new suit. The messenger returns the favor by giving Peck his Old World costume, and Peck finds himself possessed by the spirit of the clothing. When he puts on the refugee's suit, Peck goes outside and sees the essence of his chrome-plated suburb–his neighbor giving her rocks a second coat of pink paint. As Eli, dressed in the ragged hand-me-downs, goes to see his newborn son at the hospital, his friends deal with him the only way they can: they declare him crazy, and the story ends with him going under from the effects of a hastily administered sedative. This story is close in tone to the mystical otherworldliness of Bernard Malamud's stories in *The Magic Barrel* (1958).

Another story of the odd-man-out is "The Conversion of the Jews," in which the hero, a twelve-year-old bar mitzvah student, begins to question the values of his religion and ultimately the powers of God himself. The antagonists are the boy, Ozzie Freedman, and his rabbi, Marvin Binder, whose names suggest their opposite approaches to life. Binder can provide nothing but unexamined answers to Ozzie's questions, while Ozzie is continually looking for something more. Ozzie wants to know why, for example, the Virgin Birth can be an impossibility for a God who can create the world in six days. Binder can respond only with exasperation and a call to Ozzie's parents. Finally Ozzie forces the rabbi and the rest of the community to assent to his beliefs by climbing to the roof of the synagogue and threatening to jump. Only when he extracts a promise that no one will ever hit anyone over a question of religion does Ozzie come down, jump-

ing into the waiting firemen's net. Unlike Neil Klugman, Ozzie has the courage of his convictions and ends the story a free man.

The most complex story in the collection is the often-anthologized "Defender of the Faith," which concerns Sheldon Grossbart, an army recruit who uses his Jewish heritage to weasel concessions from his Jewish sergeant, Nathan Marx. Although Marx sees through most of Grossbart's tricks, at least after the fact, he lets him get away with them, primarily because he is trying to recover the humanity he feels has been lost in his front-line battle experiences. When Grossbart goes beyond hustling favors to wangle the only stateside assignment among a group of men who are being sent to fight in the Pacific, Marx uses his influence and a Grossbart-like reliance on the Jewish "underground" to send Grossbart with the others to take his chances in the Pacific. Roth brilliantly sets up the mixed motivations for Marx's decision so that Marx can never be certain whether he has sent Grossbart out of spiteful vengeance or a need to see that justice is done. Marx has spent his whole stateside tour trying to relearn his grandmother's dictum that "mercy overrides justice" only to find that sometimes a man must opt for the more difficult choice of justice. In making this decision, Marx becomes the real defender of the faith–faith in human responsibility– and replaces Grossbart, whose nominal defense of his Jewish faith is simply a way to get favors and take care of himself.

After the almost unanimous praise for *Goodbye, Columbus,* Roth's second book, *Letting Go* (1962), was met with muted hostility and faint praise. Most reviewers granted Roth his undeniable eye for detail and his ear for real conversation but felt that these talents had been wasted in a large, overwritten novel. *Letting Go* is a deliberately Jamesian novel, a bleak comedy of manners in which the narrator, Gabe Wallach, has to learn the value of getting involved and also of getting out of involvements. James's *Portrait of a Lady* becomes a significant stage property in the novel–a letter from Wallach's mother is left, and a kind of Isabel Archer character, Libby Herz, reads it at an opportune moment. In addition, Wallach's Ph.D. dissertation is on James. If Libby finds the Jewish world of her husband Paul as much of an alien land as Isabel Archer finds Europe, then Wallach's most significant problems seem closest to those of Lambert Strether in *The Ambassadors:* Wallach tries to help out in other people's affairs without fully committing himself to anyone or anything.

The novel follows Wallach's relationships with three women: Marge Howells, a student of his with no problems other than a boring Midwestern upbringing; Martha Regenhart, a life-battered divorcée; and most important, Libby Herz, the troubled wife of a friend of his. As will be the case with many of Roth's heroes, Wallach is a man for whom life has not created many natural disasters, and he will, therefore, have to create his own problems and test his own limits. As the novel opens, he is a graduate student but one well off enough to have no need of cashing the checks his father sends him and intellectually fluent enough not to have to struggle to get a job. Later, he does just as well teaching at college. In this he is contrasted with Paul Herz, for whom everything goes wrong. Herz is a man with a talent for misery, who wanders around in a hand-me-down coat, the smell of egg salad sandwiches wafting up from the briefcase carrying his unfinished novel-dissertation. Herz gets a job on an auto assembly line and almost immediately injures his hand. He finds the crisis of trying to get his wife an abortion confused by two men who are arguing over how to divide the profits on a stock of remaindered underwear that one has sold.

Wallach sees himself as a humanist and is proud of his clash with the faculty members who concern themselves with form and punctuation, but his humanism is less valid when concerned with real life. His affair with Marge Howells, a girl with perfect teeth who is "in revolt against Kenosha, Wisconsin," is recorded primarily to show Gabe's natural proclivity to withdraw from any human relationship at the first sign of commitment on his side. Roth gives simultaneous examples of this character flaw when he places Wallach in his father's dental office with his father working on his teeth. Wallach thinks "I could have reached up and pulled him down and kissed him. But would he understand that I was not prepared to surrender my life to his? He was a wholehearted man, and such people are hard to kiss half-heartedly." Once his teeth are clean, Wallach calls Marge long-distance and breaks off his affair using his need to be with his father as an excuse for not returning to Chicago. Wallach is as halfhearted with her as he is with his father.

Wallach is filled with guilt about his inability to get involved, and he compensates for his lack of feeling with a superabundance of charity. He helps people, using tremendous energy but lit-

tle emotional commitment. His help usually causes further trouble, particularly when he tries to straighten out the troubled marriage of the Herzes. Early in the novel he tells himself "I had no business in the lives of these people and that I would not come back, no matter who invited me." Nonetheless, he feels guilty when his help does not increase the love and understanding in the Herz household, and he goes off to New York to reconcile Paul's parents to the idea that their son has married a Gentile. He tries to conduct a dignified conversation with Paul's mother, who talks to him while simultaneously giving her husband in the bathroom instructions for dealing with his constipation. The scene is one of many in the novel in which some minor concern undercuts the seriousness of the business at hand and often sabotages the hero's attempt to get the business of helping others done. Later, the toilet-training of a young child will interrupt Wallach's attempt to find an adoptive child for the Herzes.

In his involvement with Martha Regenhart, Wallach seems at first kind and considerate. Going beyond being merely a lover, he pays his share of the rent and food and acts as a father to her children. While this is going on, however, he never gives up his own unused apartment. He panics both when Martha lets her ex-husband take her children, leaving himself and Martha the freedom to become totally involved, and also when Martha seems ready to dismiss totally her most persistent other suitor, leaving Wallach as the man to marry her. Although Wallach sees himself as a man of sensitivity, he is instead a fault-finder who uses fine perceptions about the motivations of others to mask his boorishness. When his planned dinner for the Herzes turns into a disaster, he blames Martha for dressing the wrong way, he blames the Herzes for acting too genteelly poor, but does not admit that his subconscious motivation is both to fracture his relationship with Martha and to impress Libby with his freedom and suave worldliness.

In the most Jamesian inversion in the book, Wallach's greatest moral flaw turns out to be his failure to seduce his friend's wife. He grants Libby a stolen kiss early in the novel but then pulls back. Wallach gives Libby just enough support to allow her to question the value of staying with her doomed-to-failure husband, but he does not dare to take the step, adultery, which would free her. Wallach attempts to make up for his lack of emotional courage by working—as he sees it, crusading—to acquire a child for the couple to adopt and fill the emptiness he has helped build into Libby's life. Gabriel Wallach is ultimately satisfied with this substitution of help for commitment and feels that his name, that of the angel, is as fitting for him as is his favorite song, "Earth Angel."

Roth continued his analysis of people enamored of their own perfection in his next novel, *When She Was Good*–one of whose working titles was *Saint Lucy*. In *When She Was Good* (1967) Roth invades the American heartland the way Alexander Portnoy does when he goes off to visit his all-American girlfriend, Kay Campbell. Portnoy is somewhat disappointed not to find in the Midwest the narrowmindedness of a Sinclair Lewis or Sherwood Anderson novel, but Roth finds closed minds and a desperate lack of freedom in Liberty Center. Many reviewers noted that Roth seemed to be trying to prove that he could write about some other milieu than the urban Jewish settings that had been his forte, but far more important, although not noteworthy at the time, is that Lucy Nelson, the heroine of *When She Was Good*, remains one of the few three-dimensional female characters in Roth's writing.

Reviews were mixed, but most of the negative views saw the heroine as obsessive, deserving the condemnation of the novel's most despicable character, Julian Sowerby, who calls her "A little ball-breaker of a bitch. That's the saint you are, kiddo–Saint Ball-breaker." The problem for both the other characters in the novel and for the reviewers is that Lucy is not only an idealist, she is a female. Like Gabe Wallach in *Letting Go*, there is a good deal of snobbery about Lucy Nelson's attempt to improve everybody else, but Gabe draws nowhere the amount of hostility, apparently because he is a man. Lucy is a perfectionist who becomes outraged by the mediocrity, particularly the moral mediocrity, of others. She uses truth like a club, only to discover that no one in Liberty Center wants to hear it. For example, she fights back against her husband's uncle Julian, who has in effect stolen her child, by correctly accusing him of adultery but discovers that everyone, including his daughter and his wife, already knows about it. What she discovers is that the truth makes no one free in Liberty Center.

When She Was Good is the only one of Roth's novels which gives a woman an independent existence, that is, not simply a role, no matter how vividly drawn, in the life of a man. Roth begins by recording the history of the two previous generations of Lucy's family so that it is clear how she came to be the woman she is. From her grandfather, Willard Carroll, she has inherited a sense of civilized values, but unlike Willard, she has not learned to moderate these values in the face of human weakness. Willard is a figure of honesty and perspicacity, but he is willing to excuse the flaws of others. This attitude looks like compassion but may well be weakness. For example, he continually makes excuses for Lucy's father, Whitey, in the hopes that Whitey will reform, but by taking Whitey and his family into his home, Willard effectively robs his son-in-law of the motivation to reform. Willard constantly pleads for goodness, but as his wife reminds him, he is no hero: "You are not Abraham Lincoln. You are the assistant Postmaster in Liberty Center."

Lucy has no such sense of her limits. As a teenager, she becomes a Catholic and dreams of becoming St. Teresa, but she gives this up when she finds that the passive goodness of the saint is not enough and calls for the police to keep her drunk father from attacking her mother. She had "dedicated herself to a life of submission, humility, silence and suffering.... After calling upon Saint Teresa of Lisieux and Our Lord–and getting no reply–she called the police."

The main action of the novel details the collapse of Lucy's marriage to Roy Bassett, an ineffectual dreamer whom she married because she was pregnant. Roy dreams of becoming an important man but ends up with the absurd role of assistant to the "society" photographer in Fort Kean. Lucy tries to pierce Roy's empty dreams so that he might take steps to fulfill himself, but her self-righteousness only drives him and their four-year-old son out of the house. After a frantic and fruitless attempt to recover her family, Lucy walks off into the snow at Passion Paradise, where she and Roy first became involved, and there she dies of exposure.

Like Emma Bovary or Hedda Gabler, Lucy Nelson expects others to live up to her romantic high standards, particularly her obsession with truth. The weakness of the novel lies in the absence of a suitable foil for Lucy. Both her husband and her father are spineless in their own ways, and her grandfather's passive endorsement of goodness does not offer a valid alternative to Lucy's moral militancy. Only Julian Sowerby faces up to Lucy, but his responses are so crass as to make her courage in the face of them meaningless.

Furthermore, Lucy's monolithic, saintlike goodness prevents her from facing any moral crises or spiritual dilemmas. She locks her father out of the house, ignoring the fact that her weak, sentimental mother would rather have him back than have him good; she fights to get her son back but only to prove herself right–never does she weigh the importance of having him back against the importance of being right. The novel, therefore, though a fascinating portrait of the growth of an obsessive personality, fails to raise the central issues in the struggle of a morally superior person against a world of mediocrity.

Among the artifacts discovered by Alexander Portnoy in his sister's room is a copy of *A Portrait of the Artist as a Young Man; Portnoy's Complaint* (1969) does for the American Jewish bildungsroman what Joyce did for Irish Catholicism. Like Stephen Dedalus, Portnoy yearns for freedom from the repressive laws of his youth–and like Dedalus, Portnoy feels love as well as revulsion for that youth. In Portnoy's case, the laws are those of Jewish domesticity imposed by a mother whose domineering exterior hides a mass of guilt and fear. Her rules–eat your vegetables, beware of polio, don't fool around with shiksas, don't feel innocent when you can feel guilty–are the manifestation of a classic superego. Portnoy grows up to be not an artist but an Assistant Commissioner of Human Opportunity, and as such he becomes the Rothian hero–the man who helps those less fortunate than himself, without ever really getting involved with them. Little is seen of Portnoy's professional role, but his involvement with women, Gentiles all (until the last few pages), is based on the same condescending need to improve the other person, combined with a fear of total commitment. Portnoy claims that it is the pull of freedom that makes him avoid complete involvement, but it is fear, guilt, and a desire to avenge his father's powerlessness in Anglo-Saxon America. Portnoy searches endlessly for girls he can improve, the prime example being Monkey, an ignorant but passionate model from the coalfields of West Virginia. When the girls do not respond sufficiently to his tutelage, he has a reason for leaving them. Typically his response to their flaws is disproportionate. He leaves Monkey largely because of her illiteracy, the documentary evidence being her dreadfully misspelled note to her maid, but he forgets that she has been brought to orgasm by his recitation of Yeats's "Leda and the Swan," surely an example of a higher literacy. Portnoy gives all of the women type names such as "the Pumpkin" or "the Pilgrim," which stereotypes each as a certain

kind of American conquest for him. In doing this, he ignores their humanity: each is of interest only as she becomes an extension of Portnoy.

The source of Portnoy's repression is his parents. His father is an ineffectual insurance salesman who lives in fear of the home office and its WASP managers and suffers through a lifetime of constipation. His mother, Sophie, on the other hand, seems in complete control of her environment. Not only does she impress young Portnoy with all kinds of repressive fears and compulsions toward neatness and cleanliness, but she continually strives to impress him with her patience and generosity. It is no wonder that Portnoy seeks women as unlike his mother as can be imagined, and yet it is also not surprising that he is disappointed when they are not like her.

In his youth, Portnoy's desperate search for freedom is centered around masturbation, an activity both prohibited and also exclusively devoted to the service of the id rather than the superego. The strategy does not work, however, because it only wraps Portnoy further in self and because it is never carried out without guilt. Eventually Portnoy finds himself masturbating in public places, like buses, which indicates a subconscious hope that he might get caught.

As Portnoy matures, sex with the forbidden Gentile takes the place of masturbation but does not improve upon it: the girl remains a projection of Portnoy's ego, and when she has her own personality, he strives to make her as much like himself as he can. When Portnoy finally goes to Israel hoping to break out of his mold of seeking forbidden sex, the results are no better. Portnoy has become conditioned to a sense of impurity in his sexual gratification. Without it, he becomes impotent.

Portnoy's Complaint is a hilariously funny novel that is significant for its use of obscenity as part of its intrinsic meaning. Roth says "the book isn't full of dirty words because 'that's the way people talk;'" rather Portnoy, "is obscene because he wants to be saved." For Portnoy, obscenity is a violation of everything his mother stands for, and he hopes that by using this language, he can free himself from her influence. Like Stephen Dedalus, for whom the thought of death without a Catholic afterlife is a similar obscenity, he can never be free.

In an interview following the publication of *Our Gang* (1971), Roth reveals that the immediate reason for writing this political satire was Richard Nixon's decision to free William Calley from the stockade at the same time that he was siding with anti-abortion groups whose battle cry was "the right to life." Roth says "what that statement of his on Calley 'made perfectly clear' was that if it seemed to him in the interest of his career, he would sink to *anything*. If 50.1 percent of the voters wanted to make a hero out of a convicted multiple-murderer, then maybe there was something in it–for him." The resultant book is a series of satirical sketches which show the Nixon mentality at work in many public situations: news conferences, skull sessions, formal speeches, and finally, after the protagonist dies, on the comeback trail campaigning against Satan in Hell. Many of Roth's heroes struggle between their real selves and the fiction they have created about themselves, but Trick E. Dixon and, Roth suggests, Nixon himself, have only the rhetorical persona left.

The two epigraphs of *Our Gang* invite comparison to Swift and Orwell, and it is here that the book both stands and falls. The influence of Swift's *A Modest Proposal* is pervasive, and, like Swift, Roth is brilliant at building flawless logic on a basically absurd principle. The chain of logic remains intact whether the hero is distinguishing between troublemakers among fetuses, those who kick their mothers, and rank-and-file fetuses, the silent majority who merely move in the womb; or justifying an American invasion of Denmark on the grounds that we ought to possess Elsinore Castle because Shakespeare's play about it is in English, the American language. Not only is the Nixonian logic worked out to its absurd extreme, but the rhetoric is a deft parody of Nixon's style. What Roth hasn't learned from Swift is the devastating understatement that can deliver the most scathing attack without a touch of rant.

In an interview about the novel, Roth argues that *A Modest Proposal* would have been regarded in bad taste in its day, but he doesn't see that he is talking about the idea behind the satire, that Irish babies be used for food, not about the style which is like the persona, "modest." Precisely because it proposes the most unholy of solutions in the most timorous of accents does *A Modest Proposal* succeed in revealing the horrific mentality of those who can think this way. *Our Gang* is too shrill, and the bombast undercuts the attempt to reproduce Swiftian savagery. The chapter in which Dixon compiles his enemies list and proposes the extermination of the Boy Scouts is a good example of this rhetorical overkill. Only in

the final chapter, where Dixon campaigns in Hell and tries to prove that Satan does not know as much about evil as he does, does the irony reach Swiftian proportion: "Much as I respect and admire his lies, I don't think that lies are something to stand on. I think they are something to build on." What more need be said about the ambitions of evil men?

No novel of Roth's has caused as much consternation about the proper critical evaluation, about how to get a grasp on it, as has *The Breast* (1972), a story of metamorphosis in which the hero, David Kepesh, finds himself transformed into a massive female breast. The novel has been seen as an overextended single joke, whose tour de force qualities belong in a short story rather than a novel, and much critical rage would have been deflected if the work had appeared in a magazine as a long short story. Other reviewers saw the novel as a brilliant conception whose implementation had not been carried out properly. Finally some critics, including the novelists John Gardner and Margaret Drabble, saw the work as a worthy successor to the stories of Gogol and Kafka from which it germinated. R. Z. Sheppard said that Roth had outflanked reality without writing a dirty joke and found the work "more touchingly human than funny, whether read as a fable or credo." Sheppard comes close to Roth's own statement of his intentions. Roth, like Kepesh himself, notes the similarity to Kafka's story, "The Metamorphosis," and insists that the book must be taken seriously as a psychological study of the character and not as a symbolic statement about sexuality. "Not all the ingenuity of all the English teachers in all the English departments in America can put David Kepesh together again. . . . There is only the unrelenting education in his own misfortune. What he learns in the end is that, whatever else it is, it is the real thing: he *is* a breast, and must act accordingly."

What is significant about Kepesh is what he has lost–everything that has identified him in the past, everything that has made him a man–and he must come to terms with this loss in some way. His problem is how to maintain his continuity as a man and as a human being once he no longer has a man's body. Kepesh imagines completely radical solutions to his problem–sexual intercourse using his nipple and exploitation of his condition for financial gain–which call for making himself a breast rather than a man. What stops him is his fear that he might be separating himself from his own past and his own kind.

Almost as interesting as Kepesh's struggles with his identity are the reactions of those who have to deal with him. For the most part, the reactions are a commonplace sympathy that seems to signify an absurd emptiness in the lives of those who are afraid to deal with the absurdity of Kepesh's condition. Kepesh's friend and fellow academic, Schonbrunn, can do no more than visit and send a nice gift–a recording of Olivier's *Hamlet*–while Kepesh's father visits him as he would any other sick relative and regales him with tales of pregnancies, weddings, expensive caterers, and other everyday happenings. Only Kepesh's lover, Claire Ovington, seems to be able to accept Kepesh's condition for what it is, but she does not or cannot go beyond Kepesh's perceptions of his state.

Ultimately, then, it is up to Kepesh himself to face what has happened to him, and he finds himself in the paradoxical situation of not only separating dream from reality but also having the need to find himself mad rather than sane. Kepesh is a teacher of comparative literature, and it is easier for him to make intellectual sense of his going mad than it is to face the fact of his breast-reality. He posits a "mammary envy" which has manifested itself in the belief that he is a breast, and even a condition of "literary envy" where the critic out-creates his subject–by becoming a breast, he rationalizes he has out-Kafkaed Kafka. All of this is insufficient–the reality is not to be explained away, only lived, and it is by the very ordinariness of his comforters that Kepesh finally realizes that he is not mad, but far more frightening, sane. The callousness of Schonbrunn, the domesticity of his father, even the concern of Claire have none of the stuff of madness about them. The novel works only if the reader believes that Kepesh has indeed turned into a breast, and it is a tribute to Roth's skills that he can present the psychological portrait of a man in this state without resorting to teasing questions of whether this is dream or reality as does Gogol, for example, in his story, "The Nose," in which a man loses his nose and finds it walking about by itself. Kepesh may wonder if he is mad or dreaming, but the reader never does; he knows that the hero *has* become a breast.

Roth's next novel, *The Great American Novel* (1973), is, like Bernard Malamud's *The Natural* (1952) and Robert Coover's *The Universal Baseball Association* (1968), an attempt to mythologize the great American pastime. Although the comic touch is masterful, the mythologizing is uncertain. Roth does not stick to a central myth as does Malamud with the Wasteland motif or Coover with the Creation myth, nor does he, like Coover, get into the process of mythopoeia itself. Roth's symbols are rather superficial and dependent largely upon wordplay rather than intrinsic value. This facet of the novel may well be deliberate since the novel is a parody not only of great American (and English) novels but also the myth criticism of such novels.

The novel, after a long, playful prologue that talks about other great American novels as predecessors to this one, records the history of a third major baseball league, the Patriot, and in particular, the fate of one of its teams, the hapless Ruppert Mundy's, a team of misfits created out of the few men who are left in America during World War II. The Mundy's (named ironically for Jacob Ruppert, the brewing heir who was owner of the New York Yankees during their glory years and for the team's first owner, Glorius Mundy, whose name is associated with the Latin motto for faded greatness–*sic transit gloria mundi*) have seen better days and have become the only permanent road team in the league. In their mundane existence the Mundy's are quite clearly an image of the ordinary American who is manipulated by financial interests–the League owners–beyond his reach.

One long chapter is devoted to the biographies of these wonders. They include a fourteen-year-old second baseman who is so wet behind the ears that the only nickname he has earned is Nickname; a one-legged catcher, Hot Ptah, whose great achievement is his mastery of obscene behind-the-plate chatter; and Bud Parusha, the one-armed outfielder who takes the ball out of his glove with his teeth and who occasionally gets it stuck in his mouth, causing inside-the-park home runs. Amongst these grotesques exists the perfect specimen of an athlete, Roland Agni (named for the proud hero of *The Song of Roland* and for Christ as sacrificial lamb). Roland has been relegated to the Mundy's by his father, who insists that his boy bat eighth and receive the lowest salary in order to chastise his pride.

A major chapter is built around an allegorical conflict of good and evil in which two midgets struggle against each other. As usual in this novel, it is the malicious one who is victorious. Roth has a hilarious examination of the rights of midgets which is used to establish the grounds for the conflict. One of the midgets is Bob Yamm, whose job is to do nothing but get walks.

Yamm is a perfect human being, with a perfect doll-like wife, who meets his match in the person of a pitcher his own size, another midget named O. K. Ockatur. Yamm, despite his perfect nature, knows he does not exist except as a midget but asserts his personal identity when for the first time in his career, he disobeys the coach's orders, swings, and is hit in the face and blinded by Ockatur's pitch.

Yamm's self-assertion and sacrifice are paralleled by Roland Agni's. Roland, desperate to be traded, works out a deal to lead the always underdog Mundy's to a series of victories so that a seventeen-year-old genius can bet on them and win. Roland feeds his hopeless teammates scientifically developed Wheaties that really are the "breakfast of champions," but in a fit of honesty, he omits the dishonest breakfast cereal, the team loses, Isaac Ellis loses a quarter of a million dollars, and Roland is stuck with the Mundy's. Roland, like Achilles, sulks in his tent, but when he is finally convinced to win one for the losers of the world, he is shot for his troubles, the victim of a Communist plot.

The investigation of the death of Roland that closes the novel is a parody of the work of the various commissions that probed the death of John F. Kennedy. In *The Great American Novel*, Roland Agni is the victim of a plot of incredible complexity whose ramifications are so high-reaching that the authorities find it necessary to expunge completely the record of the league, which is the reason that no one knows of its existence any longer.

In *My Life as a Man* (1974) Roth attempts to spell out what has continually obsessed his fiction—the difference between living one's life and living a fictional version of one's life. In this case there is a playful reflex back at Roth himself. Roth is writing from the Yaddo Writers' Colony about Peter Tarnapol writing from the Quahsai Writers' Colony about a fictional character of his, Nathan Zuckerman. Zuckerman is involved in several love affairs that in some way reflect Tarnapol's life and behavior. *My Life as a Man* consists of two long short stories whose hero is Zuckerman and then Tarnapol's true story in which the failed writer tries to use his own stories to make sense of his life. The difficulty is that the stories, despite the many parallels between Zuckerman's life and Tarnapol's, are too neat and orderly to tell the novelist what is wrong with his own life.

The stories are collectively entitled "useful fictions," suggesting that Tarnapol can learn some-

thing about himself by reading or at least writing these stories. This is Tarnapol's first and biggest mistake, because seen this way the stories are useless. The first Zuckerman story, "Salad Days," finds Zuckerman torn between two loves: his teacher, Caroline Benson, who is the essence of the spirit, and Sharon Shatsky, who is the flesh. It is easy enough for Tarnapol to perceive the dichotomy and understand why neither woman can completely satisfy Zuckerman, but that is just the point: reality never allegorizes itself so neatly. The fiction, then, far from being useful, encourages Tarnapol to categorize women where no such boundaries exist.

The second Zuckerman story offers a somewhat more complex heroine, but Zuckerman's relationship to her is no more complicated. The story, "Courting Disaster," tells of Zuckerman's courtship of and marriage to Lydia Ketterer, whose primary appeal to him is that she has lived a life of immense suffering, degradation, and brutality. Since literary theory has taught him to equate degradation with realism, Zuckerman courts Lydia for a taste of reality, but he finds that loving her is no more real than his books were. Zuckerman marries Lydia to become her savior, and sex with her soon becomes merely an expression of his "goodness," and a fake one at that. After Lydia's suicide, Zuckerman runs off with his near-idiot stepdaughter, Monica ("Moonie"), for exactly the opposite reason he had married her mother—for no reason at all. He sees such a liaison as a sign of absolute existential commitment, since it has no purpose. Once this theoretical stance is perceived, however, the relationship becomes just as fake as that with Moonie's mother.

The two stories, then, set up neat dichotomies by which to measure Zuckerman's behavior and mark his failures. No such neatness exists in the real life of Tarnapol, whose problem is to discover why he has married Maureen, a castrating bitch, and why, after four years of separation, he cannot ignore her. Like Lydia, Maureen is a sufferer who needs to be saved, this time from the disasters of two marriages—one to a brute and one to a homosexual. Since Tarnapol has learned from Zuckerman the foolishness of playing savior, this does not seem to be his hang-up. Maureen is a vampirelike presence who gives meaning to her life by taking away Tarnapol's existence, and it is this that obsesses Tarnapol. Maureen does literally bite him, and four years later he is still talking about getting her fangs out of him. What he doesn't see is that his real role is not to be savior, but victim. Maureen gives him what every writer with a block needs–a reason for failure other than his own inability to write: How can he finish his novel of high seriousness with her literally and figuratively sucking the blood out of him?

Tarnapol's story also includes his affair with Susan McCall, the ideal woman, like Claire Ovington in *The Breast* and *The Professor of Desire*. She has everything he wants–money, position, love to offer–but he cannot remove the shadow of the vampire, nor ultimately does he want to. Susan is a place of recovery, an island of absolute tranquillity, that he cannot stand partly because he needs something on which to blame his failure but more importantly because, being a writer, he requires crisis. As Tarnapol's brother Moe notes, the great novels of the kind he is trying to write, Bellow's *Herzog* (1964) and Mailer's *An American Dream* (1965), require a castrating bitch, a Madeleine Herzog or a Deborah Rojack. Tarnapol is caught in a dilemma–he cannot write his novel with Maureen, and without her he has no subject because his novel is ultimately to be about his own suffering.

The Professor of Desire (1977) tells the early history of David Kepesh, the man who is turned into a breast in *The Breast*. In a recent interview in the *New York Times Book Review*, Roth denies that *The Professor of Desire* was meant to be an antecedent in the sense that it explains why Kepesh became a breast or even that the psychology is continuous from novel to novel. Rather, he says, he had sketched a brief history of Kepesh in *The Breast*, and in the new novel he has brought that history forth fully articulated. The title of the new novel indicates a dichotomy in the personality that is never fully restored. Most mundanely, the title indicates Kepesh's occupation. He is a teacher of comparative literature, whose favorite course in erotic literature he calls Desire 341. As such, the novel is a fascinating and rare account of an academic who cares passionately about his subject and reveals unabashedly why Kepesh loves Chekhov and particularly Kafka. One might compare this facet of the novel to the depiction of S. Levin in Bernard Malamud's *A New Life* (1961), where Levin's love of literature is a given rather than a thing felt and understood.

The title also indicates the split in the personality of Kepesh. He is one who professes–i.e., verbally affirms his allegiance–to desire, an emotion that has nothing to do with verbal affirmation.

Kepesh is a man who would like to live with his body and tries sincerely to do so, but at every turn he finds himself analyzing what his body, and more importantly, what his emotions are doing.

Although the novel covers vast geographic space, including two trips by Kepesh to Europe and the flight of his wife to Hong Kong, it ends some thirty miles from where it begins, as Kepesh spends an idyllic summer with his mistress in a place not far from the Catskill resort where he grew up. In a long, moving self-analysis, Kepesh discovers how far he has come in his life and paradoxically how little he has changed.

In the prologuelike description of his early years in his father's hotel, the Hungarian Royale, the reader is introduced to Kepesh's first mentor, Herbie Bratasky, the hotel's social director. Bratasky's greatest talent is his ability to imitate the sound of bodily functions, particularly those related to the bathroom. Kepesh's life's task will be to free himself from Bratasky's mimesis of life, i.e., conscious playing at desire which has the appearance of the real thing.

This is not to say that Kepesh's sex life is fantasized; far from it. Nonetheless, one finds that no matter how involved Kepesh is in sex, he is always viewing it at a distance, always thinking what else it might be. For example, in his first lengthy erotic involvement in London with two Swedish girls, Kepesh watches one of them approach mental collapse from trying to be sexually abandoned. After, she returns to Sweden dreaming of the middle-class virtues of love and marriage, leaving Kepesh with the roommate. This girl is totally involved in sex and degradation, but once Kepesh discovers that there is no more "more" they can achieve, he sends her away and returns to the United States. This is the typical Roth hero, who both desires the ultimate and runs from it when he has found it.

The same duality destroys Kepesh's marriage, although the fault is not his alone. Kepesh's wife, Helen, is a man-eating bitch like Maureen Tarnapol, but much of the failure of the marriage comes from Kepesh's need to categorize Helen, to treat her as a character in some novel he knows. He sees her earlier romance with an older man as a variation on *Anna Karenina*, with her loving the Karenin-figure, not the romantic young Vronsky. Kepesh cannot deal with this twist on his literary preconceptions and half drives Helen away. He sees in Helen the self-denial and sensuousness of Anna, but this means he also believes and therefore silently promotes (to justify his theory) her deathless passion for the other man. Helen eventually goes off to Hong Kong to seek her first love, and the marriage falls apart.

After a period of despair Kepesh finds the perfect woman, Claire Ovington, a creature of adequate, but not overwhelming, passion, with whom he takes off on a romantic holiday to Europe. Even having all he could want, Kepesh's imagination will not be still. He calls up the memory of the Swedish girl, now more powerful than when she was present, and finds Claire lacking in passion. He manages to cope with this crisis by visiting the grave of Kafka, and in a brilliant dream sequence he meets an ancient crone who is the whore of Kafka. In the dream the Czech tour guide turns out to be Kepesh's old mentor, Herbie Bratasky. In addition to being the comic epitome of all grasping tour guide scenes, the dream gathers all the attitudes that control Kepesh's life. For five dollars Kepesh is able to see the old whore's sex, perhaps the one solid reality in all the metaphysical meanderings of Kafka's life. The dream seems to say the same thing about Kepesh's relation to sex. His life has been determined almost totally in relation to sex, and yet sex itself is less important than the constructs he has built around it. Nonetheless, without the thing itself the constructs would be worthless. As the dream closes, Kepesh sees the old whore's tongue, "the pulp of the fruit, still red."

The image seems to suggest that the very core of desire will never fade, but the close of the novel casts a good deal of doubt upon this notion. Kepesh returns with Claire to the environs of his youth, and in the presence of his father and his father's friend, he meditates on the nature of his life and upon the gradual dissipation of desire. The father's friend, Mr. Barbatnik, the survivor of every conceivable evil including the concentration camps, starts Kepesh's train of thought. If Barbatnik can outlive all that horror, then he, Kepesh, can outlive all this love and desire. Once again, Kepesh finds his life controlled by his theory of life. The more he tries to think about an answer to the feeling that all this will pass away, the more the feeling increases. Desperately he puts his mouth to the breast of Claire, who is lying asleep in bed with him, but the final result is not given: Will the theory destroy desire or can desire overcome the professor in him?

Nathan Zuckerman, the hero of Roth's 1979 novel, *The Ghost Writer,* finds two possible courses open to the great novelist. He can either retire from the literary and social community and devote himself totally to his art like the master E. I. Lonoff, or he can become like the literary lion Felix Abravanel–sleek with adulation, wealth, and beautiful mistresses. In *The Ghost Writer* Zuckerman chooses Lonoff's way. Many critics have speculated on the similarity of Lonoff to Malamud (and to a lesser extent, Malamud's own master, Isaac Bashevis Singer) and of Abravanel's similarity to Saul Bellow and/or Norman Mailer. None of these identifications is completely off the mark (Lonoff as Malamud is particularly valid), but in fact the Jewish-American novelist closest to both Lonoff and Abravanel is Roth himself. He has trod the path of self-imposed exile and lived the life of celebrity and continues to do both. So, in fact, will Zuckerman.

Zuckerman is also the hero of *Zuckerman Unbound* (1981), where he tries the Abravanel path of celebrity. Though the characterization is not entirely consistent in these three incarnations, Zuckerman, a surrogate for Roth (though not an autobiographical figure), tells us a great deal about the life of a novelist at different points in his career.

In each case, Zuckerman's fate concerns itself with the way art impinges on life and life does the same to art. Of this issue Roth has said, "My obsession for the last seven or eight years has been the uses to which literature has been put in this country. The writer in his isolation publishes a book, the book goes out into the world and the strangest things begin to happen." In both novels, Zuckerman has written a work which has gone out into the world only to offend Zuckerman's family, friends, and neighbors. In *The Ghost Writer* the offending work is a short story not unlike Roth's "Defender of the Faith" or "Epstein" (both about obnoxious Jews).

In *The Ghost Writer,* Zuckerman goes off to the Berkshires, hoping to find a spiritual father in Lonoff, a painstaking creator of brilliant parables in the style of Russian masters such as Anton Chekhov and Isaak Babel. Zuckerman seeks a surrogate father because his own father, a well-meaning, loving podiatrist, has refused to see the aesthetic virtues in Zuckerman's story "Higher Education," which uses an old family quarrel to show grasping, greedy Jews. Though the ambience of Lonoff's fiction is Jewish American, the issue he raises of the conflict of art and life is

Jamesian. Consequently, the stories of Henry James are among the significant literary ghosts that inhabit the novel.

The primary analogues are two of James's stories, "The Lesson of the Master" and "The Middle Years." In "The Lesson of the Master" a young writer named Paul Overt seeks out his literary hero, Henry St. George, only to find him looking disappointingly like a "lucky stockbroker." St. George is artistically exhausted and advises Overt not to waste his energies by falling in love with and marrying Marian Fancourt, a beautiful young woman of their mutual acquaintance. Life–the business of being a husband and father–drains the artist. Better to leave life behind and create the perfect work of art. Overt follows his master's lesson, goes off to write his novel (we never know if it is great) and returns to find that St. George's wife has died and that St. George is about to marry Marian himself. Only then does Overt realize the terrible price he has paid for his art.

Like James's young hero, Zuckerman is rather disappointed in his first meeting with the master. Lonoff seems discontent not only with his life but with his art. The pursuit of perfection has become for him an act of verbal juggling. "I turn sentences around," says Lonoff. "That's my life." Lonoff's wife, ironically named Hope, is at the point of leaving him. She is tired of having to provide the atmosphere of passive perfection in which the pursuit of literary perfection is to thrive. Furthermore, she has to compete for his meager affections with Amy Bellette, a former student who sees in Lonoff both a love object and a father figure. Like Marian Fancourt in "The Lesson of the Master," Amy becomes the focal point of the conflicting ideals of master and pupil.

In "The Middle Years," Dr. Hugh, a young physician and literary enthusiast, meets his favorite novelist, Dencombe, the author of *The Middle Years*. In pursuing the dying Dencombe and his art, the doctor neglects his only patient, a wealthy countess who had planned to leave him her fortune. Ultimately, his choice of Dencombe costs him his fortune, but he accepts the consequences with equanimity. "I chose to accept, whatever they might be, the consequences of my infatuation," he tells Dencombe. "It's your own fault if I can't get your things out of my head."

Like Dr. Hugh, Zuckerman is ready to give up everything–success, life, home–for the chance to live Lonoff's life of art. Ironically, Zuckerman is standing on Lonoff's copy of the stories of Henry James (so he can listen at the ceiling to the conversation in the room above), when he overhears Amy offer herself to Lonoff. The great man rejects her advances and can satisfy her only by doing an imitation of Jimmy Durante. When a Jewish artist is reduced to doing a vaudeville routine, and of a big-nosed Italian at that, he has turned his life into mockery for the sake of his art. Zuckerman is sanguine about this folly, however, and sees Lonoff's performance as "mad, heroic restraint."

The thought of Amy Bellette has sent Zuckerman reeling, however, and in an imaginative tour de force he gives the exotic young woman a past. Zuckerman convinces himself that Amy is none other than Anne Frank, whose diary made her Saint Anne of the Holocaust. Zuckerman posits that Anne Frank survived in the confusion at the end of the war but decided that the impact of her story–the message that her family died because they were Jews, even though they thought of themselves as Dutch–would be lost if she were no longer a martyr. Roth is at his best in creating this fictional continuation of Anne Frank's life.

Zuckerman soon cheapens his dream. He sees Bellette/Frank as the way out of his conflicts at home, out of his father's insistence that he is betraying his race, out of the ridiculous questions of Judge Leopold Wapter, Newark's most illustrious Jewish citizen. Judge Wapter has sent him a questionnaire which includes such leading questions as "Do you practice Judaism? If so, how? If not, what credentials qualify you for writing about Jewish life for national magazines?," "What in your character makes you associate so much of life's ugliness with Jewish people?," and "Can you honestly say there is anything in your short story that would not warm the heart of a Julius Streicher or a Joseph Goebbels?"

Well, Zuckerman has the answer for philistines like Wapter. He will marry Anne Frank. Let Judge Wapter question that! He can picture the moment when he announces his engagement to his parents: " 'Nathan, is she Jewish?' 'Yes, she is.' 'But who is she?' 'Anne Frank.' " The moment would be a triumph no doubt, but this imagined victory is simply beating Wapter at his own game. Wapter invokes the ghosts of the Holocaust to damn Zuckerman, and Zuckerman, just as unthinkingly, uses those same ghosts to call down a blessing on his own head. His "marriage" to St. Anne Frank would make it impossible for Wapter to condemn him, but Zuckerman has not really countered the charges leveled against him in the questionnaire. Wapter, after all, is saying that literature matters in the real world. His sensibility may be coarse and his morality superficial, but his objections will not be whisked away simply by waving an icon in front of them.

In the end both Zuckerman and Lonoff lose Amy. Zuckerman's "Has anyone ever told you you look like Anne Frank?" is just as hollow as it sounds, and Amy ignores his attempt at flirtation. Amy also refuses to accept Lonoff from his wife's hands. Hope's warning ("She can be ready to begin boring you as soon as I'm out the door . . . and get everything ready to make you happy and then see the look on your stone face when you come in at night and sit down at the table") may have some influence on her leaving, but his rejection of Amy on the night before seems to be the major reason. Hope also walks out on Lonoff, and he goes out into the snow in pursuit of his Hope. It seems as if Lonoff's wife will return, but nothing will change. Zuckerman will probably treat the marriage with more sanctity than it deserves and praise Hope as a saint. If he writes the story, Zuckerman will call it "Married to Tolstoy."

If the life of the hermit is perilous, so is the life of the literary celebrity. In *Zuckerman Unbound* Roth deals with the tribulations brought to Nathan Zuckerman by the success of his notorious novel *Carnovsky*. The situation is based in some measure on Roth's phenomenal success and attendant problems following the publication of *Portnoy's Complaint*. Zuckerman suffers under the watchful eye of Brahmin money managers, English custom tailors, and even an aging ingenue, who happens to be Fidel Castro's mistress. None of these minor demons, however, can compare with Zuckerman's personal dybbuk, a former quiz-show contestant named Alvin Pepler.

Pepler is modeled in part upon Teddy Nadler, the postal clerk with a photographic memory who won thousands of dollars before the scandals closed the big-money quiz shows in the late fifties. Like the real-life Nadler, Roth's Pepler catches facts like flypaper. Unlike Nadler, Pepler is a Jew and a landsman of Zuckerman's from his old Newark neighborhood. When Pepler first latches on to him, Zuckerman sees him merely as one of the annoying appurtenances of fame, those talentless would-be writers who come waving manuscripts in the famous author's face.

Pepler is more; he is Zuckerman's alter ego. If the novelist locked in his study is the spirit of the imagination, then Pepler with his undigested information is his polar opposite, the man of fact, and both dwell on the edges of the real world. Zuckerman wonders if either of them lives *dans le vrai* (in reality).

One of the possibilities that Zuckerman has to face is that Pepler is just as real as he is, or less optimistically, that he is as unreal as Pepler. Pepler even was for three weeks a celebrity as great as Zuckerman when he was the quiz-show champion. At first, Pepler just seems to want what most people want from celebrated writers—help with a manuscript, advice about publishing, and criticism—criticism that, of course, will go unheard.

Little by little, Zuckerman attributes all sorts of powers to Pepler and his facts. This becomes particularly striking once Pepler turns against him. Pepler first approaches Zuckerman as his redeemer, the man who can tell the world how the quiz show's producers (both Jews) refused to let him remain champion because the American television audience would not be happy with a Jewish champion. The fix was on. And in a reverse of the mythology of the scandals, Pepler was the first to cheat by agreeing to lose in exchange for promises of a career in television—promises that were later broken.

When Zuckerman shows no interest in his cause, Pepler turns accuser—first charging Zuckerman with anti-Semitism and then with a greater crime among writers, plagiarism. Pepler accuses Zuckerman not of stealing his manuscript but of stealing his life. He has taken Pepler's personality and put it between the covers of a book called *Carnovsky* instead of *Pepler*. Zuckerman has achieved what most writers long for, a reader who identifies completely with one of his characters. Instead of cheering Zuckerman up, Pepler's total involvement makes the author's life a horror. Pepler haunts him, lies to him, bullies him, and then sends him a semen-soaked handkerchief (Zuckerman's handkerchief, which Pepler had stolen), proof-positive that the masturbating hero of *Carnovsky* is really Pepler. Not even Othello had so much trouble with his own handkerchief.

One of the many paradoxes of the novel is that the fact-catcher Pepler leads a fictional life, while Zuckerman's life is mired in facts. Pepler invents an entire Broadway production company working on the musical version of the "Alvin Pepler Story," while Zuckerman finds that the only thing he still has in common with his last ex-wife is the Xerox machine in their bathroom.

Celebrity in America brings out more than screwball fans; it brings out honest-to-God crazies. Zuckerman has achieved a measure of fame smaller than John and Robert Kennedy and Martin Luther King, Jr., but he has his own threatening phone calls. In this case, the caller threatens to kidnap Zuckerman's mother. Is it Pepler? An unknown crank? Or just paranoia? Zuckerman never finds out. What he does find out is that books do not confine themselves to the study but make their way into the real world and have consequences there. Zuckerman tells the threatening caller that he has been watching too many bad movies, to which his tormentor replies, "Could be, Zuck. Haw, haw, haw. Also real life." In a world where Jack Ruby murders the murderer of a president before a live television audience, the boundaries of life and art have been curiously blurred. The Kennedy assassinations have long held a fascination for Roth, and a friend of his has said, "Long before the Kennedys were assassinated, he'd been waiting for the bullet."

Carnovsky, then, does not bring harm to his mother, but it does destroy Zuckerman's last day with his father. His father had seen the book as mercilessly satiric of his family, and there is the expected talk that the book has killed him. The old man has been paralyzed by a stroke, but manages to mouth a last word that seems to be "bastard!" and seems to be aimed at Zuckerman. At least, it seems so to Zuckerman. Zuckerman's brother, a dentist (the fate of Jewish boys who cannot make it as doctors), and a man who wanted a life in the theater but settled for the conventional and the ordinary, tries to convince Zuckerman that their father could not have said that as his last word to his son. Zuckerman is not convinced. If this rejection is the price he must pay for his art, so be it.

The novel's title refers to Zuckerman's freeing himself from all the bonds that tie one to life. Each untying is done at the cost of terrible pain, but there is no other way. Zuckerman ends his relationship with his father, discovers he no longer can stand the spiritual dishonesty of his smiling brother or the honest virtue of his ex-wife, and loses his mistress to Fidel Castro. In a scene as wrenching as the death of his father, Zuckerman returns to his old neighborhood in Newark, the source of most of his fiction, only to find it a burned-out slum. When Zuckerman has unbound himself from this last tie, the past, he is free. The book does not speculate on what

Zuckerman will do with this freedom. Roth's next book suggests that he is not as free as his hero.

Roth, in fact, seems to be unable to free himself from the terrible curse of "Zuckermanity." His next book, *The Anatomy Lesson* (1983), is that most irritating of novels, the writer's block book. In it, Roth's alter ego Zuckerman finds himself unable to write; in addition he is suffering from back-neck pains that seem a direct result of his block. Zuckerman reviews his affairs with four women, all richly characterized, but none capable of lifting the block off the man who has betrayed his mother by writing the infamous *Carnovsky*.

Much of the book consists of Zuckerman's attack on the critic, Milton Appel, who wrote a scathing review of Zuckerman's output ten years earlier. Appel is, in fact, Irving Howe, whose devastating article, "Philip Roth Reconsidered," appeared a decade before *The Anatomy Lesson*. Howe's article lambasted Roth for wasting his talent and for the innate vulgarity of *Portnoy's Complaint*. Although one could consider that Roth's ability to joke about the article means that he is over its sting, he is more than a little defensive in writing almost an entire novel to deal with it. Not only does Zuckerman compose an answer to Appel, he talks with Appel on the telephone (Appel comes across rather sane and courtly), and he then pretends to be Appel. Zuckerman goes around claiming he is Appel, no longer a critic, but Appel the pornographer, the editor of a raunchy new rival to *Playboy* called *Lickety Split*. Despite whatever obscenity he then attributes to Appel, the issue remains the same as it always is in Roth's work: which alienated Jew has remained most faithful in spirit to Judaism.

The Anatomy Lesson takes its name from a painting by Rembrandt. A close look at the painting offers many insights into what the novel is about. In the painting several clearly middle-aged students (they were, in fact, members of the corporation of surgeons who commissioned the painting) watch their master dissect the left hand of a corpse that is flat on its back. All of the students wear lace collars, and one has his in the form of a particularly high ruff. The painting becomes a symbol for Zuckerman. Though he has one aspect of the students when the novel begins, a cervical collar that looks like the Renaissance ruff, he is much closer to the corpse. His left (writing) hand, like the corpse's, is exposed and useless due to his block and, like the corpse, he spends most of his time flat on his back.

The odd fact of the students in Rembrandt's painting being middle-aged turns out to fit perfectly with the conclusion of the novel. *The Anatomy Lesson* finally turns on the long-standing stereotype about Jewish mothers and their sons. Zuckerman, despite having achieved great fame as a novelist, has never been able to please his mother because of his anti-Jewish subject matter. In an attempt to right this wrong, he goes off to Chicago, at age forty, to become what all Jewish mothers want their sons to become: a doctor. A freak accident breaks Zuckerman's jaw, and he winds up in the hospital, not as a student, but as a patient. With his jaw wired shut, Zuckerman is forced to write the most elementary questions with a magic marker. His writer's block is slowly lifted. Eventually he finds himself wandering around the hospital as a quasi-intern who offers spiritual solace to patients worse off than he. For the first time in the novel, he is able to understand that his pain is miniscule compared to the pain to be found everywhere in the world. It is not clear if he will be able to follow the first, or perhaps last, rule of such would-be doctors: physician heal thyself.

If Zuckerman is almost a corpse in *The Anatomy Lesson*, he comes even closer in *The Counterlife* (1986). This novel, like *My Life as a Man*, is a novel within a novel, only here the fiction is still in draft status so that the characters still have their "real" names. Two-thirds of *The Counterlife* purport to be the story of Henry Zuckerman (Nathan's brother), an utterly conventional dentist from suburban New Jersey, who first rebels against his conformity and then dies when he opts for heart surgery rather than live with the heart medicine that makes him impotent. In this aspect of the novel, Nathan appears as a sympathetic figure who attempts to save his brother from destroying himself, first by unconventional affairs and then as a member of a radically militant kibbutz in Israel.

The reader discovers, however, that what appears to be the novel turns out to be part of a manuscript discovered by *Henry* Zuckerman among his brother's papers, when *Nathan* dies from the heart operation necessary to save *his* virility. Henry is so angry with Nathan's using his life and fictionalizing–that is, falsifying–it, that he destroys all of the manuscript (all that the reader has thus far read) leaving only a chapter which has nothing to do with him. The counterlife then becomes the revision that the artist makes in the lives that come under his scrutiny. In this case,

however, the real liver of the life transformed has his revenge since he is able to destroy the fiction that has been made out of his life. The irony's irony is that the Zuckerman novel, destroyed in Henry's life, exists and is in print because it is really Roth's novel.

Such paradoxes help make this novel part of Roth's attempt to move into the deconstructionist camp of contemporary French criticism. One of the characters carries around copies of *Tel Quel, the* journal of deconstruction, a school of criticism that argues that every philosophy carries within it the rationale for its own deconstruction. In the novel, Nathan Zuckerman gets into philosophical or moral arguments in which traditional reasoning is turned inside out until the pulling of a single thread can destroy the entire fabric. Among the arguments are those of an aggressive Zionist who believes that the only way that Jews can survive is to forget the Holocaust, that the only way Zuckerman can truly be a Jew is to live with his Christian wife and actively participate in Christmas service in a Christian church, that the only way for a militant kibbutznik to reach harmony with the Arabs is to remain violent toward them.

The novel is a dazzling interplay of old and brilliantly new intellectual argument. Never has Roth made dialectic so sharp and bristly as in this novel, when he takes arguments to places where they have never been. The problem, or perhaps the explanation, is that the deconstructionist mood does for intellect what Roth's heroes have always done to sex: gotten them very involved without any true commitment. Since every brilliant argument in this novel will lead to its own destruction, none of them really matter, and after a while the reader gets tired of following their intricacy if there is only finally cleverness and not wisdom to be gleaned. The stimulated but exhausted reader feels like lying back and smoking a cigarette.

Bibliography:

Bernard F. Rodgers, Jr., *Philip Roth: A Bibliography* (Metuchen, N.J.: Scarecrow, 1974).
  An elaborate annotated bibliography.

References:

Irving Buchen, "*Portnoy's Complaint* of the Rooster's Kvetch," *Studies in the Twentieth Century*, 6 (Fall 1970): 97-107.
  Portnoy's Complaint is compared to Norman Podhoretz's *Making It* (1968) as examples of

"kvetching," here seen as a kind of whining confession.

Stanley Cooperman, "Philip Roth: 'Old Jacob's Eye' With a Squint," *Twentieth Century Literature*, 19 (July 1973): 203-216.
Discusses the early novels, emphasizing the moral choices that must be made by the heroes.

Irving and Harriet Deer, "Philip Roth and the Crisis in American Fiction," *Minnesota Review*, 6 (Winter 1966): 353-360.
Roth's heroes are seen struggling against the alienation of modern society.

John Ditsky, "Roth, Updike, and the High Expense of Spirit," *University of Windsor Review*, 5 (Fall 1969): 111-120.
A comparison of *Portnoy's Complaint* and John Updike's *Couples* (1968) as analyses of modern sexual despair.

John Gardner, "Review of *The Breast*," *New York Times Book Review*, 17 September 1972, pp. 3, 10.
Emphasizes Roth's Kafkaesque ability to make the most absurd premise seem realistic.

Lois G. Gordon, " 'Portnoy's Complaint': Coming of Age in Jersey City," *Literature and Psychology*, 19, 3-4 (1969): 57-60.
Discusses the dualities in *Portnoy's Complaint* in terms of Freudian psychology.

Allen Guttman, *The Jewish Writer in America: Assimilation and the Crisis of Identity* (New York: Oxford University Press, 1971).
Discusses Roth's struggle with the problems of assimilation–the attempt of Jews to Americanize themselves–without cutting themselves off from their Jewish roots.

Baruch Hochman, "Child and Man in Philip Roth," *Midstream*, 13 (December 1967): 68-76.
A largely negative analysis of Roth's early fiction, arguing that Roth has become trapped in the rhetoric of Jewish boys rebelling against their fathers.

Irving Howe, "Philip Roth Reconsidered," *Commentary*, 54 (December 1972): 69-77.

A review so devastating that Roth writes a whole novel, *The Anatomy Lesson* (in which Howe is called Martin Appel) to refute it; sees Roth's talent wasted in novels that are little more than skits; Portnoy's vulgarity draws most of Howe's ire.

Judith Jones and Guinavera Nance, *Philip Roth* (New York: Ungar, 1981).
Studies the conflicts both in Roth's heroes, especially between intellectuality and sexuality, and in Roth himself, often about the terribly high price of his fame or notoriety.

Alice Kaminsky, "Philip Roth's Professor Kepesh and the 'Reality Principle,' " *Denver Quarterly*, 13, no. 2 (1978): 41-54.
Examines the relationship of realism and fantasy in *The Professor of Desire* and *The Breast*.

Alfred Kazin, *Contemporaries* (Boston: Little, Brown, 1962), pp. 258-262.
Somewhat grudging praise of *Goodbye, Columbus*; sees Roth making the moral issues too neat in most of the stories.

Bernice Kliman, "Names in *Portnoy's Complaint*," *Critique*, 14, 3 (1973): 16-24.
Interprets the symbolism of names in *Portnoy's Complaint*.

Kliman, "Women in Roth's Fiction," *Nassau Review*, 3, no. 4 (1978): 75-88.
Sees Roth's heroes as unable to deal with women because their relationships are always limited by gender-based stereotypes.

Hermione Lee, *Philip Roth* (London: Methuen, 1982).
Though this is an introductory study, Lee provides an incisive look at Roth's mediation between interior and exterior milieus, i.e., the minds of his characters and the world they live in.

Judith Lee, "Flights of Fancy," *Chicago Review*, 31, no. 4 (1980): 46-52.
Discusses how Zuckerman's imagination takes him beyond the dichotomy of life and art that he finds in the fiction of Henry James.

John Leonard, "Cheever to Roth to Malamud," *Atlantic*, 231 (June 1973): 112-116.

Compares *The Great American Novel* favorably with other modern baseball-as-America novels: Bernard Malamud's *The Natural* (1952), Mark Harris's *Bang the Drum Slowly* (1956), and Robert Coover's *The Universal Baseball Association* (1968); Leonard praises Roth's ability to invent an entire fictional world.

Mordecai Levine, "Philip Roth and American Judaism," *College Language Association Journal*, 14 (December 1970): 163-170.
This article's attack on Roth's Jewish self-loathing makes it the kind that Nathan Zuckerman tries to defend himself against in the continuing saga of "*Carnovsky*"— bashing that has occupied Roth since *Zuckerman Unbound*.

Saul Maloff, "The Uses of Adversity," *Commonweal*, 106 (19 November 1979): 628-631.
Sees *The Ghost Writer* as Roth's most mature work, elegantly coming to terms with the conflicts of life and art that had produced so many wounds in the earlier work.

John McDaniel, *The Fiction of Philip Roth* (Haddonfield, N.J.: Haddonfield House, 1974).
A look at Roth's fiction in relation to the Jewish-American school anchored by Bellow and Malamud.

Sanford Pinsker, *The Comedy That "Hoits"* (Columbia: University of Missouri Press, 1975).
An elaborate discussion of literary influences and symbolism in Roth.

Pinsker, ed., *Critical Essays on Philip Roth* (Boston: G. K. Hall, 1982).
A collection of reviews and substantial articles; the reviews deal with individual works and the articles with broader issues.

Bernard F. Rodgers, Jr., *Philip Roth* (Boston: Twayne, 1978).
A solid introduction to the early work.

Theodore Solotaroff, "Philip Roth and the Jewish Moralists," *Chicago Review*, 13 (Winter 1959): 87-99.
An important early article, the first to see Roth as an emerging force in Jewish moral fiction.

Patricia Spacks, "About Portnoy," *Yale Review*, 58 (June 1969): 623-635.
Puts Portnoy in the tradition of the *picaro*, the comic adventurer who continually wanders into absurd situations which require *ad hoc* moral decisions.

Tony Tanner, *City of Words: American Fiction 1950-1970* (New York: Harper & Row, 1971).
Sees Roth's eye for the infinitesimal sexual detail of adolescence as first a blessing then a curse, as his fiction becomes increasingly mired in a morass of small perversions.

Ruth Wisse, *The Schlemiel as Modern Hero* (Chicago: University of Chicago Press, 1971).
Sees Portnoy as a reaction against the *schlemiel* (unworldly fool) literature it resembles since the laughter in the book increases the pain of Jewish existence rather than defusing it.

Papers:
The major collection of Roth's literary manuscripts and correspondence is at the Library of Congress; see "Philip Roth Papers," *Quarterly Journal of the Library of Congress*, 27 (1970): 343-344.

William Styron

This entry was updated by Keen Butterworth (University of South Carolina) from his entries in DLB 2, American Novelists Since World War II *and* DLB Yearbook 1980.

Places	Camp Lejeune, N.C. Tidewater, Va.	Parris Island, S.C. New York City	Italy Poland
Influences and Relationships	William Faulkner Thomas Wolfe Robert Penn Warren	John Dos Passos Albert Camus James Jones	Peter Matthiessen James Baldwin John Phillips
Literary Movements and Forms	Realism	Existentialism	
Major Themes	Revolt Guilt Moral Responsibility	Identity Alienation Redemption Sexuality	Love Initiation Racial Conflict Cultural Breakdown
Cultural and Artistic Influences	Music	Movies	Psychology
Social and Economic Influences	Slavery Racism World War II	Militarism The Holocaust	Cultural Disintegration

BIRTH: Newport News, Virginia, 11 June 1925, to William Clark and Pauline Abraham Styron.

EDUCATION: Christchurch Preparatory School; Davidson College, 1942-1943; A.B., Duke University, 1947; New School for Social Research, 1947.

MARRIAGE: 4 May 1953 to Rose Burgunder; children: Susanna, Paola, Thomas, and Alexandra.

AWARDS: American Academy of Arts and Letters Prix de Rome for *Lie Down in Darkness*, 1952; Pulitzer Prize for *The Confessions of Nat Turner*, 1968; Howells Medal of American Academy of Arts and Letters, 1970.

BOOKS: *Lie Down in Darkness* (Indianapolis: Bobbs-Merrill, 1951; London: Hamish Hamilton, 1952);

The Long March (New York: Random House, 1956; London: Hamish Hamilton, 1961);

Set This House on Fire (New York: Random House, 1960; London: Hamish Hamilton, 1961);

The Confessions of Nat Turner (New York: Random House, 1967; London: Cape, 1968);

In the Clap Shack (New York: Random House, 1973);

Admiral Robert Penn Warren and the Snows of Winter (Winston-Salem, N.C.: Palaemon, 1978);

Sophie's Choice (New York: Random House, 1979; London: Cape, 1979);

Shadrack (Los Angeles: Sylvester & Orphanos, 1979);

The Message of Auschwitz (Blacksburg, Va.: Press de la Warr, 1979);

This Quiet Dust and Other Writings (New York: Random House, 1982);

As He Lay Dead, A Bitter Grief (New York: Albondocani Press, 1983).

OTHER: "Autumn," in *One and Twenty: Duke Narrative and Verse, 1924-1945*, edited by William Blackburn (Durham: Duke University Press, 1945), pp. 36-53;

"The Long Dark Road," in *One and Twenty: Duke Narrative and Verse, 1924-1945*, edited by Blackburn (Durham: Duke University Press, 1945), pp. 266-280;

"A Moment in Trieste," in *American Vanguard*, edited by Don Wolfe (Ithaca, N.Y.: Cornell University Press, 1948), pp. 241-247;

"The Enormous Window," in *1950 American Vanguard*, edited by Charles I. Glicksberg (New York: New School for Social Research, 1950), pp. 71-89;

Introduction to *Best Short Stories from "The Paris Review"* (New York: Dutton, 1959), pp. 9-16;

"Writers under Twenty-five," in *Under Twenty-five: Duke Narrative and Verse, 1945-1962*, edited by Blackburn (Durham: Duke University Press, 1963), pp. 3-8.

PERIODICAL PUBLICATIONS:
FICTION
"Set This House on Fire," *Esquire*, 51 (June 1959): 128ff.;

"The McCabes," *Paris Review*, 6 (Autumn / Winter 1959-1960): 12-28;

"Home from St. Andrews," *Esquire*, 53 (May 1960): 147-148ff.;

"Runaway," *Partisan Review*, 33 (Fall 1966): 574-582;

"Virginia: 1831," *Paris Review*, 9 (Winter 1966): 13-45;

"The Confessions of Nat Turner," *Harper's*, 235 (September 1967): 51-102;

"Novel's Climax: The Night of the Honed Axes," *Life*, 63 (13 October 1967): 54-60;

"Marriott, the Marine," *Esquire*, 76 (September 1971): 101-104ff.;

"The Suicide Run," *American Poetry Review*, 3 (May / June 1974): 20-22;

"The Seduction of Leslie," *Esquire*, 86 (September 1976): 92-96ff.;

"The Force of Her Happiness," *The Archive* (Duke Univ.), 89 (Spring 1977): 94-114;

"My Life as a Publisher," *Esquire*, 89 (14 March 1978): 71-79;

"Shadrack," *Esquire*, 90 (21 November 1978): 82-96;

"Love Day," *Esquire*, 104 (August 1985): 94-96ff.
NONFICTION
"William Styron," *New York Herald Tribune Book Review*, 7 October 1951, p. 26;

"Letter to an Editor," *Paris Review*, 1 (Spring 1953): 9-13;

"The Prevalence of Wonders," *Nation*, 176 (2 May 1953): 370-371;

"The Paris Review," *Harper's Bazaar*, 87 (August 1953): 122, 173;

"What's Wrong with the American Novel?," *American Scholar*, 24 (Autumn 1955): 464-503;

"If You Write for Television...," *New Republic*, 140 (6 April 1959): 16;

"Mrs. Aadland's Little Girl, Beverly," *Esquire*, 56 (November 1961): 142, 189-191;

William Styron (photo copyright © 1979 by Mark Morrow)

"The Death-in-Life of Benjamin Reid," *Esquire*, 57 (February 1962): 114, 141-145;

"Role of the Writer in America," *Michigan's Voices*, 2 (Spring 1962): 7-10;

"As He Lay Dead, A Bitter Grief," *Life*, 53 (20 July 1962): 39-42;

"Aftermath of Benjamin Reid," *Esquire*, 58 (November 1962): 79ff.;

"Two Writers Talk It Over," *Esquire*, 60 (July 1963): 57-59;

"This Quiet Dust," *Harper's*, 230 (April 1965): 135-146;

"Truth and Nat Turner: An Exchange—William Styron Replies," *Nation*, 206 (22 April 1968): 544-547;

"Oldest America," *McCall's*, 95 (July 1968): 94, 123;

"Symposium: Violence in Literature," *American Scholar*, 37 (Summer 1968): 482-496;

"In the Jungle," *New York Review of Books* (26 September 1968): 11-13;

"My Generation," *Esquire*, 70 (October 1968): 123-124;

"On Creativity," *Playboy*, 15 (December 1968): 138;

"The Uses of History in Fiction," *Southern Literary Journal*, 1 (Spring 1969): 57-90;

"Kuznetsov's Confession," *New York Times*, 14 September 1969, IV: 13;

"Dead!," by Styron and John Phillips, *Esquire*, 80 (December 1973): 161-168ff.;

"Auschwitz's Message," *New York Times*, 25 June 1974, p. 37;

"William Styron's Afterword to *The Long March*," *Mississippi Quarterly*, 28 (Spring 1975): 185-189;

"A Friend's Farewell to James Jones," *New York*, 10 (6 June 1977): 40-41;

"Race Is the Plague of Civilization: An Author's View," *U.S. News and World Report*, 88 (28 January 1980): 65-66;

"Almost a Rhodes Scholar: A Personal Reminiscence," *South Atlantic Bulletin*, 45 (May 1980): 1-6;

"In Praise of Vineyard Haven," *New York Times Magazine*, 15 June 1980, p. 30;

"Children of Brief Sunshine," *Architectural Digest*, 41 (March 1984): 32ff.;

"Historic Houses: Thomas Wolfe Remembered," *Architectural Digest*, 41 (October 1984): 194-200.

The critics received *Lie Down in Darkness* (1951) as an auspicious first novel, perhaps the best to appear since World War II. If reminiscent of Faulkner, its style was distinctly the author's own; its psychological insights, accurate; and its moral vision, mature. It was, in fact, an astonishingly good novel for an author only twenty-six at the time of its publication. William Styron was immediately placed in the top rank of writers of his generation; he was awarded the Prix de Rome; and his subsequent work was awaited anxiously by critics and readers alike. The wait was a long one. Between 1951 and the appearance of his second novel, *Set This House on Fire*, in 1960, Styron's only published fiction was a novella, *The Long March* (1956), and an excerpted episode from his work in progress. When *Set This House on Fire* finally appeared, it was not well received, primarily because the story seemed to sprawl out of control, with wildly allegorical episodes obviously satirical in intent. It was not the kind of book *Lie Down in Darkness* had led readers to expect. However, the poetic power of description and the dramatic power of narration and characterization were evident, more refined, and the story was far less derivative than the first novel. Some felt that this was the book Styron needed to get out of his system before going on to his best work. Again the public waited—seven years this time, filled with a trickle of essays, reviews, and excerpts from work in progress—for the appearance of the next novel. When *The Confessions of Nat Turner* was published in 1967, the critics generally agreed that this one had been worth the long wait. Styron had found a subject for which his style and moral vision were perfectly suited. The novel received a great deal of publicity and favorable criticism, and Styron was awarded the Pulitzer Prize in 1968.

After *The Confessions of Nat Turner*, Styron began work on a novel about the military, "The Way of the Warrior." Excerpts appeared in *Esquire* and *American Poetry Review*, but the project ceased to compel Styron and he put it aside. In 1973 he published *In the Clap Shack*, a play that had been produced by the Yale Repertory Theatre the previous year. He also began work on *Sophie's Choice*, two excerpts of which appeared in *Esquire* before its publication in 1979. The novel received mixed reviews, but has been an extremely popular best-seller; it was also the first of Styron's fiction to be made into a movie. Since *Sophie's Choice*, Styron has returned to "The Way of the Warrior" and hopes to have it ready for publication in the near future.

Styron's production of novels has been slow, particularly compared to the pace of most of his contemporaries. He began writing *Lie Down in Darkness* in 1947, and, in the face of a tendency among American critics to measure an artist not only by the quality of his work but by the quantity as well, he has produced only four full-length novels in thirty-nine years. It is significant that Styron has resisted the pressure to produce more rapidly, for it is improbable that he could turn out the high quality work that he has at a faster rate. Styron has limited his production, but his labors are evident in the highly polished prose of all his work.

This polish, as well as power, in Styron's writing has been recognized since the publication of *Lie Down in Darkness*, and Styron has generally been accorded a place among the most accomplished stylists of contemporary American letters. The similarities between *Lie Down in Darkness* and Faulkner's fiction have caused many to see Styron as a southern writer, even as Faulkner's literary heir. Malcolm Cowley even suggested that in some ways Styron had improved on Faulkner's handling of several motifs. There is much in the novel—its setting, its characters, its themes—to indicate that Styron was consciously working in the tradition of Faulkner, Wolfe, and Warren, but, given Styron's southern background, this was to be expected.

Styron's father, William Clark Styron, was a North Carolinian, a marine engineer whose career had taken him to Newport News, Virginia. Styron grew up there on the banks of the James, and when his mother, Pauline Margaret Abraham Styron, died in 1938, Styron's father sent him off to Christchurch, an Episcopal preparatory school for boys on the south bank of the Rappahannock. The school was not as elite as several other of the Virginia prep schools, but it was respectable and it carried on the traditions of the Tidewater gentry. Styron also attended two prominent southern colleges: he spent one year at Davidson before transferring to Duke in 1943.

Despite his frequent use of southern characters and settings, Styron stated in an interview early in his career that he did not consider himself a writer of the southern school. Of course he had been influenced by Faulkner, Warren, and Katherine Anne Porter, but so had nearly every other American writer of his generation. And he has pointed out other influences which he considers as important as the southern ones: Fitzgerald and Dos Passos in America; Conrad and Joyce in

Britain; Flaubert, Dostoyevski, Tolstoy, and Camus on the Continent. (These, of course, are the modern influences. Among the traditional ones he has indicated are the Bible, Shakespeare, Marlowe, Donne, and Blake.)

Styron's apprenticeship as a writer began during his college years. Although he had made early ventures into fiction, they were the usual boyhood attempts at story telling, and he did not consider writing as a career until he began studying with Professor William M. Blackburn at Duke University. Blackburn published two of Styron's stories, "Autumn" and "The Long Dark Road," in his 1945 anthology of Duke narrative and verse and urged him to continue his writing. Styron's education was interrupted by a stint in the Marine Corps toward the end of the war. However, he returned to Duke, and after his graduation in 1947 went to New York to work as a reader for McGraw-Hill; but he disliked the job immensely and left the company after four months. In the same year he enrolled in Hiram Haydn's short-story course at the New School for Social Research. Haydn saw that Styron was not comfortable with the constrictions of the short-story form and suggested that he try writing a novel. As a consequence Styron began work on *Lie Down in Darkness*. Even though he published two more short stories, in *American Vanguard* ("A Moment in Trieste," 1948, and "The Enormous Window," 1950), he must have found Haydn's advice good, for he published no more stories until 1985, when "Love Day" appeared in the August issue of *Esquire:* the short fiction that appeared in magazines between 1950 and 1985 was excerpted from his novels in progress. However, Styron did not find novel writing easy. He has said recently that he was not mature enough, or did not know enough in 1947 to write the story. But his experiences over the next two or three years, during which he established a bohemian existence in Greenwich Village and later spent a period of artistic exile in Brooklyn, provided him with what he needed, and he was able to finish the novel in 1950.

Lie Down in Darkness is an impressive book, much better than Styron's four early short stories—indicative of his talent but clearly apprentice work—would have led one to expect. Styron's greatest problem in his short stories had been with characterization, but the expansive form of the novel allowed him to create interesting, fully developed characters. His talent for poetic description, which had been evident in his apprentice work, was further developed and refined in the novel.

And the story is replete with vividly presented and memorable scenes. It is an emotionally charged book: Styron has said that he wrote his heart into it, that he had been more completely absorbed in its creation than he was with any of his later works. But it is a young man's book, and it has flaws which result from its youthful subjectivity: the imagery at times is too personal, and the metaphors sometimes do not carry the load Styron wished them to carry. In short, the physical matter was not shaped quite well enough to a metaphysical purpose. For instance, Styron opens the book with an interesting strategy to involve the reader directly in the story, to invite him inward through the frame: he does this by projecting a train trip from Richmond to Port Warwick, and he places the reader ("you") on the train; then he describes the passengers, the landscape of passage, and the entry into the town. This device is quite personal, not only because Styron speaks directly to the reader, but also because it is apparently Styron himself who is taking the final leg of a trip from New York to Port Warwick to tell the story of the Loftis family. (This becomes apparent in the final passage of the book when a train leaves Port Warwick headed toward Richmond and the North–evidently with Styron returning to New York after having told the story.) It is an effective device and an appropriate one for a novel which requires a very subjective involvement in its action. Ultimately, however, it must be considered extraneous because it does not integrate with the literal or metaphorical concerns of the story.

Another problem is Styron's having Peyton Loftis commit suicide on the day the United States dropped the first atom bomb on Japan. A coincidence of this sort must mean something, but what it means is not apparent. The novel is certainly not concerned with politics; in fact, the characters, caught up in their own personal problems, are nearly oblivious to the war. Thus the coincidence must be considered gratuitous, a misdirected attempt to give another dimension to the novel.

These are artistic flaws, certainly, the kinds of flaws that reveal themselves only after one has finished the novel. Yet, in spite of its flaws, *Lie Down in Darkness* has worn well over the nearly forty years since its publication. It has been republished in several paperback editions and is probably the most often taught of Styron's novels in college English courses.

Styron has said that after the idea for the book came to him, the most difficult technical problem he faced was the handling of time. His solution was to present the action within the frame of a single day, then fill in the necessary background through a series of flashbacks. The day which frames the story is that of Peyton's funeral. As the narrative begins, Milton Loftis, her father; Dolly Bonner, his mistress; Ella Swan, the family servant; and the undertaker and his understrapper are waiting on a sultry August day at the Port Warwick train station for the arrival of Peyton's body. During the course of the novel the body arrives, is carried, despite a series of automotive mishaps, to the graveyard, and is buried. But this is only the aftermath; the climax of the story has already occurred, and most of the novel is occupied with explaining how the characters arrived at this dreadful state of affairs. One of the most impressive aspects of the book is how well Styron handles the shifts in time and makes the present situation a believable outcome of the history he presents through the flashbacks. He evokes a sense of inevitability, an essential element of the tragic mode. And, indeed, the novel is a tragedy, not in the classical or Elizabethan sense, perhaps, for every age dictates its own terms for tragedy, but certainly in the tradition of *Sister Carrie* (1900), *The Great Gatsby* (1925), and *The Sound and the Fury* (1929).

The central and most fully developed character of the novel is Milton Loftis, and essentially the tragedy is his, for although it is Peyton who comes to a tragic end when she flings herself, naked, from the window of a Harlem sweatshop, it is Milton who must mourn and acknowledge his large share of responsibility for her suicide. He has spoiled her and almost literally stifled her to death with love. Milton is a charming and handsome man, but a feckless one. Once an ambitious young lawyer with political aspirations, he has slowly let his law practice dissipate until he makes barely enough for his family's subsistence and depends on the inheritance of his wife, Helen, for the amenities. Helen, whose father and model of manhood had been an army officer, a man of strength and authority, reacts to Milton's ineffectuality early in their marriage and begins to withdraw from him. The affection she withdraws from Milton is transferred to Maudie, their retarded daughter. In reaction, Milton lavishes his love on their other child, the normal and lovely Peyton. Thus the family is polarized—and neither parent is equipped to deal with the problem.

Helen becomes unreasonably jealous of Peyton, and her incipient emotional imbalance is aggravated into a psychotic rigidity. Milton, who still loves his wife, would like to reconcile their marriage but finds he cannot cope with Helen's frigid inaccessibility. Consequently, he turns more to Peyton and whiskey and finally initiates an affair with Dolly Bonner, the sensual and willing wife of an acquaintance. The situation is untenable yet irresolvable, and herein lies the tragedy of the book, for Peyton, who is not only beautiful but intelligent, and possesses a great potential for love and life, must grow up in and is finally destroyed by this fractured world. No matter how she tries to escape it—at college in the mountains of Virginia, in the homes of friends during the summers, or, finally, by rebelling against not only her family but the entire culture of her childhood by going to New York and marrying a Jewish artist—she cannot. She must finally admit both her hatred for her mother and incestuous love for her father and, what is more damaging to her psyche, that she suffers from the same weaknesses as they—her father's promiscuity and dependence on alcohol and her mother's insane jealousy and vindictiveness.

Lie Down in Darkness is a deterministically pessimistic novel. Peyton, Helen, and Milton are trapped by circumstance and biology, and there is no salvation available to them through a society whose selfishness and hedonism Styron captures vividly at Peyton's wedding reception. Nor is salvation available through religion, the ineffectuality of which is manifest in the Episcopal minister, Carey Carr, and the charlatanism of Daddy Faith. Nor is there salvation in love in a world that has forgotten love's proper forms. If there is any indication of hope in the world of this novel, it lies with two characters: Peyton's Jewish husband, Harry Miller, who can love and knows its proper meaning even though he cannot save the already doomed Peyton; and the Loftis's black servant La Ruth—not Ella Swan, who is as much as the whites a victim of a false respectability and who is hoodwinked by the religious huckster Daddy Faith. La Ruth, Ella's simple daughter, loved Peyton simply for what she was. Though neither Harry nor La Ruth can save her, they can mourn her death honestly and without self-pity.

Much has been made of Styron's indebtedness to Faulkner in *Lie Down in Darkness*, particularly to *The Sound and the Fury* and *As I Lay Dying* (1930). Styron has admitted that before he wrote the novel he had gorged himself on Faulkner's

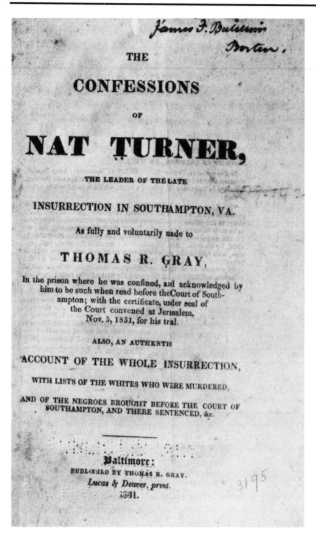

Title page for the 1831 account of the slave rebellion which served as the basis for Styron's controversial 1967 novel of the same title (courtesy of Manuscript Division, Library of Congress)

works. But, in fact, Faulkner is not the only modern American author to whom Styron is indebted. The country club life of Port Warwick and the several parties are reminiscent of Fitzgerald, and there are similarities in the characterizations of Milton Loftis and Dick Diver of *Tender Is the Night* (1934). Furthermore, Peyton's experiences in New York are certainly indebted to Dos Passos's *Manhattan Transfer* (1925). Perhaps Styron would have been well advised to have avoided close parallels with Faulkner. But he never follows Faulkner or his other sources slavishly. Even where the parallels are closest, as in the similarities between the final section of *Lie Down in Darkness* and the Dilsey section of *The Sound and the Fury*, Styron has put the material to his own use—the differences in his treatment are

more significant than the similarities. And if Styron is to be accused of stealing from Faulkner, it should be pointed out that Faulkner seems to have stolen from Styron also: in *The Mansion* (1959), Linda Snopes's journey to New York and her marriage to a Jew who becomes involved in the Spanish civil war certainly owe something to Peyton's experiences.

In 1950, shortly after *Lie Down in Darkness* had been accepted for publication by Bobbs-Merrill, Styron was recalled to active service by the Marine Corps because of the United States' involvement in Korea. It was a traumatic experience for him, he has said, and for those others like him who had remained in the inactive reserve after World War II. They had believed their ordeals in Europe and the Pacific were to end war for a long time to come. They had fallen back into the comparatively careless routines of civilian life; many had families and businesses; but suddenly here they were again back in uniform, torn from their families, their businesses disrupted. Styron had neither wife nor business, but he did have a craft and he resented bitterly finding himself again at Camp Lejeune, North Carolina, reft of his artist's life in Greenwich Village, away from the literary circles of New York. There he was, instead, making a forced march through the fierce summer heat of coastal Carolina. When he was released from the Marines the following year, he decided to write about that experience, to capture the bitterness and frustration that he and his fellow reservists had felt. The result was *The Long March*, published in 1956.

Styron has said that of all his work this novella was perhaps the easiest for him to write, that once he got started it seemed almost to write itself. He wrote the entire story in about six weeks in Paris in the summer of 1952. His facility is explained largely by the fact that *The Long March* is really an extended short story rather than a novel. It is concerned with a single event, and the history of the characters is not particularly important to understanding their behavior during the course of the story. That is not to say that it is merely an exposé of military life or simply an effort on Styron's part to purge himself of his bitterness. Styron has transmuted his experience and given it a larger significance: the story becomes a metaphor for the human condition itself, and its complexity derives from symbolic interaction rather than from psychological development. In fact, the story has a classical neatness and efficiency, for its form and execution owe a large debt to Sophoclean drama.

There are three major characters: Lieutenant Culver, from whose point of view most of the action is seen; Captain Mannix, a Jew from Brooklyn, who is the protagonist of the story; and Colonel Templeton, the battalion commander, a regular officer who believes in putting his troops through hell to prepare them for combat. As the novel begins, the bodies of eight dead marines lie strewn about the pine woods. Two mortar shells have misfired during an exercise and fallen among the troops. Culver, who has not witnessed the incident but arrives on the scene to observe the aftermath, stumbles away from the corpses to retch in the leaves nearby. Thus the tone of the novel is set. Shortly after, Colonel Templeton orders a forced march for his battalion–thirty-six miles back to base. The march would be ordeal enough for seasoned troops, but these are reserves, still poorly conditioned, and even though the march is to begin at night, it will extend through the torturous heat of the following day. There is the usual bitching among the troops, but most, like Culver, accept the inevitability of the march and reconcile themselves to the protracted suffering of their impending ordeal. Mannix, however, having already shown signs of incipient rebellion, decides that he will not accept lightly what he considers an inhuman abuse of authority. Since overt revolt would be senselessly futile, Mannix inverts his rebellion: he promises himself that he will complete the march at all costs and warns the company he commands that it, to a man, must complete the march also. For Mannix, the march becomes a contest with Templeton, in which he defies the colonel's authority by following his commands to the letter. It is a familiar form of rebellion, a childish defiance, but it is the only form available to Mannix in these circumstances. The situation is aggravated when Mannix finds a nail protruding into his boot, which during the course of the march punctures his foot and causes it to swell. Mannix hobbles on through the night and the next day, exhorting his men to do the same. And increasingly he makes his defiance known to Templeton. The story reaches its climax when Templeton, seeing Mannix's condition, orders him to board a truck. But Mannix will have none of it: he speaks his contempt for the colonel and disobeys his command by continuing the march. Templeton has no choice save to order him court-martialed. Though Mannix completes the thirty-six miles

himself, he relents, at Culver's prompting, in his demands on his company and allows those who are exhausted or injured to ride into camp on trucks provided for that purpose.

The focus of the story is the conflict between Mannix, the individual, and Templeton, the figure of authority and representative of the system. Culver functions merely as a control figure, an observer who is not directly involved in the conflict, whose normality provides a point of reference, and whose sensitivity to what he witnesses informs and gives meaning to the action. Although Culver does not join Mannix's revolt, he sympathizes with it; yet he also senses the paradox and irony of Mannix's position. He can see what Mannix fails to see: that Templeton is indifferent to Mannix's rebellion so long as it does not directly challenge his own authority. Further, Culver realizes that Mannix's particular form of rebellion has turned him into a tyrant even more inflexible than Templeton himself. Only after his confrontation with Templeton does Mannix's humanity return. He is purged of his rage and is able to perceive his situation objectively once again.

The Long March suggests two important sources in myth. The first is implied by Mannix's swollen foot: he is Oedipus; Templeton, Laius. Of course, the parallels are only loose ones, and the implications of the Oedipal motif are more Freudian than classical. Yet the meaning is the same as Sophocles': a search for evil always leads back to oneself. The other myth suggested is that of Sisyphus, particularly in Camus's redaction and interpretation. Again the parallels are loose, but the march is much like Sisyphus's task of rolling the stone uphill. Both are senseless, absurd, but inescapable. If a man accepts the task unquestioned, he is less than a man. Only by questioning, seeing the task for what it really is, and then, paradoxically, rebelling against his condition by accepting it, can man assert his dignity in the face of absurdity and become the moral creature he is capable of being. Both parallels imply that Mannix's rebellion is metaphorically a metaphysical revolt against a universe that makes no sense, which seems even inimical to man: eight men die for no reason; a battalion must walk thirty-six torturous miles while trucks that could carry them follow, empty, at the rear. And as Culver lies awake in the radio tent, he hears only static, the chaotic sounds of a universe without an understandable message, interrupted occasionally by the puny voices of men. The final scene of the book, however, is not a despairing one. Back at the BOQ, now confined to quarters, Mannix prepares to shower–a physical cleansing to signify the emotional and spiritual ones he has just undergone. As he limps toward the bath, he passes a black maid, who sees his suffering and sympathizes with him. "You poor man. . . . Do it hurt?" she says. Mannix stops, his towel falls from around his waist, and standing naked to the world he says, without self-pity, "Deed it does." The southern black and the Jew–both know suffering and can understand one another. In American Indian myth an old woman says, "It is best we die forever, so that we can feel sorry for each other." In order to comprehend that old woman's meaning one must meet the reality of man's condition head on, must understand suffering and futility before he can rise above it and sympathize with his fellow creatures: it seems that Mannix and the black maid have.

When Styron was released from active duty in 1951, he returned to New York. In 1952, having won the Prix de Rome, Styron left for Europe. In Paris he helped found the *Paris Review*, which began publication in spring 1953. In Rome, in May 1953, he married Rose Burgunder, and the next year they returned to America, to Roxbury, Connecticut, where Styron began work on *Set This House on Fire*. For the scenes of this novel he drew on his boyhood experiences at Christchurch School in Virginia, his bohemian life in Greenwich Village, and his sojourn in Europe, particularly his brief visit in 1953 to Rapallo, Italy, where the American movie *Beat the Devil* was on location. Styron worked hard on the book for the next six years, but when it was published in 1960, it was not well received. And even though a few have admired and defended it over the last thirty years, it is still generally considered the least successful of his novels. Styron himself has indicated, however, that it is, perhaps, his favorite. In this novel he seems to have given his imagination freer rein than he had in *Lie Down in Darkness* or *The Long March*, or would in *Nat Turner* or *Sophie's Choice*. Perhaps it is an apparent looseness, a tendency to wild flights of imagination, that has caused critics to overlook the very solid basic structure of the novel.

Set This House on Fire was Styron's first book to use the first-person narrator, an important development in his technique since all of his subsequent work has been in the first person also. Although there are elements of satire in his earlier work, the dominant mode is that of tragedy; in

Set This House on Fire satire prevails, and the mode is that of tragicomedy.

Peter Leverett, the narrator, tells the story by recounting conversations which took place between himself and Cass Kinsolving at Cass's home in Charleston, South Carolina. There, over a period of several weeks, they reconstruct the events at Sambuco, where Cass has killed Mason Flagg. In the course of their conversation Peter reveals that he had known Mason since boyhood, when they attended prep school together in Virginia. Mason is an intruder, a northerner whose wealthy father has bought an old plantation on the York River near Gloucester. Mason's looks, money, and self-assurance attract Peter and they become friends, but Peter soon learns that Mason is a liar and a coward. Finally, Mason is dismissed from the school for seducing a half-witted thirteen-year-old girl in the chapel. After the war Peter encounters Mason again in New York, and the two spend a sybaritic week together. Here Peter learns a great deal more about Mason's compulsive lying and shallowness, even though he is still attracted by Mason's glib charm. Peter's final encounter with Mason is in Sambuco, where Mason has invited him for a visit. When Peter arrives he finds an American movie company on location, many of the principals staying in Mason's rented palace. Peter enters this scene of frivolous and hedonistic chaos to renew their friendship, but within twenty-four hours Mason is dead, apparently by suicide; the movie company has abruptly departed; and Peter is left to clean up the mess.

In contrast to Peter's normality, Cass is a guilt-ridden expatriate painter. A North Carolina country boy whose parents were killed when he was a child, he has been raised by a poor uncle near Wilmington. During the war he saw action with the Marines in the Pacific, an experience that triggered his mental breakdown. After psychiatric treatment by the navy, Cass studies painting, marries a pretty, guileless Catholic girl, and moves to Paris to practice his art. But Cass's guilt, the source of which he does not yet recognize, drives him to incessant drinking, and he does little painting. Finally, he moves his family, which by now includes children, southward, ending in Sambuco, where he establishes residence. Here he meets Mason and, later, Peter. Mason takes advantage of Cass's alcoholism, uses him, and finally degrades him publicly. Cass, in his drunken masochism, seems to enjoy this degradation, but when Mason rapes and, Cass believes, fatally beats the Italian girl with whom Cass has fallen in love, Cass chases Mason down, smashes his head with a rock, and throws him from a precipice.

This is the sprawling and complex story Peter and Cass reconstruct. In some ways their collaboration is like that of Quentin Compson and Shreve McCannon in *Absalom, Absalom!* (1936), but the similarity is only superficial, for Peter and Cass are piecing together things they know from their own past, not hypothesizing about someone else's. A more important parallel exists between Peter and Nick Carraway of *The Great Gatsby*. They are both observer-narrators only peripherally involved in the action. They have similar backgrounds, and their moral sensibilities are basically the same. Styron has drawn on Fitzgerald in this way, it seems, to call our attention to the parallels between Jay Gatsby and Mason Flagg, not that they are alike–both represent rather what their creators saw as the prevailing American sensibility of their time. Mason is a degraded Gatsby, because Styron sees the American dream of the post-World War II era as a degraded dream. He has ensured in other ways that the reader does not miss this point. For instance, Mason Flagg's surname itself associates him with American ideals. His connection with Hollywood (his father's money was made in the movie distribution business) associates him with that materialistic-fantasy aspect of modern American life. Furthermore, Mason's interest in the arts and his pose as a playwright are entirely superficial–Mason says he believes that art has no future. Even his interest in jazz is faddish. He is a racist. He is obsessed with sex–but sex for Mason exists outside the context of love. It is, he says, the new frontier, a thing to be pursued for itself. The significant thing to note is that with this burden of symbolism, Mason is less than a real character: he is a villain. And this, too, is a part of Styron's strategy. When Mason is killed the reader is glad that he is dead. This is a necessary characteristic of tragicomedy.

Cass, the hero, on the other hand, is a very real character. He is a complicated bundle of faults and virtues. His greatest virtue is his sense of integrity: he is earnest in whatever he does, even his drinking and fornication. He is also a country boy, whereas Mason is an urbanite, and this seems to be one key to the difference in their values. Since Cass hates everything in American life that Mason stands for, particularly its self-indulgent and cosmetic affluence, he attempts to

escape it by expatriating himself in Europe. But, of course, he cannot, since in the post-World War II world America is everywhere. For Cass, America is not only external–it is internal as well: he carries America around in him, both the bad and the good of it. Cass is living off America when he accepts his pension checks; he is also living off the spoils of capitalism when he uses his wife's earnings from her inheritance. He carries also the guilt of the racism of his youth, a guilt he attempts to expiate by helping the peasants at Tramonti. Styron thus develops this irony: in trying to escape America, Cass is trying to escape himself–through expatriatism, through alcohol and hallucination, and, finally, by trying to recapture a prelapsarian world with Francesca, the innocent and beautiful Italian girl Mason rapes. But Cass's integrity, engendered by his puritan, rural-American background, will not let him escape; therefore, he must finally come to terms with his guilt or be destroyed. By killing Mason, Cass takes the first step toward his salvation. Metaphorically, by destroying the symbol of all he hates in American life, he accepts the burden of guilt for it. This becomes apparent when Luigi, the Italian policeman, will not let Cass expiate his crime by confessing it publicly. When Luigi reveals that it is not Mason but Saverio, the half-wit, who has killed Francesca, it is clear that Mason as a symbol of evil is merely a chimera–it is the human condition itself that is at fault, not Mason and his ilk. Thus, what Cass accepts finally is humanity, his own as well as others'–the burden of an imperfect world. This does not mean, however, that he must accept it indiscriminately. When he returns to America, he chooses to live in old Charleston, a city of tradition. He becomes a cartoonist, satirizing, we assume, from the vantage point of his hard-earned knowledge, those things which he finds repulsive and ludicrous in American life.

After *Set This House on Fire*, Styron turned to a subject that had been on his mind since his studies with Hiram Haydn in the 1940s. In 1831 in Southampton County, Virginia, Nat Turner led the most successful slave rebellion in United States history. However, the rebellion was aborted, and Turner was captured, tried, and executed. Although Turner's full confession, which included some important autobiography, was published in the same year, little was known about the man. Styron felt that this was promising material for fictional treatment, but in the 1950s he was not ready to tackle the subject. The racial tensions of the 1960s, however, started Styron thinking about the rebellion again, and he decided to write Turner's story. At first he thought the material would make at most a novella, and he wrote what is now part 1 of the book. The story was obviously incomplete and seemed to demand full novelistic treatment. Styron decided to reconstruct Nat's past to account for the man who led the bloody insurrection and who met his death with equanimity. He would use the few facts that were known about Turner, and for the rest he would allow his imagination free rein. He worked on the novel over the next several years, publishing excerpts and an essay, "This Quiet Dust" (*Harper's*, 1965), about his researches in Southampton County, as he worked toward completion.

The novel was published, with much fanfare, in 1967 and was favorably received by critics and the public. Many considered its appearance the literary event of the decade. Shortly thereafter, however, a reaction developed in the black intellectual community and to some extent among white liberals. In 1968 a collection of essay attacks on the novel was published under the title *William Styron's Nat Turner: Ten Black Writers Respond*. The charges against Styron were many. He was accused of falsifying details of Turner's life, ignoring known facts, misrepresenting the institution of slavery, and, ultimately, of misrepresenting Turner himself. Styron was condemned as a racist and for his audacity in trying to write from a black man's (and a slave's, besides) point of view. Styron, who was not a racist and whose intention was to bridge the gap between the races, was disturbed and thrown off balance. He answered the attacks as best he could. He argued for his interpretation of the slave society, and he was supported by such noted historians as Eugene Genovese and C. Vann Woodward. He also argued for his use of the known facts of Turner's life, and in 1971 Seymour Gross and Eileen Bender published a well-researched article in *American Quarterly* which defended the factual accuracy of Styron's treatment. For several years criticism of the novel was polarized and sidetracked: the book was being considered as history rather than fiction, although it was evident that many of the blacks were also criticizing it as propaganda–or, rather, for its not being propaganda. They wanted Turner presented as a heroic figure–Styron had presented him as a human being. They wanted a militant slave population–Styron had presented them as docile, or at least subdued; and historical research has generally supported Styron's view.

Although Styron's choice of a historical subject for his novel and his calling it "a meditation on history" suggest that it is in some way a historical study, *Nat Turner* is fiction, and it must be judged as such. Those who have read the 1831 *Confessions* know that Styron's Nat is not Turner. Turner was a narrow fanatic; Nat has poetic and moral breadth. Nat is not only the main character–his is the book's controlling vision.

At the center of Nat's psychological development is his relationship with his white owners. Styron has pointed out, and this is supported by the surviving statements of slaves themselves, that those who were treated with the most indulgence were the very slaves who rebelled or ran away. Nat is a precocious child, and because his mother is a house servant of a liberal and benevolent master, his precocity is discovered early. The master, Samuel Turner, has his family teach Nat to read; in adolescence Nat is taught carpentry. Turner's idea is to prepare Nat for freedom. He is a well-intentioned master, but he is also a naive, idealistic one; and what he accomplishes in essence is placing Nat in racial limbo. Nat's accomplishments and position on the plantation have separated him from his fellow blacks, yet he cannot enter the world of the whites except on their limited terms. But Nat accepts this ambivalent position in plantation society because his callowness allows him to believe that his promised emancipation will solve his problems. When the plantation fails and Turner puts Nat into the Reverend Epps's hands, Nat is abruptly awakened to the reality of the slave's true condition. He is worked at menial tasks until he is numb; and Epps, whom Turner has misjudged, sells him, rather than free him as Turner had directed.

During his childhood, Nat, cut off from the other slaves and without a father, naturally adopts the Turners as substitute family and as role models. He comes to scorn the field slaves for their squalid living and ignorance. As a consequence, even when he is forced among his fellow blacks, he is never able to accept them as fellow creatures. Those few he does befriend he attempts to reshape through training and education into suitable companions. More damaging to his development, he is cut off from sexual contact with women–from those of his own race by his scorn, and from the white women by the codes of society. His masturbatory fantasies are filled with white women, not black ones. (The only sexual contact Styron allows Nat is a homosexual one with Willis, a boy Nat has groomed to meet his own standards of behavior.) Eventually this isolation from his own race and his adulation of the whites causes in Nat a traumatic sense of betrayal. His idealized concept of womanhood is shattered when he overhears its embodiment, Emmeline Turner, cursing and fornicating with her cousin in the bushes. When Turner surreptitiously sells Nat's friend Willis, Nat is abject in his disillusionment. The ultimate betrayal comes when Turner delivers Nat into the clutches of Epps. Nat is so outraged that he swears never to think of Turner again.

Nat's life with the Turners is definitive: his Bible reading, his isolation, his celibacy, his betrayals have turned him inward upon himself; and after Epps sells him, he realizes that the freedom he had expected is lost forever. These are the factors that eventually cause Nat to conceive of the rebellion. The vengeance of the Old Testament God becomes the vengeance Nat envisions himself wreaking on the white community that has caused his suffering. The more ascetic Nat becomes, the more powerful his vision and his desire to destroy the whites. And because he has gained the confidence of the slaves in the community through his preaching, he is able to put his plan into effect.

Styron's use of psychology is convincing. Given the circumstances of Nat's life, his insurrection was inevitable. Nat has absorbed during his life with the Turners their humanistic idealism, along with a concept of love. Though he tries to ignore these qualities in himself, tries to sublimate them to his vengeance, he never can.' Styron manifests this theme through earthy imagery associated with the body and its functions: defecation, urination, the smells of sweat and secretion, fornication, the details of death. The effect of this imagery is to ground the book solidly in the physical world of human flesh, a world that Nat's dehumanizing idealism would like to escape. Nat cannot accept his body because he cannot accept the human condition itself. On the other hand, Nat's need to love finds an outlet in Margaret Whitehead. She, unlike Emmeline Turner, is a worthy object of his love. His relationship to her, however, is complex: he hates her for her whiteness but loves her for herself; yet her whiteness is symbolic of her purity, which he loves, and he hates her for the degradation of his sexual attraction to her. His attitude toward her is as ambivalent as post-Freudian psychology can make it. But ultimately her symbolism becomes very simple: she represents love. Styron has said that the

movement of the book is from Old Testament to New Testament. In these terms it is a movement from vengeance to love–from Yahweh to Christ. And though Margaret is not Christ, she is a sacrificial figure. She is the only person Nat kills. Through her he sins, yet is paradoxically purged of sin. And through her he is finally redeemed. The terms of their relationship are solidly in the tradition of romantic love, which holds that the souls of lovers who have been separated in this life by insurmountable obstacles will be joined in a spiritual realm beyond this world. At the end of the book Nat believes he is going to join Margaret: he has not recovered God, but he has discovered Love.

On a metaphorical level, *Nat Turner* is as much about the condition of modern man as any other of Styron's novels. Analogically, Nat's world is the modern world in its instability. Economic forces have disrupted a formerly stable society. And Nat's life has a universal quality–in childhood we feel restricted, enslaved, and we look forward to the freedom of adulthood; but that freedom never comes, for, like Nat, we are enslaved by other masters. We stand cowed before them–or we rebel. The rebellion is ultimately against the human condition itself. It may, through knowledge gained by suffering, reconcile us to our condition, as it does Mannix and Cass; or it may destroy us if it is too extreme, as it does Peyton and Nat. But there is a difference between Peyton's end and Nat's. Although Nat is not reconciled to this life–for he says he would do it all again–he is redeemed by love, and that is an important difference.

After *Nat Turner* Styron began work on a novel to be entitled "The Way of the Warrior," about a professional marine officer, a Virginian and VMI graduate, who maintains an interest in the liberal arts and wants to humanize the armed services through reform. However, Styron gave the novel up, he says, because the material ceased to move him. In 1971 Styron began work on a play, *In the Clap Shack*, based on his experiences at Parris Island. It was first presented on 15 December 1972 at the Yale Repertory Theatre in New Haven. Although several critics liked the play, Clive Barnes wrote an unfavorable review of the performance and seems to have killed any chances the play had of going to New York. As Styron has said, a play is a collaborative enterprise of playwright, director, and actors. Perhaps flaws in the original production caused the play's lack of success. (Styron has said that the lead was not cast properly, although he liked several of the other roles.) But it seems that the play itself must bear the final responsibility. The scene of the play is the urological ward of a hospital on a marine base in the South. The year is 1943. The main character is a young marine, Magruder, who has been confined to the "clap shack" by mistake. Because an acute case of trench mouth has caused a positive reading on his Wasserman test, he is believed to have a rampant case of syphilis. The error is finally discovered, but not before Magruder has suffered considerable anguish. When he learns that he is well, that really he has never been "sick," he rebels against the system and its representative–the perverted doctor who is responsible for his suffering–by speaking his anger. As a consequence, he is court-martialed, but he is willing to pay that price to have his say. Magruder is another of Styron's rebels. But Magruder's rebellion is not convincing, because there is too little preparation for it, and when it comes, it seems out of character. It appears that Styron's imagination needs room to work itself out: the compression of drama does not suit his talent. Even though the play has some fine comic moments, the comedy is undermined by its serious concerns: the racial conflict, the rigid institution, inhuman technology, perverted authority, and the pervasive "sickness" of society itself. In short, it is too busy with these various themes to succeed as drama. *In the Clap Shack* is more interesting as a microcosmic study of Styron's novelistic work than it is as a self-contained work of art.

During 1973 Styron collaborated with John Phillips on a screenplay, "Dead!" (published in the December 1973 issue of *Esquire*), about the murder of Albert Snyder by his wife Ruth and her lover Judd Gray, which had caused a sensation in 1927. The treatment is similar to James M. Cain's in *The Postman Always Rings Twice* (1934), and is of little interest to a study of Styron's artistic development, except to indicate his continuing involvement in the issue of capital punishment.

In the early 1970s, when Styron's interest in "The Way of the Warrior" began to lag, he had a dream-vision of a Polish girl he had known in Brooklyn in the late 1940s. There was nothing mystical about the dream, he says, but he realized it was a kind of artistic mandate to give up the military novel and work on her story, which he tentatively titled "Sophie's Choice: A Memory." For the next five years he worked almost constantly on the manuscript, interrupted only by a trip to Po-

land to do research and to get a feel for the country in which much of the action is set. Styron completed the manuscript late in 1978, and it was published as *Sophie's Choice* in June 1979. The reviews were mixed. Edith Milton, in the *Yale Review*, found it "an ambiguous, masterful, and enormously satisfying novel." Paul Gray, the reviewer for *Time*, called it an impressive achievement. Philip Leon, in the *Virginia Quarterly Review*, also found it masterful and impressive. In *Atlantic* Benjamin DeMott said that although the book was serious to the core, it failed to take command of the reader: it was an "overreaching blockbuster." John Gardner, in the *New York Times Book Review*, stated that although it was in many ways a masterful and moving book, he was not persuaded by it and that the devices of the southern gothic novel were inappropriate to the treatment of the Holocaust. The anonymous reviewer for the *New Yorker* found it overwrought: its style and lectures reduced Sophie's story to theory. Alvin Rosenburg, in *Midstream*, stated that, from the Jewish point of view, Styron had written not so much a novel of the Holocaust, but a "spoof of the same."

Such diverse responses were to be expected for a book as complex as *Sophie's Choice*. The use of narrative suspension and the sheer length of the book make heavy demands on its readers, particularly those who want Styron to "get on with the story." Because the subject matter, the Holocaust, is one of the most horrifying and perplexing moral problems of modern history, it was inevitable that the novel evoke contradictory responses. There has been no concerted attack on the novel (like that of *William Styron's Nat Turner: Ten Black Writers Respond*), but Rosenburg's review in *Midstream* is an example of the type of reaction Styron expected. Although Styron researched the Holocaust as thoroughly as he thought necessary for his purposes, *Sophie's Choice* is a work of fiction and must be approached as such. Styron needed only to provide a credible account of one individual's experience of the Holocaust to satisfy the artistic demands of the story: whether or not it convinces us as a valid and moving projection of human experience is the question, not its historical accuracy.

First, one must see that, despite its title, *Sophie's Choice* is Stingo's story, not Sophie's. The controlling vision is his, and all the strands of the novel are important because of their effect on him. He is the center: thus he provides the novel's structural coherence. Furthermore, it is an initiation story. Stingo is just out of college: his formal education is complete; now he must confront the world and come to terms with it. But if we see Stingo as an isolated individual, we miss the great importance of the novel. Stingo, besides being a believable fictional creation, is also representative of a whole generation of Americans. World War II had altered significantly the relationship of the United States to the rest of the world. It had become the world's major power. The lingering isolationist attitudes fostered by the Monroe Doctrine were effectively brought to an end, because the United States had assumed an international position of political and moral responsibility. The war also changed relationships within the country. It accelerated industrial and urban growth and promoted a new mobility of the population. Life all over the country became more uniform, and American experience became national, rather than regional. *Sophie's Choice* is about the period immediately following the war, and it captures in a vital way the process of change American attitudes had to undergo to reflect these new conditions.

By taking up residence among the Jews in Brooklyn, Stingo metaphorically enters the international experience, since the Jews are the most extensive coherent cosmopolitan culture. And by confronting the Holocaust through Sophie, and through his reading on the subject, he attempts to understand one of the greatest moral problems of the modern world.

But Stingo has other problems to face as well–the personal ones of a young man entering the adult world. These are primarily social and sexual. His social education is manifested in his relationships with Farrell at McGraw-Hill, Nathan Landau, Sophie, Leslie Lapidus, and the other minor characters who inhabit the book. For Stingo it is primarily a matter of adjusting himself to a new social milieu with different attitudes from the one he had left in the South. His sexual education is determined by his encounters with the Jewish "princess" Leslie Lapidus, the "Southern belle" Mary Alice Grimball, and, most importantly, Sophie. Some reviewers and readers have objected to the heavy sexual emphasis of the novel as being irrelevant to its main concerns. But if we see Stingo as the central figure, they are certainly not irrelevant. His personal social and sexual problems make him come alive as a fictional creation. If Stingo's problems were only of a metaphysical and higher moral nature, his characterization would be incomplete–he would be a

flat, theoretical character indeed. As Styron has pointed out, Stingo's masturbatory fantasies and sexual frustrations are just the kind that the sexual and emotional stinginess of the late 1940s and 1950s caused. Through Leslie and Mary Alice, Styron plants the novel solidly in the ground of its times. One must also see that the sexual, emotional, moral, and metaphysical concerns of the novel come together in Sophie. Thus the final consummation of Stingo's sexual drives by Sophie has a structural and metaphorical function. It is through Sophie's revelation of her experiences that Stingo is able to see the magnitude of evil represented by the Holocaust. Through Sophie's (and his own) relationship with the attractive but psychotic Nathan, Stingo learns firsthand about love, hate, and anguish. Since Sophie serves in this way as the vehicle through which Stingo learns about the world on a number of levels, it is appropriate that she initiate him into manhood by giving him his first complete sexual experience.

Besides the digressive sexual episodes concerning Leslie and Mary Alice, there is also the digression about the slave Artiste and the fifty-five-hundred-dollar bequest that resulted from his sale, part of which supports Stingo while he is working on his novel. To some this material has seemed irrelevant. But seen from Stingo's point of view, it is quite relevant. In dealing with the evil and guilt Sophie reveals in her conversations about her early life and her experiences at Auschwitz, Stingo must reach into his own personal and cultural past for an analogy to help him understand the things she tells him. The closest analogies he can find to the concentration camps and racial hatred of the Nazis are slavery and the whites' hatred of blacks he has witnessed in his own past. The stories of Artiste, of Nat Turner, and of Bobby Weed, the modern victim of southern racial hatred, all help him to understand the Holocaust. The analogies are not exact, but they are close. Moreover, Styron's use of psychology here is quite valid. Whenever humans encounter the new, they must draw analogies from their own experience to help them understand it. The gestalt furnished by the analogy is necessary before the particularities of the new can be studied and sorted.

It is interesting to note in this connection that Styron originally intended to make "Shadrack," which appeared in *Esquire* (November 1978), part of *Sophie's Choice*. The story establishes the narrator's personal contact with a black who had lived in slavery. But Styron decided that it did not belong–probably because its rather sentimental treatment was inappropriate to the tone of the novel. Also, its inclusion would have given too much emphasis to the theme of slavery and, thus, reduced the weight of Sophie's ordeal.

Two other aspects of *Sophie's Choice* need comment here. The first is the characterization of Nathan, which some readers have criticized because the reasons for his "paranoid schizophrenia" are never adequately explained. They fail to see that that is precisely Styron's strategy. Nathan represents on an individual level the "paranoid schizophrenia" that can beset society at large. Nathan's disease is equivalent to that which led to Nazism in Germany. The German culture was intelligent and capable of great love and the creation of great beauty (as represented in the novel by their music)–but they proved also capable of the greatest evil. Nathan, likewise, is intelligent, capable of great love and the appreciation, if not the creation, of great beauty; but he is also capable of hatred, persecution, and destructive evil. Neither Nathan nor German history can be explained by laws of cause and effect. They are part of the inexplicable mystery of existence.

The other aspect that needs comment is the novel's title. It refers on one level to the choice given Sophie at Auschwitz between sending her son or her daughter to the gas chambers. On a more important level it refers to her choice to commit suicide with Nathan. But by extension it also refers to Stingo: he has the choice of whether to reject or accept life, whether to live or die. His symbolic rebirth at the end of the novel on the beach at Coney Island, where he emerges from the sand the children have covered him with while he slept, indicates his decision. He has looked into the face of the Gorgon of life through the mirror-shield of Sophie. He does not understand it, but he now knows its terms. He knows the depths of ugliness and horror and the exquisite heights of beauty and love. And he chooses to accept it, a choice available to all men. Thus, through the title and its implications Styron indicates his belief that man is a morally free creature: he is free to choose. He may choose to commit the most horrifying of evils; but he may also choose to work for the greatest good. What he must not do is convince himself, as the German Commandant Höss does, that he has no choice. If he does, he has already committed himself to evil.

Since *Sophie's Choice* Styron has returned to work on "The Way of the Warrior." He feels that he has now worked out the structural and thematic problems that had caused his "writer's block" in the early 1970s. The two published excerpts from the novel ("Marriott, the Marine," *Esquire*, 1971, and "The Suicide Run," *American Poetry Review*, 1974) indicate that it is a first-person narrative, drawn apparently from Styron's experiences at Camp Lejeune in 1951. Styron's only other published fiction since *Sophie's Choice* is "Love Day," which appeared in the August 1985 issue of *Esquire*. Its narrator is Stingo (of *Sophie's Choice*). The action is set on a troop ship off Okinawa in 1945 on the day of the United States' invasion of the island. The story plays off the irony of the military's designation of the invasion day as "Love Day" against the marines' intense hatred of the Japanese, whom they curse as they watch a kamikaze pilot destroy one of their neighboring ships.

Bibliographies:

James L. W. West III, *William Styron: A Descriptive Bibliography* (Boston: G. K. Hall, 1977).
    A detailed primary bibliography with an introduction by Styron.

Philip W. Leon, *William Styron: An Annotated Bibliography of Criticism* (Westport, Conn.: Greenwood Press, 1978).
    Lists primary and secondary sources and includes an index of nonliterary references to Styron in the *New York Times*.

Jackson Bryer and Mary Beth Hatem, *William Styron: A Reference Guide* (Boston: G. K. Hall, 1978).
    Lists writings about Styron from 1946 to 1978, by year, with annotations.

References:

Arthur D. Casciato and James L. W. West III, eds., *Critical Essays on William Styron* (Boston: G. K. Hall, 1982).
    A collection of important biographical, critical, and textual essays on Styron.

John H. Clark, ed., *William Styron's Nat Turner: Ten Black Writers Respond* (Boston: Beacon, 1968).
    A collection of essay attacks on Styron's treatment of Turner and the slave rebellion of 1831.

John Kenny Crane, *The Root of all Evil: The Thematic Unity of William Styron's Fiction* (Columbia: University of South Carolina Press, 1984).
   The best full treatment of Styron to date: a study of the structural evolution of Styron's novels.

John B. Duff and Peter M. Mitchell, eds., *The Nat Turner Rebellion: The Historical Event and the Modern Controversy* (New York: Harper & Row, 1971).
   A collection of essays by historians and literary critics about the rebellion and Styron's treatment of it: includes an essay by Styron.

Robert H. Fossum, *William Styron: A Critical Essay* (Grand Rapids, Mich.: Eerdmans, 1968).
   A short study of Styron's first four novels from an existentialist perspective.

Melvin J. Friedman, *William Styron* (Bowling Green, Ohio: Bowling Green University Popular Press, 1974).
   An examination of Styron's thematic and technical debts to his American and French predecessors.

Friedman and Irving Malin, eds., *William Styron's The Confessions of Nat Turner: A Critical Handbook* (Belmont, Cal.: Wadsworth, 1970).
   A valuable collection of essays about Styron's most controversial novel.

David D. Galloway, *The Absurd Hero in American Fiction* (Austin: University of Texas Press, 1966).
   A study of Styron's first three novels from an existentialist perspective.

Cooper R. Macklin, *William Styron* (Austin, Tex.: Steck-Vaughn, 1969).
   A short essay containing a biographical sketch and a reading of Styron's first four novels as distinctly southern.

Robert K. Morris and Irving Malin, eds., *The Achievement of William Styron*, revised edition (Athens: University of Georgia Press, 1981).
   Contains important essays on Styron, an interview, and the most up-to-date bibliography of writings on Styron.

Richard Pearce, *William Styron* (Minneapolis: University of Minnesota Press, 1971).
   A pamphlet study of Styron's development through the first four novels, which sees *The Long March* as thematically central to the other work.

Marc L. Ratner, *William Styron* (New York: Twayne, 1972).
   Contains a brief biographical treatment and a critical overview of the first four novels.

John Updike

This entry was updated by Donald J. Greiner (University of South Carolina) from his entries in DLB 5, American Poets After World War II, DLB Yearbook 1980, *and* DLB Yearbook 1982.

Places	Shillington, Penn. Harvard University	New York City	Ipswich, Mass.
Influences and Relationships	Nathaniel Hawthorne Henry James Vladimir Nabokov	Karl Barth Søren Kierkegaard	James Thurber E. B. White

Literary Movements and Forms	The Literary
	   Essay
	Realism
		The Short Story
		Light Verse
			Self-Reflexive
			   Prose

Major Themes	Adultery and
	   Transgression
	Small-Town
	   America
		Mortality and
		   Loss
		Family
			The Value of
			   Mundane Details
			Religion

Cultural and Artistic Influences	Paul Cézanne and
	   Jan Vermeer
	Sports
		Secularization of
		   America
		J. S. Bach
			Existentialism
			Orthodox Christianity

Social and Economic Influences	The Presidency of
	   Dwight D.
	   Eisenhower
		The Assassination of
		   John F. Kennedy
			The Depression

See also the Updike entry in DLB 2, American Novelists since World War II.

BIRTH: Shillington, Pennsylvania, 18 March 1932 to Wesley R. and Linda G. Hoyer Updike.

EDUCATION: A.B., Harvard University, 1954; study on Knox Fellowship at the Ruskin School of Drawing and Fine Arts in Oxford, England, 1954-1955.

MARRIAGES: 26 June 1953 to Mary Entwistle Pennington (divorced); children: Elizabeth Pennington, David Hoyer, Michael John, and Miranda. 30 September 1977 to Martha Ruggles Bernhard.

AWARDS AND HONORS: Guggenheim Fellowship, 1959; Rosenthal Foundation Award, National Institute of Arts and Letters for *The Poorhouse Fair*, 1960; National Book Award in Fiction for *The Centaur*, 1964; elected, National Institute of Arts and Letters, 1964; O. Henry Prize for "The Bulgarian Poetess," 1966; elected, American Academy of Arts and Letters, 1977; Pulitzer Prize in Fiction for *Rabbit Is Rich*, 1982; National Book Critics Circle Award for Fiction for *Rabbit Is Rich*, 1982; American Book Award for Fiction for *Rabbit Is Rich*, 1982; National Book Critics Circle Award for Criticism for *Hugging the Shore*, 1983.

BOOKS: *The Carpentered Hen and Other Tame Creatures* (New York: Harper, 1958); republished as *Hoping for a Hoopoe* (London: Gollancz, 1959);
The Poorhouse Fair (New York: Knopf, 1959; London: Gollancz, 1959);
The Same Door (New York: Knopf, 1959; London: Deutsch, 1962);
Rabbit, Run (New York: Knopf, 1960; London: Deutsch, 1961);
The Magic Flute (New York: Knopf, 1962; London: Deutsch & Ward, 1964);
Pigeon Feathers (New York: Knopf, 1962; London: Deutsch, 1962);
The Centaur (New York: Knopf, 1963; London: Deutsch, 1963);
Telephone Poles and Other Poems (New York: Knopf, 1963; London: Deutsch, 1964);
Olinger Stories (New York: Vintage, 1964);
The Ring (New York: Knopf, 1964);
Assorted Prose (New York: Knopf, 1965; London: Deutsch, 1965);

John Updike (Gale International Portrait Gallery)

A Child's Calendar (New York: Knopf, 1965);
Of the Farm (New York: Knopf, 1965; London: Deutsch, 1966);
Verse (Greenwich, Conn.: Fawcett, 1965);
The Music School (New York: Knopf, 1966; London: Deutsch, 1967);
Couples (New York: Knopf, 1968; London: Deutsch, 1968);
Midpoint and Other Poems (New York: Knopf, 1969; London: Deutsch, 1969);
Bottom's Dream (New York: Knopf, 1969);
Bech: A Book (New York: Knopf, 1970; London: Deutsch, 1970);
Rabbit Redux (New York: Knopf, 1971; London: Deutsch, 1972);
Seventy Poems (London: Penguin, 1972);
Museums and Women (New York: Knopf, 1972; London: Deutsch, 1973);
Buchanan Dying (New York: Knopf, 1974; London: Deutsch, 1974);
A Month of Sundays (New York: Knopf, 1975; London: Deutsch, 1975);
Picked-Up Pieces (New York: Knopf, 1975; London: Deutsch, 1976);
Marry Me: A Romance (New York: Knopf, 1976; London: Deutsch, 1977);

Tossing and Turning (New York: Knopf, 1977; London: Deutsch, 1977);

The Coup (New York: Knopf, 1978; London: Deutsch, 1979);

Too Far to Go (New York: Fawcett Crest, 1979); republished as *Your Lover Just Called* (Harmondsworth: Penguin, 1980);

Problems and Other Stories (New York: Knopf, 1979; London: Deutsch, 1980);

Rabbit Is Rich (New York: Knopf, 1981; London: Deutsch, 1982);

Bech Is Back (New York: Knopf, 1982; London: Deutsch, 1983);

Hugging the Shore (New York: Knopf, 1983; London: Deutsch, 1984);

The Witches of Eastwick (New York: Knopf, 1984; London: Deutsch, 1984);

Facing Nature (New York: Knopf, 1985; London: Deutsch, 1986).

A reader would be hard pressed to name a contemporary author other than John Updike who is more in tune with the way most Americans live. Unconcerned with apocalypse in his fiction, undeterred by the universal absurdity that threatens to negate the bravest and the best, Updike writes about little people leading little lives. Man, wife, home, children, job—these mundane concerns have rested at the heart of his art since he published his first book, a volume of poetry entitled *The Carpentered Hen and Other Tame Creatures* in 1958, and they have continued to help him dissect, lovingly and clearly, the daily routine of middle America in small town and suburb.

War is generally not an issue for Updike, and neither are the problems of space weapons, worldwide hunger, or the fouling of the planet. The concerns in Updike's writing do not make front-page news. But the concerns do matter, because Updike knows that "something fierce goes on in homes." He may not write about murder and mayhem and madness, but in an exquisitely lyrical style that even his detractors admire, he probes the crises that sear the human spirit: how does a man cling to a mistress when he fears leaving his wife; how does he explain his guilt to his children when he knows that love is all that matters; how does he get his life going again when the applause heaped on him in high school has shattered into silence; how does he fill the void when religious faith seems faltering and false; and how does he grow along with his children who, overnight, seem to know more but care less?

Moralist, stylist, chronicler of the American middle class, Updike investigates the inner lives of families and the common details that define them. He knows that the insignificant particulars of a life are both signs of God's handiwork and hints of man's needs: finely crafted furniture, a carefully mown field, a perfect tee shot, a groping prayer, and, unfortunately, the halting march toward death.

Updike can tell of these lives because he has been there. Born on 18 March 1932 in Shillington, Pennsylvania, during the Great Depression, Updike grew up an only child in a relatively poor family. His father, Wesley R. Updike, taught science in the local high school, but at age thirteen Updike, his father, and his mother, Linda G. Hoyer Updike, moved from the town to a farm from which they had to commute daily. His memoir "The Dogwood Tree: A Boyhood" (*Assorted Prose*, 1965) captures the centrality of his Shillington years, and he has since implied that the loneliness uncovered by the move to the farm fired his imagination.

He now jokingly confesses that part of his adolescent imaginings were devoted to the problem of "how to get out of here," and his exquisitely paced short stories "A Sense of Shelter" and "Flight" (*Pigeon Feathers*, 1962) examine the contradictory urges that define most high school students: longing to break free from home yet fearing the flight itself. Updike "flew" imaginatively through the cartoons and fiction in the *New Yorker*, and physically when he won a scholarship to Harvard University. His lifelong commitment to style, to the sheer sound of words artfully selected and rhythmically grouped to suggest resonance and tone, was developed at Harvard. While an undergraduate English major, he drew cartoons and wrote for the *Harvard Lampoon*, which he later edited; and after he graduated summa cum laude in 1954, he studied for one year on a Knox Fellowship at the Ruskin School of Drawing and Fine Arts in Oxford, England.

Updike has revealed that his true ambition was to be a cartoonist, if not for Walt Disney then at least for the *New Yorker:* "What I have become is a sorry shadow of those high hopes." Still the beginnings of his career as a writer are associated with the *New Yorker*, for that magazine published his first professional story, "Friends from Philadelphia," on 30 October 1954. Following his return from Oxford in 1955, he joined the staff of the *New Yorker*, and for the next two years he contributed to the "Talk of the Town" column. Although he ended his formal ties with the magazine's editorial staff in 1957 and moved to Ipswich, Massachusetts, to concentrate on writing, he continued his relationship with the periodical, which has been publishing his poems, stories, essays, and reviews regularly for more than three decades. The move from New York to Ipswich brought the anticipated results, for by 1959 Updike had had three books published: *The Carpentered Hen and Other Tame Creatures*, *The Poorhouse Fair* (1959), and *The Same Door* (1959).

Critical recognition soon followed. In 1959 he was awarded a Guggenheim Fellowship, and then the Rosenthal Foundation Award of the National Institute of Arts and Letters for *The Poorhouse Fair* in 1960; his novel *The Centaur* (1963) won the National Book Award in Fiction in 1964; his short stories have been honored with O. Henry Awards; and he was elected to the National Institute of Arts and Letters in 1964, and to the American Academy of Arts and Letters in 1977. His novel *Rabbit Is Rich* (1981) won the Pulitzer Prize, the National Book Critics Circle Award, and an American Book Award; and his massive collection of essays, *Hugging the Shore* (1983), won the National Book Critics Circle Award for Criticism.

Although his popular reputation rests primarily on his novels, Updike is a master of four genres: novel, short story, poetry, and essay. In each case his care for the rhythms of language shapes his dismay at the secularization of life, but this is not to suggest that he writes in the 1980s the way he began in the 1950s. Committed in his novels, for example, to the realistic depiction of mundane affairs, he has nevertheless written about the comic intransigence of language in *A Month of Sundays* (1975), about the way that language controls both culture and global politics in *The Coup* (1978), and about the fine line between fantasy and reality in *The Witches of Eastwick* (1984), a humorous novel that is closer to the magical realism of contemporary Latin American authors than to Updike's earlier work.

Similar variations mark the development of his short fiction. The most accomplished American short-story writer since John O'Hara, Updike has moved from the nostalgia of *The Same Door* and some of the tales in *Pigeon Feathers* to the lyrical meditation of such stories as "Wife-wooing" (*Pigeon Feathers*) and "The Music School" (*The Music School*, 1966), toward the irony of *Museums and Women* (1972) and *Problems and Other Stories* (1979). His decades-long love affair with this pecu-

liarly American genre has helped changed the shape of the short story, for the narrative element associated with the tales in *The Same Door* is often subordinated to a lyrical, meditative use of language in later pieces. The general topic is diminishment, and the reader of Updike's short-story collections will note how the loss of the high-school years in *The Same Door* and *Pigeon Feathers* gives way to the loss of family through betrayal and divorce in *The Music School* and *Museums and Women*, which looks toward, in *Problems*, the declining potency brought on by the specter of loss of life. Updike stirs the emotions while he challenges the intellect.

Varied interests also direct his poetry. Blessed with a sense of humor and thus able to laugh at the flaws of life and the foibles of language, Updike has always been intrigued by the intricate verbal demands of light verse. Indeed most of the poems in *The Carpentered Hen and Other Tame Creatures* and the first half of *Telephone Poles and Other Poems* (1963) sparkle with linguistic wit. But while Updike has maintained his joyous appreciation of the playfulness of words in his later volumes of verse, he has altered his emphasis. The decline of religious sureties is a prominent consideration in *Telephone Poles and Other Poems* and *Midpoint and Other Poems* (1969), and the diminishment of life itself results in the somber tone of many of the poems in *Tossing and Turning* (1977). The odes to natural processes in *Facing Nature* (1985) are challenging displays of intellect and humor, but they also indicate, however indirectly, the inadequacy of mankind before the inexorable increments of nonhuman otherness.

Updike formally discusses many of these concerns in the fourth genre at which he excels–the essay. *Assorted Prose*, *Picked-Up Pieces* (1975), and *Hugging the Shore* illustrate not only a curious mind but also an astonishing range of interests: small-town America, Central Park, baseball, mimesis, Hawthorne, and the general state of the art of fiction are just a few of the topics that engage his delighted enthusiasm for the things of his world. Yet as with all his work, significant changes have developed in his essays since *Assorted Prose*. Largely a collection of parodies, occasional pieces that Updike wrote for the "Talk of the Town" section of the *New Yorker*, autobiographical memoirs, and reviews, *Assorted Prose* is primarily notable for four distinguished essays: "The Dogwood Tree: A Boyhood"; "Hub Fans Bid Kid Adieu," a justly famous account of Ted Williams's last baseball game for the Boston Red Sox; "Faith in Search of Understanding," an analysis of Karl Barth's rigorously conservative theology; and "More Love in the Western World," an essay on the history of romantic love in literature. *Picked-Up Pieces*, on the other hand, is necessary reading for the student of Updike primarily because it includes his speeches on the genre of fiction and his essay-reviews of the work of many non-American authors in which he develops his understanding of mimesis. European writers continue to hold Updike's focus in *Hugging the Shore*, but in this collection he discusses for the first time some of his American predecessors: Walt Whitman, Nathaniel Hawthorne, and Herman Melville. His interest in American literature also often prompts him to invoke the achievement of Henry James when evaluating the books of other writers.

The concerns that Updike elaborates in his essays shape the themes that he develops in his novels: spiritual malaise, the glory of common details, the shrinking of the family center, the enticing lure of adultery, and the ever-beckoning shadow of decay. His first novel, *The Poorhouse Fair*, is a case in point. Unlike most beginning authors who write about youthful initiation from the perspective of personal experience tentatively explored, Updike considers the plight of old folks in a charity home who have no place to turn except toward death. Published in 1959, *The Poorhouse Fair* is set in the imagined future of the 1970s as Updike predicts a welfare society where all needs are met but spiritual health. Writing in the lyrical style that would become the hallmark of his achievement, he exposes the potential sterility of a nation that supplies everything except the right to be eccentric, individual, and alone.

Detailing the one day in the county poorhouse when the inmates are permitted to hold a fair for the citizens of the town, the novel centers on the conflict between Conner, the efficient administrator, and Hook, the aging ward. The problem is not that Conner fails to care but that he fails to see. He can offer blankets for the beds and food for the table, but he cannot understand that marking the rocking chairs with nameplates denies the individuality of choice. The former schoolteacher Hook senses that "not busyness but belief" is the issue, that belief means not only that God dwells in both telephone poles and trees but that faith inspires the craftsmanship which shapes everything from handcarved furniture to the nation itself. What happens to the

soul of a country, asks Updike, when machine-sewn blankets count for more than hand-stitched quilts? On the day of the fair, the poorhouse inmates show off their carved peachstones and trinkets, and Updike celebrates their feeble yet stubborn rebellion against manufactured welfare and impersonal regard.

Announcing his presence in American fiction with an admirable first novel of verbal skill and significant concerns, Updike also previewed a theme that would become increasingly important in his canon: the necessity for belief—for faith—above all else. An informal student of modern theology, he has shaped his own religious thought from the strict tenets of Karl Barth and his predecessor Kierkegaard. Drawn especially to Barth's insistence that God is "Wholly Other," that man cannot reach God and that only God can touch man, Updike stresses Barth's call for belief. Hook has this belief and thus a faith that permits him to maintain calm in the face of care. Harry "Rabbit" Angstrom has belief, too, but he lacks Hook's capacity for thought.

Rabbit, Run (1960), the first of the Rabbit chronicle that includes *Rabbit Redux* (1971) and *Rabbit Is Rich*, continues to be Updike's most shocking novel, but many of its themes are variations of those initiated in *The Poorhouse Fair*. Although Rabbit is only twenty-six while Hook is ninety, both sense and despair over the dead ends of their lives. Both also accept Barth's notion of religious commitment. But whereas Hook possesses the serenity that comes with age and the ability to articulate his faith, Rabbit reveals the uncertainty of youth and the inability to express his fear.

Named by Stanley Edgar Hyman as "the most gifted novelist of his generation," Updike began to fill the void left by the decline of Faulkner and Hemingway. But while initiated readers responded to Updike's lush style and sympathetic probing of the pain of American life, the general public was shocked by Rabbit's sexual exploits and his wife's accidental drowning of their baby. *Rabbit, Run* continues to disturb readers because of Updike's skill at generating sympathy for a troubling young man who inadvertently causes pain. Updike takes a common American experience—the graduation from high school of a star athlete who has no life to lead once the applause diminishes and the headlines fade—and turns it into a subtle exposé of the frailty of the American dream.

Rabbit's dilemma has occupied Updike for his entire career (see, for example, "Ex-Basketball Player" in *The Carpentered Hen* and "Ace in the Hole" in *The Same Door*), and it is now clear that he has written a saga of middle-class America. Not liking what he has but not knowing what he wants, Rabbit is a decent, unintelligent man who finds that the momentum which sustained him during his basketball years has slowed to a crawl in a dingy apartment where the dinner is always late and the wife has stopped being pretty. Written entirely in the present tense–an unusual technique in American fiction–and thus stressing the immediacy of Rabbit's crisis, the novel details the sterility of a society that offers television sets and cars but ignores spiritual malaise and belief.

Bewildered by her husband's restless agony, by his inarticulate need to run, Janice personifies all that clogs Rabbit's life. Updike's astonishing facility with language is used not only to suggest Rabbit's need for order and style but also to describe the junk that surrounds him via Janice: dirty ashtrays, droning television sets, disorganized closets. All she wants is for him to be like other husbands, to give in to the nine-to-five routine of selling Magi-peelers in the local dimestore, but Rabbit senses that loss of life's momentum means loss of life itself. So he runs.

And as he runs he becomes Updike's religious quester, momentarily stalled between the right way (Janice) and the good way (freedom), but determined to save himself despite the consequences. The Reverend Jack Eccles tries to help him, but Updike shows that Eccles lacks Rabbit's Barthian sense of belief, that in his passion for good works Eccles is a cousin of Conner in *The Poorhouse Fair*. When the frustrated Eccles badgers Rabbit to explain what he wants, all the inarticulate quester can do is hit a perfect tee shot on the golf course, point to the fluidity and grace of the soaring ball, and shout, "That's it!" The last word of the novel–"Runs."–suggests Rabbit's inability to find that grace.

A decade later, in 1971, Updike reintroduced Rabbit at age thirty-six. In *Rabbit Redux* ("Rabbit led back"), however, the junk of ashtrays and closets that Harry has run from earlier is replaced by national events that threaten to overwhelm him: Vietnam, the civil rights movement, and the drug culture. Framing these disasters–as Rabbit considers them to be–is the excitement of the first moon shot; but try as he might to turn the space flight into a metaphor for his own

need to soar, gracefully and far, he understands that the moon adventure is sterile, merely a triumph of impersonal technology making contact with a dead rock. In *Rabbit Redux* Harry's dash for open territory has taught him that America no longer promises places to run to, so he returns to his dingy house in the plastic suburb.

What he finds is a metaphor for the upheaval of the 1960s: Janice has left him for a lover, although she would come home if Harry would ask; his son, Nelson, is suddenly a teenager who needs and deserves guidance; a hippie girl and a black Vietnam vet, both drug-crazed, invade his house; and Rabbit finds himself succumbing to physical sloppiness and spiritual despair. The fire that destroys the Angstrom house at the end is Updike's ironic apocalypse, his signal that nothing earth-shattering is going to happen to Rabbit, that Rabbit will have to rebuild his little life by himself. Rabbit attempts to rebound when, in the final scene–all but forgetting his earlier need for grace–he leads Janice to a motel. The last words of the novel–"Sleeps. O.K.?"–are a long way from "Runs."

Rabbit Redux is the least stimulating of the Rabbit tales, for Harry is a better character when he quests instead of halts. But the third Rabbit novel, *Rabbit Is Rich*, is one of Updike's best, and it was published within a year of a resurrection of another of Updike's favorite characters, Henry Bech, in *Bech Is Back* (1982). Read together as the latest installments in Updike's continuing sagas, the two novels illustrate the expanse of his range: Rabbit sells Toyotas; Bech writes books.

Each Rabbit novel records the tone of a decade. *Rabbit Is Rich* is about the 1970s, and the rainbow that Harry chases in the 1950s and 1960s has shrunk as the American dream goes sour with the bad taste of middle age and aimless youth. Farmland turns to shopping malls; overflowing garbage cans stand beside unsuccessful plywood restaurants; and people reel from a combination of less energy and higher prices. Now forty-six years old, Rabbit does not blame anyone for *Skylab*'s falling or Exxon's greed, but death leers on the horizon, and he is afraid of running out of gas. When Rabbit looks over his shoulder at the glory of early fame too easily won on the basketball court and thinks of himself as "king of the lot" and "the star and spear point" of the flourishing Toyota dealership his family owns, the reader knows that he has not changed much from the man whose value system was defined in terms of athletic prowess.

On the third Wednesday of every August the inhabitants of a
mansion-turned-poorhouse in central New Jersey hold their annual
fair; this novel describes a fair that occurs about twenty years
from now, when the United States has changed less drastically than
~~you might think.~~ *is generally predicted.* We travel from morning to night via the minds of
a score of characters: Conner, the Prefect, whose dedication to the
ideal of a socialist-materialist paradise is little short of saintly
and who (does indeed), at the book's climax, endure a brief martyrdom;
Hook, a didactic nonagenarian fiercely loyal to the Bible and the
Democratic party; Gregg, an ex-electrician still electric with spite;
Lucas, a man of more domestic preoccupations; Amy Mortis and
Elizabeth Heinemann, women whose prophecies and visions fall dis-
regarded ~~among~~ the male debates; Ted and Buddy, two youthful products
of their time; and, in the end, the bourgeois, middle-aged crowd that
comes to the fair. Animals haunt the landscape, and inanimate objects --
a sandstone wall, a row of horsechestnut trees, a pile of pebbles --
strain wordlessly toward the humans, who act out their quarrels of
tradition versus progress, benevolence versus pride, on a ground riddled
with omens and overborne by a massive, variable sky. The author seems
to separate sense and existence; the chatter of the mob that comes to
the fair in its sense illustrates the national decay that obsesses the
pensioners, yet in its existence, isolated by bits in the air, shares
with grass (and) stones a ~~maximum~~ positive, even cheering, _anima_. While
The Poorhouse Fair, insofar as it regrets the apparent decline of
patriotism, handcraft, and religion, carries a conservative message,
its technique is unorthodox; without much regard for fictional
conventions, (the author) attempts to locate, in the ambiguous area between farce
and melodrama, reality's own tone.

*Typescript page for Updike's first novel, about a society in which all physical needs are met at the expense of spirtual health
(Houghton Library, Harvard University; courtesy of the author)*

But he has changed some: golf has replaced basketball, and he rumbles rather than runs with a forty-two-inch waist and a tendency to avoid mirrors when he used to love reflections of himself. Still Rabbit is rich in the ironic sense of being able to afford cashews instead of peanuts. Life is sweet. For the first time in twenty-five years he is happy to be alive, even happy with his marriage to Janice. Deserted by Harry in the first Rabbit novel and deserting him in the second, Janice fits snugly into a middle-age routine, plays tennis at the country club, and, says Rabbit, "never looked sharper." She still drinks too much, and she rarely serves meals on time, but she finally enjoys sex and even manages now and then to stand up to her husband.

Despite Janice, golf, and money, Rabbit needs to run, not as fast and not as far, but somewhere. He muses on "the entire squeezed and cut-down shape of his life," and he realizes that middle age is upon him, a time when dreams decline to awareness of limits and stomachs take on a noticeable sag. The strained jollity of the country-club set, "the kind of crowd that will do a marriage in if you let it," makes him uneasy, but his flight in this novel is not as urgent as it is in *Rabbit, Run* and thus not as poignant. He knows that he is a "soft and a broad target."

Aiming at the target is his son, Nelson, twenty-two years old, a surly college dropout, and, in Rabbit's eyes, "humpbacked and mean, a rat going out to be drowned." Hitchhiking home to a hurry-up marriage to a pregnant secretary, Nelson wants a job at Rabbit's Toyota dealership. Updike sketches the father-son tension with superb detail so that the reader understands Rabbit's lament: "How can you respect the world when you see it's being run by a bunch of kids turned old?" But that old bunch was once Rabbit's bunch, and Nelson will be right behind them. He is tired of being young, but he doesn't know how to grow up. Nelson lacks fluidity and grace. Sympathy for his fear of being trapped is not easy because, unlike his father, he has no intuitive sense of joy, no yearning. His wife is correct: he is a spoiled bully. Nelson runs but without Rabbit's faith; the son runs from while the father runs toward.

Later Rabbit "glimpses the truth that to be rich is to be robbed, to be rich is to be poor." In part he means spiritually poor, though he would not say it that way, so he and Janice break from his mother-in-law and buy their own home. Maybe his rainbow is in the suburbs. He still longs for a world without ruts, but God has become a "raisin lost under the car seat." In the earlier novels Rabbit runs toward transcendence, toward what he calls "it," but now he has only a vacation in the Caribbean to rejuvenate him. There, engaged in wife-swapping where he once pursued life's rhythm, he even misses his dream girl when he is paired with his second choice. Sex is part of Rabbit's scampering, his questing, as Updike established years ago.

Rabbit returns home to find his son drifted back to college but his granddaughter born. The birth calms him for a moment, soothes his undefined sense of unsettledness, but he knows that it is also a giant step toward extinction: mortality looms beyond the middle years.

It is sad to think of death setting its snare for Rabbit Angstrom, because after three decades and three long novels he has joined the pantheon of American literary heroes. Yet a glimpse of final defeat is the price to be paid for membership in that exclusive club. Like Natty Bumppo, Ahab, Huck Finn, Gatsby, Ike McCaslin, Holden Caulfield, and many others before him, Harry is learning that no matter how far he runs in space, he cannot outrace time.

Henry Bech has all but stopped running. In *Bech Is Back* Henry returns to the literary scene with a new wife and a new novel, but his old bewilderment is still intact. His former mistress knows that his book is lousy, but the ad-fed public adores it anyway. Henry suspects that her judgment is correct; yet after suffering through a silence lasting more than a decade, he wonders how he can reject the royalties and the fanfare, since he has poured enough sex and violence into his latest novel to guarantee a best-seller all but created by media hype. Silence, he reasons, offers only limited rewards.

Bech is Updike's favorite writer, a character who promises to have the longevity of Rabbit in the Updike canon and who allows Updike the opportunity to work out the frustrations that inevitably trap the successful artist in America. When last seen in *Bech: A Book* (1970), Bech had published enough fiction to shape a reputation with the intelligentsia, had fallen into the hell of writer's block that, ironically, increased his reputation, and had emerged as a kind of artifact that Uncle Sam paraded around the globe to fulfill various cultural exchanges. Bech is Updike's joke on himself. More to the point, he is also Updike's joke on the discouraging hoopla with which Americans surround their authors in order to worship not the writing but the writer.

The laughs begin on the first page of *Bech: A Book*. There Updike reveals a letter to himself from Bech in which Bech says, with his ego showing, "Well, if you must commit the artistic indecency of writing about a writer, better I suppose about me than about you." The laughs continued through the 1970s when Updike kept up the charade of Henry Bech as real author by publishing bogus interviews between Bech and himself in the *New York Times*.

Yet there is a serious tone to the laughter. The jokes about Bech may illustrate the appalling way America treats its authors, but Updike is just as concerned with the fate that dooms so many American writers to lesser and lesser achievement. While the royalty checks jump to six figures and the talk show appearances multiply, the quality of the writing diminishes. In 1974 Updike said in a speech entitled "Why Write?": *"To remain interested—of American novelists, only Henry James continued in old age to advance his art."*

How right he is—but only up to a point. Those who care about American fiction many now place Updike's name beside James's. The point is not that he rivals James but that unlike Hawthorne and Melville, unlike Twain and Hemingway, unlike arguably, even Faulkner, Updike has continued to advance his art.

Henry Bech is not so lucky. In *Bech Is Back* irony irritates his life. Even enduring reputation smarts: "Though Henry Bech, the author, in his middle years had all but ceased to write, his books continued, as if ironically, to live, to cast shuddering shadows toward the center of his life, where that thing called his reputation cowered." This sentence begins the book, and one thinks immediately of Bech's fellow author J. D. Salinger. But Salinger's silence seems noble. Rejecting the show biz of big-time publishing, he may be writing his books only for himself. Bech's silence is more demeaning. Languishing in the success of his first novel, he is paralyzed by an old-fashioned writer's block. Silent before his public for almost fifteen years, Bech has become, to his dismay, a kind of myth.

But silence does not mean invisibility. If Americans cannot recognize true artists, they are proficient at worshiping stars. Rather than let Henry suffer privately from his inability to write, they send him around the world again to give speeches on "The Cultural Situation of the Ameri-

can Writer" and inadvertently to act the patsy to third-world audiences who use literature for political ends.

Henry's travels are the slowest part of *Bech Is Back*, but the entire book is a delight. Rebounding, for example, from the disillusion of meeting an avid collector who hoards Bech's novels for their potential value on the rare-book market, Henry agrees for a price to sign his name to 28,500 of his books. Transported to a balmy island for the chore and ministered to by his mistress, Bech confronts a stunning silence: he cannot even write his own name.

When he finally does dodge the spotlight for a moment and inches his way toward true literary recognition, he is selected for, of all things, the Melville Medal, "awarded every five years to that American author who has maintained the most meaningful silence." This kind of humor sparkles throughout *Bech Is Back*. Success, it seems, is unavoidable. Marrying his mistress's sister and moving to her family home in Ossining, he gives in to his wife's nudges to free his blocked inspiration with pep talks, changes the working title of his novel in progress from *Think Big* to *Easy Money*, and accepts the degradation of advertising's stranglehold on literature when Madison Avenue turns the book into a best-seller. "Bech is back," scream the hucksters, but, Henry and Updike muse, at what cost? Lionized as the latest rage, surrounded by New York's prettiest at a gaudy white-on-white party, he closes with a word that typifies the entire experience: "unclean."

For all Bech's troubles, however, one hopes that he will rebound again in ten years or so. For Updike has more to say about the paradox that afflicts writers: their craving for applause and their need for privacy. The conflict between easy money and noble silence is deadly to American artists. Rather than pontificate about this cultural trap in ponderous essays, Updike uses sharp wit and evocative prose to create a memorable character who lives the dilemma.

Standing between the silent but articulate Bech and the questing but inarticulate Rabbit are Updike's family novels (*The Centaur;* and *Of the Farm*, 1965); his marriage novels (*Couples*, 1968; *A Month of Sundays; Marry Me: A Romance*, 1976; and *The Witches of Eastwick*); and his unexpected novel about language and Africa (*The Coup*). Updike has occasionally named the award-winning *The Centaur* his favorite. One can see why. Beautifully written and imaginatively conceived, *The Cen-*

taur is an homage to his father, Wesley Updike, who sacrificed his own dreams to keep his family together during the disruptive trauma of the Great Depression.

Interestingly, Updike originally thought of *The Centaur* as a contrasting companion to *Rabbit, Run*. Both novels suggest that the threat of death can be defined as a loss of grace before an onslaught of the mundane yet overwhelming details that any head of a family faces in his daily routine; but whereas Harry scampers from drudgery in pursuit of "it," George Caldwell plods painfully through the snow to escort his teenaged son Peter back home. Harry is a rabbit while Caldwell is a horse, and the story of his sacrifice is a modern tale of heroism.

Told from Peter's perspective while he is a middle-aged, second-rate painter in New York, *The Centaur* develops in a complicated manner along two parallel lines of narration. The first is the realistic level as Peter recalls his high-school days in Olinger, Pennsylvania, and the agony that his mocked and martyred father suffers while teaching science to uncaring clods. The second is the mythic level as Peter adapts the Greek tale of Chiron, the centaur injured in war but beloved by Zeus, to highlight Caldwell's heroism. Dreading the shrinking of his future by the dispiriting grind of the high school and the destruction of his body by disease, Caldwell bravely yet comically bumbles his way through the day, unselfishly giving himself, unaware that the unruly students love him. Mocked, jeered, and metaphorically shot through his ankle with the "arrow" of laughter, Caldwell rarely challenges his duty and never dodges his fate.

The primary question in the novel, then, is not whether Caldwell will succumb to routine duties but whether Peter will step toward a creative life. Updike's style works its magical best in *The Centaur* as Peter's reminiscence transforms ancient Olympus into modern Olinger via lyrical descriptions of love, uncertainty, and fear. The epigraph from Karl Barth once again recalls Updike's insistence on the tenet of belief, and at the end of the novel George Caldwell trudges back through the snow toward his high school in order to guarantee the stability his son needs while growing up. Peter's narration is both an expression of gratitude and his greatest "painting," and the reader suspects that Peter is ready now to break out of his skepticism, ready now to live.

Of the Farm is the companion novel to *The Centaur*. Although the characters' names are changed, the situations are similar: both novels explore how a middle-aged son comes to terms with an aging parent who has personal myths of the family's past. The focus in *Of the Farm*, however, is on the mother, and Mrs. Robinson (whose husband is named George) is one of Updike's most intricately conceived characters. Strong, willful, jealous, brave, and afraid, Mrs. Robinson is an old woman who fears that death will beckon before her grown son, Joey, can fulfill the myth that she has dreamed for him and that he resists. She has set her life on his becoming a poet and a protector of her farm, but Joey has fled her distorting myth for a career in advertising and the concrete of New York. This short but highly charged novel is a psychological thriller that takes place during one weekend when Joey brings his second wife, Peggy, and his stepson to the farm for Mrs. Robinson's blessing.

He does not get it. In many ways *Of the Farm* is about the failure of forgiveness: Joey blames his mother for ruining his first marriage and threatening his second; Mrs. Robinson blames Peggy for enticing her son beyond poetry and the farm with the lure of uninhibited sexuality; and Peggy blames Mrs. Robinson for destroying Joey's father by forcing him to move to the lonely farm.

Framing these crosscurrents of guilt and fear is the counterpoint between the weakness of the son's resolve and the strength of the mother's myth. Joey admits that he is weak, that he has turned to Peggy's earthy sexuality as a substitute for the farm: "My wife is a field." But he also understands the force of his mother's ability to reshape her past to accommodate her present. Trapped within her warping myth of the farm as a "people sanctuary," he falls victim once again and betrays Peggy to Mrs. Robinson's disparaging dismissal. Listening to a sermon in which the minister quotes Barth on the notion that women are "an appeal to the kindness of Man," Joey must realize that he has fallen short. Unlike Peter Caldwell in *The Centaur*, he cannot use the proven glory of his command of words (the novel itself) to illuminate the potential glory of his own life.

Updike's marriage novels continue his probing of the relationship between the physical and the spiritual, but in these particular books he wonders whether sexuality can fill the void left by the decline of faith in the "post-pill paradise." In the short story "The Music School," for example, the narrator muses, "We are all pilgrims, faltering toward divorce." Separation seems the ironic goal of Updike's married couples. But the reader should understand that although adultery is a consequence, unbridled sensuality is not the issue. Like Rabbit and Bech, the men in these novels fear for the loss of their souls, and when they fail to find assurance in religion, they look to the carnal for the promise that they will never die.

The fate of Piet Hanema in *Couples* is an example. A builder who, like Hook, appreciates the strength of Calvinism and the permanence of fine carpentry, Piet becomes afraid when he suspects the inability of contemporary religious practices to hold back the darkness of his doubt. Thus when he abandons wife Angela (angel) for mistress Foxy (animal), he knows that his search for love triggers his fall to the world. Like the falls suffered by Hawthorne's characters (for example, in *The Marble Faun*), however, his plunge from grace may mean the fulfillment of his humanity. Piet's predicament is the most complex of the various adulteries in *Couples*, and the novel itself is Updike's most detailed evocation of the microcosm of the middle-class suburb. The reader must thus be careful to keep the lyrical descriptions of sex from obscuring the seriousness of Updike's concern for the ineffectuality of religion.

Updike's uncertainty about the value of Piet's effort is reflected in *Marry Me: A Romance*, a novel that exchanges the realism of *Couples* for the fable of Hawthorne, what the earlier author called "romance." Clearly not meant to be realistic, *Marry Me* proposes three illusory endings to Jerry Conant's adulterous affair with Sally, but in each case Jerry is still searching for assurance–be it spiritual or physical–that his life matters. Exclaiming that "I am married to my death," he cannot understand his wife Ruth's calm in the face of mortality. Neither can he understand how Ruth's own adulterous affair causes her blossoming as a woman. Although relatively slight as a novel, *Marry Me* contains Updike's finest portrait of a woman in Ruth. She, too, remains trapped by the Puritan insistence on the separation of the body and the soul, and her quest for love and selfhood parallels Jerry's quest for faith.

If *Marry Me* is the slightest of the marriage novels, and *Couples* the most famous, *A Month of Sundays* is the most important. It is also the most difficult, the most comic, and the most ignored. Once again openly bowing to Hawthorne, Updike places his minister, Tom Marshfield (the echo of Dimmesdale is clear), in an omega-shaped motel in the desert to which he has been

banished for seducing his organist, and in which he is to write a journal about his spiritual recovery. Marshfield has as much trouble with the intransigence of his language as with the flimsiness of his vows, and much of the comedy in this rich novel derives from the inadvertent puns and Freudian slips that he finds himself writing. Language, suggests Updike, is just as troubling to master as faith, and *A Month of Sundays* is on one level a novel about an author writing a novel in which the novelist is the main character.

But the comedy also has its serious side, for Marshfield is another of Updike's Barthian believers. Armed with his faith, aware of the weakness of his flesh, the wayward minister is convinced (as is Updike) that body and soul must be reunited if belief is to survive in a secular world. He pursues this conviction through a progression of often specious theological speculations and a longing for physical contact with women. His final affair with the mysteriously silent Ms. Prynne (a modern Hester) signals his success, and the novel ends with a serious prayer shaped by a comic embrace of the flesh.

The comedy is even more raucous in *The Witches of Eastwick*, a novel that lacks the weight of *A Month of Sundays* but that extends Updike's novelistic experiments beyond his earlier commitment to realism. Tennis balls turn into animals, and suburban witches cast a spell of adultery, but the novel is finally a celebration of duty and art. The time is the late 1960s, the place is Rhode Island, and the witches are three thirtyish mothers who have divorced their husbands in the name of womanhood and freedom. Updike's sense of history sets the frame. Famous at its founding as a refuge for liberal believers looking to escape the rigors of Massachusetts Puritanism, Rhode Island was once described by Cotton Mather as the "fag end of creation." Anne Hutchinson, banished to Rhode Island in 1637, hoped to found a covenant of grace there, but today's witches of Eastwick have established instead a coven of evil.

Jane, Sukie, and Alexandra shrink from the word "man" as an "assertive" noun that can negate the peaceful aura of a calm morning. "Man" carries such dreary connotations for the three divorced woman that they deny witchhood to a friend merely because she still has a husband. "Magic," writes Updike, "occurs all around us as nature seeks and finds the inevitable forms," and for much of the novel the inevitable form for the three liberated witches is freedom from "the armor of patriarchal protector" in the hope of indulging the fecundity women think they will find when single.

Alexandra, for example, becomes a witch when, in her middle thirties, she realizes she has a right to exist, not as "an afterthought and companion–a bent rib"–and thus less than man, but as "the mainstay of the continuing Creation, as the daughter of a daughter." Her initial tricks are often the result of "maternal wrath," and she argues that "a conspiracy of women upholds the world."

But if all this sounds good to today's housewife, consider Updike's irony: becoming a witch frees Alexandra only from the obligations of wearing high-heeled shoes and controlling her weight. Blooming selfhood has its foolish extremes, too. As the narrator wryly says, "This was an era of many proclaimed rights." Updike's bemused tone directs the first half of the novel: "Being divorced in a small town is a little like playing Monopoly; eventually you land on all the properties."

In the post-Christian era, promiscuity is no more than a game. The only burnings these witches suffer are a hot bath with a ridiculous devil and "the tongues of indignant opinion." Although these witches are a long way from Cotton Mather's scorched victims, they initially earn Updike's concern as well as laughter. When frustrated housewives receive Tofrinal from doctors and / or from ministers, domestic rebellion is just around the next corner, coming home with the children.

The complications begin when Darryl Van Horne, an unmarried, monied musician and dabbler in science, moves to Eastwick. In the waning 1960s, a time that the narrator calls "this hazy late age of declining doctrine," the wealthy lord of the underworld easily makes his way. He may be ineffective and New York vulgar, but he fascinates the locals. Van Horne is, after all, their dark prince, the odd defiler who does not bother with God.

But Updike finally sympathizes not with the sexy witches and their mysterious mentor but with the anonymous citizens who plod "through their civic and Christian duties." While Van Horne sardonically collects the "permanized garbage" of the culture as mocking works of sculpture, the dutiful suburbanites have to live with the junk. The devil in the novel is not godless science but ministers who exchange belief for the latest college course, dropouts who do not wash

and cannot think, and wives who save the world but ruin their homes.

The Witches of Eastwick laughs at these absurdities until a murder and suicide change the tone. Satire and sadness mix. Updike has written a novel of ebb and flow, spring and fall, life and death; a novel in which evil seems so potent that nothing can combat it except art. In an age of little faith, Bach counts for more than Vietnam marches, Cézanne for more than nuclear protests. Love, too, matters. Feminists will howl, but the witches regain normality when they find new husbands.

Updike's commitment to art and duty reaches a comic climax in *The Coup*. Africa has long been for Updike "an invitation to the imagination": "I've always been attracted to hidden corners." Drawing on that strange land as "the emptiest part of the world I could think of," he made *The Coup* a novel with noticeable though not dramatic differences from his other fiction. The most obvious difference is that the land of Kush is a long way from the lawns of suburbia. In addition, *The Coup* has a comic tone sustained largely by the sardonic observations of the narrator, Colonel Ellellou. Ellellou describes Kush, for example, as a constitutional monarchy "with the constitution suspended and the monarch deposed." Among Kush's natural resources, which seem largely to be comprised of drought and desert, is what Ellellou calls "the ample treasury of diseases." Finally the narrator's conscious manipulation of narrative voice is distinctive in the Updike canon. Colonel Hakim Felix Ellellou, the recently ousted president of Kush, tells of his presidency primarily in the third person even while he is very much aware of the first person who experienced the events. A narrator watching his own presence in the tale, he interrupts his story, for example, to comment on how his manuscript is blurred in places by a wet ring from a glass of Fanta.

Part of the comedy, then, results from Ellellou's distancing himself from himself with the device of third-person narration and yet relying on first person when convenient: "There are two selves: the one who acts, and the 'I' who experiences. This latter is passive even in a whirlwind of the former's making, passive and guiltless and astonished. The historical performer bearing the name Ellellou was no less mysterious to me than to the American press. . . . " The point is that Ellellou writes his story as much to find out who he is, to distinguish public mask from private man, as to explain the coup that has forced him to take up his pen. He understands now that the "he" carried the "I" here and there, and that the "I" never knew why but submitted. As a result, the "I" suffers the effects of the "he's" actions. A man of disguises and anonymous travels throughout Kush, he is a leader whose "domicilic policy is apparently to be in no place at any specific time." Even his languages are "clumsy masks" that "his thoughts must put on."

Ellelloû is a mystical leader without pragmatic talent because he believes primarily in "the idea of Kush." Yet one of his problems is that his obsession with his country is but the other side of his distrust of the world, which nurtures his determination to burn food offered by bungling America while his people go hungry. A true son of the Third World, he understands how gifts bring men who in turn bring oppression, but his hatred of America is comically undercut by the clichés of revolution in his speeches. In light of the childish rhetoric of the Iranian Revolution, Updike's portrait of the Islamic nationalist is especially interesting. America, for example, is "that fountainhead of obscenity and glut," but in Kush "the land itself is forgetful, an evaporating pan out of which all things human rise into blue invisibility."

The first meeting between Ellelloû and a goodwill bureaucrat from America is simultaneously ludicrous and pointed. Updike's two-pronged satire of the misguided American gift of a mountain of Trix cereal and potato chips to drought-stricken Kushites and of the indignant Ellelloû, who burns both the junk food and the bureaucrat, is a comic set piece that underscores how America's mindless need to be loved and the Third World's rigid ideology clash while people starve. One is reminded of Updike's earlier story "I Am, Dying, Egypt, Dying" (*Museums and Women*) with its portrait of the benign, rich American who cannot return the affection he seeks.

The comedy of this ideological sparring match depends upon the speech of the antagonists. Full of pop slang and bureaucratese, the American urges, "These cats are *starving*. The whole world knows it, you can see 'em starve on the six o'clock news every night. The American people want to help. We know this country's socialist and xenophobic." Ellelloû's response is little better: "Offer your own blacks freedom before you pile boxes of carcinogenic trash on the holy soil of Kush!" Updike's control of speech tones and language is so superb in *The Coup* that in

one sense language itself is the hero of the novel.

Style is the triumph of *The Coup*, the primary means by which Updike makes fun not only of America's need to help despite its vexation by Vietnam and President Nixon but also indirectly of President Carter's fortune in peanuts. Typical of the comic tone is the following comment by one of Ellelloû's advisers when he learns that the national fad of dieting in America has caused a drop in consumption of peanut butter and a corresponding increase in the exporting of peanuts: "Nothing more clearly advertises the American decline and coming collapse than this imperative need, contrary to all imperialist principles, to export raw materials." The laughter cuts both ways, for American peanuts on the open market threaten Kush's own crop of peanuts, which it must sell to purchase Czech dynamos. Updike understands that the intricacies of shifting political alliances often depend upon the supply of hardly strategic items like peanut oil, so he creates Ellelloû, an African revolutionary educated in America, a leader who despises the United States as a meddling superparanoid, to personify these contradictions which may be ridiculous but which are nevertheless lethal.

Longing to find a mystical cause for Kush's deprivation, Ellelloû travels the country only to collide with his Americanized side in a metropolis of McDonald's and Coke. On his final journey through Kush, he stumbles into a surprise, a bustling, illegal city named for him. Drugstores sell deodorant ("God sees the soul; men smell the flesh"), women wear miniskirts and halters, and the people go western. Ready capital and comfort undermine Spartan tradition and myth. In this plastic town, with its commitment to upward mobility and declining quality, Ellelloû discovers that *he* is considered the curse on Kush. The coup achieved, he takes refuge as a short-order cook and parking attendant, searching the newspapers for news of himself, before accepting exile in France to write *The Coup*. The last lines reemphasize his dual narrative perspective: "He is writing his memoirs. No, I should put it more precisely: Colonel Ellelloû is rumored to be working on his memoirs."

Black Muslims, prejudiced whites, doublespeak bureaucrats, liberal college students, revolutionary Africans, dull Russians—all are targets for Updike's comic darts. His love for caricatures and parodies, for James Thurber and Max Beerbohm, once manifested in his boyhood desire to

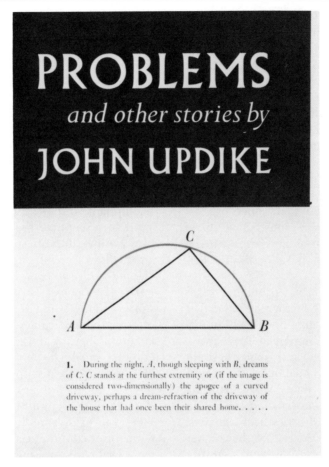

PROBLEMS
and other stories by
JOHN UPDIKE

1. During the night, *A*, though sleeping with *B*, dreams of *C*. *C* stands at the furthest extremity or (if the image is considered two-dimensionally) the apogee of a curved driveway, perhaps a dream-refraction of the driveway of the house that had once been their shared home. . . . .

Dust jacket for the 1979 volume of short stories in which Updike confronts the "specter of domestic loss"

draw cartoons for the *New Yorker*, works itself out in *The Coup*.

Despite the triumph of his African novel, Updike remains fascinated primarily by the intricate workings of the American family. His short stories illustrate the interest. Beginning with *The Same Door*, he has traced the changing curve of the stability of family life. Read as a whole, his short-story volumes offer a social commentary on American domesticity since mid century, and while the prose is always lyrical and the observation always sharp, a tone of sadness—wistfulness—prevails. For Updike shows in his tales that the instability of the family reflects the shakiness of the nation, and the nostalgia associated with *The Same Door* and *Pigeon Feathers* finally gives way to irony and the specter of mortality in *Problems*.

An important example in *Problems* is the end of "Separating" as the father Richard Maple tells his oldest son about the impending divorce. When the son asks "Why," the query cuts Richard to the quick. Facing a darkness that is suddenly grim, he realizes that he has no answer:

"*Why*. It was a whistle of wind in a crack, a knife thrust, a window thrown open on emptiness. The white face was gone, the darkness was featureless. Richard had forgotten why." Depicting that one lapse of memory, Updike dissects the breakdown of traditional values that seemed permanent in the 1950s and became baffling in the 1970s. Paul Theroux writes, "Updike is one of the few people around who has given subtle expression to what others have dismissed and cheapened by assuming it is a nightmare." The point is well taken. No American author is currently writing about the mystery of family with such patience and grace as John Updike.

Problems is largely a gathering of stories abut such trauma. Teenaged sons criticize the rest of the family, daughters go away to live with red-bearded harpsichord makers, unhappy fathers forget why, and guilt creeps through suburbia. The stories were written from 1971 to 1978, a period of unsettling family conditions for Updike himself. Although the tales are not autobiography, the specter of domestic loss, of love moving forward from all sides toward a contact barely reached, hovers around most of them. It is not that love is denied but that it is difficult to sustain. Updike supplies a definition in "Love Song, for a Moog Synthesizer": "love must attach to what we cannot help–the involuntary, the telltale, the fatal. Otherwise, the reasonableness and the mercy that would make our lives decent and orderly would overpower love, crush it, root it out. . . . " These stories detail the problems suffered when the threats to love do not stay hidden behind the bedroom wall. As Updike writes in the author's note, "Seven years since my last short-story collection? There must have been problems. . . . the collection as a whole, with the curve of sad time it subtends, is dedicated lovingly" to his children.

The plunge to domestic problems takes place immediately, for in "Commercial," the first story, Updike contrasts the manufactured familial snugness of a television commercial for natural gas with the calm, unspoken, and finally hesitant familial tension of a suburban home. "Commercial" is vintage Updike in many ways. Nothing "happens": a husband, having watched the ad for natural gas late at night, shuffles and urinates, tosses and turns, tries to doze. Yet the reader knows that all is not well: the husband's fretfulness, the wife's sleepiness, the cold room. The little details are exact: the cat's need to go out, the noise of the hampster's wheel. The prose is exquisite: "The sharp bright wires of noise etched on darkness dull down into gray threads, an indistinct blanket." And the saving grace of comedy occurs here and there: "GRANDMOTHERLINESS massages her from all sides, like the brushes of a car wash." Tone is finally all. In eight pages Updike conveys the bewilderment of sadness, the bleakness of loss. The implied question is why can't the long years of the man's domestic life equal the thirty seconds of the commercial's ideal family? The particulars behind this question are not important, but the final word of the story is: "Nothing."

Other stories touch on the unspectacular but felt burden of religious belief in a secular community: the comic allegory "Minutes of the Last Meeting" and the thoughtful "Believers." "How to Love America and Leave It at the Same Time," a lyrical meditation reminiscent of the stories in *The Music School*, contrasts with Nabokov's satire of motelville in *Lolita:* "America is a vast conspiracy to make you happy." The most unusual stories are "Augustine's Concubine," a meditation in

defense of the saint's mistress which recalls the less successful "Four Sides of One Story" (*The Music School*), and "The Man Who Loved Extinct Mammals," a comic tale of the relationships between love and extinction which echoes "The Baluchitherium" (*Museums and Women*) and which has in it the following metaphor, an example of Updike's sparkling language: "And the child's voice, so sensible and simple up to this point, generated a catch, tears, premonitions of eternal loss; the gaudy parade of eternal loss was about to turn the corner, cymbals clanging, trombones triumphant, and enter her mind."

But except for the two stories about the Maples family, the finest tale in *Problems* is "The Gun Shop." With touches of *The Centaur*, "Home" (*Pigeon Feathers*), and "Leaving Church Early" (*Tossing and Turning*), "The Gun Shop" is a story of fathers and sons filled with the gestures of domestic particulars that Updike at his best details with delicacy and care. In this portrait of generations, in which the unnecessary tension caused by a grandson's disappointment with a malfunctioning .22 rifle is eased into harmony, Updike shows the ambiguities of love that bind grandfather, son, grandson, and surrogate father into a moment of communication free of the embarrassment that close proximity always nurtures.

"The Gun Shop" is not a lyrical meditation as are, say, "Leaves" and "The Music School" (*The Music School*); that is, dialogue, characterization, and pacing instead of meditative prose carry the burden. Yet nuance takes the place of overt drama as Updike writes of the complications encountered when a country-bred but city-dwelling father brings his city-bred son back to the farmhouse of his parents. To the father, the farm is a field of memories and echoes, but to the son it is a promise of experience: he is always permitted to shoot the old Remington .22 following Thanksgiving dinner. Updike focuses on the contrasts between the ways fathers handle sons. Aware that his own tendency to respond to his son's distress with gentle irony is a reaction against his own father's embarrassing habit of good-humored acceptance, the father watches as the grandfather turns the boy's disappointment into the expectation of adventure. The grandfather knows just the man to fix the rifle.

Dutch, the gunsmith, is the hero of the tale, a man to be admired and loved, for although gruff and grimy and direct, he is an artist with machine tools, a country-bred man who can both repair the firing pin and communicate with a stranger's boy familiar with the language of skiing and golf but not of gun shops. The father is out of place in the shop. Rejecting the grandfather's life of blundering forays and unexpected breakdowns, he has made his life in Boston a model of propriety and caution. He says all the wrong things in the gun shop, makes all the wrong gestures. The grandfather makes most of the right ones. With the insight of a man who is open to the world, the grandfather knows that the grandson is like Dutch and that even the father should have had Dutch for a parent. The rare combination of love and skill emanates from the gunsmith. The story ends with the father remembering his childhood and the son firing the rifle. Pride and relief are heard in the father's final laugh. The irreconcilable tensions between generations of a family will never completely dissolve, but for the moment communication offers its balm.

None of these touches is forced, for "The Gun Shop" is a story not of commentary but of reverberation. Nor does the father have an epiphany that promises to narrow the distance between his son and himself. His retort to his wife's comment that he is too hard on the boy shows that the lesson in the gun shop is observed but not absorbed: "My father was nice to me, and what did it get him?" Indeed the final paragraph suggests that the son is on the verge of his own rebellion. But for the moment, at least, the family holds on, as it does in another story, "Son," where the boy is the family's "visitor" and "prisoner." Fathers always fail their children, who are always beautiful.

It is not outrageous to say that *Problems* will eventually be judged as one of the major collections of American short stories published in the twentieth century. John Romano supports this opinion: "*Problems and Other Stories* won't be surpassed by any collection of short fiction in the next year, and perhaps not in the next 10. Its satisfactions are profound, and the proper emotion is one of gratitude that such a splendid artistic intelligence has been brought to bear on some of the important afflictions of our times." Updike remains our foremost family chronicler because he understands that little incidents, grace notes as it were, make up the true drama of a home. The woman in "Nevada" who cries out "that it was nobody's *fault*, that there was nothing he could *do*, just let her *alone*" is a more convincing snapshot of a troubled wife than a dozen descriptions of women who survive on tranquilizers and thoughts of sui-

cide. In this sense, *Problems* is a volume of middle age. Wives' accusations are "moralistic" reflexes, and husbands' responses are full of "predictable mockery." As Updike writes in "The Egg Race," "The stratum of middle age has its insignia, its clues, its distinguishing emotional artifacts." Unlike *The Same Door* and *Pigeon Feathers*, which focus on the nostalgia felt for a time left far behind with the dogwood tree and youth, this collection is closer to *Museums and Women*, which details the love that lingers after the marriage goes bad. Not every story is about family, and not every story is about loss, but the fact remains that *Problems* reemphasizes Updike's move in his fiction from pastoral Olinger, Pennsylvania, to suburban Tarbox, Massachusetts. He took this step a long time ago, of course. The difference is that whereas in *Museums and Women* he occasionally glances back over his shoulder at the tranquil, "voluptuous" 1950s, at a time "when everyone was pregnant," in *Problems* his stories document the plunge into middle age when wives and husbands finally separate, when children unexpectedly grow up, when "the soul grows calluses," and when guilt, oddly, both lacerates and soothes.

Similar variations direct Updike's poetry except that the comic element is more pronounced in the verse than in the tales. Updike takes his poems seriously, as much more than diversions between completing one novel and planning the next, but the public wrongly defines his poetry merely as light verse in the spirit of Ogden Nash. This misconception is unfortunate, for his collections of poems show a change in tone and mood from the humor of *The Carpentered Hen*, through the lyrics of *Telephone Poles* and the autobiographical poems of *Midpoint*, to the meditations on death in *Tossing and Turning* and the celebration of nature in *Facing Nature*. This is not to say that he abandons humor after *The Carpentered Hen* but only to suggest that the poems of comic rhyme and verbal pyrotechnics are but one side of Updike the poet. The place to begin a reading of his verse is not with *The Carpentered Hen*, but with his essay "Rhyming Max," a review of Max Beerbohm's parodies first published in the *New Yorker* (7 March 1964) before being collected in *Assorted Prose*.

Understanding Beerbohm's verse parodies to be a kind of verbal cartooning, he points to the art of rhyme as an agency of comedy. Replete with regularity and rigidity, rhyme reflects the mechanical action that Henri Bergson termed a primary cause of laughter. Updike writes, "By rhyming, language calls attention to its own mechanical nature and relieves the represented reality of seriousness." Assonance and alliteration perform a similar function and join rhyme as means by which man asserts control over things. Light verse for Updike "tends the thin flame of formal magic and tempers the inhuman darkness of reality with the comedy of human artifice. . . . it lessens the gravity of its subject." *The Carpentered Hen* illustrates his argument. Beneath his celebration of the delightful artificiality of words is a respect for language itself.

Many of these early poems take to task the inane writing of journalists, advertisers, and editors. Combining verbal acrobatics such as puns, and traditional stanza forms organized with amusing twists, he often parodies the venerable art of the occasional poem when he appends to many of the verses prose statements usually lifted verbatim from an ad or editorial. Thus "Duet, with Muffled Brake Drums" pokes fun at an advertisement in the *New Yorker* claiming that the meeting of Rolls and Royce made engineering history, while "An Ode: Fired into Being by Life's 48-Star Editorial, 'Wanted: An American Novel' " comically exposes the muddled thinking of those who argue that the Great American Novel may be written to order to reflect the surface prosperity of the 1950s. Quoting parts of the editorial, and designating sections of his poem as strophe, antistrophe, and epode (parts of the Pindaric ode), he writes a parody of inspiration.

Not all of the poems are this amusing. As if foreshadowing the more somber poetry of his later collections, Updike also includes serious pieces of social observation like "Ex-Basketball Player" and "Tao in the Yankee Stadium Bleachers." These poems illustrate his lifelong interest in sports, but more important, they comment upon the ephemeral nature of physical prowess, reputation, and life itself. Readers of the story "Ace in the Hole" (*The Same Door*) and the novel *Rabbit, Run* will recognize the situation in "Ex-Basketball Player" as Updike describes the plight of the aging athlete whose current circumstances no longer equal the glory of past headlines. "Tao in the Yankee Stadium Bleachers" is a better poem, which muses on the proposition that "Distance brings proportion." Referring to passages of Eastern philosophy such as the dead rule longer than any king, Updike couches his thoughts on mutability in a metaphor of athletics. The inner journey is "unjudgeably long," and

every man eventually flies out while small boys in the grandstands wait to take their places.

These two poems look forward to the short stories in which Updike effectively comments upon the sense of diminishment and loss that age inexorably brings. Yet the dominant tone of *The Carpentered Hen* is not melancholy but joy. The book appropriately ends with the twelve-page poem "A Cheerful Alphabet," which is an updated *McGuffey's Reader* designed to teach his son the wonder of a versatile vocabulary. *A* stands no longer for the apple of sin and Eden but for the still lifes of Paul Cézanne. Designating *T* for trivet, for example, and *X* for xyster, Updike shows that alphabets can be cheerful and that language is alive.

His witty efforts to guard language from the stultifying effects of jargon and cliché, a primary feature of *The Carpentered Hen*, are continued in the first half of *Telephone Poles*. The occasional poem is again parodied, as in "Recital," which quotes a headline in the *New York Times*, "Roger Bobo Gives Recital on Tuba," and which goes on to play with the outrageous rhymes associated with light verse. For all of the pleasures of the light verse, however, *Telephone Poles* is a significant collection primarily because of the serious lyrics in the second half. These poems treat many of the themes that readers of Updike's fiction have come to expect: the attractions of memory, the threat of mutability, and the pleasure of the mundane. As Updike writes in the foreword to *Olinger Stories* (1964), he needs the "quiet but tireless goodness that things at rest, like a brick wall or a small stone, seem to affirm." These poems look more to Shillington than to Ipswich as if he were trying to secure a still point before facing the changes of middle age. A testimony to his close observation of common things, the volume illustrates his statement that "a trolley car has as much right to be there, in terms of aesthetics, as a tree."

The title poem is the center of the collection. Praising the relative permanence of man-made objects and their place in the modern imagination, Updike writes, "The Nature of our construction is in every way / A better fit than the Nature it displaces." He does not mean that trees, for example, are less valuable than telephone poles, but that poles testify to man's ingenuity in meeting his needs in the natural world, which must endure the yearly cycle of death and rebirth. Telephone poles may not offer much shade, but unlike elms they are both stable and utilitarian. Since their "fearsome crowns" at the top may literally "stun us to stone," the poles also serve as updated versions of ancient myths, in this case the myth of Gorgons' heads.

Perhaps the best poem in *Telephone Poles* is "Seven Stanzas at Easter." Noting how contemporary man is caught between the demands of reason and faith, Updike insists that the miracle of Resurrection must withstand the challenge by the mind if the Church is to survive: "Make no mistake: if He rose at all / it was as His body." The dilemma is nicely suggested in the key word *if* and in the speaker's description of the miracle in the rational discourse of scientific language. *If* Christ rose, He did so not metaphorically but literally. Symbols may not replace fact as the cornerstone of faith. The poet's uncertain tone reflects the predicament of intelligent modern man who would believe even while he doubts.

Updike's most ambitious collection of poems is *Midpoint*. Published when the poet was thirty-seven years old, the title poem is a forty-one page analysis of his life to age thirty-five, midpoint in the biblical span of three score and ten years. "Midpoint" is an impressive combination of autobiography, homage to past poets (Dante, Spenser, Pope, Whitman, and Pound), scientific knowledge, experimental typography, and comic tone. Defining the intellectual bearings of his first thirty-five years in order to prepare for the second half of his life, Updike explains that the poem is both "a joke on the antique genre of the long poem" and "an earnest meditation on the mysteries of the ego." "Midpoint" is not entirely successful because the parts are more impressive than the whole, but it must be read carefully by those interested in Updike's career.

The poem is too long and complex for a thorough analysis here, but some observations may be made. The general movement illustrates the poet's growth from youthful solipsism to an acceptance of his connection with all of humanity. *Point* is the key word both thematically and in terms of the poem's arrangement, for Updike not only shows that he needs an acceptable point of view to understand his relationship with the highpoints of man's history, but he also fills the second canto with a maze of dots that take shape as photographs from his family album when held at arm's length.

From his mid-life perspective, he understands that as a child he saw himself as the most prominent point in a radius of dots all secondary to him. Each person may view his experience

from a single point of view at a given moment in his life, but the solipsism of the child must be toned down if he is to accept his place in the world. The pointillistic photographs illustrate his most immediate connection–the family–and the opening line parodies Whitman's celebration of self: "Of nothing but me, me / –all wrong, all wrong–." Whitman may be a significant dot in the myriad points of Updike's past, but nineteenth-century beliefs are not necessarily reliable for a twentieth-century man. The importance of appropriate points is again established in the third canto about the composition of solids, which Updike now understands to be made up of compressed particles and dots. Finally he accepts the truth that identity depends upon love and the willingness to see life as a progression toward a metaphorical point that clears the vision of the eye / I.

Three other sections join the title poem to make up *Midpoint*: "Poems," "Love Poems," and "Light Verse." Of the three, "Love Poems" is the most impressive, because the mixed emotions of desire and guilt that are a hallmark of Updike's best short stories are poignantly expressed. These poems reflect what the shift from remembering his past to concentrating on his present has meant to his imagination.

Updike's recognition in *Midpoint* that he is on the down side of what he calls the "Hills of Life" forms the emotional center of *Tossing and Turning*, his best volume of poetry. He does not abandon the subject of his past, as the fine "Leaving Church Early" shows, but he focuses more than ever on the challenges of success and suburbia. The persistence of memory, a primary factor in his earlier poems and tales, gives way to the encroachment of age. The title of the collection suggests his restlessness, and a line from "Sleepless in Scarsdale" describes his dilemma: "Prosperity has stolen stupor from me."

Two of the three long poems in *Tossing and Turning* recall boyhood in Shillington and youth at Harvard: "Leaving Church Early" and "Apologies to Harvard," the Harvard Phi Beta Kappa Poem for 1973. The aloneness that later becomes insomnia is detailed in the former as Updike describes the absence of communication in his family "kept home by poverty, / with nowhere else to go." The need to forgive is a condition of their misery. The latter poem may be read along with "The Christian Roommates," a story from *The Music School*, as one of Updike's few accounts of university days.

Dust jacket for Updike's 1982 novel about a disillusioned author and his attempts to cope with writer's block and middle age

Yet the best poems in *Tossing and Turning* are the shorter lyrics in which Updike acknowledges his step across midpoint in the direction of what he metaphorically calls "Nandi." Surrounded in suburbia by the trappings of material success and a happy family, he nevertheless finds himself restless and afraid. The stupor that prosperity steals has a double meaning. He cannot find the stupor he needs to sleep because his life is now "too clean," and his success has lulled him into a stupor that clouds his artistic vision, his spiritual sustenance. Too much success "pollutes the tunnel of silence."

It also makes him afraid. More than any of the other collections, *Tossing and Turning* shows the poet's uncertainty about death and annihilation. In "You Who Swim" and "Bath After Sailing," two of his finest poems, Updike uses water to illustrate the unbeatable immensity of nonhuman otherness. The former is a sixteen-line description of his lover, who is such an expert at the dead man's float that she seems at home on both land and water. She splashes and plays and excels at love, but death lurks just out of sight.

The final line–"We swim our dead men's lives"– suggests that all men return to the water that made them. The fear is just as great in "Bath After Sailing." Safely back from another confrontation with the deep, the poet is aware of the ironic change from overwhelming ocean to soothing tub. The "timeless weight" of the sea may threaten, and the gentle swell of the bath may cleanse, but the tub so resembles a coffin that his fingertips shriveled by the water remind him of death. The last trip to the final destination is described in "Heading for Nandi" as the lonely poet takes a night flight across the endless ocean.

Not all the poems in *Tossing and Turning* are as bleak, for Updike also includes a section of light verse that recalls the verbal antics and dedication to a lively language that characterize *The Carpentered Hen*. Burlesques like "The Cars of Caracas" and "Insomnia the Gem of the Ocean" are fun to read. But the public's misconception of Updike the poet as a mere versifier of witty rhymes and sparkling puns could be corrected by close reading of his best poems, especially the second half of *Telephone Poles* and most of *Tossing and Turning*.

The light verse placed at the end of *Facing Nature* similarly recalls the linguistic fun of *The Carpentered Hen*, but in his latest collection of poetry Updike searches primarily for a balance between dread and desire. The sonnets in this volume meditate on mutability and death, but these inexorable laws of nature are then celebrated in "Seven Odes to Seven Natural Processes" in which Updike suggests that nature's "rot," "evaporation," and "fragmentation" are inextricable from nature's "growth," "crystallization," and "healing." Death and life are one. In these challenging odes, Updike reveals intellectual curiosity and verbal precision to hint that the order of art reflects the wholeness of nature.

Supporting Updike's achievement in poetry, short stories, and novels is a body of essays large and varied enough to fill three volumes. Including everything from parodies and autobiography to celebrations of baseball and golf, and erudite ruminations on the practice of fiction, Updike's collections of nonfiction testify to a lively mind joyously receptive to worldly vagaries and little details. What finally amazes the reader is the range of his curiosity, a range illustrated by the heart of each volume: the essay-reviews.

Beginning with *Assorted Prose* and *Picked-Up Pieces* and expanding in *Hugging the Shore*, Updike has assembled a substantial body of commentary on authors that not only directly investigates the literature of his day but also indirectly analyzes his own writing. The award-winning *Hugging the Shore* shows him at his best as one of the few men of letters who can write intelligently about Edmund Wilson and Nabokov, Henry Green and Iris Murdoch, Saul Bellow and Kurt Vonnegut, Celine and Pinget, Calvino and Günter Grass, Karl Barth and Paul Tillich, Roland Barthes and Levi-Straus. Few other contemporary writers can clarify so much or can help the reader see relations among so many branches of knowledge. Few except Updike have managed such enthusiasm for the life of the mind and continued to comment sanely and generously on artists who do not write or think the way he does.

As *Hugging the Shore* illustrates, Updike is primarily an appreciator. Not driven to possess his subject with an academic thoroughness, he nevertheless responds with such knowledge and wit that he cannot be dismissed as a dilettante. In *Hugging the Shore*, he writes about theology, New England churches, and—incredibly—more than 130 authors with so much tact that the reader feels comfortable in the presence of his sparkling mind.

He does not rant and rave, he does not scold and scorn, and he does not stumble into the trap that ensnares many critics and makes them unable to treat other authors' books as anything except disappointing versions of what they themselves might have written. The hallmark of *Hugging the Shore* is sympathy for the writer's dilemma, concern for the writer's chore. About Nabokov, Updike writes, "He asked, then, of his own art and the art of others a something extra—a flourish of mimetic magic or deceptive doubleness—that was supernatural and surreal in the root sense of these degraded words." About Muriel Spark and Iris Murdoch: "The two of them together reappropriate for their generation Shakespeare's legacy of dark comedy, of deceptions and enchantments, of shuddering contrivance, of deep personal forces held trembling in a skein of sociable truces." Such sympathy abounds.

Yet for all the joy of reading this book, the initiated reader might squirm just a bit. Updike's insistence on realism echoes throughout. It is not that he regards realism as a literary convention like romanticism or modernism but that he somehow drags in his acknowledged Christian perspective and affirms the marriage of realism and morality. Of Italo Calvino's fiction, for example, he writes, "There is little that sticks in the mind as involuntarily real, as having been other than intellectually achieved." Updike clearly prefers the touch of grace gained by hard contact with the real. His uneasiness with writers who stress the play of language over the reflection of the world is disquieting.

Especially rewarding are three longish lectures on three American giants, Hawthorne, Whitman, and Melville, which, he explains, were undertaken to "educate the speaker as much as the audience." That one comment perhaps best catches the spirit of *Hugging the Shore*. Updike learns as he reads and does not pontificate as he writes.

One is finally grateful for such gems as "A sensation of blasphemous overlapping, of some vast substance chemically betraying itself, is central to the Gothic tradition of which Hawthorne's tales are lovely late blooms." The question of religious belief not only unites the lectures on Hawthorne, Whitman, and Melville but also defines Updike's attitude toward his own life and art. A believer himself, he is drawn as if by paradox to the shudder of Melville's uncertainty: "Moby Dick represents the utter blank horror of the universe if Godless, a horror so awesome as to excite worship."

There are those who argue that Updike does not demand enough in his essays, that he refuses to ask hard questions. However, to insist on more than the enormous amount that he already offers is to require academic specialization from one of America's finest creative writers. The happy union of lyrical prose and intellectual probing that is the highlight of his fiction shows itself everywhere in his nonfiction. John Updike may hug the shore in his criticism, but he remains one of the most perceptive men of letters in America since Edmund Wilson and Henry James.

Bibliographies:

C. Clarke Taylor, *John Updike: A Bibliography* (Kent, Ohio: Kent State University Press, 1968).
Lists primary and secondary materials, but is valuable primarily for the listing of Updike's uncollected work from 1949 through July 1967; annotated.

B. A. Sokoloff and David E. Arnason, *John Updike: A Comprehensive Bibliography* (Norwood, Penn.: Norwood Editions, 1972).
Omits *Bottom's Dream* (1969) and is unannotated, but has good listing of Updike's uncollected material; primary and secondary.

Arlin G. Myer and Michael A. Olivas, "Criticism of John Updike: A Selected Checklist," *Modern Fiction Studies*, 20 (Spring 1974): 121-133.
Good listing of secondary material through 1973.

Olivas, *An Annotated Bibliography of John Updike Criticism 1967-1973, and A Checklist of His Works* (New York: Garland, 1975).
Designed as a supplement to Taylor; primary and secondary with helpful annotations.

Ray A. Roberts, "John Updike: A Bibliographical Checklist," *American Book Collector*, 1, new series (January-February 1980): 5-12, 40-44; (March-April 1980): 39-47.

Indispensable listing of primary material, including Updike's numerous limited and signed items.

Donald J. Greiner, "Selected Checklist," in his *The Other John Updike: Poems / Short Stories / Prose / Play* (Athens: Ohio University Press, 1981).
Lists the place and date of first publication of Updike's poems, short stories, essays, and reviews through 1977; primary.

References:

Rachael C. Burchard, *John Updike: Yea Sayings* (Carbondale: Southern Illinois University Press, 1971).
Elementary overview from the perspective of affirmative Christianity.

Robert Detweiler, *John Updike*, revised edition (New York: Twayne, 1984).
Excellent introduction with short discussion of Updike's major work.

Donald J. Greiner, *Adultery in the American Novel: Updike, James, and Hawthorne* (Columbia: University of South Carolina Press, 1985).
First major discussion of Updike's adaptation from Hawthorne and James of the themes of sin, guilt, and belief.

Greiner, *John Updike's Novels* (Athens: Ohio University Press, 1984).
In-depth analysis of Updike's novels through *Rabbit Is Rich*.

Greiner, *The Other John Updike: Poems / Short Stories / Prose / Play* (Athens: Ohio University Press, 1981).
First major analysis of Updike's non-novel writing, with discussions of crosscurrents among the works, and commentary on the reception of the various books.

Alice and Kenneth Hamilton, *The Elements of John Updike* (Grand Rapids, Mich.: Eerdmans, 1970).
Valuable sourcebook of allusions and symbols from a religious point of view.

George Hunt, *John Updike and the Three Great Secret Things: Sex, Religion, and Art* (Grand Rapids, Mich.: Eerdmans, 1980).

The most informed discussion to date of Updike's use of Kierkegaard and Karl Barth.

William R. Macnaughton, ed., *Critical Essays on John Updike* (Boston: G. K. Hall, 1982).
Excellent collection of overviews.

Joyce B. Markle, *Fighters and Lovers: Theme in the Novels of John Updike* (New York: New York University Press, 1973).
Helpful thematic approach to Updike's novels through *Rabbit Redux*.

Charles Thomas Samuels, *John Updike* (Minneapolis: University of Minnesota Press, 1969).
Pamphlet-length introduction to Updike's early work.

Larry E. Taylor, *Pastoral and Anti-Pastoral Patterns in John Updike's Fiction* (Carbondale: Southern Illinois University Press, 1971).
Excellent analysis of Updike's adaptation of the pastoral tradition in literature from 300 B.C.; especially appropriate to a reading of *The Centaur*.

David Thorburn and Howard Eiland, eds., *John Updike: A Collection of Critical Essays* (Englewood Cliffs, N.J.: Prentice-Hall, 1979).
Helpful collection of reviews and chapters from books noted above.

Suzanne Henning Uphaus, *John Updike* (New York: Ungar, 1980).
Useful short discussions of Updike's major work for the beginning reader.

Edward P. Vargo, *Rainstorms and Fire: Ritual in the Novels of John Updike* (Port Washington, N.Y.: Kennikat Press, 1973).
Examines Updike's novels from the perspective of sacrament and myth.

Kurt Vonnegut, Jr.

This entry was updated by Peter J. Reed (University of Minnesota) from his entries in DLB 2, American Novelists Since World War II and DLB Yearbook 1980.

Places	Indianapolis Ithaca, N.Y. Dresden	Schenectady, N.Y. Cape Cod, Mass. Chicago	Galapagos Islands Haiti

Influences and Relationships	Louis-Ferdinand
	  Céline
	H. L. Mencken
		Jonathan Swift
		Mark Twain
		Voltaire
			Robert Louis
			  Stevenson

Literary Movements and Forms	Science Fiction Satire	Dystopian Fiction Postmodernism	Black Humor Surrealism
Major Themes	War and Peace Social Justice Family Mental Illness	Evolution Author's Role in Society	Human Decency Atheism Religion
Cultural and Artistic Influences	German Heritage Journalism	Anthropology Biochemistry	Architecture Comedians
Social and Economic Influences	The Depression World War II	Vietnam War Extended Family	Censorship

BIRTH: Indianapolis, Indiana, 11 November 1922 to Kurt and Edith Lieber Vonnegut.

EDUCATION: Cornell University, 1940-1942, 1945; University of Chicago, 1945-1947, M.A. (anthropology), awarded, 1971.

MARRIAGES: 1 September 1945 to Jane Marie Cox (divorced); children: Mark, Nannette, Edith. November 1979 to Jill Krementz (divorced); child: Lily (adopted).

AWARDS AND HONORS: Guggenheim Fellowship, 1967; National Institute of Arts and Letters grant, 1970; Litt.D, Indiana University, 1973; Litt.D., Hobart and William Smith Colleges, 1974; elected vice-president, National Institute of Arts and Letters, 1975; Emmy for Outstanding Children's Program for "Displaced Person," 1985; Bronze Medallion, Guild Hall, 1986.

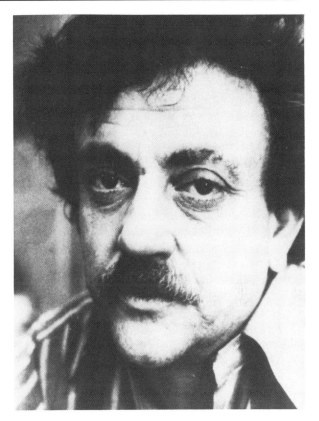

Kurt Vonnegut (Wide World Photos)

BOOKS: *Player Piano* (New York: Scribners, 1952; London: Macmillan, 1953);
The Sirens of Titan (New York: Dell, 1959; London: Gollancz, 1962);
Canary in a Cat House (Greenwich, Conn.: Fawcett Gold Medal, 1961);
Mother Night (Greenwich, Conn.: Fawcett Gold Medal, 1962; London: Cape, 1968);
Cat's Cradle (New York, Chicago & San Francisco: Holt, Rinehart & Winston, 1963; London: Gollancz, 1963);
God Bless You, Mr. Rosewater, or Pearls Before Swine (New York, Chicago & San Francisco: Holt, Rinehart & Winston, 1965; London: Cape, 1965);
Welcome to the Monkey House (New York: Seymour Lawrence / Delacorte, 1968; London: Cape, 1969);
Slaughterhouse-Five, or The Children's Crusade (New York: Seymour Lawrence / Delacorte, 1969; London: Cape, 1970);
Happy Birthday, Wanda June (New York: Seymour Lawrence / Delacorte, 1971; London: Cape, 1973);
Between Time and Timbuktu (New York: Seymour Lawrence / Delacorte, 1972; St. Albans, U.K.: Panther, 1975);
Breakfast of Champions: Goodbye Blue Monday! (New York: Seymour Lawrence / Delacorte, 1973; London: Cape, 1973);
Wampeters, Foma & Granfalloons (Opinions) (New York: Seymour Lawrence / Delacorte, 1974; London: Cape, 1975);

Slapstick, or Lonesome No More (New York: Seymour Lawrence / Delacorte, 1976; London: Cape, 1977);
Jailbird (New York: Seymour Lawrence / Delacorte, 1979; London: Cape, 1979);
Sun Moon Star, by Vonnegut and Ivan Chermayeff (New York: Harper & Row, 1980);
Palm Sunday (New York: Seymour Lawrence / Delacorte, 1981);
Deadeye Dick (New York: Delacorte / Seymour Lawrence, 1982);
Galapagos (New York: Delacorte / Seymour Lawrence, 1985);
Bluebeard (New York: Delacorte, 1987).

PLAY PRODUCTIONS: *Happy Birthday, Wanda June*, New York, Theater de Lys, 7 October 1970;
God Bless You, Mr. Rosewater, New York, Entermedia Theatre, 11 October 1979.

TELEVISION: *Between Time and Timbuktu, or Prometheus Five: A Space Fantasy*, National Educational Network, 1972.

As of 1987 Kurt Vonnegut's work includes twelve novels, a play and a television play, two collections of short stories, two collections of essays, and a miscellany of uncollected shorter pieces of fiction and nonfiction. He is himself the subject of a number of books, critical articles, theses, and dissertations, as well as many reviews, interviews, and features in the popular press. Although he began publishing in 1950, it was really in the 1960s that he made his impact. His immediate appeal was to youth, partly because he espoused pacifism in the era of the Vietnam War. Besides peace, Vonnegut speaks of everyone's need for treatment with decency, respect, and compassion in a lonely, incomprehensible world. While his plots often seem pessimistic they are nevertheless funny, and he has been called a black humorist. He also has been tagged a science-fiction writer, a satirist, and a surrealist, but perhaps he might better be seen as using all of these techniques. Since the mid 1960s this combination has evolved into what is often called "postmodernism."

The release of the film *Slaughterhouse-Five* in 1972 completed the emergence of Kurt Vonnegut, Jr., from the obscurity of ten years before to a level of fame rivaled by few contemporary American authors. From 1950 to 1960 he remained virtually a literary unknown, despite stories in large-circulation glossy magazines and two novels; from 1960 to 1970 his following swelled from a loyal but small "underground" coterie to a steadily expanding college-age audience to encompass finally a broad, heterogeneous, and perhaps truly national readership. Now it is accurate to speak of his appeal as international. That an international audience should develop is appropriate, for although in some ways, such as in his humor, he seems particularly American, and although he has been an astute observer and diagnostician of the American scene, Vonnegut's perspective remains essentially international. He makes it clear that he distrusts nationalism. He is the product of an era in which world war and nuclear explosion have made most parochial nationalism obsolete, in which humans have for the first time seen their own planet from space and recognized the imperative of mutual dependence. Yet Vonnegut's vision must surely be shaped by more humble influences. For, to return to *Slaughterhouse-Five*, the special anguish that Vonnegut felt over the firebombing of Dresden arose partly from his peculiar situation of being under attack by his own forces and sharing

the sufferings of his "enemies," and in part from the fact that his own family was of German origin. Family remains an important concept for Vonnegut, from his assertion of the family's value for the individual, to his belief that we must all see ourselves as part of a larger human family. It is in family, then, that we can look for the beginnings of much that emerges later in his fiction.

Vonnegut's ancestors were prominent members of Indianapolis's large German-American community. Vonnegut's grandfather, Bernard Vonnegut, and his father, Kurt, were both architects and men of artistic sensibility, while on the Lieber side came prosperity from a successful brewery. Edith Lieber married Kurt Vonnegut, the author's father, on 22 November 1913, and for a short time they lived well.

The outbreak of World War I seriously changed the fortunes of the family. Vonnegut speaks of the impact of the war and of its residual anti-German feelings on his family in the opening of *Slapstick*. He dwells there on the psychological and cultural effects of being treated with prejudice and suspicion and of having a native language and artistic tradition denied. After the war the family suffered economically as well. First Prohibition effectively ended all income from the brewing of beer. Then the Depression meant a drastic slowdown in the construction of houses—and in the need for architects to design them. For the ten years before World War II, Vonnegut's father was almost constantly unemployed. By that time there were three children: Bernard was born in 1914, Alice in 1917, and Kurt, Jr., in 1922. For the two elder children there were at first governesses and then private schools, but Kurt, Jr., went to public schools.

In 1940 Vonnegut went to Cornell University to major in biochemistry. By the beginning of his sophomore year he was writing for the student newspaper, the *Cornell Sun*, where several of his articles opposed American entry into the war. In particular he appealed for rationality and humanity in resisting German-baiting jingoism or any such talk that exalts brutality in the name of patriotism. But the Japanese attack on Pearl Harbor lessened his reservations about the war, and Vonnegut volunteered for military service in January 1943. Though he was at first rejected for health reasons, he finally entered the army in March, knowing that descendants of his great-grandfather were German officers.

Meanwhile, the problems faced by Vonnegut's parents mounted. In 1941 they moved to a new, smaller house designed and built by Kurt, Sr., in the northern suburbs of Indianapolis. Vonnegut's father is described as having become increasingly fatalistic about the ruin of his career. Vonnegut's mother also found their sinking fortunes hard to endure. She tried to make money by writing short stories, and when this failed she became prone to depression. In 1944 Vonnegut obtained special leave to return home for Mother's Day. The night before he arrived, his mother took an overdose of sleeping pills and died in her sleep.

In the Battle of the Bulge, Vonnegut was among large numbers of Americans taken prisoner. He was sent to Dresden where, like Billy Pilgrim in *Slaughterhouse-Five* (1969), he worked making a diet supplement for pregnant women. On 13 February, Royal Air Force bombers made a heavy raid on Dresden which was continued during the following day by the United States Air Force. Through this devastating raid Vonnegut, again like Billy Pilgrim, was sheltered in a meat storage cellar below a slaughterhouse. The devastation brought on Dresden was almost total, as the compounded fires became one huge conflagration. The horrors intensified when the prisoners were employed to dig through the rubble for corpses.

It is commonplace for critics to dwell on the effects of the Dresden firebombing in Vonnegut's work, but he has denied that his war experiences were pivotal:

> The importance of Dresden in my life has been considerably exaggerated because my book about it became a best seller. If the book hadn't been a best seller, it would seem like a very minor experience in my life. And I don't think people's lives are changed by short-term events like that. Dresden was astonishing, but experiences can be astonishing without changing you. It did make me feel sort of like I'd paid my dues—being as hungry as I was for as [sic] long as I was in prison camp. Hunger is a normal experience for a human being, but not for a middle-class American human being. I was phenomenally hungry for about six months.

In April 1945 Soviet troops occupied Dresden, and Vonnegut was liberated and repatriated to the United States where he was awarded the Purple Heart. On 1 September he married Jane Marie Cox and that fall enrolled at the University of Chicago to study anthropology. During 1946 he supplemented his family income by working as a police reporter for the Chicago City News Bureau. In the following year he finished his M.A. thesis, "Fluctuations Between Good and Evil in Simple Tales," only to have it unanimously rejected by the faculty of the Chicago anthropology department. In 1971 the anthropology department accepted *Cat's Cradle* (1963) in lieu of a thesis, and he was awarded the degree.

In 1947 one of the more important episodes in Vonnegut's life began. He went to work for General Electric Research Laboratory in Schenectady, New York, as a public relations writer. Vonnegut draws directly on this experience in several of his works, perhaps most conspicuously in the story "Deer in the Works" and his first novel, *Player Piano*. The Ilium of the latter is an ironically named parody of Schenectady, and the Ilium Works a hyperbolically rendered version of the General Electric plant. Vonnegut worked at writing in Schenectady, at first trying unsuccessfully to recount some aspect of his Dresden experience. Success came in 1949 with the acceptance of his first short story, "Report on the Barnhouse Effect," which appeared in the February 1950 *Collier's*, soon to be followed by others and by *Player Piano*. In 1951 Vonnegut took the decisive step; he resigned his job with General Electric and moved to Provincetown, Massachusetts (and later to West Barnstable), to devote himself to full-time writing.

The short stories that Vonnegut wrote during these early years of his career were quite widely varied in nature and subject. He was to speak of them later as inconsequential works written to support himself while he wrote novels. Whether he really thought so lightly of them is uncertain, but it is true that he achieved commercial success with the short stories almost instantly, whereas it would be almost twenty years before he began to earn much from his novels. *Collier's*, *Ladies' Home Journal*, *Cosmopolitan*, *Esquire*, and *Saturday Evening Post* were among the prominent magazines which published stories by Vonnegut during the 1950s. Although several of these stories used Vonnegut's knowledge of science or technology, few would qualify as science fiction. Rather, they represent the author's attempt to relate a world he has experienced, one in which technology plays a large and daily-increasing role. The stories which have such technology-related plots are generally set in recognizable, mundane worlds rather than the exotic settings frequently common to science fiction. Their purpose often seems to be, in fact, to cause reflection on what the impact of technological innovations might be on the daily lives of ordinary people. In "EPICAC," for instance, the developing trend toward having computers do everything for us is taken to the extreme when EPICAC's operator uses the machine to help him win a woman's affections with love poetry. The message about the dehumanization of modern man is delivered through an ironic reversal: the computer "humanizes," falls in love, despairs, and commits suicide.

Vonnegut later had a few short stories published in *Galaxy Science Fiction* and *Magazine of Fantasy and Science Fiction*, which, along with the technological content of other stories and of *Player Piano*, helped earn him the label of science-fiction writer. A glance at stories like "Long Walk to Forever," "Miss Temptation," "Next Door," "More Stately Mansions," or "The Hyannis Port Story" reveals this generalized label as misleading. While Vonnegut's work for General Electric, his earlier education, and perhaps his scientist brother are evident in some stories, at least equally evident is a reportorial sense for human interest. The stories often deal with quite ordinary lives, which are perceived with a mix of compassion and ironic humor, and, in the end, extol homespun middle-class values. In fact his inclusion of the technological, especially in the earlier stories and *Player Piano*, is not a reaching toward the exotic but a continuation of his concern with the level of reality which touches many daily lives. "I supposed," he has said of *Player Piano*, "that I was writing a novel about life, about things I could not avoid seeing and hearing in Schenectady, a very real town, awkwardly set in the gruesome now."

In *Player Piano* (1952) Schenectady becomes the Ilium of a fictional, if still gruesome, future. The General Electric plant has become the great Ilium Works, one-time home of Edison but now under the direction of Paul Proteus. In his late thirties, Proteus is still on the way up and at the opening of the novel appears poised between the decision to push for the next promotion or to succumb to a troubling malaise which makes him question not just the promotion but even his present status. A visit by an old friend proves crucial in deciding which way Proteus will go. Ed Finnerty is a contemporary who has also been an engineer and manager and who has received rapid promotions. Yet now he has actually quit the company. More dramatically, he effectively

has rejected the whole social system and soon becomes a sought-after outlaw. Proteus dismisses the course of the outspoken, hard-drinking, and grubby Irishman as too extreme. Yet through Finnerty, Proteus is introduced to persons and circumstances which lead to his rejecting the company and the system, and ultimately to his leading an armed rebellion. The rebellion fails, but in the novel's terms, that may be less important than the fact that Proteus does not fail himself. In the end he achieves much self-perception and makes a stand for his values.

Though Proteus's decision to turn against the company clearly has a relationship to Vonnegut's life in the period preceding the novel, equating Vonnegut with Proteus alone might be misleading. Like many good writers, Vonnegut writes a part of himself into various characters; there is obviously a great deal of the Ed Finnerty in Vonnegut. Finnerty is the practical joker, the iconoclast, the one who loves fun and life and freedom, and all these things characterize Vonnegut, too. A key event in the novel concerns a cat which tries to escape from the fully automated Ilium factory. At the last it scales a high fence, is killed by the electrified wires at the top, and falls "dead and smoking, but outside." Proteus and Finnerty fight to escape that fence, and although they appear to be condemned to death, they are outside the confines of the moribund, mechanized society at the end.

By using the name "Ilium," Vonnegut invites an ironic contrast between modern cities like Schenectady (or the Utopian vision of what technology can make them) and the Troy of Homer. The name "Proteus," from the god who could change his appearance at will, shows the same interest in myth and the ironic use of names. Vonnegut continues to make much play with the use of names in later fiction. Sometimes they are, as here, allusive, sometimes punning, and often satirical. *Player Piano* contains a good deal of satire—of the army, of the business leader's retreat, of college "amateur" athletics, to name a few—which underlines its serious purpose as social commentary. Certainly the depiction of what happens to persons deprived of useful social function, of the psychological cost to the individual of utopian schemes to make the masses placidly happy, serves as a kind of sociological editorializing.

While the satire entertains and at the same time carries the novel's message, there is besides something about *Player Piano* which other anti-utopian or satiric novels often lack and which be-comes more evident in Vonnegut's later works. There is a personal touch, an element of human warmth, even the suggestion of authorial concern in the kind of novel which is often distanced, objective-seeming, and generalized. In part that human touch shows up in the faltering uncer-tainty of Paul Proteus, in his yearning for some-thing earthy and homey. Perhaps Paul's urge to-ward the old Gottwald farm owes much to the impulse that led Vonnegut away from General Electric and Schenectady to a big old house on Cape Cod. Certainly something like Paul's nostal-gia for a time when social values were different and seemed to offer the individual more sense of belonging emerges frequently both in Vonnegut's fiction and in what he has said in interviews. And yet another personal touch in this novel which re-curs is talk of the writer and his place in society. In *Player Piano*, of course, the writer is satirized–he has let his wife go on the street rather than give up his artistic integrity by writing what the market demands. Obviously the treatment of this writer involves some self-parody in its mockery, yet the satire also works in the other direction at the expense of the commercial and philistine ele-ments of society which can make a writer's life mis-ery. Writers, almost invariably suggesting some form of self-parody, appear in many of Von-negut's novels. The self-deprecating humor, com-passion, nostalgia, and hint of long-suffering fatal-ism heard in the narrative voice of *Player Piano* become recognizable as Vonnegut's characteristic tone.

Player Piano attracted no critical acclaim at publication and to this day seldom wins praise equal to that reserved for some subsequent nov-els. During the seven years that lapsed between the publication of *Player Piano* and the appear-ance of *The Sirens of Titan*, Vonnegut worked on another never-to-be-finished novel, "Upstairs and Downstairs," wrote short stories, and sought to supplement his income with activities such as open-ing a Saab dealership and writing advertising copy. In 1957 his father died of lung cancer, and this is reported to have caused a writing block which lasted for a year. Another death which pro-foundly affected him was that of his sister, Alice. This coincided closely with the death of her hus-band (as recounted in the introduction to *Slap-stick*) and led to Vonnegut's adopting three of his four nephews.

By the late 1950s some of the magazines such as *Collier's*, which had formed a ready mar-

ket for Vonnegut's stories, were struggling. Partly because of this change, Vonnegut turned to writ-ing novels for the paperback market. *The Sirens of Titan*, which does have certain affinities with the "space opera," further added to the branding of Vonnegut as a science-fiction writer. He was not anxious to be so categorized, wishing rather to be recognized as someone who wrote about contem-porary existence in realistic terms–which in-cluded taking into account scientific and techno-logical advances and their intrusions into the average citizen's life. In that respect there is little doubt Vonnegut felt much of what he has Eliot Rosewater voice: "I love you sons of bitches," Eliot says to science-fiction writers. "You're the only ones who'll talk about the *really* terrific changes going on . . . the only ones with guts enough to *really* care about the future, who *really* notice what machines do to us, what cities do to us. . . ." At the same time, Vonnegut saw the classi-fication as an impediment and a kind of discrimi-nation, remarking subsequently that the critics who put him in the science-fiction drawer often subsequently mistook that drawer for a urinal. (*Player Piano* had been reprinted by Bantam in 1954 as *Utopia 14*.)

The Sirens of Titan (1959) has won the re-spect of many readers, some of whom regard it as the author's best book. It is basically the story of a playboy millionaire, Malachi Constant, who is told he will become a space traveler–and does, even though he has no real wish to. He is whisked off by Martians with a society woman named Beatrice Rumfoord. Despite their mutual contempt, they conceive a child, a son they call Chrono. After a brutal period of victimization on Mars and years trapped on Mercury, Malachi at last returns to earth. There he is hailed by the new religion, the Church of God the Utterly Indif-ferent, as the long-promised Space Wanderer when he speaks the foretold words, "I was a vic-tim of a series of accidents, as are we all." Soon after, however, he is made the religion's scape-goat, reviled, and hurled back into space. He ends his days, as has been promised from the start, on Titan, in the company of Beatrice, Chrono, and a Tralfamadorian robot named Salo. There the once-embittered Chrono joins the beautiful giant bluebirds and learns to thank his parents for the gift of life, Beatrice turns from resenting having been used all her life to being glad she was of some use, and the egocentrically loveless Malachi learns the value of loving "whoever is around to be loved." He also learns, to his dismay, that the earth and all its civilizations are no more than a message center for the Tralfamadorians. Stonehenge, for example, is a kind of note telling Salo that a missing part is on the way.

This second novel contains much that is repeated or amplified in subsequent novels. Simple repetitions include Tralfamadorians (although they change in appearance and nature) and the Rumfoord family, while conceptions like that of nonlinear time ("everything that ever has been always will be, and everything that ever will be always has been"), of the futility of searching for existential meaning outside of self when the answer can only be found within, or of the superiority of a charitable love between any or all humans to a narrower conjugal love also reappear with variation. The relationship between Malachi and Beatrice goes beyond the commonplace inadequacies of the Paul-Anita marriage of *Player Piano*. An important conception of love is affirmed through them. And yet there is really no romantic love story here, and Beatrice hardly emerges as a fully developed female character. In later years Vonnegut was to admit that neither a real woman nor a romantic love relationship has appeared in his novels. Father and son relationships reemerge, as, in a lesser way, does the role of the writer. Once again the main character becomes involved in a form of quest for meaning in his own life and undergoes several stages of change in himself, coming to a level of understanding he lacked at the outset. While the protagonist changes, however, there is a sense that the world cannot be changed, that existence is governed by inevitability. Despite the strong element of fatalism in the book, it contains more humor than *Player Piano*. *The Sirens of Titan* is rich in contrasts, its humor and its pathos mutually sharpened by their juxtaposition, its portrayals of scarcely relieved suffering and the cold wastes of space heightening its affirmation of the joy of life and the value of love.

For all this, and for all its subsequent recognition, *The Sirens of Titan* brought no great change to Vonnegut's reputation. In the meantime, however, Vonnegut had signed a two-book contract with Fawcett, a paperback house, which was to cover *Canary in a Cat House* and *Mother Night*. *Canary in a Cat House* (1961) was a collection of twelve short stories previously published in magazines between 1950 and 1958. This collection quickly went out of print, though all but one of

the stories were reprinted in *Welcome to the Monkey House*.

The second book of the Fawcett contract was *Mother Night* (1962), the story of an American playwright with a German wife living in Germany before World War II. Howard W. Campbell, Jr., is persuaded to remain in Germany during the war as an American agent. His cover involves becoming a Nazi propagandist, in which role he remains hated and hunted after the war without being able to reveal his other identity as spy. Caught and tried by the Israelis, he appears to be saved when his American control breaks all security to verify Campbell's secret activity, but then Campbell apparently commits suicide. The novel represents his memoirs written during those final days in an Israeli prison. What troubles Campbell most is a search for his own true identity; was he really the Nazi or really the spy? Vonnegut supplied the novel with a simple moral when he added an introduction to it in 1966: "We are what we pretend to be, so we must be careful about what we pretend to be."

In its plot, *Mother Night* is strikingly different from the two previous novels. *Player Piano* and *The Sirens of Titan*, of course, are widely different, but they share such basic plot elements as the use of a fictional future and an emphasis on technology. *Mother Night* has no future, no technology, nothing science fictional. It is the first of the novels to be written with a first-person narrator, and that helps to deepen the characterization of the protagonist and to intensify the inward reaching, on both his part and the author's, that goes on in this book. Partly for these reasons, *Mother Night* has been seen as "different" by several commentators and is regarded by many as marking a transition in Vonnegut's work or as being his best. Vonnegut himself admits to the book's difference, partly because at the time his head was filled with the work of the British playwright Harold Pinter, "so I was rather gloomy as I finished up the book," and partly "because of the war and because of my German background, and that sort of thing." Despite these differences, there are nevertheless strong lines of continuity to the other stories. Campbell becomes the most intense rendition yet of the protagonist in quest of meaning in an absurd world. Like his predecessors he begins as a rather shallow and unappealing person who suffers and learns and finally becomes a character who has won our involvement if not our affection. Like the others he feels the desire to call "Olly-olly-ox-in-free" and resign from life, but like them he finds that he cannot. Typically, the point of resignation seems to be a necessary step toward a limited recognition of his relationship to life. Since Campbell is a writer, the writers-and-artists theme receives more extensive treatment than ever in *Mother Night*. In particular it is with the writer as deceiver, the creator of fictional worlds who makes his audiences believe, that Vonnegut seems most concerned here. Ironically, Campbell himself has difficulty deciding what is true.

Cat's Cradle, the next novel, appeared in 1963 in hardcover, thanks largely to the efforts of Samuel Stewart, who had recently joined Holt, Rinehart and Winston. The return to hardcover would eventually mean that Vonnegut's work would be taken seriously, but *Cat's Cradle* was another of those works which reviewers could classify as science fiction. The story focuses on the three children of a scientist named Felix Hoenikker who, Vonnegut says, owes much of his characterization to Dr. Irving Langmuir, a researcher at General Electric in Schenectady. Thus when in the story Hoenikker leaves a tip for his wife under his breakfast plate, or when he becomes preoccupied with whether turtles buckle or compress their spines when they retract their heads, it is because Langmuir is reputed to have done both those things. Likewise the central plot device of the novel, *ice-nine*, owes its existence to the same source. Vonnegut tells the story that when H. G. Wells, the British novelist who wrote some compelling science fiction, came to visit the Schenectady laboratory

> Langmuir thought he might entertain Wells with an idea for a science-fiction story—about a form of ice that was stable at room temperature. Wells was uninterested, or at least never used the idea. And then Wells died, and then, finally, Langmuir died. I thought to myself: "Finders, keepers—the idea is mine." Langmuir, incidentally, was the first scientist in private industry to win a Nobel Prize.

Ice-nine becomes the cause of the end of the world. The narrator of *Cat's Cradle*, who calls himself John or Jonah, has set out originally to write a book called *The Day the World Ended*, meaning his subject to be the day Hiroshima was atom-bombed. In this concern with bombings and apocalyptic ends, one senses that Vonnegut is edging closer to talking about Dresden.

With the use of the General Electric laboratory, Langmuir, and the Dresden experience all

evident, it is apparent that *Cat's Cradle* continues Vonnegut's tendency to become increasingly autobiographical in his novels. There is other evidence of that, too. Hoenikker resembles other father-figures in Vonnegut and may owe almost as much to Kurt, Sr., as to Langmuir. Like the Vonnegut family, Hoenikker's three children include an older son who is a scientist, a tall middle daughter, and a younger son who joins Delta Upsilon. In this there is a correspondence between Vonneguts and Hoenikkers. And once again Vonnegut makes the writer within the novel the focus of some self-deprecating humor. Jonah becomes a follower of Bokonon, who is also a writer and who warns, "All the truths you are about to read are shameless lies." The writer-as-deceiver theme moves a step beyond *Mother Night*.

In 1965 Holt, Rinehart and Winston published a second Vonnegut novel in hardcover, *God Bless You, Mr. Rosewater*, the story of a shell-shocked multimillionaire who seeks to realize the motto: "Goddamn it, you've got to be kind." Many have seen that motto as the essence of Vonnegut. What the novel reveals, however, is that even such a simple sounding objective becomes difficult and complicated in the contemporary world. Eliot Rosewater makes an interesting variation on the Vonnegut protagonist for he, under the kinds of stresses that drive the others to the point of resignation, falls into a Lear-like madness. Sanity and questions of what constitutes insanity in an absurd environment become fully developed theses in this novel. There is another semi-autobiographical, tongue-in-cheek portrait of the writer in *Rosewater*, too. This comes in the figure of Kilgore Trout, perhaps the most famous of all Vonnegut's characters. He is a science-fiction writer who has published countless stories—which are frequently shelved with pornography—and who remains destitute and unknown while working at various menial jobs. Trout is, as Vonnegut has admitted, a vision of what the author feared he might become. Another previously seen theme, the great raid at Dresden, is also touched on several times, and at one point Rosewater hallucinates that Indianapolis is consumed in a Dresden-style firestorm.

It might seem that at this point Vonnegut's career should have reached a plateau from which to launch the final climb to success. He had written three of the four novels most often named as his best (*The Sirens of Titan, Mother Night*, and *God Bless You, Mr. Rosewater*—the other would be

Slaughterhouse-Five) and had returned to publication in hardcover. Yet in fact his situation was far from ideal. The once-remunerative short-story market was gone, his science-fiction reputation was keeping him from being seriously reviewed, the two hardcover novels had sold only a few thousand copies, and the only work he had left in print was *Rosewater*. Besides having his own three children to provide for, he had adopted three of his sister Alice's four sons. It was in this situation that Vonnegut accepted an appointment at the Writers Workshop at the University of Iowa. The position brought him into contact with other writers and with students and faculty, with consequences which Jerome Klinkowitz has described:

> The first result for Vonnegut's own writing was a startling self-consciousness. For earlier novels, *Cat's Cradle* in particular, his publishers had warned him not to use his own name or personality in fiction. In Iowa City Vonnegut learned there were no real reasons not to, and so for the hardcover issue of *Mother Night* he added a personal preface about his own involvement with "the Nazi monkey-business." For the first time in print, he told about the Dresden massacre and his own act of witness to it. Two years later, as he left Iowa City, Vonnegut added a confessional preface to his story collection *Welcome to the Monkey House*, which explained much about how his own personality expressed itself in stories and novels. And by then he had figured out *Slaughterhouse-Five*.

By the time he left Iowa in 1967, the upturn was under way. His "underground" following, mainly among college students, was beginning to break through to a larger audience, Dell and Avon republished his novels in paperback, Harper and Row republished *Mother Night*, and Holt, Rinehart and Winston reprinted *Player Piano*–all this in 1966 and 1967.

Vonnegut, meanwhile, had not ceased writing shorter prose entirely as his production of novels increased. Rather, in the mid 1960s, he began to write more short pieces of other kinds than the now largely marketless short stories, including essays, reviews, short travel accounts, and human-interest stories. "Brief Encounters on the Inland Waterway" (1966) recounts a journey from Massachusetts to Florida on the Kennedy yacht crewing for their captain, Frank Wirtanen (whose name had been borrowed for the character of an American intelligence officer in *Mother Night*). "Oversexed in Indianapolis" (1970) is a review of a novel written by another graduate of

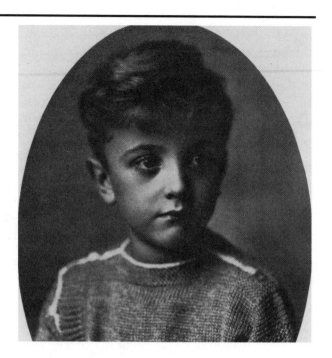

Vonnegut around the age of four

Shortridge High School, *Going All the Way* by Dan Wakefield. A couple of pieces in 1969 deal with witnessing the launching of space rockets. Many of these were later to be collected in *Wampeters, Foma & Granfalloons*, published in 1974. A characteristic of this short nonfiction is that Vonnegut frequently includes himself directly, just as he starts to in his novels from about 1966 onward. He may write reportage, but he lets us know who is reporting and how he feels about what he is reporting. One of the most interesting aspects of this material for the reader becomes the emergent relationship between observer / writer and subject. Vonnegut's association with the short story was far from over, however, and he prepared and introduced a new collection which was published in 1968 by Seymour Lawrence /Delacorte. *Welcome to the Monkey House* included eleven of the stories from *Canary in a Cat House*, plus fourteen more.

The year he left Iowa, Vonnegut visited Dresden with the assistance of a Guggenheim Fellowship, gathering material for the novel on that experience which was to emerge as *Slaughterhouse-Five*. In the course of preparing the novel, Vonnegut visited his old friend Bernard O'Hare, who had been a scout, then a prisoner, with him in Germany, and who is now an attorney in Pennsylvania, to see if together they could uncover more specific recollections. It was then, as Vonnegut notes in the introduction to *Slaughterhouse-Five* (1969), that Mary O'Hare objected to the conception of the story which seemed to be afoot as something that could be turned into a movie starring John Wayne and Frank Sinatra. Vonnegut comments, "She freed me to write about what infants we really were: 17, 18, 19, 20, 21. We were baby-faced, and as a prisoner of war I don't think I had to shave very often. I don't recall that was a problem." The description fits the kind of character Vonnegut places at the center of the novel; the bemused, "eager to please," naive Billy Pilgrim. Many things which happened to Vonnegut are made to happen to Billy Pilgrim. He gets caught up in the Battle of the Bulge, wanders between the lines searching for his own forces, meets up with some other Americans, is taken prisoner, spends a long time packed in cattle cars with little food and sleeping standing up, becomes employed in Dresden making a vitamin-supplemented malt syrup for pregnant women, escapes the great air raid of 13 February by taking shelter in a meat storage locker deep underground, comes up to be used by the Germans in digging corpses from the ruins of the city, and finally is repatriated. All of that happened to Kurt Vonnegut, too, although the specific details of biography and novel sometimes vary. Many other things happen to Billy Pilgrim, of course, which Vonnegut has never claimed happened to him: he visits Tralfamadore, he "time trips" into the future and back, he becomes a kind of preacher. Yet through these multiple roles and situations, Billy Pilgrim's characterization retains a thread of consistency, and he emerges as a modern Everyman who is part innocent, part fool, part victim. He becomes a pilgrim who is lost, an innocent Jesus who suffers without having a purpose, and yet, like the other protagonists, through losing all, even at times his wits, he comes in the end to a species of knowledge that brings him the ability to live in peace with a world whose madness and cruelty were epitomized in the blasting of Dresden. Perhaps the most striking thing is that in this book in which Vonnegut at last confronts the Dresden experience, the dominant tones are not of anger or bitterness nor even of pain so much as of compassion and sorrow.

Slaughterhouse-Five fascinates not just in its content but in the ways in which it is put together. There are multiple plot lines, just as there were in *Player Piano*, but here their interrelationship is much more complicated in that it is temporal as well as spatial. On the title page Vonnegut describes the novel as "somewhat in

the telegraphic schizophrenic manner of tales from the planet Tralfamadore, where the flying saucers come from." Later the Tralfamadorian novel is described as being made up of "clumps of symbols" each of which "is a brief, urgent message," which the Tralfamadorians read simultaneously rather than consecutively. That seems to be almost what Vonnegut attempts in constantly juxtaposing brief scenes from different plot lines, places, and times, all of which flow together to cohere at the focal event, time, and place: Dresden. Vonnegut integrates himself into the novel more directly and extensively than in any previous book. The whole story is framed by the autobiographical beginning and ending, so that from the mind of the author we are "merged," as it were, into the world of the novel. And that relationship is maintained throughout with interjected moments where Vonnegut appears as a character, noting, "That was me," or, "I said that." And finally, the novel integrates a great deal that has gone before, from familiar characters, names, and places to catchphrases, ideas, and themes. This well-constructed work seems to pull together all that Vonnegut had been reaching toward in the previous novels.

Slaughterhouse-Five enjoyed a greater commercial success than had any of the previous novels. By then Vonnegut was emerging from the "underground" of a largely youthful audience to a wider recognition. Much of the developing interest in Vonnegut was not simply with the literary man but with the social observer and commentator on life as a popular philosopher. Many of his views struck a sympathetic chord in this era of the Vietnam War, not as merely relating to war itself but to such issues as overpopulation, ecology preservation, and consumer protection, which were also enjoying popularity. This popularity was to grow even greater in the next few years, hastened in part by the making of the film *Slaughterhouse-Five*. He now became much more the public figure. In 1969, for example, he was invited to a symposium on the novel at Brown University; in the following year he gave the commencement address to the graduating class of Bennington College, won a grant from the National Institute of Arts and Letters, and spent a term teaching creative writing at Harvard University. In January of 1970, he flew into Biafra, a part of Nigeria fighting for independence, accompanying an aircraft load of medical supplies and food. Scarcely was his visit over when Biafra fell. His moving account of the suffering of the

Biafrans and of the beauty and strength of their family system was published in *McCall's* (and later included in *Wampeters, Foma & Granfalloons*), though these impressions emerge most profoundly in *Slapstick*.

Despite success and recognition, Vonnegut experienced a rather troubled phase in his life, marked by some severe depression. Possibly contributing may have been the fact that now at last the Dresden book was finished, perhaps leaving the kind of flatness which often follows the attainment of a goal. Perhaps he had, in effect, purged himself of the major motivational drive for his writing. Factors which he has mentioned himself include his children's ages, now all leaving or having left home, and his own age, approaching fifty. And Vonnegut seems to have been uncomfortable with his newfound popularity and visibility. Doubtless he was glad to escape the Kilgore Trout fate he earlier had feared, yet the new role imposed strains, too. Vonnegut discusses that problem (largely through making Trout suddenly rich and famous) and others reflecting this troubled period in his life in *Breakfast of Champions*, a book already begun but not to be finished and published until 1973.

Saying that he was dissatisfied with insubstantial characters who existed only on paper and that he would therefore write no more novels, Vonnegut cast about for a new direction. He found solid characters and a new family to replace his own dissolving one in the theatre. On 7 October 1970, his play *Happy Birthday, Wanda June* opened on Broadway and was to run until 14 March 1971. It was based on a play he had written some fifteen years earlier, derived from two attitudes. One is an impatience with the figure of the Hemingway-type hero who demonstrates his manhood by killing beautiful and rare animals that never harmed him and by abusing women. The other is an interest in Penelope of Homer's *Odyssey*, one of the works included in the Great Books program which Vonnegut and his wife had conducted on Cape Cod. Indeed the original play carried the title "Penelope." *Slaughterhouse-Five* makes the point that all people need to feel they retain some dignity; *Wanda June* shows a proud "hero" whose false sense of dignity denies any kind of dignity to women, non-white races, and a good many other men.

By 1971 he had moved, alone, to New York. The next year saw the performance on public television of a ninety-minute screenplay, *Between Time and Timbuktu*, which collects scenes, charac-

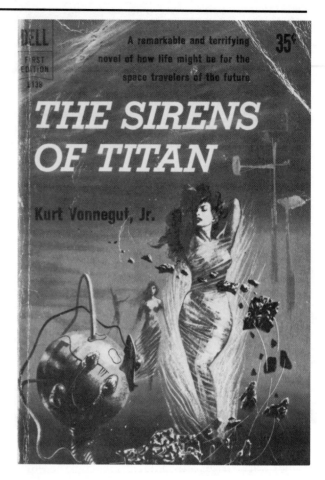

Cover for Vonnegut's 1959 novel about a playboy millionaire and a proper society woman kidnapped by Martians

ters, and themes from various pieces of Vonnegut's work. Like *Happy Birthday, Wanda June*, it was also published in the same year that it was performed, by Seymour Lawrence /Delacorte.

Breakfast of Champions, which appeared in 1973 but had been begun soon after *Slaughterhouse-Five* and had been laid aside, marked its author's return to the novel. Theater and screen were appealing and interesting, but for Vonnegut they imposed an important limitation; they made it much harder for him to appear as a character in his work. In the preface to *Between Time and Timbuktu*, he says, "I want to be a character in all of my works. . . . I have always rigged my stories so as to include myself, and I can't stop now. And I do this so slyly, as do most novelists, that the author *can't* be put on film." Vonnegut puts himself very firmly into this novel, for he appears directly in it as both character and author. He appears as Philboyd Studge, the "author" of this novel which details how Dwayne Hoover, a Pontiac dealer, runs amok after reading a science-fiction novel by Kilgore Trout, another Vonnegut surrogate. The subtitle *Goodbye Blue Monday!* suggests the author's reemergence here from a period of malaise and uncertainty, and that he is indeed writing the book as a fiftieth birthday present to himself. He also claims that the book clears all the clutter of the past from his mind, including his old characters. Indeed Vonnegut casts Kilgore Trout loose, as indeed he must, with a degree of regret on both sides. Trout's last request is "Make me young!" But the young Vonnegut and the Vonnegut who might have become a Kilgore Trout are gone. Instead Vonnegut has to grapple with the problem of the now famous and "fabulously-well-to-do" Kilgore Trout, of having people take what was only "solipsistic whimsey" as gospel. For good measure, Vonnegut tosses more "solipsistic whimsey" into the book in the form of drawings which adorn nearly every page.

Although it drew frequently unfavorable reviews, *Breakfast of Champions* became Vonnegut's greatest publishing success to that date, with a first printing of one hundred thousand copies. His popularity was now at its height, and he had achieved more serious critical and scholarly recognition as well. Two critical quarterlies, *Summary* and *Critique*, ran special Vonnegut numbers in 1971, and two book-length studies, *Writers for the 'Seventies: Kurt Vonnegut, Jr.*, by Peter Reed and *The Vonnegut Statement*, edited by Jerome Klinkowitz and John Somer, came out of academe. Vonnegut won honorary degrees from Indiana University (1973) and Hobart and William Smith College (1974), appointment as Distinguished Professor of English Prose by the City University of New York (Fall 1973–he left in February 1974), and election to vice-president of the National Institute of Arts and Letters (1975).

While *Breakfast of Champions* seemed quite different from most of the fiction that had gone before it, *Slapstick* (1976) appears to reach back in thought if not in style. It is the memoir of Dr. Wilbur Daffodil-11 Swain, a 100-year-old ex-president, who with his twin sister has written the most popular child-care book ever. His presidential program consists of giving everyone new middle names so that they will become part of elaborate extended families. Unfortunately, a plague and other disasters turn the United States into an anarchic collection of states and make the plan and the presidency meaningless. The book in its grotesque way is meant as a tribute to Vonnegut's sister, Alice. Its dominant theme is suggested by the subtitle *Lonesome No More!* In the introduc-

tion Vonnegut talks about that large old German family in Indianapolis from which he is descended and how it gave love and comfort and stability to its members. Once most Americans had such families, but now the generations are separated, and the remaining nuclear family is overloaded with the burdens once assumed by a larger and more heterogenous group. The main problem with modern Americans, he concludes, is that they are lonely. This is an old theme, though it has not been quite so overt before, having taken the form of people feeling purposeless and therefore unwanted.

Breakfast of Champions talked of people as slaves and robots, and of how once they are so viewed they lose value to themselves and to others. *Slapstick* also has slaves, human robots as it were, and characters who are not valued because they are hideous freaks. In big families–or in artificial extended families, such as Vonnegut proposes here–such people are still loved, valued, and cared for.

Slapstick is dedicated to Laurel and Hardy, and here, too, the book reaches back. Vonnegut speaks of the importance of Laurel and Hardy and contemporary comedians of radio and film to people during the Depression and therefore to himself in his formative years. One might recall how he wrote a joke column in his college newspaper, and that he has referred to his novels as mosaics built out of numerous small tiles, each tile a joke.

The 1970s proved difficult years for Vonnegut creatively. Speaking of the problems of revitalizing himself as a writer, in a 1976 interview Kurt Vonnegut told Robert Short: "I think it's just Puritanism now that keeps me writing, as I simply . . . I don't know, whatever I was born to do I completed after I completed *Slaughterhouse-Five*. After that, I just had to start a new career somehow, you know. All I say is that I have a feeling of *completion* after that. . . . It's just something was finished when I finished that." This was just before the publication of *Slapstick* (in October 1976) and before work on the next new novel, *Jailbird* (1979). Subsequently, his literary career became recharged, and he has undertaken a number of other activities.

The focus of Vonnegut's "new career" became New York City, where he lived with his second wife, photographer Jill Krementz, whom he married in November 1979, and their adopted daughter, Lily. He finds stimulation in the city, often enjoying its architectural treasures with an eye trained by his architect father. New York figures in *Jailbird* as much as Vonnegut's native Indiana does in some of his earlier books. With his literary reputation established, he has become something of a celebrity, a sought-after name. He made appearances on behalf of the 1980 presidential campaign of Rep. John Anderson, for instance, and his feature "How to Write with Style," presented nationally in a magazine advertisement, was applauded by English teachers.

Even Vonnegut's doodles have undergone artistic growth. He calls his drawings "felt tip calligraphs." He told *Horizon* (October 1980), "The human face is the most interesting of all forms. So I've just made abstracts of all these faces. Because that's how we go through life, reading faces very quickly." He reports having sold one of his drawings for $850–"That was great. It was my first sale."–and held a one-man exhibition at the Margo Feiden Galleries in New York in October 1980.

One other venture saw a kind of return to Indiana–to the Rosewater County of *God Bless You, Mr. Rosewater*. He presented the stage rights to this novel to his daughter Edith as a birthday present, and she produced a musical version of it. That this novel would lend itself to adaptation as a *musical* surprised many, but the outcome, with book, lyrics, and direction by Howard Ackman and music by Alan Menken, was delightful. With Frederick Coffin in the title role and Janie Sell as Sylvia, the play opened at the Entermedia Theatre, New York, on 11 October 1979, to generally favorable reviews, but it had trouble attracting the kind of audiences that might have taken it to Broadway.

Jailbird superficially resembles a return to "mainstream Vonnegut," sharing more with the first five novels than with those which have followed *Slaughterhouse-Five*. The novel, or its prologue, even begins with the announcement, "Yes– Kilgore Trout is back again." It echoes *God Bless You, Mr. Rosewater* in its heavy emphasis on economics and *Mother Night* in its prison-confession personal narration. In fact, however, its characteristics tie it to the later period and point toward a process of continuing evolution in Vonnegut's use of the novel form.

The prologue recalls a day in 1945 when Vonnegut, freshly returned from the European war, met with his father, his Uncle Alex, and a union officer named Powers Hapgood to discuss his finding work with a union. In 1927 Hapgood had led demonstrations at the executions of

Nicola Sacco and Bartolomeo Vanzetti, anarchists who ended up being sent to the electric chair for crimes to which another man confessed. Sacco and Vanzetti are woven through the novel as symbols of the injustices inherent in our economic system, while Hapgood serves as the prototype for one of the novel's fictional characters, Kenneth Whistler, who affirms the Sermon on the Mount as the basis of an answering morality.

The second half of the prologue moves from the reality of actual history to the creation of a fictional reality as the premise of the novel. It tells the story of the McCones, a family of rich industrialists. Alexander McCone selects his chauffeur's son as a protégé, offering him wealth, privilege, and a Harvard education. To fit the part, the boy's name is changed from Walter Stankiewicz to Walter Starbuck. He becomes the central character and narrator of the novel and the jailbird of the title.

While at Harvard, Starbuck turns toward socialism and the example of Kenneth Whistler and consequently loses McCone's patronage. His career as a government bureaucrat crumbles soon after he exposes his friend Leland Clewes to the House Committee on Un-American Activities as a former Communist. Years later, when he becomes President, former committee member Richard Nixon calls Starbuck to the White House to serve as Special Adviser on Youth Affairs. Subsequently a trunk stowed in Starbuck's subbasement office turns out to be filled with cash, and he goes to jail as a Watergate co-conspirator.

Although it is punctuated by constant flashbacks, the plot begins with Starbuck's release from jail. His unpromising start as a free man is transformed by a fairy godmother–in a modern variant of the medieval knightly test of kindness to an ugly hag. A decrepit shopping-bag lady who befriends him on a New York street corner turns out to be Mary Kathleen O'Looney, a sweetheart from his Harvard days. More than that, Mary Kathleen in fact is Mrs. Jack Graham, reclusive owner of the RAMJAC Corporation, the largest conglomerate in the country. The reunion is short-lived as Mary Kathleen soon dies after a traffic accident, but for two years Walter manages to conceal her death and to direct RAMJAC. The discovery of what he has done sends Starbuck back to jail, where, at sixty-six, he writes the memoir that becomes this novel. RAMJAC, having been left by Mary Kathleen to the people of the United States, is dismantled by the government and sold off to foreign-owned or Mafia-controlled conglomerates.

As is typical of Vonnegut's novels, the mosaic of vignettes, jokes, sketches, and analyses supersedes the importance of a story line per se. Vonnegut observed this direction in his fiction in the 1976 interview with Robert Short: "There'll be more and more to complain about in my fiction. People will say it's not fiction any more, it's editorializing. And, you know, the stories are getting sketchier and sketchier and sketchier. But I like stories because they allow you to digress. I'm not capable of logic, really a paragraph to paragraph logic. And so the story form allows me to just make statements that I know intuitively are true. I can't begin to buttress with arguments." In part, as Vonnegut says, these novels are less narrative and more editorial in nature. Also, like the "nonfiction novel" (for example, Truman Capote's *In Cold Blood* or Norman Mailer's *Armies of the Night*), which creates a fiction out of a "real" historical event, his novels acknowledge the unreality of the factual and the inevitability of reality's being given artistic form in its recounting. At the same time, there is recognition of the fictiveness of fiction. Reader and writer both know that while a novel is being told as if it were reality, it remains a fiction. Our era finds itself uncomfortable with artifice presented as reality, so the sculptor in metal may leave girders showing to reveal the true artistic medium. Vonnegut exposes authorial presence and acknowledges the fictiveness of his novels most dramatically by the inclusion of himself in *Slaughterhouse-Five*—"That was me"—and his direct involvement as character-author in *Breakfast of Champions*.

Such direct authorial declaration, and the mixes of documentary and fantasy, comic distortion and social realism, science fiction and history—even to the mix of real and fictional person in the index—typifies the chopped-up and mixed character of postmodern fiction. In its constant shifts of mood, time, place, form, and point of view, postmodernism tries to avoid imposing an artificial order upon the world it depicts. Postmodernists reject the implication in earlier writing that pattern *can* be found in the chaos, that the world, however absurd it may appear, is explainable. Even depicting life in a narrative sequence implies cause and effect rather than randomness or chance. Postmodernists try not to make the contingency of life comfortable simply in the process of narrating it, hence their concern with constant shifts and changes which keep us off guard. Vonnegut has moved increasingly in this direction. As he said much earlier, "Some writers try to make order out of chaos. I try to make chaos out of order." The postmodernist does this believing that that "order" is a false imposition upon the true nature of a contingent world.

Nevertheless, some clear themes emerge in *Jailbird*. The central theme concerns economics–the effects of an economic system on a nation and the individuals within. As elsewhere in his novels (especially *God Bless You, Mr. Rosewater*), he examines the politics and economics which precede and follow the Great Depression, that event which transformed the fortunes of his family and left a lasting impression on Vonnegut. All the documentary elements, like the Sacco and Vanzetti executions, authenticate the context the novel creates. Even the years are capitalized and characterized–"Nineteen-hundred and Twenty-nine wrecked the American economy"–like people who shape events and help fix the inexorability of life. The times themselves have personalities which we cannot escape, so that the 1930s can persuade Starbuck to embrace communism and the 1950s can persecute him for it.

Once again Vonnegut's universe seems almost mechanistic and devoid of free will. The individual remains powerless in the face of uncontrollable forces, taking comfort from minor victories, like Starbuck's last consolation: "At least I don't smoke anymore." Mary Kathleen assembles the largest conglomerate, yet her attempt to redistribute wealth fails. Government and corporations alike seem fixed in their established courses, becoming part of an undeviating cosmos rather than human instruments to contend with it. People are left to face life as they might play a chess game, asking the questions *Jailbird*'s players taunt each other with: "Have you played this game before?" "Is this a trap?"

Vonnegut shows that our society remains one where the pathetic shopping-bag lady coexists with the conglomerate. A central symbol in the book is that of the dining room of the Hotel Arapahoe, to which Walter goes during the Depression. Restaurant and hotel are under separate control; the hotel has become derelict while within it the restaurant glitters affluently. Again a Vonnegut fantasy "editorializes" on the cruel disparities of real life.

How does Watergate fit into this? Vonnegut has always been topical, and perhaps this story is in part a commentary on all the self-justifying books written by Watergate jailbirds. Starbuck, of course, does not try to justify himself even though he seems to have been, like so many of Vonnegut's protagonists, "a victim of a series of accidents." Even while Vonnegut obviously sees Watergate as a frightening aberration, *Jailbird* suggests it is almost inevitable in a system where governments, agencies, and politicians—like corporations, divisions, and company officers—seek endlessly expanded power without due regard for human welfare.

After *Jailbird* Vonnegut wrote the text for a children's book called *Sun Moon Star* (1980), a Christmas story recounting the first visual perceptions of the baby Creator of the Universe. This new treatment of an age-old story is paired with striking color illustrations by Ivan Chermayeff.

In 1981 *Palm Sunday*, a collection of assorted short pieces, appeared. Among these are his self-interview for the *Paris Review*, his short story "The Big Space Fuck," and his Palm Sunday sermon as delivered at Saint Clement's Episcopal Church, New York, on 30 March 1980. Contributions by other hands include "An Account of the Ancestry of Kurt Vonnegut, Jr.," by his uncle, John Rauch, two songs by the Statler Brothers, a letter by his daughter Nannette, and a speech by his great-grandfather, Clemens Vonnegut. These, along with many other letters, book reviews or introductions, speeches, and even a musical script, are linked together by what he calls "connective tissue." These commentaries seem a logical outgrowth of the conversational introductions to Vonnegut's later novels and read much like them. The book is Vonnegut's most complete autobiographical statement to date, revealing more of his life and background than anything previous, yet it is "complete" primarily in the breadth of topics on which it reveals his thinking. *Palm Sunday* is a treasure trove for Vonnegut devotees, but its humor and thoughtfulness, applied with characteristic freshness to so many aspects of contemporary life, give it broad appeal.

Deadeye Dick (1982), Vonnegut's tenth novel, came out shortly after his sixtieth birthday. There is less direct infusion of autobiographical fact or authorial voice than in many of the previous novels, almost as if the highly autobiographical *Palm Sunday* had paved the way. *Deadeye Dick*'s unusually short introduction contains little personal rumination. The story is not "framed" by authorial declaration or punctuated by interjection, as in *Slaughterhouse-Five*, but the introduction *does*

announce the way in which this book fictionalizes autobiography.

> "I will explain the main symbols in this book.
> "There is an unappreciated, empty arts center in the shape of a sphere. This is my head as my sixtieth birthday beckons me.
> "There is a neutron bomb explosion in a populated area. This is the disappearance of so many people I cared about in Indianapolis when I was starting out to be a writer. Indianapolis is there, but the people are gone.
> "Haiti is New York City, where I live now.
> "The neutered pharmacist who tells the tale is my declining sexuality. The crime he committed in childhood is all the bad things I have done."

In effect the events and characters of the book are frequently metaphorical equivalents of those in Vonnegut's life. He gives us a warning about that, too: "This is fiction, not history, so it should not be used as a reference book."

The narrator is Rudy Waltz, who when only twelve years old accidentally shoots a pregnant woman a mile away (hence his nickname "Deadeye Dick") and is further traumatized by the brutality of the police force and the psychological disintegration of his parents. Rudy's father, Otto, has studied art but essentially has lived a life of self-indulgence on an inherited fortune. His mother seems even more indulged and helpless, so that when the family loses everything in a lawsuit, Rudy becomes the parents' servant, cook, and nursemaid. He has a brother, but Felix has left home, advancing to ever-higher positions until the day he gets fired from the presidency of NBC. That coincides with Rudy's going to New York with a play he has written (which bombs on its opening night).

The remaining important character is Celia Hildreth. In high school she has great beauty but a distaste for the kind of male attention it brings. By her mid forties she has succumbed to amphetamine addiction and looks awful. Her decline echoes that of Mary Kathleen O'Looney from *Jailbird*, much as Rudy's humming haplessness reminds us of Walter Starbuck. Eventually Celia marries a Pontiac dealer, Dwayne Hoover, has a child, then commits suicide by swallowing Drano.

Introducing the characters is easier than describing this novel's plot. Vonnegut largely has moved beyond the kind of plot that is tied to traditional realism. As Jerry Klinkowitz observes in his book *Kurt Vonnegut* (Methuen, 1982), "Reminding the reader that fictions are provisional realities and not bedrock truths is the essence of Vonnegut's work: his one enduring theme and the metafictional center for each of his novels." *Deadeye Dick* has few of the "bedrock truths" on which a conventionally realistic plot might rest. It abounds in the provisional realities of fictions, however, as there are multiple levels of fictions. Author, narrator, and characters invent their own descriptions of what life feels like to them.

That emphasis–on what life *feels* like, on subjective impressions of reality–is underlined in the way Rudy describes life: "I was a wisp of undifferentiated nothingness, and then a little peephole opened quite suddenly. Light and sound poured in. Voices began to describe me and my surroundings. Nothing they said could be appealed." Throughout the novel people's peepholes open (in birth) and voices go on describing them until their peepholes close. Sometimes the fictions those voices invent hardly fit the character. Rudy never even sees the woman he shoots, but Midland City people call him "Deadeye Dick" for most of his life. Rudy himself also invents fictions. Besides writing his play based on the life of his father's old friend, he punctuates his narration with "playlets," dramatic scenes which reenact key episodes between the people in his life.

Beyond that, Rudy believes (as Vonnegut has suggested himself previously) that people make their lives stories. "We all see our lives as stories, it seems to me, and I am convinced that psychologists and sociologists and historians and so on would find it useful to acknowledge that." In general he suspects that a good deal of mischief results from people's trying to invent themselves interesting fictions.

Deadeye Dick itself is a fiction inhabiting a fiction. As if to emphasize the point about fiction's being only a "provisional reality," this novel is set, in effect, in another one–*Breakfast of Champions*. Names, places, dates, events are all the same from that novel to this. Celia Hildreth becomes Celia Hoover, Dwayne's wife, the one with the homosexual son Bunny, who kills herself by imbibing Drano. There is the same Keedsler Automobile Works, and Pefkos and Hooblers and Barrys, etc. (There are also odds and ends from other books–names like Ulm and Rudy and the RAMJAC Corporation.)

The highpoint of all this metafiction comes when, at Celia's funeral, Rudy finds himself smiling: "I glanced around to see if anyone had no-

ticed. One person had. He was at the other end of our pew, and he did not look away when I caught him gazing at me. He went right on gazing, and it was I who faced forward again. I had not recognized him. He was wearing large sunglasses with mirrored lenses. He could have been anyone." He isn't "anyone," of course. He is Kurt Vonnegut, author and character, as he appears in *Breakfast of Champions*.

Vonnegut has made himself a character in this story in other ways, too. Rudy is ten years younger than Vonnegut, so that he goes through some experiences that might be equivalents of the author's own a decade later. For example, Rudy's play runs in New York in 1960, Vonnegut's *Happy Birthday, Wanda June* in 1970. Rudy's great shock, the shooting, comes when he is twelve; the suicide of Vonnegut's mother when he is twenty-two. (Vonnegut even contrives these events to occur on the same date; the second Sunday, the 14th, of May, 1944.) Rudy's play bombs catastrophically on 14 February; Dresden, as Vonnegut records in *Slaughterhouse-Five*, was bombed on the night of 13 February.

Like the events, the characters are reinventions of those in Vonnegut's life. The mother whose "story ended when she married the handsomest rich man in town" and can't cope with crumbling fortunes later might stand for his own mother, as might Celia in her suicide. Elsewhere, however, Celia seems to represent his sister, Alice, especially in completing the threesome with Rudy and Felix, who, like Vonnegut's brother Bernard, is seven years senior. Vonnegut reinvents versions of this threesome in book after book.

While Vonnegut clearly is engaged in a new fiction for his life, one should remember his admonition that this "is fiction, not history," and not read it simply as a roman à clef. More important is how Vonnegut uses this autobiographical material–the fictionalizing process at work in this particular novel and, more broadly, in the continuation of his canon. That is a process which has seen Vonnegut evolving new descriptions of what experience feels like to him and new forms of the novel to match our culture's changing ways of understanding itself.

A curiosity of this book is the inclusion of recipes. Some of the recipes seem hilarious simply in the telling, others by their context. In some ways the recipes are reminiscent of the calypsos in *Cat's Cradle*. There are other echoes, too, especially in the general notion that language itself fic-

Dust jacket for Vonnegut's 1965 novel which questions the nature of sanity and madness in an absurd world

tionalizes. In *Deadeye Dick*, for instance, Haitian Creole is presented as having only a present tense, so that time and existence are transformed by the telling, as in this discussion of Rudy's late father:

"He is dead?" he said in Creole.
"He is dead," I agreed. . . .
"What does he do?" he said.
"He paints," I said.
"I like him," he said.

Deadeye Dick must be one of Vonnegut's funniest books, noticeably lacking the bleakness imparted to *Slapstick* by deformed characters and blasted landscapes. Its critical acclaim was qualified. For some, the experiments in form were a distraction, the echoes of previous work mistaken for mere repetition, and the lack of an engrossing, connected plot line a limitation. Technically it remains one of Vonnegut's most innovative books, however, and for that reason, as well as the autobiographical elements, may actually grow in interest.

Galapagos (1985), the eleventh novel, comes thirty-three years after his first, *Player Piano*. Three years in the making, it shows the labor in a polish and density that bespeak an experienced craftsman. But while *Galapagos* has a smooth fluidity it contains much of the wacky wit and irreverent imagination one expects of Vonnegut.

For this novel Vonnegut takes as his mantra Darwin and the evolutionary theory of natural selection. The story comes in two parts, "The Thing Was" and "And the Thing Became." The thirty-eight chapters of the first part trace the baroque interplay of the random and the inevitable whereby a cast of ten comes to be the Noah's Ark of human survival. The fourteen chapters of the second part take these people to Santa Rosalia, one of the Galapagos Islands. They evade the insidious virus which ends the human race, not in the usual apocalyptic bang but in the whimper of infertility. (That the fifty-two chapters equal the weeks of the year fits much else in this book which at every turn manifests evolution over periods of time.)

A million years later humans have evolved to have fur, flippers, and streamlined heads like seals. This is a consequence of a typical mix of freak circumstance and gradual adapting. The fur comes from a genetic mutation caused by the atom bomb dropped on Hiroshima; the flippers and smaller heads evolve as humans are forced to become seaborne fish hunters. They are much happier, of course, because without hands they cannot use tools or weapons. And they have shed the huge, overactive brains which invented lies and caused trouble and which were as burdensome (and probably as lethal) to humans as the vast antlers of the long-extinct Irish elk.

The theme of evolution permeates the book. It certainly governs the form. Vonnegut has described his books as mosaics in which each tile is a joke. That fits here, too, as chapter after chapter ends with the punch line of a joke. But each joke evolves from the last, and the larger joke of the whole situation—be it the first step of selecting the final ten survivors and getting them to the island, or the evolution one million years on—evolves out of a sea of coincidence and happenstance, as if everything conspires to thwart an inevitable destiny.

The longer, first part of the book seems at first somewhat confusing because of this technique. There are so many names and complications. But this confusion of characters and events proves effective. It shows us something about evolution: that it is not all triumph of the fittest or grand design, but that it sifts itself out of chance and coincidence. Life's evolutionary processes, Vonnegut insists, are contingent.

Evolution may seem like a curious topic to invent a novel around, but Darwin has always fascinated Vonnegut. He has obviously never liked "survival of the fittest" (a precept he casts some doubt upon) where every death is a triumph of progress. He clearly dislikes any doctrine which might be used even to imply that there is justification for the subjugation of the weak. Vonnegut has always had a warm heart for animals (in his high school writing he borrowed the nom de plume "Ferdy" from that wonderful children's book *Ferdinand the Bull*) and has frequently drawn on the deep impressions made by a visit to the Galapagos.

As a locus, though, evolution offers Vonnegut a long-term viewpoint from which to look at human endeavors with his characteristic mix of detached amusement and compassion, despite seeing cause for despair. After all, he takes as his epigraph Anne Frank's stubborn assertion: "In spite of every thing, I still believe people are really good at heart."

Another evolution in *Galapagos* comes in narration. Vonnegut does not enter this novel to speak directly, as he does in many previous novels. Instead his narrator turns out to be the son of his fictional alter ego, the science-fiction writer Kilgore Trout. This metafictional device makes it as if Vonnegut's novel has evolved out of his earlier writing, as if characters from the fiction are making more fiction. That implies the contemporary perception of the artist as a product of his or her art, rather than the traditional opposite view. And Vonnegut uses other techniques associated with postmodernism: fragmentation through short chapters and subdivisions; shifts in setting, time, and character; random, noncausal events; Darwin biography mixed with Trout science fiction; and allusions to the author's earlier fiction. It is a form, in short, which embodies the idea expressed in its content; that evolution is shaped by contingency.

Vonnegut frequently has used distancing devices like looking at earth through the eyes of an extraterrestrial or from another planet, or assessing our society from the perspective of another age or culture. Those distances are used with great accentuation in *Galapagos*. Human social behavior is measured against timeless evolutionary adaptations. The narrator views all from the perspective of the year A.D. 1001986. As a result, Vonnegut achieves the kinds of distances and fresh perspectives that Jonathan Swift created through remote locations and changing scales in *Gulliver's Travels*. He thus examines current issues like the imbalances of the world's economies or the dangers implicit in accelerating armaments procurements in striking new terms.

One way in which Vonnegut sees his work is as being a scientist who begins by asking "What if ?" The scientist conducts experiments to see what might happen given certain conditions. So can the writer, says Vonnegut, and he enjoys this because it is also a playful process. In *Slapstick* he asks, "What if gravity were not a *constant* force?" In *Galapagos* he asks, "What if all the humans died except an isolated group? How would they evolve?" Or, "All the world's wealth is really contained in pieces of paper. What if they were all called in at once and their real value demanded?" There is, as he has admitted, a certain sophomoric naivete about such questions, but that is the source of their freshness and vigor. *Galapagos* shows that, though in his sixties, Vonnegut still has that lively irreverence. It fuels his humor and arms his attacks on the platitudes and conventional wisdom which so frequently prove specious. He thus refuses to become fossilized in acquiescence to standard thinking.

In fact, the arrogance of humanity's self-assurance in its own intelligence and its dogmatic opinionation are above all what this book warns against. That arrogance emerges in the self-righteousness with which people will impose opinions, subjugate others, abuse animals, and devastate the planet. Even the arrogant assumption that humans will end the world with their own weapons is undercut when they are brought to extinction by a humble virus. Out of the adolescent irreverence, finally, emerges the kindly but rather weary avuncular voice, so frequent in Vonnegut's work, which speaks the novel's moral warnings.

Galapagos has been well received, generally. Vonnegut's own view is that he remains popular with a wide readership on the one hand (since even his earlier books have remained good sellers) and respected by literary scholars and academic writers on the other, but is resisted by some reviewers in the popular presses. Evidence supports this: some magazine and newspaper reviews were grudging about *Galapagos* and Vonnegut generally, but he continues to be taught, anthologized, and written about in the universities, where *Galapagos* often won praise. Some reviewers, including novelist John Irving, have called *Galapagos* Vonnegut's best novel ever; more have said it is his best since *Slaughterhouse-Five*, and it won conspicuously favorable assessments in the British press.

Published in 1987, *Bluebeard* is Vonnegut's twelfth novel. As its subtitle announces, it is "The Autobiography of Rabo Karabekian (1916-1988)." Karabekian previously appears as the painter who attends the Midland City Arts Fair in *Breakfast of Champions*. There his painting consists of a plain canvas with a single vertical stripe which represents "the unwavering band of light" which is the unique individual core of each human. While Karabekian is dismissed in that novel as "a vain and weak and trashy man," he nevertheless provides the affirmation which breaks the narrator out of his bleak view of a mechanic world in which people are little more than robots.

In *Bluebeard* Karabekian is not at all the abrasive, self-assured snob he was in *Breakfast of Champions*. He is a one-eyed veteran and widower, most of whose friends have died (frequently by suicide) and whose paintings have quite literally fallen apart, so that if he is remembered at all it is as an object of derision. His one friend, Paul Slazinger, is an unsuccessful novelist who takes advantage of the comforts of Rabo's home in East Hampton. Until, that is, the summer of 1987

when Karabekian encounters Circe Berman, a forty-three-year-old widow who invites herself into his life and home and urges him to write an autobiography. These three characters are the principal occupants of the "present" in this novel.

Bluebeard divides between Karabekian's autobiography and the present in which he is writing it. To a degree the two accounts are complementary, and they are punctuated by signals like "Back to the Great Depression" or "To return to the past." Inevitably the autobiography and the diary of the present converge at the end.

Karabekian's parents escaped the Turkish massacre of the Armenians and made their way to California, where Rabo was raised. After high school he goes to New York to become the apprentice of Dan Gregory, an illustrator famous for the photographic accuracy of his work. Karabekian is evicted, not for his philandering with Gregory's mistress Marilee Kemp but for being caught by the great man coming out of the Museum of Modern Art. The war intervenes, and when Karabekian returns to painting it is as a member of the abstract expressionist school. Rabo rolls a commercial wall paint, Sateen Dura-Luxe, onto huge canvases, and then applies vertical strips of tape. Sateen Dura-Luxe does not live up to its promises of longevity, and years later Rabo's paintings literally self-destruct. By this time he has retired to East Hampton, where he becomes a reclusive widower until the arrival of Circe.

Essentially two worlds dominate this novel. One is the world of art, or specifically of painting, and the other is a world of massacre and war. From the account of the Karabekians' escape from the Turkish massacre of the Armenians to the references to World War II, there is a backdrop of violence and inhumanity which sets in context the dialogue between representational and expressionist painting in this novel. It suggests that these modern horrors are in part responsible for the rise of abstract expressionism. While Vonnegut himself professes to be not much drawn to the abstract expressionists, he presents a case for their technique in an article in *Esquire* (December 1983) called "Jack the Dripper." In it he asks, "could any moralists have called for a more apt reaction by painters to World War II, to the death camps and Hiroshima and all the rest of it, than pictures without persons or artifacts, without even allusions to the blessings of Nature? A full moon, after all, had come to be known as 'a bomber's moon.' "... It had seemed impossible that any real artist could honorably create harmonious pictures for a European and North American civilization whose principal industry had become the manufacture of ruins and cripples and corpses." Jackson Pollock's answer had been to turn inward to make an expression of the unconscious. Rabo's vertical tapes which represent the "souls" of beings presumably seek to evade the corrupted physical world in the same way.

What comment is made on these paintings, then, by the fact that they fall apart? Perhaps there is parody in the portrayal of Rabo, just as there is in the characterization of Kilgore Trout. Perhaps both embody an element of self-parody by Vonnegut, too, partly expressing fears for the future of his own work or reputation. Certainly Vonnegut has struggled, like the Pollock he describes, to find an appropriate form after the horrors he experienced in the war. He also has called the book which describes those horrors, *Slaughterhouse-Five*, a failure.

If abstract expressionism is treated with a degree of parody, so is representational art. The accounts of literal representation being taken to the extreme that the copy can be taken for the original, culminating in forgery, are an undercutting of the insistence on realism. Nevertheless Vonnegut does appear to be making a case for the value of learning the skills of one's medium. What the novel also seems to show is that such skill does not always guarantee success: Rabo's friend Terry Kitchen simply blasts away with an industrial spray-rig. Similarly Circe Berman, writing as Polly Madison, enjoys vast sales with her juvenile romances while Paul Slazinger labors in obscurity.

The allusive title obviously refers to the folktale of Bluebeard, who forebade each of his wives in turn to enter one chamber of his castle. That prohibition proved irresistible, and when each wife entered she found there the remains of her predecessors and a foretaste of her own doom. In Vonnegut's tale, the forbidden room is the potato barn behind Karabekian's East Hampton home. Yet in the end Rabo opens this willingly to Circe, and it holds no horrors for her. It turns out to contain a sixty-four by eight-foot painting. It depicts a scene Rabo recalls from the end of the war when refugees, soldiers, released prisoners, and others by the thousand found themselves all together in one valley. The painting is perfect representationalism, each of its many characters depicted with photographical accuracy and

each having his or her own story (which Rabo is glad to tell). A curiosity is that the only young and healthy women are depicted hiding in root cellars. This is because they know the conquering armies are advancing and they will all be raped. The painting is called "Now It's the Women's Turn."

That title, then, is a revelation of horror to come for women, much like the ending of the old folktale. That kind of horror is ever present in this novel, from the murder of Armenian women and children by the Turks, to Dan Gregory's battering of Marilee, to Marilee's telling of being raped by the football team after her junior prom, to the women she later employs in her Italian villa who have all been brutalized by men during the war. Indeed Marilee becomes the voice of this novel's pacifist and feminist conscience. She sees war as "always men against women, with the men only pretending to fight among themselves." Men plant mines, women plant seeds. And indeed in this book the women *are* the nurturers, and the postwar men are all, like Rabo, Paul, and the suicidal abstract expressionists, damaged, inadequate, and self-destructive. In that context "Now It's the Women's Turn" could have completely different implications. It could be seen as addressing that sea of war-dislocated souls and saying, "Now it is time women had a turn running things. Men have wrought war. Perhaps women will do better."

Certainly the strongest characters in this book are women, even though women, including Circe and Marilee, are frequently victims. Marilee has been responsible for Rabo's start in art and nurtures his growth; Circe brings a washed-up recluse back to life, to sharing his art and to writing an autobiography. Many of the men in the novel are physically or emotionally crippled. Several commit suicide, as did some of the abstract expressionists in reality, and others are impaired, as is the one-eyed Rabo. Such men as are hale and hearty are real-life dictators like Mussolini or bullies like Gregory. It is the male-dominated, phallocentric patriarchy run down. Women are exploited in it, and most men are left crippled and inadequate by it. It is epitomized in war, yet war is also the sign of its failure. Perhaps, *Bluebeard* seems to be saying, we are due for that new androgynous world where art can once again tell its human story. In this sense the novel extends a feminist theme also strongly present in *Galapagos*.

Vonnegut has long entertained a strong interest in the visual arts and quite frequently relates the problems of the writer to those of the painter. *Bluebeard* is especially interesting from that perspective. It is characteristic Vonnegut in its attention to themes of war and suffering, of neurosis and suicide, and of failed marriages and reclusive widowers. It is also typical in its inclusion of commentary on the contemporary social scene, much of it deprecatory and cynical. Yet the tone of the novel is predominantly affirmative. Its relationships are mostly positive, much of its humor is lighthearted, and its ending is strongly upbeat. The life-affirming energies within the story seem to survive despite the lethal forces. The image of jewels spilling from the mouth of a dead person, like fruit from a cornucopia, recurs in the novel. It is a fitting one in a book where new life—and new art—comes out of death and destruction. Fittingly Rabo ends his autobiography by saying: "Oh, happy Meat. Oh, happy Soul. Oh, happy Rabo Karabekian."

Vonnegut has become an increasingly venerated figure on the American literary scene. He is well attended on lecture tours, a frequent guest on television talk shows, and his name enough of a household word to make him a popular figure for social columns in the glossies or interviews in airline magazines. He has been prominent in the international writers organization, PEN, and much involved in efforts to protect First Amendment rights of speech. He was even accorded a "Man of the Year" award by his old employer and subject of satire, General Electric.

Bibliography:

Jerome Klinkowitz and Asa B. Pieratt, *Kurt Vonnegut, Jr.: A Descriptive Bibliography and Annotated Secondary Checklist* (Hamden, Conn.: Archon Books, 1974).
Excellent bibliography of Vonnegut's works, with information about editions, variations, etc., and listing of secondary sources to that time.

References:

Richard Giannone, *Vonnegut: A Preface to His Novels* (Port Washington, N.Y.: Kennikat, 1977).
Fine study traces the development of Vonnegut as a novelist through *Slapstick*.

David H. Goldsmith, *Kurt Vonnegut: Fantasist of Fire and Ice* (Bowling Green, Ohio: Bowling Green University Popular Press, 1972).

An early, short overview of Vonnegut's work up to *Slaughterhouse-Five*.

Charles B. Harris, *Contemporary American Novelists of the Absurd* (New Haven, Conn.: College & University Press, 1971), pp. 51-75.
Of interest in placing Vonnegut among contemporaries in this prominent strain of recent American fiction.

Jerome Klinkowitz, *Kurt Vonnegut* (London & New York: Methuen, 1982).
Vonnegut as contemporary writer viewed from the perspectives of more recent literary theory; includes works up to *Palm Sunday* and *Jailbird*.

Klinkowitz and Donald Lawler, *Vonnegut in America* (New York: Delacorte / Seymour Lawrence, 1977).
A collection of essays by various authorities which updates *The Vonnegut Statement*, biography, and bibliography.

Klinkowitz and John Somer, *The Vonnegut Statement* (New York: Delacorte / Seymour Lawrence, 1973).
Useful collection of essays on life and works, including early writing, with fine bibliography for that date.

James Lundquist, *Kurt Vonnegut* (New York: Ungar, 1977).
This book considers Vonnegut's ironic humor, his vision of the world, and the techniques used to express them.

Clark Mayo, *Kurt Vonnegut: The Gospel from Outer Space* (San Bernardino, Cal.: Borgo Press, 1977).
Sixty-five pages on Vonnegut's fiction up to *Jailbird*, with emphasis on its use of science-fiction origins.

Peter J. Reed, *Kurt Vonnegut, Jr.* (New York: Crowell, 1976).
Most extensive treatment to date of first six novels.

Reed, "Kurt Vonnegut," in *American Writers*, supplement 2, volume 2 (New York: Scribners, 1981), pp. 753-783.
Compressed coverage of life and works, including *Slapstick*.

Stanley Schatt, *Kurt Vonnegut, Jr.* (Boston: Twayne, 1977).
Serious book-length study of Vonnegut's works and emerging style up through *Jailbird*.

Robert Short, *Something to Believe In: Is Kurt Vonnegut the Exorcist of Jesus Christ Superstar?* (New York: Harper & Row, 1976).
Vonnegut as popular culture moralist; contains interview.

Tony Tanner, "The Uncertain Messenger: A Study of the Novels of Kurt Vonnegut, Jr.," *Critical Quarterly*, 11 (Winter 1969): 297-315.
Landmark early article calling attention to Vonnegut by a British critic who is a foremost authority on contemporary fiction.

"Vonnegut," *Critique*, 12, 3 (1971), special Vonnegut number, with bibliography.
First extended attention to Vonnegut by a serious critical quarterly; four formative articles and a bibliography.

Alice Walker

This entry was updated by Laura Zaidman (University of South Carolina at Sumter) from the entry by Barbara T. Christian (University of California, Berkeley) in DLB 33, Afro-American Fiction Writers After 1955.

Places	Eatonville, Ga. Atlanta Africa	New York City Jackson, Miss. San Francisco	Bronxville, N.Y.

Influences and Relationships	Gloria Steinem
	 Robert Allen
	 Jean Toomer
	 Flannery O'Connor
		Zora Neale
		   Hurston
		 Gabriel García
		   Márquez
			Anna Akhmatova
			 Okotp'tek
			 Muriel Rukeyser

Literary Movements and Forms	Feminist Literature Black Literature "Womanist" Prose	Southern Literature Confessional Poetry Revolutionary Poetry	Autobiographical Essays Epistolary Novels

Major Themes	Southern Black
	   Life
	 Freedom from
	   Oppression
		Violence
		 Spirituality
		 Civil Rights
		 Family Relationships
			Social Change
			 The Inner Lives
			   of Women
			 Alienation

Cultural and Artistic Influences	Afro-American
	   Heritage
	 Women's Creativity
		Sewing, Quilting,
		   and Gardening
			Haiku
			 Black Dialect

Social and Economic Influences	Sexual Politics Poverty Slavery	Racism Social Injustice	Black Power Movement

See also the Walker entry in DLB 6, *American Novelists Since World War II, Second Series.*

BIRTH: Eatonton, Georgia, 9 February 1944, to Willie Lee and Minnie Tallulah Grant Walker.

EDUCATION: Spelman College, 1961-1963; B.A., Sarah Lawrence College, 1965.

MARRIAGE: 17 March 1967 to Melvyn Roseman Leventhal (divorced); child: Rebecca Grant.

AWARDS AND HONORS: National Endowment for the Arts Grant, 1969; Southern Regional Council Lillian Smith Award for *Revolutionary Petunias*, 1973; Richard and Hinda Rosenthal Foundation Award for *In Love & Trouble*, 1974; Guggenheim Award, 1977-1978; Pulitzer Prize for *The Color Purple*, 1983; American Book Award for *The Color Purple*, 1983.

BOOKS: *Once: Poems* (New York: Harcourt, Brace & World, 1968);
The Third Life of Grange Copeland (New York: Harcourt Brace Jovanovich, 1970);
Five Poems (Detroit: Broadside Press, 1972);
In Love & Trouble: Stories of Black Women (New York: Harcourt Brace Jovanovich, 1973);
Revolutionary Petunias & Other Poems (New York: Harcourt Brace Jovanovich, 1973);
Langston Hughes, American Poet (New York: Crowell, 1974);
Meridian (New York: Harcourt Brace Jovanovich, 1976);
Good Night Willie Lee, I'll See You in the Morning (New York: Dial, 1979);
You Can't Keep A Good Woman Down: Stories (New York: Harcourt Brace Jovanovich, 1981; London: Women's Press, 1982);
The Color Purple (New York: Harcourt Brace Jovanovich, 1982; London: Women's Press, 1983);
In Search of Our Mothers' Gardens: Womanist Prose (New York: Harcourt Brace Jovanovich, 1983);
Horses Make a Landscape Look More Beautiful: Poems (San Diego: Harcourt Brace Jovanovich, 1984);
To Hell with Dying, illustrated by Catherine Deeter (San Diego: Harcourt Brace Jovanovich, 1987);
Living by the Word: Selected Writings 1973-1987 (San Diego: Harcourt Brace Jovanovich, 1988);

Alice Walker (photo copyright © 1989 by Jim Marshall)

The Temple of My Familiar (San Diego: Harcourt Brace Jovanovich, 1989).

OTHER: *I Love Myself When I Am Laughing . . . and Then Again When I Am Looking Mean and Impressive: A Zora Neale Hurston Reader*, edited by Walker (Old Westbury, N.Y.: Feminist Press, 1979);
"*One* Child of One's Own: A Meaningful Digression Within The Work[s]," in *The Writer on Her Work*, edited by Janet Sternburg (New York: Norton, 1980), pp. 121-140.

SELECTED PERIODICAL PUBLICATIONS: "In Search of Our Mothers' Gardens," *Ms.*, 2 (May 1974): 64-70;
"In Search of Zora Neale Hurston," *Ms.*, 3 (March 1975): 74-79, 85-89;
"Beyond the Peacock: The Reconstruction of Flannery O'Connor," *Ms.*, 3 (December 1975): 77-79, 102-106;
"Lulls—A Native Daughter Returns to the South," *Ms.*, 5 (January 1977): 58-61, 89-90;

"When Women Confront Porn at Home," *Ms.*, 8 (February 1980): 67, 69-70, 75-76;

"Embracing the Dark and the Light," *Essence*, 13 (July 1982): 67, 114-121;

"Finding Celie's Voice," *Ms.*, 14 (December 1985): 71-72, 96;

"Am I Blue?," *Ms.*, 15 (July 1986): 29-30;

"In the Closet of the Soul," *Ms.*, 15 (November 1986): 32-35;

"Oppressed Hair Puts a Ceiling on the Brain," *Ms.*, 16 (June 1988): 52-53.

Since 1968 when *Once*, her first work, was published, Alice Walker has sought to bring closer that day for which her maternal ancestors waited–"a day when the unknown thing that was in them would be known." In five collections of poetry, two volumes of short stories, four novels, and many essays, she has expressed with graceful and devastating clarity the relationship between the degree of freedom black women have within and beyond their communities and the "survival whole" of black people. Her particular angle of vision is sharpened by her use of the history of black people in this country, and therefore of the South, where they were most brutally enslaved. A southerner, she also presents that land as the place from which their specific characteristics of survival and creativity have sprung. Her works confront the pain and struggle of black people's history, which for her has resulted in a deeply spiritual tradition. In articulating that tradition, she has found that the creativity of black women, and the extent to which they are permitted to exercise it, is a measure of the health of the entire society.

A writer who admits to "a rage to defy / the order of the stars / despite their pretty patterns," Walker consistently approaches the "forbidden" in society as a route to the truth. Perhaps the most controversial of her subjects is her insistence on investigating the relationships between black women and men, black parents and children, with unwavering honesty. A womanist (her term for a black feminist), Walker has, more than any contemporary writer in America, exposed the "twin afflictions" that beset black women: the sexism and racism that historically and presently restrict their lives. Walker develops literary forms (for example, her concept of quilting, her use of folk language) that are based on the creative legacy left her by her ancestors. But that heritage is not only a source of her forms. Most important for Walker is its essence: that spirituality is the

basis of the valuable and therefore of art. Unlike the stereotype of the socially conscious writer, she asserts "the importance of diving through politics and social forces to dig into the essential spirituality of individual persons." Her work then, though clearly political in its thrust, expands that quality to mean personal inner change as a crucial aspect of radical social change. Stylistically her work is based on the idea that "a people's dreams, imaginings, rituals, legends ... are known to contain the accumulated collective reality of the people themselves." In spite of the problems her works expose, she is essentially optimistic. Walker's work proceeds from her belief in human potential and desire for change.

Her belief in the relationship between personal and social change, her awareness that struggle and spirituality are primary characteristics of black southern folk tradition, and her sense of that unknown thing in her ancestors that yearns to be articulated are not solely intellectual concepts for Alice Walker. They are part of her own personal history.

She was born 9 February 1944, the youngest of the eight children of Willie Lee and Minnie Tallulah Grant Walker, sharecroppers from Eatonton, Georgia. She grew up in that small town at a time when many blacks, like her parents, worked in the fields for a pittance and when whites exerted control over practically every aspect of black life. Her childhood was filled with stories of past lynchings, and like other southern black children she found "at 12 that the same little white girls who had been her playmates were suddenly to be called 'miss.' " The young Walker was certainly affected by the pervasiveness of the violent racist system of the South, especially its impact on black families. In an interview in *Library Journal* (15 June 1970) she explained how this relationship affected her first novel, *The Third Life of Grange Copeland* (1970): "I was curious to know why people in families (specifically black families) are often cruel to each other and how much of this cruelty is caused by outside forces such as various social injustices, segregation, unemployment, etc."

Perhaps Walker was particularly attuned to the relationship between social forces and personal development because at a young age she lived through the feeling of being an outcast. At eight she lost the sight of her right eye when one of her older brothers accidentally shot her with a BB gun. Her eye was covered by a scar until she was fourteen, when a relatively simple operation corrected the disfigurement which made her feel ugly; for years she feared she would lose the sight of the other eye. This experience caused her to notice relationships more fully. For that reason, she also began to keep a notebook in which she wrote poems, often in the fields where she had some privacy. Her writings seem indelibly marked by these years, for she focuses sharply on relationships, not only between people but also between human beings and nature. Her sense of being different probably contributed to her treading forbidden paths. Receiving a "rehabilitation scholarship" from Georgia and being valedictorian of her senior class enabled her to attend Spelman College, where she studied for two years.

Although to some extent the child Walker felt separate, she was also a part of a community which nurtured her. In spite of the oppressiveness of the racist southern system, she had many excellent teachers. They saved her from "feeling alone; from worrying that the world she was stretching to find might not exist." And they lent her books, for her a necessary element in her development: "Books became my world because the world I was in was very hard." Her community, as well as her teachers, knew the importance of education. The men of Eatonton built what the schools needed, and parents raised money to keep them going.

At an early age, Walker saw the black people working together to accomplish goals necessary to their survival and development. Despite the limits imposed upon them, they felt responsible for each other. In one of her essays she recalls that growing up in the South, a black might be afraid of whites but not of blacks. As a little girl, she walked and played with black convicts who were accused of murder. This sense of "One Life" that black people share, their belief that they are a community with a functional history and culture, is, for Walker, one reason for the persistence of struggle characteristic of black southern tradition. It is not so much the grand sweep of history or the artifacts created as it is the relations of people to each other: young to old, parent to child, man to woman, that make up that heritage–a theme that Walker has treated persistently in her works.

As influential as her community was, the person who seems to have shaped her the most was her mother. Walker has often said that the stories she now tells are her mother's stories and that she has absorbed something of the urgency of her mother that her story be told. Walker's writings are an example of what her mother and others like her might have created if they were not the "mules of the world" and had had the opportunity to write, paint, or carve their own expressions. Yet, although these women did not have access to art forms, they did create in whatever forms were allowed them. In her essay "In Search of Our Mothers' Gardens," Walker illuminates this legacy of creativity as one of the spiritual bases of her own art:

> I notice that it is only when my mother is working in her flowers that she is radiant, almost to the point of being invisible–except as Creator: hand and eye. She is involved in work her soul must have. Ordering the universe in the image of her personal concept of Beauty.

> Her face, as she prepares the Art that is her gift, is a legacy of respect she leaves to me, for all that illuminates and cherishes life. She has handed down respect for the possibilities–and the will to grasp them.

Walker's mother created art as part of her daily life as a maid raising eight children. Although their society denied them the access to most of the means of creation and legislated that only a few cultivated souls could produce art, these women used quilting, gardening, cooking, and sewing to order their universe in the image of their personal concepts of beauty. Such a legacy has given Walker insight not only into the lives of black women but into the essential nature of art as a human process of illuminating and cherishing life. Walker was later to say that "if art doesn't make us better, then what on earth is it for?"

The mother also passed on to the daughter another quality that marks her art. Her mother and her aunts were the most independent people the child knew. Like the character Aunt Jimmy in Toni Morrison's *The Bluest Eye*, these women fished, hunted, worked like any man, and dressed as fine as any woman. Their sense of their own completeness certainly helped to instill the quality of assurance in the young Walker that she would need in order to be a black woman writer in America: "Unlike many women who were told throughout their adolescence they must marry, I was never told by my mother or anyone of her sisters it was something I need even think about. It is because of them, I know women can do anything and that one's sexuality is not affected by one's work."

Many critics have commented on Walker's apparently natural quality of authority as a writer, her assurance with words. Walker possesses this quality because of the experience of her maternal ancestors. Because they were not seen as women in American society with the characteristics that that definition designated, they had to do everything–and therefore knew they could do everything. Walker uses a variation on this theme in *Meridian* (1976) by speculating as to what black women will decide to do when they have a choice.

Walker's college years, first at Spelman in Atlanta, then at Sarah Lawrence in New York, also played a part in shaping the writer she would become. What she learned at these two very different institutions is indicative of her character and would influence her work. At that time Spelman was, in many ways, dedicated to turning black girls into ladies. However, during Walker's years there the atmosphere of the school was strongly affected by the civil rights movement, what Walker calls "the Southern Revolution." She grew to worship the young leaders of SNCC (Student Nonviolent Coordinating Committee)–John Lewis, Ruby Davis Robinson, and Julian Bond–and participated in civil rights demonstrations. She says of this period: "Everyone was beautiful, because everyone was conquering fear by holding the hands of the person next to them." Her experience, so strongly felt, is distilled in many of the poems of *Once*, in short stories such as "The Welcome Table," and most emphatically in *Meridian*. Throughout the novel the Sojourner tree is a striking symbol of struggle, apparent death, and rejuvenation. Years before she wrote *Meridian*, Walker evoked this memory of her years at Spelman: "Then, of course, the cherry trees–cut down now I think–that were always blooming away while we–young and bursting with fear and determination to change our world–thought beyond our fervid singing, of death."

The cherry trees, as the symbol of nature's constant thriving, the analysis of the relationship between violence and revolution, the paradox of life-giving death, the probing of the concept of womanhood as it was viewed by the college in the novel–all these are derived from Walker's years at Spelman. And the archives at the oldest college for black women would be the source of her portrayal in *The Color Purple* (1982) of Nettie, the southern black woman who went to Africa as

a missionary. Spelman's tradition helped Walker define southern black women and their role in society.

At Sarah Lawrence College in Bronxville, New York, Walker began her writing career. In an attempt to understand the recurrent dreams of suicide that she had had since she was eight, she studied the philosophers' positions on suicide, "because by that time it did not seem frightening or even odd–but only inevitable." An experience she had during her senior year put the conclusion to a test and resulted in the writing of *Once*.

During the previous summer she had become pregnant and had traveled to Africa. "I felt at the mercy of everything, including my body, which I had learned to accept as a kind of casing over which I considered my real self " and "began to understand how alone woman is, because of her body." She decided that if she failed to find an abortionist she would kill herself. A decision of such finality caused her to review her relationship with her mother, father, siblings, and community. She realized that her family would be hurt to hear of her death while they would be ashamed if they discovered she was pregnant. During the time while she waiting anxiously for her friends to find an abortionist, she began writing *Once*. After she was "saved," she wrote without stopping, stuffing each completed poem under the door of Muriel Rukeyser, because "someone had to read them." Her first published poems (about love, death, Africa, and the civil rights movement) and her first published story, "To Hell With Dying" (about an old man saved from death many times by the love of his neighbor's children), grew out of her gladness that she was alive.

Walker's peculiar point of view on specific social issues in her large body of work can be traced to pivotal experiences she had in her college years that heightened her awareness of the position of blacks and women in society. At Spelman she confronted the concept of the "lady," which clashed with her experience of her mother's and aunts' lives. She was also absorbed in the civil rights movement, in which many people risked death. Meaningful struggle for more life was necessarily connected to death. It was also clear to her that if black women were to participate effectively in that movement, they could not be restricted by a definition of woman that denied them their full potential. Black people's struggle to be free then could not be separated from

Dust jacket for Walker's first novel, in which she examines the ways racism undermines traditional gender roles in black families

the necessity for black women to be free enough to struggle–a theme that Walker probes in her second novel, *Meridian.*

At Sarah Lawrence she discovered in her pregnancy the aloneness of woman in her body, the extreme result of which could also be death. In this crisis, she was saved by other women who knew that they too could be in her place, and she recognized the different standards of acceptance for women and men within her own family as well as the outer society. This social definition of woman meant her experience was not just a private one–thus her public acknowledgment of her pregnancy and abortion as the impetus for *Once.* Like other women in the 1970s, this and other peculiarly female experiences would result in Walker's recognition that she had to unite with other women to raise society's consciousness. As *The Third Life of Grange Copeland* (1970) and *In Love & Trouble* (1973) illustrate, Walker insisted that sexism existed in the black community and was not an issue only for white women. Most black

leaders focused only on racism and considered her position to be practically heresy. She also dramatized in her works the relationship between sexism and racism as a mode of oppression that restricted the lives of all women and men. Her experiences at Spelman and Sarah Lawrence deepened her understanding of the interconnectedness of pivotal struggles for freedom in America.

At the core of her perception of these two experiences is the risk of death that one takes in society just to be oneself if that self is not the norm. This sense of the danger involved in being the "other" seems to be connected to her childhood accident and the recurrent dreams of suicide that followed it. In all these instances, Walker's response was the desire for death, then anger, followed by introspection, and finally the insistence on being all of one's self, no matter what the cost. Thus the confrontation with death led to a struggle for a more genuine and free life, a paradox that Walker explores profoundly in many of her works.

During her college years, Walker deepened her knowledge of other writers. Books continued to be an integral part of her life. Her response to other writers has been extremely important to her literary development, as illustrated by the epigraphs for her books–excerpts from the Russian woman poet Akhmatova, the African poet Okotp'tek, the native American seer Black Elk, and the German poet Rainer Maria Rilke. And her essays–"In Search of Our Mothers' Gardens," "*One* Child of One's Own," and "In Search of Zora Neale Hurston"–use the insights of many women writers to illuminate the creativity of black women. Walker sees herself as part of an international community of writers from whom she learns and to whom she continually responds. This quality of hers is worth noting since white American society often views the black writer as separate from American literature and therefore from all other literature, despite the reciprocal impact black writers have had with other writers of the world. Like Richard Wright, Walker claims insights of the entire world of writers as connected to her own.

The writers who have influenced Walker indicate her preoccupations. In her sophomore year she read every Russian writer she could get her hands on, for it seemed to her that "Russia must have something floating about in the air that writers breathe from the time they are born." What most impressed her was the ability of Tolstoy, Dostoyevski, Turgenev, Gorki, and Gogol to render the tone of their entire society while penetrating the essential spirit of individuals: the scope, depth, and sounding of the genuine common in all people. This configuration of qualities certainly marks Walker's fiction, for there is always an interrelation between the lives of the black women she portrays, the values of the entire society, and essential spiritual questions that are asked in every human society.

Walker is also drawn to writers who are not afraid of fantasy, myth, and mystery, qualities that inspired her in the works of African writers Okotp'tek (author of her favorite modern poem, "Song of Lowino"); Elechi Amadi, whose *Concubine* she calls a perfect story; Camara Laye and Bessie Head. Like Black Elk, whose vision permeates *Meridian*, and Gabriel García Márquez, the South American novelist, these writers seem to Walker to be "like musicians: at one with their cultures and their historical subconscious."

Though not in concert with their own cultures, the German writers Rilke and Hesse insisted on loving "those questions like locked rooms / full of treasures / to which [their] blind / and groping key / does not yet fit." Like them, Walker believes that the artist "must be free to explore, otherwise she or he will never discover what is needed (by everyone) to be known." She has successfully applied their questions to American black women.

The quality of mystery is especially evident in the poetry that has nurtured Walker: the Japanese haiku poets; E. E. Cummings, Emily Dickinson, and William Carlos Williams; Ovid and Catullus; Okotp'tek; Gwendolyn Brooks, Arna Bontemps, and Jean Toomer. Though they come from vastly different cultures and periods in history, they all are passionate in their perception of the many, sometimes contradictory, meanings of experience, and in the way language can evoke the complexity of life. Most of these poets share another quality: an economical yet sensual style. Walker clearly prefers this approach to language. The process of stripping off layers and honing down to the core is apparent in her fiction as well as her poetry.

Two other groups of writers had enormous influence on Walker: black writers, especially women, and women writers of other cultures. They often have a view of the world that illuminates and records aspects of experience unknown to or interpreted differently by men and/ or whites; furthermore, they often write against

great social barriers, sometimes internalized as their own psychological conflicts. Walker has been influenced by Virginia Woolf (especially *A Room of One's Own*), the Brontës, Doris Lessing, and Kate Chopin, because "their characters can always envision a solution, an evolution to higher consciousness on the part of society, even when society itself cannot." Perhaps that belief in the possibility of change is related to retention of their own humanity despite the impact of oppressive forces. The same belief that human beings can evolve is central to Walker's two favorite books by black writers, Jean Toomer's *Cane* and Zora Neale Hurston's *Their Eyes Were Watching God*. Although Walker has been critical of Toomer's attempt to be "just an American," she emphasizes these two writers' expression of an essential quality from their African heritage–animism, "a belief that makes it possible to view all creation as living, as being inhabited by spirit." As a result these books are infused with the historical unconscious of black people in this country. But because of these writers' radical exploration of society and their expression of a belief contrary to the American worldview, they were criticized or ignored by their own communities.

But Walker not only claims these writers as nurturers of her own creativity, she is an activist in restoring their works to the reading public. In particular her sense of the precarious position of the black woman writer in a racist, male-dominated society is dramatized in her successful attempt to rescue Zora Neale Hurston's works from oblivion. Walker did not discover this writer until she was in her twenties, working on the short story "The Revenge of Hannah Kemhuff." Appalled that no one had told her about this literary ancestor, Walker recognized the incredible loss, particularly to black women, that the silence about Hurston's works represented.

In pursuit of her own literary sources, Walker saw that as part of their tradition, black women writers have explored the relationship between sexism and racism and therefore have been a threat to established literary norms in both black and white society. By placing a tombstone on Hurston's unmarked grave and writing about it in "In Search of Zora Neale Hurston" (1975), by teaching courses on black women writers–a result of which was the essay "In Search of Our Mothers' Gardens" (1974)–and by editing *I Love Myself When I Am Laughing . . . and Then Again When I Am Looking Mean and Impressive* (1979), an anthology of Hurston's works,

Walker was not only thanking her literary ancestor, she was also acknowledging the tradition of black women writers and insisting that black women themselves would have to safeguard their own creative legacy. Her example has helped to encourage and support a generation of black feminist writers.

In an interview in the early 1970s, Walker made the connection between the fate of past black women writers and the attitudes that she herself had begun to encounter: "There are two reasons why the black woman writer is not taken as seriously as the black male writer. One is that she is a woman. Critics seem unusually ill-equipped to intelligently discuss and analyze the works of black women. Generally they do not even make the attempt; they prefer, rather, to talk about the lives of black women writers, not about what they write. And since black women writers are not, it would seem, very likeable (until recently they were the least willing worshippers of male supremacy) comments about them tend to be cruel."

After Walker graduated from Sarah Lawrence in 1965, she spent a brief time in New York's Lower East Side, an experience which formed the basis for certain sections of *Meridian* and her controversial story about interracial rape, "Advancing Luna–and Ida B. Wells." Because of her commitment to the southern revolution, however, she soon returned to the South. From 1967 to 1974 she worked in Mississippi in voter registration and welfare rights. During that time she married Mel Leventhal, a white civil rights lawyer. For many years critics, particularly black male critics, had a tendency to focus on her marriage rather than on her work. Walker points out that these critics were "themselves frequently interracially married who moreover hung on every word from Richard Wright, Jean Toomer, Langston Hughes, James Baldwin, John A. Williams and LeRoi Jones, to name a few; all of whom were at some time in their lives interracially connected. . . . I, a black woman, had dared to exercise the same prerogative as they."

In Mississippi Walker collected folklore from ordinary black women and recorded the details of their everyday lives. Doubtless this activity deepened the knowledge she had acquired of how southern black women saw themselves and their communities and how they contended with the conventions that limited their lives. In her essays during these years she articulated the cycle of works which she would complete in the next decade. "In Search of Our Mothers' Gardens" de-

Dust jacket for the 1976 novel in which Walker challenges the myths surrounding black motherhood

picts three types of black women: the physically and psychologically abused women; the exceptional black women torn by "contrary instincts," who, in order to try to fulfill their creativity, are forced to repress the sources from which it comes; and the new black women who can freely re-create themselves out of the legacy of their maternal ancestors. Throughout her fictional works, Walker presents glimpses of all types while intensely focusing on one. In *The Third Life of Grange Copeland* Walker shows how the racist fabric of the South affects the black family. Because society thwarts the Copeland men in their drive for control of their lives–the American definition of manhood–they vent their frustrations by inflicting violence on their wives. Because the Copeland women, too, are thwarted in their desire to be "women" in society–that is, to be taken care of– one finally kills herself, and the other is killed by her husband when she tries to take care of their family. In each case the children are not so much a source of the mother's strength as they are victims. Mothers, then, are not always respected in black society, nor are they always victorious. Her characterization of Mem and Margaret Copeland as physically and psychologically abused black women leads her to the characterization of Ruth Copeland as a black woman who may be able to re-create herself whole. Walker insists that an understanding of the "herstory" of black women and the lives they are actually living is critical to growth and transformation.

Her first collection of short stories, *In Love & Trouble*, demonstrates this dual commitment, from Roselily, the poor mother of illegitimate children whose marriage to a Black Muslim is seen by most as a triumphant deliverance from her backward condition, but who knows that she will still be confined, to Maggie in "Everyday Use," who is not knowledgeable about the new "blackness" but truly understands heritage because through her quilting she loves the people who have passed unto her a tradition of caring. Most of the protagonists in this volume are southern black women who, often against their own conscious wills in the face of pain, abuse, even death, challenge the conventions of sex, race, and age that attempt to restrict them. As a result, *In Love & Trouble* seemed heretical to some black male critics, for it clearly proclaims the violent effects of sexism and racism as evils against which black women must struggle within black society.

The title poem of Walker's second book of poetry, *Revolutionary Petunias & Other Poems* (1973), also reflects her Mississippi years. Its central character, Sammy Lou, typifies the black woman of whom "revolutionaries" are often contemptuous. Sammy Lou prays to the Lord, is against violence, names her children after presidents, even loves flowers, a misdirected use of time and energy according to the political figures of the day. Yet she insists on righteousness, on justice even to the point of dangerous action, for she kills the white man who has killed her husband—a rebellious act that inspires folk songs about her. Walker sees the many Sammy Lous as part of an ongoing revolution: "Any black revolution, instead of calling her incorrect will have to honor her single act of rebellion."

Revolutionary Petunias is also about the apparent decline of the southern revolution, about that time when the external activism of the movement could not be sustained, when it became necessary for those who continued to struggle to clarify for themselves the difference between rhetoric and

principle. Walker says that "in a way the whole book is a celebration of people who will not cram themselves into any ideological or racial mold. . . . They are aware that the visions that created them were all towards a future when all people—and flowers too—can bloom. They require that in the midst of the bloodiest battles or revolution this thought not be forgotten."

A black woman married to a white man and living in Mississippi; a writer committed to exposing the violence caused by sexism, racism, and the exploitation of the poor; a thinker who refuses to accept unquestioningly that violence is essential to revolution and who focuses on the importance of beauty in the lives of everyone; a political activist who insists that the history of ordinary, seemingly backward, folk is the underpinning of the contemporary movement for social change—Alice Walker continued to walk forbidden paths.

Her inquiry into the lives of southern black women affected Walker's craft as well as her subject matter. During this period she paid careful attention to the "low" arts—quilting, gardening, cooking—the only forms through which most black women could express their creativity. Her fiction of this period has at the core of its craft the technique of quilting—the use of recurring economical patterns to create a synthesis of the bits and pieces of life into a work of functional beauty.

Meridian is such a work. Walker demonstrates the relationship between the history of ordinary black folk, particularly women, and the philosophical character Meridian, whose question—when is it necessary, when is it right, to kill?—provides the central theme of the novel. Walker's quilting of intersecting and recurring motifs stresses on the one hand the fragmentation of life caused by the unnatural ideologies of sexism and racism and, on the other, the natural unity of life as expressed in nature itself, in music, and in the love of human beings for each other. Also, *Meridian* proves how important the subject of motherhood is to Walker. Since black women are primarily glorified as mothers in their own communities and debased as mammies in white society, it is almost impossible to explore their lives in the past or in the present without examining the many ramifications that that role has meant for them.

Meridian's quest for wholeness begins with her feelings of inadequacy in living up to the myth of black motherhood. Again, Walker challenges a prevalent myth. She presents a major character who gives up her son (an act no black woman should do willingly) and has her tubes tied after a painful abortion, because she does not think she can fulfill the responsibilities of motherhood. Presenting this controversial series of actions, Walker heightens the restrictiveness of the role. While society deifies motherhood, it places little value on children, especially black children, or on mothers, especially black mothers. In fact, it often punishes mothers for being mothers by restricting their development. Walker also broadens the definition of mother as more than biological. Meridian attains the state of motherhood because she believes so profoundly in the sacredness of all life that she takes responsibility for the lives of all the people. Her aborted motherhood yields a perspective on life–that of "expanding her mind with action."

While Walker challenges the monumental myth of black motherhood in *Meridian*, she also maintains the importance of the perspective and culture that that historical role has given women. In her essay "*One* Child of One's Own" (1980) she questions the idea that some white American feminists were proposing–that motherhood is in and of itself an evil for women. The essay has as its central theme the writer as mother, a crucial question of the 1970s, when many women protested through books such as Tillie Olsen's *Silences* that women have traditionally had to choose between being mothers and being creative in the arts. Walker gave birth to her daughter, Rebecca, three days after finishing her first novel in 1969. Her child awakened in her fears about the changes in her life: "Well, I wondered, with great fear, where is the split in me now? What is the damage. . . . Was I, as a writer, done for?" Walker explains that her fear and the fears of other women like her are not based on primal truth but on a social definition of woman. Without those social and psychological limits, knowledge, rather than damage, could come from being a mother: "My child's birth was the incomparable gift of seeing the world at quite a different angle than before and judging it by standards far beyond my natural life." That new perspective has strengthened Walker's commitment to an international women's movement that works for all women, all children, and against all injustice. The two major injustices that affect her life and the lives of other black women are sexist and racist behavior–even from their most natural allies, black men and other women, whatever

their race. Walker concludes that it is not her child who restricts her but the social system within which she lives: "It is not my child who tells me I have no femaleness white women must affirm; not my child who says I have no rights black men or women must respect."

"*One* Child of One's Own" was written while Alice Walker was living in New York City. For the latter half of the 1970s she taught at various northern colleges and universities, communicating to others the long tradition of black women writers. During these years when the women's movement in the Northeast was so visible, she encountered resistance among some white feminists to recognize black women as women and as a vital part of the history of feminism. She also encountered the same resistance among black women to see themselves not only as black but also as women with all of the responsibility worldwide that such conscious assertion would entail. In "*One* Child of One's Own," one of her most important essays, Walker clarifies for black women the long tradition of black feminism that is often conveniently forgotten and confronts white women with the racism poisoning the women's movement. Her analysis leads her to a principle that she, as well as others, can use in this complicated society:

> What was required of women of color, was to learn to distinguish between who was the real feminist and who was not, and to exert energy in feminist collaborations only when there is little risk of wasting it. The rigors of this discernment will inevitably keep throwing women of color back upon themselves, where there is, indeed, so much work, of a feminist nature, to be done. . . . To the extent that black women disassociate themselves from the women's movement, they abandon their responsibilities to women throughout the world. This is a serious abdication from and misuse of radical black herstorical tradition: Harriet Tubman, Sojourner, Ida B. Wells and Fannie Lou Hamer would not have liked it. Nor do I.

Along with a vocal movement of other women of color, Walker has raised questions about the relationship of woman to her world that would have been unasked only a few decades before. What these writers are demonstrating in their works is that the relationships between persons are politically critical and might, in fact, be a major determinant of the relationship of the people to the state.

Walker's third work of poetry, *Good Night Willie Lee, I'll See You in the Morning* (1979), is permeated with political concerns. Like *Revolutionary Petunias*, it is about the vital connection between love and lasting change, though now the emphasis is on the changing of love relationships between women and men as the foundation for a radical and irreversible transformation in society. Walker presents her inner process of demystifying love, especially for women, as a disease or a total giving up of self. Without going through this process, the poet at her deepest level will be trapped by these pervasive societal definitions. Walker constructs a more healthy definition of love based on cherishing self, for only through self-love can the self be preserved. Yet she maintains the need to give herself without giving up self as part of the true interconnectedness of all.

The movement of *Good Night Willie Lee, I'll See You in the Morning* is instructive for an understanding of Walker's process in all her work. The title refers to the last farewell her mother gave her father at his funeral. Her parents' love, though it might have been troubled, was Walker's first experience of love between woman and man. Using this frame, Walker moves through a five-part journey from a night of loss to a morning of hope based on a deeper understanding of love. The poet begins with the pain of a love that has declined into disease ("Did This Happen to Your Mother? Did Your Sister Throw Up a Lot?"). She takes a stand on the inviolability of her self ("On Stripping Bark From Myself"), which allows her to ask questions about her commitment to a wider love, a radical change in society, in "Facing the Way." In becoming able to act because she loves, she analyzes in "Early Losses" those historical losses and scars that may impede love, and forgives herself and others in the final section, "Forgiveness." Through this process she is able to love and to insist on being loved without possessiveness or fear. Particularly striking is that black women, their history, and their understanding of love are Walker's primary guides.

Published in 1981, Walker's second collection of short stories, *You Can't Keep A Good Woman Down*, was called her most blatant womanist book to date. Walker delved into polemical feminist issues of the 1970s—abortion, sadomasochism, pornography, interracial rape—which she analyzed from the perspective that intimate relationships are both personal and political. For example, "Porn" describes the connection between a black man who prides himself on his sexual tech-

nique and a black woman who is "liberated," makes her own money, lives separately from her lover, and values her women friends. Walker focuses on the man's use of pornographic fantasies and the woman's reaction to them. She explores the way his fantasies underline his inability to make love to this woman with whatever flaws might result because of his need to prove his superiority through his sexuality. His fantasies, as perceived by the woman, degrade her, him, and other people they know, for his porn collection uses stereotypes of black and white men and women. Her awareness of the insidiousness of his collection destroys the sexual pleasure she had believed they were sharing. Like "Porn," many of the stories in this volume show the connection between racist and sexist stereotypes, particularly in the area of sexuality, and reveal how it affects the quality of black women's lives.

You Can't Keep A Good Woman Down attempts a womanist technique as well as subject matter. Many of the stories are not classic in form—that is, they are not presented as finished, objective products. Rather, the author's subjective positions are obvious, and the stories are presented as in process. Feminist thinkers of the 1970s asserted a link between process (the unraveling of thought and feeling) and the way women perceive the world. Walker experiments with this technique as a more honest and vital rendering of the truth. Her technique is especially evident in "Advancing Luna–and Ida B. Wells," a story about a young southern black woman's growing understanding of the complexity of interracial rape. Because of the historical connection between rape and lynching, sex and race, that continues even today, the author cannot end her story conclusively. Walker discloses her own thought processes in two endings–"After Thoughts" and "Discarded Notes and Postscripts."

You Can't Keep A Good Woman Down is clearly different in subject matter and style from Walker's previous works but shares with them her fundamental values. This book proves the extent to which black women are free to pursue their own selfhood in a society permeated by sexism and racism. But while the protagonists of *In Love & Trouble* wage their struggle in spite of themselves, the heroines of *You Can't Keep A Good Woman Down* consciously challenge conventions. Published eight years apart, these two collections are rooted in the same perspective yet demonstrate a clear progression of theme. Though the stories of *You Can't Keep A Good Woman Down* are contemporary in subject matter, they proceed, like *Meridian*, from the deeply felt history of black women.

Walker's third novel, *The Color Purple*, exemplifies her belief that history is a necessary element of depth, that nothing is a product of the immediate present. Walker finished the novel after she and her husband divorced in 1977, and she moved to San Francisco. But she started writing it in New York City, where she says her major character, a rural early-twentieth-century southern black woman, seemed to elude her. It was not until she got a place in the country outside San Francisco that her characters' spirit and their language came rushing out. Critics agree that the superb black folk speech resonates with a history of feeling and experience that is specifically Afro-American.

As in Walker's other two novels, this work spans generations of one poor rural black family in the South. Again, the image of quilting is central to its concept. Yet this novel further develops Walker's womanist process. It is written as a series of letters, reminding us that letters, along with diaries, were the dominant mode of expression allowed women in the West. In using the epistolary style, Walker is able to combine the subjective and the objective. As Celie, the main character, records the details of her life, she does so in images and in language that express the impact of oppression on her spirit as well as her resistance to it. Walker's subject matter is also emphatically womanist, for the emphases in *The Color Purple* are on the oppression black women experience in their relationships with black men and the sisterhood they must share with each other in order to liberate themselves. As a vehicle for these themes, two sisters' letters–Celie's to God, Nettie's to Celie, and finally Celie's to Nettie– provide the novel's form. Form and content, then, are inseparable.

Walker continues to explore "forbidden" sexual themes, as she did in *You Can't Keep A Good Woman Down*. In *The Color Purple* she focuses on incest in a black family and portrays a lesbian relationship as natural and liberating. Like many of the protagonists in her short stories, the heroine triumphs despite the tremendous odds against her. In an interview in *California Living*, Walker reveals that Celie was based on the story of her great-grandmother, who at twelve was raped and abused. Though the story ends happily, Walker does not flinch from presenting the sexual abuse, the wife beatings, and the violence that Celie undergoes in a society that demeans her as a

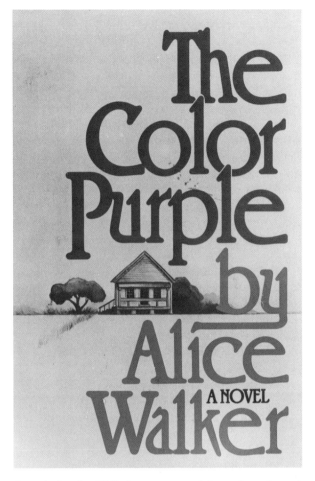

Dust jacket for Walker's most successful novel to date, the story of an oppressed black woman who finds independence through an affair with her husband's mistress, a roadhouse singer

woman. As in all of her works, violence is a result of the unnatural ideologies of sexism and racism. Though many readers and critics would prefer to ignore it, Walker has always insisted on exposing the violence inflicted upon black women's bodies and spirits.

In *The Color Purple* Walker adds another dimension to the sexism black women experience. Through Nettie, who escapes her condition to become a missionary, Walker describes the subordination of women to men in Africa. She therefore suggests that sexism for black women does not derive from racism, though it is qualitatively affected by it. "We're going to have to debunk the myth that Africa is a haven for black people– especially black women. We've been the mule of the world there and the mule of the world here." Nettie's letters also provide other dimensions of history. They graphically demonstrate black Americans' knowledge of their ancestral link to

Africa—which, contrary to American myth, predates the black power movement of the 1960s—and they emphasize concrete ways in which colonization disrupts African life and values.

The Color Purple is remarkable in language, radical themes, and technique. Perhaps even more than Walker's other works, it especially affirms that the most abused woman can transform herself. It completes the cycle Walker announced a decade ago: the survival and liberation of black women through the strength and wisdom of others.

Walker reached a much larger audience for her message with the popular 1985 film adaptation of *The Color Purple*. She wrote a rough draft for the screenplay and worked closely with director Steven Spielberg and producer Quincy Jones, trusting them to remain faithful to her work. The movie catalyzed Walker's rise to even greater national literary prominence and has attracted more attention to her recent fiction and nonfiction.

Horses Make a Landscape Look More Beautiful: Poems (1984) contains powerful works about social and private topics: celebrating the simple joys of life and love, lambasting the cruelty of racism and evil in world politics, and sharing her delight in her daughter. Her poems have been linked not only to the tradition of Whitman in her love of ordinary humanity with its pleasures and pains, but also to the work of Langston Hughes in her cheerful yet sad music. "Each One, Pull One" explains the absolute necessity for the writer to write; the book's final poem advocates saving the world through love: "This could be our revolution: / To love what is plentiful / as much as / what's scarce." One is reminded of Walker's remarks that she writes to pay "homage to people I love, the people who are thought to be dumb and backward but who were the ones who first taught me to see beauty" and that "writing poetry is my way of celebrating with the world that I had not committed suicide the evening before." Reviewers have criticized some poems here as too polemical and dogmatic but have praised others for their remarkable wisdom and sweetness.

To Hell with Dying (1987), Walker's first published story and the final selection of *In Love & Trouble*, has been revived as an illustrated children's book. Even though the *Bulletin of the Center for Children's Books* labels it for grades two to five, it presents an adult's perspective of a poignant childhood memory. Its large picture-

book format, with stylized, bright illustrations, conflicts with the adult nature of the story with references to Mr. Sweet Little's drinking, and questioning his wife's fidelity. Teenage readers may appreciate the sensitive story of friendship and death, of life's mystery, and the magical healing power of love. The story is narrated by a woman who recalls fondly how family friend Mr. Sweet, on the brink of death many times, would be revived by her brother and her when their father would say to him: " 'To hell with dying, man, these children want Mr. Sweet' "—their cue to revive him with their affectionate hugs, kisses, and tickling. Years later, on Mr. Sweet's ninetieth birthday, the narrator, now twenty-four and finishing her doctorate, is summoned home. She finds the frail Mr. Sweet again on his deathbed, but she cannot revive her "first love" this time. Images of fragrant yellow roses and the quilt on the old-fashioned bed reinforce the legacy of the past and the sweet miracle of life itself.

Living by the Word: Selected Writings 1973-1987 (1988) contains a wide range of articles focusing on social and political issues—race, gender, sexuality, and political freedom—as well as Walker's life and the lives of family, ancestors, and friends. She shares her observations from journeys to China, Bali, and Jamaica, comments on San Francisco's lesbian and gay communities and on the filming of *The Color Purple*, and offers insights from her psychic journeys that link her with the universal spirit. The essays affirm that all people and the earth sustaining them are interconnected spiritually.

Walker's frequent contributions to *Ms.* have allowed readers to keep in touch with her after *The Color Purple*. In the December 1985 issue she explains how Celie's voice expresses, from the character's viewpoint, the brutal sexual and emotional violence she suffers; this folk idiom also validates Celie's existence and conveys her evolving growth. Responding to criticism that the novel is too sexually explicit and degrading to blacks, Walker says that racist stereotypes of blacks should be exposed, not suppressed. She defends also the illiterate speech: "If we kill off the *sound* of our ancestors, the major portion of us, all that is past, is history, is human being, is lost and we become historically and spiritually thin, a mere shadow of who we were, on the earth." In another essay (*Ms.*, June 1988) she describes how her hair put a "ceiling" on her brain, oppressing her (with seven or eight hours of braiding and four to seven hours of unbraiding) and stifling her creativity. In her fortieth year a break-through occurred: she realized that her hair wanted to be left alone to be as it was, and thus, after a long period of restlessness came a new spiritual growth. She has remarked that her hair is like life itself–"undeniably knotty," yet "perfect." This acceptance of her natural self, in fact, relates to her fourth novel, into which she channeled her newfound creative inspiration and energy.

   The Temple of My Familiar (1989), which Walker calls a "romance of the last 500,000 years," continues the theme of *The Color Purple*–that racism and sexism oppress black women and men. Comparisons to Walker's masterpiece are inevitable, especially with references to Celie and Shug. Some believe *The Temple of My Familiar*, with its moralizing, lacks the strength and unity of *The Color Purple;* however, others who have enjoyed Walker's previous work will praise this most ambitious, inspiring, rich panorama of much that is familiar in the evolution of her writing.

   With interwoven relationships and previous lives spanning huge distances (from northern California to an island off South Carolina to Africa) and eras (from prehistoric time to the modern), Walker skillfully weaves together the stories of three couples. Celie's granddaughter, Fanny, finds her true self by tracing her dreams' archetypal memories of African origins. Her ex-husband Suwelo (born Louis), a history professor who believes history is built on white men's lies, leaves academia for carpentry, renounces his philandering, and is reunited with Fanny in separate wings of a bird-shaped house. Another couple (rather, threesome) are Carlotta, her husband Arveyda, and her mother, Zedé, who becomes Arveyda's lover. Coincidentally, both Fanny and Carlotta leave university positions as professors of women's studies to lead freer lives. The third couple, most integral to the novel, are Miss Lissie and Mr. Hal; Lissie's narratives cover incarnations as a white man, many enslaved black women–even a lion. Wise from these past lives, she can recall not only prehistoric times when people lived peacefully with "animal familiars" but also the times of war and slavery–and thus we experience the brutal dominance by a white patriarchal society as Africa, cradle of civilization, was raped by greedy Europeans and Africans.

   Walker's message in this novel, articulated in "The Gospel According to Shug," is one of inner peace and harmony with the world. Some

will say this cosmic vision of beauty, creativity, and love–being at one with the universe–is too idealistic to be possible; others will strive to realize Walker's dream. In interviews she speaks reverently of her growth as a person and a writer, having discovered the "goddess" in herself and coming to terms with what is important in her life, considering life too precious to waste on trivialities.

   Having lived in California since 1978, Walker admits that being a black southern woman has greatly influenced her writing because she is greatly affected by the land and natural things. As she writes in *In Search of Our Mothers' Gardens*, "Guided by my heritage of a love of beauty and a respect for strength–in search of my mother's garden, I found my own."

Interviews:

John O'Brien, *Interviews With Black Writers* (New York: Liveright, 1973), pp. 186-221.

Jessica Harris, "Interview with Alice Walker," *Essence*, 7 (July 1976).

Mary Helen Washington, "Her Mother's Gifts," *Ms.*, 10 (June 1982): 38.

Pam Abramson, "Alice Walker Makes the Big Time with Black Folk Talk," *California Living* (15 August 1982): 16-20.

Claudia Tate, "Alice Walker," in *Black Women Writers at Work*, edited by Tate (New York: Continuum, 1983), pp. 175-187.

References:

David Bradley, "Telling the Black Woman's Story," *New York Times Magazine*, 8 January 1984, pp. 24ff.
   Discusses the various images of women in Walker's work.

Trudy Bloser Bush, "Transforming Vision: Alice Walker and Zora Neale Hurston," *Christian Century*, 105 (16 November 1988): 1035-1039.
   Compares Walker's black women characters with those of her literary mentor, Zora Neale Hurston, in Hurston's *Their Eyes Were Watching God*.

J. M. Coetzee, "The Beginnings of (Wo)man in Africa," *New York Times Book Review*, 30 April 1989, p. 7.
Reads *The Temple of My Familiar* as a fable exploring the inner lives of contemporary black Americans.

Robert Coles, "To Try Men's Souls," *New Yorker*, 47 (27 February 1971): 104-106.
Praises the skillful characterizations in *The Third Life of Grange Copeland* but criticizes the violence of Brownfield's family relationships.

Michael Dirda, "In Praise of Poetry," *Book World Washington Post Book World*, 9 December 1979, p. 11.
Suggests the poems in *Good Night Willie Lee, I'll See You in the Morning* are allegorical in their morals about parents, friends, lovers, and black history.

Susan Dworkin, "The Strange and Wonderful Story of the Making of 'The Color Purple,'" *Ms.*, 14 (December 1985): 66-70, 94-95.
Provides interesting background on how Walker's novel was adapted into the movie.

Peter Erickson, "'Cast Out Alone / To Heal / And Re-Create / Ourselves': Family-Based Identity in the Work of Alice Walker," *CLA Journal*, 23 (September 1979): 71-94.
Discusses the dynamics of family relationships in *The Third Life of Grange Copeland, Meridian*, and "A Sudden Trip Home in the Spring."

Trudier Harris, "On 'The Color Purple,' Stereotypes, and Silence," *Black American Literature Forum*, 18 (Winter 1984): 155-161.
Argues that *The Color Purple* should not be canonized because it perpetuates negative stereotypes about blacks, and that its fairy-tale elements betray its message of good over evil by affirming silence in the face of violence and violation.

Lisel Mueller, Review of Walker's *Once: Poems, Poetry* (February 1971): 328-329.
Compares the poems to haiku in their economy yet credits them with having the power to shock in their very personal, sharp observations.

Alan Nadel, "Reading the Body: Alice Walker's *Meridian* and the Archeology of Self," *Modern Fiction Studies*, 34 (Spring 1988): 55-68.
Uses a structuralist approach to analyze Meridian Hill's personal development and self-sacrifice.

Bettye J. Parker-Smith, "Alice Walker's Women: In Search of Some Peace of Mind," in *Black Women Writers, 1950-1980: A Critical Evaluation*, edited by Mari Evans (Garden City, N.Y.: Doubleday, 1984), pp. 478-493.
Posits that *The Color Purple* glorifies and elevates black women to the height of sovereignty as they find God in themselves and are robed in purple majesty.

Noel Perrin, Review of Walker's *Living by the Word: Selected Writings 1973-1987*, *New York Times Book Review*, 5 June 1988, p. 42.
Considers Walker's chronicles of both her physical journeys and her spiritual journey to be successful.

Marge Piercy, Review of Walker's *Meridian*, *New York Times Book Review*, 23 May 1976, pp. 135-136.
Views Meridian as saint, making real the concept of holiness and commitment to the civil rights movement.

Darryl Pinckney, "Black Victims, Black Villains: *The Color Purple* and Reckless Eyeballing," *New York Review of Books*, 34 (29 January 1987): 17-20.
Attributes the popular appeal of *The Color Purple* to its reconciliation of black and white feminists and its welcome departure from the revolutionary rhetoric of black men.

Katha Pollitt, "Stretching the Short Story," *New York Times Book Review*, 24 May 1981, pp. 9, 15.
Sees Walker's "fictional-essayistic hybrid" stories in *You Can't Keep A Good Woman Down* as too biased in their sympathetic treatment of black women exclusively and too unfocused in their loose ends, yet praises the storyteller's power and passion.

Peter S. Prescott, "A Long Road to Liberation," *Newsweek*, 99 (21 June 1982): 67-68.

Views the theme of redemptive love in *The Color Purple* as requiring female bonding that liberates women from predatory men.

L. M. Rosenberg, Review of Walker's *Horses Make a Landscape Look More Beautiful: Poems, New York Times Book Review*, 7 April 1985, p. 12.
Discusses the virtues and flaws of the poems, concluding that Walker's canon has been generally overpraised by people who admire her work.

Daniel W. Ross, "Celie in the Looking Glass: The Desire for Selfhood in *The Color Purple*," *Modern Fiction Studies*, 34 (Spring 1988): 69-84.
Discusses Celie's struggle for self-identity through the novel's mirror imagery.

Frank W. Shelton, "Alienation and Integration in Alice Walker's *The Color Purple*," *CLA Journal*, 28 (June 1985): 382-392.
Traces three patterns of alienation (men-women, women-women, and human-nature) and shows how Walker resolves the conflicts.

Barbara Smith, "The Souls of Black Women," *Ms.*, 2 (February 1974): 42-43, 78.
Attributes the pain, violence, and absence of love in the lives of women in *In Love & Trouble* to racism.

Dinitia Smith, " 'Celie, You a Tree,' " *Nation*, 235 (4 September 1982): 181-183.
Finds the vivid language and theme of women's relationships as the novel's strengths, and the occasional didacticism and unrealistic character changes as its weaknesses.

George Stade, "Womanist Fiction and Male Characters," *Partisan Review*, 52, no. 3 (1985): 264-270.
Argues that Walker's "womanist prose" in *The Color Purple* is really female chauvinism that flaunts the superiority of women's virtues over men's vices.

Gloria Steinem, "Do You Know This Woman? She Knows You: A Profile of Alice Walker,"

Ms., 10 (June 1982): 35-37, 89-94.
Asserts that *The Color Purple* touches a diverse audience with its universal, inner moral values of dignity, balance, and autonomy.

Robert Towers, "Good Men Are Hard to Find," *New York Review of Books*, 29 (12 August 1982): 35-36.
Faults *The Color Purple* for melodramatic plot revelations and feminist bias, yet praises the poignant poetic rhythms of the black folk idiom.

Mary Helen Washington, "An Essay on Alice Walker," in *Sturdy Black Bridges: Visions of Black Women in Literature*, edited by Roseann P. Bell, Bettye J. Parker, and Beverly Guy-Sheftall (New York: Anchor Books, 1979), pp. 133-149.
Asserts that Walker is an "apologist and chronicler" for black women, portraying their evolution from victimization to liberation as seen in three cycles through several works.

Mel Watkins, "Some Letters Went to God," *New York Times Book Review*, 25 July 1982, p. 7.
Analyzes the authenticity of the folk voice in Celie's letters, revealing her sharper observations and more lyrical cadence as she evolves.

Richard Wesley, " 'The Color Purple' Debate: Reading Between the lines," *Ms.*, 15 (September 1986): 62, 90-92.
A black male critic defends Walker's artistic right to portray black men as oppressors on the grounds that she does not intend to stereotype all black men this way.

Valerie Wilson, Review of Walker's *To Hell with Dying, New York Times Book Review*, 14 August 1988, p. 28.
Refutes the appropriateness of this story, narrated from an adult's perspective, as a children's book.

Robert Penn Warren

This entry was updated by Victor Strandberg (Duke University) from his entry in DLB *48, American Poets, 1880-1945, Second Series and the entry by Everett Wilkie (University of South Carolina) and Josephine Helterman in* DLB *2, American Novelists Since World War II.*

Places	Vanderbilt University Berkeley (University of California)	Tennessee Kentucky Louisiana	Vermont Italy Yale University
Influences and Relationships	John Crowe Ransom Allen Tate T. S. Eliot Thomas Hardy	Dante Shakespeare Herman Melville Cleanth Brooks	William James Joseph Conrad William Faulkner
Literary Movements and Forms	The Fugitives / Agrarians The New Criticism	Realism Naturalism Existentialism	Transcendentalism / Romanticism
Major Themes	Solipsism vs. Community Determinism vs. Responsibility	Man's Fall vs. Redemption The Nature of Time	Guilt vs. Innocence Identity Pantheism
Cultural and Artistic Influences	History Pragmatism Pluralism	Empiricism Jungian Psychology Southern Renascence	Modernism Postmodernism
Social and Economic Influences	Civil War Populism	The New Deal Old South	New South Integration

See also the Warren entry in DLB Yearbook 1980.

BIRTH: Guthrie, Kentucky, 24 April 1905, to Robert Franklin and Ruth Penn Warren.

EDUCATION: B.A., Vanderbilt University, 1925; M.A., University of California at Berkeley, 1927; Yale University, 1927-1928; B.Litt., Oxford University, 1930.

MARRIAGES: 12 September 1930 to Emma Brescia (divorced). 7 December 1952 to Eleanor Clark; children: Rosanna, Gabriel Penn.

AWARDS AND HONORS: Rhodes Scholarship, 1928; Houghton Mifflin Literary Fellowship for *Night Rider*, 1936; Guggenheim Fellowships, 1939-1940, 1947-1948; Shelley Memorial Award, 1943; Consultant in Poetry, Library of Congress, 1944-1945; Pulitzer Prize for *All the King's Men*, 1947; D.Litt, University of Louisville, 1949; L.H.D., Kenyon College, 1952; D.Litt., University of Kentucky, 1955; D.Litt., Colby College, 1956; Edna St. Vincent Millay Memorial Award (American Poetry Society), 1958; National Book Award for *Promises*, 1958; Pulitzer Prize for *Promises*, 1958; D.Litt., Swarthmore College, 1958; D.Litt., Yale University, 1959; LL.D., University of Bridgeport, 1965; Bollingen Prize in Poetry, 1966-1967; D.Litt., Fairfield University, 1969; Van Wyck Brooks Award for Poetry, 1970; National Medal for Literature, 1970; D.Litt., Wesleyan University, 1970; D.Litt., Harvard University, 1973; D.Litt., Southwestern at Memphis, 1974; D.Litt., University of the South, 1974; D.Litt., University of New Haven, 1974; Emerson-Thoreau Award (American Academy of Arts and Sciences), 1975; D.Litt., Johns Hopkins University, 1975; Copernicus Award (American Academy of Poets), 1976; Pulitzer Prize for *Now and Then*, 1979; Harriet Monroe Award for Poetry, 1979; Common Wealth Award, 1980; Presidential Medal of Freedom, 1980; Prize Fellowship, MacArthur Foundation, 1981; Poet Laureate of the United States, 1986.

BOOKS: *John Brown: The Making of a Martyr* (New York: Payson & Clarke, 1929);
Thirty-Six Poems (New York: Alcestis Press, 1935);
An Approach to Literature, by Warren, Cleanth Brooks, and John Thibault Purser (Baton Rouge: Louisiana State University Press, 1936);

Night Rider (Boston: Houghton Mifflin, 1939; London: Eyre & Spottiswoode, 1940);
Eleven Poems on the Same Theme (Norfolk, Conn.: New Directions, 1942);
At Heaven's Gate (New York: Harcourt, Brace, 1943; London: Eyre & Spottiswoode, 1943);
Selected Poems, 1923-1943 (New York: Harcourt, Brace, 1944; London: Fortune Press, 1951);
All the King's Men (New York: Harcourt, Brace, 1946; abridged edition, London: Eyre & Spottiswoode, 1948);
Blackberry Winter (Cummington, Mass.: Cummington Press, 1946);
The Circus in the Attic and Other Stories (New York: Harcourt, Brace, 1947; London: Eyre & Spottiswoode, 1952);
Modern Rhetoric, by Warren and Brooks (New York: Harcourt, Brace, 1949);
World Enough and Time: A Romantic Novel (New York: Random House, 1950; London: Eyre & Spottiswoode, 1951);
Fundamentals of Good Writing, by Warren and Brooks (New York: Harcourt, Brace, 1950; London: Dobson, 1952);
Brother to Dragons: A Tale in Verse and Voices (New York: Random House, 1953; London: Eyre & Spottiswoode, 1954; new version, New York: Random House, 1979);
Band of Angels (New York: Random House, 1955; London: Eyre & Spottiswoode, 1956);
Segregation: The Inner Conflict in the South (New York: Random House, 1956; London: Eyre & Spottiswoode, 1957);
To a Little Girl, One Year Old, In a Ruined Fortress (New Haven: Yale School of Design, 1956?);
Promises: Poems 1954-1956 (New York: Random House, 1957; London: Eyre & Spottiswoode, 1959);
Selected Essays (New York: Random House, 1958; London: Eyre & Spottiswoode, 1964);
Remember the Alamo (New York: Random House, 1958);
How Texas Won Her Freedom (San Jacinto Monument, Tex.: San Jacinto Museum of History, 1959);
The Cave (New York: Random House, 1959; London: Eyre & Spottiswoode, 1959);
The Gods of Mount Olympus (New York: Random House, 1959; London: Muller, 1962);
All the King's Men (A Play) (New York: Random House, 1960);
You, Emperors, and Others: Poems 1957-1960 (New York: Random House, 1960);

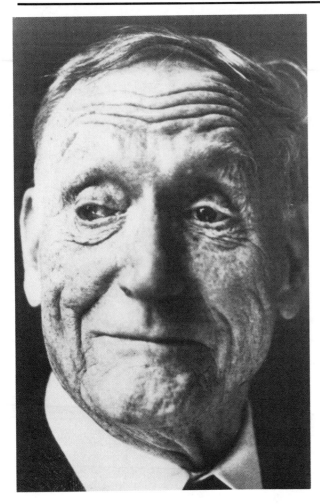

Robert Penn Warren (photo by Robert A. Ballard, Jr.)

The Legacy of the Civil War: Meditations on the Centennial (New York: Random House, 1961);

Wilderness: A Tale of the Civil War (New York: Random House, 1961; London: Eyre & Spottiswoode, 1962);

Flood: A Romance of Our Time (New York: Random House, 1964; London: Collins, 1964);

Who Speaks for the Negro? (New York: Random House, 1965);

A Plea in Mitigation: Modern Poetry and the End of an Era (Macon, Ga.: Wesleyan College, 1966);

Selected Poems: New and Old, 1923-1966 (New York: Random House, 1966);

Incarnations: Poems 1966-1968 (New York: Random House, 1968; London: Allen, 1970);

Audubon: A Vision (New York: Random House, 1969);

Homage to Theodore Dreiser: August 27, 1871-December 28, 1945, On the Centennial of His Birth (New York: Random House, 1971);

Meet Me in the Green Glen (New York: Random House, 1971; London: Secker & Warburg, 1972);

Or Else: Poem / Poems 1968-1974 (New York: Random House, 1974);

Democracy and Poetry (Cambridge: Harvard University Press, 1975);

Selected Poems: 1923-1975 (New York: Random House, 1977; London: Secker & Warburg, 1977);

A Place to Come To (New York: Random House, 1977; London: Secker & Warburg, 1977);

Now and Then: Poems 1976-1978 (New York: Random House, 1978);

Being Here: Poetry 1977-1980 (New York: Random House, 1980; London: Secker & Warburg, 1980);

Jefferson Davis Gets His Citizenship Back (Lexington: University Press of Kentucky, 1980);

Rumor Verified: Poems 1979-1980 (New York: Random House, 1981; London: Secker & Warburg, 1982);

Chief Joseph of the Nez Perce (New York: Random House, 1983);

New and Selected Poems 1923-1985 (New York: Random House, 1985);

Portrait of a Father (Lexington: University of Kentucky Press, 1988);

New and Selected Essays (New York: Random House, 1989).

OTHER: "The Briar Patch," in *I'll Take My Stand: The South and the Agrarian Tradition*, by Twelve Southerners (New York: Harper, 1930);

A Southern Harvest: Short Stories by Southern Writers, edited by Warren (Boston: Houghton Mifflin, 1937);

Understanding Poetry: An Anthology for College Students, edited by Warren and Cleanth Brooks (New York: Holt, 1938; fourth edition, New York: Holt, Rinehart & Winston, 1976);

Understanding Fiction, edited by Warren and Brooks (New York: Crofts, 1943; third edition, Englewood Cliffs, N.J.: Prentice-Hall, 1976);

"A Poem of Pure Imagination: An Experiment in Reading," in *The Rime of the Ancient Mariner*, by Samuel Taylor Coleridge (New York: Reynal & Hitchcock, 1946), pp. 59-117;

An Anthology of Stories from the Southern Review, edited by Warren and Brooks (Baton Rouge: Louisiana State University Press, 1953);

Short Story Masterpieces, edited by Warren and Albert Erskine (New York: Dell, 1954);

Six Centuries of Great Poetry: From Chaucer to Yeats, edited by Warren and Erskine (New York: Dell, 1955);

A New Southern Harvest, edited by Warren and Erskine (New York: Bantam, 1957);

The Scope of Fiction, edited by Warren and Brooks (New York: Appleton-Century-Crofts, 1960);

Dennis Devlin, *Selected Poems*, edited by Warren and Allen Tate (New York: Holt, Rinehart & Winston, 1963);

Faulkner: A Collection of Critical Essays, edited by Warren (Englewood Cliffs, N.J.: Prentice-Hall, 1966);

Randall Jarrell: 1914-1965, edited by Warren, Robert Lowell, and Peter Taylor (New York: Farrar, Straus & Giroux, 1967);

Selected Poems of Herman Melville: A Reader's Edition, edited by Warren (New York: Random House, 1970);

John Greenleaf Whittier's Poetry, edited by Warren (Minneapolis: University of Minnesota Press, 1971);

American Literature: The Makers and the Making, 2 volumes, edited by Warren, Brooks, and R. W. B. Lewis (New York: St. Martin's Press, 1973).

Robert Penn Warren's reputation as one of the most versatile and talented of America's men of letters has grown steadily since the publication of his first work in 1929. Although he achieved instant recognition among scholars as a critic, poet, and essayist, popular acceptance of his work was not forthcoming until the 1946 publication of *All the King's Men*. As Leonard Casper and Charles Bohner have noted, this situation was the probable result of financial disasters at home and wartime conditions abroad. Warren's first book, *John Brown: The Making of a Martyr* (1929), reached bookstores during the stock-market crash; *Night Rider* (1939) was published as Hitler entered Prague; and *At Heaven's Gate* (1943) was largely ignored at the height of America's military involvement in Europe during World War II. Over nearly sixty years he has published some fourteen volumes of verse interspersed with eleven books of fiction, a dozen books of nonfiction prose, and numerous essays and textbooks. This prolific creativity has arguably made Warren his nation's foremost living man of letters–"America's Dean of Letters," according to a 25 August 1980 *Newsweek* essay.

Far from imagining such a future, Warren, the son of Robert Franklin and Ruth Penn Warren, grew up in the small town of Guthrie, Kentucky, wanting to be a sea captain. After dividing his boyhood years between his grandfather's farm in summer and his family home during school terms, he obtained an appointment to enroll as a naval cadet at Annapolis. While he was waiting for the appointment to become active, however, a serious eye injury changed his plans, and he instead matriculated at Vanderbilt University in 1921 with the intention of becoming an electrical engineer.

During his freshman year an English course with John Crowe Ransom along with the influence of Allen Tate, an older student whom he met early in 1923, combined to kindle Warren's passion for literature, leading him to become part of Nashville's Fugitive group, so named after their literary magazine of the mid 1920s. During these formative years Tate and Ransom helped shape Warren's poetic style both through their own examples (Ransom's verse being especially instructive) and through their respective affinities. Ransom's taste for traditional poets from the metaphysical school to A. E. Housman and Thomas Hardy left its mark on many of Warren's earlier poems. "The Garden," for example, shows Andrew Marvell's strong influence in its imagery, style, and tone; and "Love's Parable" develops a central metaphor as elaborately as a conceit of John Donne's while using consciously archaic diction: "As kingdoms after civil broil, / Long faction-bit and sore unmanned, / Unlaced, unthewed by lawless toil. . . ."

Likewise, Allen Tate's affinities with modern experimenters such as Hart Crane and T. S. Eliot proved influential early on. After *The Waste Land* was published late in 1922, Warren drew its scenes on his dormitory wall (Tate was most impressed by the rat crawling through vegetation); he later claimed in a 1970 interview that he and most of his college literary circle had soon learned the poem by heart. "To a Face in a Crowd," the earliest of his poems to survive into later volumes (it terminates all four of the *Selected Poems*), clearly displays the influence of Eliot in its theme of alienation (implicit in the title), its imagery of the futile quest for meaning ("we . . . weary nomads in this desert"), its dread of mortality ("I was afraid"), and its mood of world-weariness rendered in memorable sound play: "how black and turbulent the blood / Will beat through iron chambers of the brain."

Within a few years Warren's two most ambitious early poems were to show a more sophisticated level of apprenticeship to Eliot: "Kentucky Mountain Farm" for its form (in five segments) and imagery (including a death by water), and "The Return: An Elegy" for its mood and prosody.

After graduating summa cum laude from Vanderbilt in 1925, Warren went for graduate study to the University of California at Berkeley, where he met his wife-to-be Emma Brescia but found the program of literary studies unfulfilling compared with the excitement of his Fugitive circle at Vanderbilt. He therefore headed East, first to Yale and then on a Rhodes Scholarship to Oxford University in England, where he worked on his first book, *John Brown: The Making of a Martyr*. This portrayal of Brown as a bloody fanatic who had coldly slaughtered several entire families in the name of the abolitionist ideal prior to Harpers Ferry was the precursor to a memorable series of similar characters in Warren's fiction and poetry, including Adam Stanton in *All the King's Men* and Lilburne Lewis in *Brother to Dragons* (1953).

Returning from Oxford in 1930 to marry Emma Brescia and take up a teaching career, Warren found positions as an assistant professor at Southwestern at Memphis (now Rhodes College, 1930-1931) and as an acting assistant professor at Vanderbilt (1931-1934). In autumn 1934 he went on to Louisiana State University, where, with Cleanth Brooks and Charles W. Pipkin, he founded the *Southern Review* in 1935 and where his collaboration with Brooks also produced several textbooks of landmark importance for their propagation of the so-called New Criticism—an approach to literature stressing analysis of the formal elements making up the work of art. The most important of these books was *Understanding Poetry* (1938), which brought the New Criticism into thousands of college classrooms over the next several decades.

With his first novel, *Night Rider*, Warren took historical facts and created a fictional context for the interpretation and redefinition of an event, a pattern which was to become the hallmark of his fiction. Set in Kentucky in the first years of the twentieth century, the novel offers a vivid picture, with moralistic overtones, of the Association formed by local tobacco growers in an attempt to wrest higher prices from the large tobacco companies. When non-Association farmers accept only slightly higher prices for their tobacco, the Association's "night riders," a secret organization using Ku Klux Klan tactics, retaliate by destroying the unfortunate farmers' crops.

Warren's novel, superficially a story of only regional implications, invites interpretations of universal scope in its portrayal of attorney and night rider Percy Munn ("Mr. Munn" throughout the novel), a modern man in search of selfhood. Barnett Guttenburg emphasizes, "He is not Man, but Munn," a distinction which in Munn's mind exempts him from the problems of this world. Even when all his pretenses are stripped away and he stares directly into the existential void, Munn cannot clearly perceive his moral dilemma. For Warren, selfhood is achieved when man looks into the void and accepts his Sartrian responsibility, thereby having knowledge of it in a manner reminiscent of the "Fortunate Fall."

The traditional dichotomies of light / dark and good / evil are woven into the fabric of the novel in such a manner that they become the compelling metaphors in the work. Darkness and evil are represented in Mr. Munn, and his consistent refusal to respond to the knowledge symbolized in the light imagery leads to his ultimate destruction "in the woods, the absorbing darkness." His refusal naturally colors all he perceives. Thus, May, who is basically innocent, is raped by Munn in the night, an extension of the violence still raging in him after he has committed a murder. Even Lucille Christian, whose name means "Light of Christ," is perverted in Munn's own mind into a creature of the night, one identified "with all the small night noises." It is Munn's resounding rejection of knowledge and its responsibility that leads to his violent deeds and his violent death. Despite the existential overtones, living by the sword brings its promised conclusions, and, ultimately, Munn must inherit man's fate.

Despite his outstanding success in letters, Warren was not promoted to full professor at Louisiana State University, and so he accepted a position as professor of English at the University of Minnesota in 1942. Here, after completing his *Selected Poems, 1923-1943* (1944), he devoted the remainder of the decade to writing several major prose works, including the novels *All the King's Men* and *World Enough and Time* (1950).

Warren's second novel, *At Heaven's Gate*, bridges the simple chronology of *Night Rider* and the more elaborate time juxtapositions of *All the King's Men*. Although his more complex structural techniques do not approach the maturity of his craft in *All the King's Men*, they do anticipate his extensive use of flashback and demonstrate his experimentation with second-person narration. In this second novel Warren counterpoints time past with time present to emphasize the futility of defining oneself through an alter ego. Set in Tennessee in the 1920s, *At Heaven's Gate* is based on the career of Luke Lea, a wealthy and unscrupulous financier prominent during Warren's undergraduate years at Vanderbilt. Like Lea, Warren's Bogan Murdock, with his corrupt machinations, represents to the Agrarian mind the evils of a spiritually empty urban world. Contrasted to Murdock is Ashby Wyndham, a farmer and visionary, whose combination of stoicism and traditional Christianity provides Agrarianism's answer to the corruptions of a modern age. One must, as Wyndham's life makes clear, not only accept oneself, but other people, and also recognize the legitimacy of their existence.

Warren's most celebrated novel is *All the King's Men*, which was made into a movie in 1949. This work, which has received the bulk of critical attention given Warren's novels, is based on the life of Huey Long, the celebrated Louisiana governor who rose to national prominence through his populist politics, only to be gunned down in mid career by Dr. Carl A. Weiss, who acted from motives still unclear. Warren has denied that the novel is based directly on Long, insisting instead that Long's story simply gave him the "line of thinking and feeling" he used to construct the novel.

As he often does, Warren shifts the natural historical focus of the story. *All the King's Men* does not concentrate on Willie Stark (Long's counterpart), but rather on Jack Burden, the governor's sycophant who does much of Stark's gumshoe work. As Stark requires one manipulation after another, Burden always rises to the occasion. It is Burden's gradual realization of his own true position and the consequences of his actions that lead to his heightened, more nearly correct perception of his role in this life.

The temptation is to point to the role of lies and deceit in this novel; however, it is not deceit per se which is the book's basis, but rather the uses to which truth may be legitimately put. Burden's major task is not to fabricate lies, but to discover truth and to put it into the hands of those who can use it to their own ends and to the purposes of their political ideology.

Burden has, for the most part, lived his life believing he is exempt from both time and respon-

sibility. His explanation for the events of this world is "The Big Twitch," or alternately, "The Big Sleep." He is slow to perceive causal relationships between what he does and ensuing events and ascribes chains of events to the Twitch itself rather than to anything he does, where the responsibility properly belongs. It may be that no greater force does shape this world; however, as Burden discovers, that fact does not exempt him from responsibility for what he does. Nor is he exempt from time, as he initially believes. All his actions are on a continuum of existence, and Burden must gradually realize that all his beliefs have no validity in the face of certain realities, of which time is the most real of all.

The complex interweavings of several dimensions of time reinforce Burden's realizations. *All the King's Men* is a masterpiece of narrative technique. The flashbacks reinforce the idea that all existence is on the continuum Burden seeks so desperately to avoid or escape and that events of the past reach forward to shape present events, which will themselves have ramifications in the future. However, it is also clear in the technique that time will not save one, either; it always comes at that moment when one's time in this world ceases.

The so-called Kentucky Tragedy forms the basis for *World Enough and Time* (1950), although Warren expertly moves the tale from the melodramatic confines often given it by other writers to a realm of universal significance. In many respects the physical details remain the same, and Warren loudly echoes his source. For example, the historic Colonel Sharp becomes Colonel Fort; Jeroboam Beauchamp becomes Jeremiah Beaumont; and both tales are set in Kentucky during the first quarter of the nineteenth century. But Warren managed to imbue the old story with new life and to expand his fictional version of it far beyond the original boundaries.

The point of view from which the story is told is crucial to the success of the novel. Rather than permitting one of the characters to control the narrative, Warren places that role in the hands of an unnamed historian who has discovered the truth of the matter among the papers of the now dead Wilkie Barron, a principal in the novel. The crucial document is Jeremiah's diary, from which the bulk of the information is derived; however, its contents are not served up in a raw, undigested state. Rather, the scholarly narrator chooses which elements to show us and connects the parts with his own comments, which give insight into the moral dilemmas posed by the history.

This technique gives Warren three stages of control over the vocabulary, that element upon which the success of such a narrative must rest. The first stage, that of the primary sources such as the diary and letters, reflects the preoccupations and concerns of the characters, who themselves are not totally blind to the implications of their deeds and whose developing awareness the reader may view. The second stage, that of the connecting passages, allows the impartial observer to correct the characters' impressions and to become involved himself, to a certain extent, in the incredible tale of love, revenge, and politics he has discovered, and of which "We have what is left, the lies and half-lies and the truths and half-truths." The interplay between the narrator and the characters forms one of the salient features of the novel's technique. Of most importance is the third level of vocabulary, that which describes all of life, including that with which the reader might describe his own. One is not particularly inclined to see his own life in terms of "blood," "revenge," or "murder," as is the case in this novel; however, everyone may well question the consequences of his actions and the horrible weight which they often compel him to bear, as when Beaumont, reflecting on the enormity of his deeds, sums up the response in his journal entry for 20 October: "Drunk." He later concludes, "It is the crime of self, the crime of life. The crime is I."

During this period Warren produced, as well, important essays in literary criticism such as his classic book-length interpretation of Coleridge, "A Poem of Pure Imagination: An Experiment in Reading" (published in a 1946 edition of *The Rime of the Ancient Mariner*), and pioneering studies of Joseph Conrad, Ernest Hemingway, William Faulkner, Robert Frost, Herman Melville, Katherine Anne Porter, and Eudora Welty. In addition to their many penetrating and original insights, these essays furnish significant revelations concerning Warren's own practice as a creative writer. His essay on Conrad (collected in *Selected Essays*, 1958), for example, contains a statement of purpose applicable to every particle of Warren's own literary creation: "The philosophical novelist, or poet, is one for whom the documentation of the world is constantly striving to rise to the level of generalization about values, for whom the image strives to rise to symbol, for whom images always fall into a dialectical configu-

ration, for whom the urgency of experience, no matter how vividly and strongly experience may enchant, is the urgency to know the meaning of experience." The essays on Porter and Welty have an even more direct relevance to Warren's poetry, in that Welty's "A Still Moment," together with a word of advice from Porter, combined to form the genesis of Warren's *Audubon: A Vision* (1969), published some twenty-five years later.

In 1950 Warren's acceptance of a professorship at Yale University coincided shortly thereafter with divorce from Emma Brescia (1951) and marriage to the writer Eleanor Clark (1952), by whom he fathered his only two children, Rosanna (1953) and Gabriel Penn (1955). Since then Warren has divided his habitation between his home in Fairfield, Connecticut, a former barn in which he personally did much of the renovation in carpentry and stone work, and his summer home in Stratton, Vermont. These settings, together with his frequent sojourns with his family in France and Italy, have provided a vital stimulus to much of Warren's verse since *Brother to Dragons* in 1953.

Brother to Dragons, the most ambitious long poem in Warren's fourteen volumes of poetry, is generally seen as a watershed separating his traditional, formally disciplined earlier verse from the later volumes, which display the loosening effects that were becoming generally prevalent in American poetry of the 1950s. Among those loosening effects was a more open use of his own persona in the later poetry, once he had broken away from the "impersonality of art" doctrine by installing "R. P. W." as a major character in *Brother to Dragons*. It should be remarked, however, that the loosening effects in Warren's later style, though extending far enough to encompass free verse, generally coexist with a continuing respect for traditional forms. From first to last, Warren's verse comprises a virtual catalogue of modified conventions, from the epic grasp of *Brother to Dragons* to the nursery rhymes in *You, Emperors, and Others: Poems 1957-1960* (1960). Sonnets, terza rima, iambic couplets, rhyming quatrains, sestinas, quasi-Spenserian stanzas, and various combinations thereof characterize Warren's style in virtually all his volumes of poetry.

Within this great range of styles, however, a fundamental coherence in the development of Warren's themes gives his poetic opus an underlying unity reminiscent of William Faulkner's remark that "not only each book had to have a design but the whole output or sum of an artist's work had to have a design." In Warren's verse this total design may in the end justify reference to another eminent quotation, Eliot's assertion that "We must know all of Shakespeare's work in order to know any of it." Something similar may be said of the poetry of Robert Penn Warren.

The master theme that unifies Warren's fourteen volumes of verse published over six decades is the neoromantic trauma of the Fall–considered as a philosophical and psychological phenomenon–along with a gradually evolving set of redemptive possibilities. In retrospect, it can be seen that this subject matter has extended across Warren's poetic opus within the frame of three overlapping phases. Using mainly lyrical form, the poetry of the first phase–the 1920s and 1930s–depicts the Fall in the usual fashion: original innocence, characterized by delight in one's being within the kingdom of nature, yielding to a forced, one-way passage into a world ruined by time, loss, and evil, the naturalistic Waste Land promulgated in the writings of Eliot and Hemingway. At times, Warren employs a frankly Wordsworthian manner, as in "Letter from a Coward to a Hero" (*Thirty-Six Poems*, 1935): "The scenes of childhood were splendid, / And the light that there attended, / But is rescinded: / The cedar, / The lichened rocks, / The thicket where I saw the fox, / And where I swam, the river." Elsewhere, somewhat like Robert Frost, he makes nearly obsessive use of an autumnal setting as a seasonal pun for the theme of losses–in "Late Subterfuge" and "Garden Waters," for example, as well as "The Garden" and "Aged Man Surveys Past Time" (all in *Thirty-Six Poems*). And as these poems of passage proliferate, Eliot continues to manifest his spectral presence; for example, a phrase lifted from "Gerontion"–"fractured atoms"–appears in the *Kentucky Mountain Farm* segment entitled "At the Hour of the Breaking of the Rocks" (*Thirty-Six Poems*).

To the irony and regret of this "Paradise Lost" perspective, Warren adds still deeper trauma through bringing the Fall to bear upon the inner psyche. Repeatedly in his verse the lapsarian experience precipitates a division within the psyche between a fleeing anima figure, representing the lost child-self, and a fallen persona that is left behind to cope as best it can with its inner vacancy and its ruined environment. In "Man Coming of Age" (*Thirty-Six Poems*) the lost self is "That frail reproachful *alter ego*" who, harking back toward "a season greener and of more love," flees the approach of his lapsed, autumn-

bound doppelgänger as the poem ends. In other poems, the fleeing anima takes a nonhuman form, like the doe escaping the hunt in "Eidolon" and the hawk sailing into the sunset (Warren's most frequent version of this motif) at the end of "Picnic Remembered." The often-anthologized poem "Bearded Oaks" (*Eleven Poems on the Same Theme*, 1942), which portrays the state of being dead in terms of undersea imagery (like Eliot's "Death by Water" in *The Waste Land*), illustrates the bankrupt condition of the fallen self without its anima. Here, pursuing their intent to "spare an hour's term / To practice for eternity," the two lovers maintain absolute silence and total stasis in a sea-bottom setting, where "Dark is unrocking, unrippling, still." To this scene, the upper, living world contributes just so much sediment: "Passion and slaughter, ruth, decay / Descend, minutely whispering down, / Silted down swaying streams."

Further exacerbating this postlapsarian sense of fragmentation–of being separated from one's deepest self, from nature, from the world of the living–is the motif of broken relationships that extends through these poems. Portrayed at times in terms of society at large, as in two poems in *Thirty-Six Poems*–"Pondy Woods" (where a killer flees the manhunt) and "History" (whose present generation disgraces the noble dream of its pioneer ancestors)–this theme of alienation most commonly affects intimate relationships, such as that between mother and son in "The Return: An Elegy" (*Thirty-Six Poems*) and "Revelation" (*Eleven Poems on the Same Theme*). Most often, it dissolves the bond between lovers, thereby promoting an ultimate expression of the "Paradise Remembered" sensibility. In their depictions of this subject, poems such as "Monologue [as opposed to Dialogue] at Midnight," "Love's Parable," and "Picnic Remembered" (all in *Eleven Poems on the Same Theme*) anticipate the broken romance between Anne Stanton and Jack Burden after their one Edenic summer in *All the King's Men*–itself a title whose reference to Humpty Dumpty implies the "Great Fall" from innocence suffered by all the book's main characters.

Extending its ruinous sway in this fashion, the first phase of Warren's verse culminates at last in the five-poem sequence, "Mexico Is a Foreign Country: Five Studies in Naturalism" (*Selected Poems, 1923-1943*). Like his predecessor John Brown, or like the bloody ideologues who were precipitating global war at the time the poem was written, the political fanatic in poem one, "Butterflies Over the Map," seeks relief from his intolerable inner vacancy by committing slaughter while "robbed in the pure / Idea." By comparison, the ragged beggar sitting passively in poem two, "The World Comes Galloping: A True Story," is a figure of wisdom and dignity. For the speaker of these poems, the world's fragmentation widens from the human dimension in poem three, "Small Soldiers with Drum in Large Landscape" (their drumbeat accentuates his solitude: "And I and I, and they are they, / And *this* is *this*, and *that* is *that*"), to the theological level in poem five, "The Mango on the Mango Tree," where God the "Great Schismatic" is to blame for "the Babel curse by which we live." To the craving for communion in this poem there is no answer but fantasy—"And I could leap and laugh and sing . . . and everything / Take hands with us and pace the music in a ring."

Reversing the biblical analogue, the second phase of Warren's verse—that of the 1940s and 1950s—moves from the theme of the Fall to that of "Original Sin," which Warren defines (in his essay on Coleridge) as "original with the sinner and . . . of his will." Here the bifurcation of the psyche precipitated by the lapsarian experience brings on a crisis of identity that necessitates the addition of dramatic and narrative elements to Warren's earlier elegiac-lyric mode. Extending from *Eleven Poems on the Same Theme* through "The Ballad of Billie Potts" (in *Selected Poems, 1923-1943*), *Brother to Dragons*, *Promises: Poems 1954-1956* (1957), and *You, Emperors, and Others*, this phase of Warren's verse dramatizes the lost alter ego of prelapsarian innocence being supplanted by a fearsome new identity, a figure of innate evil rising up with hatchet in hand—like Big Billie Potts or Lilburne Lewis—to answer the fallen self's yearning for definition. In terms of Jungian archetypes, the "undiscovered self" or "shadow" (comparable to Freud's id) thus replaces the lost child-self, or anima; and the poems of Warren's middle period become a sort of psychodrama in which a sanctimonious surface ego (whom Warren calls "you") attempts to repudiate any consanguinity with its polluted Jungian shadow.

In the most original of the *Eleven Poems on the Same Theme*—"End of Season," "Original Sin: A Short Story," "Crime," "Pursuit," and "Terror"—"you" is portrayed in headlong flight from this bestial doppelgänger, but the pursuit is relentless. Hence the "Terror" of that last title: there is no preserving of "innocence." In "End of Season"

the persona takes refuge in a beach resort whose quasi-baptismal rites of play offer a cleansed new identity. (John the Baptist, Ponce de Leon, and Dante add to the ironic "new life" motif in this stanza.) The undersea realm renders protection in lines of rich sound texture—"deep and wide-eyed, dive / Down the glaucous glimmer where no voice can visit"—but the past self is a relentless pursuer: "But the mail lurks in the box at the house where you live." In "Crime" another passage of arresting aural effects describes the polluted self as a corpse showing alarming signs of resurrection from the secret place where "you" had buried it: "though the seasons stammer / Past pulse in the throat of the field-lark, / Still memory drips, a pipe in the cellar-dark, / And in its hutch and hole . . . / The cold heart heaves like a toad, and lifts its brow. . . ." In "Terror" the "clean" part of the self strives mightily to maintain its sanctity, as "you now, guiltless, sink / To rest in lobbies, or pace gardens. . . ," but the world-wide outpouring of depravity in this poem, embodied in the figures of Mussolini, Hitler, Stalin, and Franco, makes innocence an increasingly untenable concept, as "you" admit in the closing comparison between "you" (vis-à-vis the shadow) and Macbeth "the criminal king" (vis-à-vis Duncan): "the conscience-stricken stare / Kisses the terror; for you see an empty chair."

This effort of "you" to escape or renounce its fallen shadow self creates the central drama of Warren's subsequent four volumes. In "The Ballad of Billie Potts" Little Billie's "original sin"—his attempt to ambush and murder a wayfarer—precipitates first his loss of Eden ("the green / World, land of the innocent bough"—a reference to Eden's Tree) and then his loss of the anima, whose departure "like the cicada had left . . . / The old shell of self, thin, ghostly, translucent, light as air." Flight to the West gives Billie "another name and another face," but the insufficiency of this new identity imposes the vacancy of "you" upon the runaway, bringing him home at last in search of the missing anima:

> Though the letter always came and you lovers were
>   always true,
> Though you always received the respect due to
>   your position,
> Though your hand never failed of its cunning and
>   your glands always
>   thoroughly knew their business,
> Though your conscience was easy and you were as-
>   sured of your innocence.

> You became gradually aware that something was
>   missing from the picture,
> And upon closer inspection exclaimed: "Why, I'm
>   not in it at all!"
> Which was perfectly true.
>
> Therefore you tried to remember when you last
>   had
> Whatever it was you had lost,
> And you decided to retrace your steps from that
>   point[.]

So Billie returns home and drinks at the spring where his ghostly reflection in the dark may yet harbor the child-self that was lost so long ago:

> But perhaps what you lost was lost in the pool long
>   ago
> When childlike you lost it and then in your inno-
>   cence rose to go
> After kneeling, as now, with your thirst beneath the
>   leaves:
> And years it lies here and dreams in the depth and
>   grieves,
> More faithful than mother or father in the light or
>   dark of the leaves.

For the fallen psyche, what rises up from the dark is not the innocent child-self, however, but rather the father "Who is evil and ignorant and old." After the hatchet stroke of Big Billie–"What gift–oh, father, father–from that dis-severing hand?"–Little Billie's death ("the patrimony of your crime") leaves "you" to carry the search for true selfhood to its momentous conclusion.

For its visionary power, its vividness of image, and its appeal to the ear, that conclusion (in the closing lines of "The Ballad of Billie Potts") marks a pinnacle of achievement rarely equaled and never surpassed in Warren's other poetry:

> The bee knows, and the eel's cold ganglia burn,
> And the sad head lifting to the long return,
> Through brumal deeps, in the great unsolsticed
>   coil,
> Carries its knowledge, navigator without star,
> And under the stars, pure in its clamorous toil,
> The goose hoots north where the starlit marshes
>   are.
> The salmon heaves at the fall, and, wanderer, you
> Heave at the great fall of Time, and, gorgeous,
>   gleam
> In the powerful arc, and anger and outrage like
>   dew,

> In your plunge, fling, and plunge to the thunder-
>   ous stream:
> Back to the silence, back to the pool, back
> To the high pool, motionless, and the unmur-
>   muring dream.

As though to illustrate the Coleridgean reconciliation of opposites, "you" (the lapsarian ego) are here reconciled with the shadow self represented in the multitude of animal faces–faces that call up such precursors as the "old horse" and "old hound" that "you" locked out in "Original Sin: A Short Story." In their compulsive movement homeward, driven by intuitions of subhuman or prehuman origin, they manifest Carl Gustav Jung's insight that the collective unconscious is "the only accessible source of religious experience." Using expressly religious diction and imagery, the coda to "The Ballad of Billie Potts" opens up two specific religious possibilities–the lapsarian ego's recovery of "innocence" through a shared identity with these questing creatures ("Brother to pinion and the pious fin that cleave / Their innocence of air and the disinfectant flood") –and, a crucial tenet in any religious attitude, the sacramental acceptance of one's mortality:

> The hour is late,
> The scene familiar even in shadow,
> The transaction brief,
> And you, wanderer, back,
> After the striving and the wind's word,
> To kneel
> Here in the sacramental silence of evening
> At the feet of the old man
> Who is evil and ignorant and old[.]

Because this moment is so crucial in Warren's total poetic vision–it initiates the third major phase in his design, that which postulates a kind of redemption from the Fall–its philosophical groundwork requires some exposition from two of Warren's seminal prose writings. The first of these is Warren's essay on *The Rime of the Ancient Mariner*, which he had already begun to contemplate at the time he was writing this poem. While speaking of Coleridge, Warren defines the nature and purpose of poetry in terms directly applicable to his own practice. Calling poetry "a myth of the unity of being" and "a glorious synthesis in which all breaches would be healed and all malice reconciled," he quotes Coleridge's celebrated definition of the Imagination for confirmation of his inferences: "It dissolves, diffuses, dissipates in order to recreate: ... at all events it struggles to idealize and to unify." This unification may begin on the psychological level–"We know by creating, and one of the things we create is the Self "–but ultimately it entails theological consequences. The "imagination shows us how Nature participates in God," Warren says; and the poet who apprehends this truth–whether Coleridge or Warren–then promulgates "the theme of sacramental vision," which is "the sense of the 'One Life' in which all creation participates." From such a sacramental vision, the wanderer in "The Ballad of Billie Potts" derives a sense of final identity that transcends the fragmentation, the "original sin," and the fear of mortality which the Fall had precipitated.

Further illumination of this central design of Warren's poetry may be found in "Knowledge and the Image of Man," an essay whose publication date (1955) suggests that it is the poet's retrospective on his mythopoeic construction. "Man eats of the tree of knowledge, and falls," Warren writes. "But if he takes another bite, he may get at least a sort of redemption." For Warren this redemption does not postulate a convert's withdrawal from the world of the "unclean," as orthodoxy teaches; it rather requires an opposite process of union between oneself and the whole of reality: "[Man is] in the world with continual and intimate interpenetration, an inevitable osmosis of being, which in the end . . . affirms his identity." From the reconciliation of opposites that this vision permits, merging "the ugly with the beautiful, the slayer with the slain," Warren's figures of grace may derive "such a sublimation that the world which once provoked . . . fear and disgust may now be totally loved." Moreover, as against the unconscious innocence of the Eden period, the redemptive knowledge that is attained through this osmosis of being is the more precious for being willed and earned: "Man can return to his lost unity, and if that return is fitful and precarious, if the foliage and flower of the innocent garden are now somewhat browned by a late season, all is the more precious for the fact, for what is now achieved has been achieved by a growth of moral awareness. . . ."

Although Warren's system of ideas was essentially complete with "The Ballad of Billie Potts," he has renewed and reinvigorated his fundamental themes in his later poetry by bringing on vast stretches of freshly imagined material–"willing," as he says in his tribute to Conrad, "to go naked into the pit, again and again, to make the same old struggle for his truth." About half of War-

Eleanor Clark (photo by Ellen Levine)

ren's total body of verse, written over six decades, relates to the theme of the Fall, or forced passage into a ruined world; against this background he has played off the other two themes–reconciliation between the ego and its shadow, and between the self and the whole of reality–in a continuous dialectical tension.

In *Brother to Dragons*, it is Thomas Jefferson and his nephew Lilburne Lewis who act out this drama of reconciliation between the "innocent" surface ego and its bestial shadow. Drawn from the Book of Job–the story of another "innocent" character who eventually comes to say, "Behold, I am vile"–the poem's title refers primarily to Lilburne's vivisection of a slave in retaliation for a minor transgression, an actual incident in the family history that Jefferson was never known to mention in speech or writing. In the poem Jefferson's disillusion at this betrayal of his humanistic idealism generates variations upon the "brother to dragons" motif such as his cacophonous description of the minotaur: "In the blind dark, hock-deep in ordure, its beard / And shag foul-scabbed, and when the hoof heaves– / Listen! the foulness sucks like mire. / The beast waits. He is . . . / Our brother, our darling brother." That this president, probably the only genius ever to hold the office, should state such sentiments bespeaks a national Fall from innocence appropriate to the poem's biblical analogue. But here again, as in "The Ballad of Billie Potts," the shadow self offers redemptive affinities with the whole of reality which are inaccessible to the surface ego. Thus, as Jefferson downgrades the human image toward these bestial archetypes, dragon and minotaur, R. P. W. in contrary fashion upgrades the beastly toward the human level. The giant snake that rears up "taller / Than any man" from the ruins of the Lewis home thereby assumes a demeanor more humane than reptilian in R. P. W.'s view of it: "then / The bloat head sagged an inch, the tongue withdrew, / And on the top of that strong stalk the head / Wagged slow, benevolent and sad and sage, / As though it understood our human pitifulness / And forgave all, and asked forgiveness, too." Likewise, the Mississippi catfish, though its "brute face / Is the face of the last torturer," enjoys an immersion in nature of quasi-religious dimensions: "The catfish is in the Mississippi and / The Mississippi is in the catfish and / Under the ice both are at one with God. / Would that we were!"

Described by Hyatt Waggoner in his *American Poets: From Puritans to the Present* (1968) as "certainly a central *document* in American poetry," *Brother to Dragons* has elicited responses ranging from encomiastic to contemptuous. When it first appeared, Parker Tyler complained that the poem is "full . . . of ideological axes" (*Poetry*, December 1953), and Hugh Kenner said its style "resembles that of a Kentucky preacher hypostatizing Sin" (*Hudson Review*, Winter 1954). But other poets found it admirable. Robert Lowell, saying he had read the work three times through without stopping, found it "superior to any of the larger works of Browning" (*Kenyon Review*, Autumn 1953); Delmore Schwartz thought it "most remarkable as a sustained whole" (*New Republic*, 14 September 1953); and Randall Jarrell called it "an event, a great one" (*New York Times Book Review*, 23 August 1953). In 1979 Warren published a rewritten version of *Brother to Dragons*, revising the characterization (Jefferson, for one thing, is less vitriolic), recasting the form (in five segments), and generally doing away with "the blank verse trap," as the poet later called it. Although the later version is more economical than the first, it retains the most skillful passages, like the coming of the annus mirabilis and R. P. W.'s long closing meditation, virtually intact.

Warren's 1955 novel, *Band of Angels*, is rich in complex ironies and sudden reversals of fortune. Told from the first-person view of Amantha Starr, the tale explores the painful acquisition of the answer to the question "Who am I?" as Amantha's fortunes sink when she is gradually caught up in the lost cause of the Old South, at first by no fault of her own, later by a deliberate choice on her part. It is a world where nothing is really as it seems and Amantha has stripped away from her the physical attributes by which she formerly defined her own nature and the meaning of existence. It is a world of masks.

The question "Who is everybody else?" is posed as well and becomes a significant feature in the novel. Amantha's father, though he tries to protect and educate her, ends up laying a trap for her by concealing her birth and then by failing to rectify the deceit before his death. The kindly Hamish Bond, who at first pities her and to whom she becomes devoted, in fact uses her instead of feeling any true affection for her. He was previously a dealer in slaves. Seth Parker, a wild-eyed idealist at Oberlin, where Amantha was taught "the vanity of this, our perishing world," eventually deserts his calling to follow the lures of this world instead. Finally, Tobias Sears, a Union officer, marries her, and, after some wandering, both real and symbolic, the couple begins to resolve the problems of identity which have plagued them. It is in this resolution that the key to the novel lies. Amantha learns that she is the only one in this world who can solve the problems of self-knowledge in a manner that gives them meaning to her own life.

In a world of pretending it is important that one not pretend, for such action is only deceptive and self-defeating. Amantha runs speedily from her own origins but finds that they pursue faster than she can escape and must, as everyone must, come to grips with the reality of who she really is. The slave mentality is not only symbolic, it is real, and even the emancipation following the Civil War does not set Amantha free; only she can do that, for freedom is a relative concept, not truly dependent upon circumstances of birth or position. This world is not constituted of bands of angels, only bands of humans struggling on the face of this earth. God is not coming to set you free; there is no one to do that "except yourself."

In his prizewinning volume *Promises: Poems 1954-1956*, Warren's belated experience of fatherhood revives a lyric strain, as he fills the two sequences dedicated to his son and daughter with sonnets, ballads, lullabies, and other harmonic forms. In substance, however, his theme of the Fall is still very much in evidence. The five-poem sequence dedicated to Rosanna, "To a Little Girl, One Year Old, in a Ruined Fortress," creates a dialectic tension between the melancholia of the narrator, thinking of "The malfeasance of nature or the filth of fate" ("The Child Next Door"), and the prelapsarian delight of his daughter: "And you sing as though human need / Were not for perfection" ("The Flower"). The "Promises" sequence addressed to Gabriel includes episodes of "Original Sin," such as a father's slaughter of all his children ("School Lesson Based on Word of Tragic Death of Entire Gillum Family") and a grandfather's culpability in a legalized lynching ("Court-Martial"). Probably Warren's most obsessive image of a fallen soul is the tragically rootless wandering bum in "Dark Night of the Soul," a character transposed into poetry from his most widely admired short story, *Blackberry Winter* (1946). But in "Dragon Country: To Jacob Boehme," the poet argues the "fortunate fall" idea that the world's evil–the dragon–gives life its truest meaning: "in church fools pray only that the Beast depart. / / But if the Beast were withdrawn now, life might dwindle again / To the ennui, the pleasure, and the night sweat, known in the time before / Necessity of truth had trodden the land. . . ." Also counteracting the Fall are the epiphanies in *Promises* emanating from the world's beauty ("Gold Glade") and from a boy's first experience of shared work ("Boy's Will, Joyful Labor Without Pay, and Harvest Home–1918").

For its visionary power, the most original and momentous poem in *Promises* is "Ballad of a Sweet Dream of Peace," a sequence of seven lyrics in which a brash young fellow (resembling "you") is forcibly initiated into the next world through the ministrations of a skeletal granny. Reminiscent of Cass Mastern's cosmic web in *All the King's Men*, the guide's assertion that "all Time is a dream, and we're all one Flesh, at last" promulgates the Osmosis of Being in this setting, as do the spectral hogs that embody the "one Flesh" principle.

The 1959 novel *The Cave*, based on the real story of Floyd Collins, is not so much the story of Jasper Harrick, who is trapped in a cave that he was exploring, as it is the tale of his rescuers. Warren is able to explore not only the individual consciousnesses of each character, but also to re-veal the groping and struggling of the entire community as it wrestles with its own preoccupations and helplessness in the face of disaster.

This work is unusual among novels in that the main character and object of the rescue is never seen or heard from. Trapped far below ground, he is never reached alive, despite false reports from the cowardly, grandstanding Isaac Sumpter, and dies alone and unrelieved in the darkness of his underground tomb. Although he is lost from view, his plight is never forgotten and serves as a foil to the machinations of the would-be rescuers whose lives are revealed through their schemings.

The novel is explicitly a tale of knowledge, self-discovery, and communal responsibility. The epigraph of the novel links the story to a scene in Plato's *The Republic*, the famous metaphor of the cave. The question naturally arises whether any of the characters in the novel have struggled up the long road to the pure sunlight and to real appreciation of reality, or whether they have simply perverted the concepts of truth and justice to make them fit their own ends. Thus, the cave metaphor operates on two levels in the novel. The first is the obvious one of Jasper trapped below, with no one above of sufficient fortitude or knowledge to save him. The second level is that of the metaphysical cave in which the whole community and all mankind are trapped. In reality, it is not Jasper who is trapped, it is everyone else. They are chained and unable to glimpse anything but the most perverted images of reality, like Isaac, who ends up pursuing money and makes publicity for himself from Jasper's plight.

In many respects, the knowledge gained is of a negative nature; it is not so much the knowledge of what we are, but rather the realization of what we are not. This is knowledge gained by the process of elimination rather than an aggressive examination of the human condition. After Jasper is declared dead, the crowd goes off into an orgy of drinking and intercourse. The commissioner observes, "They have enthusiasm." The lieutenant replies: "It is the same old kind . . . Red-eye and nookie. They are also enthusiastic about not being dead in the ground." As Plato makes clear, and Warren with him, knowledge is a hurtful thing and often odious to him who acquires it. It is far simpler to stare at the shadows of reality dancing before our eyes than to see it revealed clearly in the bright light of perfect truth.

You, Emperors, and Others concludes the poems about "you" that had commenced two decades earlier in *Eleven Poems on the Same Theme*. In the "Garland for You" sequence a new intensity is manifest in the postlapsarian psychodrama. "Man in the Street," for example, portrays a young man with "eyes big as saucers" who simply cannot accept the fallen world: "I see facts I can't refute– / Winners and losers, / Pickers and choosers . . . / And my poor head, it spins like a top." Although the poem's headnote relates Jesus to this world ("Raise the stone, and there thou shalt find me"), the young man prefers the Christianity of the flight reflex: "And I go to prepare a place for you, / For this location will never do." Another notable instance of the flight reflex is "The Letter About Money, Love, or Other Comfort, If Any," in which "you" first revert to the anima-self of childhood ("crooning among the ruined lilies to a teddy bear, not what a grown man ought / / To be doing past midnight") and finally lapse back into primal bestiality ("you, like an animal, / will crouch among the black boulders . . . / / waiting for hunger to drive you down to forage . . ."). The emperors–two of the worst, Domitian and Tiberius–add further instruction to "you" about innate depravity ("Let's stop horsing around–it's not Domitian, it's you / We mean . . .").

The most moving poems in this volume are the "Mortmain" sequence about the death of the poet's father. Here, poised between his small son's and his father's life spans, the speaker stares "Down the tube and darkening corridor of Time" to glimpse a scene from his father's boyhood: "The boy, / With imperial calm, crosses a space, rejoins / The shadow of woods, but pauses, turns, grins once, / And is gone . . ." ("A Vision: Circa 1880"). Poem four of this sequence, "In the Turpitude of Time: N.D.," recalls the "One Life" theme at the end of "The Ballad of Billie Potts" while also anticipating later poems such as "Trying to Tell You Something" (*Selected Poems: 1923-1975*, 1977): "Can we–oh, could we only– know / What annelid and osprey know, / And the stone, night-long, groans to divulge? / If only we could, then that star / That dawnward slants might sing to our human ear. . . ."

The 1966 *Selected Poems* opens with a section entitled "Tale of Time: New Poems 1960-1966." Here Warren's growing preference for poem sequences–a reminder of his comment that he stopped writing short stories because they kept turning into poems–resulted in six such arrangements that subsume nearly the whole collection. (The only separate poem is "Shoes in the Rain Jun-

gle," an early protest against the war in Vietnam.) Through five of the six sequences the Tale of Time is the familiar story of the Fall retold as individual history. "Notes on a Life to be Lived," somewhat like *Promises*, juxtaposes the postlapsarian narrator's fear ("Stargazing"), grief ("Blow, West Wind"), and regret against various anima figures: the prelapsarian lad in "Little Boy and Lost Shoe," the fetus rapt in its "pulse and warm slosh of / . . . unbreathing bouillon" in "Vision under the October Mountain," the eagle "climbing / The light above the mountain" in "Composition in Gold and Red-Gold," and the speaker's small son in "Ways of Day": "I watch you at your sunlight play. / Teach me, my son, the ways of day." "Tale of Time," the title sequence, recalls that supreme trauma in any man's life, the death of a mother–in this case amplified by the additional death of an ancillary mother figure, the family's black servant. Tracing the mother's life from an Edenic girlhood ("What Were You Thinking, Dear Mother?") to her funeral ("What Happened?"), "Tale of Time" fashions for this occasion a new formulation of the Osmosis of Being concept, reminiscent of the hogs' feast in "Ballad of a Sweet Dream of Peace"; "the solution is: You / Must eat the dead./ You must eat them completely, bone, blood, flesh, gristle. . . ." The "Homage to Emerson, On Night Flight to New York" sequence juxtaposes the great figure of transcendentalist prophecy– who said that there was no Fall, that man is an incarnation of God living in nature, the divine kingdom–against a series of postlapsarian images: "The Wart," "The Spider," masturbation, drunkenness, fear of flying, urban filth, the inhuman immensity of nature. "The Day Dr. Knox Did It" (committed suicide) uses its setting of August 1914 as a paradigm of lost innocence reaching from the boy-witness to the Western world. The discovery of "original sin" on the narrator's part–his confession that "I have lied, . . . committed / adultery, and for a passing pleasure / . . . inflicted death on flies"–completes the experience of the Fall: "for there is / / no water to wash the world away. / We are the world, and it is too late / to pretend we are children at dusk watching fireflies." In the "Holy Writ" sequence Warren's theme of "original sin" informs the first poem, "Elijah on Mount Carmel," in that the slaughter of the priests of Baal precipitates psychopathic frenzy–suggestive of Warren's first murderous fanatic, John Brown–in God's prophet: "he screamed, / Screaming in glory / Like / A bursting blood blister." The other biblical episode, "Saul at Gilboa," is probably the grimmest instance of postlapsarian trauma in all Warren's poetry. Here the prophet Samuel anoints Israel's first king only to witness, later, the anointed head lying severed from its torso, which, with "a stake/ Thrust upward to twist the gut-tangle, towered/ Above the wall of Beth-shan." Saul's prelapsarian innocence during the anointing–"How beautiful are the young, walking!"–is all the more unbearable in this hindsight: "through/The enormous hollow of my head, History/Whistles like a wind...." Yet the "Tale of Time" section ends in "Delight," a sequence of seven short, exquisitely musical lyrics about the world's redemptive beauty.

Two remaining books of the 1960s, *Incarnations: Poems 1966-1968* (1968) and *Audubon: A Vision*, counter-balance morbidity versus delight. *Incarnations*, as its title implies, takes up the "One Flesh" theme of "The Ballad of Billie Potts" and *Promises*, drawing support for the concept from a biblical epigraph: "Yet now our flesh is as the flesh of our brethren.–*Nehemiah* 5.5" The flesh in *Incarnations* is greatly various: animal ("The Red Mullet"), human ("Internal Injuries," about a dying convict and an old woman struck by an automobile), and even vegetable ("The Ivy"). What binds most of these poems into unity is the premise of limitation: to be incarnated as a man is to be conscious of time, death, and separation from the "One Flesh" ideal. "Myth on Mediterranean Beach: Aphrodite as Logos" is particularly effective in its portrayal of Aphrodite as a humpbacked old crone whose fleshy decay represents the Logos (Truth) principle: "The breasts hang down like saddle-bags, / To balance the hump the belly sags...." Rising from the sea "In Botticellean parody," she "passes the lovers, one by one, / / And passing, draws their dreams away,/ And leaves them naked to the day." Several poems of "delight" counteract this mood, including "The Faring" (in a style reminiscent of Old English poetry), "The Enclave," and "Skiers," but *Incarnations* ends with two images of limitation: fog, a recurring image of being dead in Warren's later verse; and, in the fog, a crow call, evoking the problem of solipsism: "crow, / Come back, I would hear your voice: / / That much, at least, in this whiteness."

Initially, *Audubon* too seems morbid, describing an attempted murder that is punished by the hanging of the perpetrators. But, as Allen Shepherd has shown, Warren departed sharply from

John James Audubon's *Ornithological Biography* (1831-1839), where the great naturalist, saved from murder by a band of vigilantes, was "well-pleased" at seeing the "infernal hag" who tried to kill him hanged for her turpitude. The poem instead imputes to Audubon a profound empathy with the old woman, whose willfulness during her hanging evokes something close to a mystical experience in the observer: "The face, / Eyes, a-glare, jaws clenched, now growing black ... had achieved, / It seemed to him, a new dimension of beauty." This beauty of human character, like the beauty of Audubon's birds, has the effect of reversing the Fall, imparting to Audubon that perfected contentedness with himself ("Simply ... as he was / ... The blessedness!") and with the surrounding world that is normally reserved to prelapsarian innocence. Even his own mortality is easily accepted in this spirit, and the Osmosis of Being becomes immanent ("Thinks / How thin is the membrane between himself and the world"). In the end the poem's narrator (Warren's persona) takes instruction from this figure of grace, emulating Audubon's life-joy as he hears the geese flying North (the anima returning): "Tell me a story of deep delight."

Warren's remarkable late-flowering of creativity, compared by George Palmer Garrett, Jr., to that of Pablo Picasso, Igor Stravinsky, and William Butler Yeats, produced four more volumes in the 1970s, as the poet was settling into his eighth decade. Subtitled *Poem / Poems 1968-1974*, *Or Else* (1974) takes as its epigraph a verse from Psalm 78 that identifies Jehovah's succor of Israel with the modern poet-prophet's mission: "He clave the rocks in the wilderness, and gave them drink as out of the great depths." The dialectic between rocks / wilderness and drink in *Or Else* begins in poem one with the ominous image of Time the Devourer: "the sun, / Beyond the western ridge of black-burnt pine stubs like / A snaggery of rotten shark teeth, sinks...." Poem two, "Natural History," counteracts this mood with a visionary portrayal of death as a benign absorption into nature. Here the spectral old couple's nakedness implies a return to Edenic innocence, and their embodiment in rain and flowers signifies the Osmosis of Being perfectly: "In the rain the naked old father is dancing.... / Her breath is sweet as bruised violets, and her smile sways like daffodils reflected in a brook." A similar counterpoint juxtaposes the two artists in "Homage to Theodore Dreiser"–a soul damned by his knowledge of his own and the world's evil–

and "Flaubert in Egypt," in which Gustave Flaubert's life is redeemed by his intense experience of the world's beauty: "his heart / burst with a solemn thanksgiving to God for / the fact he could perceive the worth of the / world with such joy. / / Years later, death near, he remembered the palm fronds– / how black against a bright sky!" At the close of *Or Else*, two verbal paintings represent the terminal instance of this juxtaposition. In "Birth of Love" a man, "all / History dissolving from him, is / Nothing but an eye. Is an eye only. Sees," as he is absorbed totally into the spectacle of his beloved bathing, "A white stalk from which the face flowers gravely toward the high sky." This epiphany yields in the next poem, however, to a description of death as "A Problem in Spatial Composition." Here Warren's long-standing image of the anima as a hawk disappearing into darkness at sunset occurs in a newly pictographic fashion, with the patterning of words on the page providing a visual image of the bird's descent:

All is ready.

The hawk,
Entering the composition at the upper left frame
Of the window, glides,
In the pellucid ease of thought and at
His breathless angle,
Down.

Breaks speed.
Hangs with a slight lift and hover.
Makes contact[.]

Though few in number, the new poems in *Selected Poems: 1923-1975* include several memorable achievements. Gathered under the title, "Can I See Arcturus From Where I Stand?–Poems 1975," these ten poems subserve that collective title in their recurring reach toward transcendence ("Arcturus") from a generally postlapsarian environment ("Where I Stand"). The opening poem, "A Way to Love God," depicts the dialectical conflict between the world's immanent beauty and its appalling turpitude through sudden contrast in sound and image patterns: "the sea's virgin bosom unveiled / To give suck to the wavering serpent of the moon; and / In the distance, in *plaza, piazza, place, platz,* and square, / Boot heels, like history being born, on cobbles bang." The closing memory of sheep standing in fog ("Their eyes / Stared into nothingness") amplifies the poem's title: waiting quietly for death is A Way to Love

God. "Evening Hawk" recalls a familiar anima image–the bird "climbing the last light / Who knows neither Time nor error"–and sharply contrasts its inaccessible realm of transcendence ("The star / Is steady, like Plato, over the mountain") against the fallen world, where one might "hear / The earth grind on its axis, or history/ Drip in darkness like a leaking pipe in the cellar." Two other poems about loss and fragmentation, "Answer to Prayer" (a "paradise past" poem about a lost romance) and "Brotherhood in Pain" (a paradox defining loneliness as the deepest human bond), add resonance to perhaps the finest postlapsarian poem in this collection, "Loss, of Perhaps Love, in Our World of Contingency." Trying to isolate the exact lapsarian moment, when the "Loss, of Perhaps Love" of the world occurred, this poem moves backward from the present moment, epitomized in the image of a ruined bum sliding shoe soles on the pavement, and forward from the prelapsarian memory of "the dapple / Of sunlight on the bathroom floor while your mother / Bathed you."

This poem's concluding line, "We must learn to live in the world," states simply enough the prevailing issue of Warren's postlapsarian poetry. Total immersion in the world's beauty, like that portrayed in "Trying to Tell You Something," is one way of addressing this issue; but Warren's most distinctive and, in the "Arcturus" collection, most ambitious response to the problem is the final and longest poem of the group, "Old Nigger on One-Mule Cart Encountered Late at Night When Driving Home from Party in the Back Country." Like Audubon, the Old Nigger becomes in the end a figure of grace and an alter ego for Warren's persona, despite the barriers imposed by race, class, age, education, and–since their near-collision–time and distance. "Brother Rebuker, my Philosopher past all / Casuistry," the Old Nigger reconciles "Arcturus" and "Where I Stand" within the vast embrace of his final attitude: "Between cart and shack, / [he] Pauses to make water, and while / The soft, plopping sound in deep dust continues, his face / Is lifted into starlight, calm as prayer."

Warren's latest novel, *A Place to Come To* (1977), is in many respects his most personal. The story of a renowned medieval scholar who has come far from his humble beginnings in Dugton, Alabama, the novel poses many of the questions Warren has explored in his earlier works and shows the futility of seeking to escape the past and the flux of time. The work is apparently autobiographical to a certain extent, and Warren's use of history in this case seems to lean heavily on his own experiences as a scholar and teacher.

The main character, Jed Tewksbury, narrates the story in the first person, and everything is filtered through his enlightened, though somewhat confused, view of the world and the events that have shaped his life. Whereas Jack Burden in *All the King's Men* ascribed events to "The Big Twitch," Jed sees the world in terms of "The Great Avalanche" or what might be called the "Great Dong Theory." Jed's father died in a particularly obscene accident, and as the story of his death passed in local legend, Jed found he could not escape it and eventually tried to sublimate the effects of the incident by telling the tale, complete with gestures, to his friends at parties. All of his maneuverings, however, prove futile, for his past continues to come back on him when he least suspects it, and it is not until he integrates his heritage into his life that he can hope to find some peace with himself and the world.

The narrative technique of the novel is a complex web of narrative-within-narrative and flashbacks, which reinforces the awful presence of the past. Moreover, Jed's work as a medievalist makes him even more sharply aware of the past, for he not only wonders why a man who is supposedly in control of his life prefers such ancient history, but he also sees in the medieval texts situations and phrases which apply to his present condition. One may not, as Jed learns, live his life divorced from what has come before. As he states early in the novel: "Something is going on and will not stop. You are outside the going on, and you are, at the same time, inside the going on. In fact, the going on is what you are. Until you can understand that these things are different but are the same, you know nothing about the nature of life. I proclaim this." The narrative technique is itself a "going on" that embodies the complexities of Jed's experiences.

The novel clearly expounds an existential view of existence. In one of the more moving passages, Jed's wife concludes even as she dies that there is no God. Indeed there is no God in this work except the one of knowledge and knowing, from whom Jed constantly turns his face. Even as Jed struggles to persuade his lover, whom he first met in high school, to leave her husband, the chiming of the clock interrupts his speech, "words fraught with the authority of passion," and he feels that each of them is "like a grasshop-

per that, impaled on a boy's fishhook, is swung out, twitching, kicking, spitting, and gesticulating, over the dark water." Only Jed's gradual realization and acceptance of his condition in a world where all time is realized in the present allow him to view the world with the dispassionate sobriety required truly to know one's condition.

Now and Then: Poems 1976-1978 (1978), the volume that earned Warren his second Pulitzer Prize for poetry, adumbrates the theme of the Fall in its title–the *Now* of lapsarian consciousness being played off against the *Then* of Edenic memory. In general, the *Then* motif occurs in the opening ("Nostalgic") cluster of poems, while the *Now* preoccupies the second ("Speculative") collection, but several of the finest poems weave the *Now* and *Then* together. The book's opening poem "American Portrait: Old Style," accomplishes this design by juxtaposing the youth and the old age of "K.," a boyhood friend who had figured into one of Warren's early short stories, "Goodwood Comes Back." The paradise past of K.'s youth, now resembling "a vision still clinging to plaster / Set by Piero della Francesca," allowed him to "float / With a singular joy and silence, / In his cloud of bird dogs, like angels, / With their eyes on his eyes like God, / And the sun on his uncut hair bright. . . ." Later a big-league pitcher, until ruined by booze, K. now, "some sixty / Years blown like a hurricane past," has deteriorated into a pathetic ruin of a man, illustrating "How the teeth in Time's jaw all snag backward / And whatever enters therein / Has less hope of remission than shark-meat." The poem's closing summation, "And I love the world even in my anger," suggests the dialectic of moods that the rest of the volume amplifies.

The biblical epigraph of *Now and Then*– ". . . let the inhabitants of the rock sing . . ." (Isaiah 42:11)–also announces this dialectical pattern through its contrast between the noun "rock" (a Waste Land analogue) and the verb "sing." Among the poems that sing most lyrically of nature's beauty are "Star-Fall," "Code Book Lost," and "Dream of a Dream": "Moonlight stumbles with bright heel / In the stream, and the stones sing. . . ." The poems of the contrary "rock" mentality, such as "Waiting," "Sister Water," and "Last Laugh," lead to a deepening of the speaker's hunger for his lost anima. In "Ah, Anima!," where a storm's ruinous aftermath is "a metaphor for your soul . . . in the hurricane of Time," the vacancy of the fallen self prompts the vain wish "that you, even in the wrack and pelt

YOU SORT OLD LETTERS

Some are pure business, land deals, receipts, a contract,
Bank statements, dead policies, demand for some payment.
But a beach-party invite! -- yes, that tease of a hostess and you,
Withdrawn behind dunes, lay, the laughing far, and for contact
 With your tongue and teeth, she let you loosen a breast.
You left town soon after -- now wonder what might have that gay meant.

Suppose you hadn't left town -- well, she's dead anyway.
Three divorces, three children, all born for the sludge of the pit.
To Number One married, a nice guy, when you crept off to the dunes,
 And she gasped, "Bite harder -- hard!" And you did, in the glare of day.
Scrambling up, she cried, "Oh, don't you hate me --" kept like a child.
You patted, caressed, cuddled, kissed her. She said, "I'm a shit."

Do you seem to remember that for a moment your heart stirred?
You ... remember ... the ... hand ... shook up
With a likker-head plumber who now and then jolt or two to the jaw,
Then slammed her the works, blood on her swollen lips -- as you've heard.
You married late -- and now in this mass of old papers
The words: "You were smart to blow town. Keep your pecker up."

Signed only: "Yours -- maybe." Then: "P.S. what might have been?"
Yes, she had everything -- money, looks, breeding, a charm
Of defenseless appeal -- the last what trapped, no doubt, the
The three men middle-age fell ... three near middle-aged fall
... she threw all away, as you thought, and by struggling sank deeper in
A slough of self-hate But you're no psychiatrist,
And couldn't say what or why, as you lay by the warm

And delicious body you loved, in the dark ashamed
Of recurring speculations, as though this
Betrayed your love. Years passed. The end, your heard was sleeping pills.
You felt some confusion, or guilt, but how could you be blamed? -- Even if,
Even if, knees grinding sand, sun once smote your bare back, or once in
Or once in dream, lips, bloody, lifted for your kiss.

                    Robert Penn Warren

Revised typescript for "You Sort Old Letters" (courtesy of the author) of gray light, / / Had run forth, screaming . . . to leave / / The husk behind, and leap / Into the blind and antiseptic anger of air." "Heart of Autumn"–a notably imagistic postlapsarian title–closes *Now and Then* with an extraordinary expression of this anima-hunger in a speaker who stands watching a flock of geese fly South:

> and I stand, my face lifted now skyward,
> Hearing the high beat, my arms outstretched in the tingling
> Process of transformation, and soon tough legs,
>
> With folded feet, trail in the sounding vacuum of passage,
> And my heart is impacted with a fierce impulse
> To unwordable utterance–
> Toward sunset, at a great height.

Being Here: Poetry 1977-1980 (1980), dedicated to Warren's grandfather, begins with three epigraphs about Time, the last of which is Warren's own formulation: "Time is the dimension in which God strives to define His own Being." For the poet, memory is the dimension of Time in which the attempt to define *his* Being occurs, creating most of these poems in the process. This gathering of memories begins with a prefatory poem, "October Picnic Long Ago," that portrays the poet-persona as a seven-year-old safely ensconced within his nuclear family. As against this fragile prelapsarian moment, section one counterposes early episodes of lost innocence. Death and funerals–including his mother's funeral in "Grackles, Goodbye"–are landmarks of initiation here, but almost as traumatic is the first awareness of solipsism. In the opening poem, "Speleology," the solitude of self in the cave–"I dared not move in darkness so absolute. / I thought: *This is me.* Thought: *Me–who am I?*"–precipitates a wish for self-transcendence ("to be, in the end, part of all"), a motif that recurs in "Boyhood in Tobacco Country" ("I . . . try / To forget my own name and be part of the world") and in "Platonic Drowse" ("your body began to flow / On every side into distance, / . . . / / Leaving only the steady but pulsing / Germ-flame of your Being. . . ."). Section two portrays the emergence of the poet's artistic purpose, which in "Youthful Truth-seeker, Half-Naked, at Night, Running down Beach South of San Francisco," evokes a strong biblical analogy: "You dream that somewhere, somehow, you may embrace / The world in its fullness and threat, and feel, like Jacob, at last / The merciless grasp of unwordable grace."

Skillful appeals to the eye and ear characterize this section ("the glutted owl makes utterance," "Scraggle and brush broken through, snow-shower jarred loose / To drape shoulders. . . ."), but not all its poems record Nature's beauty; "Sila" concludes section two with the remembered mercy killing, by knife blade, of a wounded deer. Section three focuses upon the religious imagination, beginning and ending with the imagery of the Cross–the speaker mounting a cross in the first instance and erecting a grave marker for a drowned monkey in the other. Guilt, like that of Warren's "Original Sin" poems, proves a recurrent theme here, linking together the callous decapitation of kittens in "Dream, Dump-Heap, and Civilization," the killing of snakes for sport in "Deep–Deeper Down," a clandestine romance in "Vision," a giant boulder poised to overrun a valley "like God's wrath" in "Globe of Gneiss," and the color white as a cover for guilt in "Function of Blizzard." And the summoning of the dead–"Each wants to know if you remember a name"–adds another religious dimension in "Better Than Counting Sheep." Section four, focusing on the inadequacy of communication, begins with a similar séance ("Truth is the long soliloquy / Of the dead all their long night") and goes on to counterpose the silence of Nature in "No Bird Does Call" and "Language Barrier" against indecipherable or fragmentary speech in "What Is the Voice That Speaks?" and "Lesson in History." Section five concludes *Being Here* by gathering up the book's themes in a dialectical configuration. "Eagle Descending," an anima poem dedicated "To a Dead Friend," evokes a vision of mortality that advances upon the persona himself in "Acquaintance with Time in Early Autumn." Here, watching a leaf "Release / Its tiny claw-hooks, and trust / A shining destiny," he sees it instead "descend to water I know is black." This less-than-benign paradigm of his own death leads to a moment of theomachy–"and I hate God"–which appears to be strengthened by other postlapsarian poems such as "Ballad of Your Puzzlement" ("He picks the scab of his heart"), "Trips to California" (during the Dust Bowl disaster), and "Auto-da-Fé" ("stench of meat burned: / Dresden and Tokyo, and screams / In the Wilderness . . ."). On the other hand, the Osmosis of Being transpires in "Antimony: Time and Identity," where, in a canoe at night, "As consciousness outward seeps, the dark seeps in. / As the self dissolves . . . / . . . / / I wonder if this is I." And the epiphanies in "Synonyms" and "Night

Walking" affirm that "beauty is one word for reality" ("Synonyms"). In "Passers-By on Snowy Night," the last poem of *Being Here*, the lyrically rhyming quatrains restate earlier themes (such as *the moon, skull-white*" evoking nature's beauty and threat) while balancing the theme of isolation against its motif of the encounter. Here the essential purpose of poetry seems implicit in this partial release from solipsism: *"Alone, / I wish you well in your night / As I pass you in my own."*

Rumor Verified: Poems 1979-1980 (1981) derives its distinctive unity and power from the intensity of its meditations and mortality–a natural theme in the poet's eighth decade. The ramifications of the subject include the expiring of a day in "Sunset Scrupulously Observed" ("The evening slowly, soundlessly, closes. Like / An eyelid."); a bird smashed bloodily in "Going West" (it is going West on a car windshield); a horse being devoured by crows and vultures in "Dead Horse in Field," its missing eyes enabling it to "more readily see / Down the track of pure and eternal darkness"; the deaths of friends in "Minneapolis Story" and "Small Eternity"; the obituary of an old girlfriend, "photograph unrecognizable," in "Afterward"; and the death of the poet's father in "One I Knew" and "Questions You Must Learn to Live Past." In this last poem, the memory of father's deathbed (played off against seeing "your own child, that first morning, wait / / For the school bus") calls forth a prospect of the speaker's own impending future, "when / After the fable of summer, a lithe sinuosity / / Slips down to curl in some dark, wintry hole, with no dream."

In relating this central subject of *Rumor Verified* to himself, the Warren persona retains a characteristically dialectical range of responses. "Rumor Verified," the book's title poem, appears to imply some mode of death as the subject of its "rumor"–the death of an old identity if not physical death. "Since the rumor has been verified, you can, at least, / Disappear," the poems begins; "you" can now abandon the carefully cultivated persona of public life in favor of some new possibilities, such as becoming a guerrilla fighter in a Third World country. But in the end, there is no escaping "the terror / Of knowledge"–in this instance, a knowledge of limitations sufficient to transform an old idiom into an ominous pun: "you are simply a man, with a man's dead reckoning, nothing more." The dead reckoning of "Convergences" somewhat resembles Edwin Arlington Robinson's "The Man Against the Sky" in its portrayal of a distant figure disappearing into a railroad tunnel: "Now I saw him a half-mile back, / / A dot in the distance of sun / Where two gleaming rails become one / / To impale him in the black throat / Of a tunnel that sucked all to naught." Another poem, "Immanence," has the persona foreseeing his own death even more nihilistically; he "will, into / / The black conduit of Nature's Repackaging System, be sucked. / But that possibility is simply too distressing / / To– even–be considered." Yet other poems in the "But Also" section conceive of death as a welcome absorption into larger being reminiscent of the son's return "home" at the end of "The Ballad of Billie Potts." "What Voice at Moth-Hour" depicts its twilight scene in such tones of invitation: *"It's late! Come home."* Likewise, "Gasp-Glory of Gold Light" evokes the osmosis of being through a quasi-romantic apprehension of Nature so annealing that "The Self flows away into the unbruised / Guiltlessness of no-Self," and one may "try to think, at the same moment, / Of the living and the dead." And "English Cocker: Old and Blind" describes the blind creature's descent of the stairs–"At the edge of each step one paw suspended in air"–as representing the One Flesh concept impinging against mortality: "But you remember how you last saw / Him hesitate in his whirling dark, one paw / / Suspended above the abyss at the edge of the stair, / And . . . you knew in him / The kinship of all flesh defined by a halting paradigm."

"Fear and Trembling," the concluding section of *Rumor Verified*, begins, in "If Ever," with a formulation of this dialectical tension: "Do contradictory / Voices now at midnight utter / Doom–or promise?" One of the contradictory voices, in "Have You Ever Eaten Stars?," describes how a field of wild mushrooms suddenly– like Wordsworth's daffodils–entrances the speaker: "There, by a deer trail, by deer dung nourished, / Burst the gleam, rain-summoned, / Of bright golden chanterelles. / However briefly, however small and restricted, here was / A glade-burst of glory." Gathered to be eaten, these starlike plants also nourish, metaphorically, the poet's appetite for epiphanies: "What can you do with stars, or glory? / . . . Eat. Swallow. Absorb. . . . / Let brain glow / In its own midnight of darkness, / . . . let the heart / Rejoice." The contrary voice, in "Afterward," fastens with Melvillean brooding upon the "polar / Icecap stretching forever in light of gray-green ambiguousness, / And, lulled by jet-hum, [you] wondered if this / Is the only image of eternity." A "nameless skull"–suggesting the final meaning of the title "Afterward"–poses the riddle of mortality in a radically stoic question: the skull, "In the moonlit desert, smiles, having been / So long alone. After all, are you ready / To return the smile?" Set off by itself in a "Coda" to *Rumor Verified*, "Fear and Trembling" recalls the two poems that began the book by comprising its "Prologue." The first of these, "Chthonian Revelation: A Myth," is a strikingly Edenic love poem set against a Mediterranean seacoast. The other poem, "Looking Northward, Aegeanward: Nestlings on Seacliff," describes the tenacity of new life in a harsh environment: "From huddle of trash, dried droppings, and eggshell, lifts / . . . The pink corolla of beak-gape, the blind yearning lifeward." In "Fear and Trembling" those earlier seasons of love and vitality give way to autumnal meditation, not only about the speaker's impending transition–"The gold leaf–is it whirled in anguish or ecstasy skyward?"–but also about the efficacy of turning one's past life into poems. "It is time to meditate on what the season has meant," the first stanza posits, but it is hard to meditate as the seasonal metaphor takes a more ominous coloring: "Can one, in fact . . . find his own voice in the towering gust now from northward?" In the end, a sacrifice of self ("the death of ambition") precipitates the new life of poetic resurrection: "only at death of ambition does the deep / Energy crack crust, spurt, forth, and leap / / From grottoes, dark– and from the caverned enchainment."

In 1983 Warren's abiding interest in American history was manifested in a new book-length narrative poem, *Chief Joseph of the Nez Perce* (subtitled *Who Called Themselves the Nimipu "The Real People"*). Focusing on the War of 1877, in which Chief Joseph resisted efforts, in violation of several treaties, of the U.S. government to relocate his people, the poem re-creates the long trek of the Indians through Idaho and Montana until their valiant and resourceful band was overcome by superior force. Told partly by the poet and partly in the native eloquence of Chief Joseph's own voice, the narrative also draws upon a broad range of contemporary documents for added resonance. Thus the sympathy of Presidents Jefferson and Grant for the Indians is set against Charles Dickens's contempt for these "savages" and the satisfaction expressed in an Oregon newspaper when a party of miners returned from an expedition "with twenty scalps and some plunder. The miners are well." The Indians' achieve-

ment of glory despite military defeat is nicely encompassed in two quotations from Gen. William Tecumseh Sherman, whose words at the outset serve as an epigraph: "The more we can kill this year, the less will have to be killed the next war." In the end he wrote: "The Indians throughout have displayed a courage and skill that elicited universal praise; they abstained from scalping; let captive women go free . . . they fought with almost scientific skill."

Wallace Stevens's remark that a poet reveals his personality in his choice of a subject has interesting implications in this instance. Warren's lifelong effort to revise Americans' perception of their past frequently has taken the form of reversing the traditional assignment of guilt and innocence: John Brown, in Warren's first book, was a murderous fanatic, while the Secession's leader, in the recent *Jefferson Davis Gets His Citizenship Back* (1980), was a high-minded gentleman. But Warren's purpose is not merely to expose, once again, the moral turpitude of the victorious Northern politicians and generals; his deeper interest lies in his affinities with the aging Indian leader. Chief Joseph's devout attitude toward nature (reminiscent of Warren's Audubon), his strong loyalty to the father figure ("I prayed / That my father . . . / Might find some worth in a act of mine, / However slight"), and his posture in facing old age ("A dying animal humped with no motion under / Darkness of skies that reach out forever")–these are deeply felt themes of Warren's later poetry. And perhaps the quest for religious meaning is the final affinity between Chief Joseph and his commemorator: "But what is a man? An autumn-tossed aspen, / Pony-fart in the wind, the melting of snow-slush? / Yes, that is all. Unless–unless– / We can learn to live the Great Spirit's meaning. . . ."

On 24 April 1985–the poet's eightieth birthday–Random House published Warren's fourth volume of selected poems (*New and Selected Poems 1923-1985*). Although too few poems are republished here from his earlier volumes, this book's new poems–gathered in a section entitled "Altitudes and Extensions 1980-1985"–are an important addition to Warren's poetic oeuvre. The "Extensions" of his title encompass large horizons in both geography and time, represented by poems such as "Minnesota Recollection," "Arizona Midnight," "Far West Once," "Winter Wheat: Oklahoma," and "Old-Time Childhood in Kentucky." This last poem, evoking the octogenarian poet's octogenarian grandfather, indicates the great range of personally felt time in this collection (which is dedicated to Warren's infant granddaughter). Perhaps the most striking achievement of this collection relates to the other key word in its title, "Altitudes." From the first poem, "Three Darknesses," to the terminal "Myth of Mountain Sunrise" a dialectical pattern of images gradually produces an extraordinary final effect of rejuvenation. At one pole of the dialectic are numerous intimations of mortality in such poems as "Mortal Limit," "Old Dog Dead," "Rumor at Twilight," "Last Walk of Season," and "Sunset." At the other pole are the poems of virtually pantheistic affinities with nature (reminding us of Chief Joseph and Audubon yet again), such as "Caribou," "Hope," "Why You Climbed Up," and "First Moment of Autumn Recognized." Initially rejuvenation appears hopelessly remote as the speaker (at the end of "Three Darknesses") compares his stay in the hospital to "A dress rehearsal / . . . for / The real thing. Later. Ten years? Fifteen?" Even here the "Altitudes" suggest a presence, however, in the miniature form of a background image in the television movie the patient is watching: "Far beyond / All the world, the mountains lift. . . . / . . . They float / In that unnamable altitude of white light." Reappearing with increasing imminence at various points in the collection (in "Last Walk of Season," "If Snakes Were Blue," "Wind and Gibbon," "Delusion—No!"), the mountains are animate in the end, infused by the poet's vitalistic vision: "The mountain dimly wakes, stretches itself on windlessness. Feels its deepest chasm, waking, yawn." Ending the poem ("Myth of Mountain Sunrise") and the collection is one of the most striking images in all Warren's verse as the mountain birch assumes an erotic stance toward the rising sun, her lover:

> Think of a girl-shape, birch-white sapling, rising now
> From ankle-deep brook-stones, head back-flung, eyes closed in first beam,
> While hair—long, water-roped, past curve, coign, sway that no geometries know—
> Spreads end-thin, to define fruit-swell of haunches, tingle of hand-hold.
> The sun blazes over the peak. That will be the old tale told.

For its originality, its visionary power, and its technical virtuosity, poetry such as this seems to justify Warren's comment in the *Georgia Review* for Summer 1982 that "I've done some of my best poems in the last few years." Concerning his

work as a whole, perhaps the best summary of Warren's poetic career is his own statement of purpose from his Jefferson Lecture in the Humanities, published as *Democracy and Poetry* in 1975. Beginning in his foreword with "the notion of the self as the central fact of 'poetry,' " Warren later explains that "only insofar as the work [of art] establishes and expresses a self can it engage us." Ultimately, "the work itself represents the author's adventures in selfhood," he goes on to observe; and in the end Warren's concept of creating selfhood serves to describe the design of his sixty years of poetic practice: "we may declare that the self is a style of being, continually expanding in a vital process of definition, affirmation, revision, and growth, a process that is the image, we may say, of the life process. . . ." The shelf of books in which Warren has recorded that life process has now become, by general consensus, a major document in American poetry. Given the magnitude and excellence of his achievement, it seems singularly appropriate that in February 1986 the Librarian of Congress, Daniel J. Boorstin, designated Robert Penn Warren the first official Poet Laureate of the United States of America.

Interviews:

Robert Penn Warren Talking: Interviews 1950-1978, edited by Floyd C. Watkins and John T. Hiers (New York: Random House, 1980).
Reprints eighteen interviews covering Warren's most productive three decades, including televised sessions with Bill Moyers, Edwin Newman, and Dick Cavett.

Bibliography:

James A. Grimshaw, Jr., *Robert Penn Warren: A Descriptive Bibliography 1922-1979* (Charlottesville: University Press of Virginia, 1981).
Definitive coverage of all the writings by and about Warren for a fifty-five-year period, from his college years into his mid seventies.

Biography:

Floyd C. Watkins, *Then & Now: The Personal Past in the Poetry of Robert Penn Warren* (Lexington: University Press of Kentucky, 1982).
The only biography of Warren that exists, focusing mostly on Warren's life into his twenties and correlating biographical information with specific episodes in many of Warren's poems.

References:

Walter Berger, *A Southern Renascence Man: Views of Robert Penn Warren* (Baton Rouge: Louisiana State University Press, 1984).
Includes essays by distinguished authors Louis Rubin, Jr., Madison Jones, Harold Bloom, and James Dickey on Warren as poet, novelist, critic, and historian.

Charles Bohner, *Robert Penn Warren* (New York: Twayne, 1964; revised edition, 1981).
A gracefully written, knowledgeable general introduction to Warren's whole literary corpus up to 1980.

John M. Bradbury, *The Fugitives: A Critical Account* (Chapel Hill: University of North Carolina Press, 1958), pp. 172-255.
A sophisticated, well-researched study of the literary group which made up Warren's creative milieu during and after his formative years at Vanderbilt University in the 1920s, with special focus on John Crowe Ransom, Allen Tate, and Warren.

John Burt, *Robert Penn Warren and American Idealism* (New Haven: Yale University Press, 1988).
Studies the dialectic between American idealism (especially the Transcendentalist heritage) and pragmatism that translates into the theme of romance versus realism in Warren's writing–particularly his writings with historical subject matter (*John Brown, Brother to Dragons, Audubon, All the King's Men*).

Leonard Casper, *Robert Penn Warren: The Dark and Bloody Ground* (Seattle: University of Washington Press, 1960).
This first book-length study of Warren's work correlates the themes and images of his earlier fiction and poetry–especially the motifs of guilt, complicity, and redemption.

William Bedford Clark, ed., *Critical Essays on Robert Penn Warren* (Boston: Twayne, 1981).
Twenty book reviews (from *John Brown*, 1929, to *Brother to Dragons*, revised 1979), an interview with Warren, and nine essays by major Warren scholars.

D. M. Dooley, "The Persona RPW in Warren's *Brother to Dragons*," *Mississippi Quarterly*, 25 (Winter 1971-1972): 19-30.

Analyzes the subtle changes in the persona of Warren which parallel the more obvious transformation of Thomas Jefferson from a voice of cynicism to an exponent of reconciliation.

Richard Gray, ed., *Robert Penn Warren: A Collection of Critical Essays* (Englewood Cliffs, N.J.: Prentice-Hall, 1980).
Seventeen essays by noted scholars, mostly about specific novels but including several essays about Warren's poetry and criticism.

James A. Grimshaw, Jr., ed., *Robert Penn Warren's Brother to Dragons: A Discussion* (Baton Rouge: Louisiana State University Press, 1983).
A collection of essays by Warren scholars that consider both the original version of *Brother to Dragons* (1953) and the extensively rewritten 1979 version.

Grimshaw, Jr., *Time's Glory: Original Essays on Robert Penn Warren* (Conway: University of Central Arkansas Press, 1986).
New essays on Warren's work, mostly on his fiction but including one on Warren's final book of poems and one on the writer's historical sensibility.

James H. Justus, *The Achievement of Robert Penn Warren* (Baton Rouge: Louisiana State University Press, 1981).
The most recent and most ambitious overview of Warren's whole corpus of fiction, poetry, and nonfiction prose, this book is the best general study yet to appear; it is particularly helpful for its perceptive analyses of Warren's fiction.

John L. Longley, Jr., ed., *Robert Penn Warren: A Collection of Critical Essays* (New York: New York University Press, 1965).
A gathering of essays written by scholars of a generation ago, giving an overview of Warren from the then-prevalent school of modernism, as contrasted with our contemporary postmodernism.

Neil Nakadate, ed., *Robert Penn Warren: Critical Perspectives* (Lexington: University Press of Kentucky, 1981).
Collects twelve essays by eminent scholars on Warren's fiction and ten essays on his po-

etry; two of the essays are by Warren himself about *All the King's Men* and *Brother to Dragons*.

Katherine Snipes, *Robert Penn Warren* (New York: Ungar, 1983).
A perceptive discussion of Warren's fiction and poetry, divided into six chapters organized by his periods of creativity.

Victor Strandberg, *The Poetic Vision of Robert Penn Warren* (Lexington: University Press of Kentucky, 1977).
An overview and close analysis of the themes and image patterns that unify Warren's poetic corpus over a half-century of creativity.

Strandberg, "Warren's Poetic Vision: A Reading of *Now and Then*," *Southern Review*, new series 16 (Winter 1980): 18-45.

An intensive analysis of the volume of poems that won Warren the Pultizer Prize for 1977.

Floyd C. Watkins, "Billie Potts at the Fall of Time," *Mississippi Quarterly*, 11 (Winter 1958): 19-28.
A careful philosophical analysis of the poem that was as important in Warren's poetic development as "Tintern Abbey" was for Wordsworth.

Papers:
Most of Warren's manuscripts and letters are on deposit in the Beinecke Library at Yale University; the Margaret I. King Library, Special Collections and Archives, at the University of Kentucky in Lexington; and the *Southern Review* files at Louisiana State University in Baton Rouge.

Contributors

Brian Attebery..*College of Idaho*
Nancy Barendse ....*University of South Carolina*
Alex Bateman ....*University of South Carolina*
Ronald Baughman ....*University of South Carolina*
Beverly Spears Blackmon..................................*Francis Marion College*
Susan L. Blake..*Lafayette College*
Ashley Brown ....*University of South Carolina*
Philip M. Bufithis..*Shepherd College*
Keen Butterworth ....*University of South Carolina*
Keith E. Byerman ....*University of Texas*
Ann Charters ....*University of Connecticut*
Barbara T. Christian ....*University of California, Berkeley*
Mildred Louise Culp...*Seattle, Washington*
Mary Doll...*Fulton, New York*
Virginia Dumont...*Francis Marion College*
Sarah English ....*Meredith College*
Paula R. Feldman ....*University of South Carolina*
John Gerlach..*Cleveland State University*
Andrew Gordon...*University of Florida*
Donald J. Greiner...*University of South Carolina*
Jeffrey Helterman ....*University of South Carolina*
Josephine Helterman ....*Columbia, South Carolina*
Robert Hill..*Clemson University*
Elizabeth B. House ....*Augusta College*
Sylvia Patterson Iskander ....*University of Southwestern Louisiana*
Michael Joslin ....*University of South Carolina*
Brooks Landon ....*University of Iowa*
J. Michael Lennon ....*Sangamon State University*
Carol MacCurdy ....*University of Southwestern Louisiana*
Brett C. Millier ....*Middlebury College*
Robert M. Nelson...*University of Richmond*
Peter J. Reed..*University of Minnesota*
Victor Strandberg ....*Duke University*
Stephen L. Tanner ....*University of Idaho*
Margaret A. Van Antwerp...............................*Columbia, South Carolina*
Joseph Wenke ....*University of Connecticut*
Holly Mims Wescott ....*Francis Marion College*
Alden Whitman ....*South Hampton, New York*
Everett Wilkie..*University of South Carolina*
Gary K. Wolfe..*Roosevelt University*
Laura Zaidman ....*University of South Carolina at Sumter*

Concise Dictionary of American Literary Biography Cumulative Index

Cumulative Index

Cumulative Index

Cumulative Index

Cumulative Index

80: *Restoration and Eighteenth-Century Dramatists,* First Series, edited by Paula R. Backscheider (1989)

81: *Austrian Fiction Writers, 1875-1913,* edited by James Hardin and Donald G. Daviau (1989)

82: *Chicano Writers,* First Series, edited by Francisco A. Lomelí and Carl R. Shirley (1989)

83: *French Novelists Since 1960,* edited by Catharine Savage Brosman (1989)

84: *Restoration and Eighteenth-Century Dramatists,* Second Series, edited by Paula R. Backscheider (1989)

85: *Austrian Fiction Writers After 1914,* edited by James Hardin and Donald G. Daviau (1989)

86: *American Short-Story Writers, 1910-1945,* First Series, edited by Bobby Ellen Kimbel (1989)

87: *British Mystery and Thriller Writers Since 1940,* First Series, edited by Bernard Benstock and Thomas F. Staley (1989)

88: *Canadian Writers, 1920-1959,* Second Series, edited by W. H. New (1989)

89: *Restoration and Eighteenth-Century Dramatists,* Third Series, edited by Paula R. Backscheider (1989)

90: *German Writers in the Age of Goethe, 1789-1832,* edited by James Hardin and Christoph E. Schweitzer (1989)

91: *American Magazine Journalists, 1900-1960,* First Series, edited by Sam G. Riley (1990)

92: *Canadian Writers, 1890-1920,* edited by W. H. New (1990)

93: *British Romantic Poets, 1789-1832,* First Series, edited by John R. Greenfield (1990)

94: *German Writers in the Age of Goethe: Sturm und Drang to Classicism,* edited by James Hardin and Christoph E. Schweitzer (1990)

95: *Eighteenth-Century British Poets,* First Series, edited by John Sitter (1990)

96: *British Romantic Poets, 1789-1832,* Second Series, edited by John R. Greenfield (1990)

97: *German Writers from the Enlightenment to Sturm und Drang, 1720-1764,* edited by James Hardin and Christoph E. Schweitzer (1990)

98: *Modern British Essayists,* First Series, edited by Robert Beum (1990)

99: *Canadian Writers Before 1890,* edited by W. H. New (1990)

100: *Modern British Essayists,* Second Series, edited by Robert Beum (1990)

101: *British Prose Writers, 1660-1800,* First Series, edited by Donald T. Siebert (1991)

102: *American Short-Story Writers, 1910-1945,* Second Series, edited by Bobby Ellen Kimbel (1991)

103: *American Literary Biographers,* First Series, edited by Steven Serafin (1991)

Documentary Series

1: *Sherwood Anderson, Willa Cather, John Dos Passos, Theodore Dreiser, F. Scott Fitzgerald, Ernest Hemingway, Sinclair Lewis,* edited by Margaret A. Van Antwerp (1982)

2: *James Gould Cozzens, James T. Farrell, William Faulkner, John O'Hara, John Steinbeck, Thomas Wolfe, Richard Wright,* edited by Margaret A. Van Antwerp (1982)

3: *Saul Bellow, Jack Kerouac, Norman Mailer, Vladimir Nabokov, John Updike, Kurt Vonnegut,* edited by Mary Bruccoli (1983)

4: *Tennessee Williams,* edited by Margaret A. Van Antwerp and Sally Johns (1984)

5: *American Transcendentalists,* edited by Joel Myerson (1988)

6: *Hardboiled Mystery Writers,* edited by Matthew J. Bruccoli and Richard Layman (1989)

7: *Modern American Poets,* edited by Karen L. Rood (1989)

8: *The Black Aesthetic Movement,* edited by Jeffrey Louis Decker (1991)

Yearbooks

1980, edited by Karen L. Rood, Jean W. Ross, and Richard Ziegfeld (1981)

1981, edited by Karen L. Rood, Jean W. Ross, and Richard Ziegfeld (1982)

1982, edited by Richard Ziegfeld; associate editors: Jean W. Ross and Lynne C. Zeigler (1983)